Advances in Human-Robot Interaction

Edited by

Vladimir A. Kulyukin

Advances in Human-Robot Interaction

Edited by Vladimir A. Kulyukin

Republished by InTech

Janeza Trdine 9, 51000 Rijeka, Croatia

Technical Editor Teodora Smiljanic

Additional hard copies can be obtained from orders@intechopen.com

Advances in Human-Robot Interaction, Edited by Vladimir A. Kulyukin
p. cm.
ISBN 978-953-307-020-9

For EU product safety concerns:
IN TECH d.o.o., Prolaz Marije Krucifikse Kozulić 3, 51000 Rijeka, Croatia,
info@intechopen.com or visit our website at intechopen.com.

Meet the editor

Vladimir A. Kulyukin is currently an Associate Professor of Computer Science at Utah State University. Kulyukin's research focuses on wavelet algorithms for video and audio l^2 (Z) data

Preface

Rapid advances in the field of robotics have made it possible to use robots not just in industrial automation but also in entertainment, rehabilitation, and home service. Since robots will likely affect many aspects of human existence, fundamental questions of human-robot interaction must be formulated and, if at all possible, resolved. Some of these questions are addressed in this collection of papers by leading HRI researchers.

Readers may take several paths through the book. Those who are interested in personal robots may wish to read Chapters 1, 4, and 7. Multi-modal interfaces are discussed in Chapters 1 and 14. Readers who wish to learn more about knowledge engineering and sensors may want to take a look at Chapters 2 and 3. Emotional modeling is covered in Chapters 4, 8, 9, 16, 18. Various approaches to socially interactive robots and service robots are offered and evaluated in Chapters 7, 9, 13, 14, 16, 18, 20. Chapter 5 is devoted to smart environments and ubiquitous computing. Chapter 6 focuses on multi-robot systems. Android robots are the topic of Chapters 8 and 12. Chapters 6, 10, 11, 15 discuss performance measurements. Chapters 10 and 12 may be beneficial to readers interested in human motion modeling. Haptic and natural language interfaces are the topics of Chapters 11 and 14, respectively. Military robotics is discussed in Chapter 15. Chapter 17 is on cognitive modeling. Chapter 19 focuses on robot navigation. Chapters 13 and 20 cover several HRI issues in assistive technology and rehabilitation. For convenience of reference, each chapter is briefly summarized below.

In Chapter 1, Mamiko Sakata, Mieko Marumo, and Kozaburo Hachimura contribute to the investigation of non-verbal communication with personal robots. The objective of their research is the study of the mechanisms to express personality through body motions and the classification of motion types that personal robots should be given in order to make them express specific personality or emotional impressions. The researchers employ motion-capturing techniques for obtaining human body movements from the motions of Nihon-buyo, a traditional Japanese dance. They argue that dance, as a motion form, allows for more artistic body motions compared to everyday human body motions and makes it easier to discriminate emotional factors that personal robots should be capable of displaying in the future.

In Chapter 2, Atilla Elçi and Behnam Rahnama address the problem of giving autonomous robots a sense of self, immediate ambience, and mission. Specific techniques are discussed to endow robots with self-localization, detection and correction of course deviation errors, faster and more reliable identification of friend or foe, simultaneous localization and mapping in unfamiliar environments. The researchers argue that advanced robots should be able to reason about the environments in which they operate. They introduce the concept of Semantic Intelligence (SI) and attempt to distinguish it from traditional AI.

In Chapter 3, Xianming Ye, Byungjune Choi, Hyouk Ryeol Choi, and Sungchul Kang propose a compact handheld pen-type texture sensor for the measurement of fine texture. The proposed texture sensor is designed with a metal contact probe and can measure the roughness and frictional properties of a surface. The sensor reduces the size of contact area and separates the normal stimuli from tangential ones, which facilitates the interpretation of the relation between dynamic responses and the surface texture. 3D contact forces can be used to estimate the surface profile in the path of exploration.

In Chapter 4, Sébastien Saint-Aimé, Brigitte Le-Pévédic, and Dominique Duhaut investigate the question of how to create robots capable of behavior enhancement through interaction with humans. They propose the minimal number of degrees of freedom necessary for a companion robot to express six primary emotions. They propose iCrace, a computational model of emotional reasoning, and describe experiments to validate several hypotheses about the length and speed of robotic expressions, methods of information processing, response consistency, and emotion recognition.

In Chapter 5, Takeshi Sasaki, Yoshihisa Toshima, Mihoko Niitsuma and Hideki Hashimoto investigate how human users can interact with smart environments or, as they call them, iSpaces (intelligent spaces). They propose two human-iSpace interfaces – a spatial memory and a whistle interface. The spatial memory uses three-dimensional positions. When a user specifies digital information that indicates a position in the space, the system associates the 3D position with that information. The whistle interface uses the frequency of a human whistling as a trigger to call a service. This interface is claimed to work well in noisy environments, because whistles are easily detectable. They describe an information display system using a pan-tilt projector. The system consists of a projector and a pan-tilt enabled stand. The system can project an image toward any position. They present experimental results with the developed system.

In Chapter 6, Jijun Wang and Michael Lewis presents an extension of Crandall's Neglect Tolerance model. Neglect tolerance estimates a period of time when human intervention ends but before a performance measure drops below an acceptable threshold. In this period, the operator can perform other tasks. If the operator works with other robots over this time period neglect tolerance can be extended to estimate the overall number of robots under the operator's control. The researchers' main objective is to develop a computational model that accommodates both coordination demands and heterogeneity in robotic teams. They present an extension of Neglect Tolerance model in section and a multi-robot system simulator that they used in validation experiments. The experiments attempt to measure coordination demand under strong and weak cooperation conditions.

In Chapter 7, Kazuki Kobayashi and Seiji Yamada consider the situation in which a human cooperates with a service robot, such as a sweeping robot or a pet robot. Service robots often need users' assistance when they encounter difficulties that they cannot overcome independently. One example given in this chapter is a sweeping robot unable to navigate around a table or a chair and needing the user's assistance to move the obstacle out of its way. The problem is how to enable a robot to inform its user that it needs help. They propose a novel method for making a robot to express its internal state (referred to as robot's mind) to request users' help. Robots can express their minds both verbally and non-verbally.

The proposed non-verbal expression centers around movement based on motion overlap (MO) that enables the robot to move in a way that the user narrows down possible responses and acts appropriately. The researchers describe an implementation on a real mobile robot and discuss experiments with participants to evaluate the implementation's effectiveness.

In Chapter 8, Takashi Minato and Hiroshi Ishiguro present a study human-like robotic motion during interaction with other people. They experiment with an android endowed with motion variety. They hypothesize that if a person attributes a cause of motion variety in an android to the android's mental states, physical states, and the social situations, the person has more humanlike impression toward the android. Their chapter focuses on intentional motion caused by the social relationship between two agents. They consider the specific case when one agent reaches out and touches another person. They present a psychological experiment in which participants watch an android touch a human or an object and report their impressions.

In Chapter 9, Kazuhiro Taniguchi, Atsushi Nishikawa, Tomohiro Sugino, Sayaka Aoyagi, Mitsugu Sekimoto, Shuji Takiguchi, Kazuyuki Okada, Morito Monden, and Fumio Miyazaki propose a method for objectively evaluating psychological stress in humans who interact with robots. The researchers argue that there is a large disparity between the image of robots from popular fiction and their actual appearance in real life. Therefore, to facilitate human-robot interaction, we need not only to improve the robot's physical and intellectual abilities but also find effective ways of evaluating the psychological stress experienced by humans when they interact with robots. The authors evaluate human stress with acceleration pulse waveforms and saliva constituents of a surgeon using a surgical assistant robot.

In Chapter 10, Woong Choi, Tadao Isaka, Hiroyuki Sekiguchi, and Kozaburo Hachimura give a quantitative analysis of leg movements. They use simultaneous measurements of body motion and electromyograms to assess biophysical information. The investigators used two expert Japanese traditional dancers as subjects of their experiments. The experiments show that a more experienced dancer has the effective co-contraction of antagonistic muscles of the knee and ankle and less center of gravity transfer than a less experienced dancer. An observation is made that the more experienced dancer can efficiently perform dance leg movements with less electromyogramic activity than the less experienced counterpart.

In Chapter 11, Tsuneo Yoshikawa, Masanao Koeda and Munetaka Sugihashi propose to define handedness as an important factor in designing tools and devices that are to be handled by people using their hands. The researchers propose a quantitative method for evaluating quantitatively the handedness and dexterity of a person on the basis of the person's performance in test tasks (accurate positioning, accurate force control, and skillful manipulation) in the virtual world by using haptic virtual reality technology. Factor scores are obtained for the right and left hands of each subject and the subject's degree of handedness is defined as the difference of these factor scores. The investigators evaluated the proposed method with ten subjects and found that it was consistent with the measurements obtained from the traditional laterality quotient method.

In Chapter 12, Tomoo Takeguchi, Minako Ohashi and Jaeho Kim argue that service robots may have to walk along with humans for special care. In this situation, a robot must be able to walk like a human and to sense how the human walks. The researchers analyze

3D walking with rolling motion. The 3D modeling and simulation analysis were performed to find better walking conditions and structural parameters. The investigators describe a 3D passive dynamic walker that was manufactured to analyze the passive dynamic walking experimentally.

In Chapter 13, Yasuhisa Hirata, Takuya Iwano, Masaya Tajika and Kazuhiro Kosuge propose a wearable walking support system, called Wearable Walking Helper, which is capable of supporting walking activity without using biological signals. The support moment of the joints of the user is computed by the system using an approximated human model of four-link open chain mechanism on the sagittal plane. The system consists of knee orthosis, prismatic actuator, and various sensors. The knee joint of the orthosis has one degree of freedom and rotates around the center of the knee joint of the user on sagittal plane. The knee joint is a geared dual hinge joint. The prismatic actuator includes a DC motor and a ball screw. The device generates support moment around the user's knee joint.

In Chapter 14, Tetsushi Oka introduces the concept of a multimodal command language to direct home-use robots. The author introduces RUNA (Robot Users' Natural Command Language). RUNA is a multimodal command language for directing home-use robots. It is designed to allow the user to robots by using hand gestures or pressing remote control buttons. The language consists of grammar rules and words for spoken commands based on the Japanese language. It also includes non-verbal events, such as touch actions, button press actions, and single-hand and double-hand gestures. The proposed command language is sufficiently flexible in that the user can specify action types (walk, turn, switchon, push, and moveto) and action parameters (speed, direction, device, and goal) by using both spoken words and nonverbal messages.

In Chapter 15, Jessie Chen examines if and how aided target recognition (AiTR) cueing capabilities facilitate multitasking (including operating a robot) by gunners in a military tank crew station environment. The author investigates if gunners can perform their primary task of maintaining local security while they are performing two secondary tasks of managing a robot and communicating with fellow crew members. Two simulating experiments are presented. The findings suggest reliable automation, such as AiTR, for one task benefits not only the automated task but also the concurrent tasks.

In Chapter 16, Eun-Sook Jee, Yong-Jeon Cheong, Chong Hui Kim, Dong-Soo Kwon, and Hisato Kobayashi investigate the process of emotional sound production in order to enable robots to express emotion effectively and to facilitate the interaction between humans and robots. They use the explicit or implicit link between emotional characteristics and musical parameters to compose six emotional sounds: happiness, sadness, fear, joy, shyness, and irritation. The sounds are analyzed to identify a method to improve a robot's emotional expressiveness. To synchronize emotional sounds with robotic movements and gestures, the emotional sounds are divided into several segments in accordance with musical structure. The researchers argue that the existence of repeatable sound segments enable robots to better synchronize their behaviors with sounds.

In Chapter 17, Eiji Hayashi discusses a Consciousness-based Architecture (CBA) that has been synthesized based on a mechanistic expression model of animal consciousness and behavior advocated by the Vietnamese philosopher Tran Duc Thao. CBA has an evaluation function for behavior selection and controls the agent's behavior. The author argues that it is difficult for a robot to behave autonomously if the robot relies exclusively on the CBA. To achieve such autonomous behavior, it is necessary to continuously produce behavior in the robot and to change the robot's consciousness level. The research proposes a motivation model to induce conscious, autonomous changes in behavior. The model is combined with the CBA. The motivation model serves an input to the CBA. The modified CBA was implemented in a Conscious Behavior Robot (Conbe-I). The Conbe-I is a robotic arm with a hand consisting of three fingers in which a small monocular CCD camera is installed. A study of the robot's behavior is presented.

In Chapter 18, Anja Austermann and Seiji Yamada argue that learning robots can use the feedback from their users as a basis for learning and adapting to their users' preferences. The researchers investigate how to enable a robot to learn to understand natural, multimodal approving or disapproving feedback given in response to the robot's moves. They present and evaluate a method for learning a user's feedback for human-robot interaction. Feedback from the user comes in the form of speech, prosody, and touch. These types of feedback are found to be sufficiently reliable for teaching a robot by reinforcement learning.

In Chapter 19, Kohji Kamejima introduces fractal representation of the maneuvering affordance on the randomness ineluctably distributed in naturally complex scenes. The author describes a method to extract scale shift of random patterns from scene image and to match it to the a priori direction of a roadway. Based on scale space analysis, the probability of capturing not-yet-identified fractal attractors is generated within the roadway pattern to be detected. Such an in-situ design process yields anticipative models for road following process. The randomness-based approach yields a design framework for machine perception sharing man-readable information, i.e., natural complexity of textures and chromatic distributions.

In Chapter 20, Vladimir Kulyukin and Chaitanya Gharpure describe their work on robot-assisted shopping for the blind and visually impaired. In their previous research, the researchers developed RoboCart, a robotic shopping cart for the visually impaired. The researchers focus on how blind shoppers can select a product from the repository of thousands of products, thereby communicating the target destination to RobotCart. This task becomes time critical in opportunistic grocery shopping when the shopper does not have a prepared list of products. Three intent communication modalities (typing, speech, and browsing) are evaluated in experiments with 5 blind and 5 sighted, blindfolded participants on a public online database of 11,147 household products. The mean selection time differed significantly among the three modalities, but the modality differences did not vary significantly between blind and sighted, blindfolded groups, nor among individual participants.

Editor

Vladimir A. Kulyukin
Department of Computer Science,
Utah State University
USA

Contents

1

Motion Feature Quantification of Different Roles in *Nihon-Buyo* Dance

Mamiko Sakata, Mieko Marumo, and Kozaburo Hachimura
Doshisha University, Nihon University, Ritsumeikan University
Japan

1. Introduction

As the development of smart biped robots has been thriving, research and development of personal robots with unique personalities will become an important issue in the next decade. For instance, we might want to have robots capable of affording us pleasure by chatting, singing or joking with us in our homes. Most of these functions are realized by verbal communications. However, motion of a whole body, namely non-verbal communication, also plays an important role.

We can get information concerning the personality of a subject when we observe his or her body motion. We may receive various impressions through their body motions. This means that human body movements convey emotion and the personality of the individual. Personality might be the involuntary and continuous expression of emotions, which are peculiar to an individual.

The aim of our research is to investigate the mechanism of expressing personality through body motions, the mechanism of how we get emotional impressions from body motions, and finally to investigate what kind of motion we should give robots in order to make them express specific personality and/or emotional impressions.

For this purpose, we employ Kansei information processing techniques, motion capturing, feature extraction from motion data and some statistical analyses, including regression analysis. The word "Kansei" is a Japanese word which is used to express some terms like "feeling" and "sensibility" in English. Kansei information processing is a method of extracting some features which are related to Kansei conveyed by the media we receive or, in contrast, a method of adding or generating some Kansei features to media produced by computers.

In Kansei-related research, some types of psychological experiments are indispensable in order to measure the Kansei factor which humans receive. With this methodology we can measure quantitatively, for instance, the effect of a color, or combination of colors, on an observer.

We employ motion-capturing techniques for obtaining human body movements, which has become common among the communities of film and CG animation production. Several systems are commercially available nowadays.

For this investigation, we used the motions of *Nihon-buyo*, which is a Japanese traditional dance. The reasons why we chose this type of traditional dance form are as follows: First and most importantly, we are conducting research on digitally archiving traditional Japanese dancing, and we are well accustomed with this kind of dance [1, 2]. Secondly, dance in general provides us with much more artistic body motions compared to the human body motions found in our everyday lives, and it should be rather easy to find and discriminate emotional factors in dance movements. In contrast, it is hard to distinctively find and discriminate subtle emotional factors in ordinary body motions.

2. Related works

Some of the related research investigating the relationship between body motion and emotion will be reviewed below.

We have already conducted research in which we used intentionally generated typical body motions with seven different emotions called the "7 motives." The relationship between the physical characteristics of body motion and the impressions has been studied [3].

Nakata et al. investigated the relationship between body motion and emotional impressions by using a simple, pet-like toy robot capable of swinging its hands and head [4]. The motions were generated with a control program, and the change of joint angles could be measured. They used angular velocities and accelerations as motion features. A factor analysis was used for finding the relationship between these features and the Kansei evaluation obtained by human observers. In this research, a theory called LMA, Laban Motion Analysis, was used for characterizing motions. However, since the motions they dealt with were very simple, this model could not be directly applied to human body motions during dance.

LMA theory was also applied to the analysis of body motion [5]. In this case, human body motions during dance, specifically ballet, have been analyzed, and labels indicating LMA features have been attached to motions in each frame. The motion was obtained using a motion-capture system, and some LMA elements have been obtained by analyzing the change of spatial volume which a person produces during dance. The results obtained with this program have been compared with the results obtained by a LMA specialist.

The theory of LMA was also applied in [6], in which modification of neutral motions of CG character animation was done using the concept of LMA Effort and Shape factors in order to add some emotional features to the motion.

Although LMA is a powerful framework for evaluating human body motions qualitatively [5], we think it is not universally applicable, but that some kinds of experimental psychological evaluations are required for its reinforcement.

Motions of Japanese folk dance [7] were analyzed, and fundamental body motion segments and style factors expressing personal characteristics were extracted. Then new realistic motions were generated by adding style factors to the neutral fundamental motions displayed with CG animation. A psychological evaluation was not conducted in this research.

Neutral fundamental motions, such as those motions used when one picks up a glass and takes a drink of water, were modified by applying some transformations to the speed (timing) and amplitude (range) of motion for generating motions with emotions in CG [8]. However, the body motions used were simple.

A psychological investigation was performed to determine what the principal factors were for determining the emotions attached to motions [9]. In this research, by using LEDs attached to several body parts, e.g. head, shoulder, elbows, ankles and hands, motions were analyzed. The result was that the velocity of these body parts had a strong relationship with the emotions expressed by the motions. The results are convincing, but more elaborate analysis of body motions might be required.

A method for extracting Kansei information from a video silhouette image of the body was developed [10]. In this case, the analysis method based on LMA was also implemented. However, the motion of each individual body part was not considered in this research.

3. *Nihon- Buyo* and the work *Hokushu*

The origin of *Nihon-buyo* can be traced back to the early *Edo* period, i.e. early 17t century. Its style matured during the peaceful *Edo* period, which lasted for almost 300 years. Literally interpreted, *Nihon-buyo* means "Japanese dance," but there are many dance forms in Japan other than *Nihon-buyo*. Different from folk dances, *Nihon-buyo* is a sophisticated and stylized dance performance, and its choreography has been maintained by the professional school systems peculiar to the Japanese culture. This differentiates *Nihon-buyo* from other popular folk dances in Japan, which are voluntarily maintained by the general population. The choreography of many *Nihon-buyo* is strongly related to the narratives, which are sung by choruses. Their subjects are taken from legendary tales or popular affairs.

We used a special work of *Nihon-buyo* named *Hokushu* in which a single player performs multiple roles or characters with different personalities successively. The work, often hailed as one of the most elaborately developed dances, depicts the changing seasons and seasonal events as well as the many peoples who come and go in the licensed "red-light district" during the *Edo* era. Despite the name, used here due to the lack of an appropriate English term, the area was a highly sophisticaed, high-class venue for social interaction and entertainment, where *daimyo*, or feudal lords, would often entertain themselves. It is synonymous with "*Yoshiwara*." *Edo* was a typical class society, and people depicted in the play belong to several different social classes and occupations.

In our experiment described below, a female dancer played both female and male characters, although it is sometimes performed by a male dancer. It is said that the *Hokushu* performance requires professional skills and that it is difficult for most people, let alone novices, to portray the many roles in dance form. The play we used for our analysis was performed by a talented, professional dancer.

The *Hokushu* is performed with no particular costume or special hand props, except for just a single folding fan. Photos in Table 1 show a dancer wearing traditional Japanese attire, which is still worn today on formal occasions.

4. Motion capture and the method of analysis

We have used an optical motion capture system (Motion Analysis Corporation, EvaRT with Eagle and Hawk cameras) to measure the body motions of this dance. Figure 1 shows a scene of motion captured in our studio. Reflective markers are attached to the joints of the dancer's body, and several high-precision and high-speed video cameras are used to track the motion.

In our case, 32 markers were put on the dancer's body, and the movement was measured with 10 cameras (see Figure 2). The acquired data can be observed as a time series of three-dimensional coordinate values (x, y, z) of each marker in each frame (frame rate is 60 fps).

Role		Duration	Explanation	Photos
Name	Gender			
Yukyaku	Male	2 sec.	Visitor at a licensed red-light district	
Tayu	Female	35 sec.	"*Geisha*" in the highest rank	
Hokan	Male	9 sec.	Professional entertainer, Comedian	
Bushi	Male	5 sec.	Bureaucrat, "*Samurai*"	
Mago	Male	5 sec.	Horse driver, Coachman	
Shonin	Male	5 sec.	Merchant, Businessman	
Yujo	Female	5 sec.	"*Geisha*"	
Enja	Female	6 sec.	Neutral character, Dancer	

Table 1. Multiple roles performed by a dancer

Fig. 1. Motion capture

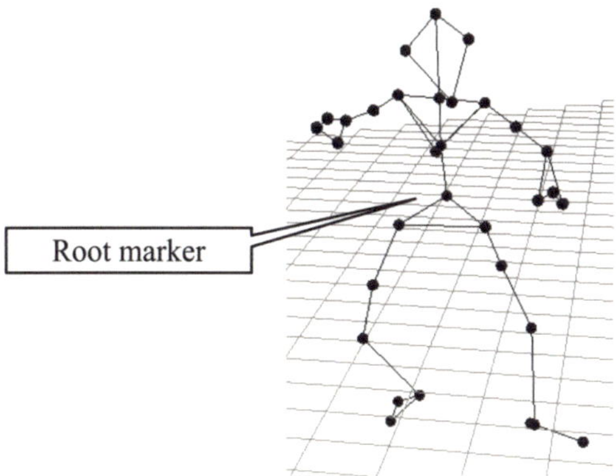

Fig. 2. Positions of markers

5. Psychological rating experiments

In order to examine what type of impression is perceived from the body movement of the eight characters in *Hokushu*, we first conducted a psychological rating experiment using the stick figure animation (see Figure 3) of the motion capture data. Thirty-four observers (21 men and 13 women) participated in this experiment. The mean and the standard deviation of age among the 34 observers are 21.7 and 2.73 respectively. They had no experience in dance performances of any kind and no particular knowledge about this particular dance and the Japanese traditional culture. The animation was projected on a 50-inch display with no sound. Stick-like figure animation and muted audio were used to allow the audience to focus on the Kansei expressed through the body movements alone, discarding other factors, e.g. facial expression, costume, music, etc.

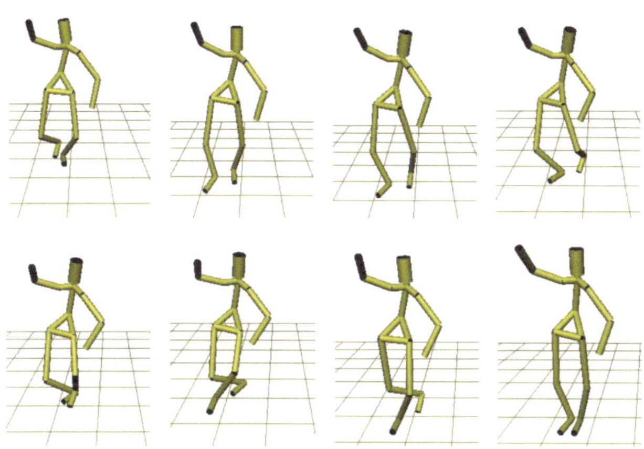

Fig. 3. Stick figure animation used in the experiment

After each movement was shown, the observers were asked to answer the questions on the response sheets. In this rating, we employed the Semantic Differential questionnaire. In the Semantic Differential questionnaire, 18 image-word pairs, which are shown in Table 2, were used for rating the movements. We selected these 18 word pairs, which we considered suitable for the evaluation of human body motions, from the list presented by Osgood [11].

The observers rated the impression of the movement by placing checks in each word pair scale on a sheet.
The rating was done on a scale ranking from 1 to 7. Rank 1 is assigned to the left-hand word of each word pair and 7 for the right-hand word as shown in Table 2. Using this rating, we obtained a numerical value representing an impression for each of the body motions from each subject. Table 3 shows the results of the experiment, in which mean values of the rating scores were obtained from all of the subjects for each image-word pair obtained from the eight motions listed.

	1 2 3 4 5 6 7	
Light	--+--+--+--+--+--+--+--	Dark
Strong	--+--+--+--+--+--+--+--	Weak
Complex	--+--+--+--+--+--+--+--	Simple
Sharp	--+--+--+--+--+--+--+--	Blunt
Hard	--+--+--+--+--+--+--+--	Soft
Excitable	--+--+--+--+--+--+--+--	Calm
Straight	--+--+--+--+--+--+--+--	Curved
Graceful	--+--+--+--+--+--+--+--	Awkward
Serious	--+--+--+--+--+--+--+--	Humorous
Stable	--+--+--+--+--+--+--+--	Changeable
Beautiful	--+--+--+--+--+--+--+--	Ugly
Pleasurable	-+--+--+--+--+--+--+--	Painful
Large	--+--+--+--+--+--+--+--	Small
Colorful	--+--+--+--+--+--+--+--	Colorless
Noble	--+--+--+--+--+--+--+--	Vulgar
Cheerful	--+--+--+--+--+--+--+--	Gloomy
Masculine	--+--+--+--+--+--+--+--	Feminine
Angular	--+--+--+--+--+--+--+--	Rounded

Table 2. 18 image-word pairs

Image-word pairs	*Yukyaku*	*Tayu*	*Hokan*	*Bushi*	*Mago*	*Shonin*	*Yujo*	*Enja*
Light-Dark	2.62	5.21	4.15	4.79	3.47	1.91	2.97	4.74
Strong-Weak	3.26	3.62	4.76	4.38	4.74	3.29	4.26	3.35
Complex-Simple	5.29	3.09	4.03	5.41	3.97	3.94	4.00	5.09
Sharp-Blunt	3.62	4.62	4.62	5.15	4.76	3.76	3.94	3.26
Hard-Soft	4.65	3.26	4.85	4.12	5.06	5.53	5.24	2.97
Excitable-Calm	3.94	5.82	5.29	5.88	4.21	2.97	3.82	5.26
Straight-Curved	3.29	4.24	4.65	3.88	5.59	5.06	5.06	2.21
Graceful-Awkward	3.41	2.74	3.18	3.06	4.97	4.74	3.12	2.76
Serious-Humorous	3.82	2.68	3.62	3.18	5.29	6.00	3.79	2.21
Stable-Changeable	3.06	3.29	3.47	2.79	5.24	4.44	3.71	2.26
Beautiful-Ugly	3.09	3.12	3.47	3.59	4.50	4.12	2.88	3.09
Pleasurable-Painful	3.29	5.00	3.85	4.44	3.32	2.06	3.32	4.32
Large-Small	3.18	3.91	4.79	4.65	4.68	2.76	3.65	4.09
Colorful-Colorless	3.47	4.68	4.38	5.42	4.38	3.03	2.91	4.74
Noble-Vulgar	3.44	2.76	3.56	3.59	4.94	4.76	3.38	2.91
Cheerful-Gloomy	3.03	4.97	3.82	4.85	3.62	1.76	3.38	4.65
Masculine-Feminine	3.62	3.94	5.00	3.56	3.38	2.44	5.76	3.38
Angular-Rounded	4.06	3.97	5.00	4.21	5.12	5.06	5.29	2.79

Table 3. Mean values of scores in 18 image-word pairs

Then we applied a principal component analysis, PCA, (based on a correlation matrix) to the mean value of the rating value shown in Table 3 and obtained the principal component matrix. Four significant principal components were extracted, which are PC1-PC4 shown in Table 4.
Table 4 shows the values of factor loading of each word pair to four principal components, and the shaded areas in the table indicate the significant image-word pair ratings to each principal component, whose magnitude is larger than 0.6. In the shaded area in the PC1 column, we can find the word pairs "excitable-calm," "pleasurable-painful" and "cheerful-gloomy," etc., which are often used to represent activity. Hence, it is interpreted that PC1 is a variable related to the "activity" behind the motion. Similarly, PC2 is related to "potency," because we can find the word pairs "sharp-blunt," "strong-weak" and "large-small" in that column. For each PC3 and PC4, only a single word pair, "masculine-feminine" and "complex-simple" respectively, is found. Therefore, we could interpret PC3 as a variable related to "gender" and PC4 as being related to "complexity."

	PC1	PC2	PC3	PC4
Light-Dark	-0.884	0.413	0.105	-0.174
Strong-Weak	0.076	0.897	-0.240	0.332
Complex-Simple	-0.272	-0.341	0.370	0.805
Sharp-Blunt	-0.083	0.912	0.049	0.002
Hard-Soft	0.908	0.125	-0.259	0.277
Excitable-Calm	-0.886	0.426	0.091	-0.045
Straight-Curved	0.733	0.580	-0.275	-0.193
Graceful-Awkward	0.886	0.179	0.398	-0.042
Serious-Humorous	0.978	0.099	0.171	-0.018
Stable-Changeable	0.849	0.421	0.042	-0.232
Beautiful-Ugly	0.637	0.478	0.596	-0.038
Pleasurable-Painful	-0.930	0.301	-0.022	-0.168
Large-Small	-0.435	0.815	0.076	0.264
Colorful-Colorless	-0.714	0.508	0.474	0.050
Noble-Vulgar	0.872	0.283	0.378	0.105
Cheerful-Gloomy	-0.905	0.379	0.051	-0.071
Masculine-Feminine	-0.206	0.240	-0.916	0.200
Angular-Rounded	0.774	0.447	-0.417	0.062
Eigenvalue	9.669	4.397	2.294	1.122
Variance (%)	53.715	78.140	90.885	97.120

Table 4. Results of PCA for the rating experiment

Consequently, we can conclude that we recognize the characteristics of motions of *Hokushu* based on these four aspects: activity, potency, gender and complexity.
Figure 4 is a plot of the principal component score of each motion datum. Observing Figure 4, we can see that, for instance, a motion of *Shonin* is active, strong and masculine, a motion of *Tayu* inactive and complex and a motion of *Yujo* feminine.
By this analysis, the impressional features of each motion were clarified. However, the impressional features obtained so far by the experiment were based on the subjective perception of the observers. We then had to examine the relationship between the subjective feature perceived by the observers and the physical characteristics of body movements.

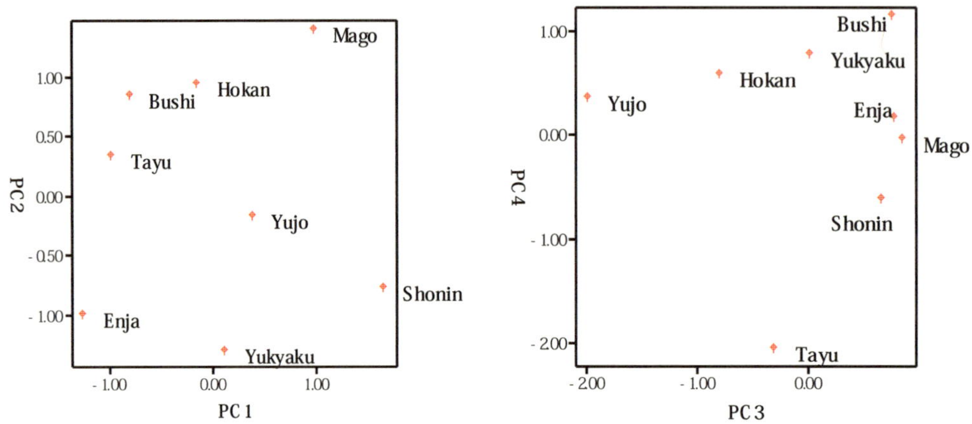

(a) PC1 vs PC2 (b) PC3 vs PC4

Fig. 4. Plot of PCA score for each motion

6. Feature values for body motion

In this research, we extracted 22 physical parameters from the motion capture data. These parameters consist of four types. One is related to the velocities of certain body parts, namely, the velocities of the head, the left and right hands, the waist and the left and right feet.

The second parameter is related to the shape of the body: angle of the left and right knees. The third category is related to the size of the body: the area span of the body, which is the size of the space occupied by the body, and the height of the waist. The last parameter is related to smoothness: acceleration of waist motion.

As stated earlier in Section II, it was found that the velocity of body parts, especially end effectors, had a strong relationship with the emotions expressed by motions [9]. Looking at this result, we mainly focused on the velocity (actual magnitudes of velocities) of end effectors. In addition to these velocity features, we also used several features related to the shape of the body, size of the body and size of the space occupied by the body. In order to evaluate the smoothness of the whole body motion, we used the acceleration of the motion of the waist.

Velocities of end effectors are calculated by using relative coordinates measured from the origin placed at the root marker shown in Figure 2. Contrastingly, the velocity and acceleration of the waist is calculated in the absolute coordinate system.

Mean values and standard deviation (SD) values of these physical parameters were used for the feature values representing human body motions. We simply disregarded the variation in time of these values during the motion by taking an average and an SD. However, we also found that these kinds of simple feature values gave fairly satisfactory results in the recognition of dance body motion, which was used for our dance collaboration system [12].

We also applied a principal component analysis (based on a correlation matrix) for these physical parameters to obtain a principal component matrix. Four principal components were extracted, which are shown as PC1 through PC4 in Table 5.

By observing Table 5, it can be understood that PC1 correlates to "speed," PC2 the "height of the waist (angle of the knees)," PC3 the "area of the body" and PC4 the "variation of height of the waist." Figure 5 is a plot showing the principal component scores of our motion data.

	PC1	PC2	PC3	PC4
Mean velocity of the head	0.808	-0.344	0.036	0.427
Mean velocity of the left hand	0.928	0.325	-0.037	-0.094
Mean velocity of the right hand	0.850	0.467	-0.094	-0.208
Mean velocity of the waist	0.783	-0.511	0.138	0.295
Mean velocity of the left foot	0.541	-0.649	0.337	0.231
Mean velocity of the right foot	0.905	0.066	-0.118	-0.072
SD velocity of the head	0.431	-0.460	0.599	-0.046
SD velocity of the left hand	0.747	0.496	0.101	-0.397
SD velocity of the right hand	0.778	0.525	0.038	-0.311
SD velocity of the waist	0.586	-0.572	0.461	-0.053
SD velocity of the left foot	0.657	-0.686	0.035	0.159
SD velocity of the right foot	0.902	-0.275	-0.212	-0.011
Mean angle of the left knee	0.164	0.748	0.592	0.235
Mean angle of the right knee	0.113	0.923	0.334	0.086
SD angle of the left knee	0.070	0.562	-0.330	0.715
SD angle of the right knee	-0.014	0.893	-0.023	0.382
Mean area of the body	0.771	0.123	-0.558	-0.085
SD area of the body	0.742	0.224	-0.555	-0.257
Mean height of the waist	-0.046	-0.837	-0.530	-0.053
SD height of the waist	0.295	-0.006	-0.284	0.598
Mean acceleration of the waist	0.952	0.139	-0.088	0.186
SD acceleration of the waist	0.924	0.043	0.336	-0.073
Eigenvalue	9.939	6.048	2.458	1.857
Variance (%)	45.177	72.669	83.843	92.285

Table 5. Result of PCA for motion feature values

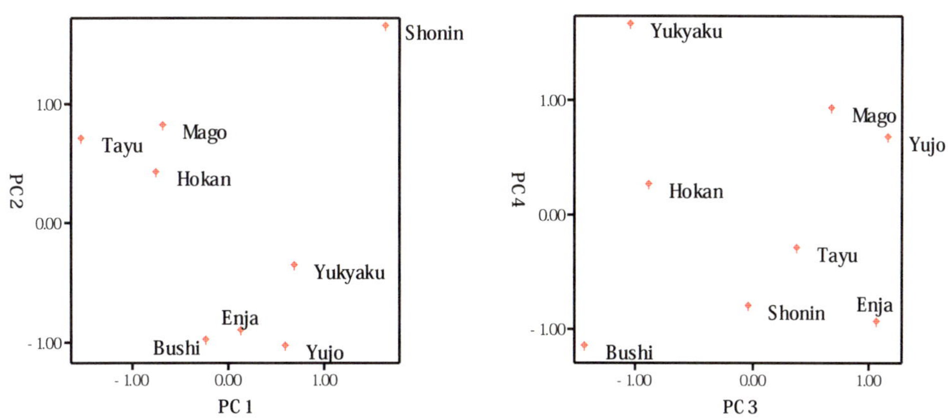

(a) PC1 vs PC2 (b) PC3 vs PC4

Fig. 5. Plot of PCA score for motion feature values

7. Multiple regression analysis

We investigated the regression between the impression and the physical feature values of movements. In the multiple regression analysis, we set the physical feature values obtained from our motion capture data as independent variables and the principal component scores of impressions determined by observers (for example, PC1: activity, PC2: potency, etc.) as dependent variables (by the stepwise procedure). Table 6 shows the results of the analysis, standardized coefficients ($p<0.05$) and the scores of adjusted R^2.

Dependent Variables	Independent Variables	Standardized Coefficients	Adjusted R^2
PC1 (Activity)	Mean acceleration of the waist	0.642**	0.840
	SD angle of the right knee	0.586*	
PC2 (Potency)	SD velocity of the waist	-0.596**	0.907
	SD height of the waist	-0.487*	
	SD velocity of the left hand	-0.344*	
PC3 (Gender)			
PC4 (Complexity)	Mean height of the waist	0.770*	0.525

*…$p<0.05$, **…$p<0.01$

Table 6. Result of multiple regression analysis

As a result, three regression models with high significance were obtained, except for PC3 (significance level $p<0.05$).

From this result of our regression analysis, we found that the physical motion feature that contributes to "activity" is <Mean acceleration of the waist> and <SD angle of the right knee>. Similarly, <SD velocity of the waist>, <SD height of the waist> and <SD velocity of the left hand> contribute to the property of "potency," whereas <Mean height of the waist> is a factor of "complexity."

The result shows that impressions obtained from body motions mainly stem from motions located at some specific body parts, especially impressions concerning "activity," "potency" and "complexity," which can be estimated from motions of the waist, knees and hands. The result may apply only to the target dance motion used in this study, but it is a convincing result in that this kind of analysis can be used for extracting impressions from motion.

Although, as stated earlier, we found a factor related to "gender" in psychological experiments, we could not find any regression model for "gender" with a sufficient level of significance this time. We should have employed other physical parameters that can explain "gender" qualities, for instance, smoothness of movements, etc. This is left for further investigation.

At this time, we did not use the variables obtained by the PCA described in the previous section as the independent variables, because we could not find any significant regression model in this case. However, the regression analysis using the original 22 physical feature values is rather useful for understanding the direct relationship between physical body motions and emotions or personalities.

8. Discussion and conclusion

This research was intended to investigate the relationship between body motions and Kansei, or emotional features, conveyed by the motions. The very special dance work in which a single performer plays several different roles or characters has been used for the subject of the investigation.

Through a psychological rating experiment observing a CG character animation in an abstract representation, we found that the observer recognized the impressional factors of the body motions of each individual character or role based on four aspects: (1) activity, (2) potency, (3) gender and (4) complexity of the motions.

In this research, psychological rating experiments were done by using stick-figure CG animation characters generated from the motion captured data. Although pure physical body motion is subjected to analysis, excluding the effects of the gender of a performer, facial expressions and costumes, we found that the personalities (including gender and social class) of the characters played by the dancer were expressed well.

Also, some physical factors which contribute to the specific impressions of the motions were revealed, and a model showing the relationship between them was derived.

These results could be applied to producing a robot or CG character animation with a personality. Until now, many attempts have been made to add or enhance the emotional expression of robots using linguistic communication, some simple body motions, e.g. nodding, and facial expressions. Also, changing the design or shape of robots might be a simple way of providing a robot with a personality. However, we could not find much research on giving robots personalities through body motions.

We think that changing the personalities of robots by changing their body motions and changing the emotional expressions relayed through the robot's body motions are very promising areas for further investigation.

Future work includes (1) the study of body motions of other dance styles, e.g. contemporary dance, (2) investigation of other models besides the linear regression models, e.g. use of neural networks, and (3) use of physical feature values which take the variation in time into account.

9. Acknowledgments

This work was supported in part by the Global COE Program and Grant-in-Aid for Scientific Research (A) No. 18200020 and (B) Nos. 16300035 and 19300031 of the Ministry of Education, Culture, Sports, Science and Technology, Japan.

The authors would like to express their sincere gratitude to Ms. Daizo Hanayagi for her cooperation with our research. Thanks are also due to Dr. Woong Choi for his kind help in motion capturing and the students at the Hachimura laboratory for their help in the post-processing of our motion data.

10. References

Amaya, K., Bruderlin, A., Calvert, T. (1996). Emotion from Motion, *Proc. Graphics Interface 1996*, pp.222-229.

Camurri, A., Hashimoto, S., Suzuki, K, and Trocca, R. (1999). KANSEI Analysis of Dance Performance, *Proc. IEEE SMC '99 Conference*, Vol. 4, pp.327-332.

Chi, D., Costa, M., and Zhao, L., et al. (2000). The EMOTE Model for Effort and Shape, *ACM SIGGRAPH'00 Proceedings*, pp.173-182.

Hachimura, K., Takashina, K., and Yoshimura, M. (2005). Analysis and Evaluation of Dancing Movement Based on LMA, *Proc. 2005 IEEE International Workshop on Robots and Human Interactive Communication*, pp.294-299.

Hachimura, K. (2006). Digital Archiving of Dancing, *Review of the National Center for Digitization*, Vol.8, pp.51-66.

Nakata, T., Mori, T., and Sato, T. (2002). Analysis of Impression of Robot Bodily Expression, *Journal of Robotics and Mechatronics*, Vol.14, No.1, pp.27-36.

Nakazawa, A., Nakaoka, S., Shiratori, T., and Ikeuchi, K. (2003). Analysis and Synthesis of Human Dance Motions, *Proc. IEEE Conf. on Multisensor Fusion and Integration for Intelligent Systems 2003*, pp.83-88.

Osgood, C. E. et al. (1957) The measurement of meaning, U. of Illinois Press.

Paterson, H., Pollick, F., and Stanford, A. (2001). The Role of Velocity in Affect Discrimination, *Proc. 23rd Annual Conference of the Cognitive Scinece Society*, pp.756-761.

Sakata, M., Hachimura, K.. (2007). KANSEI Information Processing of Human Body Movement, *Human Interface, Part I, HCII2007* (Smith and Salvendy eds.), LNCS 4557, pp.930-939.

Tsuruta, S., Kawauchi, Y., Choi, W., and Hachimrua, K. (2007). Real-Time Recognition of Body Motion for Virtual Dance Collaboration System, *Proc.17th Int. Conf. on Artificial Reality and Telexistance*, pp.23-30.

Yoshimura, M., Hachimura, K., and Marumo, Yuka. (2006). Comparison of Structural Variables with Spatio-temporal Variables Concerning the Identification of Okuri Class and Player in Japanese Traditional Dancing, *Proc. ICPR06*, Vol.3, pp.308-311.

2

Towards Semantically Intelligent Robots

Atilla Elçi and Behnam Rahnama
Eastern Mediterranean University
North Cyprus

1. Introduction

Approaches are needed for providing advanced autonomous wheeled robots with a sense of self, immediate ambience, and mission. The following list of abilities would form the desired feature set of such approaches: self-localization, detection and correction of course deviation errors, faster and more reliable identification of friend or foe, simultaneous localization and mapping in uncharted environments without necessarily depending on external assistance, and being able to serve as web services. Situations, where enhanced robots with such rich feature sets come to play, span competitions such as line following, cooperative mini sumo fighting, and cooperative labyrinth discovery. In this chapter we look into how such features may be realized towards creating intelligent robots.

Currently through-cell localization in robots mainly relies on availability of shaft-encoders. In this regard, we would like to firstly present a simple-to-implement through-cell localization approach for robots even without a shaft-encoder in order to empower them to traverse approximately on the desired course (curve or linear) and end up registered properly at the desired target position. Researchers have presented ways including fuzzy- and neural-based control systems for correcting the navigation deviation error. By providing a formulation for deviation error, especially during turning curves, and then applying reverse formulation to correct it, our self-corrective gyroscope-accelerometer-encoder cascade control system adjusts the robot even more. When the robot detects that it has yawed off course, the system affects the requisite maneuvering and its timing in order to correct the deviation from course.

Next step is to facilitate robots with ability of Friend-or-Foe (FoF) identification for cooperative multi-robot tasks. Mini-sumo team robots are well-known case-in-point where FoF identification capability would be most welcome whereas absolute positioning of teammates is not practical. Our simple-to-implement FoF identification does not require two-way communication as it only relies on decryption of payload in one direction. It is shown that the replay attack is not feasible due to high computation complexity as the communication is encrypted and timestamp is inserted in the messages. Our hardware implementation of cooperative robots incorporates a gyroscope chipset and rotary radar which is able to sense the direction and distance to detected object. Studying dynamics of robots allows finding solutions to attack even stronger enemy from sides so they will not be able to resist. Besides, there are certain situations that robots must evade or even try escaping instead of facing a fight. Our experimental work here attempts to illustrate situations of real battlefields of cooperative mini-sumo competitions as an example of localization, mapping, and collaborative problem solving in uncharted environments.

Simultaneous localization and mapping (SLAM) is another feature we wish to discuss here. Within this respect, robots are not only able to identify friends from foes but also they construct a real-time map of the situation without use of expensive equipments as laser beam sensors or vision cells.
There have been a lot of change and improvement in robotics within current decade. Today, humanoid robots such as ASIMO are able to talk, walk, learn and communicate. On the other hand, there are new trends for self-adjustment and calibration in wheeled robots. Both humanoid and wheeled robots may be able to identify friends or foes, communicate with others, and correct deviation errors. Researchers have provided quite acceptable balance mechanisms for any type of inverted pendulum based robots from a range of humanoids holding themselves on one leg to wheeled robots standing on a wheel or two while moving. Yet they cannot jump, nor run on irregular surfaces like humans do. However, there are many other features including speech synthesizing and video processing enabled on more advanced robots.
Advanced robots should be equipped with further human-like capability to reason and base it on knowing the meaning of its surroundings. At this point, we tend to introduce the subject of Semantic Intelligence (SI) as opposed to and in augmentation of conventional artificial intelligence. Better understanding of environment, and reasoning necessarily through SI fueled by the intelligence of knowing the meaning of what goes around. In other words, SI would be enabling robots with the power of imagination as we do. As future study, we aim to shed some light on bases of robotic behavior towards thinking, learning, and imagining the way human being does through Semantic Intelligence Reasoning.
In next section, we will discuss self localization of robots with limited resources while they have neither shaft encoders nor gyroscope. Consequent section will represent more advanced family of robots where they are able to correct deviated errors with use of gyroscope, accelerometer, and shaft encoder in a triple cascaded loop. Section 4 presents our formulations and algorithms for identification of Friend or Foe and responding accordingly in battle of multi and collaborative robots. Then we will present Simultaneous Localization and Mapping for multi collaborative robots in section 5. Section 6 will cover a brief introductory on Semantic Intelligence and application example for solving a robotic problem. Finally the chapter is concluded in section 7.

2. Through-cell self-localization

Line following is one of the simplest categories of wheeled robots. Line following robots is mainly equipped with two DC motors for left and right wheels and line tracking sensors which is a set of 1 to 6 Infrared transceiver pairs. (Notice that using only one sensor to follow a line makes the robot able to only follow edge of a connected and simple path without extra loops). Microrobot Cruiser robot (Active-Robots) were selected for this section due to the simplicity of design. In addition, there is neither shaft encoder nor gyroscope on this robot. It is aimed to enable even such robots to traverse the desired curve or path.
As can be seen in Fig. 1 (A), the front side of the robot is equipped with 6 IR sensors (3 at left and at right side) each one consisting of an infrared transmitter LED and an infrared receiver transistor read by ADC port of the microcontroller. The ADC port output is a voltage between $[0, V_{max}]$ presenting the reverse relation with distance to reflector (an obstacle, for example, walls in labyrinth platform). Sensors provide V_{max} approximately when the robot so close as to touch a wall. Initial calibration may be performed by keeping

the sensors as close as possible to reflector and then recording the captured voltage. The output of 6 sensors is presented by the $[(F_l, F_r), (S_l, S_r), (B_l, B_r)]$ tuples where subscripts l and r are respectively for sensors placed at left and right side of the robot. F is for front sensor, S shows side sensor and finally B indicates the sensors installed to watch 45° towards backside of the robot on both sides (i.e. S_l is the voltage level of left side IR sensor). When a robot is in the center of a cell with approximately same distance from either side walls, we end up with $S_l \simeq S_r \simeq V_n$ s.t. $V_n \in [0, V_{max}]$. Notice that V_{max}stands for maximum voltage captured from sensors and let's assume that v_{max} represents the maximum velocity of motors.

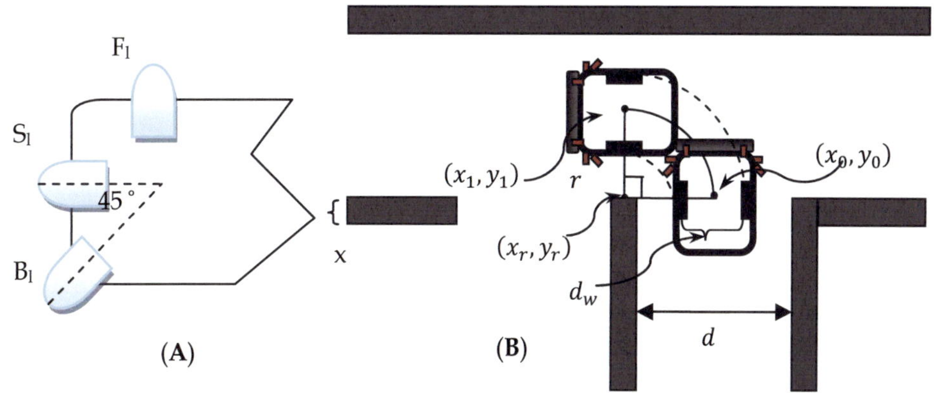

Fig. 1. left section of sensor boards of Microrobot Cruiser robot (A), and Turning left over the perimeter of the circle in a labyrinth: representation of a situation where the decision maker has decreed that the robot is to turn left (B).

For a robot turning toward a direction, its starting position is important. The radius of the curve and its length need be calculated. The main points are deciding on which curve (radius defines it) is the best choice, and when the turn has been accomplished. It is assumed that the best curve is the one which keeps the robot straddling the middle line of the next cell.

Practically, if $V_n - \alpha \le S_l \simeq S_r \le V_n + \alpha$, where α is a small threshold value and $V_a - \alpha \le B_l \simeq B_r \le V_a + \alpha$, $V_a < V_n$ then the robot continues moving straight so that $S_l \simeq 0$ or $S_r \simeq 0$ (depending on the direction of turn) until ($B_l < V_a - \alpha$ or $B_r < V_a - \alpha$). It indicates that the center of axes of wheels is approximately on (x_0, y_0). Now on the robot can start turning over the desired curve with defined radius. Therefore, it traverses a quarter of perimeter of the circle with radius r $\left(r = \frac{x}{2} + \frac{d}{2} \right)$ in which its initial point is (x_0, y_0) and its destination point is (x_1, y_1). Notice that x is the thickness of a wall and d is the distance between two walls or the cell width. We assume that $(x_0, y_0) := (0,0)$ as initial point befor turning and $(x_1, y_1) := (-r, r)$ is the point after turning left, whereas (x_1, y_1) would be (r, r) for turning right. As a result, traversed distance over the perimeter of inner and outer curves is calculated by the following formula (1). Additionally, we require adjusting the speed of motors as shown in (2); it's clear that the robot does not need shaft encoders in order to measure the traversed distance. Turning is continued until $B_l > V_a - \alpha$ (for turning left) or $B_r < V_a - \alpha$ (while turning right).

$$\begin{cases} \text{Turning Left: } P_l = 2\pi\left(r - \frac{d_w}{2}\right), P_r = 2\pi\left(r + \frac{d_w}{2}\right) \\ \text{Turning Right: } P_l = 2\pi\left(r + \frac{d_w}{2}\right), P_r = 2\pi\left(r - \frac{d_w}{2}\right) \end{cases} \tag{1}$$

$$\begin{cases} \text{Turning Left: } v_l = \frac{P_l}{P_r} v_{max}, v_r = v_{max} \\ \text{Turning Right: } v_l = v_{max}, v_r = \frac{P_r}{P_l} v_{max} \end{cases} \tag{2}$$

Now let's consider more advanced robots which are widely used in real-life where not only pushing the robot to follow a specific curve is intended but also error detection and correction is considered simultaneously. Autonomous Guided Vehicles (AGVs) are highly used everywhere. Next section presents a solution to error detection and correction in situations that the machine works properly however, problems such as slippage causes deviation.

3. Self-corrective cascaded control

Self-corrective gyroscope-accelerometer-encoder cascade control system adjusts the robot if the host vehicle deviates from its designated lane. In case the vehicle detects that it has yawed away, the system calculates a desired maneuvering moment in order to correct deviation. The calculation is simply addition/subtraction from the desired value of movement expected from shaft encoder sensors of both wheels. This is done by steering the host vehicle back on course in a direction that avoids the host vehicle's lane deviation. The system compensates for the desired yawing moment by a correction factor or a gain. Manufacturing a new generation of AGVs with ability of self-corrective gyroscope-accelerometer-encoder cascade control system will improve current AGVs and cooperative robots to overcome their major difficulties and improve their utility.

When measuring odometry errors, one must distinguish between 1) ***Systematic*** errors and 2) ***non-systematic*** errors. Systematic errors are caused by kinematic imperfections of the mobile robot (i.e. unequal wheel-diameters). Another systematic error caused in many researches is simplifying kinematic control properties by default values (i.e. $d = 0$, d is distance from new referenced point to intersection of rear wheel axis and symmetry axis of mobile robot). Extending the kinematic control into dynamics level, the majority of researchers consider the general case of $d = 0$ in dynamic model of mobile robot, whereas the restriction of I = 0 is mostly imposed by the kinematic controller (Pengcheng & Zhicheng, 2007). On the other hand, non-systematic errors may be caused by wheel-slippage or irregularities of the floor. University of Michigan Benchmark test (UMBmark), is a test method for systematic errors prescribing a simple testing procedure designed to quantitatively measure the odometric accuracy of a mobile robot (Borenstein & Feng, 1995). Non-systematic errors are more difficult to be detected. Cascade control systems for localization are more reliable in this sense.

J. Borenstein et al (Borenstein et al., 1997) defined seven categories for positioning systems based on the type of sensors used in controlling the robot. 1) ***Odometry*** is based on simple equations which hold true when wheel revolutions can be translated accurately into linear displacement relative to the floor. However, in case of wheel slippage and some other more subtle causes, wheel rotations may not translate proportionally into linear motion. The resulting errors can be categorized into one of two groups: systematic errors and non-systematic errors. 2) ***Inertial Navigation*** uses gyroscopes and accelerometers to measure rate of rotation and acceleration, respectively. Measurements are integrated once (or twice, for accelerometers) to yield position. 3) ***Magnetic Compass*** is widely used. However, the earth's magnetic field is often distorted near power lines or steel structures. Besides, the speed of measurement and accuracy is low. There are several types of magnetic compasses due to variety of physical effects related to the earth's magnetic field. Some of them include Mechanical, Fluxgate, Hall-effect, Magnetoresistive, and Magnetoelastic compasses. 4) ***Active Beacons*** navigation systems are the most common navigation aids on ships and airplanes, as well as on commercial mobile robot systems. Two different types of active beacon systems can be distinguished: trilateration that is the determination of a vehicle's position based on distance measurements to known beacon sources; and triangulation, which in this configuration there are three or more active transmitters mounted at known locations. 5) ***Global Positioning System*** (GPS) is a revolutionary technology for outdoor navigation. GPS was developed as a Joint Services Program by the Department of Defense. However, GPS is not applicable in most of robotics fields due to two reasons, firstly, unavailability of GPS signals indoor; and secondly, low accuracy in small prototype single chip GPS receivers used in cellular phones and robot boards. 6) Landmark Navigation is based on landmarks that are distinct features so a robot can recognize from its sensory input. Landmarks can be geometric shapes (e.g., rectangles, lines, circles), and they may include additional information (e.g., in the form of bar-codes). In general, landmarks have a fixed and known position, relative to which a robot can localize itself. 7) ***Model Matching*** or ***Map-based positioning***, also known as ***map matching*** is a technique in which the robot uses its sensors to create a map of its local environment. This local map is then compared to a global map previously stored in memory. If a match is found, then the robot can compute its actual position and orientation in the environment. Certainly there are lots of situations where achieving global map is unfeasible or prohibited. Therefore, solutions based on independent sensors carried on robots are more likely valued.

Some applications of cascade control can be seen in the research done by (Ke et al., 2004) where cascade control strategy of robot subsystem has been applied instead of the widely used single speed-feedback closed-loop control strategy. They provided the cascade control system such that the outer loop is to regulate speed of the wheel; the inner loop is to adjust the current passing through the DC-motor. By applying cascade control system to DC-motor, the unexpected time-delay and inaccuracy can be reduced. The dynamic features of robots motion and anti-interference of robots can be improved. At the same time, the damage of current to DC-motor can be dropped and the life span of DC-motor can be prolonged.

Various control strategies for mobile robot formations have been reported in the literature, including behavior based methods, virtual structure techniques, and leader–follower schemes (Defoort et al., 2008). Among them, the leader–follower approaches have been well recognized and become the most popular approaches.

The basic idea of this scheme is that one robot is selected as leader and is responsible for guiding the formation. The other robots, called followers, are required to track the position and orientation of the leader with some prescribed offsets. The advantage of using such a strategy is that specifying a single quantity (the leader's motion) directs the group behavior. In followers, sliding-mode formation controller is applied which is only based on the derivation of relative motion states. It eliminates the need for measurement or estimation of the absolute velocity of the leader and enables formation control using vision systems carried by the followers. However, it creates bottleneck for message passing and decision making while it can be improved by decentralized autonomous control such as in (Elçi & Rahnama, 2009) on the other hand, situations wherein the leader dies is not considered.

Other method of cascade control in robotics is with use of multi visual elements in positioning and controlling the motion of articulated arms (Lippiello et al., 2007). In a multi arm robotic cell, visual systems are usually composed of two or more cameras that can be rigidly attached to the robot end-effectors or fixed in the workspace. Hence, the use of both configurations at the same time makes the execution of complex tasks easier and offers higher flexibility in the presence of a dynamic scenario.

Cascade control for positioning is also used in Unmanned Aerial Vehicles (UAVs). A decentralized cascade control system including autopilot and trajectory control units presents more precise collision avoidance strategy (Boivin et al., 2008).

3.1 Impact and significance of self-corrective AGVs in human life

Following information on various application areas of AGVs is presented in order to highlight wide spectrum of applicability of the results of the upgraded AGVs.

3.1.1 AGVs for automobile manufacturing

Typical AGV applications in the automotive industry include automated raw material delivery, automated work in process movements between manufacturing cells, and finished goods transport. AGVs link shipping/receiving, warehousing, and production with just-in-time part deliveries that minimize line side storage requirements. AGV systems help create the fork-free manufacturing environment which many plants in the automotive industry are seeking.

3.1.2 Hospitals

Using an AGV Automated Transport System (ATS) frees hospital employees to spend a maximum amount of their time directly on patient care. It improves safety in the hospital by minimizing the potential for hospital workers to be injured pushing heavy carts. It tracks all material movements and can prioritize jobs so that the most important tasks can be completed first (for example: surgical supplies, then patient meals, then linens, then trash, etc.) The AGV can be outfitted with obstacle detection sensors which bring it to a safe stop before contacting any obstacles that might be in its path. It is reliable, safe, efficient and cost effective.

3.1.3 AGV (Automated Guided Vehicle) systems for the manufacturing industry

Timely movement of materials is a critical element to an efficient manufacturing operation. The costs associated with delivering raw materials, moving work in process and removing finished goods must be minimized while also minimizing any product damage that is the result of improper handling. An AGV system helps streamline operations while also delivering improved safety and tracking the movement of materials.

Our aim is to create a universal AGV controller board with the abilities as explained in the previous section. Manufacturing a new generation of AGVs with ability of Self-Corrective Compass Cascaded Control System will improve current AGVs to overcome difficulties mentioned earlier.

The product is a universal robot controller board which can be produced and exported worldwide. Future enhancements were taken into account as covering more servo/stepper motors for full fledged robots serving different purposes.

3.2 Cascaded control method

AGVs are widely used in production lines of factories. They mostly track a line on floor rather than being able to accurately follow dynamics of planned trajectories of start and end positions. In more advanced cases, they are equipped with a feedback control loop, which corrects the deviation errors due to movement imperfection of actuators and motors. This section presents triple feedback loops consisting of gyroscope, accelerometer, and shaft-encoder to provide self-corrective cascade control system.

A cascade control system is a multiple-loop system where the primary variable is controlled by adjusting the set point of a related secondary variable controller. The secondary variable then affects the primary variable through the process.

The primary objective in cascade control is to divide an otherwise difficult to control process into two portions, whereby a secondary control loop is formed around major disturbances thus leaving only minor disturbances to be controlled by the primary controller.

Despite the fact that first loop (which might be implemented by a PID controller) detects and corrects deviation errors in trajectory planning, however in practice there are disturbances that are generally excluded in theoretical implementations. Nevertheless, disturbances such as friction and slippage are highly important and are frequently happening in real life robotic implementations. For instance, an oily floor in factory causes AGVs to slide however, the primary control does not recognize it.

In such a scenario, Global Positioning System (GPS) is not useful either because rotational errors (without movement of the position) are not detectable. In addition, in real life examples of factories, reading GPS signals indoor is barely possible. Besides, accuracy of GPS receptors is very low in small form factor carried by tiny robots.

On the other hand, errors caused by skidding wheels while robot has not moved or parallel deviation can be detected by a ternary control loop using not only detection of movement, but also detection of acceleration towards each axis.

3.3 Feedback control mechanism:

Essentially the movement of the robot is translated in terms of number of Pulses generated from shaft-encoders connected to each wheel. The number of Steps estimates the length of movement and rotation of each wheel. However it might face with an error in movement. Therefore, the robot is deviated from the straight line. Consequently, error on both motors at the same time do not deviate the robot from the line but it causes less or more movement on that line. Therefore, the trajectory planning of the robot movement is planned as a rectangle starting from a vertex and return to the same after passing all four edges.

This path is divided into smaller sub paths based on number of traversed pulses. And at each, the magnetic angle of the robot is read using the compass module. If the robot is deviated the correct value for control algorithm is calculated to eliminate and minimize the total error.

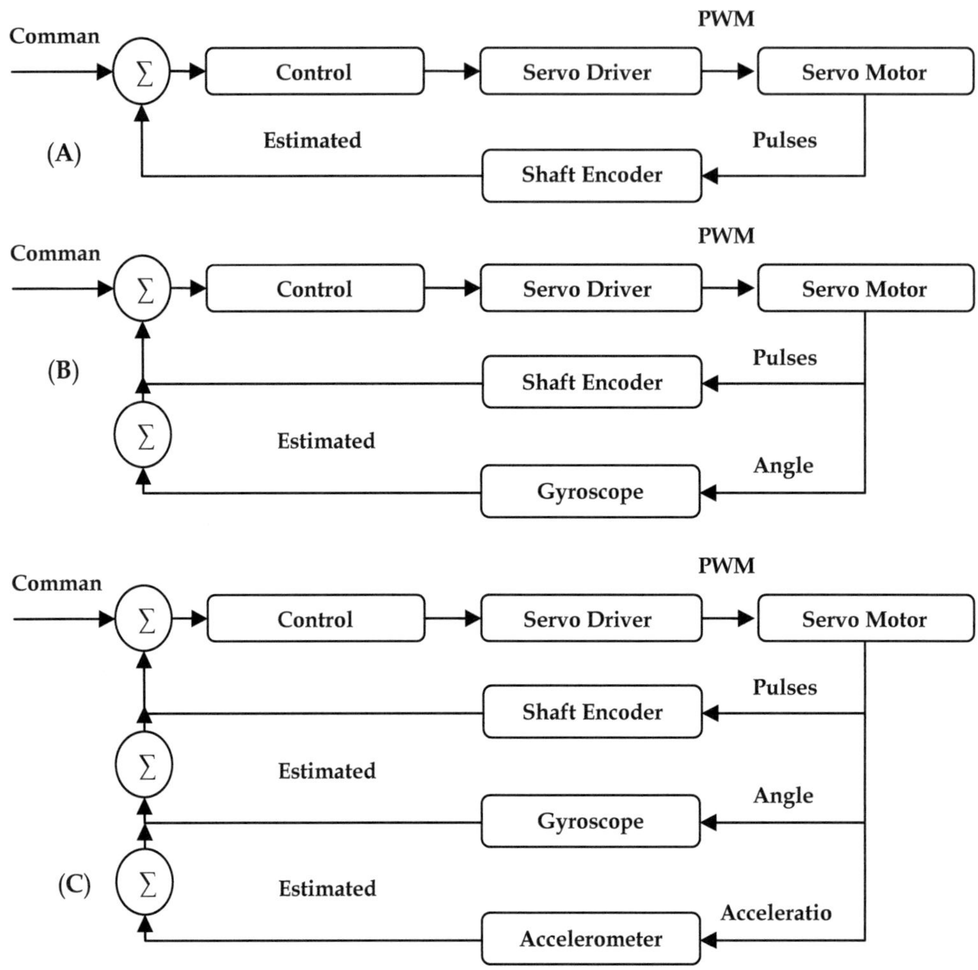

Fig. 2. Feedback control with shaft encoder (A), additional loop for gyroscope (B), and the third loop for accelerometer (C).

As shown in Fig. 2(A), the robot is only based on shaft encoder and without Gyroscope to be used in cascaded control as the second loop. The loop continues until the number of pulses coming from shaft encoders reaches the required value. For instance, the command go_forward(1 meter) will be translated as Right_Servo(CW, 1000); and Left_Servo(CCW, 1000) then the shaft encoder which triggers external interrupt routines for counting left and right pulses. The encoder value will be increased at each interrupt call until it reaches the maximum value (i.e. 1000 in above example). Then it sends a stop command to pulse generator module at control unit to stop the corresponding motor.

Such system yet is vulnerable to errors caused by the environment such as slippage while shaft encoders yet present correct movement. A command might be wasted at mechanics of motor because of voltage loss etc. in Addition, the motor might work but the wheel does not have enough friction with the floor to push the robot. Therefore, gyroscope enables the robot to understand such deviations. Fig. 2 (B) presents the cascaded control with inclusion of Gyroscope. Yet, slippages in the direction of movement while both wheels having same amount of error do not activate gyroscope. Our proposed way to detect such error is to control acceleration continuously toward direction of movement. Acceleration is zero while traversing a path on a fixed speed. Moreover, acceleration can be subtracted from output of accelerometer in situations that robot traverses a path on variable speed. Fig. 2 (C) presents the triple cascade control loop.

3.3 Practical results

In order to test the result, we developed a scenario for movement of the robot without/with triple cascade control feedback mechanism. The robot must traverse a rectangle of edge size equal to one meter and return to the home position. The error is calculated in both unmodified and modified robot assuming only one direction of rotation (CCW). Following figure presents the developed scenario.

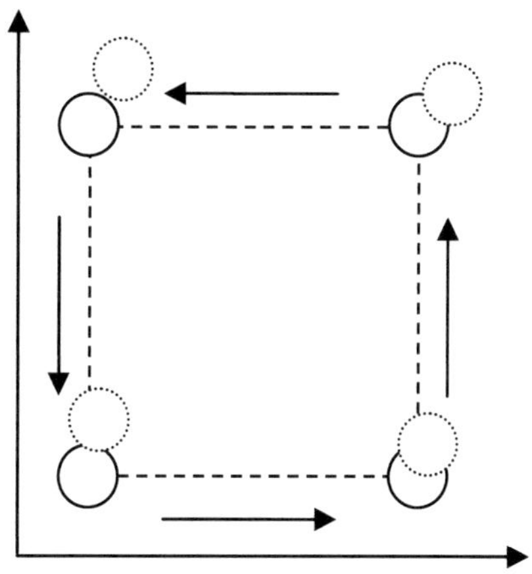

Fig. 3. Trajectory design of self-corrective cascade control robot

As shown in Fig. 4 (A), robot without second and third loop in cascade control mechanism deviates a lot from desired positions in robot trajectory. Fig. 4 (B) presents the corrected error after applying above mentioned loops to correct the deviation error.

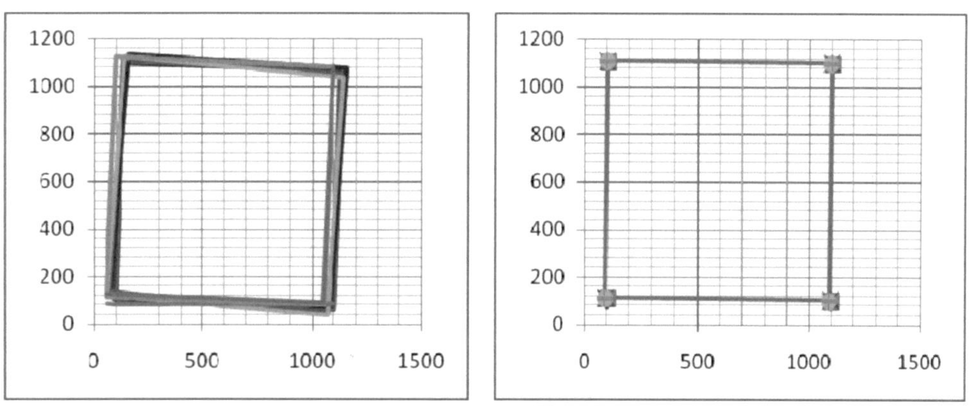

Fig. 4. Robot with only shaft encoder feedback control loop (A), and results while triple loop cascade control is applied (B).

In next section more sophisticated robots are presented while they are not only to correct the deviated errors but also they are able to identify friends from enemies in cooperative environment and help each other towards achieving the common goal.

4. Friend-or-Foe identification

In this section a novel and simple-to-implement FOF identification system is proposed. The system is composed of ultrasonic range finder rotary radar scanning the circumference for obstacles, and an infrared receiver reading encrypted echo messages propagated from omnidirectional infrared transmitter on the detected object through a fixed direction.

Each robot continuously transmits a message encrypted by a shared secret key between teammates consisting of its unique identifier and timestamp. The simplicity is due to excluding transceiver system for exchanging encoded/decoded messages. System counters replay attack by comparing the sequence of decoded timestamp. Encryption is done using a symmetric encryption technique such as RC5. The reason for selecting RC5 is its simplicity and low decryption time. Besides its hardware implementation consists of few XOR and simple basic operators which are available in all microcontrollers.

The decision making algorithm and behavioral aspects of each robot are represented as follows.

1. *Scan surrounding objects using ultrasonic sensor.*
2. *Create a record consist of distance and position for detected elements.*
3. *Fetch the queue top record and direct the rotary radar towards its position.*
4. *Listen to IR receptor within a certain period (i.e. 100 ms)*
5. *if no message is received*
   a. *Clear all records*
   b. *Attack the object*
   c. *Go to 1*
6. *Otherwise,*
   a. *Decode the message using the secret key*
   b. *If not decodable Go to 5.a*
   c. *Otherwise, register the identifier and timestamp besides position and distance for detected object*
   d. *Listen again to IR receptor within a certain period*
   e. *Decode the message using the secret key*
   f. *If not decodable Go to 5.a*
   g. *Otherwise, match the identifier and timestamp against the one kept before*
   h. *If identifier mismatches or timestamp is the same or smaller than as it was before, Go to 5.a*
   i. *Else if detected identifier is the same as the identifier of detector, Go to 5.a*
   j. *Go to 3*

It is assumed that the received message is free of noise and corrupted messages are automatically discarded. This can be done by listening for a limited number of times if message is not decodable. However, transmission is modulated on a 38 KHz IR carrier so sunlight and fluorescent light are not highly distorting the IR transmitted stream.

4.1 Hardware Implementation

Our first generation of cooperative mini sumo robot included an electronic compass instead of gyroscope and accelerometer so it was not able to detect skidding errors towards any axes without possibly the robot being rotated. Very common instance is when the robot is pushed by enemies. Fig. 5 (A) presents the first developed board being able to control two DC servomotors, communicate through wireless over 900MHz modulation, and having infrared sensors and bumpers to detect surrounding objects.

In the second design, an extension board suitable for open source Mark III mini sumo robots is presented. The Mark III Robot is the successor to the two previous robot kits designed and sold by the Portland Area Robotics Society. The base robot is serial port programmable. It includes PIC16F877 20MHz microcontroller with boot-loader which has made programming steps easier. In System Programming (ISP) is provided by boot-loader facility. It is possible to program the robot in Object Oriented PIC (OOPIC) framework. It includes controller for two DC servomotors in addition to three line following and two range finder sensors. Low-battery indicator is an extra feature provided on Mark III. However, there were few requirements to enhance the robot to fit our requirements for cooperative robotics. Wireless Communication, Ultrasonic range finder, infrared modulated transceiver, gyroscope, and acceleration sensors were added in extension board as shown in fig. 5 (B). In addition, the robot uses two GWS S03N 2BB DC servomotors each providing 70 gr.cm torques at 6v. However, the battery pack connected to motors is not regulated so it does not provide steady voltage while discharging. It effects center point of Servo calibration which effects servo proper movement. In extension board, a regulator is also included to fix the problem explained above.

Such robots are able to communicate and collaborate with each other in addition to benefitting from self-corrective cascaded control system. It can be easily used as a controller for intelligent robotics to solve a given task cooperatively by multiple robots.

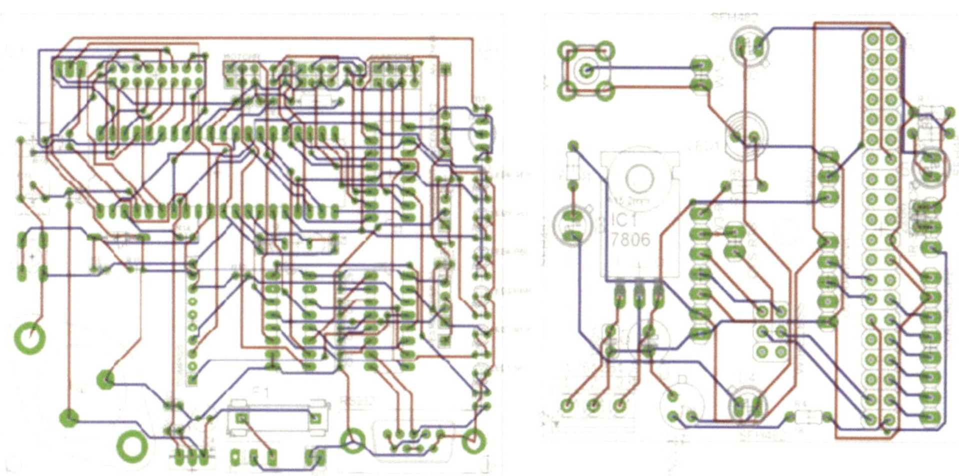

Fig. 5. The first generation of cooperative mini sumo platform robots 9×10 cm (A), and the extension board for Mark III (B).

4.2 Cipher analysis and attacking strategies

Following figure represents two of the worst cases for decision making in battlefield. These two crucial situations shown in Fig .6 includes 1) When an enemy robot masks a friend and enemy copies messages it receives from the masked friend to others so called reply attack. 2) Attacking an enemy by two robots from opposite sides

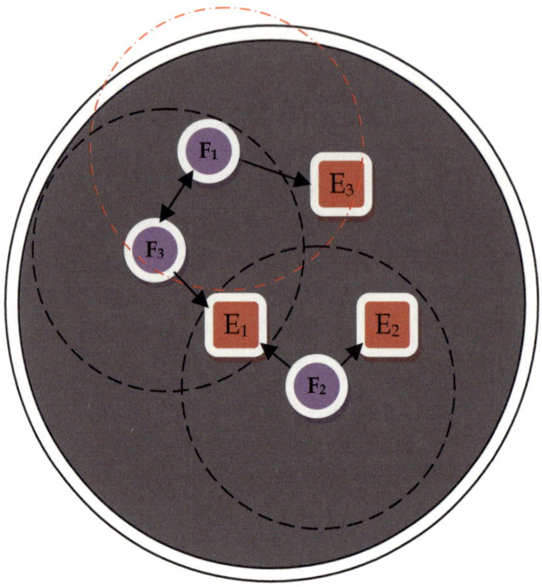

Fig. 6. An example arrangement of two teams of robots while fighting. Arrows demonstrate detection of objects.

4.2.1 Replay attack

In the first instance, E_1 stands between F_2 and F_3 covering their line of sight, so it is possible for E_1 to copy messages propagated from F_3 and replay them to F_2 and present itself as a friend and then attack against F_2. In this situation, F_2 assumes that E_1 is friend F_3 and it will be targeting the next possible enemy detected by rotary radar however it will be attacked by E_1.
Part 6.1 of the algorithm presented in Section 2 counters replay attack. In order to avoid replay attack, the timestamp included in decrypted message is compared against the one received in advance. Besides, the other friend robot receives the same copy of its own transmitted message including its identifier. Therefore it recognizes the enemy by matching and comparing the identifier of copied message with its own unique identifier. Therefore it recognizes the enemy.

4.2.2 Opposite side dual attack

According to the algorithm represented in previous section, both F_2 and F_3 start attacking E_1 from opposite sides either towards sideways of E_1, or one faces front of E_1. In both cases, they keep pushing enemy until they see the boundary so they return and start searching for other enemies. However, they either stay in this situation and challenging for a long time or one of friend robots understands that it is pushed out. It is highly possible so any of friends will be detected by other enemies and they will be pushed out. Therefore, a convincing strategy is to escape if it is not able to push. Being pushed or challenging without being able to push is simply detectable by checking gyroscope and acceleration sensors. LIS3LV02DL from free samples of ST Microelectronics single chipset gyro-acceleration sensor is used to provide movement and acceleration towards x, y, and z axes.

4.3 Strategies

Escape strategy simply consists of backing off for a period or rotating around itself with maximum speed and then moving towards a direction so it can start the algorithm from beginning or attack the enemy from a better direction.
Another upgrade in algorithm is to cancel an attack if the enemy is escaped away out of detection radios. The reason is making the system more efficient and spending time on fighting against other enemies instead of an escaping robot which might not be caught in a short while.
It is assumed that the radius of detection range is adjusted to half of radius of the platform. It is due to applying Divide and Conquer (DAC) policy within cooperative robots by assuming to solve each subset of battlefield by one of the robots. In addition it reduces the complexity and collision while communicating with other teammates. Later it is shown that the radius of detection can be dynamically changed based on real-time conditions of match.
A better but more time consuming approach is to detect all enemies in range and then decide which one to attack rather than attacking against first detected enemy. For instance, $E_1$and E_2 are in see sight of the F_2. In this situation F_2 should be intelligent enough to choose the best attack. It is highly possible for robots to be at the boundary so they cannot back off or run away. Therefore the robot has to attack to the first detected enemy asking for help from other teammates.
Determining the level of power of enemy robots helps deciding to utilize escape strategy more efficiently. The problem refers to the condition that level power of enemy robots are more than ours. Therefore, in such situation having face to face attack is not desired. Instead, the only way to remedy is to attack from wheel sides of enemy robot. Consequently finding relative movement angle of the enemy robot helps friend robots to decide whether to attack or not. Following are three main concerns.

4.3.1 Determining the level of power of enemy robots

Utilizing gyroscope and matching it with usual speed of the robot in steady state helps measuring movement toward *x,y,z* axes. See fig. 7.

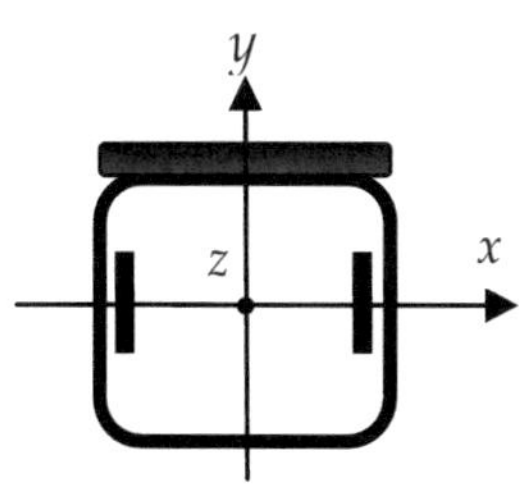

Fig. 7. The direction of axes over the robot while *y* showing the front of the robot.

Respectively A_x, A_y, A_z variables presents gyroscope values. The digital returning value from SPI port indicating gyroscope results follows $A_x, A_y, A_z \in (-512, +512)$. Attacking face to face with enemy robot is when $A_y < -\alpha, \alpha > 0$ or $A_x > \beta, \beta > 0$. While a and β are threshold values such that $A_y < -\alpha$ shows backward movement and similarly $A_x > \beta$ indicates side movements more than an acceptable threshold for skidding errors. Therefore, $A_y < -\alpha$ indicates that the level of power of the enemy is more than being able to repel against. In this case attacking sideways of enemy is needed. Respectively, the relative angle of enemy should be suitable for attack so that one side of enemy could be caught. The ultrasonic rangefinder on implemented rotary radar determines the distance to detected object. The relative angle is calculated from position of DC servomotor rotating the radar. An example is represented in Fig. 8.

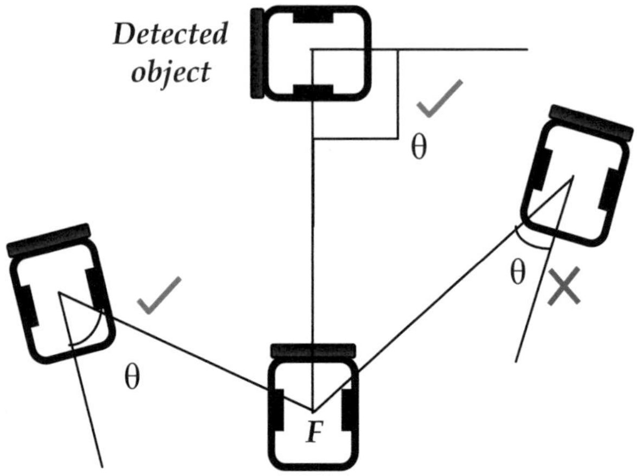

Fig. 8. θ is acceptable if $\theta > \theta_0$.

4.3.2 Determining the speed of enemy

Estimating velocity of enemy robots is done through two ways. Firstly, while the enemy attacks directly towards friend. Therefore, $v_e = \frac{l}{s}$, v_e is velocity of enemy robot, and l is the distance traversed is s seconds. Secondly, we can estimate speed of enemy robot using radar. At first detection of enemy, assuming its distance is l_1 and detecting it again in a short while as s seconds in distance l_2 with θ degrees angular rotation of rotary radar, speed can be calculated as follows using law of Cosines as shown in Fig. 9.

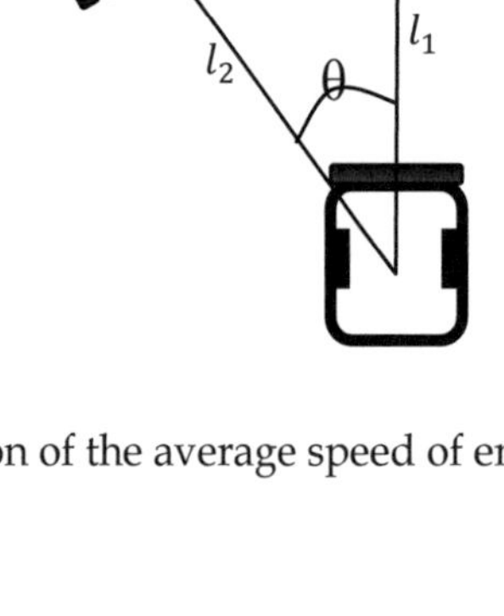

Fig. 9. Second way of calculation of the average speed of enemy.

$$l_s = \sqrt{(l_1)^2 + (l_2)^2 - 2l_1 l_2 \cos\theta}$$
$$v_e = \frac{l_s}{s}. \tag{3}$$

4.3.3 Determining the relative angle of enemy robots

The relative angle is considered in both static and dynamic situations. Static situation (see Fig. 10) is while friend robot does not move. Reversely, dynamic situation declares when friend robot is moving.

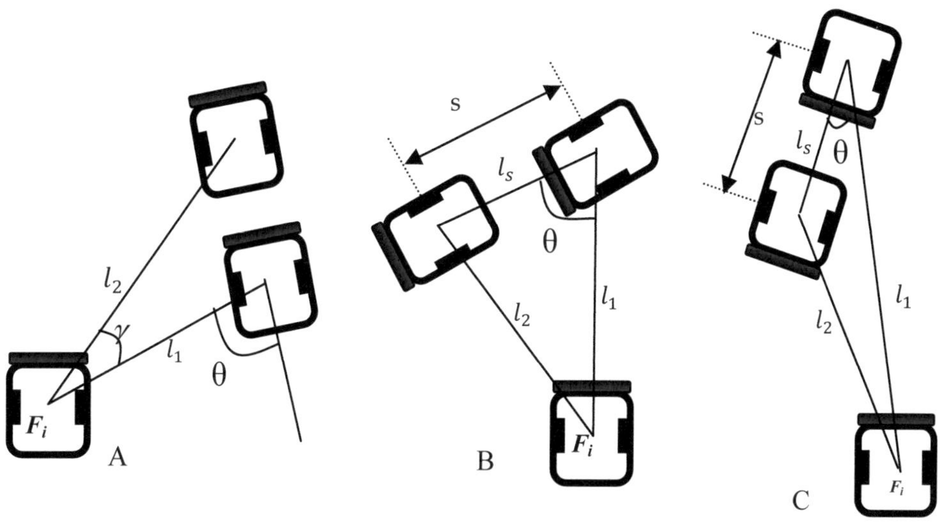

Fig. 10. While enemy is getting far from friend robot (A). The enemy gets closer with a desirable angle (B). While enemy gets closer with an angle more than threshold (C).

In fig. 10 (A) $l_2 > l_1$ then in attacking strategy it is decided to follow the enemy if it is in an acceptable range considering that the enemy would not be able to change the role of front and back side of the robot. Otherwise, leaving the target is a better decision as enemy probably has time to attack friend robot.

In fig. 10 (B) $l_2 < l_1$. $0 < \frac{l_1 - l_2}{s} < \alpha$, α is an acceptable threshold for speed of decreasing distance of enemy towards friend. Satisfying above inequality allows attacking the enemy. $l_s = v_e \cdot s$, l_s is the distance traversed by enemy robot in s seconds.

In the situation shown by fig. 10 (C) friend is not allowed to attack. Therefore execution of escape strategy is done and friend robot runs away. In other words, $\frac{l_1 - l_2}{s} > \alpha$, which shows that the enemy is in good state to attack friend.

$\bar{l} = l_1 - l_2$, $\bar{v} = \frac{\bar{l}}{s}$, $\bar{v}$ stands for velocity of enemy moving towards friend robot. Final results of static situation are as follows.

1. If $\bar{v} \cong 0$ then the movement of enemy is octagonal to our robot.
2. If $0 < \bar{v} < \alpha$ then enemy is getting close with an acceptable relative angle for friend to attack.
3. If $\bar{v} \cong v_e$ then the enemy is able to attack straight.

Next, the dynamic situation is considered. As shown in fig. 11. $l_{s_e} = v_e \cdot s$, l_{s_e} is the distance traversed by enemy in s seconds. Similarly, $l_{s_f} = v_f \cdot s$, l_{s_f} is the distance traversed by friend in s seconds. Results of dynamic situation are as follows.

If $\bar{v} < v_f$ then enemy is going far (see Fig. 11 (A)).

1. If $\bar{v} \cong v_f$ then the movement of enemy is octagonal to our robot.
2. If $v_f < \bar{v} < \alpha$ then enemy is getting closer (see Fig. 11 (B)).
3. If $\alpha < \bar{v} \leq v_f + v_e$ then the enemy is able to attack straight.

Conditions 2 and 3 are desirable to attack. However, a better strategy in condition 4 is escaping away. Condition 1 depends on the ratio of speed of friend versus speed of enemy. This ratio can be used in decision making strategy whether to attack or leave the enemy.

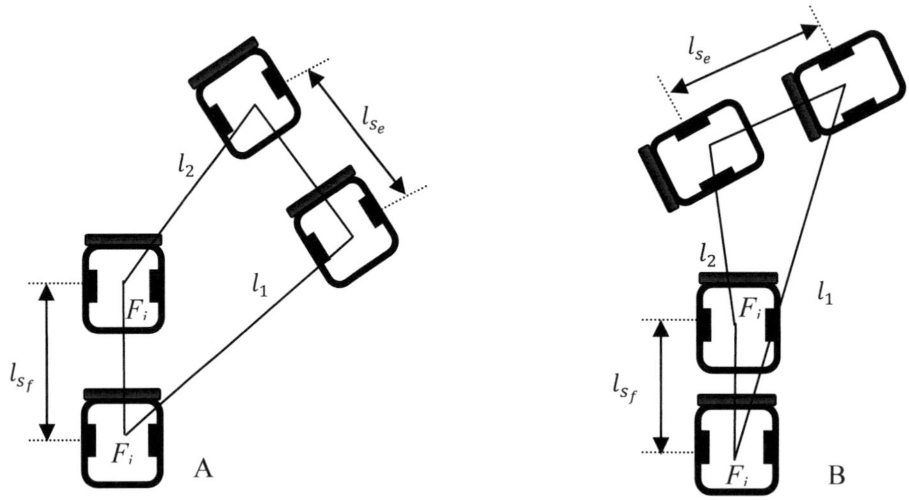

Fig. 11. $\bar{v} < v_f$ (A), and $v_f < \bar{v} < \alpha$ (B).

If the enemy comes towards friend straightly and there would be no possibility to escape, friend should start attack while announcing request for help over wireless medium. Notice, it is already known that level of power of enemy is higher than level of power of friend. Therefore more likely, friend will lose the battle. Now teammates can decide to help the challenging friend if the distance is acceptable or if friend is in the range of their radar, or leave the friend to die.

4.4 Experimental results

The developed system is tested on team of three robots. The team of enemies consists of three cooperative robots with basic abilities which include IR transceiver for FOF identification. The test is done for ten rounds. Last remaining robot(s) win the game. There were five different situations to test robots. Therefore, fifty different rounds of competition were conducted. These five situations included basic, wireless enabled, radar and wireless enabled, radar and wireless with gyroscope, and finally everything in addition to utilizing escape strategy. Wireless communication helps robots to talk to each other, share their information, and ask for help. Rotary radar is an ultrasonic range finder. Gyroscope shows movement towards all directions. Finally escape strategy is a software enhancement as mentioned in earlier section. Following figure presents five set of competitions each in ten rounds. The absolute duration for each competition resulting loss of one team is considered separately in terms of mm:ss.

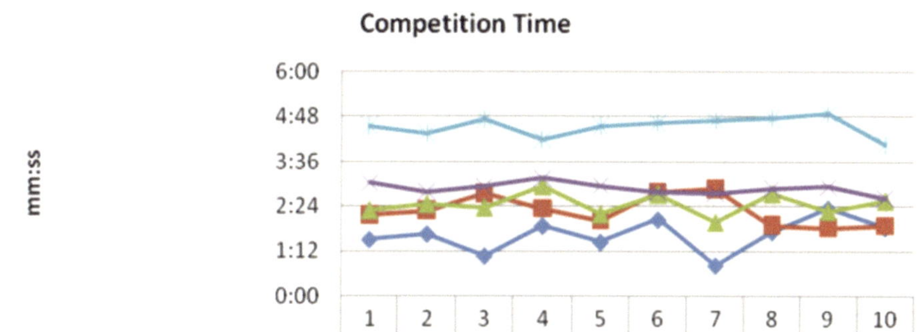

	1	2	3	4	5	6	7	8	9	10
Base	1:31	1:40	1:05	1:53	1:27	2:03	0:50	1:44	2:21	1:51
Wireless Enabled	2:10	2:17	2:44	2:20	2:01	2:47	2:52	1:54	1:50	1:53
Radar & Wireless Enabled	2:18	2:28	2:22	2:56	2:12	2:43	1:59	2:44	2:17	2:33
Wireless & Radar & Gyroscope	3:02	2:47	2:56	3:09	2:57	2:47	2:45	2:53	2:56	2:38
All with Escape Strategy Enabled	4:32	4:21	4:43	4:12	4:32	4:38	4:42	4:46	4:53	4:04

Fig. 12. Competition time for 50 different tests

5. Simultaneous localization and mapping

An unmanned aerial vehicle (UAV) is tasked to explore an unknown environment and to map the features it finds, but must do so without the use of infrastructure-based localization systems such as GPS, or any a priori terrain data. The UAV navigates using a statistical estimation technique known as simultaneous localization and mapping (SLAM) which allows for the simultaneous estimation of the location of the UAV as well as the location of the features it sees. SLAM offers a unique approach to vehicle localization with potential applications including planetary exploration, or when GPS is denied (for example under intentional GPS jamming, or applications where GPS signals cannot be reached), but more importantly can be used to augment already existing systems to improve robustness to navigation failure (Bryson & Sukkarieh, 2008)

The solution of the SLAM problem has been one of the notable successes of the robotics community over the past decade. SLAM has been formulated and solved as a theoretical problem in a number of different forms. SLAM has also been implemented in a number of different domains from indoor robots, to outdoor, underwater and airborne systems. At a theoretical and conceptual level, SLAM can now be considered a solved problem. However, substantial issues remain in practically realizing more general SLAM solutions and notably in building and using perceptually rich maps as part of a SLAM algorithm (Chanier et al., 2008) (Pathiranage et al., 2008).

The first problem is the computational complexity due to the growing state vector with each added landmark in the environment. The second problem is the data association which matches the observations and landmarks in the state vector (Temeltas & Kayak, 2008).

One key requirement for SLAM to work is that it must re observe features, and this has two effects: firstly, the improvement of the location estimate of the feature; and secondly, the improvement of the location estimate of the platform because of the statistical correlations that link the platform to the feature. So our UAV has two options; should it explore more unknown terrain to find new features, or should it revisit known features to improve localization quality. These options are instantiated into the online path planner for the UAV (Bryson & Sukkarieh, 2008).
One of the main problems with the SLAM algorithm has been the computational requirements. Although the algorithm is originally of O(N3) the complexity of the SLAM algorithm can be reduced to O(N2),N being the number of landmarks in the map. For long duration missions the number of landmarks will increase and eventually computer resources will not be sufficient to update the map in real time. This N2 scaling problem arises because each landmark is correlated to all other landmarks. The correlation appears since the observation of a new landmark is obtained with a sensor mounted on the mobile robot and thus the landmark location error will be correlated with the error in the vehicle location and the errors in other landmarks of the map. This correlation is of fundamental importance for the long-term convergence of the algorithm and needs to be maintained for the full duration of the mission (Frese, 2005).
Recently, estimation algorithms have been roughly classified according to their underlying basic principle. The most popular approaches to the SLAM problem are the extended Kalman filter (EKF-SLAM) and the Rao–Black wellized particle filter. The effectiveness of the EKF approach comes from the fact that it estimates a fully correlated posterior over feature maps and vehicle poses. EKF-SLAM permits linear approximations of the motion and the measurement models, and it assumes Gaussian representations for the probability density functions .the solution of the EKF-SLAM is inconsistent due to errors introduced during linearization, which induces inaccurate maps with filter divergence. Therefore, the consistency issue of the EKF-SLAM has attracted the attention of the research community due to its importance, and many recent research efforts have concentrated on improving the classical algorithm (Kim et al., 2008).

5.1 Proposed SLAM method

There are N robots as friends and N robots as enemies. Friends achieve the simultaneous map presenting the position of all robots. This scheme consumes ultrasonic radar, gyroscope and wireless connection. At the beginning, the radar will present position distance of any detected object within its receptive range. It is obvious that some might be masked. We consider the matrix A with two dimensions with the size $2N \times 3$ as follows.

$$A = \begin{bmatrix} ID_1 & l_1 & \theta_1 \\ ID_2 & l_2 & \theta_2 \\ \vdots & \vdots & \vdots \\ ID_{2N} & l_{2N} & \theta_{2N} \end{bmatrix}_{2N\times 3} \tag{4}$$

ID_i presents the identification of detected object i. A fixed unique identifier is given to friends in the range of 0 to $N-1$. ID_i is equal to N for foes and consequently undefined objects are tagged by $N+1$. l_i, is the distance between the robot and detected object. Therefore, it is equal to 0 for the Scanner robot. θ_i, is the angle between North Pole and the detected robot. Thus it defines the angle for scanner robot if $l_i = 0$. All equations can be upgraded so that perpendicular vector to connecting line of the wheels or front side of the robot would be considered as North Pole. For the time being let's consider the angle between front side of the robot and detected object as α_i. Then $\theta_i = (\alpha_i + \theta)$. $\theta = \theta_i$ if $l_i = 0$. α_i is in the range of 0 to +180 for counterclockwise rotation; and it is in the range of 0 to -180 for clockwise rotation. The radar initial state is as 0 position while pointing to front side of the robot. θ presents the shift from North Pole. Thus both θ and θ_i are positive when the angle is towards counterclockwise direction. Following figure presents three different situations while scanning the environment.

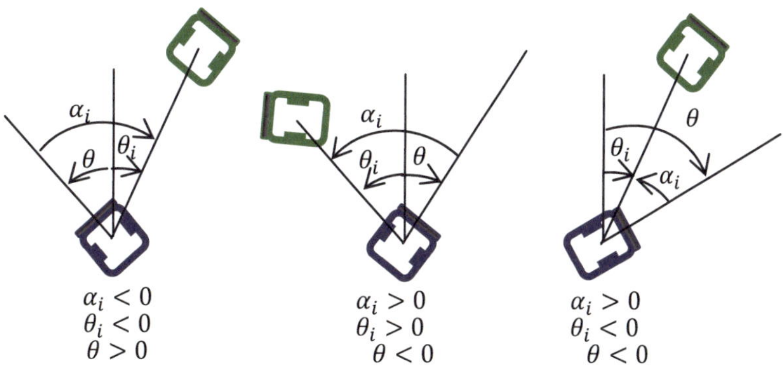

Fig. 13. Different situations while scanning the environment by ultrasonic radar

The matrix A is broadcasted and thus the most recent SLAM information is propagated among all robots. There are three conditions while aiming to find position of friends: 1) A friend is detected, 2) A friend is masked by another friend, and 3) A friend is masked by foe. First case is straightforward, therefore, second and third situations are considered as follows. In second condition, as shown in Fig. 15, the robot at the bottom of figure (scanner) cannot detect the robot which is masked behind the robot in the middle.

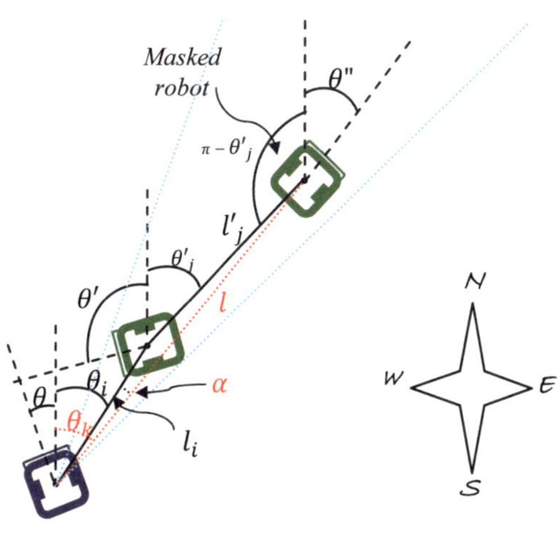

Fig. 15. A friend is masked by another friend.

In this condition l is the distance between the robot at the bottom and the masking robot. The masking robot is having θ_k degree with scanner considering to North Pole. Therefore, l and θ_k are calculated as follows.

$$l = \sqrt{(l_i)^2 + (l'_j)^2 - 2\, l_i l'_j \sin\left(\pi - \left||\theta_i| - |\theta'_j|\right|\right)}$$
$$\theta_k = \theta_i + \alpha \tag{5}$$

and, by the sine rules on triangle

$$\frac{l}{\sin\left(\pi - \left||\theta_i| - |\theta'_j|\right|\right)} = \frac{l'_j}{\sin\alpha} \Rightarrow \alpha = \sin^{-1}\left(\frac{l'_j \cdot \sin\left(\left||\theta_i| - |\theta'_j|\right|\right)}{l}\right) \tag{6}$$

then scanner robot updates l and θ_k of record corresponding to the masked robot. In third condition as seen in the following figure, two situations are considered.

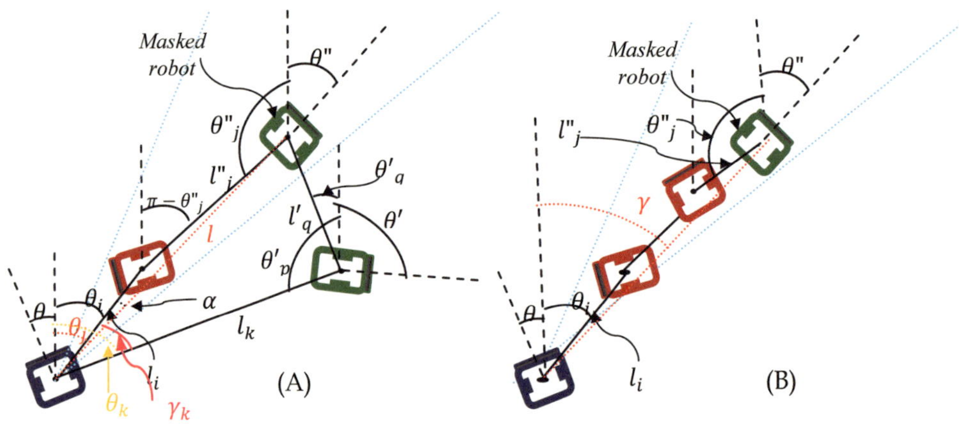

Fig. 16. Third situation while a friend is masked by an enemy. Blue robot is scanner, Friends are shown in green color, and Enemies are shown by red.

In the Fig. 16 (A) a friend is masked by an enemy. In this condition l and θ_k are calculated as there is only one enemy between scanner and the masked friend. However, Fig. 16 (B) presents a worse situation while a friend is masked by two consequent enemies. In such case calculation of SLAM will be done at another robot where both current scanner and friend are not masked by two enemies in the middle. Therefore, at least three robots are needed at each side. Consequently, l and θ_k of the masked robot are calculated accordingly.

$$l = \sqrt{(l_k)^2 + (l'_q)^2 - 2\, l_k l'_q \sin\beta}$$
$$\beta = \theta'_p - \theta'_q \tag{7}$$
$$\frac{l}{\sin\beta} = \frac{l'_q}{\sin\gamma_k} \Rightarrow \gamma_k = \sin^{-1}\left(\frac{l'_q \cdot \sin\beta}{l}\right) \Rightarrow \theta_j = \theta_k - \gamma_k$$

In case of having no friend in a proper position to solve the problem presented in Fig. 16 (B), the record and estimation of position of friends are considered. θ is known for all friends Comparing SLAM records generated at both scanner and masked robot at certain timing which is base on subtraction of timestamp of two consequent records provides an estimated record for the masked robot. The angle is approximately equal to the angle which the masking enemy (γ) exists. A very accurate detection is done by searching among θ_i and comparing them against $\pi - \theta_i$ of angle of masked friend in addition to keep tracking of previous position of friend at Δt period of time.

6. Reasoning through semantic intelligence

Semantic Web Services provide a new approach to communication, situation- and context-awareness, and knowledge representation for reasoning by multiple agents. Collaboratively working multiple robots on a mesh acting autonomously require a universal platform in order to merge data processed by each agent for perception and map building while gathering possible answers to a query.

In the foundation of semantic Web reasoning engines and communication platforms rests Open World Assumption (OWA). This is due to 'openness' of web where absence of entities being searched should not entail negative response rather simply treated as a fact "not available at the moment." While, that sets the base in anticipation of future enhancements of the fact base, it is not preferred in situations where a definitive answer is needed. Closed World Assumption (CWA) alternatively returns definitive yes/no answers even in situations where future enhancements are inevitable (Elçi et al., 2008). It is also essential to derive partial results from a set of cooperative agents/robots based on Locally Close World (LCW) settings (Doherty et al., 2000).

Robots currently apply CWA for decision making and learning. They could also utilize the huge mass of information available on semantic web in order to deduct new knowledge using standard or extended OWA. Consequently, robots cannot only cooperate and communicate using semantic Web platform but also be able to retrieve much more realistic and acceptable answers to queries. This is even more so where unsupervised learning plays the main role where our knowledge about task is incomplete; and that is true for the most of real life situations.

Systems with distributed processing and control require distributed coordination in order to achieve a shared goal. Such systems may be realized using self-actuated agents donning semantic capability such as that of an autonomous semantic agent (ASA). Implementation of an ASA (Elçi et al., 2006) as a semantic Web service possibly offered by a robot provides the required features. In a multi-agent system, one of the ASAs may indeed assume as well the duty of a common site acting as the central registry of web services in the field. We devised new software architecture for distributed environments using autonomous semantic agents (ASAs) (Elçi & Rahnama, IWSC2005, 2005). Multiple ASAs can act collaboratively serving the same goal. One of the applications ASAs can serve is Traffic network Management System (TMS).

Recent research on traffic and transport systems has been concentrated on vehicle and driver safety through fitting vehicles with onboard IT systems. TMS takes control over traffic flow and reports possible incidents in an urban area. An intersection network can then serve to improve the quality of life in mobile municipal communities (Elçi & Rahnama, 8-9 June 2006), (Takahashi et al., Dec. 2004). Traffic junctions can be replaced by MASAs rather than to be controlled through a centralized architecture. An instance of such structure is a security scenario concerning tracing and tracking of missing vehicles was considered and shown how to implement it over so called Traffic network Management and Information System (TMIS) network. Simulation results showed promising outcomes. Further research involving similar development base was also suggested (Elçi et al., TEHOSS 2006, 09-13 October 2006). Cooperatively responding to a query by intelligent intersections in TMIS is in some essential ways similar to a multi-agent robotic system discovering a way out of a labyrinth. Communication-wise, each robot should talk to its neighbors and share its information. Furthermore, we aim at effecting coordination and cooperation among MASAs towards realizing intelligent behavior in order to achieve a shared goal through processes benefiting from semantic web technologies (Elçi & Rahnama, ROMAN 2007, August 26-29, 2007) (Elçi & Rahnama, 30 Nov - 1 Dec 2006). Within this respect and for simplicity in referring to these robots, and in order to convey their capability better, we will call them as the Cooperative Labyrinth Discovery Robots (CLDRs).

Researchers have worked in various categories of cooperatively solving problems by robots. For instance, to recite a few, Takahashi et al. (Takahashi et al., Dec. 2004) studied autonomous decentralized control for formation of multiple mobile robots. They covered formulations for forming a group of robots following the same goal. Chia-How Lin et al.(Lin et al., 10-12 Oct. 2005) represented an agent-based robot control design for multi-robot cooperation in real time control. Their system is suitable for cooperative tasks with capability of controlling heterogeneous robots. Finally, Xie Yun et al. (Yun et al., 5-8 Oct. 2003) have prepared a communication protocol for their soccer robots.

In cooperative robotics, such as Cooperative Labyrinth Discovery (CLD) (Elçi & Rahnama, 30 Nov - 1 Dec 2006), (Elçi & Rahnama, 2009) in an uncharted labyrinth, conventionally, the probability and the estimation were used to select one path among a set of possible but as yet undiscovered ones. In order to overcome naïve decision making, according to (Elçi et al., 2008) a hybrid scheme is needed to serve as decision maker. Following algorithm is a revised and simplified version of the one presented at (Elci & Rahnama, 2009) to suite the limited capacity CCLDRs by dividing it into two phases running cooperative decision making on SCLDRs and local standalone decision making on CCLDRs.

Team of CLDRs consists of an SCLDR and some CCLDRs start discovering an unknown labyrinth trying to find the correct exit. (i.e. an entrance should not be distinguished as exit if it is not defined so). The only information they have is the position of entrance they start from and position of exit in labyrinth matrix but not the way through. As mentioned earlier a counter is defined for each cell presenting the number of times that a robot has visited it. Therefore, value 0 presents an undiscovered cell. In SCLDR in addition to copy of local counters, another counter indicates shared value as sum of all local counters concerning a cell.

The α / β algorithm is an undeterministic version of minimax algorithm widely used in AI. Our algorithm applies α / β algorithm as entire labyrinth data is not known for each individual. Assuming a CLDR at a junction with 4 possible ways (left, right, forward and backward), α / β finds the minimum of counter values of respected neighboring cells. For instance, assuming 3 for value of local counter of cell at left side, 4 for front and 8 for the cell at backside, and 0 for the cell at the right side, the minimum of 0, 3, 4, and 8 which is 0 (right) is chosen. Following is the detailed algorithm.

1. *CCLDR is on a cell in the labyrinth. It is to decide on its next move: advance to neighboring cell forward, left, right or backup?*
2. *Has the current cell been visited before?*
   - 2.1. *Read walls of the current cell if not visited*
   - 2.2. *Update local counter at CCLDR and request SCLDR to update the shared counter*
   - 2.3. *Request SCLDR to update shared memory of paths (Actually it is done as consequence of 1.2. at SCLDR)*
3. *Run Decision-Maker based on CWA (Local Counters) obtaining the next-move-to cell.*
   - 3.1. *Has the next-move-to cell been visited before?*
     - 3.1.1. *If yes, run shortest path algorithm*
     - 3.1.2. *Otherwise wait for the answer from SCLDR based on following situations*
       - 3.1.2.1. *Finding results of running α / β algorithm based on shared counter of visited cells*
       - 3.1.2.2. *If α / β algorithm returns more than one minimum, run OWA based on local counters*
       - 3.1.2.3. *If OWA results in an unknown answer, then infer from labyrinth ontology based on LCW by limiting shared ontology to just neighboring cells.*
       - 3.1.2.4. *If LCW reasoning contradicts CWA results, select a solution randomly or based on a move priority*
4. *Move the robot to the next-move-to position and update position value.*
5. *Check if the selected cell is an exit cell.*
   - 5.1. *If not, repeat from Step 1.*

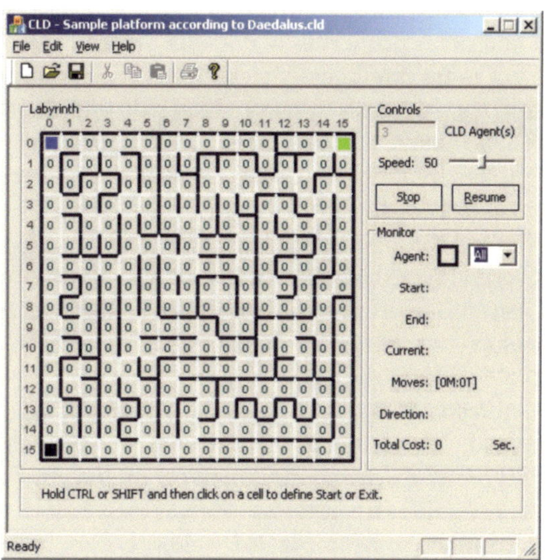

Fig. 17. Screenshot from the Semantic Intelligent Reasoning Engine on three cooperative labyrinth discovery robots.

The experience with this algorithm proved that there are some cases for which CWA alone cannot answer the query so OWA returns a better estimation of a possible answer. Therefore, utilizing open / locally-closed / open world assumptions simultaneously is necessary side-by-side. It is not possible to avoid any of the world assumptions but having them together leads to better answer sets to queries in some domains such as robotic platforms. This powers the robot with better estimation and answers where CWA alone would have returned negative result. The following screenshot presents the SI software developed to act as core of decision making according to the given algorithm.

7. Conclusion

This chapter draws a beginning to end framework for design and implementation of more intelligent robots in different aspects such as self-localization, deviated error correction, Friend or Foe identification, simultaneous localization and mapping, and finally semantic intelligence. Line-following robots were used to illustrate simple modification without necessarily hardware improvement and making them able to localize themselves while traversing a curve or a straight line. Mini-sumo robots were the example case self-corrective cascade control and friend or foe identification robots while absolute positioning of each teammate was not possible. Our designed friend or foe strategy does not require two-way communication as it only relies on decryption of payload in one direction. The replay attack is not feasible time wise as the communication is encrypted and timestamp is inserted in the messages.

There were two sets of hardware implementations for the test robots. The second version is equipped with rotary robot able to detect direction and distance to detected object in addition to gyroscope chipset. There were several facts that could be enhanced in decision making algorithm of fighter robots. There were situations that robot were losing the game against more powerful enemies. Although studying dynamics of robots allowed finding solutions to attack such enemies from sides so they will not be able to resist. There were certain situations that robots must escape instead of fighting. These states were based on the relative position, speed and other properties of enemies which could be calculated by friend robots helping them to act more intelligently in cooperative environments. Such improved robots can be used within the scope of industry standards and they that can be applied in manufacturing industries, hospitals, and automated seeking products in chain shops.

Finally, design and implementation of client cooperative labyrinth discovery robots (CCLDRs) were presented especially addressing severe restriction or lack of resources. Decision making is performed through a semantic intelligence approach incorporating Open / Locally Closed / Closed World Assumptions in its algorithm. The algorithm was retrofitted from earlier research in order to fit into limited capacities of client CLDRs. On the other hand, decision making algorithm was optimized to perform autonomously leaving only more complicated calculation to SCLDR.

CCLDR hardware architecture was enhanced by inserting an extension board accommodating modulated IR receivers for Friend or Foe determination, wireless communication capability, and allowing multiplexing of line tracing and sides detector sensor boards. Robots are able to localize themselves based on the mathematical formulations relying on distance measurements by side sensors but without needing shaft-encoders. They act as clients of more advanced CLDRs with ability of processing ontology files, and providing Semantic Web Services (SWS), etc. Within this environment, each agent is autonomous complex system acting based on its sensory input, information retrieved from other agents, and suitable form of converted ontology files from SCLDR.

8. Acknowledgement

We wish to thank Mr. Hamid Mirmohammad Sadeghi from EMU for his valuable contribution in mathematical formulating of proposed algorithms provided in this chapter.

The material in Section 3- Self-Corrective Cascaded Control was drawn from our project proposal "Self-corrective compass cascaded control system for AGVs" in the Project Competition to support young entrepreneurs by GMTGB Teknopark, Famagusta, North Cyprus. Our project proposal was awarded the fourth place on 24 October 2008.

9. References

Active-Robots. (n.d.). *Cruiser Maze Solver Robot.* (http://www.microrobot.co.kr) Retrieved 10 2008, from Active Robots: http://www.active-robots.com/products/robots/cruiser-details-2.shtml

Boivin, E., Desbiens, A., & Gagnon, E. (2008). UAV Collision Avoidance Using Cooperative Predictive Control. *16th Mediterranean Conference on Control and Automation* (pp. 683-688). Ajaccio, France: IEEE.

Borenstein, J., & Feng, L. (1995). UMBmark: a benchmark test for measuring odometry errors in mobile robots. *Presented at the 1995 SPIE Conference on Mobile Robots, Philadelphia.,* (pp. 1-12). Philadelphia.

Borenstein, J., Everett, H., Feng, L., & Wehe, D. (1997). Mobile Robot Positioning & Sensors and Techniques. *Invited paper for the Journal of Robotic Systems , 14* (Special Issue on Mobile Robots), 231-249.

Bryson, M., & Sukkarieh, S. (2008). Observability analysis and active control for airborne SLAM. *IEEE Transactions on Aerospace and Electronic Systems , 44* (1), 261-280.

Chanier, F., Checchin, P., Blanc, C., & Trassoudaine, L. (2008). LAM process using Polynomial Extended Kalman Filter: Experimental assessment. *Control, Automation, Robotics and Vision, 2008. ICARCV 2008. 10th International Conference* (pp. 365 - 370). IEEE.

Defoort, M., Floquet, T., Kokosy, A., & Perruquetti, W. (2008). Sliding-Mode Formation Control for Cooperative Autonomous Mobile Robots. *IEEE Transactions on Industrial Electronics , 55* (11), 3944 - 3953 .

Doherty, P., Lukaszewicz, W., & Szalas, A. (2000). Efficient Reasoning Using the Local Closed-World Assumption. In *Artificial Intelligence: Methodology, Systems, and Applications* (Vol. 1904, pp. 21-34). Springer Berlin / Heidelberg.

Elçi, A., & Rahnama, B. (2005). Considerations on a New Software Architecture for Distributed Environments Using Autonomous Semantic Agents. *Proc. 2nd International Workshop on Software Cybernetics, 29th IEEE COMPSAC 2005* (pp. 133-138). IEEE.

Elçi, A., & Rahnama, B. (8-9 June 2006). Intelligent Junction: Improving the Quality of Life for Mobile Citizens through better Traffic Management. *Proc. YvKB 2006.* Ankara, Turkey: TBD Publications, in Turkish.

Elçi, A., Rahnama, B., & Amintabar, A. (09-13 October 2006). Security through Traffic Network:Tracking of Missing Vehicles and Routing in TMIS using Semantic Web Services. *The Second IEEE International Conference on Technologies for Homeland Security and Safety.* Istanbul, Turkey.

Elçi, A., & Rahnama, B. (30 Nov - 1 Dec 2006). Applying Semantic Web in Engineering a Modular Architecture for Design and Implementation of a Cooperative Labyrinth Discovery Robot. *4th FAE International Symposium on Computer Science and Engineering,* (pp. 447-451). Gemikonağı, Northern Cyprus.

Elçi, A., & Rahnama, B. (December 2006). *Theory and practice of autonomous semantic agents.* MEKB-05-01 Project final report, Eastern Mediterranean University, Department of Computer Engineering and Internet Technologies Research Center.

Elçi, A., & Rahnama, B. (August 26-29, 2007). Human-Robot Interactive Communication Using Semantic Web Technologies in Design and Implementation of Collaboratively Working Robots. *In Proc. Robot Human Interactive Communication 2007.* Jeju Island, Korea: IEEE.

Elçi, A., Rahnama, B., & Kamran, S. (2008). Defining a Strategy to Select Either of Closed/Open World Assumptions on Semantic Robots. *COMPSAC2008* (pp. 417-423). Turku, Finland: IEEE.

Elçi, A., & Rahnama, B. (2009). Semantic Robotics: Cooperative Labyrinth Discovery Robots for Intelligent Environments. In A. Tolk, & L. C. Jain, *Complex Systems in Knowledge-based Environments: Theory, Models and Applications.* Berlin Heidelberg: Springer-Verlag.

Elci, A., & Rahnama, B. (2009). Towards Decidable Reasoning Using Hybrid Autoepistemic Operators. *In Special Issue on Engineering Semantic Agent Systems, with Expert Systems: The Journal of Knowledge Engineering , Accepted for publication.*

Frese, U. (2005). Treemap: An O(log n) Algorithm for Simultaneous Localization and Mapping. In *Spatial Cognition IV. Reasoning, Action, and Interaction* (Vol. 3343/2005, pp. 455-477). Lecture Notes in Computer Science, Springer Berlin / Heidelberg.

Ke, Z., Rong, X., Jian, C., & Xianhua, J. (2004). A novel approach to increase control performance of soccer robot. *Fifth World Congress on Intelligent Control and Automation, 2004. 6,* pp. 4946- 4950. Hangzhou, China: IEEE.

Kim, C., Sakthivel, R., & Chung, W. K. (2008). Unscented FastSLAM: A Robust and Efficient Solution to the SLAM Problem. *IEEE Transactions on Robotics , 24* (4), 808-820.

Lin, C.-H., Song, K.-T., & Anderson, G. T. (10-12 Oct. 2005). Agent-based robot control design for multi-robot cooperation. *In Proc. IEEE International Conference on Systems, Man and Cybernetics 2005. 1,* pp. 542-547. IEEE.

Lippiello, V., Siciliano, B., & Villani, L. (2007). Position-Based Visual Servoing in Industrial Multirobot Cells Using a Hybrid Camera Configuration. *IEEE Transactions on Robotics , 23* (1), 73 - 86.

Pathiranage, C., Watanabe, K., Jayasekara, B., & Izumi, K. (2008). Simultaneous Localization and Mapping: A Pseudolinear Kalman Filter (PLKF) Approach. *Information and Automation for Sustainability, 2008. ICIAFS 2008. 4th International Conference* (pp. 61 - 66). IEEE.

Pengcheng, C. .., & Zhicheng, J. (2007). Simulation Study on Tracking Control of Mobile Robot Based on Cascaded Adaptive Approach. *Control Conference, 2007. CCC 2007. Chinese* (pp. 339-403). Zhangjiajie, Hunan, China: IEEE.

Takahashi, H., Nishi, H., & Ohnishi, K. (Dec. 2004). Autonomous decentralized control for formation of multiple mobile robots considering ability of robot. *IEEE Transactions on Industrial Electronics , 51* (6), 1272-1279.

Temeltas, H., & Kayak, D. (2008). SLAM for robot navigation. *IEEE Aerospace and Electronic Systems Magazine , 23* (12), 16-19.

Yun, X., Yiming, Y., Zeming, D., Bingru, L., & Bo, Y. (5-8 Oct. 2003). Design and realization of communication mechanism of autonomous robot soccer based on multi-agent system. *In Proc. IEEE International Conference on Systems, Man and Cybernetics 2003. 1,* pp. 66-71. IEEE.

3

Pen-type Sensor for Surface Texture Perception

Xianming Ye[1], Byungjune Choi[1], Hyouk Ryeol Choi[1], and Sungchul Kang[2]
[1]*Sungkyunkwan University*
[2]*Korea Institute of Science and Technology*
Korea

1. Introduction

The measurements of surface properties by contact sensing have been investigated for a long time. Recent advances in tactile related applications that previously rely only on visual feedback, e.g. telepresence, interactions with objects in virtual environments, and minimally invasive surgery, have raised the requirement for the feedback of haptic information to get realistic sensations of direct contact. Surface texture is one of the most important surface properties that affect the feeling of touch. However, it is difficult to describe and measure the property of tactile texture of a surface. Unlike the measurements of texture to characterize the mechanical performance of a surface, research of measuring tactile texture is still in its initial stage, and most efforts have been spent in the developments of texture sensors.

The common methods of measurements of surface properties are based on the measurements of contact forces/pressure. For example, geometric parameters of surfaces can be estimated based on the stress map of the contact area which is measured by arrays of force sensing units. Sophisticated force-based applications can measure the contact locations, surface curvatures, edges and shapes of objects (Fearing & Binford, 1991; Heidemann & Schopfer, 2004; Murakami & Hasegawa, 2005). By measuring the dynamics of contact forces in dexterous manipulations, the incipient slip between the object and robot hands can also be detected (Tremblay & Cutkosky, 1993). However, in contrast to force-based measurements of geometry, the goal of tactile sensing is to obtain local contact parameters, such as surface roughness/ texture, the hardness/softness of object, heat transfer properties, frictional properties, the material of the object, etc.

The development of force-based texture sensors for the perception of texture is difficult because the required modalities for the characterization and measurement of surface texture are still ambiguous. Psychophysical researches showed that contact vibrations provide the most useful information for the perceptions of surface fine textures with inter-element spacing less than about 1 *mm* (Johnson & Hsiao, 1994; Hollins et al., 1998). Therefore, there are many sensors imitate the structures of the human finger by designing components of nails, bones, ridges on the sensor surfaces, multilayered sensing skin, and use different transducers embedded in the sensors to measure the stimuli of contact vibrations (Mayol-Cuevas et al., 1998; Yamada et al., 2001; Tada et al., 2003).

Based on the responses of haptic explorations, several sensors showed the ability of discriminations of different types of fine-textured surfaces. Mayol-Cuevas et al. developed a fingertip-like sensor using an electret piezoelectric microphone embedded in a rugged material as the transducer (Mayol-Cuevas et al., 1998). Contact sounds generated during sliding motions against a surface were picked up by a microphone and analyzed with FFT and learning vector quantization technique (LVQ) for texture recognition. Baglio et al. presented a tactile sensor that used bimorph piezo-ceramic actuators and sensors for stimulation and sensing of response signals (Baglio et al., 2002). By combining signal power spectral density analysis with fuzzy recognition, this system can recognize different types of materials. Fend et al. developed an active multi-whisker array modeled on the rat whisker system (Fend et al., 2003). This whisker array can discriminate different textures based on the frequency response elicited by the whiskers. Mukaibo et al. developed a finger-like multilayered texture sensor (Mukaibo et al., 2005). The sensor is able to identify the differences in roughness, softness and frictional properties of different materials and quantitatively detect the texture information of a surface. Hosoda et al. developed a soft fingertip with randomly distributed strain gauges and PVDF films (Hosoda et al., 2006). With force signals from strain gauges and the variances of the signals from the PVDF films produced by pushing and rubbing movements, this anthropomorphic fingertip can discriminate five different types of materials. In our previous research (Ye et al., 2006), a texture sensor with embedded PVDF films was developed, which can discriminate the fine textures on different types of sandpapers based on the patterns of responses in the frequency domain.

Vibration-based texture sensors have showed the ability to perceive and discriminate textures. Meaningful results having been obtained individually; however, the comparison of experimental results in terms of precision, efficiency, or even the validity, seems to be difficult. Based on previous results, it would be also difficult to define any essential requirement for texture sensing. Therefore, fundamental researches are required to understand the mechanisms of fine texture perception to which the texture perceptions to which the developments of texture sensors can be referred.

In this report we propose a sensor for the perception of surface roughness. Rather than targeting to the discrimination of perceived roughness from the point of view of sensation, efforts are made for the measurements of surface roughness profiles, with which the analysis and reconstruction of surface textures can be performed. The proposed sensor has a rigid contact probe and is able to measure the 3D contact forces applied to the probe's tip and the dynamic contact signal along the probe's axis direction. It has been used in our previous research (Ye et al., 2007). It can be discriminated from the hand-held device developed by Pai and Rizun which measures 3D accelerations and 1D contact force in the normal direction (Pai et al., 2003). The measurement of 3D contact forces offer more useful information for estimations of surface profiles and perceptions of textures.

2. Requirements for texture sensing

Because psychophysical and neurophysiological studies have showed that contact vibrations are necessary and sufficient for the perceptions of fine textures by human fingers, the dynamic sensing has been adopted for texture perceptions and techniques for analysis of time-varying signals have also been applied. Tactile texture sensors are developed by emulating the structure of the human finger; sensing processes also start with contact explorations on objects. However, the dynamic response signals are affected by the details of sensor design and the exploratory parameters (contact force, speed, etc.) as well as the surface texture itself, making it difficult to quantitatively describe the obtained texture. On the other hand, recent psychophysical studies with metal gratings showed that the groove widths between ridges have the strongest effect on the estimation of perceived roughness, and the estimated magnitudes of roughness can be described accurately as a function of groove widths and ridge widths (Yoshioka et al., 2001). This finding suggests that the perceived texture can be represented more accurately by parameters of surface profile instead of the frequency components of contact response signals.

One of the difficulties in texture sensing comes from the unquantifiable characteristics of tactile sensors. Most of tactile sensors are composed of a soft layer between the textured surface and the transducers. This soft layer is subject to all kinds of contact texture stimuli in explorations. For example, there are tangential forces and normal height variations in the contact area in the case of surface height detection. When the sensor slides onto a bump, tangential and normal stimuli are both significant. However, it is easy to draw a conclusion that the sensor characteristic is inhomogeneous if only the normal stimuli are taken into consideration. The existence of such intermediate layer makes it difficult to interpret sensor outputs with respect to surface textures. It can simplify the system design and the development of algorithm for analysis if the intermediate uncertainties of measurements can be minimized.

Another factor that makes texture sensing difficult is that the sizes of texture elements are generally smaller than the size of the contact area. Measuring a fine-textured surface with a comparatively large-sized transducer will filter out the details of texture, as illustrated in Fig. 1. The existence of an intermediate soft layer worsens this problem as the contact stimuli propagate within the layer. For the perception of fine texture, the developments of tactile sensors have to reduce the size of contact interface during explorations to preserve surface details.

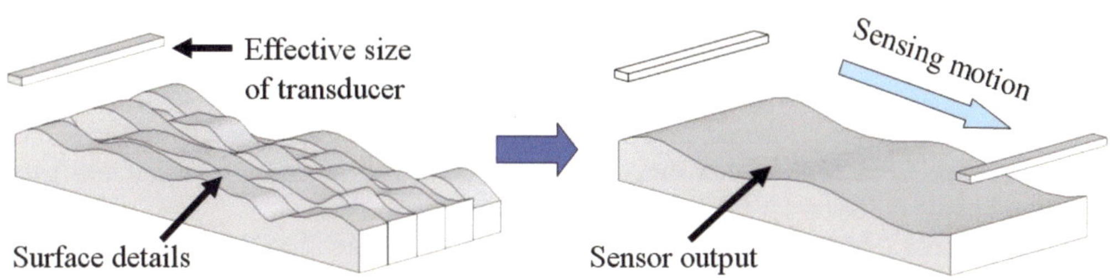

Fig. 1. The effect of large contact area on tactile sensing. The local texture details are filtered out because of the relatively large contact area.

In this report, we present a handheld pen-type texture sensor (see Fig. 2) that can satisfy the requirements described above. By using a rigid contact probe for texture sensing, the contact stimuli (static and dynamic forces) are measured with minimum distortions. The contact between the probe's hemispherical tip and the surface can be considered as a single point contact. The profile of surface in the path of exploration can be estimated based on the measurements of contact forces and the motion of the sensor.

3. Development of pen-type texture sensor

This section describes the development of a miniaturized handheld pen-type texture sensor for the perception of surface texture. The proposed pen-type sensor is capable of measuring

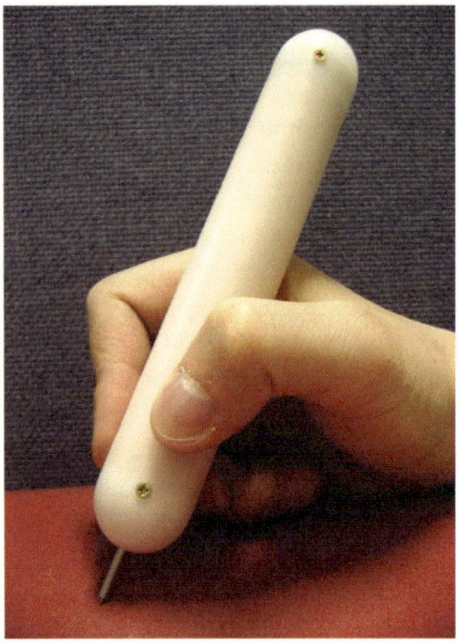

Fig. 2. The proposed handheld texture sensor for texture sensing.

3D contact forces applied at the tip and the dynamic force in the axial direction. It consists of one aluminium probe with a hemispherical tip and three kinds of sensing elements: four strain gauges, a force sensor, and a PVDF module. The structure of the sensor is shown in Fig. 3(a). Two half-bridge strain gauge circuits are used to measure the tangential forces in x- and y- directions, respectively. The rigid probe works as a cantilever in the measurements of tangential forces. The applied axial force component is measured by a pair of strain gauges which are connected to a half-bridge circuit and attached close to the supported end at opposite sides of the probe. The normal contact force in z-direction is measured by a force sensor (LPM 562 500G by Cooper Instruments & Systems) installed coaxially at the end of the probe. The force sensor also functions as an axial bearing and prevents the axial movement of the probe under the load of normal contact force.

A PVDF module (H×W×L=2.5×12×5 *mm*) is installed between the force sensor and the contact probe to measure the dynamic of force in z-direction. There is one thin PVDF film (H×W×L=0.1×1×10 *mm*) embedded in the center of a silicon layer. While the silicon layer delivers the contact force from the probe to the force sensor, the PVDF film embedded inside measures the change rate of force in its thickness direction (d_{33}). As a transducer, the PVDF film has very wide frequency range and dynamic range. Combined with the force sensor, they function similarly to the different types of receptors distributed in the fingertip skin. As a ferroelectric polymer, the PVDF film exhibits piezoelectric and pyroelectric properties. To minimize the pyroelectric effect, the temperature of the PVDF module is maintained approximately at the room temperature.

As a compact handheld device, the circuit (see Fig. 3(c)) is also included in the pen-type sensor. Common circuit modules are used in the circuit design, as shown in Fig. 3(b). A differential amplifier is used for the amplification of the output signals of the force sensor. Two half-bridge circuits are used to readout the signals from the four strain gauges, followed by proper amplifications.

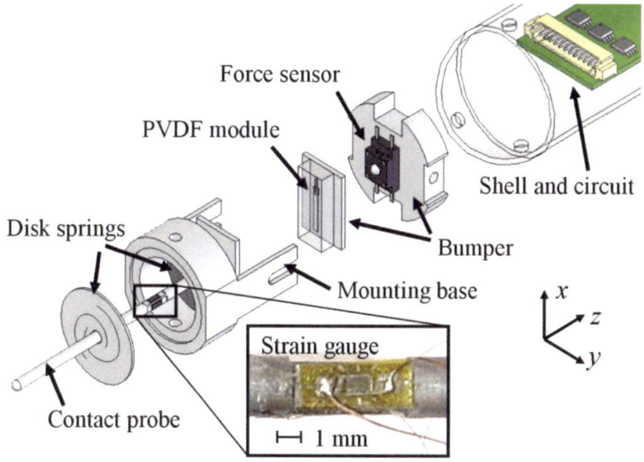

(a) The structure of sensor

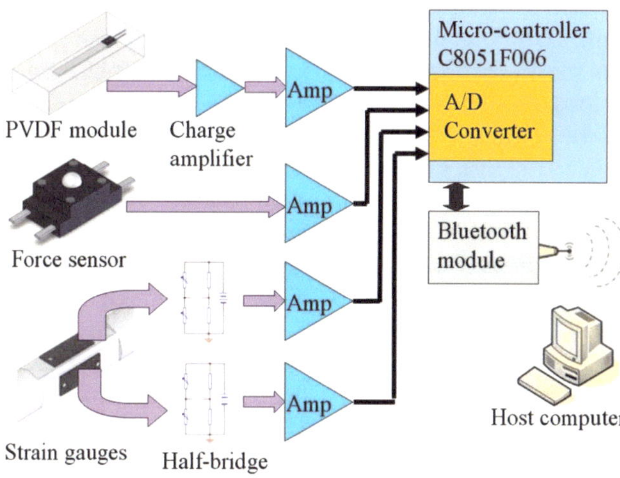

(b) Schematic diagram

(c) Circuit for signal conditioning and wireless communication

Fig. 3. The mechanical structure of pen-type texture sensor and the layout of transducers.

A charge amplifier and a second amplifier are used to read the signal of the PVDF module. These four signal channels are digitalized using the built-in A/D converter of the micro-controller and transmitted to a host computer via a Bluetooth wireless communication link. A data processing program written with MATLAB is running on the host computer to perform further signal analysis.

One more problem that should be considered is how to support the contact probe. Because the load on the probe is small, the simple and widely used bush bearing was firstly adopted. However, the outputs of the force sensor were distorted and the stimuli to the PVDF film were strongly suppressed. This is due to the static contact friction of the bush bearing. When tangential contact forces are applied at the tip of the probe, a torque about the point of bearing is introduced. To counterbalance this torque, a pair of counteractive forces is generated at the both ends of the bush. Although the sliding frictional coefficient of metal is small, such counteracting forces and the consequent sticking effects are severe enough to filter out the dynamic force.

Although the rigidity of the sensor in the probe's axial direction is large and there is no relative motion between the contact probe and the base of bearing, frictionless bearing is required in the design. Therefore, the flexure bearing is built by using a pair of disk springs for the support of the sensing probe, as shown in Fig. 4. The disk-shaped springs is made by carving involute-shaped grooves through thin copper disks. For the radial support, the equivalent model of the spring is a simple beam with force and torque loads at its ends. The probe can move freely in the disk's axial direction but be restricted in the radial direction. A pair of separated disk springs is used to counterbalance the torque introduced by the tangential contact forces. When the probe moves from its equilibrium position, a spring force proportional to the displacement is generated. This force can be calculated according to Hooke's law. Because the contact probe does not move during tactile sensing, the probe can be set to stay at its equilibrium position, and no static spring force is applied to the force sensor. However, a small preloaded spring force is intentionally applied to keep a tight contact in the axial direction between the probe, the PVDF module, and the force sensor. One disadvantage of the disk spring mechanism is its low radial stiffness, which results in the coupling effect between the measured tangential forces and the normal contact force, and therefore, a decoupling calculation is required.

(a) (b) (c)

Fig. 4. The disk spring mechanism for the supporting of the contact probe. (a) The structure of the disk spring. The probe can move (b) forward and (c) backward in the probe's axis direction.

Unlike the sensor used in our previous research (Ye et al., 2006), there is no foam layer in this design, and therefore, the contact probe exhibits higher rigidity in the normal direction. A wider signal bandwidth is expected and a higher sampling rate of A/D conversion is required. The micro-controller is able to perform A/D conversions up to 25 KHz for each of the four signal channels. However, a 3 KHz sampling rate limitation is introduced by the relatively low bitrate of the wireless communication. Explorations with reduced speeds can alleviate the effect of sampling rate limitation.

4. Experimental evaluations

This section presents the evaluation of the proposed texture sensor. For all experiments, the sensor is held by hand and perpendicular to the target surface. The contact point locates at the hemispheric end of the aluminum contact probe. Four kinds of handy materials are used for experiments: the hard surface of a desk, a mouse pad, a transparent duct tape with smooth surface and a towel. Contact forces are controlled approximately at a constant value in the same exploration. Sliding speeds are between 40 ~$60mm/s$.

4.1 Measurement of 3D contact force

The purpose of 3D contact force measurements is to evaluate the Coulomb frictional property of the surface which is calculated based on the normal forces and tangential forces. The contact force can be measured with a 3DOF force sensor, and there are many commercial force/torque sensors can be used for this purpose. However, for a small hand held device, the size constraint is critical. It is difficult to find a cheap force sensor that can satisfy all of these requirements.

The proposed texture sensor provides good results of 3D contact force measurements while maintaining a relatively small size. According to the beam theory, there are transverse coupling effects between the forces in x-, y- and z-directions. These coupling effects mean that the measured values of f_x, f_y and f_z are affected each other by the Poisson's ration of aluminium. Ideally, there is no coupling between the normal force and the tangential forces. However, the experiments showed that such coupling effect exists and becomes stronger with the increase of the applied tangential forces. This coupling effect can be explained as follows. When the torque introduced by tangential forces is totally counteracted by the pair of disk springs, the force sensor is only sensitive to the normal force f_z. In this case, however, the radial bearing rigidity provided by the disk springs is not sufficiently strong. The contact probe rotates in a small scale under the combination of bearing forces and tangential forces. Because the assembly of the sensor is tight in the axial direction, the rotations generate small displacement with respect to the force sensor, and therefore, additional axial contact force is introduced.

A correction for decoupling is required to obtain the precise values of applied contact forces. Assuming that the coupling factors are linear and can be represented by a constant value, every factor is determined by a calibration. Firstly, the amplifiers for every force components are tuned to unify three measurement channels with the 2 N contact force corresponding to the maximum voltage outputs of amplifiers. After the gain unification, forces in the full range are applied in one axial direction; the outputs of other two force components are recoded simultaneously. The relation between the coupled outputs and the applied forces is approximately linear. The coupling factors from the given component to the others are determined by the ratio of corresponding coupled outputs to the applied force. With all determined coupling factors, the contact forces are calculated as follows.

$$\begin{bmatrix} F_x \\ F_y \\ F_z \end{bmatrix} = \begin{bmatrix} 1 & -0.09 & -0.2 \\ -0.10 & 1 & -0.25 \\ -0.15 & -0.18 & 1 \end{bmatrix} \begin{bmatrix} f_x \\ f_y \\ f_z \end{bmatrix}, \tag{1}$$

where F_x, F_y and F_z are the applied forces, f_x, f_y and f_z are outputs of amplifiers. It is noticed that the decoupling matrix is not symmetric because of the sensitivities of strain gauges, which are manually attached, are not identical.

4.2 Measurement of frictional coefficient

With the normal and tangential force measurements, the Coulomb frictional coefficient can be evaluated using the equation $\mu = f / N$, where the normal contact force $N = F_z$, and the friction is the tangential force $f = \sqrt{F_x^2 + F_y^2}$.

A mouse pad and a towel were used in the experiments. Three different normal contact forces were applied for explorations on each surface. The experiments results are shown in Figs. 5(c) and 5(d). Each column in the figure is the result for one kind of normal contact force. The first row is the tangential force (frictional force) f; the second row is the normal force applied N; and the third row is the frictional coefficient calculated with equation $\mu = f / N$.

The results showed that the calculated frictional coefficient changes dynamically. This is due to the changing of applied normal forces and the uneven surface textures. Especially in the responses of scanning on the towel, an approximately constant frequency response is observed with increased normal contact forces. This is due to the regular textile texture of the towel which can be treated as a coarse texture. The calculated coefficients are similar under different normal contact forces. Furthermore, the difference between the coefficients of friction of these two materials is small, which is consistent with the feeling of exploring on both surfaces with bare fingers.

4.3 Dynamic sensing with PVDF film

The PVDF module is located between the contact probe and force sensor. Normal contact is transmitted to the force sensor via the silicon layer while the dynamic signals are picked up by the PVDF film. In this tactile sensor configuration, PVDF film is adopted because of its high sensitivity and wide bandwidth response to dynamic stimuli.

One of the known effects of measuring contact dynamic via a contact probe is the consequent low sensitivity of the system. The gains of amplifiers need to be increased several hundreds times higher than those used in our previous research (Ye et al., 2006) to generate equal amplitudes of outputs from similar inputs. This is due to two factors. Firstly, the reduced contact area indicates the reduction of the input intensity; and secondly, the use of the contact probe and the bearing disk springs attenuates the tactile stimuli, because they act as a spring-mass system with high spring constant.

4.3.1 Dynamic response of the PVDF film

To find out the respond characteristics of PVDF film, two kinds of primitive inputs were used: step change of the normal contact force F_z and tapping inputs. The results are shown in Fig. 6. The PVDF film is sensitive to stress rate, its output magnitude is proportional to the changing rates of F_z, which is qualitatively verified from the results.

(a) A mouse pad

(b) A towel

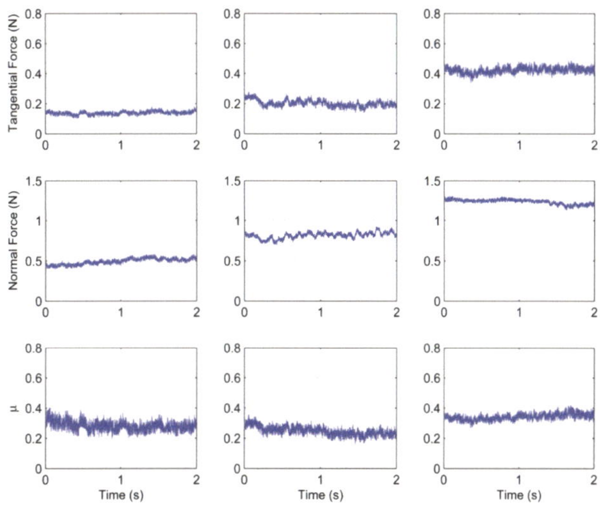

(c) Frictional coefficient of a mouse pad

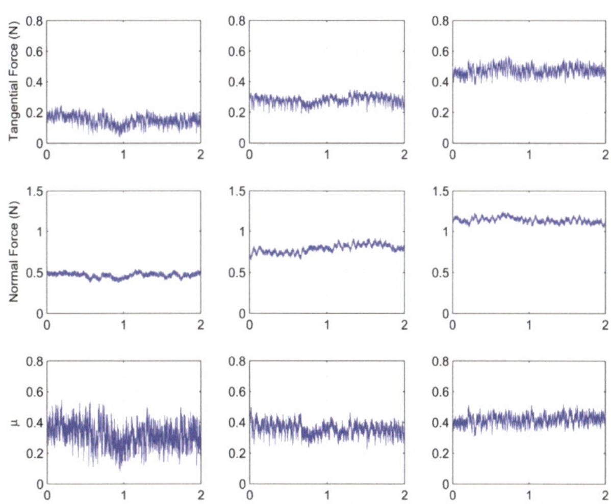

(d) Frictional coefficient of a towel

Fig. 5. The measurements of coefficient of frictional of a mouse pad and a towel with different applied normal contact forces.

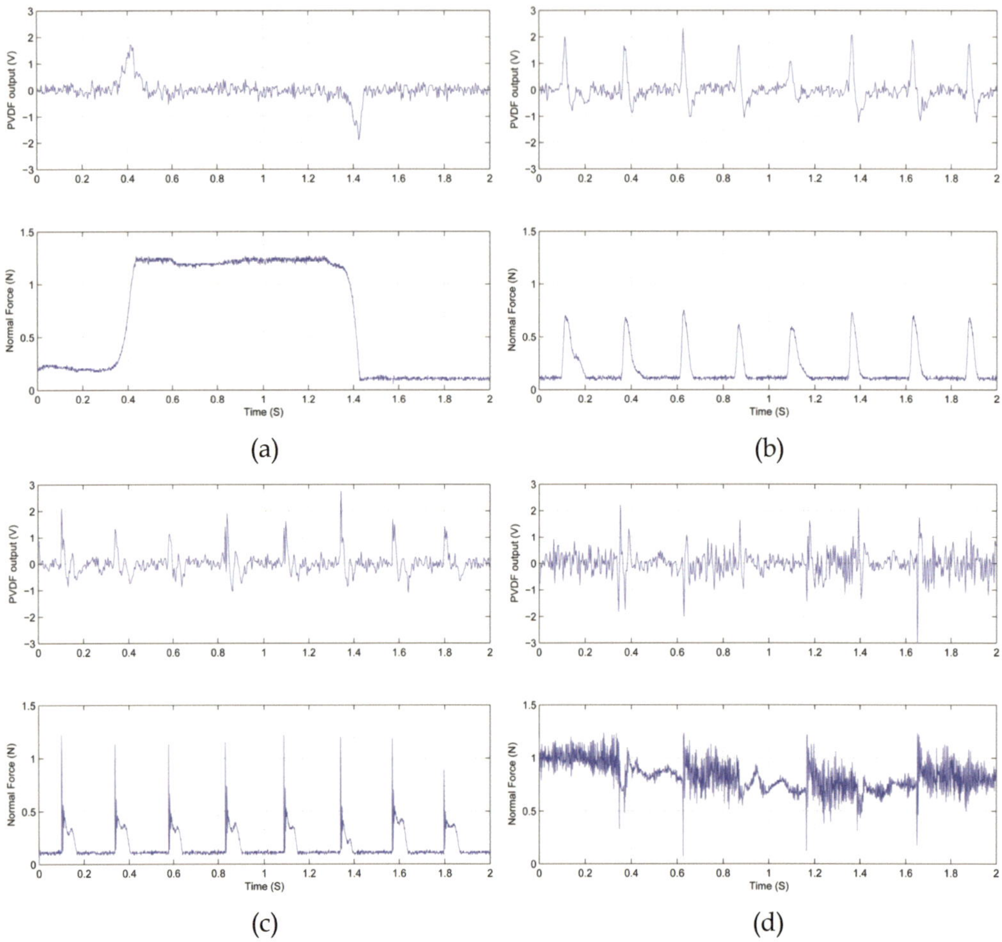

Fig. 6. The dynamic output of PVDF film vs. force sensor. (a) Response to step input of normal contact force. (b) Response to tapping against a mouse pad. (c) Response to tapping against a hard desktop. (d) Response of sliding over three bands of duct tape.

From the response of desk tapping (see Fig. 6(b) and 6(c)), both the force sensor and the PVDF film generate a high peak output at each moment of contact. For the PVDF film, the most important signal is the peak response, so it should be detected by the micro-controller. However, as mentioned in the section of sensor development, limited by the architecture of the micro-controller, A/D conversion for each channel is performed one after another at a limited sampling rate, which means that there is a conversion time delay for each signal channel.

4.3.2 Sliding response of the PVDF film

Fig. 6(d) shows the response of sliding over of three parallel bands of duct tape stuck on the desktop with intervals equal to the tape's width. Although the desktop surface is felt smooth to the human fingers, the pen-type sensor picks up the high frequency response signals because of the high rigidities of the desktop and the high axial stiffness of the sensor.

Therefore, even small height variations at the contact area can trigger strong dynamic tactile stimuli.

When the sensor is sliding on the smooth tape, its outputs indicate the change rate of the normal force and the white noise of circuit. Therefore, the outputs in this case can be considered the response of the sensor to the explorations of surface with "zero texture." When sliding on and off the edges of duct tape, the PVDF module generates much stronger responses than the force sensor, which can be used for edge detections.

5. Conclusions

In this report, a compact handheld pen-type texture sensor for the measurement of fine texture was presented. Because surface roughness and friction properties are most critical parameters in tactile texture sensing, the proposed texture sensor was designed with a metal contact probe and was able to measure the roughness and frictional properties of a surface. Using a rigid contact probe for contact explorations, the sensor can reduce the size of contact area and separate the normal stimuli from tangential ones, which facilitates the interpretation of the relation between dynamic responses and the surface texture.

As for the measured 3D contact forces, they can be used to estimate the surface profile in the path of exploration. Based in the profiles of surface, sophisticated algorithm can be applied for the analysis and restriction of textured surface. In our latest research, the proposed pen-type texture sensor was applied in the reconstruction of periodic texture with limited number of scans on the surface. The dynamic force sensing can be used for the estimation of surface texture in various ways. For example, we can use the rate of strike to represent the rate of appearance of micro peaks of surface texture that come in contact with the sensor's probe. When the amplitudes of the response signal exceed a given threshold, contact strikes are considered happened and a surface with higher rate of contact strikes during explorations can be considered as a rougher surface.

6. Acknowledgment

This work was supported partially by Korea Institute of Science and Technology under the Immersive Tangible Experience Space Technology project, and partially by the Ministry of Knowledge Economy(MKE) and Korea Institute for Advancement in Technology (KIAT) through the Workforce Development Program in Strategic Technology.

7. References

Baglio, S., Muscato, G. & Savalli, N. (2002). Tactile measuring systems for the recognition of unknown surfaces, 51(3): 522–531.

Fearing, R. S. & Binford, T. O. (1991). Using a cylindrical tactile sensor for determining curvature, 7(6): 806–817.

Fend, M., Bovet, S., Yokoi, H. & Pfeifer, R. (2003). An active artificial whisker array for texture discrimination, *Proc. IEEE/RSJ International Conference on Intelligent Robots and Systems (IROS 2003)*, Vol. 2, pp. 1044–1049.

Heidemann, G. & Schopfer, M. (2004). Dynamic tactile sensing for object identification, *Proc. IEEE International Conference on Robotics and Automation ICRA '04*, Vol. 1, pp. 813–818.

Hollins, M., Bensmaia, S. & Risner, R. (1998). The duplex theory of tactile texture perception, *Proceedings of the 14th Annual Meeting of the International Society for Psychophysics*.

Hosoda, K., Tada, Y.&Asada, M. (2006). Anthropomorphic robotic soft ngertip with randomly distributed receptors, *Robotics and Autonomous Systems* 54: 104–109.

Johnson, K. O. & Hsiao, S. S. (1994). Evaluation of the relative roles of slowly and rapidly adapting afferent fibres in roughness perception, *Canadian Journal of Physiology & Pharmacology* 72: 488–497.

Mayol-Cuevas, W. W., Juarez-Guerrero, J. & Munoz-Gutierrez, S. (1998). A first approach to tactile texture recognition, *Proc. IEEE International Conference on Systems, Man, and Cybernetics*, Vol. 5, pp. 4246–4250.

Mukaibo, Y., Shirado, H., Konyo, M. & Maeno, T. (2005). Development of a texture sensor emulating the tissue structure and perceptual mechanism of human fingers, *Proc. IEEE International Conference on Robotics and Automation ICRA 2005*, pp. 2565–2570.

Murakami, K. & Hasegawa, T. (2005). Tactile sensing of edge direction of an object with a soft fingertip contact, *Proc. IEEE International Conference on Robotics and Automation ICRA 2005*, pp. 2571–2577.

Pai, D., Pai, D. & Rizun, P. (2003). The what: a wireless haptic texture sensor, *in* P. Rizun (ed.), *Proc. 11th Symposium on Haptic Interfaces for Virtual Environment and Teleoperator Systems HAPTICS 2003*, pp. 3–9.

Tada, Y., Hosoda, K., Yamasaki, Y. & Asada, M. (2003). Sensing the texture of surfaces by anthropomorphic soft fingertips with multi-modal sensors, *Proc. IEEE/RSJ International Conference on Intelligent Robots and Systems (IROS 2003)*, Vol. 1, pp. 31–35.

Tremblay, M. R. & Cutkosky, M. R. (1993). Estimating friction using incipient slip sensing during a manipulation task, *Proc. IEEE International Conference on Robotics and Automation*, pp. 429–434.

Yamada, D., Maeno, T.&Yamada, Y. (2001). Artificial finger skin having ridges and distributed tactile sensors used for grasp force control, *Proc. IEEE/RSJ International Conference on Intelligent Robots and Systems*, Vol. 2, pp. 686–691.

Ye, X., Choi, B., Choi, H. & Kang, S. (2006). Roughness perception with tactile sensor, *1st Conference on Intelligent Robots*, Korea Robotics Society, pp. 343–348.

Ye, X., Choi, B., Choi, H. & Kang, S. (2007). Pen-type sensor for surface texture perception, *Proc. 16th IEEE International Symposium on Robot and Human interactive Communication RO-MAN 2007*, pp. 642–647.

Yoshioka, T., Gibb, B., Dorsch, A. K., Hsiao, S. S. & Johnson, K. O. (2001). Neural coding mechanisms underlying perceived roughness of finely textured surfaces, *The Journal of Neuroscience* 21(17): 6905–6916.

4

iGrace – Emotional Computational Model for EmI Companion Robot.

Sébastien Saint-Aimé and Brigitte Le-Pévédic and Dominique Duhaut
Valoria Laboratory - University of Bretagne Sud
France

1. Introduction

A new challenge in Robotics is to create systems capable of behaviour enhancement due to their interaction with humans. Research work in psychology has shown that facial expressions play an essential role in the coordination of human conversation (Boyle et al., 1994) and constitute an essential modality in human communication. Robotherapy, a field in robotics, attempts to apply the principles of social robotics to better the psychological and physiological state of the ill, the secluded, or those with physical or mental handicaps. It seems that robots can play a role of both companionship and stimulation. They must, however, be designed with a maximum of communication capacities for such a purpose. One of the first experiments in this field of robotics was carried out with elderly people in a retirement home and Paro (Shibata, 2004). These experiments clearly showed that companion robots could give a certain moral and psychological comfort to those that are most vulnerable.

In this context, the goal of the MAPH project is the realisation of a robot with the following fundamental qualities: a stuffed animal, pleasant to touch, sensors, etc. However, a robot that is too complex or too big should be avoided. The EmotiRob project, a component of the MAPH project, aims to give a robot the capacities of perception and natural language comprehension so that it can establish a formal representation of the emotional state of its interlocutor. Finally, the EmotiRob project also includes the conception of a model of the emotional states of the robot and its evolution. Following a study of the progress of research on perception and emotional synthesis, determining the most appropriate way to express emotions proved important to have a recognition rate that would be acceptable to our public. After experimentation on the subject, we have determined the minimal number of degrees of freedom necessary for a robot to express the 6 primary emotions. The second step was the definition and description of our emotional model iGrace. The experiments carried out allowed us to validate the hypotheses of the model which would be integrated into EmI - Emotional Model of Interaction. The next steps of the project will help in evaluating the robot, its expression, as well as the amount of comfort it can bring to children.

2. The MAPH project - active media for handicap

The MAPH project objective is to give comfort to vulnerable children and/or those undergoing long-term hospitalization with the help of a robot which can be used as an emotional companion. As the use of robots in a hospital environment remains limited, we have decided to opt for simplicity in the robotic architecture, thus in the emotional expression as well. The EmotiRob project, a component of the MAPH project, aims at maintaining nonverbal interaction with children between 4 and 8 years of age. As has been shown in the synopsis (see Figure 1), the project is essentially made of three main interdependent parts:

- Recognition and understanding of a child's spoken language.
- Emotional interaction between the child and the robot.
- Cognitive interaction between the child and the robot.

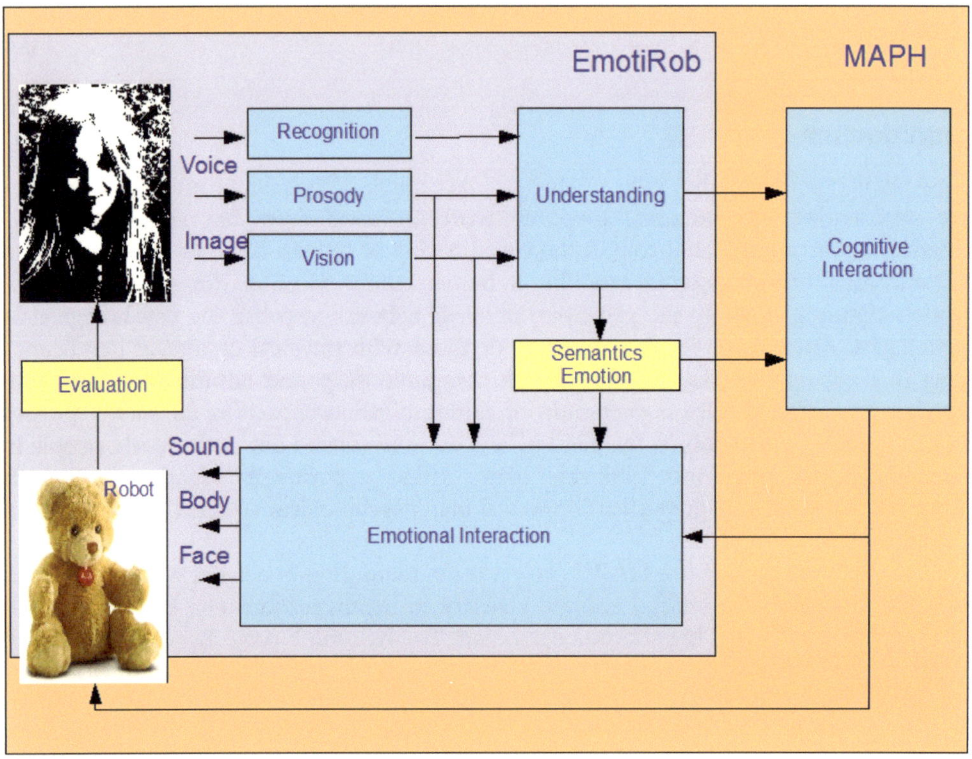

Fig. 1. General synopsis of the MAPH project

Only emotional interaction will be laid out in detail in this document.[1]

3. Emotion & interaction

3.1 Definitions

3.1.1 Emotions

For several years now, human emotion has been the source of scientific research about its definition, as well as its composition. Originally, emotion is a notion of the mind, and is, therefore, analysed and studied by psychologists and physiologists. Over time, research has

[1] For more informations about ohers parts of the project, you can visit Website: http://www-valoria.univ-ubs.fr/emotirob/

proven that human activities are influenced by emotional states. This theory opened the door to the integration of the notion of emotion into diverse activities such as communication, negotiation, learning, etc. Moreover, computer science research naturally aims to integrate the emotional aspect in its applications for better man-machine interaction. Some of the definitions that current research is based on are given in Table 1.

Authors	Definition
Descartes et al. (de Sousa, 2008)	Emotions are made up of primary emotions and are measured in function to a limited number of finite dimensions (ex. level of stimulation, intensity, pleasure or aversion, one's own intention or that of others, etc.)
Magda Arnold Arnold (1960)	An emotion is a tendency toward an object intuitively judged as good (beneficial) or away from an object intuitively judged as bad (harmful). This attraction or aversion is accompanied by a pattern of physiological changes for approaching or avoiding.
Solomon (Solomon, 1973)	Emotions are judgements characterized by their temporal mode and their content evaluation; emotions are also strategic choices in the aim to protect oneself and to increase respect of oneself (inspired by Sartre's theory, 1938 (Sartre, 1995)).
James (James, 1884) and Lange (Lange & , Trans)	Emotion is a response to physiological changes. *"... we feel sorry because we cry, angry because we strike, afraid because we tremble ... "*.
Ortony and al. Ortony & Turner (1990)	Emotions are valence reactions to events, agents or objects.
Greenspan (Greenspan, 1988)	Emotion is a conscious mental process affecting a major component of the body; it also has a lot of influence on one's thought and action, notably to plan social interaction strategies.
Lazarus (Lazarus, 1991)	He highlights that appraisals are necessary and sufficient for emotion. Adding that the notion of coping allows an individual to choose strategies to confront future problems.
Scherer (Scherer, 2005)	In general, emotion can be seen as a sort of process that involves different parts, including subjective feeling, cognition, physical expression, the tendency of action or desires, and the neurological process.

Table 1. Definitions of emotions

In the design of our iGrace model, we will define emotion as a process which characterises the whole of physiological and psychological emotions of a human being for an event at a given moment. As a process, an emotion follows an algorithm which is repeated each time an event is identified:

- Perception of the event
- Reaction to the event
- Expression of the event

3.1.2 Emotional experiences

Emotions are generally characterised by subjective experiences of certain types (Parrott, 1991). Despite the complexity of the emotions and the disagreement between theoreticians on their nature, there is a consensus on the fact that subjective experience or *"feeling"* is an important aspect in emotion for Man. According to some theoreticians, this subjective emotional experience or *"feeling"* is in part the result of internal corporal changes or the activation of *"primitive"* or *"non-cognitive"* zones of the brain. However, Parrot (Parrott, 1988) sees *"feeling"* as a result of activities in high level cerebral zones. Inexorably, emotional experience is also linked to these zones of activity.

Michelle Larivey (Larivey, 2002) determined four types of emotional experiences which represent our emotion type: simple emotions, mixed emotions, dismissed emotions, and pseudo-emotions. More detailed explications on the meaning and use of these different emotional experiences follow.

- Simple emotions: These are the only real emotions. They give us direct information on the state of our needs and how to satisfy them. Emotions are used to inform us of the state of our needs. Are they satisfied? To what extent? What need is it? It is important to recognize and feel our emotions. By letting the natural process of emotions happen, we are sure to be in control of the satisfaction of our needs.
- Mixed Emotions: These are defensive experiences that seem to be emotions. In fact, they are a mix of emotions and subterfuges which cause us to fool ourselves and our interlocutor. They try to "misinform" us (unlike simple emotions). Examples: guilt, jealousy, contempt, pity, shame, etc.
- Dismissed Emotions: These are usually corporally dominated experiences which happen when an emotion is dismissed or not expressed. The repressed emotion should be uncovered. Examples: worry, anxiety, feverishness, discomfort, emptiness, muscle tension, overexcitement, migraine, knot in one's stomach, stuttering, lump in one's throat, etc.
- Pseudo-emotions: we often mistake these for emotions, but they are concepts that give meaning to our reality, images used as metaphors, states of mind, attitudes, or assessments. In fact, they are not emotions, they are pseudo-emotions.

3.1.3 Behaviour

Like emotions, there are several different definitions of the concept of "behaviour" in the current literature (Bloch et al., 1994):

- It is a group of phenomena that can be externally observed.
- Way of being and acting of Animals and Mankind, objective manifestations of their global activity.
- Behaviour is a group of objectively observable reactions that an organism doted with a nervous system generally executes in response to stimuli from the environment, themselves being objectively observable.
- Behaviour is a reality that can be apprehended in the form of observation units and acts, the frequency and sequencing of which are likely to be modified; it translates into action the image of the situation as it is created, with its own tools, by the being that is being studied: behaviour expresses a form of representation and construction of a particular world.

Behaviour can be defined as a group of organised movements external to the organism (Castel, visité en 2009). For humans, it can be described as a group of actions and reactions (movement, physiological modification, verbal expression, etc.) of an individual in a given situation. In the rest of this paper, the behaviour of our robot will be defined as a series of actions and/or reactions to stimuli.

3.2 Founding psychological theories

3.2.1 Appraisal theory

According to the appraisal theory (Ortony et al., 1988) or the "assessment" theory, each person is always able to pick out, consciously or unconsciously, what is important to him/her in the given context (Scherer, 2005). Emotions are thus linked to one's evaluation of the environment. Therefore, emotions are reactions to events, agents or objects. The events, agents or objects are themselves assessed in accordance to goals, norms and attitudes of the person.

This theory, which is similar to a computational approach, is used in the majority of emotion modules for its generic criteria for emotion assessment. However, this process does not define the intensity of the emotions during a reaction.

3.2.2 Lazarus theory

"People are constantly evaluating relationships with the environment with respect to their implications for personal well-being." (Lazarus, 2001)

According to Lazarus (Lazarus, 1991) there are two processes which allow the individual to stabilise his/her relationship with the environment:

- Cognitive evaluation or appraisal: adaptive process which permits conserving or modifying the relationship between the agent and his/her goals, as well as the world with its restrictions, in such a way as to maintain balance. He has determined two types of evaluation:
    - Primary evaluation: represents the pertinence of an event or the congruence of an event, or not, to the goal.
    - Secondary evaluation: represents what could or should be done in response to an event.
- Adaptation or the concept of coping: includes "cognitive and behavioural efforts to manage internal or external demands that are appraised as taxing or exceeding the resources of the person" (Lazarus & Folkman, 1984). In other words, coping is a way to adapt to difficult situations. There are two types of coping:
    - Coping centred on the problem: meaning action: we try to solve the problem or deny it to reduce its effect.
    - Coping centred on emotion: meaning thought: we do not deny the events, but make an effort to emotionally respond to the problem.

3.2.3 Scherer theory

Scherer's component process model (Scherer, 2005) defines emotion as a sequence of changes in state in response to external or internal stimulation in relation to the interest of the individual. These changes take place in five organic systems:

- Cognitive: information processing. Evaluation of a stimulus by perception, memory, the prediction and evaluation of available information.
- Neurophysiological: change in the internal state.
- Motivational: response to the event by preparation of actions.
- Motor: expression and behaviour of the individual.
- Subjective feeling.

These components operate independently of each other during unemotional events, but work in unison in emergency situations or emotional events.

Scherer also focused on information processing and the evaluation of a stimulus. During an emotional process, the individual sequentially evaluates and event in function to a group of criteria or SECs (Sequential Evaluation Checks). These criteria are based on four main objectives which are subdivided into secondary objectives. The main criteria correspond to the most important information that the organism needs:

- Novelty: determine if the external or internal stimulation has changed.
- Pleasantness: determine if the event is pleasant or not and produce the appropriate approach or avoidance behaviour.
- Goal significance: determine the implications and consequences of the event. To what point will they affect my well-being or goals in the long term?
- Coping potential: determine if the individual is able to cope with the consequences or not.
- Compatibility: determine if the event is significant to personal convictions, norms, and social values.

The result of this evaluation will give the type and intensity of the emotion caused by the event. Each emotion should be able to be determined by a combination of SECs and subchecks.

3.2.4 Personality theory

The idea of personality remains rather complex and it is difficult to find a unanimous concept for all those who use it. The general idea bringing together the different visions is that it represents the whole of behaviours that make up an individual. Knowledge of one's personality allows for the prediction, with a limited margin of error, of that person's behaviour in ordinary situations, for example, professional situations. Its objective is to gain knowledge of oneself. The type of theory from analytical psychology, elaborated by psychiatrist Carl Gustav Jung Jung (1950), defines three major characteristics of the human psyche[2]:

- Introversion / Extraversion
- Intuiting / Sensing
- Thinking / Feeling

A person's preference for one of the two poles, on the three axes, gives the psychological type. This is determined by two main personality types:

- Introvert
- Extravert

There is a second series of psychological types determined by four fundamental psychological functions that can be found in the introvert, as well as the extravert:

- Sensing: "S". This process helps you obtain awareness of sensorial information and answer this information free of judgement or evaluations of it. Importance is given to experience, facts, and data.
- Intuition: "N". This process, sometimes called the sixth sense, lets you perceive abstract information, such as symbols, conceptual forms and meanings.
- Thinking: "T". This is an evaluation process of judgement based on objective criteria. It lets you make decisions based on rules and principles.

---

[2] Psyche, in analytical psychology: all of the conscious manifestations of the human personality and intellect.

- Feeling: "F". This process lets you make evaluations based on what is important to you, personal, interpersonal or universal values. This cognitive process of feeling evaluates situations and information subjectively.

From this, Myers and Briggs (Myers, 1987) added a dimension to Jung's work. This dimension judges a person's capacity for organisation and his/her aptitude in respecting the law. It added two psychological functions to those that already existed: judgement and perceiving. By reorganising these functions and preferences into four dimensions, Myers and Briggs created the Myers Briggs Type Indicator (Myers et al., 1998). The MBTI identifies 16 major personality types Cauvin & Cailloux (2005) from a pair of possible preferences for each of the four dimensions.

3.3 Computational models

3.3.1 FLAME - Fuzzy Logic Adaptive Model of Emotions

FLAME (El-Nasr et al., 2000) is a computational model of emotions based on the evaluation of events. It includes some learning components to enhance adaptation for emotion modelling. It also uses an emotion filtering component which takes motivational states into account to solve contradictory emotions. FLAME uses fuzzy logic to map events through goals to emotional intensity. The model contains three components: emotional component, learning component, and decision-making component.

3.3.2 ParlE - Adaptative Plan Based Event Appraisal Model of Emotions

ParleE (Bui et al., 2002) is a quantitative, flexible, adaptive model of emotions for a conversational agent in a multi-agent environment which has multimodal communication capacities. ParleE assesses events based on learning and a probabilistic planning algorithm. It also models personality, as well as motivational states and their role in determining the manner in which the agent experiences emotions.

Rousseau's model of personality (Rousseau, 1996) is used in this particular model, thus classifying personality into the different processes that an agent can carry out: perceiving, reasoning, learning, deciding, acting, interacting, revealing, and feeling - all the while showing emotion. However, the model lacks specifications of the exact influence of emotions on a planning process. Furthermore, the components of models of other agents seem to make the model not quite as flexible as the authors supposed.

3.3.3 Kismet - a robot with artificial emotions

This model aims at establishing interaction between a robot, Kismet (Breazeal, 2003), and a human by using the parent-child relationship during early communication as inspiration. Cynthia Breazeal, who set out this model of emotions in 2002, placed her approach in an agentbased architecture: the different components of the system function in parallel and influence each other. This model was tested with 5 primary emotions (anger, disgust, fear, sadness, happiness) and three additional ones (surprise, interest, and excitement). The personality was not modelled because this model was inspired by the parent-child relationship.

3.3.4 Greta - The dynamics of the affective state in an animated conversational agent

Aiming to create a man-machine interface based on an animated conversation agent, C. Pelachaud and I. Poggi proposed the Greta model (de Rosis et al., 2003). Their agent model includes two closely interrelated components:

- A representation of the agent's mind with a dynamic mechanism for updating.
- A translation of the agent's cognitive state through facial expressions which use various available channels (gaze direction, eyebrow shape, head direction and movement, etc.).

Although implementation of the personality application was created in their model, this idea was not clearly described. In other words, the real relationship between actual personality and emotion or influences of emotion on Greta's mind is not actually identified.

3.3.5 EMA - Emotion and Adaptation

In the EMA model (Gratch & Marsella, 2005), a triggered emotion is determined from evaluation variable values such as the desirability of the event and its probability, but also by the type of agent responsible for the event and the degree of control the agent has over the situation. There is also a casual representation between events (past, present, and future) and resulting states of the agent, as well as the agent's decision planning system which allows for the computation of variables. However, the authors do not model personality in this model.

3.3.6 GALAAD - GRAAL Affective and Logical Agent for Argumentation and Dialog

GALAAD (Adam & Evrard, 2005) is an emotional, conversational, BDI (Belief Desire Intention) agent whose architecture is based on the OCC model. Emotions influence the standard framework of a dialogue and allow for an adaptation process defined by Lazarus. The coping strategy aims at maintaining balance for the agent by reducing the intensity of negative or sensitive emotions that could cause negative effects on his/her behaviour.

Nevertheless, this model has tried to integrate actual behaviour evaluation and adaptation to the architecture of the conversational agent in the dialogue game, but it does not take personality or motivational states of the emotional rational into account.

Another model by Carole Adam is the PLEIAD model (Adam et al., 2007) which seems to be another version of GALAAD. In this model, the author concentrated on updating the knowledge base of the agent by introducing a logic demonstration and activation management model. Like GALAAD, PLEIAD does not integrate personality into their agent.

3.3.7 GRACE - Generic Robotic Architecture to Create Emotions

The generic GRACE model (Dang et al., 2008) defines its emotional process as a physiological emotional response triggered by an internal or external event. It is characterised by 7 components applying the appraisal, coping, Scherer, and personality theories. Being generic lets it incorporate the functionalities of all of the above-sited models. Moreover, it integrates an "Intuition" component, which does not exist in the other models, which allows it to obtain unforeseeable emotional reactions.

3.3.8 Comparison of models

Generally speaking, the three fundamental theories that characterise an emotional process are the appraisal theory, the coping theory, and the personality theory. In previous sections we have described the most useful computational models for our project. Table 2 shows model accordance with the fundamental theories.

Name	Model	Appraisal	Coping	Personnality
1	FLAME	Yes	Yes	No
2	ParleE	Yes	Not mentioned	Rousseau model
3	Kismet	Yes	Not mentioned	No
4	Greta	Yes	Not mentioned	Personality trait
5	EMA	Yes	Yes	No
6	GALAAD	Yes	Yes	No
7	PLEIAD	Yes	Yes	No
8	GRACE	Yes	Yes	MBTI

Table 2. Comparaison of emotional models

We have chosen to instantiate and adapt the GRACE model to our project as it is the only one to apply all three theories.

4. Robotherapy

The different studies in human-robot interaction focus on two major aspects:

- Psychological robotics: studies on the behaviour between humans and robots
- Robotherapy: use of robots as therapeutic companions for people suffering from psychological or limited physiological problems.

Robotherapy is defined as a framework of human-robot interaction with the goal to reconstruct a person's negative experiences through the development of new technological tools to create a foundation on which new positive ideas may be constructed (Libin & Libin, 2004). In other words, robotherapy offers a methodological and experimental concept which allows for the stimulation, assistance, and rehabilitation of people with physical or cognitive disorders, those with special needs, or others with physiological disabilities.

The MAPH project, which has the goal of building a robot companion, falls within the context of robotherapy for the rehabilitation and comfort of children with physical or cognitive disorders. Research has allowed for numerous robot companions having such a purpose to be created. This novel idea is based on the works carried out on a robot with a very simple architecture, but maximal expressivity.

4.1 Robots for social interaction

4.1.1 Paro

Paro (AIST, 2004) is an interactive robotic baby seal which is currently the 8th generation of a design developed by AIST in 1993. It was designed to help the elderly deal with loneliness and develop communication and affective interaction with others. It is mainly used to give companionship in Japanese retirement homes. It reacts to being touched and to the sound of voices, makes sounds, and can move its flippers, tail, as well as its eyebrows.

4.1.2 iCat

iCat (van Breemen et al., 2005) is a robot companion cat produced by the Phillips Research laboratories. It is meant to assist its user with everyday tasks such as sending messages, receiving the daily news, selecting music, pictures or videos, and even home surveillance. It can see due to cameras located behind its eyes, reacts to sound, one's voice, as well as gestures and can express itself due to 13 servomotors.

4.1.3 Kismet

Kismet (Breazeal & Scassellati, 2000) is an expressive robot developed by MIT that has perceptual modalities. Motors are used to give it facial expressions, as well as gaze and head orientation adjustment. With 15 degrees of freedom, it is capable of expressing emotions such as surprise, happiness, anger, sadness, etc.

These motor systems let it automatically adjust its visual and auditory detectors toward the stimulus source. Four Motorola 68332 microprocessors execute the perception, motivation, behaviour, motor skills, and face motor systems. The visual system is run by nine networked 400 MHZ PCs running QNX (a real-time Unix operating system). The speech synthesis is taken on by a dual 450 MHZ PC running NT, while the speech recognition runs on a 500 MHZ PC running linux.

4.1.4 Cosmobot

Cosmobot (Lathan et al., 2005; Brisben et al., 2005) is a robot developed by AnthroTonix designed to help children with developmental and behavioural disorders. It can react to movement and voice, and can also be controlled by a child-friendly keyboard called "Mission Control". It can repeat sentences, move parts of its body, as well as move forward and backward, and help the child during therapy. With a sensor-equipped glove a child can make the robot move or copy the machine's movements.

5. iGrace – computational model of emotions

To realize emotional synthesis, the first step is to establish the necessary information to understand the environment (including the interlocutor). As noted above, it is important for a robot to know how to physically express itself if it is to have non-verbal communication. However, because the interlocutor is able to communicate verbally, it is necessary to understand the main words in his/her discourse, his/her intonation, as well as his/her facial expression to grasp the emotion unveiled. We would like to be able to gather the following information:

- Discourse: even though the current systems cannot perfectly understand the range of human vocabulary and especially the discourse of an interlocutor, if the context is taken into account, some words can be processed allowing for emotional reaction. The comprehension module will enable the processing of these data to be analysed, allowing us to gather a series of information, such as the subject that is doing the action, the action, the object or subject that is undergoing the action. Moreover, by combining the acts of language, times of action, and emotional state of the interlocutor, it is possible to react without completely understanding the discourse. This reaction can still be coherent with what is said.
- The sound signal: similar to the video signal, there are 2 uses for sound. The first is to reinforce the decision taken about the emotional state of the child while speaking, as prosody is not the same for the different emotions felt while speaking. The second case is for system protection. Depending on the level of sound intensity, an appropriate reaction may be taken by the system.
- The video signal: this information is useful for 3 cases. The first is to be able to follow the child's face. During a conversation, the interlocutor could quickly be disorientated or may think that the conversation lacks interest if his/her partner is not looking at him/her. The second case allows for the affirmation of the emotional state of the child

thanks to recognized facial expression that is associated to an emotion. Finally, the signal will be very helpful in emergency situations. As children sometimes shake their toys rather roughly, it would be necessary to stop the robot from functioning during wrongful manipulation. Thus, depending on the obstruction of the camera's field of vision, the system can react in the appropriate way and will automatically go in standby mode if necessary to avoid any mechanical mishaps.

The second step helps to define the method to be used to react to the discourse and to have the appropriate expression. This step is crucial in that it helps to maintain interaction at its maximum if it is correctly carried out. The emotional interaction model iGrace (see Figure 2), which is based on the emotional model GRACE that we have designed, will allow us to reach our expectations. It is composed of 3 main modules (described in detail in the following subsections) which will be able to process the received information:

- "Input" Module
- "Emotional interaction" Module
- "Output" Module

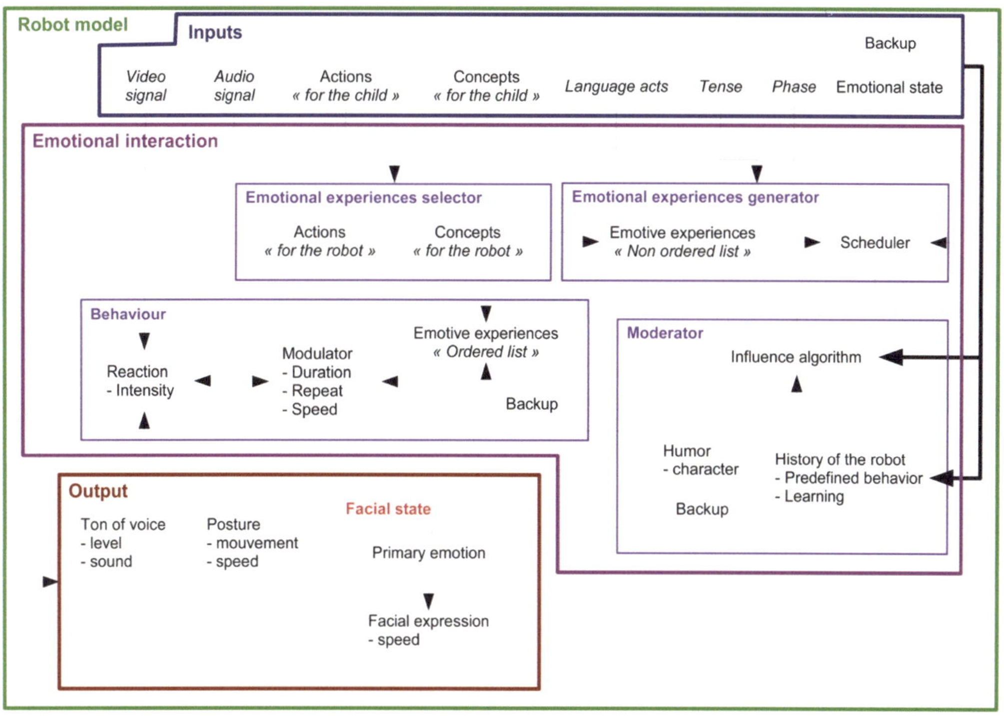

Fig. 2. Computal interaction model - iGrace

Before beginning our project, we did two experimental studies. The first experiment (Le-Pévédic et al., 2006) was carried out using the Paro robot to verify if reaction/interaction with robots depended on cultural context. This experiment pointed out that there could be mechanical problems linked to weight and autonomy, as well as interaction problems linked to the robot due to lack of emotions.

The second experiment (Petit et al., 2005) was to help us reconcile the restriction of a light, autonomous robot with understanding expression capacities. Evaluators had to select the faces that seemed to best express primary emotions among a list of 16 faces. It was one of the simplest faces that obtained the best results. With only 6 degrees of freedom (Saint-Aimé et al., 2007), it was possible to obtain a very satisfying primary emotion recognition rate.

5.1 "Input" module

This module represents the interface for communication and data exchange between the understanding module and emotional interaction module. This is where the parameters can be found, which help to obtain the information necessary to make the process go as well as possible for interaction between the child and his/her robot companion. The parameters taken into account are the following:

- Video signal: The camera, which is placed in the nose of the robot, will first help to follow the movements of the child to keep up interaction and to keep his/her attention during the interaction; this camera will also help to stop the system when the interlocutor exhibits inappropriate or unexpected behaviour.
- Sound signal: The sound system will enable understanding, as well as ensure the robot's safety. In the case of loud screams or a panic attack assimilated to a signal that is too high, the functioning of the robot will temporarily go into standby mode. The robot will automatically generate an "isolating" behaviour.
- Actions "for the child": They represent a group of actions that are characterised by verbs (ex. eat, sleep, play, etc.) which children most often use. These actions or verbs are put into a hierarchy or are organised in a tree structure.
- Concepts "for the child": These are the main themes of a child's vocabulary (ex. family, friends, school, etc.). These terms are put into a hierarchy or are organised in a tree structure with one or more levels according to the difficulty and the subtlety of reaction that we would like to create during the interaction.
- Act of language: This helps us to understand what type of discourse is being used: question, affirmation, etc., which therefore allows us to give the robot the behaviour that is most adapted to the child's discourse. Indeed, some types of discourse, such as interrogation, require a more expressive behaviour than others.
- Tense: This lets the robot situate the discourse in time to create better interaction. The past, present, and future are implemented.
- Phase: This represents the state of mind that the child is in during the discourse. Four different phases are taken into account:
  - Imaginary: language taken from his/her imagination.
  - Real: language from real life experience.
  - Imitation: the robot should imitate the child's behaviour.
  - Play: the robot will play a predefined game with the child.
- Emotional state: This provides information on the emotional state of the child during the discourse. It is represented by a vector of emotions giving the degree of implication or the recognition of each primary emotion (joy, fear, anger, surprise, sadness, disgust) on a scale of -1 to 2 (see Table 3).

These input values are recorded in a database which allows the robot to check if its behaviour is having a positive or negative effect on the child's behaviour or discourse. The objective is to increase interaction time between the child and robot companion. This comparison also enables the evolution of the history, character, and personality of the robot. This step is considered as our version of coping, see "learning" or "knowledge" of the interlocutor.

Coefficient	Definition
-1	We do not know if the emotion is implicated
0	Emotion not implicated
1	Slightly implicated emotion
2	Very implicated emotion

Table 3. Definitions of emotion vector coefficients.

5.2 "Emotional interaction" module

Due to the processed input information, the robot is able to react as naturally as possible to the child's discourse. Knowing that it is limited to only primary emotions through facial expression to maintain nonverbal discourse, we must be able to express ourselves through the other elements of the human body. To do this we decided to integrate the notion of emotional and behavioural experience into our module. The 100 emotional experiences in our database will give us a very large number of different behaviours for the model. However, we have decided, for now, to limit ourselves to only fifty entrees of emotional experience. This diversity is possible thanks to the principle of mixing emotions (Ochs et al., 2006) coupled with the dynamics of emotions (Jost, 2009). Four main elements of interaction can be found in the model:

- Moderator
- Selector of emotional experience
- Generator of emotional experience
- Behaviour

The four modules cited and described below will help us carry out the processing necessary for interaction in six steps:

1. Extraction, from list L_1, of emotional experiences linked to the personality of the robot - sub-module "Moderator"
2. Extraction, from list L_2, of emotional experiences linked to discourse - sub-module "Selector of emotional experience"
3. Extraction, from list L_3, of emotional experiences linked to the emotional state of the child during discourse - sub-module "Generator of emotional experience"
4. Fusion of lists L_1, L_2 and L_3 into L_4 and recalculation of coefficient associated to each emotional experience in function to:
    - Mood of the robot
    - Affect of discourse action
    - Phase and discourse act
    - Affect of the child's emotional state
    - Affect of discourse

    This process is carried out in the sub-module "Generator of emotional experience"
5. Extraction of best emotional experiences from list L_4 into L_5 - sub-module "Behaviour".
6. Expressions of emotions linked to chosen emotional experiences. These expressions determine the behaviour of the robot - sub-module "Behaviour".

5.2.1 Sub-module "Moderator"

It tells if the character, mood, personality, and history of the robot have an influence on its beliefs and behaviour. The personality of the robot, taken from the psychological definition, is based on the MBTI model which enables it to have a list L_1 of emotional experiences in accordance with its personality. Currently, this list is chosen in a pseudo-random way by the robot during its initialisation. It makes a choice of 10 emotional experiences from the base which represents its profile. It is important to not select a number of emotional experiences having a negative effect higher than the number that has a positive effect. This list will be weighed in function to its mood of the day, which is the only parameter that is taken into consideration for the calculation of the coefficients C_{eemo} (see equation 1) of the emotional experiences. As the development is still in progress, the other parameters are not integrated into the equation used. This list will have an influence on the behaviour it is supposed to have during the discourse.

$$
\begin{aligned}
C_{eemo} &= \begin{cases} [(1-a)\times 0] + (a \times 10) & : \text{if positive mood} \\ [(1-a)\times 10] + (a \times 0) & : \text{if negative mood} \\ 10 & : \text{if neutral mood} \end{cases} \\
a &= \begin{cases} 0 : \text{if negative affect} \\ 1 : \text{if positive affect} \end{cases}
\end{aligned} \tag{1}
$$

$$
\text{with} \left| \begin{array}{lll} C_{eemo} & : & \text{emotional experience coefficient} \\ a & : & \text{emotional experience affect} \end{array} \right.
$$

5.2.2 Sub-module "Selector of emotional experience"

This module helps give the emotional state of the robot in response to the discourse of the child. The child's discourse is represented by the list of actions and concepts that the speech understanding module can give. With this list of actions and concepts, usually represented in trio form: "concept, action, concept", the emotional vectors V_i that are associated with it can be gathered in the database. We first manually and subjectively annotated a corpus (Bassano et al., 2005) of the most common words used by children. This annotation associates an emotional vector (see Table 4) with the different words of the corpus. Each primary emotion of the vector with a coefficient C_emo between -1 and 2 represents the individual's emotional degree for the word. It is important to note that the association represents the robot's beliefs for the speech and not those of the child. Actually, the annotated coefficients are statistics. However, a learning system that will make the robot's values evolve during its lifespan is planned. The parameters that are taken into account for this evolution will mostly be based on the feedback we gather of good or bad interaction with the child during the discourse.

Word	**Vector**					
	Joy	Anger	Surprise	Disgust	Sadness	Fear
Dad (concept)	1	-1	0	0	-1	-1
Mum (concept)	1	-1	0	0	-1	-1
Sister (concept)	-1	-1	0	-1	-1	0
Kill (action)	-1	1	0	0	-1	0
Kiss (action)	1	0	0	0	-1	0
Eat (action)	1	0	0	0	-1	0
Coefficient of the vector (see Table 1): -1 :does not know; 0: no; 1: slightly; 2: a lot						

Table 4. Extracts of emotion vectors for a list of words (action or concept)

$$V(emo, C_{emo}) = \sum_{i=1}^{n} V_i . C_{emo} \tag{2}$$

with
emo	:	primary emotion
$C_{emo} > 0$	:	emotion coefficient
V	:	emotional vector
i	:	word of speech index
$n \leq 3$	:	number of word of speech

$$C_{eemo} = \frac{C_{emo} \times 50}{n} \tag{3}$$

with
C_{eemo}	:	emotional experience coefficient
$C_{emo} > 0$	:	emotion coefficient
n	:	number of word of speech

Due to these emotional vectors, that we have combined using equation 2, it is possible for us to determine list L_2 of emotional experiences that are linked to the discourse. In fact, thanks to the categorisation of emotions in layers of three that Parrot (Parrott, 2000) proposes, we can associate each emotion with emotional experiences i_{emo} (see Table 5). At that moment, unlike emotional vectors, emotional experiences are associated with no coefficient Ceemo. However, this will be determined in function to that of the emotional vector and by applying equation 3. This weighted list, which represents the emotional state of the robot during the speech, is transmitted to the "generator".

Emotion	Emotional experiences
Joy	Happiness, contentment, enchantment, euphoria, happy, etc.
Fear	Panic, anxiety, fear, fright, etc.
Anger	Rage, agitation, detest, fury, hate, etc.
Sadness	Grief, deception, depression, sorrow, etc.
Surprise	Wonder, surprise, etc.
Disguss	Nausea, contempt, etc.

Table 5. Association extracts between emotions and emotional experiences

5.2.3 Sub-module "Generator of emotional experience"

This module defines the reaction that the robot should have to the child's discourse. It is linked to all the other interaction model modules to gather a maximum amount of information and to generate the adequate behaviour(s). The information processing is done in three steps which help give a weighted emotional experience list.

The first step consists in processing the emotional state that has been observed in the child. This state is generated by a spoken discourse, prosody and will be completed in the next version of the model by facial expression recognition. It is represented by an emotional vector, similar to the one used for the words of the discourse and will have the same coefficients C_{emo}, which will help create a list L_3 of emotional experience. Coefficient C_{eemo} of emotional experiences is calculated by applying equation 4.

$$C_{eemo} = C_{emo} \times 10 \tag{4}$$

with
C_{eemo}	:	emotional experience coefficient
$C_{emo} > 0$	:	emotion coefficient

The second step consists in combing our 3 lists (moderator(L_1) + selector(L_2) + emotional state(L_3)) into L_4. The new coefficient will be calculated by adding it to each list for the same emotional experience (see equation 5).

$$L\left(eemo, C_{eemo}\right) = \sum_{i=1}^{n} L_i . C_{eemo}$$

$$\text{with} \left| \begin{array}{lll} eemo & : & \text{emotional experience} \\ C_{eemo} > 0 & : & \text{emotional experience coefficient} \\ L & : & \text{Listof emotional experiences} \\ i & : & \text{emotional experience index} \\ n & : & \text{number of emotional experiences} \end{array} \right. \quad (5)$$

The first steps carried out have first given us list L_4 of emotional experiences which can generate a behaviour. However, this list was created on data which corresponded to the different emotional states, as well as the discourse of the interlocutor, and the personality of the robot. Now, that have the data in hand, we will need to take into account the meaning of the discourse to find the appropriate behaviours. The goal of this third step is the recalculate the emotional experience coefficient (see Figure 3) in function to the new parameters.

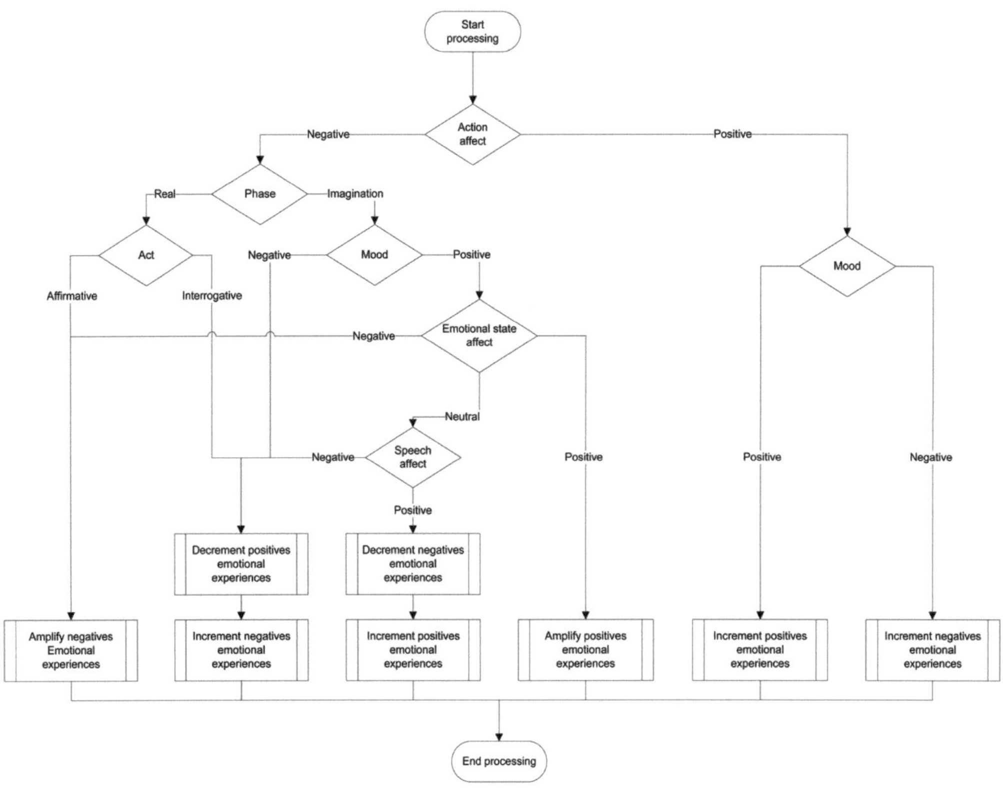

Fig. 3. Weighing of emotional experiences linked to new parameters - step 3

5.2.4 Sub-module "Behaviour"

This module lets the behavioural expression that the robot will have in response to the child's discourse be chosen. From list L_4, we have to extract emotional experiences with the best coefficient into a new list L_5. To avoid repetition, the first thing to be done was to filter the emotional experiences that had already been used for the same discourse. A historical base of behaviours associated to the discourse would help in this process. The second process is to choose N emotional experiences from the list with the best coefficients. In the case of the same coefficients, a random choice will be made. We currently have set the number of emotional experiences to be extracted to three.
Another difficulty with this module is in the dynamics of behaviour and the choice of expressions. It is important not to lose the interaction with the child by constantly repeating the same expression for a type of behaviour. The choice of a large panel of expressions will help us obtain different and unexpected interaction for the same sentence or same emotional state.

5.3 "Output" module

This module must be capable of expressing itself in function to the material characteristics it is made of: microphone/HP, motors. The behaviour comes from the emotional interaction module and will be divided into 3 main sections:

- Tone "of voice": characterized by a greater or lesser degree of audible signal and choice of sound that will be produced by the robot. Within the framework of my research, the interaction will remain non-verbal, thus the robot companion should be capable of emitting sounds on the same tone as the seal robot " Paro ". These short sounds based on the works of Kayla Cornale (Cornale, visited in 2007) with " Sounds into Syllables ", are piano notes associated to primary emotions.
- Posture: characterized by the speed and type of movement carried out by each member of the robot's body, in relation to the generated behaviour.
- Facial expression: represents the facial expressions that will be displayed on the robot's face. At the beginning or our interaction study, we mainly work with "emotional experiences". These should be translated into primary emotions afterwards, and then into facial expressions. Note that emotional experience is made up of several primary emotions.

6. Operating scenario

For this scenario, the simulator and the robot will be used for expressing emotions. This system will allow us to compare the expression of the two media. The scenario takes place in 3 phases:

- System Initialization
- Simulation Event
- Processing event
- Reaction

6.1 System initialisation

At system startup, Moderator an Outputs module initialize variables like mood, personality and emotion running the robot with values inFigure 4

6.2 Simulation event

For this phase, a sentence is pronounced into the microphone allowing the system start process. The selected phrase, extract from experiments with the robot and children in schools is: "Bouba's mother is die". From this sentence, the team of treatment and understanding of discourse selects the following words: Mum, Be, Death. From this selection, the 9 parameters of the module Inputs will be initialized as in Figure 5.

6.3 Processing event

The emotional interaction module processes the event received and generates a reaction to the speech in six steps. Each of these steps allows us to obtain a list of emotional experiences associated with a coefficient having a value between 0 and 100.

Step 1: Personality profile

This step, performed by the sub-module Moderator, produces an initial list of responses for the robot based on its personality. The list on which treatment is based is the personality profile of the robot (see Figure 4). Applying the equation 1 at this list, we get the first list of emotional experiences L_1 (see Figure 4).

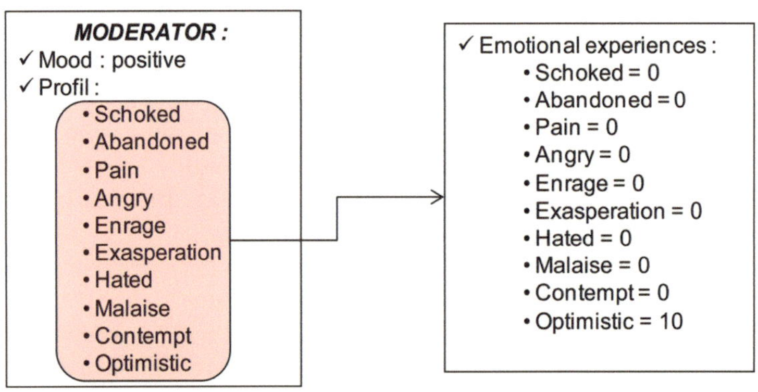

Fig. 4. List L_1 from Moderator

Step 2: Reaction to speech

This step, performed by the sub-module selector of emotional experiences, produces a list of reactions to the speech of the interlocutor. An amotional and an affect vector is associated with each concept and action of discourse, but only the emotional vector is taken into account in this step. Using the equation 2, we add the vectors coefficient for each primary common emotion. Only values greater or equal to 0 are taken into account in our calculation. In the case of joy (see Figure 5), we have: $V \cdot joie = V1 \cdot joie + V2 \cdot joie = 1 + 0$. This vector fusion allows us to get list L_2 of emotional experiences to which we apply the equation 3 to calculate the corresponding coefficients.

Step 3: Responding to the emotional state

This step, performed by the sub-module generator of emotional experiences, produces a list L_3 of emotional experiences for the emotional state of the speaker when the speech is done. The emotional state of the child being represented as a vector, we can obtain a list of emotional experiences to which we apply the equation 4 for coefficient.

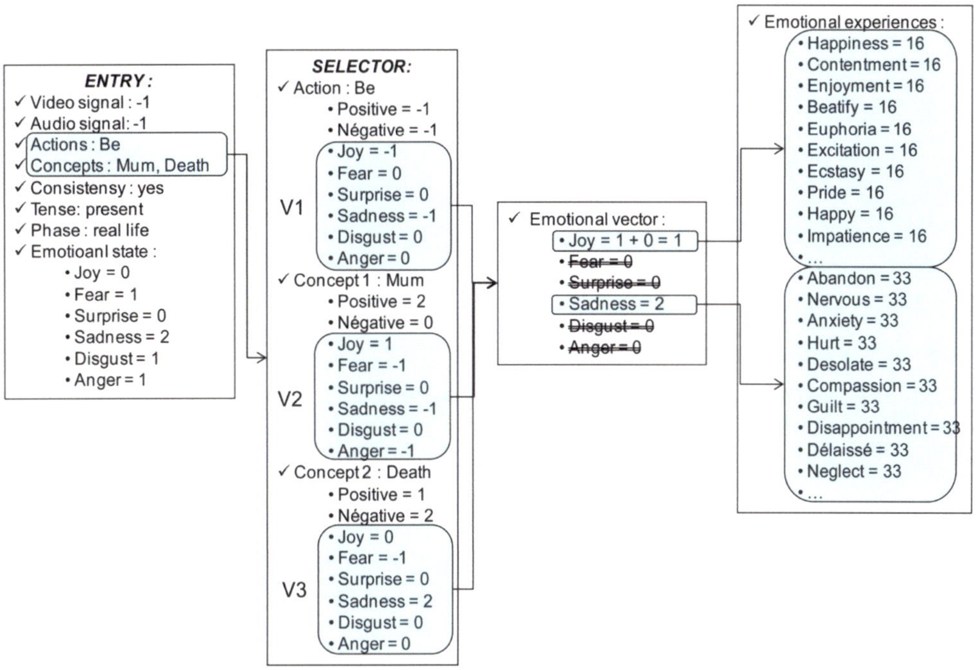

Fig. 5. List L_2 from Selector

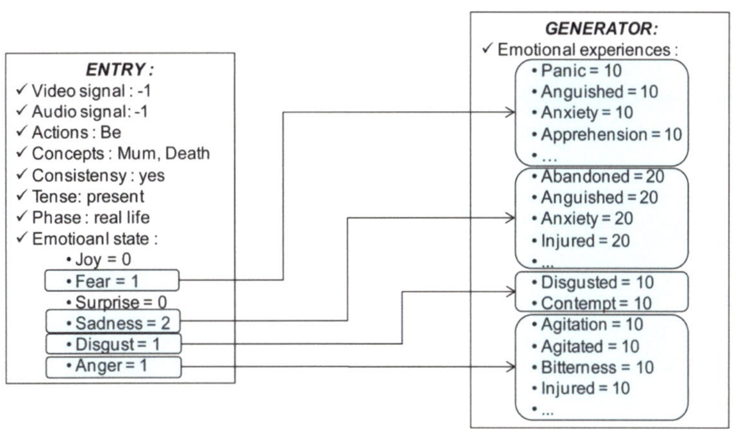

Fig. 6. List L_3 from emotional state

Step 4: Fusion of lists

This step, performed by the sub-module generator of emotional experiences, allows the fusion of all lists L_1, L_2, L_3 into L_4 and computing the new coefficient of emotional experiences by using algorith see in Figure3. The new list L_4 is see in Figure 7.

Step 5: Selection of the highest coefficients

This step, performed by the sub-module behavior, achieves the 3 best emotional experiences of the list L_4 into L_5. The list will be first reduced by deleting emotional experiences that have already been chosen for the same speech. In the case of identical coefficients, a random selection will de made.

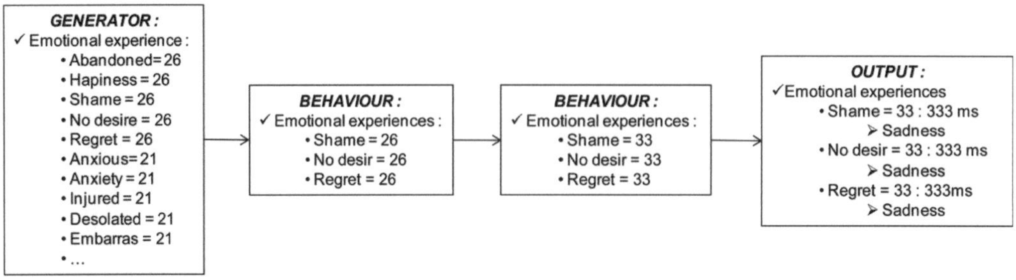

Fig. 7. From Generator to Output module - List L_4 and L_5

Step 6: Initialization parameters of expression

The last step, performed by the sub-module behavior, calculates the parameters for the expression of the reaction of the robot. We obtain the time expression in second of each emotional experience (see Figure 7).

6.4 Reaction

This last phase, carried out by the output module, simulates the robot's reaction to the speech. With the list L_5 (see Figure 7) of reaction given by the emotional interaction module. For each of the emotional experiences of the list associated with one or more emotions, we randomly choose a facial expression in the basic pattern. This will be expressed using the motor in the case of the robot or the GUI in the case of the simulator.

7. Experiments

The goal of the first experiment was to partially evaluate and validate the emotional model. For this, we start we start experiment with a small public of all ages to gather the maximum amount of information on the improvements needed for interaction. After analysis of the results, the first improvements were made. For this experiment, only the simulation interface was used.

7.0.1 Protocol

For the first step, having been carried out among a large public, it was not difficult to find volunteers. However, we limited the number to 10 people because as we have already stated, this is not the targeted public. We did not want to modify the interaction in function to remarks made by adults. The first thing that was asked was to use abstraction as the interface represented the face and behaviour of the robot, and that the rest (type of input, ergonomy, etc.) was not to be evaluated. Furthermore, these people were asked to put themselves in the place of a targeted interlocutor so as to make the most useful remarks.
To carry out the tests, we first chose a list of 4 phrases upon which the testers were to base themselves. For each one, we included the following language information:

- Time of action: present.
- Language act: affirmative.
- Discourse context: real life.

This system helped us gain precious time that each person would use to make their decisions. The phrases given were the following:

- Mum, Hug, Dad.

- Tiger, Attack, Grandma.
- Baby, Cry.
- I, Tickle, Sister.

7.1 Evaluation grid

After the distribution and explication of the evaluation grids, each person first had to go through the following steps:

1. Give an affect (positive, negative, or neutral) to each word of the phrase.
2. Define their emotional state for the discourse.
3. Predict the emotional state of the robot.

Although this step was easy to do, it was rather long to input because some people had trouble expressing their feelings. After inputting the information we could start the simulation for each phrase. We asked the users to be attentive to the robot's expression because it could not be seen again. After observation of the robot's behaviour, the users had to complete the following information:

1. Which feelings could be recognized in the behaviour, and what was their intensity on the scale: not at all, a little, a lot, do not know.
2. The average speed of the expression and length of the behaviour on a scale: too slow, slow, normal, fast, too fast.
3. Did you have the impression there was a combination of emotions? Yes or no?
4. Was the sequence of emotions natural? Yes or no?
5. Are you satisfied with the robot's behaviour? Not at all, a little, very much?

7.2 Results

The objective of this experiment was to evaluate the recognition of emotions through the simulator, and especially to determine if the response the robot will give to the speech was satisfying or not. As regards the rate of appreciation of the behaviour for each speech, 54% for at lot of satisfaction and 46% for a little, we observed that all the users found the simulator's response coherent, and thereafter admitted that they would be fully satisfied if the robot was as they were expected. The fact that testers answered about the expected emotions had an influence on overall satisfaction.

For the rate of emotions recognition, 82% in average, the figures were very satisfactory and allowed us to prepare the next evaluation on the classification of facial expressions for each primary emotion. Not all emotions are on the graph because they bore no relation to the sentences chosen. We have also been able to see that even if the results were still rather high, there were some emotions which were recognized although they were not expressed. This confirms the need to classify, and especially the fact that each expression can be a combination of emotions. The next question is to know if the satisfaction rate will be the same with the robot after the integration of the emotional model. The other results were useful for the integration of the model on the robot:

- Speed of expressions: normal with 63%
- Behaviour length: normal with 63%
- Emotional combination: yes with 67%
- Natural sequences: yes with 71%

8. EmI - robotic conception

EmI is currently in the integration and test phase for future experiments. This robot was partially conceived by the CRIIF for the elaboration of the skeleton and the first version of the covering (see Figure 8(c)). The second version (see Figure 8(d)), was made in our laboratory. We will briefly present the robotic aspect of the elaborated work while waiting for the second generation of it.

(a) Head conception (b) Body conception

(c) EmI version 1 (d) EmI version 2

Fig. 8. EmI conception

The skeleton of the head (see Figure 8(a)) is completely made of ABS and contains:

- 1 camera at nose level to follow the face and potentially for facial recognition. The camera used is a CMUCam 3.
- 6 motors creating the facial expression with 6 degrees of freedom. Two for the eyebrows, and four for the mouth. The motors used are AX-12+. This allows us to communicate digitally, and soon with wireless thanks to Zigbee, between the robot and a distant PC. Communication with the PC is done through a USB2Dynamixel adapter using a FTDI library.

The skeleton (see Figure 8(b)) of the torso is made of aluminium and allows the robot to turn its head from left to right, as well as up and down. It also permits the same movements at the waist. There are a total of 4 motors that create these movements.

Currently, communication with the robot is done through a distant PC directly hooked up to the motors. In the short term, the PC will be placed on EmI to process while allowing for interaction. The PC used will be a Fit PC Slim, at 500 Mhz, with 512 Mo of RAM and a 60 Go hard drive. The exploitation system used is Windows XP. It is possible to hook up a mouse, keyboard, and screen for modifications and to make the system evolve at any moment.

9. Conclusion and perspectives

The emotional model iGrace we propose allows to react emotionally to a speech given. The first experiment conducted on a small scale has enabled us to answer some questions such as length and speed of the robot expression, methods of information processing, consistency of response and emotion recognition on a simulator. To fully validate the model, a new large-scale experimentation will be repeated.
The 6 degrees of freedom used for the simulation give recognition rate very satisfactory. It is our responsibility now to make a similar experiment on the robot to evaluate its expressiveness. In addition, we undertook extensive research on the dynamics of emotions in order to increase the fluidity of movement and make the interaction more natural. The second experiment, with the robot, will allow to compare the recognition rate between the robot and the simulator.
The next version of EmI will integrated a new texture, camera recognition and prosody traitment. These parameters will allows us have a best recognition for emotional state of the child. Some parts of modules and su-modules of the model have to be develop for a best interaction.

10. Acknowledgements

EmotiRob is a project that is supported by ANR through the Psirob programme. The MAPH project is supported by regional funding from la rgion Martinique and la rgion Bretagne. We would like to first of all thank the different organisations for their financial support as well as their collaboration.
The authors would also like to thank all of the people who have contributed to the evaluation grids for the experiments, as well as the members of the Kerpape centre and IEA "Le Bondon" centre for their cooperation.
Finally, the authors would also like to thank all of the participants in the experiments for their time and constructive remarks.

11. References

Adam, C. & Evrard, F. (2005). Galaad: a conversational emotional agent, *Rapport de recherché IRIT/2005-24-R*, IRIT, Universit Paul Sabatier, Toulouse.

Adam, C., Herzig, A. & Longin, D. (2007). PLEIAD, un agent motionnel pour valuer la typologie OCC, *Revue d'Intelligence Artificielle, Modles multi-agents pour des environnements complexes* 21(5-6): 781–811. URL: *ftp://ftp.irit.fr/IRIT/LILAC/2007 Adam et al RIA.pdf*

AIST (2004). Seal-type robot "paro" to be marketed with best healing effect in the world. URL: *http://www.aist.go.jp/aist e/latest research/2004/20041208 2/20041208 2.html*

Arnold, M. (1960). *Emotion and personality*, Columbia University Press New York.

Bassano, D., Labrell, F., Champaud, C., Lemétayer, F. & Bonnet, P. (2005). Le dlpf: un nouvel outil pour l'évaluation du développement du langage de production en français, *Enfance* 57(2): 171–208.

Bloch, H., Chemama, R., Gallo, A., Leconte, P., Le Ny, J., Postel, J., Moscovici, S., Reuchlin, M. & Vurpillot, E. (1994). *Grand dictionnaire de la psychologie*, Larousse.

Boyle, E. A., Anderson, A. H. & Newlands, A. (1994). The effects of visibility on dialogue and performance in a cooperative problem solving task, *Language and Speech* 37(1): 1–20.

Breazeal, C. (2003). Emotion and sociable humanoid robots, *Int. J. Hum.-Comput. Stud.* 59(1-2): 119–155.

Breazeal, C. & Scassellati, B. (2000). Infant-like social interactions between a robot and a human caretaker, *Adaptative Behavior* 8(1): 49–74.

Brisben, A., Safos, C., Lockerd, A., Vice, J. & Lathan, C. (2005). The cosmobot system: Evaluating its usability in therapy sessions with children diagnosed with cerebral palsy.

Bui, T. D., Heylen, D., Poel, M. & Nijholt, A. (2002). Parlee: An adaptive plan based event appraisal model of emotions, *in* S. B. Heidelberg (ed.), *KI 2002: Advances in Artificial Intelligence*, Vol. 2479 of *Lecture Notes in Computer Science*, Springer Berlin / Heidelberg, pp. 129–143.

Cambreleng, B. (2009). Nao, un robot compagnon pour apprendre ou s'amuser. URL:http://*www.google.com/hostednews/afp/article/ALeqM5jBCTtjOmxw1ZAGOJaWNKX6itOmsA*

Castel, Y. (visité en 2009). Psychobiologie humaine. URL: *http://psychobiologie.ouvaton.org/*

Cauvin, P. & Cailloux, G. (2005). *Les types de personnalité: les comprendre et les appliquer avec le MBTI (Indicateur typologique de Myers-Briggs)*, 6 edn, ESF éditeur.

Cornale, K. (visited in 2007). Sounds into syllables. URL: *www.soundsintosyllables.com*

Dang, T.-H.-H., Letellier-Zarshenas, S. & Duhaut, D. (2008). Grace generic robotic architecture to create emotions, *Advances in Mobile Robotics: Proceedings of the Eleventh International Conference on Climbing and Walking Robots and the Support Technologies for Mobile Machines* pp. 174–181.

de Rosis, F., Pelachaud, C., Poggi, I., Carofiglio, V. & Carolis, B. D. (2003). From greta's mind to her face: modelling the dynamics of affective states in a conversational embodied agent, *International Journal of Human-Computer Studies* 59(1-2): 81–118. Applications of Affective Computing in Human-Computer Interaction.

de Sousa, R. (2008). Emotion, *in* E. N. Zalta (ed.), *The Stanford Encyclopedia of Philosophy*, fall 2008 edn.

El-Nasr, M. S., Yen, J. & Ioerger, T. R. (2000). Flame—fuzzy logic adaptive model of emotions, *Autonomous Agents and Multi-Agent Systems* 3(3): 219–257.

Gazdar, G. (1993). *The simulation of Human intelligence*, Donald Broadbent edition.

Gratch, J. & Marsella, S. (2005). Evaluating a computational model of emotion, *Autonomous Agents and Multi-Agent Systems* 11(1): 23–43.

Greenspan, P. (1988). *Emotions & reasons: an inquiry into emotional justification*, Routledge.

James,W. (1884). What is an emotion?, *Mind* 9: 188–205.

Jost, C. (2009). *Expression et dynamique des émotions. application sur un avatar virtuel*, Rapport de stage de master recherche, Université de Bretagne Sud, Vannes.

Jung, C. G. (1950). *Types psychologiques*, Georg.

Lange, C. G. & (Trans), I. A. H. (1922). *The emotions*, Williams & Wilkins Co, Baltimore, MD, US.

Larivey, M. (2002). *La puissance des émotions: Comment distinguer les vraies des fausses.*, de l'homme edn, Les éditions de l'Homme, Québec.

Lathan, C., Brisben, A. & Safos, C. (2005). Cosmobot levels the playing field for disabled children, *interactions* 12(2): 14–16.

Lazarus, R. & Folkman, S. (1984). *Stress, Appraisal, and Coping*, Springer Publishing Company. URL:*http://www.amazon.com/exec/obidos/redirect?tag=citeulike07-20&path=ASIN/0826141919*

Lazarus, R. S. (1991). *Emotion and Adaptation*, Oxford University Press, New York.

Lazarus, R. S. (2001). *Relational meaning and discrete emotions*, Oxford University Press, chapter Appraisal processes in emotion: Theory, methods, research., pp. 37–67.

Le-Pévédic, B., Shibata, T. & Duhaut, D. (2006). Etude sur paro. study of the psychological interaction between a robot and disabled children.

Libin, A. & Libin, E. (2004). Person-robot interactions from the robopsychologists' point of view: the robotic psychology and robotherapy approach, *Proceedings of the IEEE* 92(11): 1789–1803.

Myers, I. B. (1987). *Introduction to type: A description of the theory and applications of the Myers-Briggs Type Indicator*, Consulting Psychologists Press Palo Alto, Calif.

Myers, I. B., McCaulley, M. H., Quenk, N. L. & Hammer, A. L. (1998). *MBTI manual*, 3 edn, Consulting Psychologists Press.

Ochs, M., Niewiadomski, R., Pelachaud, C. & Sadek, D. (2006). Expressions intelligentes des émotions, *Revue d'Intelligence Artificielle* 20(4-5): 607–620.

Ortony, A., Clore, G. L. & Collins, A. (1988). *The Cognitive Structure of Emotions*, Cambridge University Press. URL:*http://www.amazon.com/exec/obidos/redirect?tag=citeulike07-20&path=ASIN/0521353645*

Ortony, A. & Turner, T. (1990). What's basic about basic emotions, *Psychological review* 97(3): 315–331.

Parrott, W. (1988). The role of cognition in emotional experience, *Recent Trends in Theoretical Psychology*, w. j. baker, l. p. mos, h. v. rappard and h. j. stam edn, New-York, pp. 327- 337.

Parrott,W. G. (1991). The emotional experiences of envy and jealousy, *The psychology of jealousy and envy*, p. salovey edn, chapter 1, pp. 3–30.

Parrott, W. G. (2000). *Emotions in Social Psychology*, Key Readings in Social Psychology, Psychology Press.

Peters, L. (2006). Nabaztag Wireless Communicator, *Personal Computer World* 2.

Petit, M., Pévédic, B. L. & Duhaut, D. (2005). Génération d'émotion pour le robot maph: média actif pour le handicap, *IHM: Proceedings of the 17th international conference on Francophone sur l'Interaction Homme-Machine*, Vol. 264 of *ACM International Conference Proceeding Series*, ACM, Toulouse, France, pp. 271–274.

Pransky, J. (2001). AIBO-the No. 1 selling service robot, *Industrial robot: An international journal* 28(1): 24–26.

Rousseau, D. (1996). Personality in computer characters, *In Artificial Intelligence*, AAAI Press, Portland, Oregon, pp. 38–43.

Saint-Aimé, S., Le-Pévédic, B. & Duhaut, D. (2007). Building emotions with 6 degrees of freedom, *Systems, Man and Cybernetics, 2007. ISIC. IEEE International Conference on*, pp. 942-947.

Sartre, J.-P. (1995). Esquisse d'une théorie des émotions (1938), *Herman et Cie, Paris*.

Scherer, K. R. (2005). What are emotions? and how can they be measured?, *Social Science Information* 44(4): 695–729.

Shibata, T. (2004). An overview of human interactive robots for psychological enrichment, *IEEE* 92(11): 1749–1758.

Solomon, R. C. (1973). Emotions and choice, *The Review of Metaphysics* pp. 20–41.

van Breemen, A., Yan, X. & Meerbeek, B. (2005). icat: an animated user-interface robot with personality, *AAMAS '05: Proceedings of the fourth international joint conference on Autonomous agents and multiagent systems*, ACM, New York, NY, USA, pp. 143–144.

Wilksa, Y. & Catizone, R. (2000). *Encyclopedia of Microcomputers*.

5

Human System Interaction through Distributed Devices in Intelligent Space

Takeshi Sasaki[1], Yoshihisa Toshima[2], Mihoko Niitsuma[3] and Hideki Hashimoto[1]
[1]*Institute of Industrial Science, The University of Tokyo,*
[2]*Daikin Industries, Ltd.,*
[3]*Chuo University*
Japan

1. Introduction

Intelligent Space (iSpace) is a space with ubiquitous sensors and actuators (Lee & Hashimoto, 2002). iSpace observes the space using the distributed sensors, extracts useful information from the obtained data and provides various services to the users through the actuators. iSpace can be considered as an "invisible" robot that is united with the environment since it can carry out the fundamental functions of robots - observation, recognition and actuation functions.

This type of spaces is also referred to as smart environment, smart space, intelligent environment, etc. and recently there is a growing number of research work (Cook & Das, 2004). Some smart environments are designed for supporting the users in informative ways. For example, a meeting support system (Johanson et al., 2002) and a healthcare system (Nishida et al., 2000) using distributed sensors were developed. Other smart environments are used for support of mobile robots to provide physical services. Delivery robots with ubiquitous sensory intelligence were developed in an office room (Mizoguchi et al., 1999) and a hospital (Sgorbissa & Zaccaria, 2004). The functions of mobile robot navigation including path planning (Kurabayashi et al., 2002) and localization (Han et al., 2007), (Hwang & Shih, 2009) of mobile robots were assisted by using information from distributed devices. Fig. 1 shows the configuration of our iSpace which is able to support human in both informative and physical ways.

iSpace has to recognize requests from users to provide the desired services and it is desirable that the user can request the services through natural interfaces. Therefore, a suitable human-iSpace interface is needed. Gesture recognition has been studied extensively (Mitra & Acharya, 2007) and human motions are often utilized as an interface in smart environments. A wearable interface device, named Gesture Pendant, was developed to control home information appliances (Mynatt et al, 2004). This device can recognize hand gestures using infrared illumination and a CCD camera. Gesture pads are also used as input devices (Youngblood et al, 2005). Speech recognition is considered as another promising approach for realizing an intuitive human-iSpace interface. The smart environment research project described in (Scanlon, 2004) utilizes distributed microphones to recognize spoken commands.

On the other hand, interaction can also be started by the space. If iSpace finds that a user is in trouble based on observation, for example, a mobile robot in the space would go to help the user. To realize this, human activity and behaviour recognition methods in smart environments are studied actively (Mori et al, 2007), (Oliver et al, 2004). It is also important to develop actuators including display systems, audio systems and mobile robots in order to provide services based on the observed situations.

Here both types of human-iSpace interaction mentioned above are described in the following sections. Section 2 and 3 introduce our human-iSpace interfaces - a spatial memory and a whistle interface. The spatial memory uses three-dimensional positions whereas the whistle interface utilizes frequency of sounds to activate services. Section 4 presents an information display system using a pan-tilt projector. Sections 2, 3 and 4 give also experimental results to demonstrate the developed system. Finally, a conclusion is given in section 5.

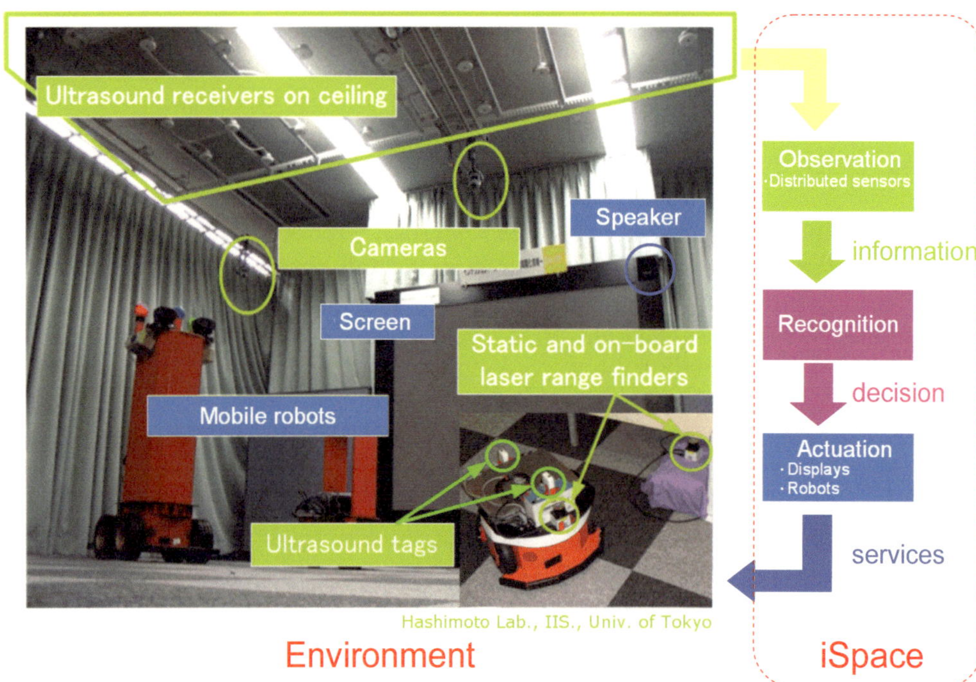

Fig. 1. Configuration of Intelligent Space

2. Spatial memory

Fig. 2 shows a schematic concept of the spatial memory. The spatial memory regards computerized information, such as digital files and commands, as externalized knowledge and enables human to store computerized information into the real world by assigning a 3-D position as the memory address. By storing computerized information into the real world, users can manipulate the information, as if they manipulated physical objects. For example, as shown in Fig. 2, conference proceedings can be organized in front of file cabinets or special memories might be stored into the second drawer from the top.

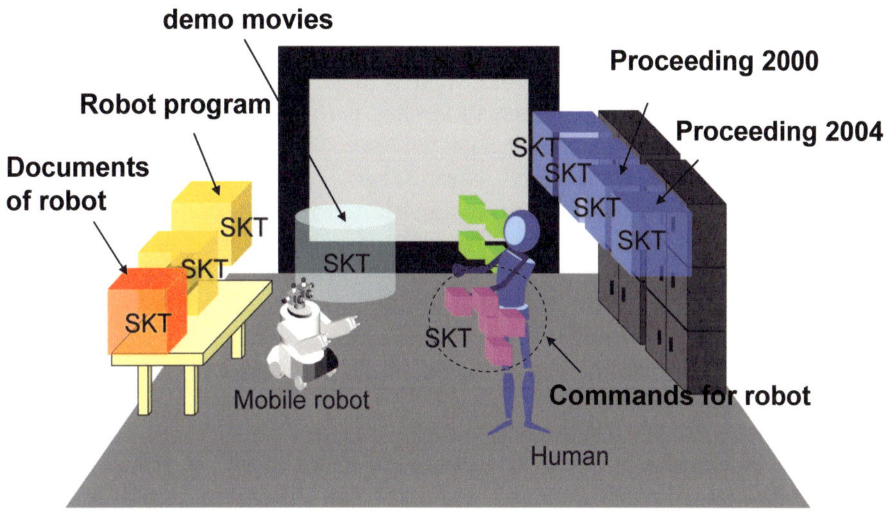

Fig. 2. Concept of the spatial memory

2.1 Definitions of terms

1) SKT (Spatial-Knowledge-Tag): We introduce a virtual tag, which associates computerized information with a spatial location. We will call them SKTs. SKT has three important parameters, namely: 1) stored computerized information; 2) 3-D position as a memory address; and 3) size of an accessible region. The details of an accessible region will be explained later. Stored computerized information is called spatial memory data.

Environmental information, such as arrangements of equipment and objects, is adopted as tags, which represent the whereabouts of externalized knowledge. Equipment placed in a working environment has visually distinguishable functions, respectively, and humans are able to recognize them easily by using their own cognitive abilities. Therefore, when real objects represent tags, they will play a role of a trigger to recall stored data and will be effective to memorize the whereabouts. In addition, the location of objects can be utilized to arrange externalized knowledge for easy recall.

There have been several approaches to associate computerized information with real objects, e.g., using Radio Frequency Identification (Kawamura et al., 2007), (Kim et al., 2005) or using 2-D barcode (Rekimoto et al. 1998). The approaches are useful to recognize the objects in a physical sense. However, there is a need to directly attach a hardware tag to each object in advance, and the user can only arrange computerized information for predetermined objects. Optional properties regarding accessibility, security, and mobility are not easily changed because they depend on hardware specifications, such as antennas or cameras.

There are two key differences between 3-D position-based method and hardware-tag-based method, such as 2-D barcodes. First, in the case of using 3-D position, we do not need to directly attach the hardware tag to each object, and therefore we can store information freely, if the position and the motion of human can be measured. Second, stored data manipulations, such as changing optional properties, are easier than using the hardware tag.

Another important aspect of our spatial memory is that the SKT can also take a human-centric approach to store the computerized information. More specifically, let us just consider the case where the coordinate frame is defined based on the human body. We can realize transformation from a human-centric coordinate frame to the real world, since the human can also take an option to carry the SKTs with his motion so that the relative position of SKTs will not be changed, for example, "my left side 2 m away to get access to file A," "my right side 10 m away to call my friend B." However, of course, if the user attaches the computerized information to a real object in the initial stage, the approach on the spatial memory needs to recognize an object with a human intuitive assist to register the object to the memory.

2) Human Indicator: The spatial memory whose address is represented by its 3-D position requires a new memory access method. In order to achieve intuitive and instantaneous access method that anyone can apply, the spatial memory adopts an indication of a human body as a memory indicator. Therefore, when using the spatial memory, a user can retrieve and store data by directly indicating the positions using his own body, for example, user's hand or user's body. The position based on the user's body used for operating the spatial memory is called a "human indicator."

However, it is impossible for a human to indicate the exact position of the spatial memory address every time. To easily and robustly access an SKT by using the human indicator, it is necessary to define an accessible region for each SKT. The accessible region is also needed for the arrangement of several SKTs by distinguishing their locations from others. The size of accessible region is determined based on the accuracy of the human indicator and its action type. For example, when using a hand for the human indicator, the user can indicate more accurately than using the body position. Therefore, a small size of accessible region can be achieved when using a hand, whereas a large one will be needed for a body human indicator.

We notice here that a guideline to determine the size of a human indicator using a hand has been obtained. In our previous work, we have investigated the accuracy of the human indicator (Niitsuma et al., 2004) using the user's hand. The accuracy is defined by the indication error, which is the distance between a spatial memory address of SKT and the human indicator. Investigations of two cases of human activities were carried out, namely: 1) the case of performing only the indication task and 2) the case of performing the indication task during another task. The results show the different margin of indication error between two cases. The accuracy of case 2 is worse than case 1 because the error margin of case 2 is larger than case 1. In order to achieve both smooth access and arrangement of several SKTs, accessible region is defined as follows. The accessible region is the sphere whose origin is located at a spatial memory address of SKT, whereas the radius is determined according to human activities: the radius in the case of just the indication task was found to be about 20 cm, and the radius in the case of indicating while performing another task was found to be about 40 cm.

3) Spatial Memory Address: As explained above, spatial memory addresses define spatial locations of computerized information in the spatial memory. Addressing method of the spatial memory system adopts a human-indicator-centered method, i.e., a position indicated by a human indicator is used for a spatial memory address. Consequently, the action for storing data into spatial memory can be carried out intuitively by pointing a spatial location as well as the action for accessing SKT. The implemented spatial memory has a 3-D coordinate system whose origin is at an arbitrary point in a space.

2.2 Usability evaluation of the spatial memory

Memorizing both the contents of SKTs and their whereabouts are required to utilize the spatial memory. If the users learn SKT positions and contents, they can get access to aimed

SKTs quickly without errors. Namely, it can be assumed that access time will be limited only by the physical access time necessary to utilize a human indicator and indicate the position of an aimed SKT. Therefore, the accessibility of the spatial memory and the effectiveness of memorizing were investigated from the viewpoint of the time needed to access SKTs.

Human subjects memorized some SKTs, which had been arranged in advance, then accessed them. The task started from the situation where each subject did not have any information about the whereabouts and ended when the subject could access all SKTs. We measured the task completion time of each subject by changing intervals of tasks; more specifically 1 h later, 3 h later, and up to 20 days later, in order to check how the subject would memorize the spatial arrangement of SKTs. We then analyzed the time variation of the task completion time. Here, the accessible region was determined as the sphere with radius of 20 cm. The experiment was carried out by six subjects (21-26 years old, science or engineering students). All subjects have used the spatial memory for about 30 min before the experiment, and they know the usage.

The details of the specified task are described as follows.

1. Initialization phase
   a) An experimenter stores seven SKTs whose spatial memory data are given by images.
2. Learning phase
   a) A subject accesses stored SKTs and memorize the contents and the whereabouts. In this step, the "access indicator" which shows colors based on the distance between the human indicator and the spatial memory address of the nearest SKT on a computer display is used.
   b) Learning is ended by the subject's decision.
3. Test phase
   a) Experimenter specifies the content of the SKT.
   b) The subject accesses the specified SKT.
   c) Phases 3-a and 3-b are repeated until all SKTs were accessed by the subject.

The task completion time from phase 2-a to phase 3-c was measured for each subject. Fig. 3 (a) shows the completion time of each subject (Subjects 1-6). The horizontal axis represents logarithmic time [h] that had passed from the experiment start time, and the vertical axis represents the completion time [s]. All subjects learned the contents and the whereabouts of seven SKTs at the first performance, which resulted in a long completion time. The completion time of the first performance of Subject 6 is the shortest because he stored all SKTs before the experiment. All subjects completed accessing all SKTs at the performance after about four weeks from the first performance as short as the second performance. Although Subject 3 required learning at the third performance, the learning time was 50% less than the first performance. After the third performance, he completed the tasks in a time as short as the other subjects did.

These results show the easiness of accessing the stored SKTs by memorizing the spatial locations because almost all subjects did not require learning of SKTs after the first performance. The completion time at the last performance of all subjects became 18-24 s, which shows that the accessibility was maintained or even improved over time.

Fig. 3 (b) shows the completion time of each subject depending on the intervals between the performances in order to investigate the effectiveness of memorizing the stored SKTs. The horizontal axis represents the logarithmic interval time [h] of task executions, and the vertical axis represents the completion time [s] of each task performance. The figure shows the completion times from the second to the last performance. In the experiment, the interval

between performances was increased according to the number of performances, although the interval time is not exactly the same among subjects. Thus, the last performances of all subjects are performed with an interval time of about 500 h (about 20 days).
The completion times of three subjects fluctuated until the first half of the experiment, where the interval time was less than 20 h. The variations of the subjects' completion time, however, decreases when the number of the execution times increase, and the completion times become shorter. Other subjects carried out the task in an almost fixed time through all performances. The time 18–24 of the last performances is close to the physically needed time to access SKTs. In addition, all subjects successfully completed getting access to all SKTs in the performance even after about 20 days from the first performance. As shown in Fig. 3 (b), the performance after 20 days is as short as the performance of 2-h duration.
The results show that the subjects were able to recall the stored SKTs without forgetting them, and accessibility of the spatial memory has been maintained or even improved even if the interval time between usages increased. Therefore, the spatial memory approach in which the access method uses the human body and the storing method tags a real environment is effective for minimizing the forgetting of stored computerized information even if time has passed since it was stored.

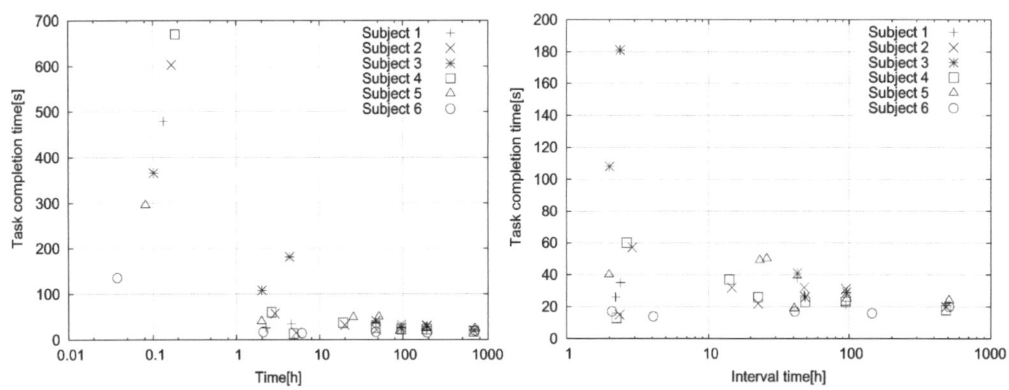

(a) (b)

Fig. 3. Result of the usability evaluation experiment (a) time variation of the task completion time of each subject, (b) task completion time focused on the task interval

2.3 Service execution using spatial memory

By storing services into a space using the spatial memory, we can execute various services in iSpace. Fig. 4 shows an example of a service execution using the spatial memory. In the example, the spatial memory is used for sending commands to a mobile robot. A "call robot" service was stored behind a user and the user called a mobile robot by indicating the position (Fig. 4 (a)-(c)). We also developed an interface to create and delete SKTs. This interface contains a speech recognition unit and SKTs can be managed using voice commands. In the example, another "call robot" service was stored in the user-specified position by using the interface (Fig. 4 (d)-(f)).

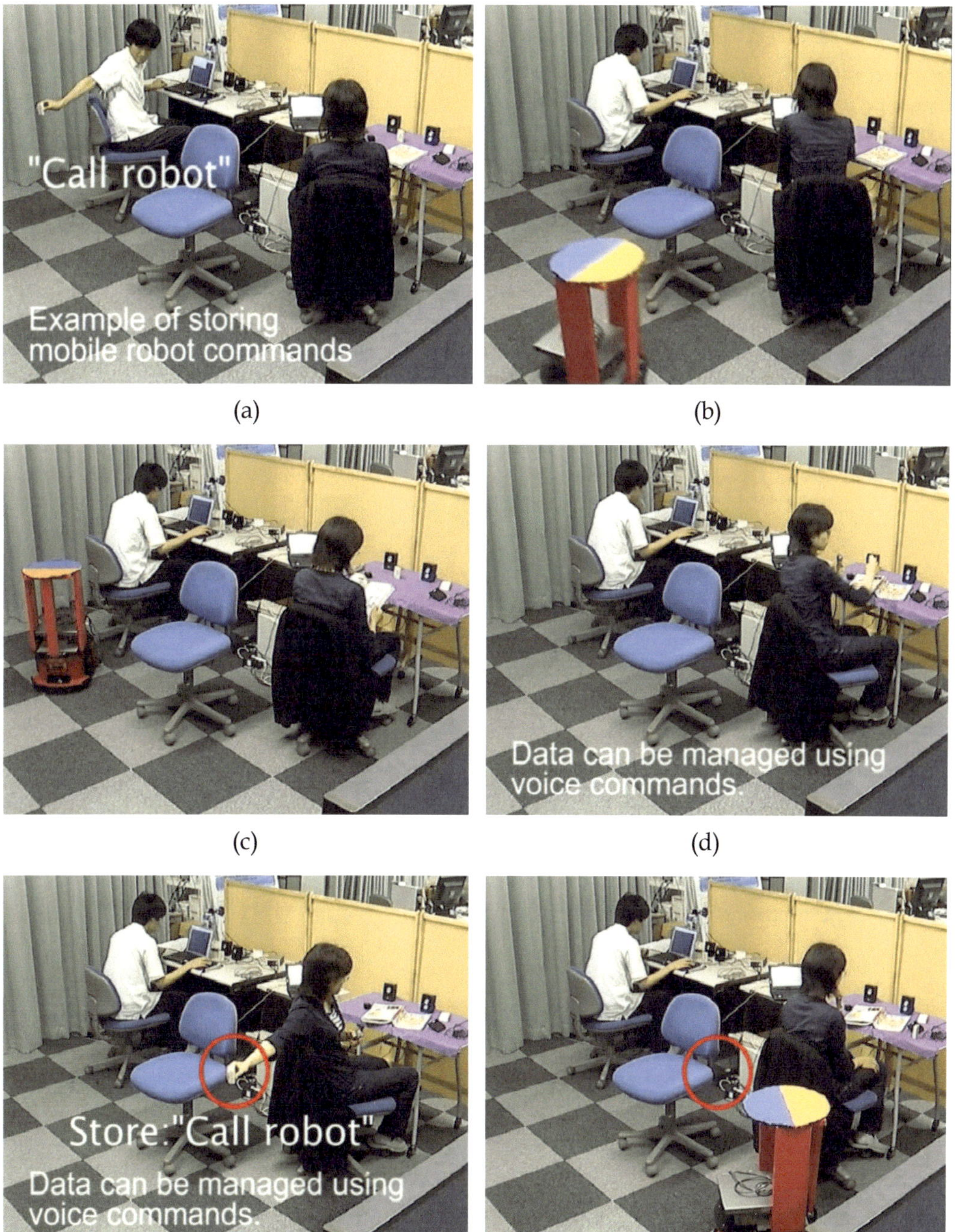

Fig. 4. Service execution using the spatial memory (a)request for "call robot" service by indicating the specified position, (b)(c)execution of "call robot" service, (d)service management by using a voice command, (e)storing the "call robot" service, (f)execution of "call robot" service

3. Sound interfaces

Sound interfaces provide another method for activating services in iSpace. Although iSpace has speech recognition units as shown in the previous section, we introduce a simple but robust sound interface using a human whistling in this section.
Here we consider the frequency of sounds as a trigger to call a service, i.e. a service is provided when the system detects a sound which has the corresponding frequency. The advantages of using a whistle as an interface are that humans do not have to carry any special devices and the range of the sound can be expanded through exercises to activate different types of services depending on the pitch. In addition, it carries a long way and can be easily detected by using distributed microphones. Fig. 5 shows an example of sound waveforms and their frequency spectrum for various sound sources obtained by Fourier analysis. As shown in Fig. 5 (d), the sound of a whistle is considered as a pure tone and easily recognized by considering the percentage of the power of the main frequency component among the total power of the sound.

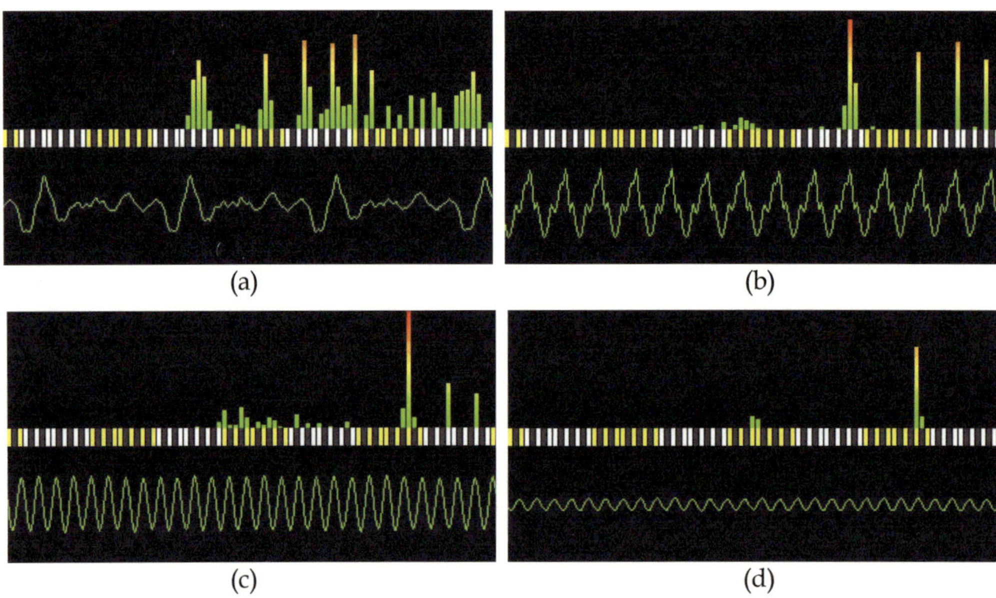

Fig. 5. Result of frequency analysis for various sound sources (a)human voice, (b)melodica, (c)metallophone, (d)human whistle

Fig. 6 shows an example of human-robot interaction through the sound interface. In this example, each sound denotes different commands and a mobile robot is controlled based on the commands. Here we tested various sound sources and played a sound of a different pitch for each source. As shown in the figure, the system detected the sound and the mobile robot generated the corresponding motion successfully. We note that as also shown in Fig. 6, since the sound of the melodica contains rather large harmonic components, the system sometimes failed to detect the sounds. On the other hand, a whistle is robustly recognized even in the presence of environmental noise.
By associating the frequency of sounds with services, this interface can be used to activate various services by the users.

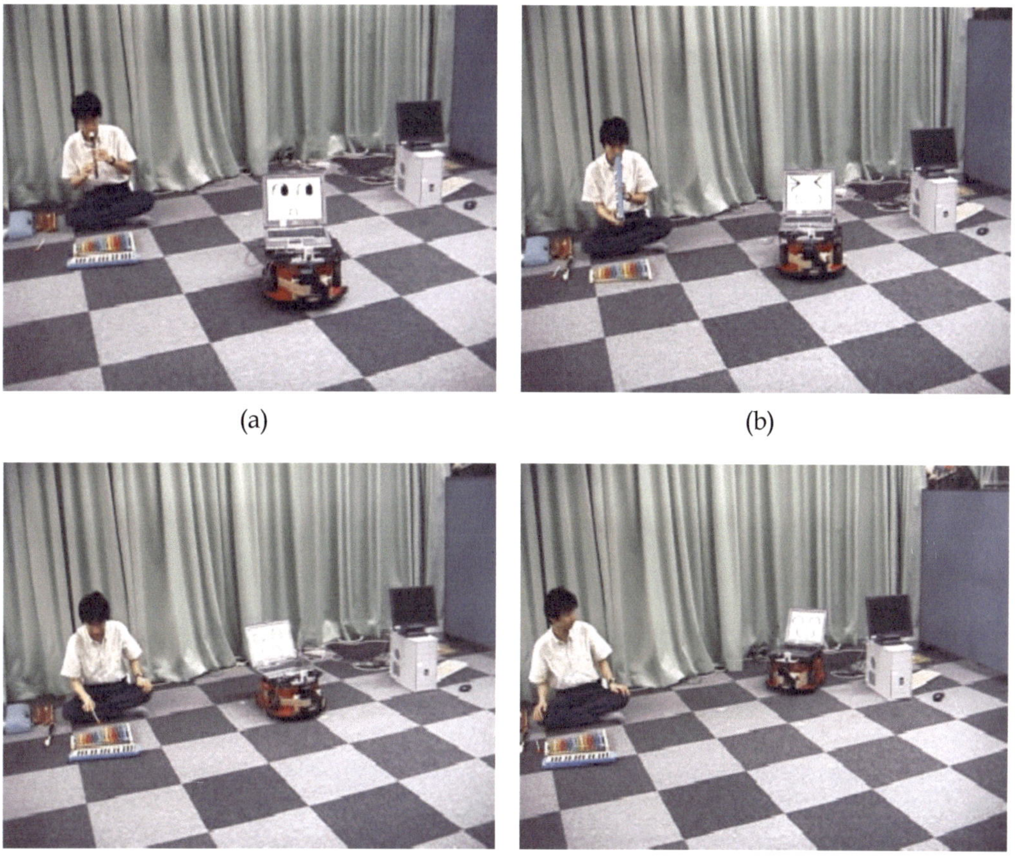

(a) (b)

(c) (d)

Fig. 6. Sending commands to a mobile robot using various sound sources (a)recorder, (b)melodica, (c)metallophone, (d)human whistle

4. Information display using a pan-tilt projector

Based on observation of users in the space, iSpace can actively provide information which is expected to be useful for the users. Here we consider an interactive information display system using visual information. The information display system uses a projector with a pan-tilt unit, which is able to project an image toward any position according to human movement in the space. By utilizing the interactive information, many applications can be developed, for example, the display of signs or marks in public spaces, or various information services in daily life.

However, main issues in active projection are distortion of the projection image and occlusion of the image. These issues are addressed in the following subsections.

4.1 Compensation of projection image

When projection direction is not orthogonal to the projection surface, projection distortion occurs. Moreover the size of the projected image depends on the distance to the projection surface. Therefore with change of the projection point it is not possible to provide a uniform image to a user. The projector provides uniform projection toward any position by compensation of the projection image by using a geometric model and inverse perspective conversion.

The resize ratio γ for compensation of the image size is given as follows.

$$\gamma(d)=W/t(d) \quad (1)$$

where d denotes distance between the projector and the projection surface, W is the desired image size and $t(d)$ is a image size on the projection surface.

Distortion is also caused by the angle between the optical axis of the projector and the projection surface. The geometrical definition is shown in Fig. 7. As shown in this figure, the pan-tilt projector projects an image toward O_p. The plane Q is the projection surface and the plane R is orthogonal to the projection direction. The points r_1 to r_4 denote the corners of the non-distorted image whereas the points q_1 to q_4 are the corresponding points on the distorted image. A relation between a point p_Q on plane Q and a point p_R on plane R is obtained based on perspective conversion:

$$\begin{bmatrix} p_Q \\ 1 \end{bmatrix} \sim \mathbf{H}_{\mathbf{QR}} \begin{bmatrix} p_R \\ 1 \end{bmatrix} \quad (2)$$

This conversion matrix $\mathbf{H}_{\mathbf{QR}}$ is a 3×3 matrix and the degree of freedom is 8. Therefore, if four or more sets of corresponding points of p_Q and p_R are given, we can identify $\mathbf{H}_{\mathbf{QR}}$ and represent image distortion. The corresponding points can be found by the intersection of the plane Q with the line through r_i from the projection origin (lens). The inverse matrix of $\mathbf{H}_{\mathbf{QR}}$ represents compensation of image distortion and we can get pre-compensated output image.

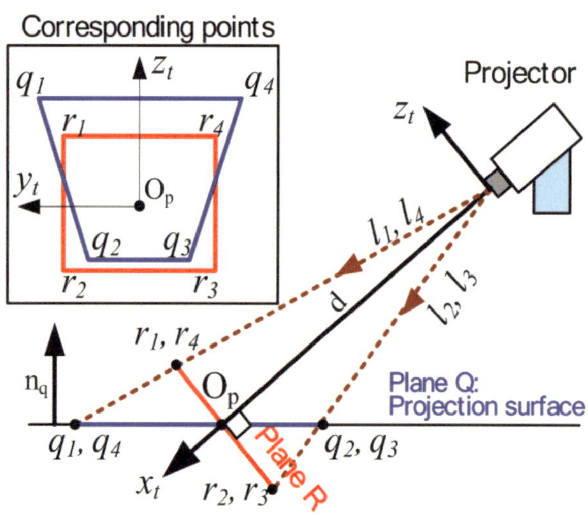

Fig. 7. Geometrical definition of image distortion

4.2 Occlusion avoidance

Projection occlusion occurs when human enters into the area where the human obstructs the projection. This problem sometimes happens in active projection due to human movement or change in projection environment. Hence, by creating an occlusion area and a human

(obstruction) model and judging whether they overlap with each other, occlusion can be detected and avoided.
We modelled the shape of projection light and human are corn and cylinder, respectively. We judge the overlap between these two models to detect occlusion. Moreover, not only humans but also other objects including chairs and tables could cause the occlusion problem. Our occlusion avoidance algorithm can be used by considering the object shape model.
The avoidance method needs to modify the projection position so that the user can easily view the image. Fig. 8 shows the determination of the modified position. In the situation that the projection position is on the left side of the human model, the projection direction is moved to the left to avoid occlusion since it requires less angular variation compared to the rightward movement. On the contrary, when the projection position is on the right side of the human model, it moves to the right for the same reason. If the calculated correction angle is greater than the limit correction angle θ_{max}, the projection position is moved away from the human.

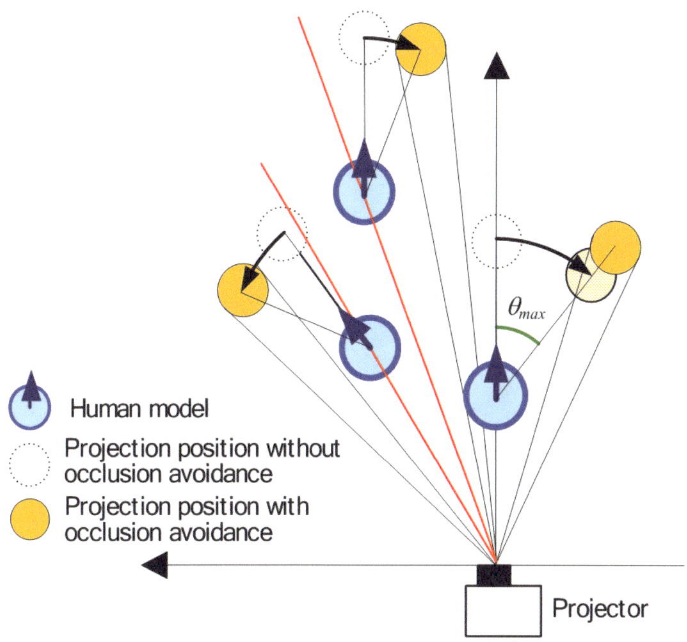

Fig. 8. Determination of the modified position for occlusion avoidance

4.3 Visitor guidance application

We developed a visitor guidance application as an example of interactive informative services. Fig. 9 shows the procedure of the visitor guidance. When iSpace detects a visitor using distributed sensors, the projector displays a guidance panel in front of the visitor. In this case, two messages "call robot" and "view map" are shown (Fig. 9 (a)(b)). If the visitor stands on the "call robot," the projector provides a message "calling robot" and a mobile robot comes toward a user (Fig. 9 (c)). On the other hand, if the visitor stands on "view map," the projector displays the map of the space in front of the visitor (Fig. 9 (d)). In addition, the projector indicates the direction of the place that is selected by the visitor (Fig. 9 (e)(f)).

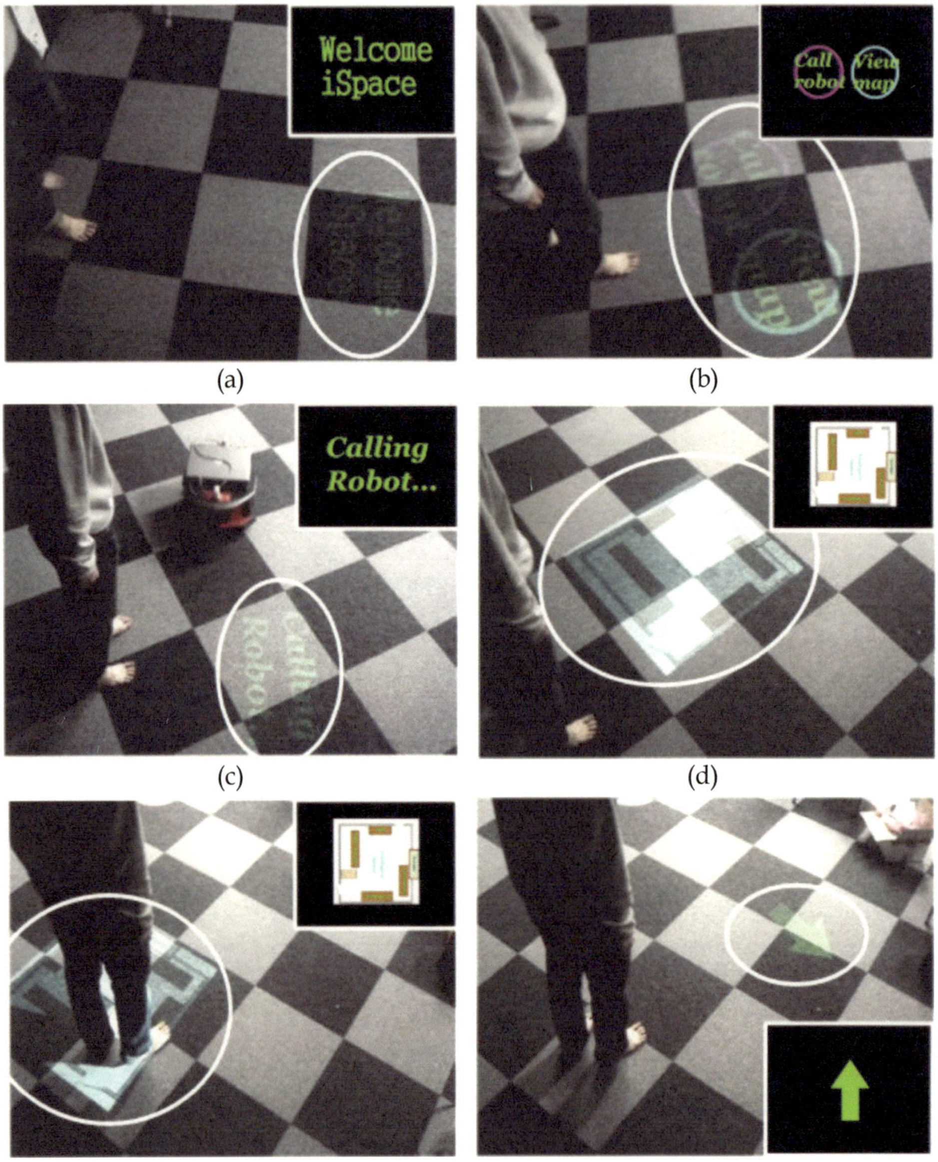

(a) (b) (c) (d) (e) (f)

Fig. 9. Guidance application using a pan-tilt projector (a)detection of a visitor, (b)display of a guidance panel (c)"call robot" service, (d)"view map" service, (e) selection of a place where the visitor wants to go (in the "view map" service), (f)indication of the direction of the place selected by the visitor (in the "view map" service)

5. Conclusion

Intelligent Space (iSpace) is an environmental system, which has multiple distributed and networked sensors and actuators. Since a variety of sensors including cameras, microphones, laser range finders and pressure sensors are taken into account as sensor devices of iSpace, the users can interact with the space in various ways.

The spatial memory was presented as an interface between users and iSpace. We adopt indication actions of users as operation methods in order to achieve an intuitive and instantaneous way that anyone can apply. A position of a part of user's body which is used for operating the spatial memory is called a human indicator. When a user specifies digital information and indicates a position in the space, the system associates the three-dimensional position with the information and manages the information as Spatial-Knowledge-Tag (SKT). Therefore, users can store and arrange computerized information such as digital files, robot commands, voice messages etc. into the real world. They can also retrieve the stored information in the same way as on storing action, i.e. indicating action.

Sound interfaces are also implemented in iSpace. The whistle interface which uses frequency of a human whistling as a trigger to call a service was introduced. Since a sound of a whistle is considered as a pure tone, the sound is easily detected by iSpace. As a result, this interface works well even in the presence of environmental noise.

An information display system was also developed to realize interactive informative services. The system consists of a projector and a pan-tilt enabled stand and is able to project an image toward any position. In addition, this system can provide easily viewable images by compensating the image distortion and avoiding occlusions.

6. References

Cook, D. J. & Das, S. K. (2004). *Smart Environments: Technologies, Protocols, and Applications (Wiley Series on Parallel and Distributed Computing)*, Wiley-Interscience, ISBN 0-471-54448-7, USA.

Han, S.; Lim, H.-S. & Lee, F.-M. (2007). An efficient localization scheme for a differential-driving mobile robot based on RFID system, *IEEE Transaction on Industrial Electronics*, Vol.54, No.6, (Dec., 2007) pp.3362–3369, ISSN 0278-0046.

Hwang, C. & Shih, C. (2009). A distributed active-vision network-space approach for the navigation of car-like wheeled robot, *IEEE Transaction on Industrial Electronics*, Vol.56, No.3, (Mar., 2009) pp.846–855, ISSN 0278-0046.

Johanson, B.; Fox, A. & Winograd, T. (2002). The Interactive Workspaces project: experiences with ubiquitous computing rooms, *IEEE Pervasive Computing*, Vol.1, No.2, (Apr.-Jun. 2002) pp.67-74, ISSN 1536-1268.

Kawamura, T; Fukuhara, T.; Takeda, H.; Kono, Y. & Kidode, M. (2007). Ubiquitous Memories: a memory externalization system using physical objects, *Personal and Ubiquitous Computing*, Vol.11, No.4, (Apr., 2007) pp.287-298, ISSN 1617-4909.

Kim, B. K.; Ohara, K.; Ohba, K.; Tanikawa, T. & Hirai, S. (2005). Design of ubiquitous functions for networked robots in the informative spaces, *Proceedings of the 2nd International Conference on Ubiquitous Robots and Ambient Intelligence*, pp.71-76, Daejeon, Korea, Nov., 2005.

Kurabayashi, D.; Kushima, T. & Asama, H. (2002). Performance of decision making: individuals and an environment, *Proceedings of the 2002 IEEE/RSJ International Conference on Intelligent Robots and Systems*, Vol.3, pp.2831-2836, ISBN 0-7803-7398-7, Lausanne, Switzerland, Sep.-Oct., 2002.

Lee, J-H. & Hashimoto, H. (2002). Intelligent Space - concept and contents, *Advanced Robotics*, Vol.16, No.3, (Apr. 2002) pp.265-280, ISSN 0169-1864.

Mitra, S. & Acharya, T. (2007). Gesture recognition: a survey, *IEEE Transactions on Systems, Man, and Cybernetics, Part C: Applications and Reviews,* Vol.37, No.3, (May 2007) pp.311-324, ISSN 1094-6977.

Mizoguchi, F.; Ohwada, H.; Nishiyama, H. & Hiraishi, H. (1999). Smart office robot collaboration based on multi-agent programming, *Artificial Intelligence,* Vol.114, No.1-2, (Oct. 1999) pp.57-94, ISSN 0004-3702.

Mori, T.; Fujii, A.; Shimosaka, M.; Noguchi, H. & Sato, T. (2007). Typical behavior patterns extraction and anomaly detection algorithm based on accumulated home sensor data, *Proceedings of the 2007 International Conference on Future Generation Communication and Networking,* Vol.2, pp.12-18, ISBN 0-7695-3048-6, Jeju Island, Korea, Dec., 2007.

Mynatt, E. D.; Melenhorst, A.-S.; Fisk, A.-D. & Rogers, W. A. (2004). Aware technologies for aging in place: understanding user needs and attitudes, *IEEE Pervasive Computing,* Vol.3, No.2, (Apr.-Jun. 2004) pp.36-41, ISSN 1536-1268.

Niitsuma, M.; Hashimoto, H. & Watanabe, A. (2004). Spatial human interface in working environment - spatial-knowledge-tags to access memory of activity, *Proceedings of the 30th Annual Conference of IEEE Industrial Electronics Society,* Vol.2, pp.1284-1288, ISBN 0-7803-8730-9, Busan, Korea, Nov., 2004.

Nishida, Y.; Hori, T.; Suehiro, T. & Hirai, S. (2000). Sensorized environment for self-communication based on observation of daily human behavior, *Proceedings of the 2000 IEEE/RSJ International Conference on Intelligent Robots and Systems,* Vol.2, pp.1364-1372, ISBN 0-7803-6348-5, Takamatsu, Japan, Nov., 2000.

Oliver, N.; Garg, A. & Horvitz, E. (2004). Layered representations for learning and inferring office activity from multiple sensory channels, *Computer Vision and Image Understanding,* Vol.96, No.2, (Nov. 2004) pp.163-180, ISSN 1077-3142.

Rekimoto, J.; Ayatsuka, Y. & Hayashi, K. (1998). Augment-able reality: situated communication through physical and digital spaces, *Proceedings of the 2nd International Symposium on Wearable Computers,* pp.68-75, ISBN 0-8186-9074-7, Pittsburgh, PA, USA, Oct., 1998.

Scanlon, L. (2004). Rethinking the computer - Project Oxygen is turning out prototype computer systems, *Technology Review,* Jul./Aug., 2004.

Sgorbissa, A. & Zaccaria, R. (2004). The artificial ecosystem: a distributed approach to service robotics, *Proceedings of the 2004 IEEE International Conference on Robotics and Automation,* Vol.4, pp.3531-3536, ISBN 0-7803-8232-3, New Orleans, LA, USA, Apr.-May, 2004.

Youngblood, G. M.; Holder, L. B. & Cook, D. J. (2005). Managing adaptive versatile environments, *Proceedings of the 3rd IEEE International Conference on Pervasive Computing and Communications,* pp.351-360, ISBN 0-7695-2299-8, Kauai Island, HI, USA, Mar., 2005.

6

Coordination Demand in Human Control of Heterogeneous Robot

Jijun Wang[1] and Michael Lewis[2]
[1]*Quantum Leap Innovations, Inc.*
[2]*University of Pittsburgh*
USA

1. Introduction

The performance of human-robot teams is complex and multifaceted reflecting the capabilities of the robots, the operator(s), and the quality of their interactions. Recent efforts to define common metrics for human-robot interaction (Steinfeld et al., 2006) have favored sets of metric classes to measure the effectiveness of the system's constituents and their interactions as well as the system's overall performance. In this chapter we follow this approach to develop measures characterizing the demand imposed by tasks requiring cooperation among heterogeneous robots.

Applications for multirobot systems (MRS) such as interplanetary construction or cooperating uninhabited aerial vehicles will require close coordination and control between human operator(s) and teams of robots in uncertain environments. Human supervision will be needed because humans must supply the perhaps changing goals that direct MRS activity. Robot autonomy will be needed because the aggregate decision making demands of a MRS are likely to exceed the cognitive capabilities of a human operator. Autonomous cooperation among robots, in particular, will likely be needed because it is these activities (Gerkey & Mataric, 2004) that theoretically impose the greatest decision making load.

Controlling multiple robots substantially increases the complexity of the operator's task because attention must constantly be shifted among robots in order to maintain situation awareness (SA) and exert control. In the simplest case an operator controls multiple independent robots interacting with each as needed. A search task in which each robot searches its own region would be of this category although minimal coordination might be required to avoid overlaps and prevent gaps in coverage. Control performance at such tasks can be characterized by the average demand of each robot on human attention (Crandal et al., 2005). Under these conditions increasing robot autonomy should allow robots to be neglected for longer periods of time making it possible for a single operator to control more robots.

Because of the need to share attention between robots in MRS, teloperation can only be used for one robot out of a team (Nielsen et al., 2003) or as a selectable mode (Parasuraman et al., 2005). Some variant of waypoint control has been used in most of the MRS studies we have reviewed (Crandal et al., 2005, Nielsen et al., 2003, Parasuraman et al., 2005, Trouvain & Wolf, 2002) with differences arising primarily in behavior upon reaching a waypoint. A more fully autonomous mode has typically been included involving things such as search of a designated area (Parasuraman et al., 2005), travel to a distant waypoint (Trouvain & Wolf, 2002), or executing prescribed behaviors (Murphy and Burke, 2005). In studies in which robots did not cooperate and had varying levels of individual autonomy (Crandal et al., 2005, Nielsen et al., 2003, Trouvain & Wolf, 2002) (team size 2-4) performance and workload were both higher at lower autonomy levels and lower at higher ones. So although increasing autonomy in these experiments reduced the cognitive load on the operator, the automation could not perform the replaced tasks as well.

For more strongly cooperative tasks and larger teams individual autonomy alone is unlikely to suffice. The round-robin control strategy used for controlling individual robots would force an operator to plan and predict actions needed for multiple joint activities and be highly susceptible to errors in prediction, synchronization or execution. Estimating the cost of this coordination, however, proves a difficult problem. Established methods of estimating MRS control difficulty, neglect tolerance and fan-out (Crandal et al., 2005) are predicated on the independence of robots and tasks. In neglect tolerance the period following the end of human intervention but preceding a decline in performance below a threshold is considered time during which the operator is free to perform other tasks. If the operator services other robots over this period the measure provides an estimate of the number of robots that might be controlled. Fan-out works from the opposite direction, adding robots and measuring performance until a plateau without further improvement is reached. Both approaches presume that operating an additional robot imposes an additive demand on cognitive resources. These measures are particularly attractive because they are based on readily observable aspects of behavior: the time an operator is engaged controlling the robot, interaction time (IT), and the time an operator is not engaged in controlling the robot, neglect time (NT).

This chapter presents an extension of Crandall's Neglect Tolerance model intended to accommodate both coordination demands (CD) and heterogeneity among robots. We describe the extension of Neglect Tolerance model in section 2. Then in section 3 we introduce the simulator and multi-robot system used in our validation experiments. Section 4 and 5 describes two experiments that attempt to manipulate and directly measure coordination demand under tight and weak cooperation conditions separately. Finally, we draw conclusion and discuss the future work in section 6.

2. Cooperation demand

If robots must cooperate to perform a task such as searching a building without redundant coverage or act together to push a block, this independence no longer holds. Where coordination demands are weak, as in the search task, the round robin strategy implicit in the additive models may still match observable performance, although the operator must now consciously deconflict search patterns to avoid redundancy. For tasks such as box pushing, coordination demands are simply too strong, forcing the operator to either control the robots simultaneously or alternate rapidly to keep them synchronized in their joint activity. In this case the decline in efficiency of a robot's actions is determined by the actions of other robots rather than decay in its own performance. Under these conditions the sequential patterns of interaction presumed by the NT and fan-out measures no longer match the task the operator must perform. To separate coordination demand (CD) from the demands of interacting with independent robots we have extended Crandall's Neglect Tolerance model by introducing the notion of occupied time (OT) as illustrated in Figure 1.

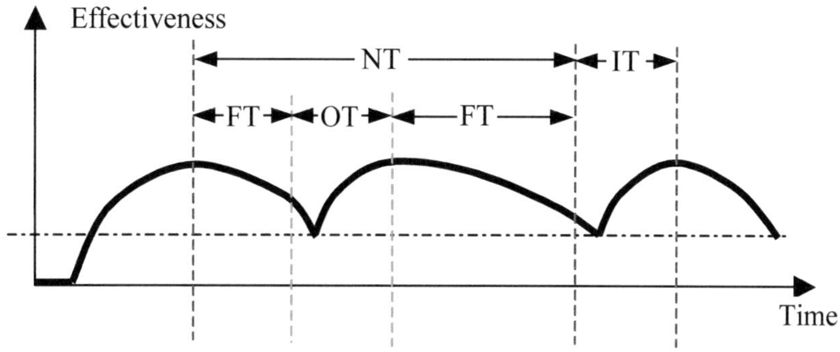

NT: Neglect Time;
FT: Free Time, time off task;
IT+OT: time on task
IT: Interaction Time;
OT: Occupied Time

Fig. 1. Extended neglect tolerance model for cooperative

The neglect tolerance model describes an operator's interaction with multiple robots as a sequence of control episodes in which an operator interacts with a robot for period IT raising its performance above some upper threshold after which the robot is neglected for the period NT until its performance deteriorates below a lower threshold when the operator must again interact with it. To accommodate dependent tasks we introduce OT to describe the time spent controlling other robots in order to synchronize their actions with those of the target robot. The episode depicted in Figure 1 starts just after the first robot is serviced. The ensuing FT preceding the interaction with a second dependent robot, the OT for robot-1 (that would contribute to IT for robot-2), and the FT following interaction with robot-2 but preceding the next interaction with robot-1 together constitute the neglect time for robot-1. Coordination demand, CD, is then defined as:

$$\mathrm{CD} = 1 - \frac{\sum FT}{NT} = \frac{\sum OT}{NT} \tag{1}$$

where, CD for a robot is the ratio between the time required to control cooperating robots and the time still available after controlling the target robot, i.e. the portion of a robot's free time that must be devoted to controlling cooperating robots. Note that the OT associated with a robot is less than or equal to NT because OT covers only that portion of NT needed for synchronization. A related measure, team attention demand (TAD), adds IT's to both numerator and denominator to provide a measure of the proportion of time devoted to the cooperative task, either performing the task or coordinating robots.

2.1 Measuring weak cooperation for heterogeneous robots

Most MRS research has investigated homogeneous robot teams where additional robots provide redundant (independent) capabilities. Differences in capabilities such as mobility or payload, however, may lead to more advantageous opportunities for cooperation among heterogeneous robots. These differences among robots in roles and other characteristics affecting IT, NT, and OT introduce additional complexity to assessing CD. Where tight cooperation is required as in the box-pushing experiment, task requirements dictate both the choice of robots and the interdependence of their actions. In the more general case

requirements for cooperation can be relaxed allowing the operator to choose the subteams of robots to be operated in a cooperative manner as well as the next robot to be operated. This general case of heterogeneous robots cooperating as needed characterizes the types of field applications our research is intended to support. To accommodate this case the Neglect Tolerance model must be further extended to measure coordination between different robot types. We describe this form of heterogeneous MRS as a MN system with M robots that belong to N robot types, and for robot type i, there are m_i robots, that is $M = \sum_{i=1}^{N} m_i$. Thus, we can denote a robot in this system as R_{ij} , where $i = [1, N]$, $j = [1, m_i]$. If we assume that the operator serially controls the robots for time T and that each robot R_{ij} is interacted with l_{ij} times, then we can represent each interaction as IT_{ijk}, where $i = [1, N]$, $j = [1, m_i]$, $k = [1, l_{ij}]$, and the following free time as FT_{ijk}, where $i = [1, N]$, $j = [1, m_i]$, $k = [1, l_{ij}]$. The total control time T_i for type i robot should then be $T_i = \sum_{j,k} \left(IT_{ijk} + FT_{ijk} \right)$. Because robots that are of the same robot type are identical, and substitution may cause uneven demand, we are only interested in measuring the average coordination demand CD_i, i=[1, N] for a robot type.
Given robots of the same type R_{ij}, j = [1, m_i], we define OT_i^* and NT_i^* as the average occupation time and interaction time in a robot control episode. Therefore, the CD_i for type i robot is

$$CD_i = \frac{1}{m_i} \sum_{j=1}^{m_i} CD_{ij} = \frac{1}{m_i} \sum_{j=1}^{m_i} \frac{l_{ij} OT_i^*}{l_{ij} NT_i^*} = \frac{OT_i^* \sum_{j=1}^{m_j} l_{ij}}{NT_i^* \sum_{j=1}^{m_j} l_{ij}}$$

Assume all the other types robots are dependent with the current type robots, then the numerator is the total interaction time of all the other robot types, i.e. $OT_i^* \sum_{j=1}^{m_j} l_{ij} = \sum_{\substack{type=1 \\ type \neq i}}^{N} IT$.

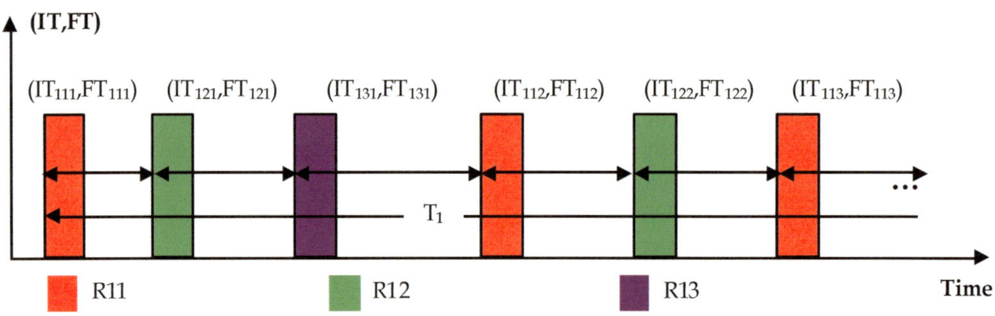

Fig. 2. Distribution of (IT, FT)

For the denominator, it is hard to directly measure NT_i^* because the system performance depends on multiple types of robots and an individual robot may cooperate with different team members over time. Because of this dependency, we cannot use individual robot's active time to approximate NT. On the other hand, the robots may be unevenly controlled. For example a robot might be controlled only once and then ignored because there is another robot of the same type that is available, so we cannot simply use the time interval between two interactions of an individual robot as NT. Considering all the robots belonging to a robot type, the population of individual robots' (IT, FT)s reveal the NT for a type of robot. Figure 2 shows an example of how robots' (IT, FT) might be distributed over task time. Because robots of the same capabilities might be used interchangeably to perform a cooperative task it is desirable to measure NT with respect to a type rather than a particular robot. In Figure 2 robots R_{11} and R_{12} have short NTs while R_{13} has an NT of indefinite length. F(IT, FT), the distribution of (IT, FT) for the robot type, shown by the arrowed lines between interactions allows an estimate of NT for a robot type that is not affected by long individual NTs such as that of R_{13}. When each robot is evenly controlled, the F(IT, NT) should be $m_i \times (IT_i, FT_i)^*$ where $(IT_i, FT_i)^*$ is the (IT, FT) for each type i robot, $(IT_i, FT_i)^* = \frac{T_i}{\sum_{j=1}^{m_i} l_{ij}}$. And when only one robot is controlled, $F(IT_i, NT_i)^*$ will be the (IT_i, FT_i) for this robot. Here, we introduce weight $w_i = \frac{\sum_{j=1}^{m_i} l_{ij}}{m_i \max_{j=1}^{m_i}(l_{ij})}$ to assess how evenly the robots are controlled. $w_i \times m_i$ is the "equivalent" number of evenly controlled robots. With the weight, we can approximate $F(IT_i, NT_i)$ as:

$$F(IT_i, NT_i) \approx w_i \times \left(m_i (IT_i, NT_i)^*\right) = \frac{\sum_{j=1}^{m_i} l_{ij}}{\max_{j=1}^{m_i}(l_{ij})} \times \frac{T_i}{\sum_{j=1}^{m_i} l_{ij}} = \frac{T_i}{\max_{j=1}^{m_i}(l_{ij})}$$

Thus, the denominator in CD_i can be calculated as:

$$NT_i^* \sum_{j=1}^{m_i} l_{ij} = \left(\frac{T_i}{\max_{j=1}^{m_i}(l_{ij})} - IT_i^* \right) \sum_{j=1}^{m_i} l_{ij} = \frac{\sum_{j=1}^{m_i} l_{ij}}{\max_{j=1}^{m_i}(l_{ij})} T_i - IT_i^* \sum_{j=1}^{m_i} l_{ij} = \frac{\sum_{j=1}^{m_i} l_{ij}}{\max_{j=1}^{m_i}(l_{ij})} T_i - \sum_{type=i} IT,$$

where $\sum_{type=i} IT$ is the total interaction time for all the type i robots.

In summary, we can compute CD_i as:

$$CD_i = \frac{\sum_{type \neq i} IT}{\frac{\sum_{j=1}^{m_i} l_{ij}}{\max_{j=1}^{m_i}(l_{ij})} T_i - \sum_{type=i} IT} \qquad (2)$$

3. Simulation environment and multirobot system

To test the usefulness of the CD measurement, we conducted two experiments to manipulate and measure coordination demand directly. In the first experiment robots perform a box pushing task in which CD is varied by control mode and robot heterogeneity.

The second experiment attempts to manipulate coordination demand by varying the proximity needed to perform a joint task in two conditions and by automating coordination within subteams in the third. Both experiments were conducted in the high fidelity USARSim robotic simulation environment we developed as a simulation of urban search and rescue (USAR) robots and environments intended as a research tool for the study of human-robot interaction (HRI) and multi-robot coordination.

3.1 USARSim

USARSim supports HRI by accurately rendering user interface elements (particularly camera video), accurately representing robot automation and behavior, and accurately representing the remote environment that links the operator's awareness with the robot's behaviors. It was built based on a multi-player game engine, UnrealEngine2, and so is well suited for simulating multiple robots. USARSim uses the Karma Physics engine to provide physics modeling, rigid-body dynamics with constraints and collision detection. It uses other game engine capabilities to simulate sensors including camera video, sonar, and laser range finder. More details about USARSim can be found at (Wang et al. 2003; Lewis et al. 2007). Validation studies showing agreement for a variety of feature extraction techniques between USARSim images and camera video are reported in (Carpin et al., 2006a), showing close agreement in detection of walls and associated Hough transforms for a simulated Hokuyo laser range finder (Carpin et al., 2005) and close agreement in behavior between USARSim models and the robots being modeled (Carpin et al., 2006b, Wang et al., 2005, Pepper et al., 2007, Taylor et al., 2007, Zaratti et al., 2006). USARSim is freely available and can be downloaded from www.sourceforge.net/projects/usarsim.

3.2 Multirobot Control System (MrCS)

A multirobot control system (MrCS), a multirobot communications and control infrastructure with accompanying user interface, was developed to conduct these experiments. The system was designed to be scalable to allow of control different numbers of robots, reconfigurable to accommodate different human-robot interfaces, and reusable to facilitate testing different control algorithms. It provides facilities for starting and controlling robots in the simulation, displaying camera and laser output, and supporting inter-robot communication through Machinetta, a distributed mutiagent system with state-of-the-art algorithms for plan instantiation, role allocation, information sharing, task deconfliction and adjustable autonomy (Scerri et al. 2004).

The user interface of MrCS is shown in Figure 8. The interface is reconfigurable to allow the user to resize the components or change the layout. Shown in the figure is a configuration that used in one of our experiments. On the upper and center portions of the left-hand side are the robot list and team map panels, which show the operator an overview of the team. The destination of each of robot is displayed on the map to help the user keep track of current plans. On the upper and center portions of the right-hand side are the camera view and mission control panels, which allow the operator to maintain situation awareness of an individual robot and to edit its exploration plan. On the mission panel, the map and all nearby robots and their destinations are represented to provide partial team awareness so that the operator can switch between contexts while moving control from one robot to another. The lower portion of the left-hand side is a teleoperation panel that allows the operator to teleoperate a robot.

4. Tight cooperation experiment

4.1 Experiment design

Finding a metric for cooperation demand (CD) is difficult because there is no widely accepted standard. In this experiment, we investigated CD by comparing performance across three conditions selected to differ substantially in their coordination demands. We selected box pushing, a typical cooperative task that requires the robots to coordinate, as our task. We define CD as the ratio between occupied time (OT), the period over which the operator is actively controlling a robot to synchronize with others, and FT+OT, the time during which he is not actively controlling the robot to perform the primary task. This measure varies between 0 for no demand to 1 for maximum demand. When an operator teleoperates the robots one by one to push the box forward, he must continuously interact with one of the robots because neglecting both would immediately stop the box. Because the task allows no free time (FT) we expect CD to be 1. However, when the user is able to issue waypoints to both robots, the operator may have FT before she must coordinate these robots again because the robots can be instructed to move simultaneously. In this case CD should be less than 1. Intermediate levels of CD should be found in comparing control of homogeneous robots with heterogeneous robots. Higher CD should be found in the heterogeneous group since the unbalanced pushes from the robots would require more frequent coordination. In the present experiment, we measured CDs under these three conditions.

Fig. 3. Box pushing task

Figure 3 shows our experiment setting simulated in USARSim. The controlled robots were either two Pioneer P2AT robots or one Pioneer P2AT and one less capable three wheeled Pioneer P2DX robot. Each robot was equipped with a GPS, a laser scanner, and a RFID reader. On the box, we mounted two RFID tags to enable the robots to sense the box's position and orientation. When a robot pushes the box, both the box and robot's orientation and speed will change. Furthermore, because of irregularities in initial conditions and accuracy of the physical simulation the robot and box are unlikely to move precisely as the operator expected. In addition, delays in receiving sensor data and executing commands were modeled presenting participants with a problem very similar to coordinating physical robots.

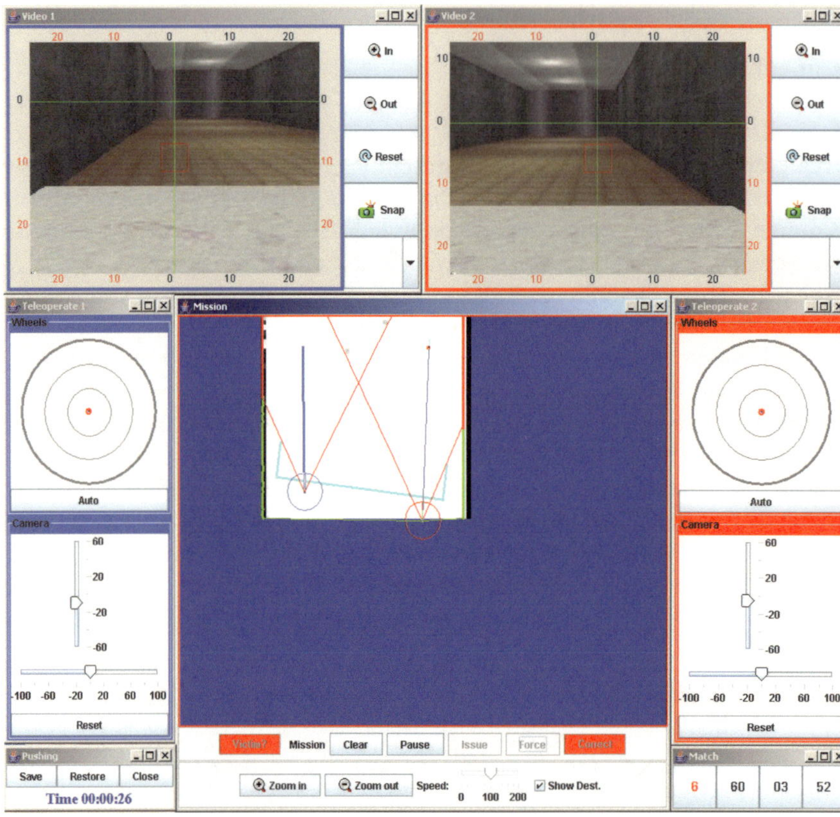

Fig. 4. GUI for box pushing task

We introduced a simple matching task as a secondary task to allow us to estimate the FT available to the operator. Participants were asked to perform this secondary task as possible when they were not occupied controlling a robot. Every operator action and periodic timestamped samples the box's moving speed were recorded for computing CD.

A within subject design was used to control for individual differences in operators' control skills and ability to use the interface. To avoid having abnormal control behavior, such as a robot bypassing the box bias the CD comparison, we added safeguards to the control system to stop the robot when it tilted the box.

The operator controlled the robots using a distributed multi-robot control system (MrCS) shown in Figure 4. On the left and right side are the teleoperation widgets that control the left and right robots separately. The bottom center is a map based control panel that allows the user to monitor the robots and issue waypoint commands on the map. On the bottom right corner is the secondary task window where the participants were asked to perform the matching task when possible.

4.2 Participants and procedure

14 paid participants, 18-57 years old were recruited from the University of Pittsburgh community. None had prior experience with robot control although most were frequent computer users. The participants' demographic information and experience are summarized in Table 1.

	Age		Gender		Education	
	18~35	>35	Male	Female	Currently/Complete Undergraduate	Currently /Complete Graduate
Participants	11	3	11	3	2	12

	Computer Usage (hours/week)				Game Playing (hours/week)			
	<1	1-5	5-10	>10	<1	1-5	5-10	>10
Participants	0	1	2	11	8	4	2	0

	Mouse Usage for Game Playing		
	Frequently	Occasionally	Never
Participants	9	4	1

Table 1. Sample demographics and experiences

The experiment started with collection of the participant's demographic data and computer experience. The participant then read standard instructions on how to control robots using the MrCS. In the following 8 minutes training session, the participant practiced each control operation and tried to push the box forward under the guidance of the experimenter. Participants then performed three testing sessions in counterbalanced order. In two of the sessions, the participants controlled two P2AT robots using teleoperation alone or a mixture of teleoperation and waypoint control. In the third session, the participants were asked to control heterogeneous robots (one P2AT and one P2DX) using a mixture of teleoperation and waypoint control. The participants were allowed eight minutes to push the box to the destination in each session. At the conclusion of the experiment participants completed a questionnaire about their experience.

4.3 Results

Figure 5 shows a time distribution of robot control commands recorded in the experiment. As we expected no free time was recorded for robots in the teleoperation condition and the longest free times were found in controlling homogeneous robots with waypoints. The box

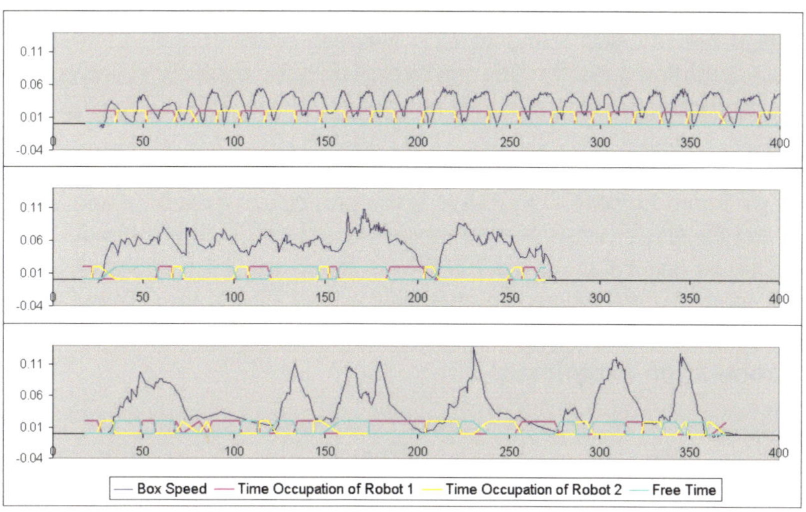

Fig. 5. The time distribution curves for teleoperation (upper) and waypoint control (middle) for homogeneous robots, and waypoint control (bottom) for heterogeneous robots

speed shown on Figure 5 is the moving speed along the hallway that reflects the interaction effectiveness (IE) of the control mode. The IE curves in this picture show the delay effect and the frequent bumping that occurred in controlling heterogeneous robots revealing the poorest cooperation performance.

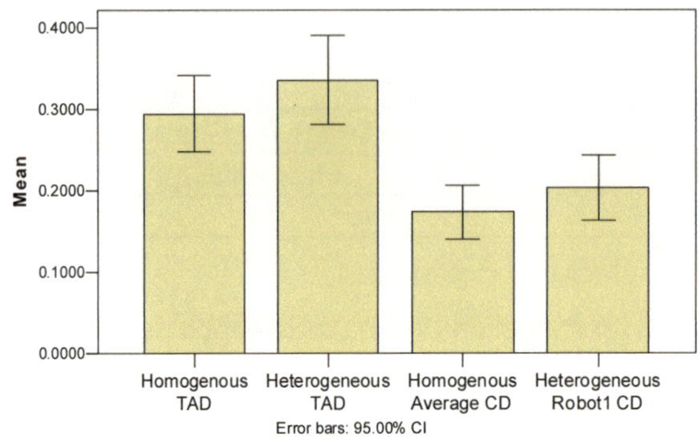

Fig. 6. Team task demand (TAD) and Cooperation demand (CD)

None of the 14 participants were able to perform the secondary task while teleoperating the robots. Hence, we uniformly find TAD = 1 and CD = 1 for both robots under this condition. Within participants comparison found that under waypoint control the team attention demand in heterogeneous robots is significantly higher than the demand in controlling homogeneous robots, $t(13) = 2.213$, $p = 0.045$ (Figure 6). No significant differences were found between the homogeneous P2AT robots in terms of the individual cooperation demand ($P = 0.2$). Since the robots are identical, we compared the average CD of the left and right robots with the CDs measured under heterogeneous condition. Two-tailed t-test shows that when a participant controlled a P2AT robot, lower CD was required in homogeneous condition than in the heterogeneous condition, $t(13) = -2.365$, $p = 0.034$. The CD required in controlling the P2DX under heterogeneous condition is marginally higher than the CD required in controlling homogenous P2ATs, $t(13) = -1.868$, $p = 0.084$ (Figure 6). Surprisingly, no significant difference was found in CDs between controlling P2AT and P2DX under heterogeneous condition ($p=0.79$). This can be explained by the three observed robot control strategies: 1) the participant always issued new waypoints to both robots when adjusting the box's movement, therefore similar CDs were found between the robots; 2) the participant tried to give short paths to the faster robot (P2DX) to balance the different speeds of the two robots, thus we found higher CD in P2AT; 3) the participant gave the same length paths to both robots and the slower robot needed more interactions because it trended to lag behind the faster robot, so lower CD for the P2AT was found for the participant. Among the 14 participants, 5 of them (36%) showed higher CD for the P2DX contrary to our expectations.

5. Weak cooperation experiment

To test the usefulness of the CD measurement for a weakly cooperative MRS, we conducted another experiment assessing coordination demand using an Urban Search And Rescue (USAR) task requiring high human involvement (Murphy and Burke, 2005) and of a complexity suitable to exercise heterogeneous robot control. In the experiment participants were asked to control explorer robots equipped with a laser range finder but no camera and inspector robots with only cameras. Finding and marking a victim required using the inspector's camera to find a victim to be marked on the map generated by the explorer. The capability of the robots and the cooperation autonomy level were used to adjust the coordination demand of the task. The experiment was conducted in simulation using USARSim and MrCS.

5.1 Experiment design

Three simulated Pioneer P2AT robots and 3 Zergs (Balakirsky et al., 2007), a small experimental robot were used. Each P2AT was equipped with a front laser scanner with 180 degree FOV and resolution of 1 degree. The Zerg was mounted with a pan-tilt camera with 45 degree FOV. The robots were capable of localization and able to communicate with other robots and control station. The P2AT served as an explorer to build the map while the Zerg could be used as an inspector to find victims using its camera. To accomplish the task the participant must coordinate these two types robot to ensure that when an inspector robot finds a victim, it is within a region mapped by an explorer robot so the position can be marked.

Fig. 7. Urban search and rescue task

Three conditions were designed to vary the coordination demand on the operator. Under condition 1, the explorer had 20 meters detection range allowing inspector robots considerable latitude in their search. Under condition 2, scanner range was reduced to 5 meters requiring closer proximity to keep the inspector within mapped areas. Under condition 3, explorer and inspector robots were paired as subteams in which the explorer robot with a sensor range of 5 meters followed its inspector robot to map areas being searched. We hypothesized that CDs for explorer and inspector robots would be more even distributed under condition-2 (short range sensor) because explorers would need to move more frequently in response to inspectors' searches than in condition-1 in which CD should be more asymmetric with explorers exerting greater demand on inspectors. We also hypothesized that lower CD would lead to higher team performance. Three equivalent damaged buildings were constructed from the same elements using different layouts. Each environment was a maze like building with obstacles, such as chairs, desks, cabinets, and bricks with 10 evenly distributed victims. A fourth environment was constructed for training. Figure 7 shows the simulated robots and environment.

A within subjects design with counterbalanced presentation was used to compare the cooperative performance across the three conditions. The same control interface shown in Figure 8 allowing participants to control robots through waypoints or teleoperation was used in all conditions.

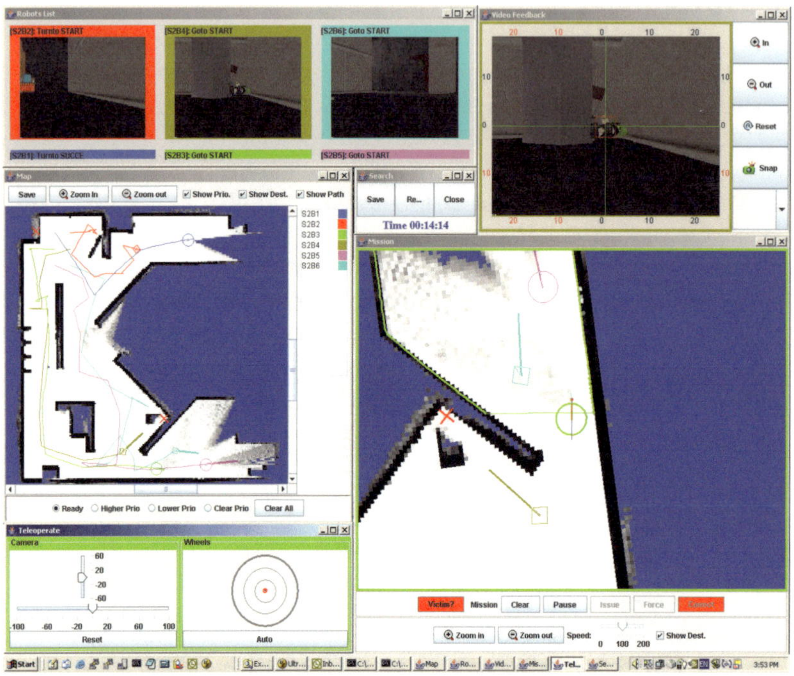

Fig. 8. GUI for urban search and rescue

5.2 Participants and procedure

19 paid participants, 19-33, years old were recruited from the University of Pittsburgh community. None had prior experience with robot control although most were frequent computer users. 6 of the participants (31.5%) reported playing computer games for more than one hour per week. The participants' demographic information and experience are summarized in Table 2.

<table>
<tr><th></th><th colspan="2">Age</th><th colspan="2">Gender</th><th colspan="4">Education</th></tr>
<tr><td></td><td>19~29</td><td>30~33</td><td>Male</td><td>Female</td><td colspan="2">Currently/Complete Undergraduate</td><td colspan="2">Currently /Complete Graduate</td></tr>
<tr><td>Participants</td><td>18</td><td>1</td><td>7</td><td>12</td><td colspan="2">11</td><td colspan="2">8</td></tr>
<tr><td></td><td colspan="4">Computer Usage (hours/week)</td><td colspan="4">Game Playing (hours/week)</td></tr>
<tr><td></td><td><1</td><td>1-5</td><td>5-10</td><td>>10</td><td><1</td><td>1-5</td><td>5-10</td><td>>10</td></tr>
<tr><td>Participants</td><td>0</td><td>1</td><td>5</td><td>13</td><td>13</td><td>4</td><td>1</td><td>1</td></tr>
<tr><td></td><td colspan="8">Mouse Usage for Game Playing</td></tr>
<tr><td></td><td colspan="3">Frequently</td><td colspan="3">Occasionally</td><td colspan="2">Never</td></tr>
<tr><td>Participants</td><td colspan="3">14</td><td colspan="3">2</td><td colspan="2">3</td></tr>
</table>

Table 2. Sample demographics and experiences

After collecting demographic data the participant read standard instructions on how to control robots via MrCS. In the following 15~20 minute training session, the participant practiced each control operation and tried to find at least one victim in the training arena under the guidance of the experimenter. Participants then began three testing sessions in counterbalanced order with each session lasting 15 minutes. At the conclusion of the experiment participants completed a questionnaire.

5.3 Results

Overall performance was measured by the number of victims found, the explored areas, and the participants' self-assessments. To examine cooperative behavior in finer detail, CDs were computed from logged data for each type robot under the three conditions. We compared the measured CDs between condition 1 (20 meters sensing range) and condition 2 (5 meters sensing range), as well as condition 2 and condition 3 (subteam). To further analyze the cooperation behaviors, we evaluated the total attention demand in robot control and control action pattern as well. Finally, we introduce control episodes showing how CDs can be used to identify and diagnose abnormal control behaviors.

1. Overall performance

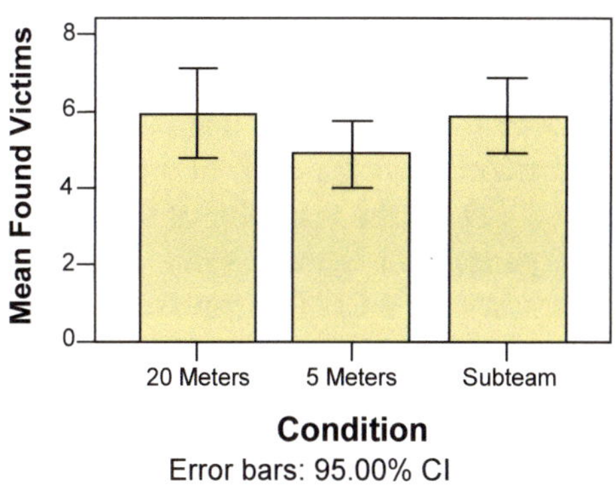

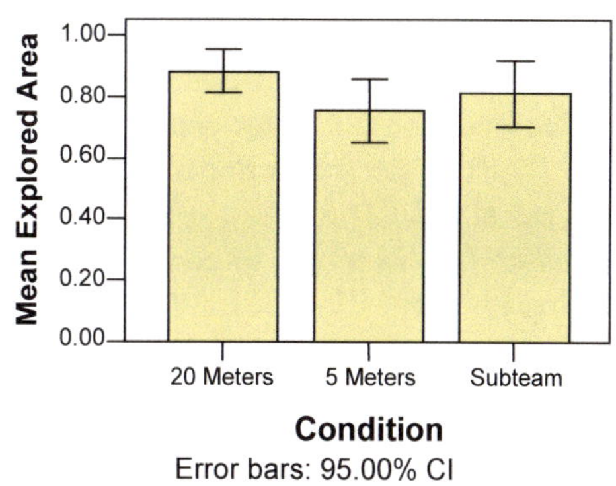

Fig. 9. Found victims (left) and explored areas (right) by mode

Examination of data showed two participants failed to perform the task satisfactorily. One commented during debriefing that she thought she was supposed to mark inspector robots rather than victims. After removing these participants a paired t-test shows that in condition-1 (20 meters range scanner) participants explored more regions, $t(16) = 3.097$, $p = 0.007$, as well as found more victims, $t(16) = 3.364$, $p = 0.004$, than under condition-2 (short range scanner). In condition-3 (automated subteam) participants found marginally more victims, $t(16) = 1.944$, $p = 0.07$, than in condition-2 (controlled cooperation) but no difference was found for the extent of regions explored (Figure 9).

In the posttest survey, 12 of the 19 (63%) participants reported they were able to control the robots although they had problems in handling some interface components, 6 of the 19 (32%) participants thought they used the interface very well, and only one participant reported it being hard to handle all the components on the user interface but still maintained she was able to control the robots. Most participants (74%) thought it was easier to coordinate inspectors with explorers with long range scanner. 12 of the 19 (63%) participants rated auto-cooperation between inspector and explorer (the subteam condition) as improving their performance, and 5 (26%) participants though auto-cooperation made no difference. Only 2 (11%) participants judged team autonomy to make things worse.

2. Coordination effort

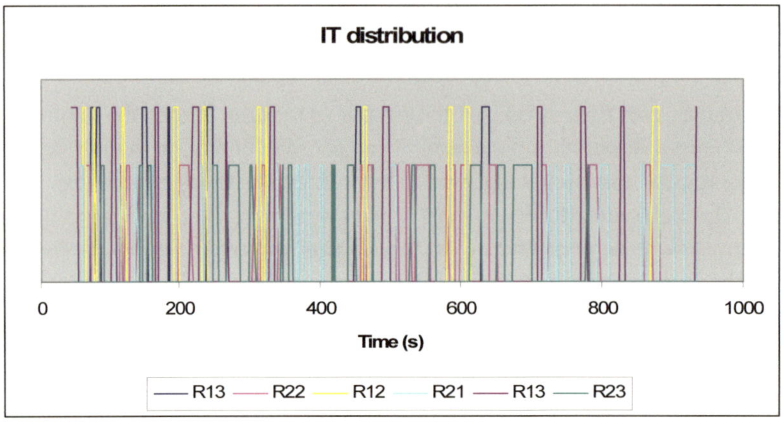

Fig. 10. Typical (IT,FT) distribution (higher line indicates the interactions of

During the experiment we logged all the control operations with timestamps. From the log file, CDs were computed for each type robot according to equation 2. Figure 10 shows a typical (IT,FT) distribution under condition 1 (20 meters sensing range) in the experiment with a calculated CD for the explorer of 0.185 and a CD for the inspector of 0.06. The low CDs reflect that in trying to control 6 robots the participant ignored some robots while attending to others. The CD for explorers is roughly twice the CD for inspectors. After the participant controlled an explorer, he needed to control an inspector multiple times or multiple inspectors since the explorer has a long detection range and large FOV. In contrast, after controlling an inspector, the participant needed less effort to coordinate explorers.

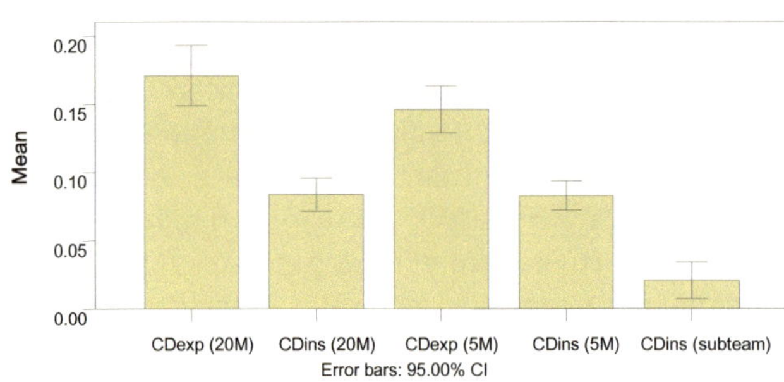

Fig. 11. CDs for each robot type

Figure 11 shows the mean of measured CDs. We predicted that when the explorer has a longer detection range, operators would need to control the inspectors more frequently to cover the mapped area. Therefore a longer detection range should lead to higher CD for explorers. This was confirmed by a two tailed t-test that found higher coordination demand,

$t(18) = 2.476$, $p = 0.023$, when participants controlled explorers with large (20 meters) sensing range.

We did not find a corresponding difference, $t(18)=.149$, $p=0.884$, between long and short detection range conditions for the CD for inspectors. This may have occurred because under these two conditions the inspectors have exactly the same capabilities and the difference in explorer detection range was not large enough to impact inspectors' CD for explorers. Under the subteam condition, the automatic cooperation within a subteam decreased or eliminated the coordination requirement when a participant controlled an inspector. Within participant comparisons shows that the measured CD of inspectors under this condition is significantly lower than the CD under condition 2 (independent control with 5 meters detection range), $t(18) = 6.957$, $p < 0.001$. Because the explorer always tries to automatically follow an inspector, we do not report CD of explorers in this condition.

As auxiliary parameters, we evaluated the total attention demand, i.e. the occupation rate of total interaction time in the whole control period, and the action pattern, the ratio of control times between inspector and explorer, as well. Total attention demand measures the team task demand, i.e.; how hard the task is. As we expected paired t-test shows that under subteam condition, participants spent less time in robot control than under short sensing range condition, $t(18)=3.423$, $p=0.003$. However, under long sensing conditions, paired t-test shows that participants spent more time controlling robots than under the short sensing condition, $t(18) = 2.059$, $p = 0.054$. This is opposite to our hypothesis that searching for victims with shorter sensing range should be harder because the robot would need to be controlled more often. Noticing that total attention demand was based on the time spent controlling not the number of times a robot was controlled we examined the number of control episodes. Under long and short sensing range conditions two tailed t-tests found participants to control explorers more times with short sensing explorers, $t(18)=2.464$, $p=.024$, with no differences found in frequency of inspector control, $p=.97$. We believe that with longer sensing explorers participants tend to issue longer paths in order to build larger maps. Because the sensing range in condition 1 is five times longer than the range in condition 2, the increased control time under the long sensing condition my overwhelm the increased explorer control times. This is partially confirmed by a paired t-test that found longer average control time for explorers and inspectors under the long detection condition, $t(18)=3.139$, $p=.006$, $t(18)=2.244$, $p=.038$, respectively. On average participants spent 1.5s and 1.0s more time in explorer and inspector control in the long range condition. The mean action patterns under long and short range scanner conditions are 2.31 and 1.9 respectively. This means that with 20 and 5 meters scanning ranges, participants controlled inspectors 2.31 and 1.9 times respectively after an explorer interaction. Within participant comparisons shows that the ratio is significantly larger under long sensing condition than under short range scanner condition, $t(18) = 2.193$, $p = 0.042$.

3. Analyzing Performance

As an example of applying CDs to analyze coordination behavior, Figure 11 shows the performance over explorer CD and total attention demand under the 20 meters sensing range condition. Three abnormal cases A, B, and C can be identified from the graph. Associating these cases with recorded map snapshots (Table 3), we observed that in case A, one robot was entangled by a desk and stuck after five minutes; in case B, two robots were controlled in the first five minutes and afterwards ignored; and in case C, the participant ignored two inspectors throughout the entire trial. Comparing with case B and C, in case A only one robot didn't function properly after five minutes.

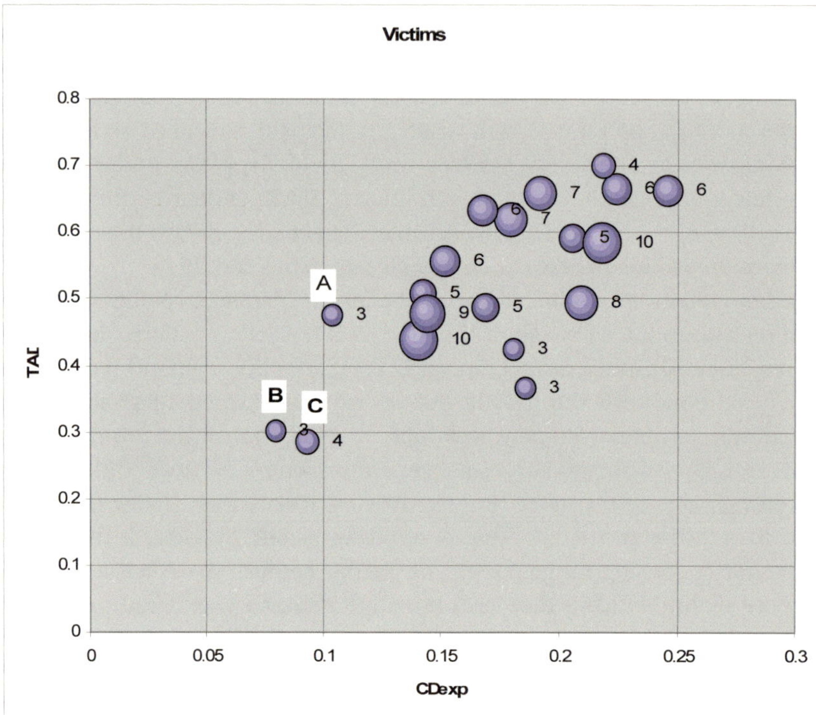

Fig. 12. Found victims distribution over CDexp and TAD

6. Conclusion

We proposed an extended Neglect Tolerance model to allow us to evaluate coordination demand in applications where an operator must coordinate multiple robots to perform dependent tasks. Results from the first experiment that required tight coordination conformed closely to our hypotheses with the teleoperation condition producing CD=1 as predicted and heterogeneous teams exerting greater demand than homogenous ones. The CD measure proved useful in identifying abnormal control behavior revealing inefficient control by one participant through irregular time distributions and close CDs for P2ATs under homogeneous and heterogeneous conditions (0.23 and 0.22), a mistake with extended recovery time (41 sec) in another, and a shift to a satisficing strategy between homogeneous and heterogeneous conditions revealed by a drop in CD (0.17 to 0.11) in a third.

As most target applications such as construction or search and rescue require weaker cooperation among heterogeneous platforms the second experiment extended NT methodology to such conditions. Results in this more complex domain were mixed. Our findings of increased CD for long sensor range may seem counter intuitive because inspectors would be expected to exert greater CD on explorers with short sensor range. Our

	5 minutes snapshot	10 minutes snapshot	15 minutes snapshot
A	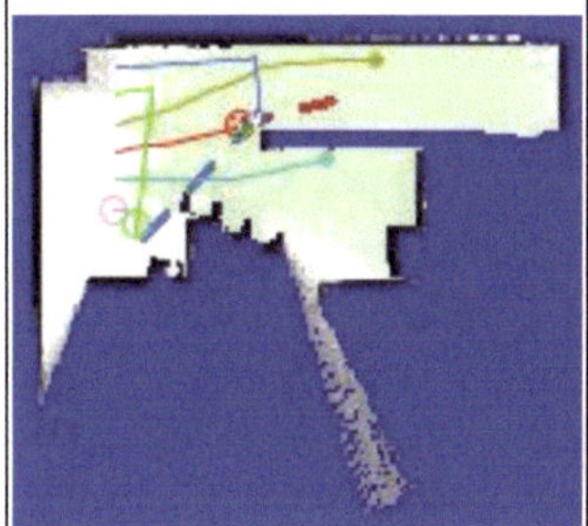	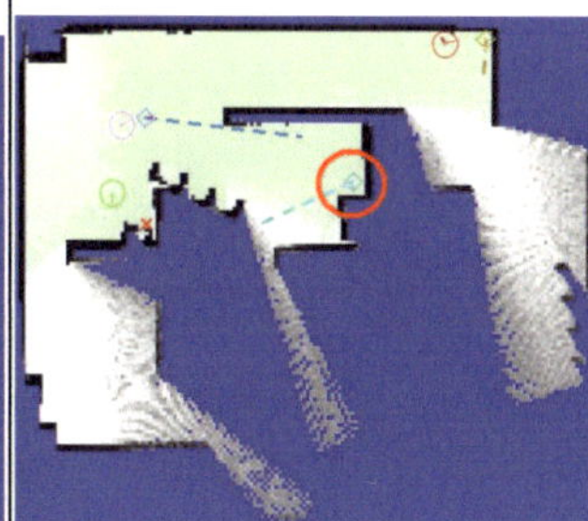 the robot on the center of the map was stuck	
B	 the two robots on the upper map were never controlled since then	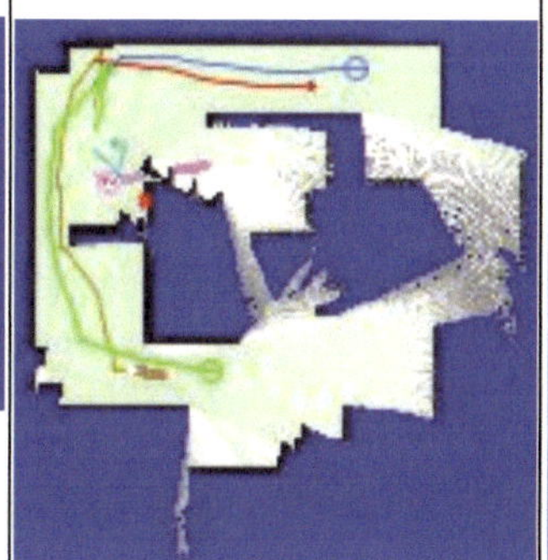	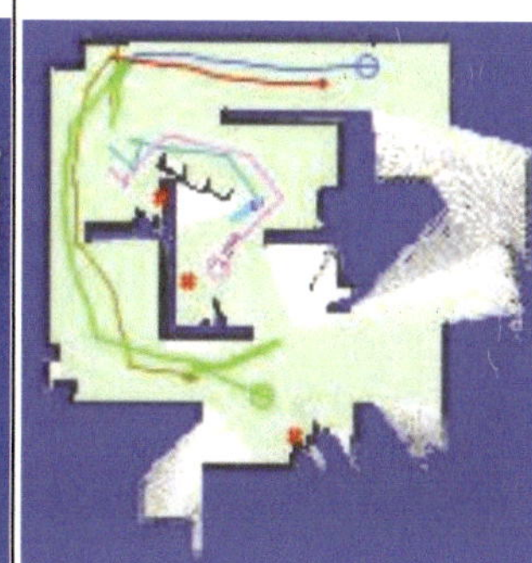
C	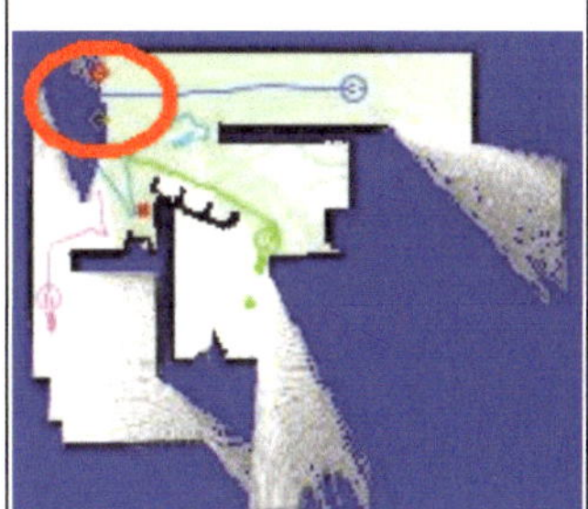 the two robots on the upper left corner were totally ignored	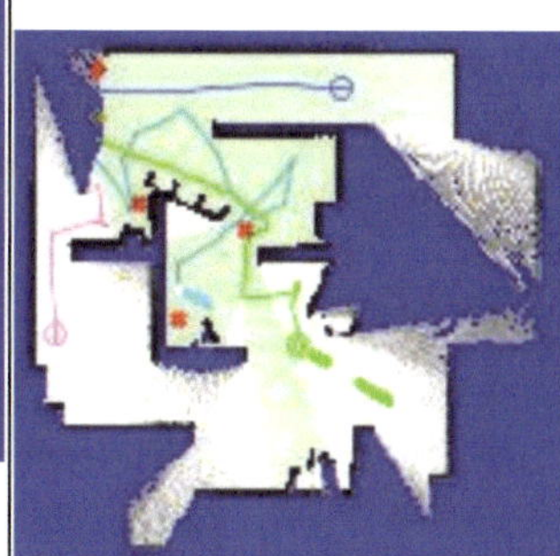	

Table 3. Map snapshots of abnormal control behaviors

data show, however, that this effect is not substantial and provide an argument for focused metrics of this sort which measure constituents of the human-robot system directly. Moreover, this experiment also shows how CD can be used to guide us to identify and analyze aberrant control behaviors.

We anticipated a correlation between found victims and the measured CDs. However, we did not find the expected relationship in this experiment. From observation of participants during the experiment we believe that high level strategies, such as choosing areas to be searched and path planning, have significant impact on the overall performance. The participants had few problems in learning to jointly control explorers and inspectors but they needed time to figure out effective strategies for performing the task. Because CD measures control behaviours not strategies these effects were not captured.

On the other hand, because the NT methodology is domain and task independent our CD measurement could be used to characterize any dependent system. For use in performance analysis, however, it must be associated with additional domain and task dependent information. As shown in our examples, combined with generated maps and traces CD provides an excellent diagnostic tool for examining performance in detail.

In the present experiment, we examined the action pattern under long and short sensing range conditions. The results reveal that it can be used as an evaluation parameter, and more important, it may guide us in the design of multiple robot systems. For instance, the observation that one explorer control action was followed on average by 2 inspector control actions may imply that the MRS should be constructed by n explorer and 2n inspectors.

In the weak cooperation experiment, the time-based assessment showed higher coordination demand under a longer sensing condition. The control times evaluation reported more control times, which implies a higher coordination demand in the shorter sensing condition. This difference illustrates how the measurement unit, control time or control times, may impact the HRI evaluation. Usually, the time-consuming operations such as teleoperation are suited to time-based assessment. In contrast, control times may provide more accurate evaluation to the one-time style operations such as command issuing. Improving the Neglect Tolerance model to suit control times based evaluation should be an area for future work.

In summary, the proposed methodology enables us evaluate weak or tight cooperation behaviors in control of heterogeneous robot teams. The time parameter based measurement makes this methodology domain independent and practical in real applications. The lack of consideration of domain, other system characteristics and information available to the operator, however, makes this metric too impoverished to use in isolation for evaluating system performance. A more complete metric for evaluating coordination demand in multirobot systems would require additional dimensions beyond time. Considering human, robot, task and world as the four elements in HRI, possible metrics might include mental demand, situation awareness, robot capability, autonomy level, overall task performance, task complexity, and world complexity.

7. References

Balakirsky, S.; Carpin, S.; Kleiner, A.; Lewis, M.; Visser, A.; Wang, J. and Zipara, V. (2007). Toward hetereogeneous robot teams for disaster mitigation: Results and performance metrics from RoboCup Rescue, *Journal of Field Robotics*, Vol. 24, No. 11-12, pp. 943-967

Carpin, S.; Wang, J.; Lewis, M.; Birk, A., and Jacoff, A. (2005). High fidelity tools for rescue robotics: Results and perspectives, *Robocup 2005 Symposium*

Carpin, S.; Stoyanov, T.; Nevatia, Y.; Lewis, M. and Wang, J. (2006a). Quantitative assessments of USARSim accuracy. *Proceedings of PerMIS'06*

Carpin, S.; Lewis, M.; Wang, J.; Balakirsky, S. and Scrapper, C. (2006b). Bridging the gap between simulation and reality in urban search and rescue. *Robocup 2006: Robot Soccer World Cup X*, Springer, Lecture Notes in Artificial Intelligence

Crandall, J.; Goodrich, M.; Olsen, D. and Nielsen, C. (2005). Validating human-robot interaction schemes in multitasking environments. *IEEE Transactions on Systems, Man, and Cybernetics, Part A*, Vol. 35, No. 4, 2005, pp. 438–449

Gerkey, B. and Mataric, M. (2004). A formal framework for the study of task allocation in multi-robot systems. *International Journal of Robotics Research*, Vol. 23, No. 9, 2004, pp. 939–954

Lewis, M.; Wang, J. & Hughes S. (2007). USARSim : Simulation for the Study of Human-Robot Interaction. *Journal of Cognitive Engineering and Decision Making*, Vol. 1, pp. 98-120

Murphy, R. and Burke, J. (2005). Up from the Rubble: Lessons Learned about HRI from Search and Rescue, *Proceedings of the 49th Annual Meetings of the Human Factors and Ergonomics Society*, Orlando, 2005

Nielsen, C.; Goodrich, M. and Crandall, J. (2003). Experiments in human-robot teams. *Proceedings of the 2002 NRL Workshop on Multi-Robot Systems*, October 2003

Parasuraman, R.; Galster, S.; Squire, P.; Furukawa, H. and Miller, C. (2005). A flexible delegation-type interface enhances system performance in human supervision of multiple robots: Empirical studies with roboflag. *IEEE Transactions on Systems, Man, and Cybernetics, Part A*, Vol. 35, No. 4, 2005, pp. 481–493

Pepper, C.; Balakirsky S. and C. Scrapper. (2007). Robot Simulation Physics Validation, *Proceedings of PerMIS'07*

Scerri, P.; Xu, Y.; Liao, E.; Lai, G.; Lewis, M. and Sycara, K. (2004). Coordinating large groups of wide area search munitions. In *Recent Developments in Cooperative Control and Optimization*, Grundel, D.; Murphey, R. and Pandalos, P. Ed., pp. 451–480, World Scientific Publishing, Singapore

Steinfeld, A.; Fong, T., Kaber, D.; Lewis, M.; Scholtz, J.; Schultz, A. and Goodrich, M. (2006). Common Metrics for Human-Robot Interaction, *Proceedings of ACM/IEEE International conference on Human-Robot Interaction*, March, 2006

Taylor, B.; Balakirsky, S.; Messina E. and Quinn. R. (2007). Design and Validation of a Whegs Robot in USARSim, *Proceedings of PerMIS'07*

Trouvain, B. and Wolf, H. (2002). Evaluation of multi-robot control and monitoring performance. *Proceedings of the 2002 IEEE Int. Workshop on Robot and Human Interactive Communication*, pp. 111–116, September 2002

Wang, J.; Lewis, M. & Gennari, J. (2003). A game engine based simulation of the NIST urban search and rescue arenas. *Proceedings of the 2003 Winter Simulation Conference*, pp. 1039-1045

Wang, J.; Lewis, M.; Hughes, S.; Koes, M. and Carpin, S. (2005). Validating USARsim for use in HRI research, *Proceedings of the 49th Annual Meeting of the Human Factors and Ergonomics Society*, pp. 457-461, Orlando, FL.

Zaratti, M.; Fratarcangeli M. and Iocchi L. (2006). A 3D Simulator of Multiple Legged Robots based on USARSim. *Robocup 2006: Robot Soccer World Cup X*, Springer, Lecture Notes in Artificial Intelligence

7

Making a Mobile Robot to Express its Mind by Motion Overlap

Kazuki Kobayashi[1] and Seiji Yamada[2]
[1]*Shinshu University,*
[2]*National Institute of Informatics*
Japan

1. Introduction

Various home robots like sweeping robots and pet robots have been developed, commercialized and now are studied for use in cooperative housework (Kobayashi & Yamada, 2005). In the near future, cooperative work of a human and a robot will be one of the most promising applications of Human-Robot Interaction research in factory, office and home. Thus interaction design between ordinary people and a robot must be very significant as well as building an intelligent robot itself. In such cooperative housework, a robot often needs users' help when they encounter difficulties that they cannot overcome by themselves. We can easily imagine many situations like that. For example, a sweeping robot can not move heavy and complexly structured obstacles, such as chairs and tables, which prevent it from doing its job and needs users' help to remove them (Fig. 1). A problem is how to enable a robot to inform its help requests to a user in cooperative work. Although we recognize that this is a quite important and practical issue for realizing cooperative work of a human user and a robot, a few studies have been done thus far in Human-Robot Interaction. In this chapter, we propose a novel method to make a mobile robot to express its internal state (called robot's *mind*) to request users' help, implement a concrete expression

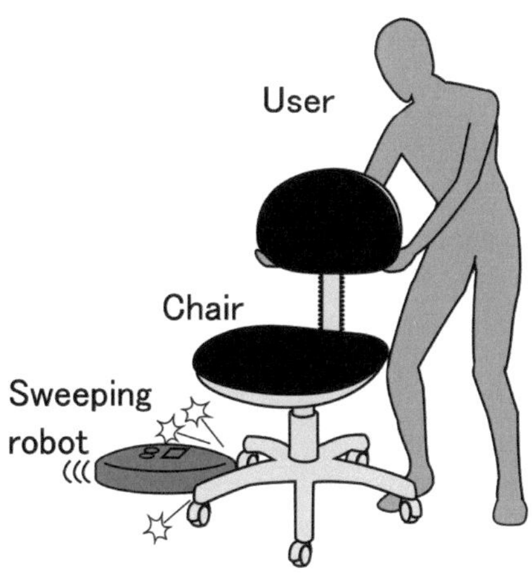

Fig. 1. A robot which needs user's help.

on a real mobile robot and conduct experiments with participants to evaluate the effectiveness.

In traditional user interface design, some studies have proposed design for electric home appliances. Norman (Norman, 1988) addressed the use of affordance (Gibson, 1979) in artifact design. Also Suchman (Suchman, 1987) studied behavior patterns of users. Users' reaction to computers (Reeves & Nass, 1996) (Katagiri & Takeuchi, 2000) is important to consider as designing artifacts. Yamauchi et al. studied function imagery of auditory signals (Yamaguchi & Iwamiya, 2005), and JIS (Japanese Industrial Standards) provides guidelines for auditory signals in consumer products for elderly people (JIS, 2002). These studies and guidelines deal with interfaces for artifacts that users operate directly themselves. These methods and guidelines assume use of an artifact directly through user control: an approach that may not necessarily work well for home robots that conduct tasks directly themselves. Robot-oriented design approaches are thus needed for home robots.

As mentioned earlier, our proposal for making a mobile robot to express its mind assumes cooperative work in which the robot needs to notify a user how to operate it and move objects blocking its operation: a trinomial relationship among the user, robot, and object. In a psychology field, the theory of mind (TOM) (Baron-Cohen, 1995) deals with such trinomial relationships. Following TOM, we term a robot's internal state *mind*, defined as its own motives, intents, or purposes and goals of behavior. We take weak AI (Searle, 1980) position: a robot can be made to act as if they had a mind.

Mental expression is designed verbally or nonverbally. If we use verbal expression, for example, we can make a robot to say "Please help me by moving this obstacle." In many similar situations in which an obstacle prevents a robot from moving, the robot may simply repeat the same speech because it cannot recognize what the obstacle is. A robot neither say "Please remove this chair" nor "Please remove this dust box". Speech conveys a unique meaning, and such repetition irritates users. Hence we study nonverbal methods such as buzzers, blinking lights, and movement, which convey ambiguous information that users can interpret as they like based on the given situation.

We consider that the motion-based approach feasibly and effectively conveys the robot's mind in an obstacle-removal task. Movement is designed based on *motion overlap* (MO) that enable a robot to move in a way that the user narrows down possible responses and acts appropriately. In an obstacle-removal task, we had the robot move *back and forth* in front of an obstacle, and conducted experiments compared MO to other nonverbal approaches. Experimental results showed that MO has potential in the design of robots for the home.

We assume that a mobile robot has a cylindrical body and expresses its mind through movement. This has advantages for developers in that a robot needs no component such as a display or a speech synthesizer, but it is difficult for the robot to express its mind in a humanly understandable manner. Below, we give an overview of studies on how a robot can express its mind nonverbally with human-like and nonhuman-like bodies.

Hadaly-2 (Hashimoto et al., 2002), Nakata's dancing robot (Nakata et al., 2002), Kobayashi's face robot (Kobayashi et al., 2003), Breazeal's Kismet (Breazeal, 2002), Kozima's Infanoid (Kozima & Yano, 2001), Robovie-III (Miyashita & Ishiguro, 2003), and Cog (Brooks et al., 1999) utilized human-like robots that easily express themselves nonverbally in a human understandable manner. The robot we are interested in, however, is nonhuman-like in shape, only having wheels for moving. We designed wheel movement to enable the robot to express its mind.

Ono et al. (Ono et al., 2000) studied how a mobile robot's familiarity influenced a user's understanding of what was on its mind. Before their experiments, participants were asked to grow a life-like virtual agent on a PC, and the agent was moved to the robot's display after the keeping. This keeping makes the robot quite familiar to a user, and they experimentally show that the familiarity made a user's accuracy of recognising robot's noisy utterance quite better. Matsumaru et al. (Matsumaru et al., 2005) developed a mobile robot that expresses its direction of movement with a laser pointer or animated eye. Komatsu (Komatsu, 2005) reported that users could infer the attitude of a machine through its beeps. Those require extra components in contrast with our proposal. The orca-like robot (Nakata et al., 1998), seal-like Paro (Wada et al., 2004)(Shibata et al., 2004), and limbless Muu (Okada et al., 2000) are efforts of familiarizing users with robots. Our study differs from these, however, in that we assume actual cooperative work between the user and robot, such as cooperative sweeping.

2. Expression of robot mind

The obstacle-removal task in which we have the robot express itself in front of an obstacle and how the robot conveys what is on its mind are explained below.

2.1 Obstacle-removal task

The situation involves a sweeping robot can not remove an obstacle, such as a chair and a dust box, that asks a user to remove it so that it can sweep the floor area where the obstacle occupied (Fig. 1). Such an obstacle-removal task serves as a general testbed for our work because it occurs frequently in cooperative tasks between a user and a robot. To execute this task, the robot needs to inform its problem to the user and ask for help. This task has been used in research on cooperative sweeping (Kobayashi & Yamada, 2005).
Obstacle-removal tasks generally accompany other robot tasks. Obstacle avoidance is essential to mobile robots such as tour guides (Burgard et al., 1998). Obstacles may be avoided by having the robot (1) avoid an obstacle autonomously, (2) remove the obstacle autonomously, or (3) get user to remove the obstacle. It is difficult for a robot to remove an obstacle autonomously because it first must decide whether it may touch the object. In practical situations, the robot avoids an obstacle either by autonomous avoidance or having a user remove it.

2.2 Motion overlap

Our design, *motion overlap*, starts when movement routinely done by a user is programmed into a robot. A user observing the robot's movement will find an analogy to human action and easily interprets the state of mind. We consider the overlap between human and robot's movement causes an overlap between the minds of the user and the robot (Fig. 2).
A human is neither a natural light emitter nor expresses his/her intention easily using nonverbal sounds. They do, however, move expressively when executing tasks. We therefore presume that a user can understand a robot's mind as naturally as another person's mind if robot movement overlaps recognizable human movement. This human understanding has been studied and reported in TOM.
As described before, nonverbal communication has alternative modalities: a robot can make a struggling movement, sound a buzzer, or blink a light. We assume movement to be better for an obstacle-removal task for the following reasons.

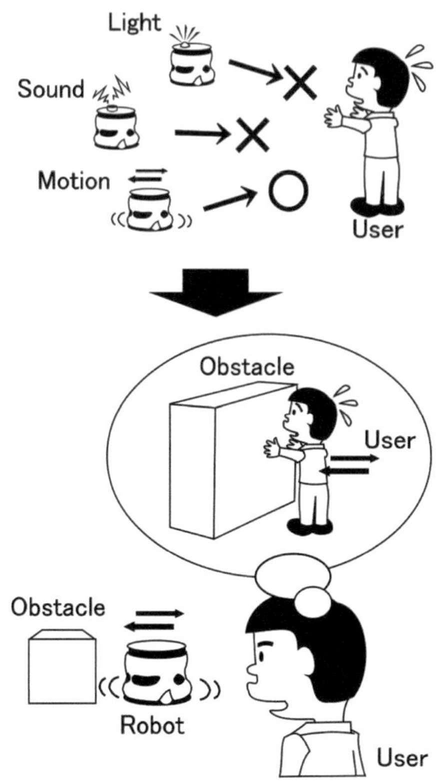

Fig. 2. Motion overlap.

- *Feasibility*: Since a robot needs to move for achieving tasks, so a motion-based approach requires no additional component such as a LED or a speaker. The additional nonverbal components make a robot quite more complicated and expensive.
- *Variation*: The motion-based approach enables us to design informational movement to suit different tasks. The variety of movements is far larger than that of sounds or light signals of other nonverbal methods.
- *Less stress*: Other nonverbal methods, particularly sound, may force a user to strong attention at a robot, causing more stress than movement. The motion-based approach avoids distracting or invasive interruption of a user who notices the movement and chooses whether or not to respond.
- *Effectiveness*: Motion-based information is intuitively more effective than other nonverbal approaches because interesting movement attracts a user to a robot without stress.

While feasibility, variety, and stress minimization of motion-based information are obviously valid, we need to verify effectiveness needs to be verified experimentally.

2.3 Implementing MO on a mobile robot

We designed robot's movements which a user can easily understand by imagining what a human may do when he/she faces with an obstacle-removal task. Imagine that you see a person who has baggage and hesitates nervously in front of a closed door. Almost all the human observers would immediately identify the problem that the person needs help to

open the door. This is a typical situation in TOM. Using similar hesitation movement could enable a robot to inform a user that it needs help.
A study on human actions in doing tasks (Suzuki & Sakai, 2001) defines hesitation as movement that suddenly stops and either changes into other movement or is suspended: a definition that *our back and forth movement* fits (Fig. 3). Seeing a robot moves back and forward in a short time in front of an obstacle should be easy for a user because a human acts similarly when they are in the same trouble.

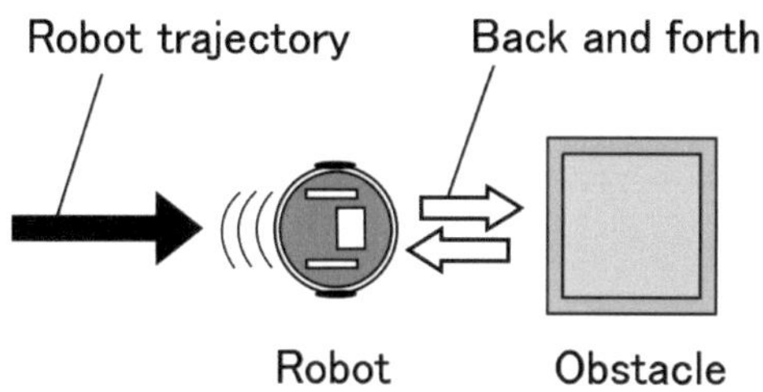

Fig. 3. Back and forth motion.

We could have tested other movement such as turning to the left and right, however back and forth movement keeps the robot from swerving from its trajectory to achieve a task. It is also easily applicable to other hardware such as manipulators. Back and forth movement is thus appropriate for an obstacle-removal task in efficiency of movement and range of application.

3. Experiments

We conducted experiments to verify the effectiveness of our motion-based approach in an obstacle-removal task, comparing the motion-based approach to two other nonverbal approaches.

3.1 Environments and a robot

Fig. 4 shows the flat experimental environment (400mm X 300mm) surrounded by a wall and containing two obstacles (white paper cups). It simulated an ordinary human work space such as a desktop. Obstacles corresponded to penholders, remote controllers, etc., and are easily moved by participants. We used a small mobile robot, KheperaII (Fig. 5), which has eight infrared proximity and ambient light sensors with up to a 100mm range, a Motorola 68331 (25 MHz) processor, 512K bytes of RAM, 512K bytes of flash ROM, and two DC brushed servomotors with incremental encoders. Its C program runs on RAM.

3.2 Robot's expressions

Participants observed the robot as it swept the floor in the experimental environment. The robot used ambiguous nonverbal expressions enabling participants to interpret them based on the situation. We designed three types of signals to inform the robot's mind to sweep the area under an obstacle or the wish for wanting user's help to remove the obstacle. It expressed by itself using one of the three following types of signals:

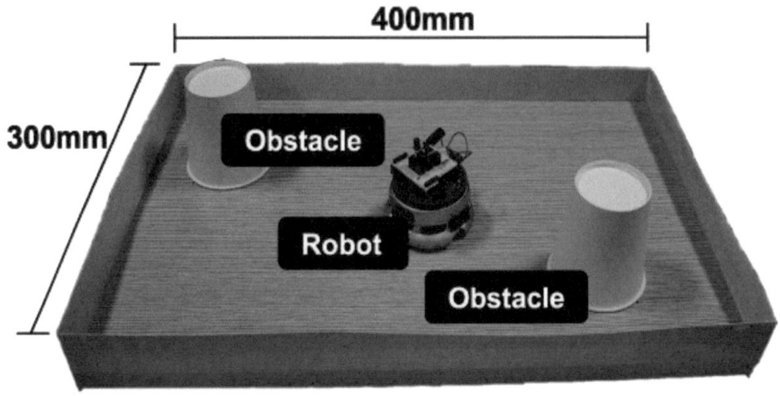

Fig. 4. An experimental environment.

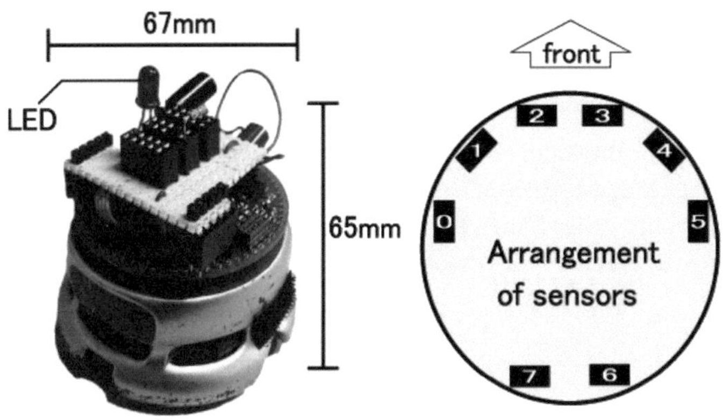

Fig. 5. KheperaII.

- **LED**: The robot's red LED (6 mm in diameter) blinks based on ISO 4982:1981 (automobile flasher pattern). The robot turns the light on and off based on the signal pattern in Fig. 6, repeating the pattern twice every 0.4 second.
- **Buzzer**: The robot beeps using a buzzer that made a sound with 3 kHz and 6 kHz peaks. The sound pattern was based on JIS:S0013 (auditory signals of consumer products intended for attracting immediate attention). As with the LED, the robot beeps at "on" and ceases at "off" (Fig. 6).
- **Back and forth motion**: The robot moves back and forward, 10 mm back and 10 mm forth based on "on" and "off" (Fig. 6).

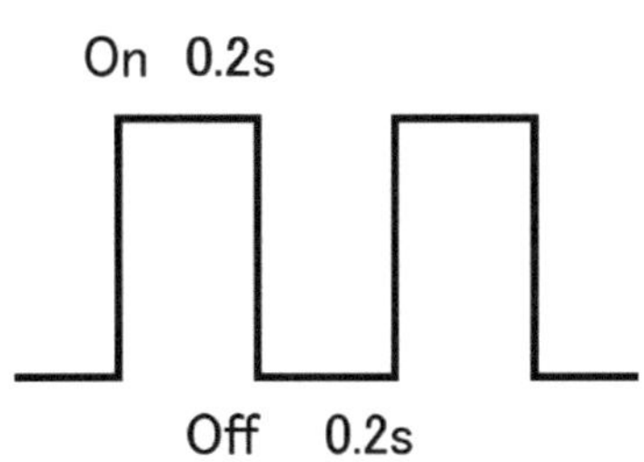

Fig. 6. Pattern of Behavior.

The LED, buzzer, and movement used the same "on" and "off" intervals. The robot stopped sweeping and performed each when it encountered an obstacle or wall, then turned left or right and moved ahead. If the robot senses an obstacle on its right (left), it makes a 120 degree turn to the left (right), repeating these actions during experiments. Note that the robot did not actually sweep up dust.

3.3 Methods

Participants were instructed that the robot represented a sweeping robot, even though it actually did not sweep. They were to imagine that the robot was cleaning the floor. They could move or touch anything in the environment, and were told to help the robot if it needed it.

Each participant conducted three trials and observed the robot moved back and forth, blinked its lights, or sounded its buzzer. The order of expressions provided to participants was random. A trial finished after the robot's third encounter with obstacles, or when the participant removed an obstacle. The participants were informed no information and interpretation about the robot's movement, blinking, or sounding.

Fig. 7 details experimental settings that include the robot's initial locations and those of objects. At the start of each experiment, the robot moved ahead, stopped in front of a wall, expressed its mind, and turned right toward obstacle A. Fig. 8 shows a series of snapshots in which a participant had interaction with a mobile robot doing back and forth. The participant sat on the chair and helped the robot on the desk.

The participants numbered 17: 11 men and six women aged 21-44 including 10 university students and seven employees. We confirmed that they had no experience in interacting with robots before.

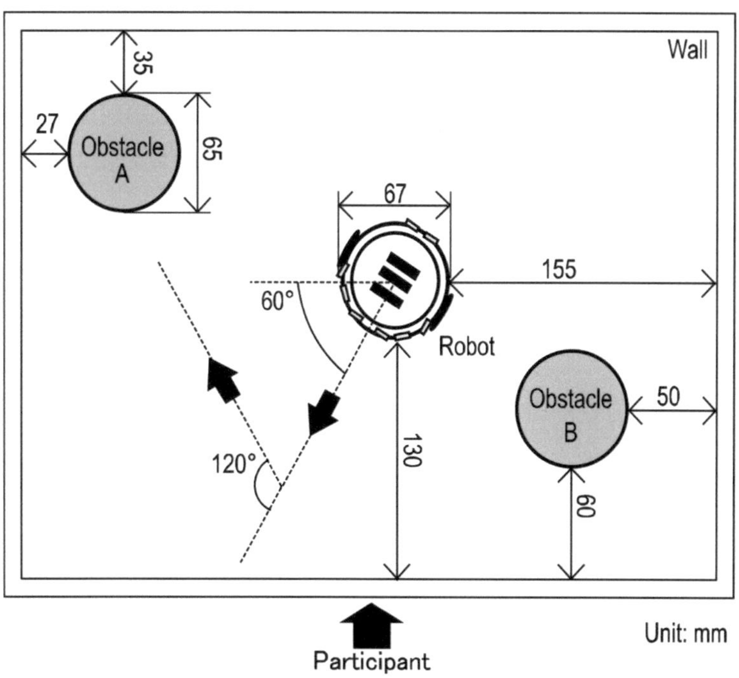

Fig. 7. Derailed experimental setup.

Fig. 8. MO experiments.

3.4 Evaluation

We used the criterion that fewer expressions were better because this would help participants understand easily what was on the robot's mind. The robot expressed itself whenever it encountered a wall or an obstacle. We counted the number of participants who moved the object just after the robot's first encounter with the object. We considered using other measurement such as the period from the beginning of the experiment to when the participant moved an obstacle, however this was difficult because the time at which the robot reached the first obstacle was different in each trial. Slippage of the robot's wheels changed its trajectory.

3.5 Results

Table 1 shows participants and behavior in the experiments. The terms with asterisks are trials in which a participant removed an obstacle. Eight of 17 participants (47%) did not move any obstacle in any experimental condition. Table 2 shows ratios of participants moving the obstacle under each condition. The ratios increased with the number of trial. This appeared more clearly under the MO condition.

ID	Age	Gender	Trial-1	Trial-2	Trial-3
1	25	M	LED*	Buzzer*	MO*
2	30	M	Buzzer	MO	LED
3	24	M	MO	LED	Buzzer
4	25	M	LED*	MO*	Buzzer*
5	23	M	Buzzer*	LED	MO*
6	43	F	MO	LED	Buzzer
7	27	M	LED	Buzzer	MO*
8	29	F	LED	MO*	Buzzer*
9	44	F	Buzzer	MO*	LED*
10	26	F	Buzzer	LED	MO*
11	29	F	MO	Buzzer	LED
12	27	M	LED	Buzzer	MO*
13	36	M	MO	LED	Buzzer
14	27	M	Buzzer	LED	MO
15	26	M	Buzzer*	MO*	LED*
16	26	M	MO	Buzzer	LED
17	21	F	LED	Buzzer	MO

Table 1. Participant behaviors.

	Trial-1	Trial-2	Trial-3
LED	33% (2/6)	0% (0/6)	40% (2/5)
Buzzer	33% (2/6)	17% (1/6)	40% (2/5)
MO	0% (0/5)	80% (4/5)	71% (5/7)

Table 2. Expressions and trials.

Fig. 9 shows ratios of participants who moved the obstacle immediately after the robot's first encounter with it. More participants responded to MO than to either the buzzer or light. We

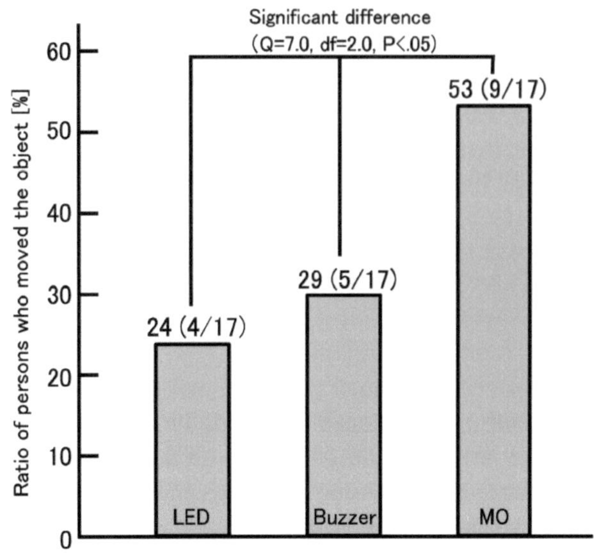

Fig. 9. Ratios of participants who moved an object.

statistically analyzed the differences in ratios among the three methods. The result of the statistical test (Cochran's Q test) showed significant differences among methods (Q = 7.0, df = 2.0, p < .05). We conducted a multiple comparison test, Holm's test, and obtained 10% level differences between MO-LED (Q = 5.0, df = 1.0, p = 0.0253, α' = 0.0345, α' is the modified significant level by Holm's test) and MO-buzzer (Q = 4.0, df = 1.0, p = 0.0455, α' = 0.0513), indicating that MO is as effective or more effective than the other two methods. In the questionnaire on experiments (Table 3), most participants said they noticed the robot's action. Table 4 shows results of the questionnaire. We asked participants why they moved the object. The purpose of our design policy corresponds to question (1). More people responded positively to question (1) for the cases of the buzzer and MO. MO achieved our objective because it caused the most participants to move the object.

4. Discussion

We discuss the effectiveness and application of MO based on experimental results.

4.1 Effectiveness of MO

We avoided using loud sounds or bright lights because they are not appropriate for a home robot. We confirmed that participants correctly noticed the robot's expression. Results of the questionnaires in Table 3 show that the expressions we designed were appropriate for experiments.

	LED	Buzzer	MO
I noticed.	15	17	16
I don't remember.	2	0	1

Table 3. The number of participants who noticed the robot's expression.

MO is not effective in any situation because Table 2 suggests the existence of a combination effect. Although the participants experienced MO in previous experiments, only 40% of them moved the obstacle in the LED-Trial3 and Buzzer-Trial3 conditions. In the MO-Trial1 condition, no participants moved the obstacle. Further study of the combination effect is thus important.

We used specific lighting and sound patterns for expressing the robot's mind, however the effects of other patterns are not known. For example, a different frequency, complex sound pattern may help a user to understand the robot's mind more easily. The expressive patterns we investigated through these experiments were just a small part of huge candidates. A more organized investigation on light and sound is thus necessary to find the optimal pattern. Our results show that conventional methods are not sufficient and that MO shows promise.

Questionnaire results (Table 4) show that many participants felt that the robot "wanted" them to move the obstacle or moved it depending on the situation. The "wanted" response reflects anthropomorphization of the robot. The "depending on the situation" response may indicate that they identified with the robot's problem. As Reeves & Nass (Reeves & Nass, 1996) and Katagiri & Takeuchi (Katagiri & Takeuchi, 2000) have noted participants exhibiting interpersonal action with a robot would not report the appropriate reason, so questionnaire results are not conclusive. However MO may encourage users to anthropomorphize robots.

	LED	Buzzer	MO
1. I felt that the robot wanted me to move it.	1	3	4
2. I moved it depending on the situation.	2	3	3
3. I don't know why I moved it.	1	1	1
4. I felt some urgency.	0	2	1
5. Other reason.	0	0	1
Total	4	9	10

Table 4. Results of the questionnaire.

Table 4 compares MO and the buzzer, which received different numbers of responses. Although fewer participants moved the obstacle after the buzzer than after MO, the buzzer had more responses in the questionnaires. The buzzer might offer highly ambiguous information in the experiments. The relationship between the degrees of ambiguity and expression is an important issue in designing robot behavior.

4.2 Coverage of MO

Results for MO were more promising results than for other nonverbal methods, however are these results general? Results directly support the generality of obstacle-removal tasks. We consider that an obstacle-removal task is a common subtask in human-robot cooperation. For other tasks without obstacle-removal, we may need to design another type of MO-based informative movement. The applicable scope for MO is thus an issue for future study.

Morris's study of human behavior suggests the applicability of MO (Morris, 1977). Morris states that human beings sometimes move preliminarily before taking action, and these preliminary movements indicate what they will do. A person gripping the arms of a chair during a conversation may be trying to end the conversation but does not wish to be rude in doing so. Such behavior is called an *intention movement* and two movements with their own rhythm, such as left-and-right rhythmic movements on a pivot chair, are called *alternating intention movement*. Human beings easily grasp each other's intent in daily life. We can consider the back and forth movement to be a form of alternating intention movement meaning that the robot wants to move forward but cannot do so. Participants in our experiments may have interpreted the robot's mind by implicitly considering its movements as alternating intention movement. Although the LED and buzzer rhythmically expressed itself, they may have been less effective than MO. Participants may not have considered them as intention movement because they were not preliminary movement --- sounding and blinking were not related to previous movement, moving forward.

If alternating intention movement works well in enabling a robot to inform a user about its mind, the robot will be able to express itself with other simple rhythmic movements, e.g., the simple left and right movements to encourage the user to help it when it loses the way. Rhythmic movement is hardware-independent and easily implemented. We believe that alternating intention movement is an important element in MO applications, and we plan to study this and evaluate its effectiveness. A general implementation for expressing robot's mind can be established through such investigations. The combination of nonverbal and verbal information is important for robot expression, and we plan to study ways to combine different expression to speed up interaction between users and robots.

4.3 Designing manual-free machines

A user needs to read the manuals of their machines or want to use them more conveniently. However, reading manuals imposes workload on the user. It would be better for a user to discover a robot's functions naturally, without reading a manual. The results of our experiments show that motion-based expression enables a user to understand the robot's mind easily. We thus consider motion-based expression to be useful for making *manual-free machines*, and we currently devising a procedure for users to discover robot's functions naturally.

The procedure is composed of three steps: (1) expression of the robot's mind, (2) responsive action of its user, and (3) reaction of the robot. The robot's functions are "discovered" when the user causality links his/her actions with the robot's actions. Our experiments show that the motion-based approach satisfies step (1) and (2) and helps humans to discover such causality relations.

5. Conclusion

We have proposed a motion-based approach for nonverbally informing a user of a robot's state of mind. Possible nonverbal approaches include movement, sound, and lights. The design we proposed, called motion overlap, enabled a robot to express human-like behavior in communicating with users.

We devised a general obstacle-removal task based on motion overlap for cooperation between a user and a robot, having the robot move back and forth to show the user that it wants an obstacle to be removed.

We conducted experiments to verify the effectiveness of motion overlap in the obstacleremoval task, comparing motion overlap to sound and lights. Experimental results showed that motion overlap encouraged most users to help the robot.

The motion-based approach will effectively express robot's mind in an obstacle-removal task and contribute to design of home robots. Our next step in this motion overlap is to combine different expressions to speed up interaction between users and robots, and to investigate other intentional movement as extension of motion overlap.

6. References

Baron-Cohen, S. (1995). *Mindblindness: An Essay on Autism and Theory of Mind*, MIT Press.

Breazeal, C. (2002). Regulation and entrainment for human-robot interaction, *International Journal of Experimental Robotics*, 21, 11-12, 883-902.

Brooks, R.; Breazeal, C.; Marjanovic, M.; Scassellati, B. & Williamson, M. (1999). The Cog Project: Building a Humanoid Robot, In: *Computation for Metaphors, Analogy and Agent*, Lecture Notes in Computer Science, Nehaniv, C. L. (Ed.), 1562, 52-87, Springer.

Burgard, W.; Cremers, A. B.; Fox, D.; Hahnel, D.; Lakemeyer, G.; Schulz, D.; Steiner, W. & Thrun, S. (1998). The Interactive Museum Tour-Guide Robot, *Proceedings of the 15th National Conference on Artificial Intelligence*, pp.11-18.

Gibson, J. J. (1979). *The Ecological Approach to Visual Perception*, Lawrence Erlbaum Associates Inc.

Hashimoto, S. et al. (2002). Humanoid Robots in Waseda University- Hadaly-2 and WABIAN, *Autonomous Robots*, 12, 1, 25-38.

Japanese Industrial Standards. (2002). JISS0013:2002 Guidelines for the elderly and people with disabilities- Auditory signals on consumer products.

Katagiri, Y. & Takeuchi, Y. (2000). Reciprocity and its Cultural Dependency in Human-Computer Interaction, In: *Affective Minds*, Hatano, G.; Okada, N. & Tanabe, H. (Eds.), 209-214, Elsevier.

Kobayashi, H.; Ichikawa, Y.; Senda, M. & Shiiba, T. (2003). Realization of Realistic and Rich Facial Expressions by Face Robot, *Proceedings of 2003 IEEE/RSJ International Conference on Intelligent Robots and Systems*, pp.1123-1128.

Kobayashi, K. & Yamada, S. (2005). Human-Robot Cooperative Sweeping by Extending Commands Embedded in Actions, *Proceedings of 2005 IEEE/RSJ International Conference on Intelligent Robots and Systems*, pp.1827-1832.

Komatsu, T. (2005). *Can we assign attitudes to a computer based on its beep sounds?, Proceedings of the Affective Interactions: The computer in the affective loop Workshop at Intelligent User Interface 2005*, pp.35-37.

Kozima, H. & Yano, H. (2001). A robot that learns to communicate with human caregivers, *Proceedings of International Workshop on Epigenetic Robotics*, pp.47-52.

Matsumaru, T.; Iwase, K.; Akiyama, K.; Kusada, T. & Ito, T. (2005). Mobile Robot with Eyeball Expression as the Preliminary-Announcement and Display of the Robot's Following Motion, *Autonomous Robots*, 18, 2, 231-246.

Miyashita, T. & Ishiguro, H. (2003). Human-like natural behavior generation based on involuntary motions for humanoid robots, *Robotics and Autonomous Systems*, 48, 4, 203-212.

Morris, D. (1977). *Manwatching*, Elsevier Publishing.

Nakata, T.; Mori, T. & Sato, T. (2002). Analysis of Impression of Robot Bodily Expression, *Journal of Robotics and Mechatronics*, 14, 1, 27-36.

Nakata, T.; Sato, T. & Mori, T. (1998). Expression of Emotion and Intention by Robot Body Movement, *Intelligent Autonomous Systems*, 5, 352--359.
Norman, D. A. (1988). *The Psychology of Everyday Things*, Basic Books.
Okada, M.; Sakamoto, S. & Suzuki, N. (2000). Muu: Artificial creatures as an embodied interface, *Proceedings of 27th International Conference on Computer Graphics and Interactive Techniques (SIGGRAPH 2000)*, the Emerging Technologies, p.91.
Ono, T.; Imai, M. & Nakatsu, R. (2000). Reading a Robot's Mind: A Model of Utterance Understanding based on the Theory of Mind Mechanism, *International Journal of Advanced Robotics*, 14, 4, 311-326.
Reeves B. & Nass, C. (1996). *The Media Equation: How People Treat Computers, Television, and New Media Like Real People and Places,* Cambridge University Press.
Searle, J. (1980). Minds, brains, and programs, *Behavioral and Brain Sciences*, 3, 3, 417-457.
Shibata, T.; Wada, K. & Tanie, K. (2004). Subjective Evaluation of Seal Robot in Brunei, *Proceedings of IEEE International Workshop on Robot and Human Interactive Communication*, pp.135-140.
Suchman, L.~A. (1987). *Plans and Situated Actions: The Problem of Human-Machine Communication,* Cambridge University Press, 1987.
Suzuki K. & Sasaki, M. (2001). The Task Constraints on Selection of Potential Units of Action: An Analysis of Microslips Observed in Everyday Task (in Japanese), *Cognitive Studies*, 8, 2, 121-138.
Wada, K.; Shibata, T.; Saito, T. & Tanie, K. (2004). Psychological and Social Effects in Long-Term Experiment of Robot Assisted Activity to Elderly People at a Health Service Facility for the Aged, Proceedings of 2004 IEEE/RSJ International Conference on Intelligent Robots and System, pp.3068--3073.
Yamauchi, K. & Iwamiya, S. (2005). Functional Imagery and Onomatopoeic Representation of Auditory Signals using Frequency-Modulated Tones, *Japanese Journal of Physiological Anthropology*, 10, 3, 115-122.

8

Generating Natural Interactive Motion in Android Based on Situation-Dependent Motion Variety

Takashi Minato and Hiroshi Ishiguro
Asada Project, ERATO, Japan Science and Technology Agency
Japan

1. Introduction

In order to develop a robot that can work in normal everyday situations, it is necessary to discover the principles relevant to establishing and maintaining social interaction between humans and robots. Even if short-term human-robot interaction can be performed by implementing simple behaviors in a robot, it remains difficult to realize long-term social interaction. We have explored the principles underlying natural human-robot communication by development of an android which closely resembles a human being, which is called an android science approach (Ishiguro, 2005).

Nass et al. (Nass et al., 1994) demonstrated that the human-computer relationship is fundamentally social and that a person's social response toward computers is automatic in social situations. It is inferred from their studies that person's interpersonal responses subconsciously expressed toward a robot (in other words, perceptual social illusion (Jacob & Jeannerod, 2005)) underlie the natural communication between the person and the robot. The condition to elicit interpersonal behavior must be related to a mechanism to support natural communication. The android science approach explores the boundary conditions to elicit subconscious interpersonal behavior toward an android from humans by investigating methods to make the android more humanlike.

Humanlike body motions are necessary to implement humanlike behavior in an android. There have been several studies on the generation of humanlike motion, including studies on a model to generate human motion trajectories based on a neurocomputational approach (Flash & Hogan, 1985; Uno et al., 1989; Kawato, 1992; Schaal & Sternad, 2001), a study on the control of a manipulator based on a model of motion trajectories of a person's arm (Kashima & Isurugi, 1998), and studies on a computer graphics (CG) animated characters, which have shown that noise in the motion makes the character's motion more humanlike (Perlin, 1995; Bodenheimer et al., 1999). These studies successfully generated a humanlike motion. However, a humanlike motion specific to communication situations has not been considered. The present study considers the human-like nature of a person's motion during interaction with other people.

A person generally does not produce exactly identical motion when he/she repeats a behavior with the same intention, as shown in Fig. 1(a). In contrast, a robot is able to repeat exactly identical motion with a purpose. A person's motion is diverse in that the motion

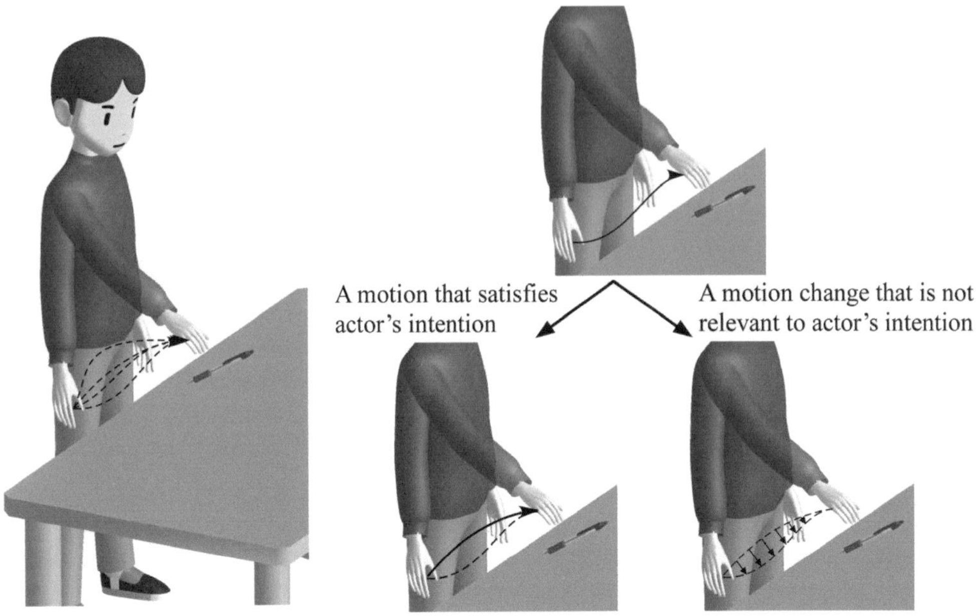

(a) An example of variation in reaching movement.

(b) An example of motion decomposition.

Fig. 1. An example of motion decomposition in a reaching movement.

varies according to noises, mental and physical states, the social situation, and so on, even if the person's intention does not change. We endow an android with motion variety in order to make the android behavior more humanlike. If a person consciously or subconsciously attributes a cause of motion variety in an android motion to such things as the android's mental states, physical states, and the social situations, the person has more humanlike impression toward the android.

We further consider the variety of human motion. We divide a person's motion into the following two components (an example is shown in Fig. 1(b)):

i. A motion that satisfies his/her intention.
ii. A motion change that is not relevant to the intention (a variation of the physical properties of the motion (i) such as its trajectory and velocity).

The motion variety described in the above means a variety in the motion change. Motion generation models involving a signal-dependent noise have been proposed in studies related to the variety of the motion change (Todorov & Jordan, 2002; Miyamoto et al., 2004). This noise-based variety cannot be controlled even if the subject consciously attempts to control or suppress this variety. In contrast, motion variety caused by such things as mental strain or hesitation can be consciously controlled. We assume that the motion variety in an intentional motion influences the human-like nature of the android behavior, even if an observed motion change caused by the variety is small.

The present chapter hypothesizes that the motion change that is not relevant to a subject's intention and can be consciously controlled influences the humanlike impression towards the subject. In particular, we focus on motion variety in an intentional motion caused by the social relationship between the subject and another person. The present chapter concretely

Fig. 2. Gestures to be modelled. A subject reaches out and touches an object or a person.

takes up the motion of a subject reaching out and touching another person. Even a simple reaching motion of a humanoid robot has not been studied with respect to how the change of its properties due to social situations affects the impression of an observer toward the robot. As an extreme case, the present chapter models the motion difference between two cases in which a subject touches another person or an inanimate object through observing the subject's behavior. We then examine how the presence of the motion variety in an android motion influences the impression toward the android. In a psychological experiment, as a third party, participants watch an android touches a person or an object and report their impressions.

2. A model of human motion variety based on differences in social situation

The present chapter hypothesizes that motion variety in an intentional motion independent of uncontrollable noise contributes to the human-like nature of the motion. In order to examine this hypothesis, we model the motion difference caused by the social relationship between two persons in the motion of one reaching out and touching the other. It is, however, difficult to control the social relationship between two persons in an experiment. As the extreme case, we consider the difference between a person-object relationship (Fig. 2, top) and an interpersonal relationship (Fig. 2, bottom). The person-object relationship is not social, but this chapter considers it as the least social relationship. We then construct a model of the difference in the subject's arm movements in these two cases.

In order to construct the model, we set up the situations shown in Fig. 2 and measured the subject's arm movements with a motion capture system (MAC 3D System, Motion Analysis Corporation). The task of the subject was to reach out with the right hand and touch a box or a female experimenter in front of the subject. The hand position of the subject was measured by attaching a marker to the back of the hand. The sampling rate was 60 Hz. The subject touched the left shoulder, nose, and forehead of the experimenter and two spots on the box, the heights of which are the same as those of the shoulder and forehead (box low and box high). The subjects were seven male students. Some of the subjects were familiar with the female experimenter and others were not. All subject touched the target in the order of box low, box high, left shoulder, nose, and forehead, once for each target (total of thirty-five trials). The subjects were told to touch the target and return their hand to the initial position.

The analysis is not for the purpose of finding differences in motion common to all subjects because the motion variation is caused by individuality in some cases. It is sufficient to find a feature to differentiate a subject-person relationship (interpersonal case) from a subject-object relationship (impersonal case) within a subject. However, if the feature is not common among the subjects, it may be difficult to obtain a common impression towards an android in the later experiment. Therefore, we attempt to find a feature that is shared by the majority of the subjects.

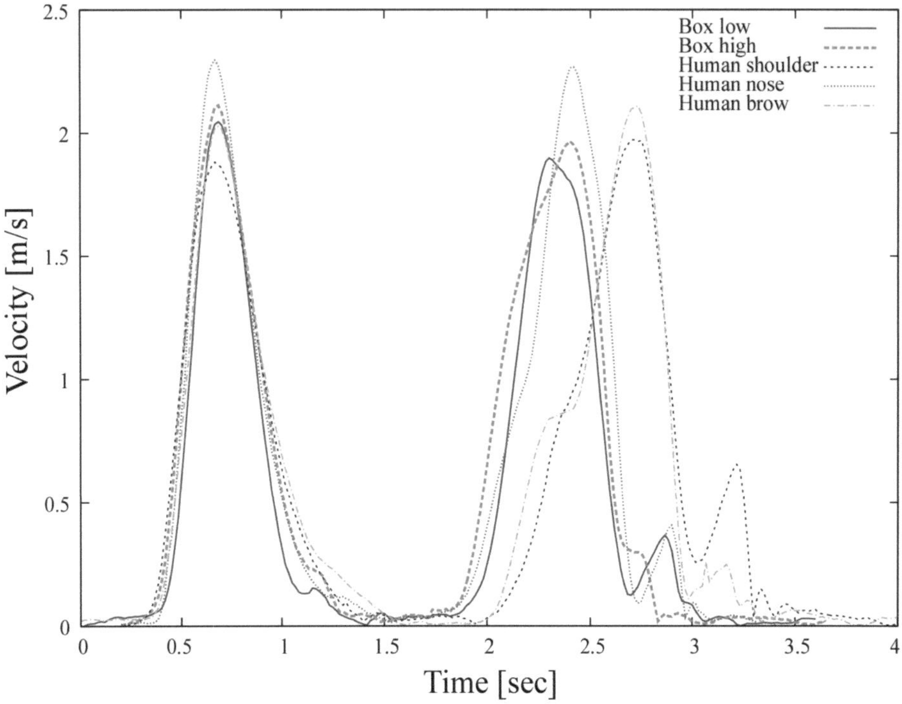

Fig. 3. An example of a subject's hand velocity (subject 1).

First, we calculated the absolute value of the hand velocity in order to facilitate the analysis. The trajectory of the hand position was smoothed by a low-pass filter, and the velocity was calculated by forward differences. We investigated the difference in the velocity profiles. As an example, the results for a typical subject are shown in Fig. 3. Each plot is the absolute value of the velocity of the hand and is shifted in time so that the times of the first peaks are the same. In each plot, the first bell-shaped curve indicates the reaching out motion, and the second bell-shaped curve indicates the returning motion. The following features were found for each subject.

- The velocity profile in the reaching phase forms a unimodal, bell-shaped curve that does not depend on the relationships (interpersonal and impersonal cases).
- The velocity profile in the returning phase varies depending on the relationships.

There were no remarkable differences in motion among the subjects that were familiar with the experimenter and the subjects that were not familiar with the experimenter. In order to examine the returning phase in detail, the horizontal and vertical components of the velocity were calculated. Figures 4 and 5 show the absolute value of the horizontal and vertical components, respectively. In all cases, the profile of the vertical component in the returning phase is a single-peak shape. This characteristic is common among all subjects. Moreover,

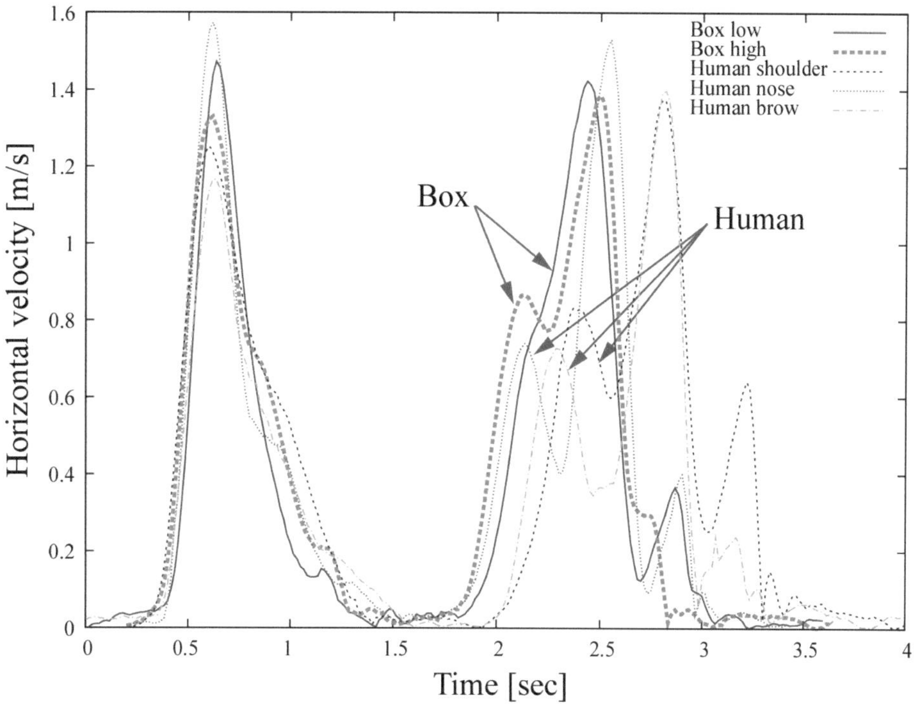

Fig. 4. Horizontal velocity of the hand (the horizontal component of the Fig. 3).

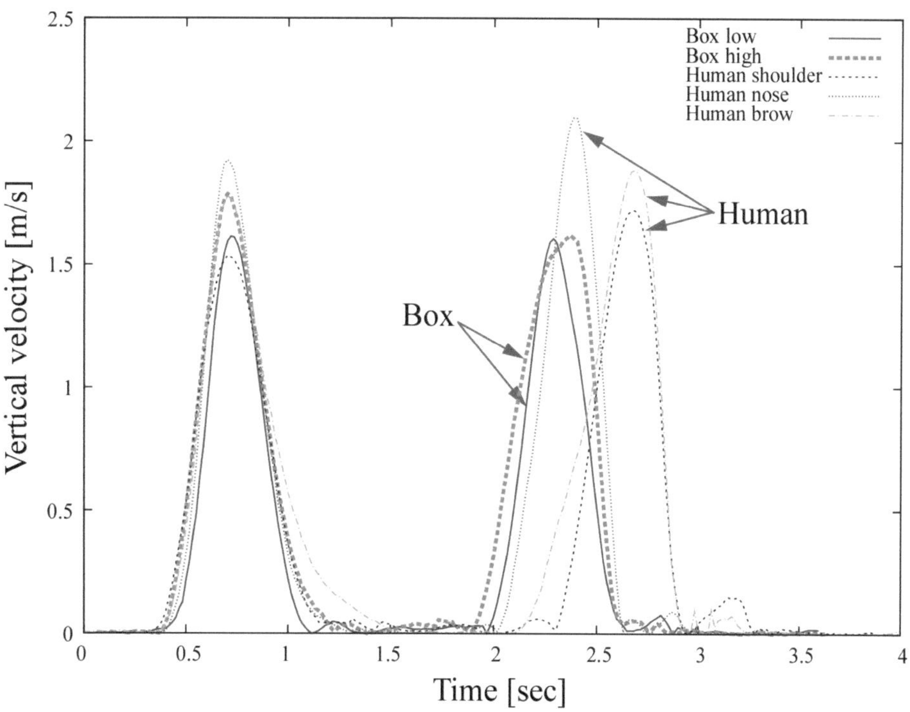

Fig. 5. Vertical velocity of the hand (the vertical component of the Fig. 3).

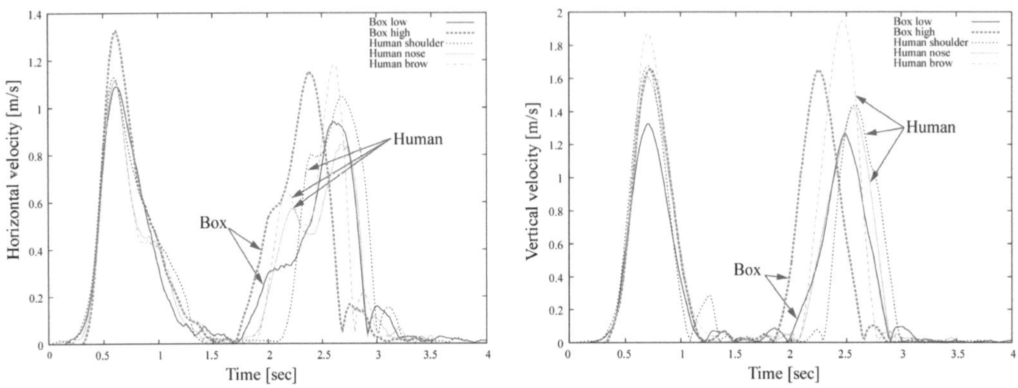

(a) Horizontal velocity (b) Vertical velocity

Fig. 6. An example of a subject's hand velocity (subject 2).

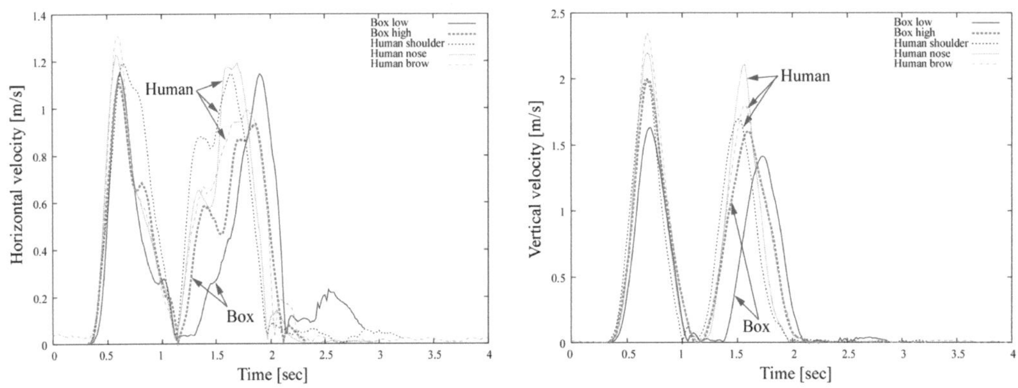

(a) Horizontal velocity (b) Vertical velocity

Fig. 7. An example of a subject's hand velocity (subject 3).

the profile of the horizontal component in the returning phase has a peak before the maximum peak. Other examples of the horizontal and vertical components are shown in Figs. 6 and 7. We can also find a similar profile of the horizontal component in these examples.

This characteristic appears 6 times among the 14 trials of the impersonal case and 18 times among the 21 trials of the interpersonal case. In other words, this characteristic appears more often in the interpersonal case than in the impersonal case. Although there is no statistically significant difference between the two cases because the number of the subjects is not sufficient, we focus on this feature in order to differentiate the interpersonal and impersonal cases. Comparing the horizontal and vertical components, the time to start increasing the vertical velocity is always later than the time to start increasing the horizontal velocity. There is a tendency for this time delay to be larger in interpersonal cases than in impersonal cases. These results suggest that, in the interpersonal case, when the subjects returned their hands, they moved their hands horizontally at first and then brought their hands down, whereas, in the impersonal case, subjects brought their hands down from the beginning. It is generally thought that a person moves his/her arm by controlling his/her

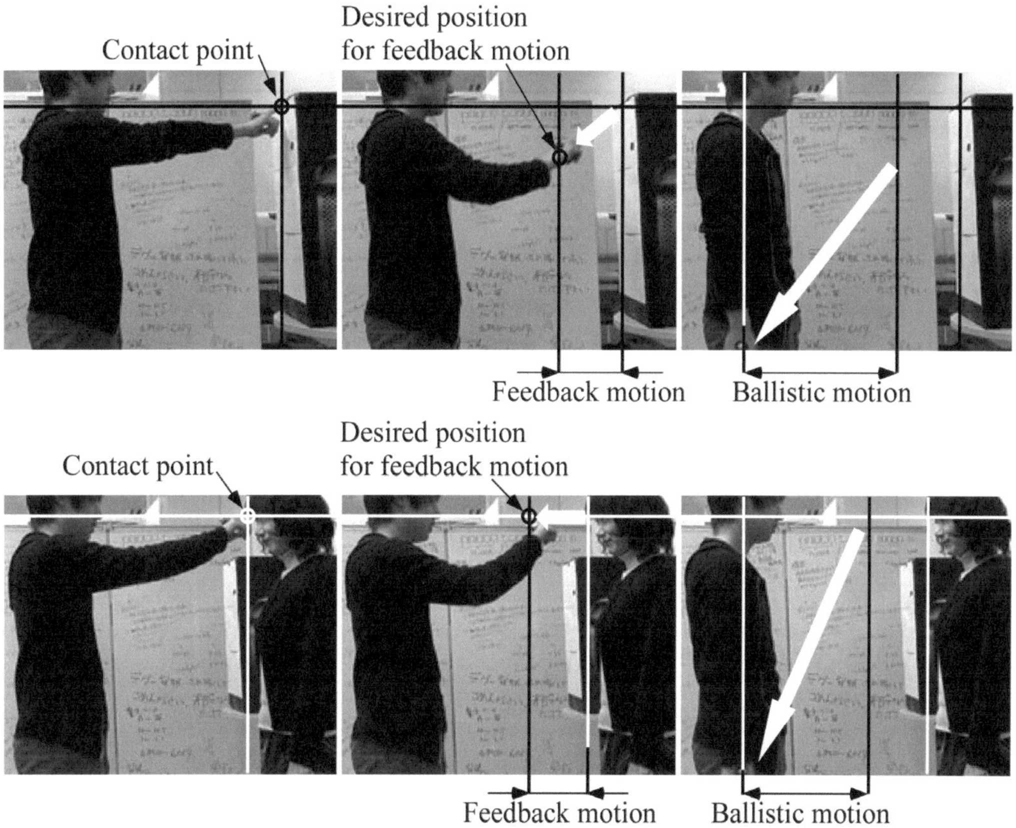

Fig. 8. The model of variation in returning phase of touching motion.

hand position initially with feedback control and then moves his/her arm in a ballistic trajectory. This difference in motion can be modelled as the difference of desired hand position of feedback control in the space close to another person (Fig. 8). To put it more concretely:

- In the impersonal case, the desired hand position is set such that the hand can be returned in the fastest path (Fig. 8, top).
- In the interpersonal case, the desired hand position is set such that the hand can move from the space in proximity to the other person along the fastest path (Fig. 8, bottom).

Although this model is specific to the motion for touching another person or a box, it can be taken as a model of human motion variety due to differences in social situation. In the next section, we examine the influence of the model on the impression towards an android.

3. Experiments

3.1 Repliee Q2 android

The android (called Repliee Q2) used in the experiment is shown in Fig. 9. The android is modelled after a Japanese woman, the standing height of which is approximately 160 cm. The skin is composed of a kind of silicone that feels like human skin. The android is driven by pneumatic actuators that give it 42 degrees of freedom from the waist up. The legs and feet are not powered. The android can neither stand up nor move from a chair. The joints driven by the pneumatic actuator has mechanical flexibility in the control thanks to the high compressibility of air. The flexibility of the joints makes for safer interaction, with movements that are generally smoother than those of other similar systems. The complicated dynamics of the air actuator make executing the trajectory tracking control difficult.

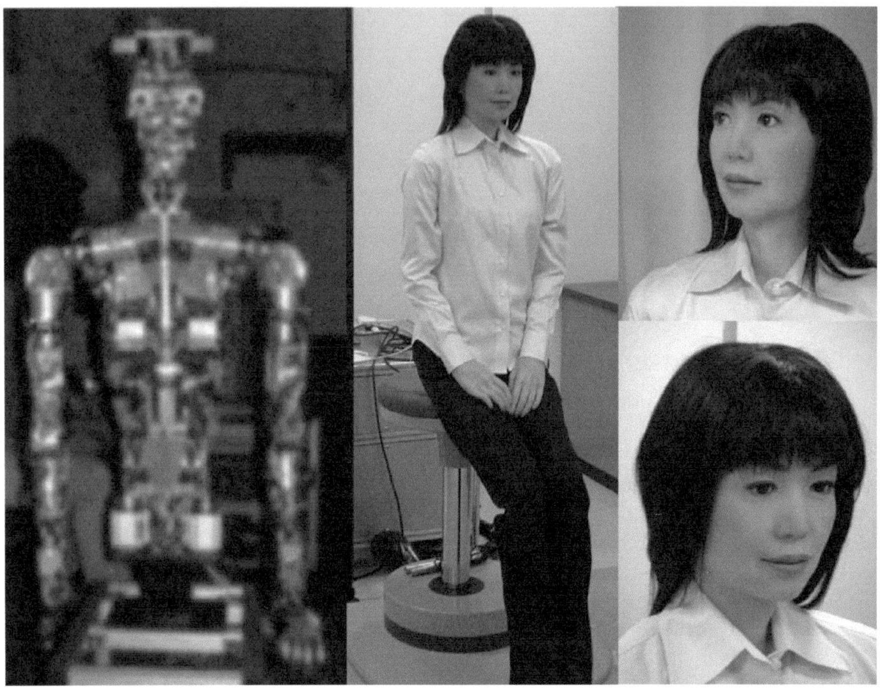

Fig. 9. "Repliee Q2" android. The left figure is blurred in order to hide the details.

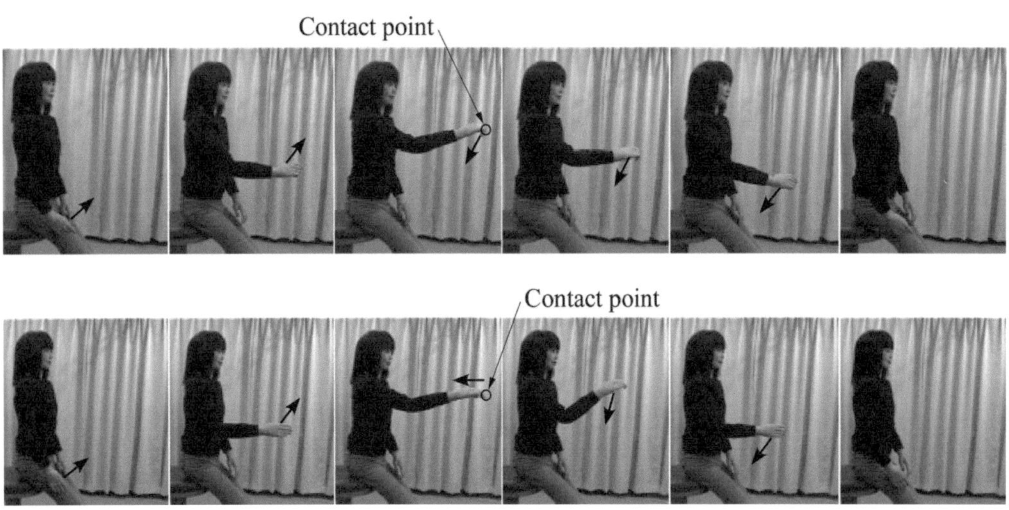

Fig. 10. Android motions generated based on the constructed model.

3.2 Method

We implemented the motion variation based on the proposed model in the Repliee Q2 android and investigated the impression toward the android from a third-person viewpoint in psychological experiments. We showed video recordings of the android motions to participants and asked them impressions toward the android. The android motions generated based on the proposed model are shown in Fig. 10. The top of the figure shows the motion in which the hand is returned along the fastest path (hereafter, motion M1). The bottom panel shows the motion in which the hand leaves from the space near the other person along the fastest path (hereafter, motion M2). The motion of reaching out was implemented according to the average motion of the subjects' reaching motions observed in the experiment described in Section 2. It is difficult to implement a quick and smooth motion in the android with a simple feedback control because the joints are driven by flexible pneumatic actuators. In order to avoid this difficulty, we implemented the motions in the android so that the speed of motion is slow. The video stimuli were made by playing videos of the android with slow motion at fast speed.

In order to examine the influence of the motion variety on the impression toward the android, we prepared three types of android, as shown in Table 1. Three androids reach out and touch persons and inanimate objects in different manners. The android in Condition A (hereafter, android A) touches persons and objects with motion M1. The android in Condition B (hereafter, android B) touches persons and objects with motion M2. The android in Condition C (hereafter, android C) touches objects with motion M1 and persons with motion M2. Conditions A and B are used to examine the impressions with respect to the androids without motion variety, and Condition C is used to examine the impressions with respect to the androids with motion variety. When the target is a person, the android touches the left shoulder of the person sitting in a face-to-face position.

	Android A	Android B	Android C
A motion with which the android touches an object	Motion M1	Motion M2	Motion M1
A motion with which the android touches a person	Motion M1	Motion M2	Motion M2

Table 1. The experimental conditions.

In each condition, a participant was presented six android motions to report the impression. The android touches three objects (a calendar, a video camera, and a small shelf) and three male persons once for each target. The six targets are shown in Fig. 11. The video stimulus is synthesized from a video recording of the android motion without the target and a video recording of the only target. The video of each motion is five seconds long. In each condition, six motions were randomly presented to a participant with a constraint in which the motion of touching an object and the motion of touching a person were alternately presented. In order to eliminate memory effect and aftereffect, a blank image was presented for two seconds between the videos, as shown in Fig. 12.

We designed a questionnaire using a five-point Likert scale with 1 = strongly disagree, 3 = neutral, and 5 = strongly agree. The aim of the questionnaire is to ask the impression of the android's human-like nature; therefore, the questionnaire asked how the android is "humanlike." It is, however, possible that the variation in the arm trajectories does not influence the impression on the human-likeness. We then prepared other six items in the

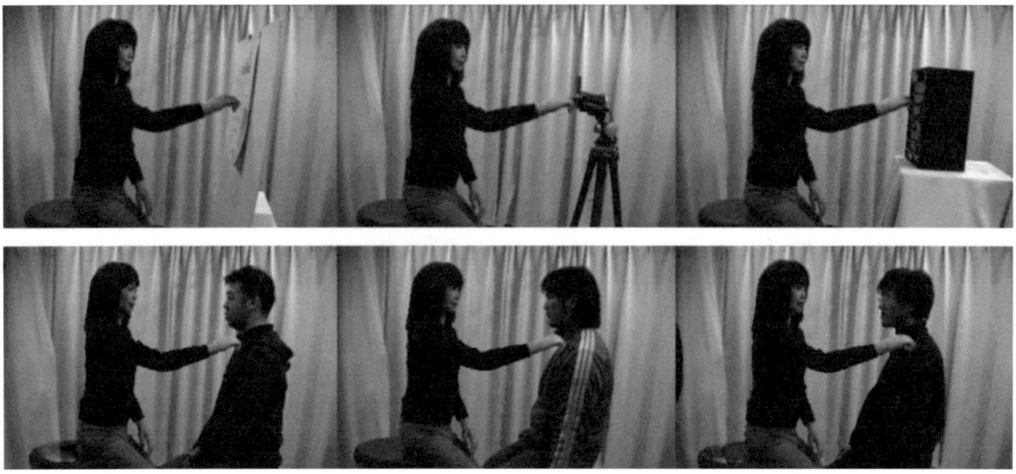

Fig. 11. The objects and persons in the video stimuli.

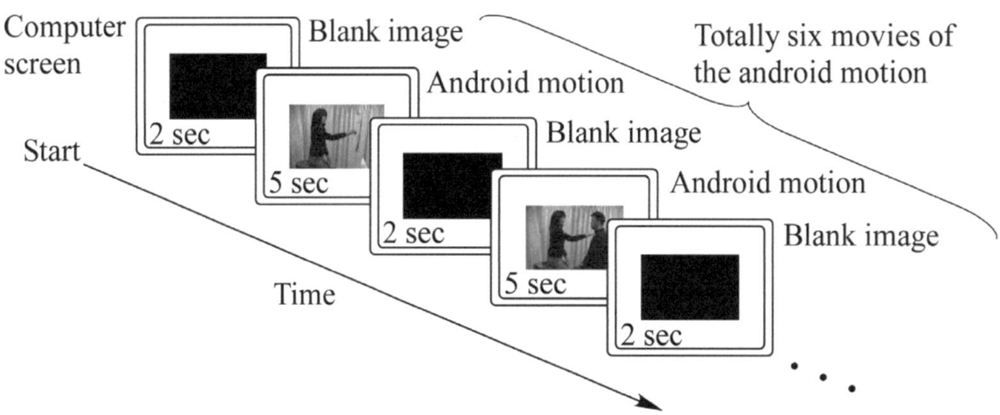

Fig. 12. The procedure to present the video stimuli.

questionnaire, which are likely influenced by the variation in the arm trajectories. The items are ``the android is (1) polite, (2) accurate, (3) intellectual, (4) conscientious, (5) friendly, (6) graceful, and (7) humanlike.'' The items are listed in random order in order to avoid the order effect, except for "humanlike," which always appears at the end of the questionnaire, because an answer to the item "humanlike" is likely to influence the responses to the other items.

3.3 Experiment 1: comparing Androids A and C

At first, we compared Androids A and C in order to investigate the influence of the presence of motion variety in the android. The expectation is that the comparison of the impressions of the human-like nature results in the following:

$$\text{Android C} > \text{Android A}.$$

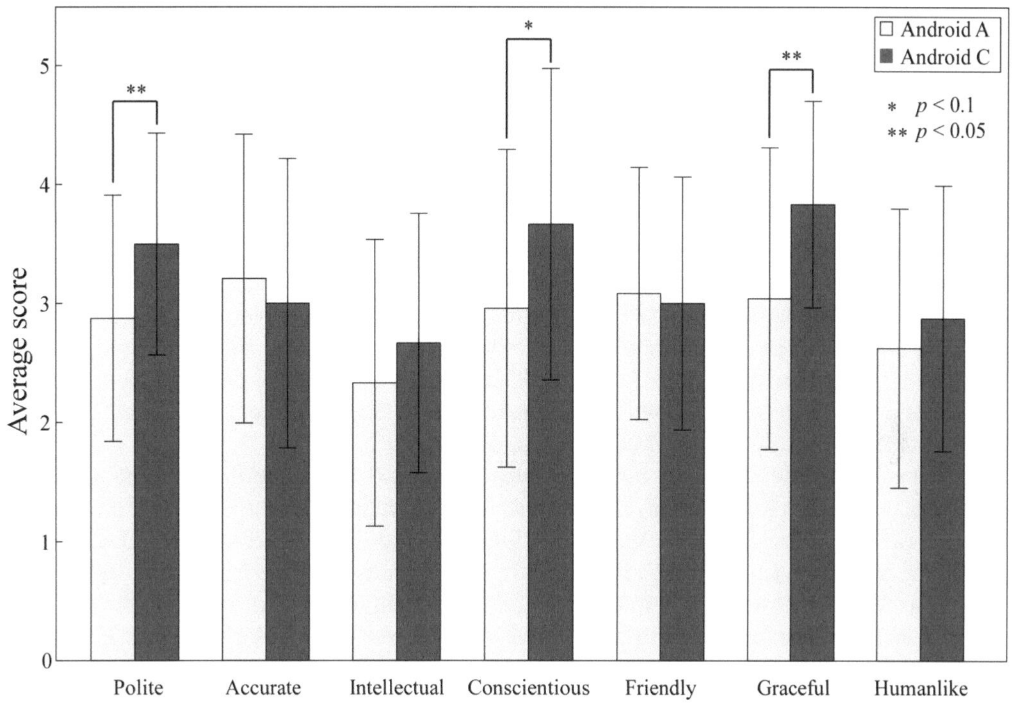

Fig. 13. The results of questionnaire about impressions towards Androids A and C.

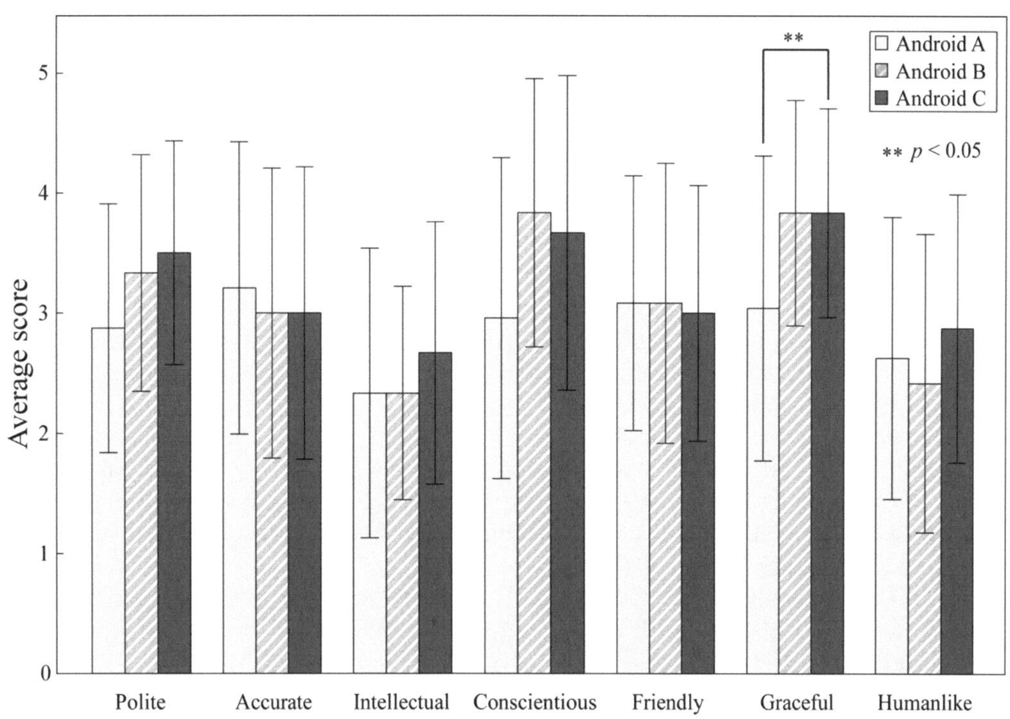

Fig. 14. The results of questionnaire about impressions towards Androids A, B, and C.

The participants were twenty-four university students (nineteen males and five females) who were familiar with the Repliee Q2 android. Each participant participated in both conditions, although the order of the conditions was changed randomly. The participant answered the questionnaire after every condition was presented.

The average scores of the impressions are shown in Fig. 13. A paired t-test revealed significant differences (p<0.05) in two conditions for the items of "polite" and "graceful," although there was no significant difference for the item "humanlike." The android behavior in which the hand quickly moves from the space in proximity to the other person likely gave an impression that the android carefully and deliberately touches the other person. It is inferred that the participants thought that the android had an intention of touching the other person carefully. It is, therefore, that the participants thought that Android C is politer and more graceful. It can be also said that the participants were consciously or subconsciously aware that Android C changed the hand trajectory from the fact that there are significant differences for some items.

Here, we consider the difference between Androids A and C. In Condition C, the android's arm trajectory varies according to the android-target relationship, and in Condition A, the android's arm trajectory does not vary according to the android-target relationship. Another difference is that, in Condition C, the android shows motion M2, which is not the case in Condition A. In other words, there is a possibility that the presence of motion M2 produced different impressions. In order to show that the different impressions are caused by the difference in social situation, it is necessary to examine the influence of motion M2. Therefore, in the next section, we conducted an additional experiment to assess the android in Condition B.

3.4 Experiment 2: comparing Androids A, B, and C

The participants in this experiment were twelve of twenty-four participants who participated in experiment 1. They were nine males and three females. Each participant was presented Android B and answered the questionnaire about it. The expectation is that the comparison of the impressions of the human-like nature results in the following:

Android C > Android A, Android B.

The average scores of the impressions toward Android B are shown in Fig. 14 by adding the result to Fig. 13. Ryan's multiple comparison test revealed a significant difference (p<0.05) between Androids A and C for the item "graceful." This is the same result as the one obtained in the experiment 1. Contrary to our expectation, however, there was no significant difference between Androids B and C.

We then considered the influence of the order of stimulus presentation. The participants of the experiment 2 assessed in order of Androids A, C, and B or C, A, and B. Hereinafter, Case O1 and Case O2 indicate the order of A→C→B and C→A→B, respectively. A repeated measures two-way ANOVA with a factor of condition order and a factor of android motion was conducted. There were significant interactions at the 5% level for the items of "intellectual", "friendly", and "humanlike" and at the 10% level for the item of "conscientious." It is possible that the effect of the android motion on the impression score depends on the order of conditions.

We divided the twelve participants into participants who participated in Case O1 (seven persons) and participants who participated in Case O2 (five persons) and analyzed their impression scores. The average impression scores obtained in Cases O1 and O2 are shown in Figs. 15 and 16, respectively. For each item, three conditions are rearranged in the order of presentation. Two tendencies can be seen in these figures:

- The scores obtained in the condition right after Condition C are smaller than those in Condition C.
- The scores obtained in the condition right after Condition A are larger than those in Condition A.

Ryan's multiple comparison test revealed several significant differences at 5% level among Androids A, B, and C as shown in Figs. 15 and 16. In particular, as expected, the score of "humanlike" for Android C is significantly larger than that for Android B in Case O1. In Case O2, the participants thought the android which touched anything with the motion M2 was more deliberate and careful than the android which touched anything with the motion M1. Furthermore, it is likely that this careful motion gave an impression that Android B was more humanlike than Android A in Case O2. However, the participants thought that Android C with motion variation was more humanlike than Android B when Android C was presented just after Android B in Case O1. It is possible that the participants think the android with the motion variation is more humanlike than the android with only the careful motion.

3.5 Summary

The experimental results showed that the variety of the android motion enhances the impression of human-like nature toward the android under the influence of the order of stimulus presentation, although the expected result (i.e., Android C is more humanlike than Androids A and B) was not obtained. In addition, the results showed that motion variety influences impressions such as "conscientious" and "graceful", which are related to the human-like nature of the android. The number of participants of the experiments was too few to compare the three conditions. The expected effect of the motion variety may be shown by an experiment with a larger number of participants.

As an example of motion variety, the present chapter examined the motion variation in which the desired hand position of feedback control varies in two ways when a person returns his/her hand after touching a target. In addition, the social relationship which causes this variation was also designed to be varied in two cases, that is, android-person and android-object relationships. This is a simple example of variety. However, more complicated motion variation can be designed, for example, by changing the causes of the variation. It is inferred that complicated variation has a different influence on the impression, although there are appropriate variations for enhancing the human-like nature. Further investigation is necessary in order to clarify what motion variety makes the android humanlike.

In Section 2, we assumed that the variation of the subject's arm motion is caused by the social relationship between the subject and the target. However, the subconscious motion variation was not verified to be due to the social situation. There is another possibility, i.e., that the variation is, for example, due to the hardness of the target, such as a hard box or a soft human body. In addition, it was not verified that the participants in Section 3 actually attributed the cause of motion variation to the social situation, although the motion variation conditionally enhanced the impression of the android's human-like nature. In other words, it is not clear that the participants think Android C socially behaves like

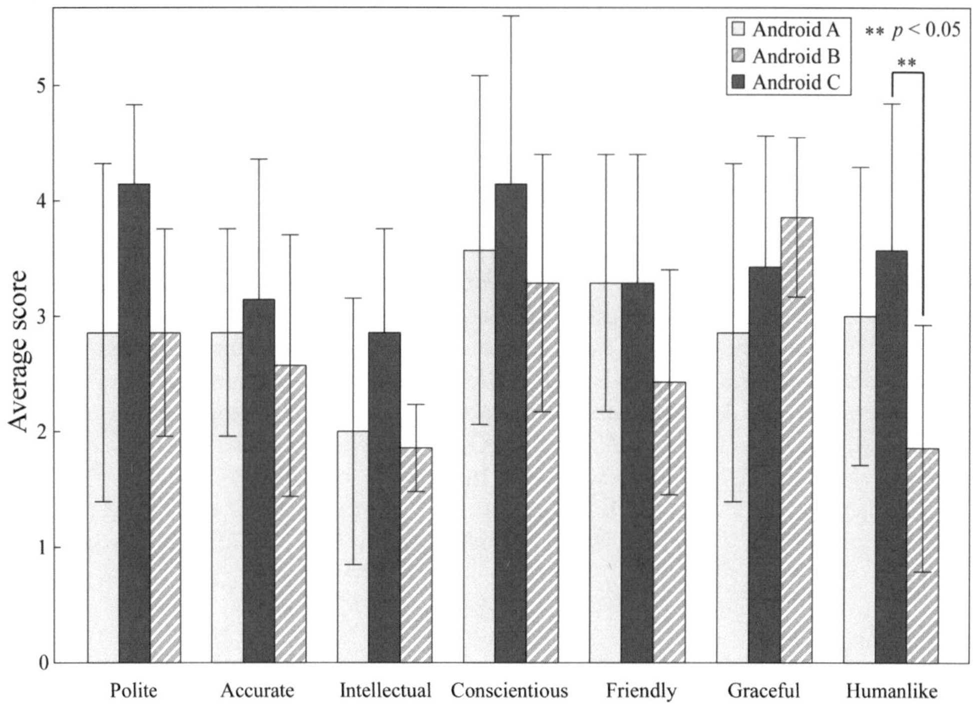

Fig. 15. Impressions of participants assessed in order of Androids A, C, and B (Case O1).

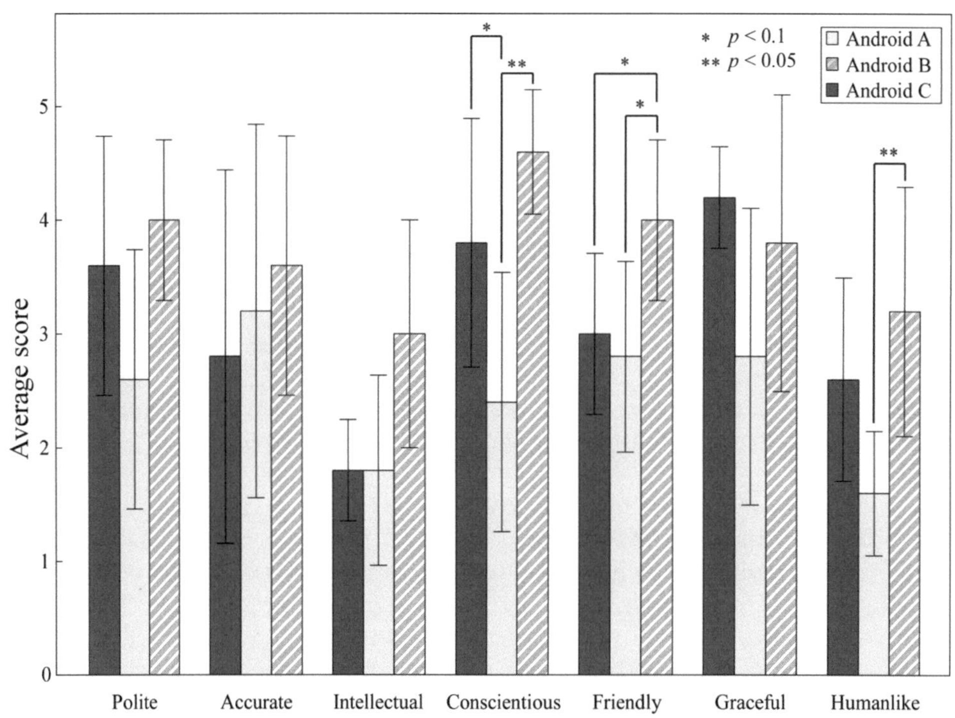

Fig. 16. Impressions of participants assessed in order of Androids C, A, and B (Case O2).

human beings. One possible design of an experiment is to compare with the android which has same motions but different motion variation, that is, the android which touches objects with motion M2 and persons with motion M1 (this manner is opposite to Android C). If this android is less humanlike than Android C, the motion variation which is congruent with that of human subjects shown in Section 2 contributes the human-likeness of the android. However, further investigation is necessary to verify whether the social relationship caused the arm motion variation observed in Section 2 and the different impressions toward the android obtained in Section 3.

4. Conclusion

We hypothesized that a motion variety that is not related to a subject's intention and can be consciously controlled influences the humanlike impression of the subject, and we assumed that this motion variety makes the android more humanlike. In order to verify this hypothesis, we constructed a model of the motion variety through the observation of persons' motions. We examined the variation in a motion of reaching out and touching another person, which occurred in different social relationships between the subject and the other person (or object). The experimental results showed that the modelled motion variety conditionally influences the impression toward the android.

The results of the present chapter are specific to the android's motion of reaching out and touching a person. The present study is a first step in the exploration of the principles for providing natural robot behaviors. The results revealed that a phenomenon whereby motion variety influences the impression towards the actor can be seen at least in certain motions of a very humanlike robot. Based on these results, it is possible to examine which aspects of the robot's appearance and motion are affected by this phenomenon. This exploration will help to clarify the principles underlying natural human-robot communication.

From the viewpoint of the robot motion design, a motion variety model is also useful. Several studies have proposed a method by which to implement humanlike motion in a humanoid robot by copying human motion as measured by a motion capture system to the robot (Riley et al., 2000; Nakaoka et al., 2003; Matsui et al. 2005). In order to make a robot motion more humanlike, it is necessary to implement a humanlike motion variation. However, it is not necessary to copy all human motions. This humanlike motion variation can be automatically generated from an original motion by the motion variety model.

5. Acknowledgements

The android robot Repliee Q2 was developed in collaboration with Kokoro Company, Ltd.

6. References

Bodenheimer, B.; Shleyfman, A. V. & Hodgins, J. K. (1999). The effects of noise on the perception of animated human running, *Computer Animation and Simulation '99: Proceedings of the Eurographics Workshop*, pp. 53-63, ISBN: 978-3-211-83392-6, Milano, Italy, Sep., 1999, Springer-Verlag.

Flash, T. & Hogan, N. (1985). The coordination of arm movements: An experimentally confirmed mathematical model, *Journal of Neuroscience*, Vol. 5, No. 7, pp. 1688-1703, 1985, ISSN: 0270-6474.

Ishiguro, H. (2005). Android science -toward a new cross-interdisciplinary framework, *Proceedings of the 12th International Symposium of Robotics Research*, San Francisco, USA, Oct., 2005.

Jacob, P. & Jeannerod, M. (2005). The motor theory of social cognition: a critique. *Trends in Cognitive Sciences*, Vol. 9, No. 1, pp. 21-25, 2005, ISSN: 1364-6613.

Kashima, T. & Isurugi, Y. (1998). Trajectory formation based on physiological characteristics of skeletal muscles, *Biological Cybernetics*, Vol. 78, No. 6, pp. 413-422, 1998, ISSN : 0340-1200.

Kawato, M. (1992). Optimization and learning in neural networks for formation and control of coordinated movement, *Attention and performance XIV*, pp. 821-849, ISBN: 978-0-262-13284-8, 1992, MIT Press.

Matsui, D.; Minato, T.; MacDorman, K. F. & Ishiguro, H. (2005). Generating natural motion in an android by mapping human motion, *Proceedings of the IEEE/RSJ International Conference on Intelligent Robot Systems*, pp. 1089-1096, ISBN: 0-7803-8912-3, Edmonton, Alberta, Canada, Aug., 2005.

Miyamoto, H.; Nakano, E.; Wolpert, D. M. & Kawato, M. (2004). Tops (task optimization in the presence of signal-dependent noise) model. *Systems and Computers in Japan*, Vol. 35, Issue 11, pp. 48-58, 2004, ISSN: 0882-1666.

Nakaoka, S.; Nakazawa, A.; Yokoi, K.; Hirukawa, H. & Ikeuchi, K. (2003). Generating whole body motions for a biped humanoid robot from captured human dances, *Proceedings of the IEEE-RAS International Conference on Robotics and Automation*, pp. 3905-3910, ISBN: 0-7803-7737-0, Taipei, Taiwan, Sep., 2003.

Nass, C.; Steuer, J. & Tauber, E. (1994). Computers are social actors, *Proceedings of the ACM Conference on Human Factors in Computing Systems*, pp. 72-78, ISBN: 0-89791-651-4, Boston, Massachusetts, USA, Apr., 1994.

Perlin, K. (1995). Real time responsive animation with personality, *IEEE Transactions on Visualization and Computer Graphics*, Vol. 1, No. 1, pp. 5-15, 1995, ISSN: 1077-2626.

Riley, M.; Ude, A. & Atkeson, C. G. (2000). Methods for motion generation and interaction with a humanoid robot: Case studies of dancing and catching, *Proceedings of AAAI/CMU Workshop on Interactive Robotics and Entertainment*, pp. 35-42, Pittsburgh, Pennsylvania, USA, Apr., 2000.

Schaal, S. & Sternad, D. (2001). Origins and violations of the 2/3 power law in rhythmic 3d movements, *Experimental Brain Research*, Vol. 136, No. 1, pp. 60-72, 2001, ISSN: 0014-4819.

Todorov, E. & Jordan, M. I. (2002). Optimal feedback control as a theory of motor coordination, *Nature Neuroscience*, Vol. 5, Issue 11, pp. 1226-1235, 2002, ISSN: 1097-6256.

Uno, Y.; Kawato, M. & Suzuki, R. (1989). Formation and control of optical trajectory in human multi-joint arm movement - minimim torque-change model, *Biological Cybernetics*, Vol. 61, No. 2, pp. 89-101, 1989, ISSN: 0340-1200.

9

Method for Objectively Evaluating Psychological Stress Resulting when Humans Interact with Robots

Kazuhiro Taniguchi[1], Atsushi Nishikawa[2], Tomohiro Sugino[3], Sayaka Aoyagi[3], Mitsugu Sekimoto[4], Shuji Takiguchi[4], Kazuyuki Okada[4], Morito Monden[4] and Fumio Miyazaki[2]

[1]*Graduate School of Engineering, The University of Tokyo*
[2]*Graduate School of Engineering Science, Osaka University*
[3]*Research & Development Division , Soiken Inc.*
[4]*Graduate School of Medicine, Osaka University*
Japan

1. Introduction

Most of us have seen robots in movies, animations and comic book stories, so the word "robot" tends to conjure up images of fictional robots rather than the real thing. The robots in Japanese cartoons such as *Astro Boy* and *Doraemon* have human-like social skills, and their physical abilities make it possible for them to live alongside humans without any difficulties. In reality, robots are quite different from these fictional creations. At least, the robots of the early 21st century are still unable to interact smoothly with humans (Norman, 2007). Due to the large disparity between the fictional image of robots and their actual appearance, people sometimes feel stressed when confronted with robots. To facilitate smoother interactions between humans and robots, we must not only to improve the intelligence and physical ability of robots, but also find some way of evaluating the psychological stress felt by humans when they have to interact with robots. To develop robots that can interact smoothly with humans, we need to be able to ascertain the psychological and physiological characteristics of humans by evaluating and analyzing the stress they experience in everyday activities, design robots based on human characteristics, and evaluate and study these robots. In short, stress evaluation is a key requirement for the realization of smooth interactions between robots and humans.

In this chapter, we discuss methods for objectively evaluating and investigating the psychological stress that people experience when interacting with robots. For the evaluation of stress, we used acceleration pulse waveforms and the saliva constituents which are biochemical stress markers. These were used to evaluate the psychological stress of a surgeon using a surgical assistant robot.

A surgical assistant robot is a robot that interacts with a surgeon and is situated in contact with the patients to provide support for surgical operations. Interaction with humans is of greater importance for surgical assistant robots than for any other type of robot. A laparoscope robot is one robot of this type that is put to practical use and is a typical example of a robot where interaction with humans is important. This is a robot that is used instead of a human camera assistant in order to hold the laparoscope in position during laparoscopic surgery (Jaspers et al., 2004). Laparoscopic surgery is a technique where surgical tools and a laparoscope are inserted into the patient's body through small holes in the abdomen, and the surgeon carries out the surgery while viewing the images from the laparoscope on a TV monitor. Laparoscopic surgery has grown rapidly in popularity in recent years, not only because it is less invasive and produces less visible scarring, but also because of its benefits in terms of healthcare economy, such as shorter patient stays. The most important characteristic of this technique is that the surgeon performs the operation while watching the video image from the laparoscope on a monitor instead of looking directly at the site of the operation. Thus, an important factor affecting the safety and smoothness of the operation is the way in which the video images are presented in a field of view suitable for the surgical operation. Manipulation of the laparoscope is not only needed for orienting the laparoscope towards the parts requiring surgery, but also for making fine adjustments to ensure that the field of view, viewing distance and so on are suitable for the surgical operation being performed. A camera assistant operates the laparoscope according to the surgeon's instructions, but must also make independent decisions on how to operate the laparoscope in line with the surgeon's intentions as the surgery progresses. Consequently even the camera assistant that operates the laparoscope must have the same level of experience in laparoscopic surgery as the surgeon. However, not many surgeons are skilled in the special techniques of laparoscopic surgery. It is therefore not uncommon for camera assistants to be inexperienced and unable to maintain a suitable field of view, thus hindering the progress of the operation. To address this problem, a laparoscope robot was developed to hold and position the laparoscope instead of a human camera assistant. Figure 1(a) shows how laparoscopic surgery is conventionally performed with a human camera assistant operating the laparoscope, and Figure 1(b) shows how laparoscopic surgery is performed using a laparoscope robot. When using a laparoscope robot, the laparoscope is held and positioned by the manipulator part of the laparoscope robot which is situated beside the surgeon and is operated by a human-machine interface based on speech recognition or the like.

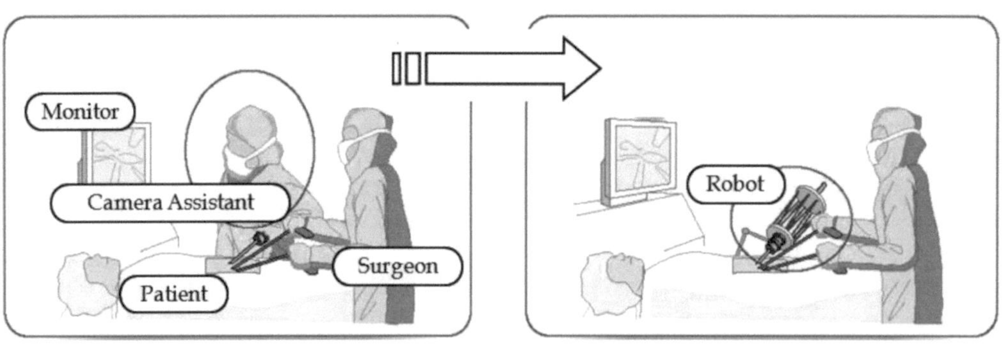

(a) (b)

Fig. 1. (a) Conventional laparoscopic surgery where the laparoscope is operated by a human camera assistant. (b) Robot-assisted surgery where the laparoscope is operated by a laparoscope robot.

Laparoscope robots have already been made commercially available and are in widespread use. These include Hitachi's Naviot™ (Kobayashi et al., 1999; Tanoue et al., 2006), the AESOP™ made in the US by Computer Motion (now known as Intuitive Surgical Inc.) (Sackier & Wang, 1994), and EndoAssist™ made by Prosurgics (Finlay, 2001). These commercial products all move according to the surgeon's instructions. Meanwhile, although still at the research stage, there are other systems in which the surgeon's movements are autonomously determined by the robot which positions the laparoscope automatically. A typical example is the laparoscope positioning system developed by Nishikawa et al. (Sekimoto et al., 2009; Nishikawa et al., 2008; Nishikawa et al., 2006).

Laparoscope robots are generally evaluated by measuring work efficiency, precision and error rates, and by using interviews and questionnaires to gather the opinions of surgeons. In cases where the interaction between laparoscope robots and the surgeons operating them resulted in bad feelings, the result was that this drawback worsened the overall performance of the system even if the robot performed excellently in all other aspects. It is therefore necessary to evaluate stress by using interviews, questionnaires and the like. However, interviews and questionnaires produce subjective results that tend to be rather vague, and it is also possible that the results are affected by the human relationship between the examiner and examinee. For the objective measurement of stress, there is growing interest in methods that use biological stress responses.

The concept of biological stress responses was defined by the physiologist Hans Selye as "the nonspecific response of the body to any demand upon it" (Selye, 1936; Selye, 1974). Since stress appears to originate from very complex mechanisms, not only do different people respond differently to stimuli, but even the same person can exhibit a range of different responses to the depending on whether the stress is comfortable or uncomfortable, psychological or physical, and so on.

In the field of physiology, biological stress responses to psychological stress stimuli take place in the autonomic nervous system and endocrine system. In biological stress responses of the autonomic nervous system, sympathetic nerves produce a very fast biological response in which the activity of sympathetic nerves takes priority, and a biophylactic mechanism acts to resist the stress stimulus. In biological stress responses of the endocrine system, processes such as hormone secretion from the adrenal cortex causes a biological response that changes the organism's internal environment so as to keep it in a suitable state.

Methods for the evaluation of biological stress responses include biochemical methods that measure stress-related substances in biological samples of blood, saliva or the like, and methods that involve performing a statistical dynamic analysis of physiological markers such as blood pressure and heart rate.

In the following section, as a typical stress evaluation technique, we describe the evaluation of stress based on biochemical markers and acceleration pulse waveforms.

2. Evaluation of stress with biochemical markers (saliva, urine)

Stress responses can be generally distinguished by two systems — the hypothalamus - sympathetic nerves - adrenal medulla system (sympathetic-adrenal-medullary axis: SAM) and the hypothalamus - pituitary - adrenal cortex system (hypothalamic-pituitary-adrenal axis: HPA). When an excessive stress is loaded, this is reflected as changes in biochemical markers in blood, urine and saliva (Figure 2).

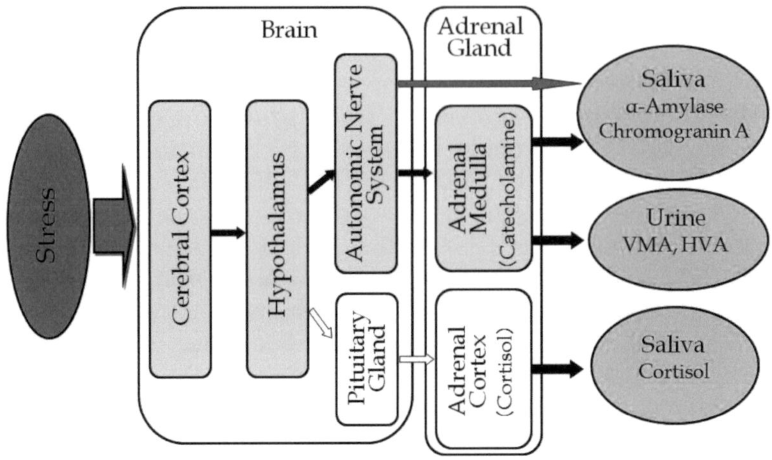

Fig. 2. Physiological reaction to stress loading

The SAM system corresponds to the response of the autonomic nervous system, where the stimulus of stress load is transmitted to the cerebral cortex and causes the catecholamines (epinephrine, norepinephrine, etc.) to be released via the hypothalamus, either directly from the autonomic nervous system or indirectly via the adrenal medulla. These catecholamines and related substances can be useful as stress markers. On the other hand, the HPA system corresponds to the response of the endocrine system, where the stress stimulus is transmitted to the cerebral cortex and causes corticotropin releasing factor (CRF) to be released from the hypothalamus, promoting the release of adrenocorticotropic hormone (ACTH) from the pituitary gland and the secretion of glucocorticoids such as cortisol from the adrenal cortex. These pituitary and adrenal cortex hormones can be also useful as stress markers.

In the case of evaluating the stress when people use robots or work together with robots, it is not recommended to use biochemical markers in blood because an invasive medical practice is accompanied to obtain blood samples. Therefore urinary and salivary markers are more suitable because of obtaining the samples by non-invasive means. In this section we discuss especially important and useful stress markers in saliva and urine.

As mentioned above, the largest merit of using urinary and salivary markers is to obtain samples by non-invasive means, but the data often have larger variation than these of blood samples with depending on the condition of the samples, so it is necessary to select suitable collecting and sampling methods for the markers being measured. Especially in the case of saliva, it is necessary to select different collecting methods according to which salivary gland the target substances are mainly secreted from (submandibular, parotid, sublingual, etc.). A suitable collecting apparatus must be selected for the markers being measured [e.g. test tube for collecting saliva samples (Salivett® Sarstedt AG & Co.) , a short straw, etc].

As possible urinary markers for the stress response of the SAM system, vanillylmanderic acid (VMA) and homovanillic acid (HVA) are recommended, which are metabolites of catecholamines, individually norepinephrine and dopamine (Frankenhaeuser et al., 1986). Norepinephrine and dopamine in blood are a direct reflection of sympathetic nerve activity, so it has been suggested that these markers make it possible to detect changes in autonomic nerve balance induced by stress loads. However, it is not easy to identify the time point at which measuring the blood concentrations of these substances, moreover the concentrations depend on the clearance from the blood (Esler et al., 1984), so catecholamines in blood have been found to be unsuitable for use as stress markers, besides the sample collection needs invasive clinical practice. Therefore it is recommended to use the urinary concentrations of VMA and HVA as stress markers. Urinary VMA and HVA have long been used as clinical markers of neuroblastomas in infancy, and measurement methods using high performance liquid chromatography (HPLC) have been established. In human studies psychological stress load (having to perform calculations and operate a PC) is given for 4 hours, the level of VMA in urine is found to increase compared with that of unstressed condition. Also, in the case of physical stress load (ergometer exercise) for 4 hours, the urinary VMA and HVA levels are found to be higher for 4 hours after the load is given. Thus in the last few years, urinary VMA and HVA have attracted attention as markers for evaluating the effect of stress-reducing foods and medicines. More recently, they have also been used to evaluate electrical appliances for reducing stress. In one report, it was confirmed that stress-related increases in urinary HVA could be suppressed by controlling the airflow of cooling air conditioners, thus confirming the use of urinary HVA. These reports suggest that urinary VMA and HVA levels are thought to be promising stress markers for surgeons using robots, and it is expected that they will lead to the creation of robots that reduce stress.

Possible markers in saliva include α-amylase and chromogranin A as stress responses to the SAM system, and cortisol as a stress response to the HPA system.

Salivary α-amylase is mainly secreted by the parotid salivary glands, and the control of these secretions is known to be regulated by sympathetic nerves (Nater et al., 2006). When a stress load is given, this can be detected as an increase in salivary α-amylase activity, but this mechanism is thought to involve two pathways – one where the autonomic nervous system acts directly on the salivary glands, and another which is mediated by the secretion of norepinephrine from the adrenal medulla. This stress response generally occurs within 10 minutes. Salivary α-amylase activity is known to have circadian rhythm, increasing from the morning until midday and decreasing at night (Nater et al., 2007). Therefore it is no problem when evaluating acute phase stress, but when evaluating sub-acute or chronic stress for several hours or longer, the control sample must be obtained at the same time of another day. Salivary α-amylase activity is confirmed to change by both physical and psychological stress load. In the clinical study for the evaluation of electrical appliances, it has been reported that under 8-hour psychological stress loading conditions, an airbag-type automated massage chair (medical appliance) can inhibit the increase in salivary α-amylase activity. Salivary α-amylase activity can be measured by using the Caraway method, which is established as a method for the clinical examination of α-amylase in blood and urine that is a highly reliable measurement system. It has also been used to evaluate stress in surgeons using laparoscope robots.

Chromogranin A is an acid glycoprotein with a molecular weight of approximately 49,000 which is separated from adrenal medulla chromaffin cells. It is known to be widely distributed the endocrine and nervous systems, and is mostly found in the adrenal medulla and pituitary gland (Winkler & Fischer-Colibrie, 1992). A characteristic of this protein is that it coexists and is co-released with catecholamine which contributes to the stress response of the SAM system, so the blood level of chromogranin A reflects the sympathetic nerve activity. Chromogranin A is also present in the ducts of the submandibular glands, and is known to be released in the saliva as a result of stress loading (Saruta et al., 2005). Salivary chromogranin A is therefore used as a stress marker. Interestingly, it has been reported that

specific changes only occur for a psychological stress load (Kanamaru et al., 2006), and in our studies we also observed changes for psychological stress loads but not for physical stress loads. The ELISA method was established for the measurement of salivary chromogranin A concentrations. Although it has not yet been demonstrated to be useful for stress evaluation electrical appliances, it is very interesting to see how salivary chromogranin A chages when using a robot.
Cortisol is released from the adrenal cortex when the pituitary is stimulated by ACTH as a stress response of the HPA system, and has been studied for a very long time as a stress marker (Levine, 1993). Since cortisol also affects the immune system and central nervous system, it is an important hormone that reflects not only stress levels but also physiological condition. Hitherto it has been used together with ACTH as a stress marker in blood. In recent years, a method has been developed for the measurement of salivary cortisol concentrations with ELISA, and this has come to be widely used as a stress marker. Salivary cortisol concentrations are of the order of a few percent compared to that in blood, but have been found to have a very strong correlation with stress. Cortisol level generally increases from 20 to 30 minutes after the application of stress load. The response time depends on the types of load, which is a slower response than the SAM system. Also, like salivary α-amylase, the salivary cortisol is known to have circadian rhythm, with a high concentration in the morning which decreases rapidly by midday, so it is essential to perform evaluations by comparing the results with a control sample. Salivary cortisol responds to both physical and psychological stress (Nozaki et al., 2009), and it has been shown that the abovementioned massage chair reduced cortisol concentrations caused by psychological stress loading. Furthermore, as introduced in this section, it is also used to evaluate the stress of surgeons when using a laparoscope robot.

3. Evaluation of stress with accelerated plethysmography

The stress response of the SAM system can be detected as a change in autonomic nerve functions by using a physiological marker. Changes in autonomic nerve function can be evaluated in various ways such as nerve impulses, electroencephalograms and electrocardiograms. Acceleration pulse waveforms are especially useful because they can be measured quickly and easily by accelerated plethysmography (Figure 3). The acceleration pulse waveform is a secondary differentiation of plethysmogram readings based on measurements of the optical absorbency of hemoglobin in peripheral blood vessels of a fingertip or other region. These waveforms have been generally used to evaluate arteriosclerosis. The *a-a* interval of the acceleration pulse waveform is strongly correlative to the *R-R* interval in an electrocardiogram in physiological aspect. The electrocardiogram *R-R* interval can be used to evaluate autonomic nerve functions by the coefficient of variation and by the frequency analysis of time-series data with maximum entropy method or fast Fourier transform method (Akselrod et al., 1985). Even in the *a-a* interval of the acceleration pulse waveform, when the coefficient of variation reflects the activity of parasympathetic nerves or by the analysis of time-series data, it is shown that the low-frequency component (LF: 0.02–0.15 Hz) mainly reflects the sympathetic nerve activity, while the high-frequency component (HF: 0.15–0.5 Hz) reflects the parasympathetic nerve activity, and it is known that the LF/HF ratio indicates the autonomic nerve functions and that LF/HF increases in stress states (when sympathetic nerves become predominant). When a physical stress load is given, it has been reported that in comparing before with after the stress load, the coefficient of variation of the *a-a* interval decreases and the LF/HF increases. These markers are often used to evaluate the stress-reducing effects of foods (Nukui et al., 2008). Recently, it has also been applied to evaluating the stress-reducing effects of electrical appliances.

It has also been found that LF/HF in the frequency analysis is related to fatigue as well as stress. The acceleration pulse waveform is useful for not only the evaluation of stress and fatigue when using electrical appliances, but also the detection of the worker's fatigue level before the start of work, it is possible to detect the worker's health condition before operating a robot.

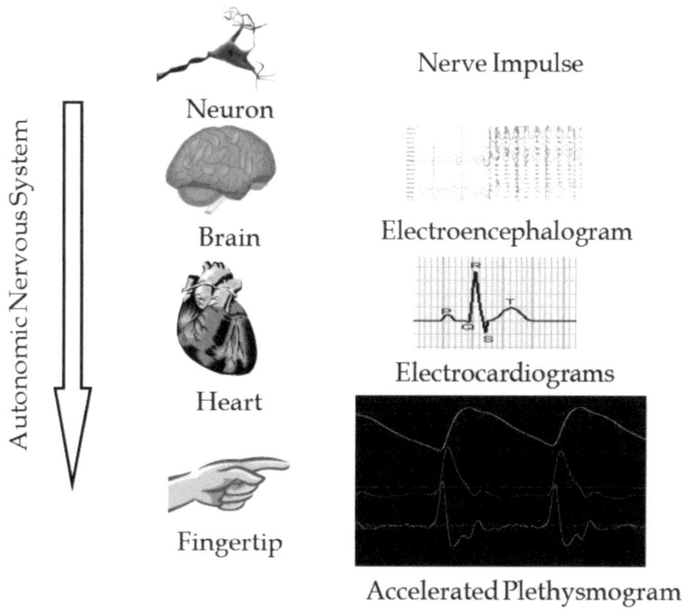

Fig. 3. Evaluation of stress based on autonomic nervous system functions

4. Objective evaluation of psychological stress by analyzing biochemical markers and acceleration pulse waveforms

In this section we describe a method for objectively evaluating psychological stress in examinees by analyzing acceleration pulse waveforms and the examinee's biochemical markers measured before and after performing a task. Saliva was used as the biochemical marker. For the acceleration pulse waveform data, we used the LF/HF ratio.

The duration of the task was set to 25 minutes. Immediately before and after the test, the examinee's saliva was sampled and acceleration pulse waveform measurements were performed.

The saliva samples were obtained by having the examinee chew the cotton swab from a saliva collection test tube (Salivette®, made by Sarstedt AG & Co.) for three minutes with the back teeth on one side of the mouth. If necessary, the saliva was stored by freezing after collection. Since the saliva constituents have circadian rhythm, in cases where multiple measurements were made on the same examinee, the saliva samples were obtained on the same day of the week and at the same time. The test subjects were also asked to chew the cotton swab with the same teeth on each occasion. The measurement of acceleration pulse waveforms was performed by attaching an infrared acceleration pulse waveform meter to the index finger and taking readings under resting conditions. The same finger was used for all measurements. The examinees were required to rest for approximately 30 minutes before starting the task. The cortisol in saliva samples was measured using a method such as ELISA. Also, the salivary α-amylase was measured using a method such as the Caraway method. The results of the salivary cortisol and α-amylase measurements are shown in Figures 4(a) and (b). Here, the subscripts "Before" and "After" indicate the results of measurements made immediately before and after performing the task. The numbers shown above the bar graphs are the measurement results or the average of multiple measurements. The results of measuring the acceleration pulse waveforms were used to calculate the LF/HF ratios, and the change before and after the task is shown in Figure 4(c) in the same way as in Figures 4(a) and (b).

Salivary cortisol, salivary α-amylase and the LF/HF ratio each have different reaction times to stress. Salivary α-amylase increases (activates) within about 10 minutes of applying a stress stimulus, whereas salivary cortisol increases (activates) roughly 20–30 minutes after applying a stress stimulus. The LF/HF ratio increases instantaneously when stress is given. By using these differences in reaction time, it is possible to estimate the stress before, during and after the task from the saliva constituents and acceleration pulse waveforms measured before and after the task lasting approximately 25 minutes as shown in Figure 5. In this Figure, the results of salivary cortisol measurements made immediately before the task (COR_{Before}) represent the stress levels 20–30 minutes before the start of the task, the results of salivary α-amylase measurements made immediately before the task (AMY_{Before}) represent the stress levels up to 10 minutes before the start of the task, the results of acceleration pulse measurements made immediately before the task (LF/HF_{Before}) represent the stress levels immediately before the start of the task, the results of salivary cortisol measurements made at the end of the task (COR_{After}) represent the stress levels in the first half of the task (20–30 minutes before the end of the task), the results of salivary α-amylase measurements made at the end of the task (AMY_{After}) represent the stress levels in the second half of the task (up to 10 minutes before the end of the task), and the results of acceleration pulse measurements made at the end of the task (LF/HF_{After}) represent the stress levels at the end of the task. By exploiting the time lags to the stress responses of each factor in this way, it is possible to estimate the stress variation over a wide period of time by making just a few measurements.

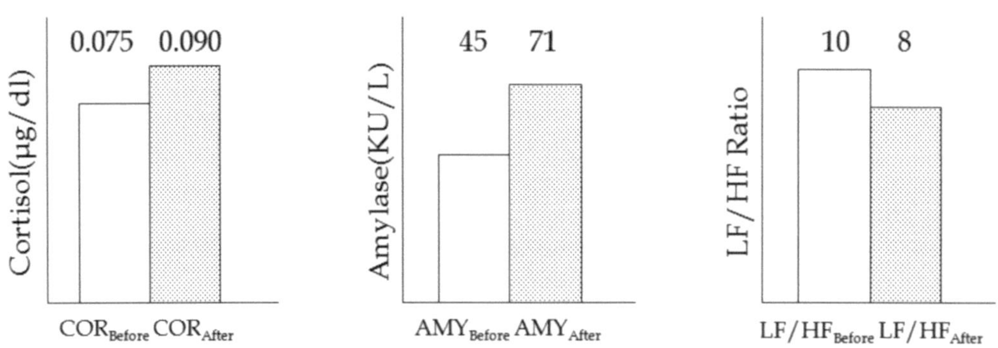

(a) Salivary cortisol levels (b) Salivary α-amylase activity levels (c) LF/HF ratios

Fig. 4. Examples of measurement results

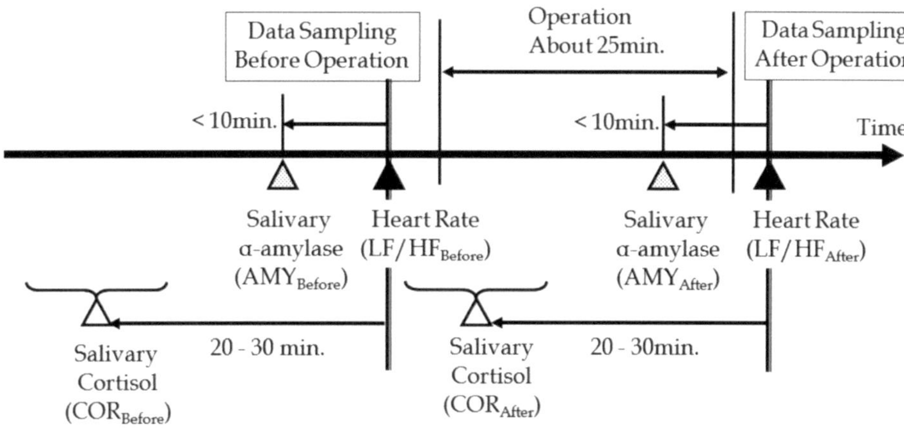

Fig. 5. Stress distribution obtained by exploiting the different stress response times of salivary constituents and acceleration pulse waveforms

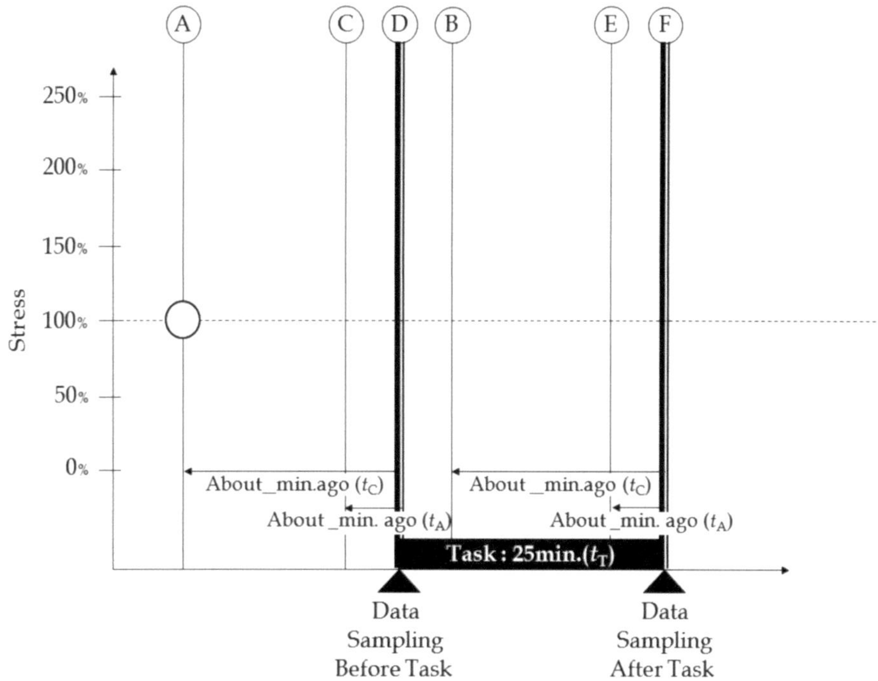

Fig. 6. Format of stress variation diagram

Next, from the results of measuring the salivary constituents and acceleration pulse waveforms, we will discuss a method for plotting a stress variation diagram depicting the temporal variation in stress. Figure 6 shows the format of a stress variation diagram. The vertical axis shows the variation of stress, with larger numbers representing higher levels of stress and smaller numbers representing lower levels of stress. Since this diagram is more concerned with changes in stress levels, the absolute values are of no great significance. The horizontal axis represents time. The task starts at point D and ends at point F. Saliva and acceleration pulse waveform data are acquired at points D and F. The stress quantities for COR_{Before}, COR_{After}, AMY_{Before}, AMY_{After}, LF/HF_{Before} and LF/HF_{After} are plotted along axes A, B, C, E, D and F respectively, and are connected by lines. Here, t_T is the task duration (25 minutes), t_C is the salivary cortisol reaction time, and t_A is the salivary α-amylase reaction time. The acceleration pulse waveform is assumed to respond instantaneously. The stress variation diagram is drawn by following the four steps shown below.

Step 1. Plot the salivary cortisol data

With regard to the salivary cortisol values measured before and after the task, COR_{Before} represents the stress state 20 to 30 minutes before the task (axis A), and COR_{After} represents the stress state 20 to 30 minutes before the end of the task (first half of the task) (axis B).

In this stress variation diagram, the COR_{Before} value is taken as a reference point (100%) as a basis for expressing subsequent stress values. First, the value of COR_{Before} is plotted at the 100% point 1 on axis A, and is denoted by γ_0 = 100%. Using Equation (1), the value of COR_{After} is converted to a percentage taking that value of COR_{Before} as 100%. This converted value γ is plotted at point 2 on axis B. A line is then drawn between points 1 and 2.

$$\gamma = \frac{COR_{After}}{COR_{Before}}\gamma_0 \tag{1}$$

Example: From Figure 4(a), the salivary cortisol value is 0.075 μg/dl before the operation and 0.090 μg/dl after the operation. From Equation (1), this corresponds to γ = 120% (a 20% increase), so the stress variation diagram starts out as shown in Figure 7.

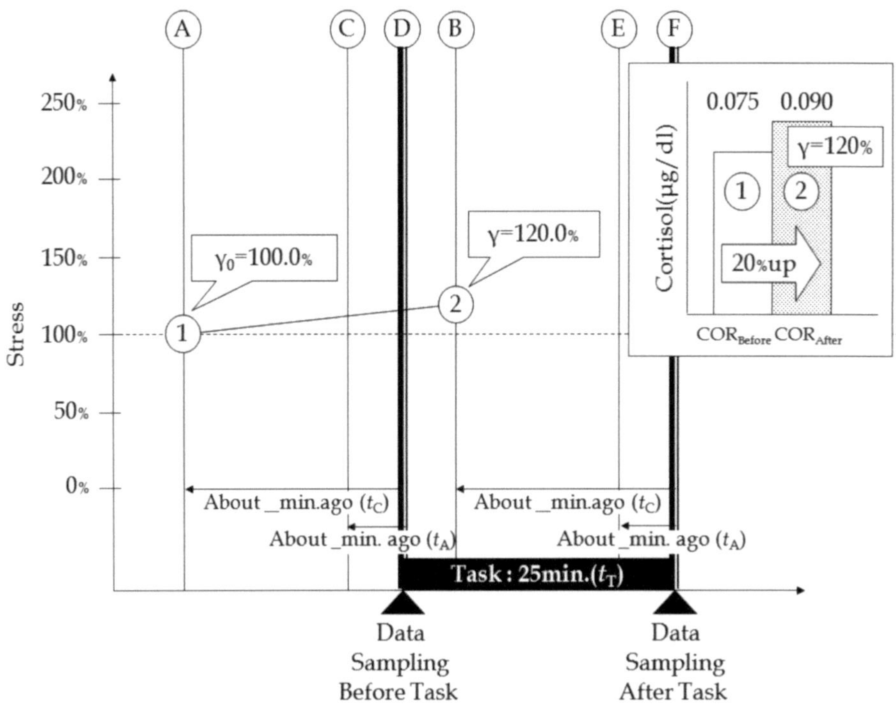

Fig. 7. Plotting the data from salivary cortisol measurements

Step 2. Plot the salivary α-amylase and LF/HF data obtained before surgery
Before the task, the examinees were assumed to be in a relaxed state with a small stress amplitude, so the point where the line drawn in step 1 intersects with axis C is assumed to correspond to AMY_{Before} and is called intersection point 3. Similarly, the point where the line drawn in step 1 intersects with axis D is assumed to correspond to LF/HF_{Before} and is called intersection point 4. In this way, intersection points 3 and 4 are points that are automatically determined from the salivary cortisol data of step 1 and the positions of axes C and D. Therefore, the value a_0 at intersection point 3 is given by Equation (2), and the value β_0 at intersection point 4 is given by Equation (3).

$$a_0 = \gamma_{Before} + \frac{t_C - t_A}{t_T}(\gamma - \gamma_0) \tag{2}$$

$$\beta_0 = \gamma_{Before} + \frac{t_C}{t_T}(\gamma - \gamma_0) \tag{3}$$

Here, the values of a_0 and β_0 are liable to be affected by the stress state before the task, so it is important that a relaxed state is maintained before the task.

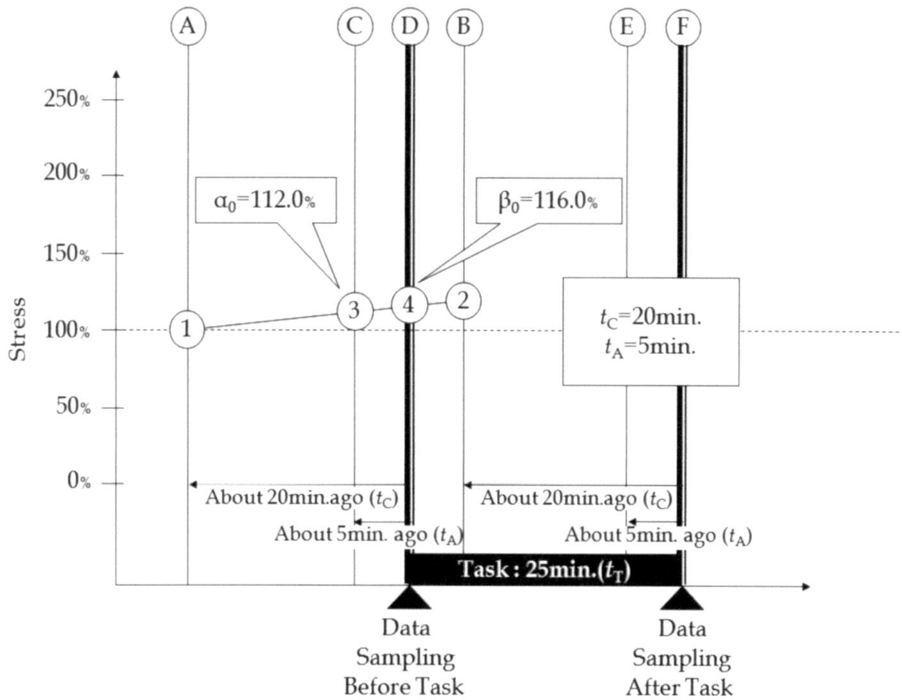

Fig. 8. Plotting the α-amylase and LF/HF data before surgery

Example: When the pre-surgery salivary α-amylase data AMY_{Before} and the pre-surgery LF/HF data LF/HF_{Before} are plotted, the stress variation diagram appears as shown in Figure 8. Here, γ_0 = 100%, γ = 120%, t_T (task duration) = 25 minutes, t_C (salivary cortisol reaction time) = 20 minutes, t_A (salivary α-amylase reaction time) = 5 minutes. Based on these values, the value a_{Before} at intersection point 3 from Equation (2) is 112.0%, and the value β_{Before} at intersection point 4 from Equation (3) is 116.0%.

Step 3. Plot the salivary α-amylase data obtained after surgery

The salivary α-amylase data AMY_{After} obtained after surgery represents the stress at point E within 10 minutes before the end of the task. This stress represents a stress quantity relative to the salivary α-amylase data AMY_{Before} obtained before surgery, so we can use Equation (4) to convert this into an increase or decrease a with respect to the base point 1. This value a is entered on axis E as intersection point 5. A line is drawn between intersection points 2 and 5.

$$a = \frac{AMY_{After}}{AMY_{Before}} a_0 \tag{4}$$

Example: From Figure 4(b), the pre- and post-surgery salivary α-amylase data AMY_{Before} and AMY_{After} have values of 45 and 71 KU/L respectively, and the value of a_0 is 112.0%. Thus from Equation (4), the value of a is 177.0%, and the resulting stress variation diagram is as shown in Figure 9.

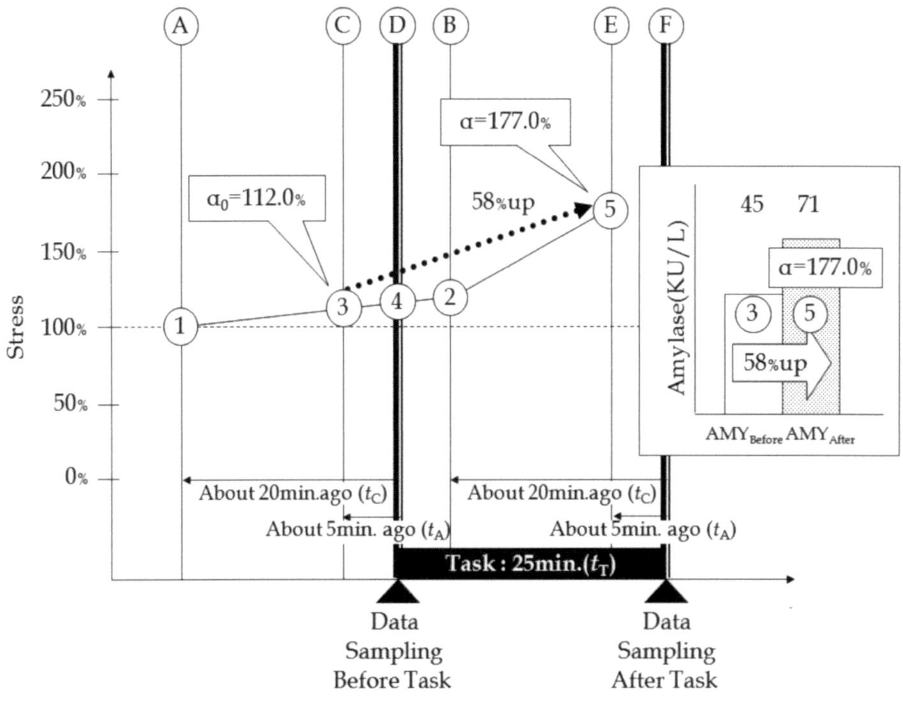

Fig. 9. Plotting the salivary α-amylase after surgery

Step 4. Plot the LF/HF data after surgery

The post-surgery LF/HF data LF/HF_{After} represents the stress level at the end of the task (point F).

This stress level represents an amount of stress relative to the pre-surgery LF/HF data LF/HF_{Before}, so Equation (5) is used to transform LF/HF_{After} into an increase or decrease β relative to the base point 1. This value β is entered on axis F as intersection point 6. A line is drawn between intersection points 5 and 6.

$$\beta = \frac{LF/HF_{After}}{LF/HF_{Before}}\beta_0 \quad (5)$$

Example: From Figure 4(c), the pre-surgery LF/HF data LF/HF_{Before} has a value of 10, the post-surgery acceleration pulse waveform data LF/HF_{After} has a value of 8, and the value of β_0 is 116.0%. Thus according to Equation (5), β is equal to 92.8%, and the stress variation diagram appears as shown in Figure 10.

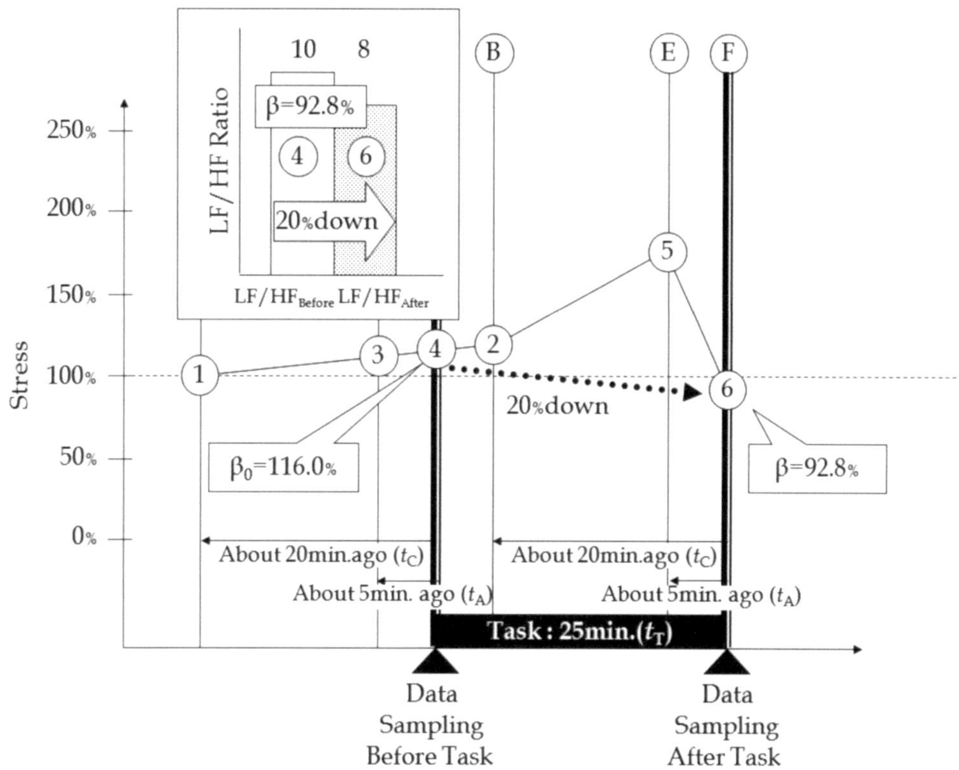

Fig. 10. Plotting the LF/HF data after surgery

By following the above procedure of steps 1 through 4, it is possible to draw a stress variation diagram.

The axes A, C and D in the stress variation diagram represent the stress values before the start of the task, axes D, B and E represent the intermediate stress levels after the start of the task, and axes E and F represent the stress levels in the second half of the task.

In the example shown in Figure 10, there is a gentle increase in stress before the start of the task, and a clear increase in stress from the beginning through to the middle of the task, but this stress is eliminated in the second half of the task.

5. A practical example of psychological stress evaluation

In this section, to illustrate how the stress variation diagrams described in section 4 can be used in practice, we show how this technique can be used in the evaluation of a laparoscopic robot. In this example, surgeons performed in-vitro laparoscopic cholecystectomy simulations using pig livers (which have an anatomically similar structure to that of human organs). These operations were performed with a laparoscope operated by a laparoscope robot, and with a laparoscope operated by a human assistant. By analyzing the surgeons' LF/HF ratio and salivary cortisol and α-amylase levels before and after each surgery, we conducted a multilateral and objective evaluation of their biological stress responses.

5.1 Laparoscope robot

For the laparoscope robot, we used the automatic laparoscope positioning system proposed by Nishikawa et al. (Nishikawa et al., 2006), which includes the ability to plan the workspace before the operation begins. This laparoscope robot is a fully autonomous system that uses a robot to hold and automatically position the laparoscope instead of a human camera assistant. The position of the laparoscope and the image zoom factor to be used during surgery are set up just before the surgery by preoperative planning whereby the surgeon selects several working area at the operation site, while at the same time determining the best image zoom factor (i.e., the distance from the working area to the laparoscope tip) for working at this position, and stores this information on a PC. Once the operation has started, the robot tracks the surgical instrument in three dimensions so that the tip of the surgical instrument remains in the center of the laparoscope image. When the tip of the surgical instrument has been positioned at the working area determined during preoperative planning, the zoom factor of the laparoscope image is automatically adjusted according to the preoperative planning. Figure 11 shows the hardware configuration of the laparoscope robot, and Figure 12 shows the control flow. The laparoscope robot consists of a manipulator, an optical three-dimensional position-measuring device (Polaris Accedo®, made by NDI Corporation), a control PC (Linux-based), a scan converter and a television monitor. The manipulator has a parallel link mechanism that uses three motors to perform positioning with three degrees of freedom. When the field of view moves to the left or right and up or down, the longitudinal position of the laparoscope camera can be adjusted to enlarge or reduce the field of view.

Fig. 11. Hardware configuration of laparoscope robot

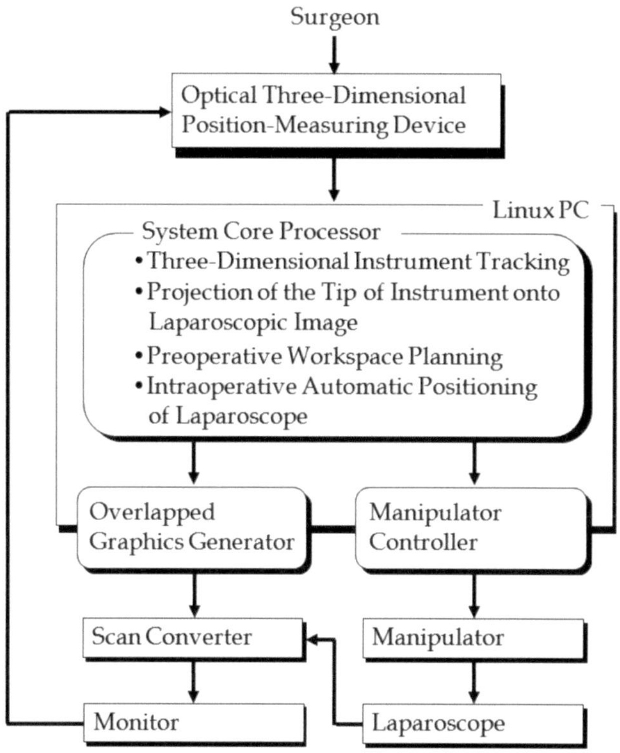

Fig. 12. Control flow of laparoscope robot

5.2 In-vitro tests

Surgeons were asked to perform in-vitro laparoscopic cholecystectomy simulations on pig livers, using either a human camera assistant or a laparoscope robot to operate the laparoscope. Before and after each operation, the surgeon's saliva was sampled and the acceleration pulse waveform was measured. The salivary cortisol and salivary α-amylase constituents of the saliva were measured. The salivary cortisol was measured by the ELISA method using reagents made by Salimetrics, and the salivary α-amylase was measured by the Caraway method using reagents made by Wako Pure Chemical Industries Ltd. The acceleration pulse waveform was measured using an Artett C acceleration pulse waveform meter made by U - Medica Inc.

For the in-vitro laparoscopic cholecystectomy simulations performed using pig livers, a fresh pig liver was placed inside a test box to represent the abdomen, and the surgeon performed a mock cholecystectomy (Figure 13). This operation is performed by the following procedure: (1) move the field of view to Calot's triangle, (2) expose and cut the cystic duct, (3) detach the gallbladder from the liver (Figure 14).

The examinees were two right-handed clinicians with extensive experience in laparoscopic cholecystectomy simulations (examinees A and B). The examinees had no previous experience in the use of laparoscope robots. In total, they performed the operation 14 times over a period of four days. The surgeon and laparoscope operator in each operation were as follows:

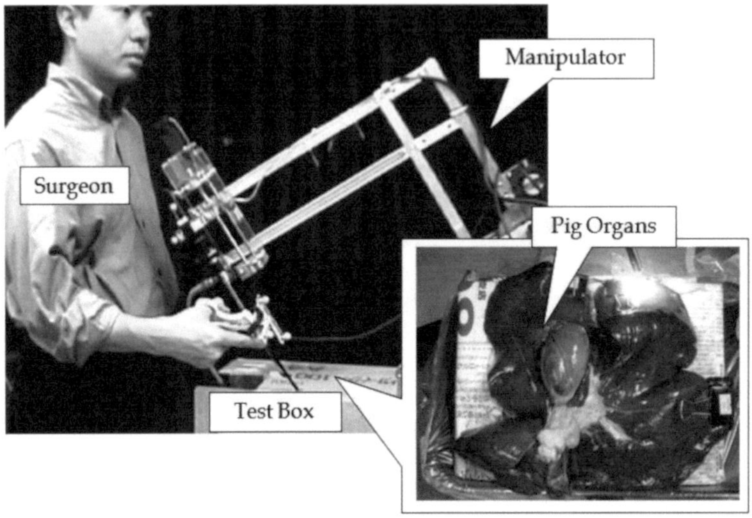

Fig. 13. Set-up of tests conducted with a laparoscope robot

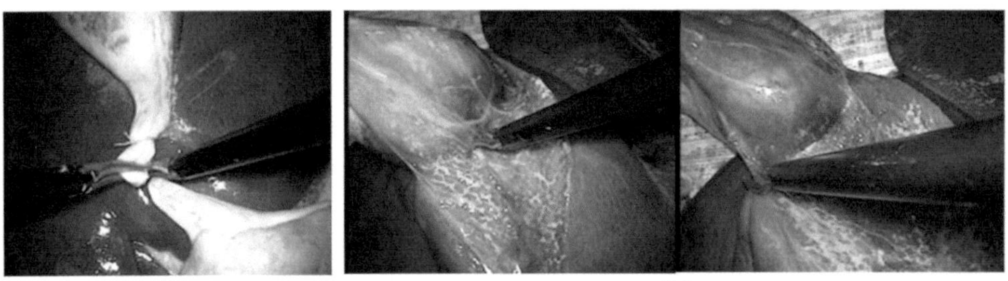

Fig. 14. Laparoscope view. (a) Moving the field of view to Calot's triangle and exposing/cutting the cystic duct. (b) Detaching the gallbladder from the liver

Day 1

(1) Surgeon: examinee A, laparoscope operator: laparoscope robot
(2) Surgeon: examinee A, laparoscope operator: examinee B
(3) Surgeon: examinee B, laparoscope operator: laparoscope robot
(4) Surgeon: examinee B, laparoscope operator: examinee A

In operations (1) and (3), we sampled the surgeon's saliva before and after the operation, and in operations (2) and (4) we sampled the saliva of both the surgeon and camera assistant. Acceleration pulse waveform measurements were not performed in operation (1).

Day 2

(5) Surgeon: examinee A, laparoscope operator: examinee B
(6) Surgeon: examinee B, laparoscope operator: laparoscope robot
(7) Surgeon: examinee B, laparoscope operator: examinee A
(8) Surgeon: examinee A, laparoscope operator: laparoscope robot

In each operation, saliva samples and acceleration pulse waveform measurements were taken from the surgeon.

Day 3

(9) Surgeon: examinee B, laparoscope operator: examinee A
(10) Surgeon: examinee A, laparoscope operator: laparoscope robot
(11) Surgeon: examinee A, laparoscope operator: examinee B
(12) Surgeon: examinee B, laparoscope operator: laparoscope robot
In operations (9) and (11) we obtained saliva samples and acceleration pulse waveform measurements from the camera assistant, and in operations (10) and (9) we obtained saliva samples and acceleration pulse waveform measurements from the surgeon.

Day 4

(13) Surgeon: examinee B, laparoscope operator: examinee A
(14) Surgeon: examinee A, laparoscope operator: examinee B
In the operations performed on day 4, we obtained saliva samples and acceleration pulse waveform measurements from the surgeon.

The above test schedule was planned to take into consideration the circadian rhythm in the substances used to evaluate psychological stress. By scheduling operations (1), (5) and (9) at the same time of day, it was possible to acquire data at the same time of day for examinee A performing the operation with a laparoscope robot and with a human camera assistant, so when making a comparative study of the data from each operation, there was no need to take into consideration the effects of circadian rhythm in the substances used to evaluate psychological stress. Similarly, operations (3), (7) and (11) were performed at the same time of day by examinee B, operations (2), (6), (10) and (13) were performed at the same time of day by both examinees, and operations (4), (8), (12) and (14) were performed at the same time of day by both examinees so that data could be collected in the same way.

The results of salivary cortisol measurements on examinees A and B before and after surgery are shown in Figures 15 and 18, and the results of salivary α-amylase measurements are shown in Figures 16 and 19. Since the results of measurements of salivary constituents were obtained by taking circadian rhythm of stress evaluation substances into consideration, the data was all processed together. Figures 17 and 20 show the results of LF/HF measurements from examinees A and B before and after the operations. Note that Figures 15 through 20 only show the data for the surgeon. The duration of the operations performed by examinees A and B are shown in Table 1 as supplementary material.

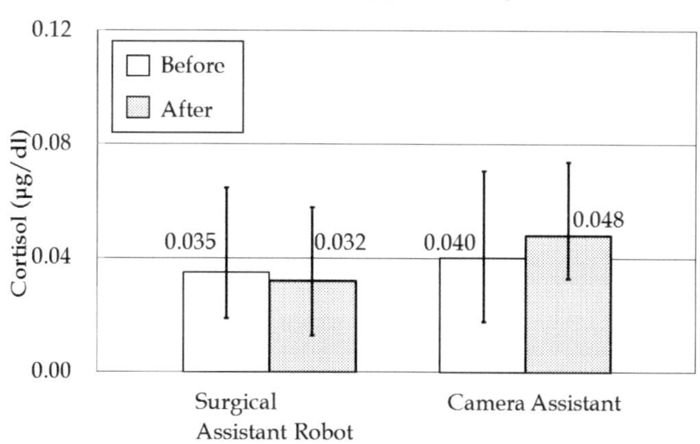

Fig. 15. Salivary cortisol levels (Examinee A)

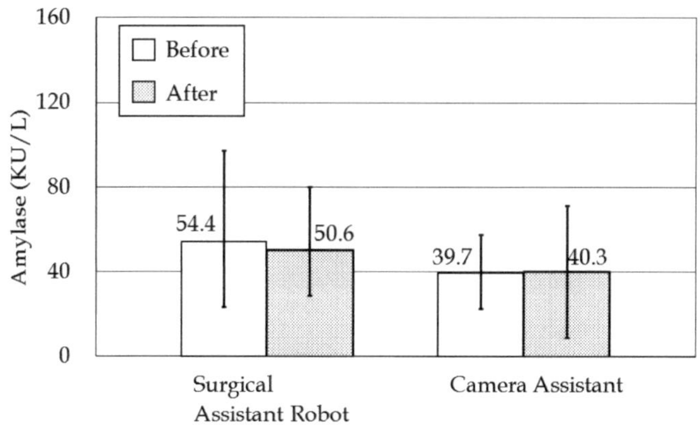

Fig.16. Salivary α-amylase activity levels (Examinee A)

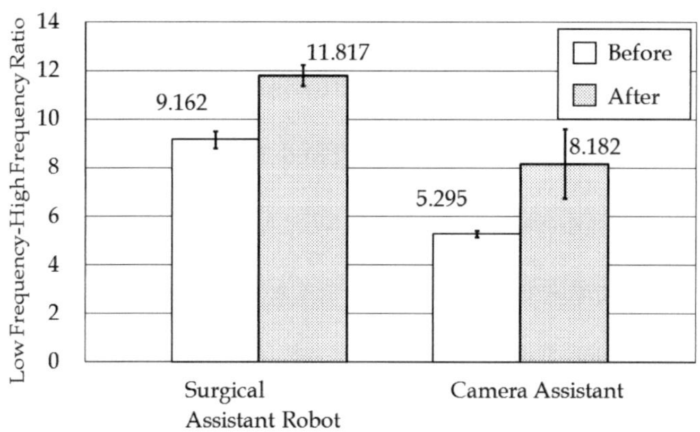

Fig. 17. LF/HF ratios (Examinee A)

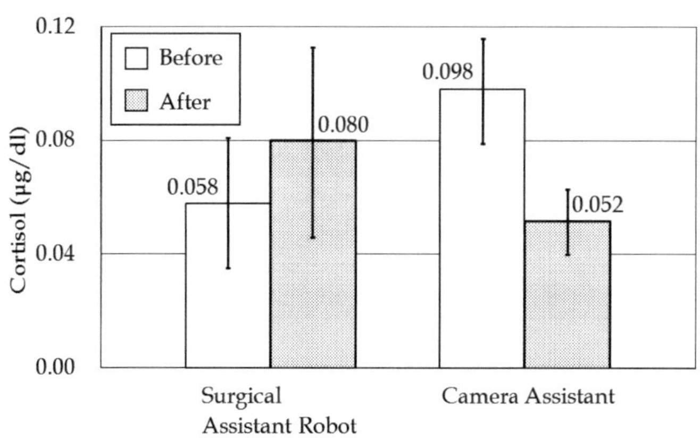

Fig. 18. Salivary cortisol levels (Examinee B)

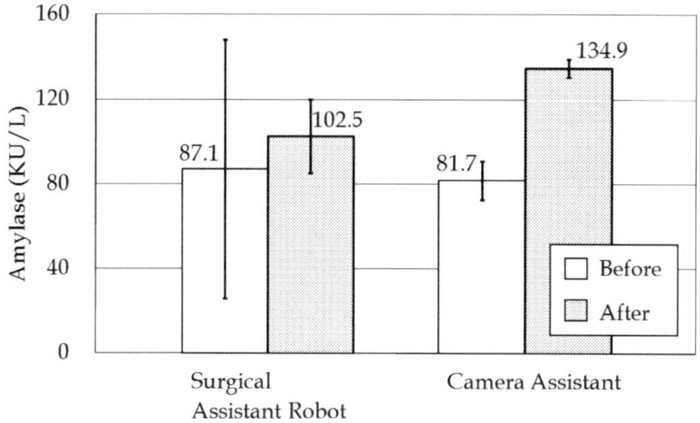

Fig. 19. Salivary α-amylase activity levels (Examinee B)

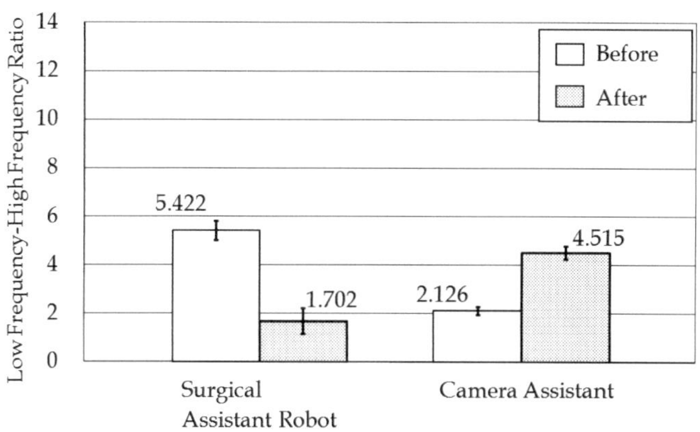

Fig. 20. LF/HF ratios (Examinee B)

		With Surgical Assistant System		With Camera Assistant	
Examinee A	Ave.	28′	13″	25′	47″
	S.D.	6′	20″	7′	5″
	Max.	34′	37″	36′	13″
	Min.	21′	57″	21′	5″
Examinee B	Ave.	20′	48″	24′	5″
	S.D.	3′	35″	7′	20″
	Max.	24′	53″	34′	25″
	Min.	18′	6″	17′	0″

Table 1. Operating times

We plotted stress variation diagrams based on the results of measuring saliva constituents and acceleration pulse waveforms shown in Figures 15 through 20 (Figures 21 and 22). Here, the task duration t_T was set to 25 minutes, the salivary cortisol reaction time was set to 20

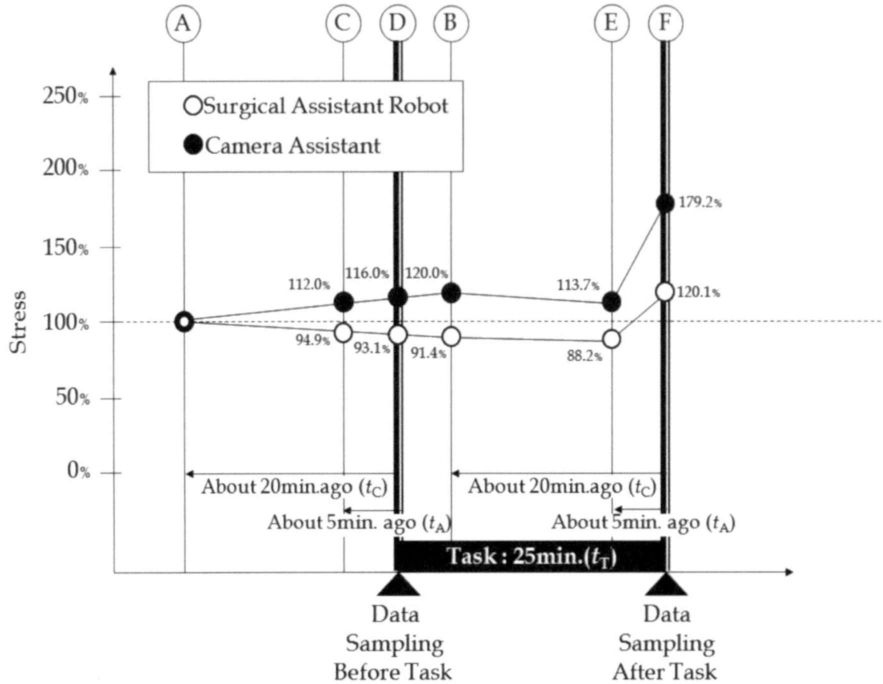

Fig. 21. Stress variation diagram for examinee A

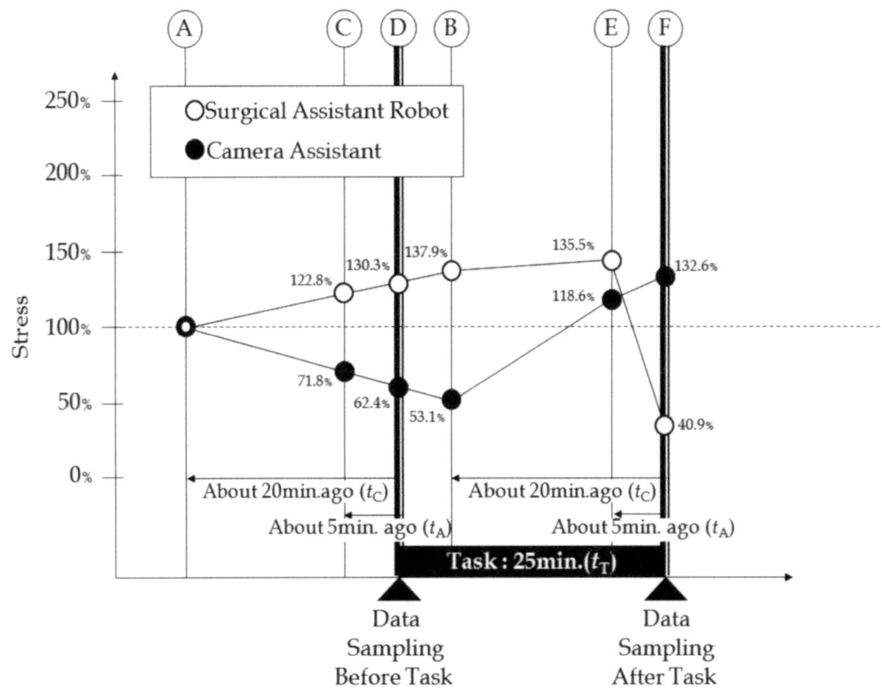

Fig. 22. Stress variation diagram for examinee B

minutes, and the salivary α-amylase reaction time t_A was set to 5 minutes. The task duration t_T can be taken as the average duration for each task as shown in Table 1. Figure 21 shows the stress variation diagrams for examinee A. This Figure shows the stress variation measured when using the laparoscope robot and when using a human camera assistant to operate the laparoscope. Figure 22 shows the corresponding results for examinee B. The line graphs shown in these Figures allow the comparative evaluation to be made between surgery with a laparoscope robot and surgery with a human camera assistant.

First of all we will consider the results for examinee A (Figure 21). Examinee A was not stressed before the operation or during the middle stages of the operation, but became stressed at the end of the operation. Examinee A was also slightly more stressed when performing the operation with a camera assistant than when performing the operation with a robot. The same can also be said of the raw data shown in Figures 15 through 17. From the salivary cortisol and salivary α-amylase results for examinee A (Figures 15 and 16), examinee A had no pronounced stress reaction in either operation. Next, from the LF/HF results (Figure 17), examinee A had a greater predominance of sympathetic nerve activity in the second half of the operation than in the first half, and tended to be slightly more stressed.

Next we will consider the results for examinee B. As Figure 22 shows, examinee B felt stressed before the operation and during the first half of the operation when using the laparoscope robot, but this stress reduced during the second half of the operation. On the other hand, when performing the operation with a human camera assistant, examinee B was not stressed before the operation, but the stress level increased as the operation began and there was no reduction of stress during the operation. Looking at the data of Figures 18 through 20 separately, in the salivary cortisol results for examinee B (Figure 18), a stress reaction occurred before the operation when using the laparoscope robot. Also, from the salivary α-amylase results (Figure 19), there was a slight stress reaction during all the operations, and the largest stress reactions were observed in operations where the laparoscope was operated by a camera assistant. When using the laparoscope robot, according to the LF/HF results (Figure 20), the sympathetic nerves are predominant around the start of the operation and suppressed at the end of the operation. On the other hand, when performing surgery using a camera assistant, the sympathetic nerves are more predominant at the end of the surgery. In other words, examinee B tended to be more stressed (tense or agitated) at the end of the operation than at the start of the operation when using a camera assistant, but tended to be more stressed at the start of the operation when using a laparoscope robot.

From the operation times shown in supplementary table 1, the style of operation was found to cause no difference in operation times, and we found it impossible to evaluate stress in terms of how long the operation took to perform.

Thus by analyzing saliva constituents and acceleration pulse waveforms, we were able to objectively evaluate the stress experienced by surgeons when performing laparoscopic surgery with a laparoscope operated by a human camera assistant and with a laparoscope operated by a laparoscope robot.

6. Conclusion

We have described a method for objectively evaluating the psychological stress experienced by people performing a task with a robot for about 25 minutes by analyzing their saliva constituents and acceleration pulse waveforms before and after the task. In particular, in this study we investigated an example where highly skilled examinees (surgeons) engaged in high-level interaction with a functionally enhanced robot (laparoscope robot) to perform a particular task (laparoscopic surgery) in a particular environment (operating theatre). A laparoscope robot is a good example of where humans and robots can interact successfully. Methods for objectively evaluating the psychological stress of humans due to interactions with robots will become increasingly important as robots become more commonplace in society. Further research will be needed to investigate stress evaluation methods that are simpler, less invasive and cheaper to implement. In the future, we plan to investigate a method for using the human herpes virus (HHV6) to evaluate long-term and chronic fatigue in surgeons, and to study an integrated stress evaluation method that combines subjective and objective stress evaluation methods.

7. Acknowledgements

This research was supported in part by "Special Coordination Funds for Promoting Science and Technology: *Yuragi* Project" of the Ministry of Education, Culture, Sports, Science and Technology, Japan, Grant-in-Aid for Scientific Research (A) (No. 19206047) of the Japan Society for the Promotion of Science.

8. References

Norman, D. (2007). *The design of future things*, Basic Books, ISBN 978-0-465-00228-3, New York.

Jaspers, J. E. N.; Breedveld, P.; Herder, J. L & Grimbergen, C. A. (2004). Camera and instrument holders and their clinical value in minimally invasive surgery. *Surg Laparosc Endosc Percutan Tech*, Vol.14, No. 3, 145–152

Kobayashi, E.; Masamune, K.; Sakuma, I.; Dohi, T. & Hashimoto, D. (1999). A New Safe Laparoscopic Manipulator System with a Five-Bar Linkage Mechanism and an Optical Zoom. *Computer Aided Surgery*, Vol.4, 182-192.

Tanoue, K.; Yasunaga, T.; Kobayashi, E.; Miyamoto, S.; Sakuma, I.; Dohi, T.; Konishi, K.; Yamaguchi, S.; Kinjo, N.; Takenaka, K.; Maehara Y. & Hashizume, M. (2006). Laparoscopic cholecystectomy using a newly developed laparoscope manipulator for 10 patients with cholelithiasis, *Surgical Endoscopy*, Vol.20, No.5, 753-756, ISSN 0930-2794 (Print) 1432-2218 (Online).

Sackier, J. M. & Wang, Y. (1994). Robotically assisted laparoscopic surgery form concept to development. *Surgical Endoscopy*, Vol.8, No.1, 63-66, ISSN 0930-2794 (Print) 1432-2218 (Online).

Wang, Y.-F.; Uecker, D. R. & Wang, Y. (1996). Choreographed Scope Maneuvering in Robotically-Assisted Laparoscopy with Active Vision Guidance, Proceedings of IEEE Workshop on Applications of Computer Vision, pp. 187-192, 0-8186-7620-5, Sarasota, FL, December, 1996

Finlay, P. A. (2001). A Robotic Camera Holder for Laparoscopy. Proceedings and Overviews of ICAR2001 Workshop 2 on Medical Robotics, in the 10th International Conference on Advanced Robotics, pp.129-132. Aug. 2001, Budapest, Hungary

Sekimoto, M.; Nishikawa, A.; Taniguchi, K.; Takiguchi, S.; Miyazaki, F.; Doki, Y. & Mori, M. (2009). Development of a Compact Laparoscope Manipulator (P-arm). *Surgical Endoscopy*, ISSN 0930-2794 (Print) 1432-2218 (Online)

Nishikawa, A; Nakagoe, H.; Taniguchi, K.; Yamada, Y.; Sekimoto, M.; Takiguchi, S.; Monden, M. & Miyazaki, F. (2008). How Does the Camera Assistant Decide the Zooming Ratio of Laparoscopic Images? – Analysis and Implementation, *Proceedings of the 11th International Conference on Medical Image Computing and Computer Assisted Intervention (MICCAI 2008)*. New York, USA, Sep.2008.

Nishikawa, A.; Ito, K.; Nakagoe, H.; Taniguchi, K.; Sekimoto, M.; Takiguchi, S.; Seki, Y.; Yasui, M.; Okada, K.; Monden, M. & Miyazaki, F. Automatic Positioning of a Laparoscope by Preoperative Workspace Planning and Intraoperative 3D Instrument Tracking, *in MICCAI2006 Workshop proceedings*, Workshop on Medical Robotics: Systems and Technology towards Open Architecture, 2006, 82-91.

Selye, H. (1936). A syndrome produced by diverse nocuous agents, Nature, Vol.138, No. 4, Jul. 1936, 32-33.

Selye, H. (1974). *Stress Without Distress*, Lippincott Williams & Wilkins, ISBN 978 - 0397010264.

Frankenhaeuser, M.; Lundberg, U.; Rauste von Wright, M.; von Wright J. & Sedvall, G. (1986). Urinary monoamine metabolites as indices of mental stress in healthy males and females. Pharmacol Biochem Behav, Vol.24, No.6. 1521-1525.

Esler, M.; Jennings, G.; Korner, P.; Blombery, P.; Sacharias, N. & Leonard, P. (1984). Measurement of total and organ-specific noreponephrine kinetics in humans, Am J Physiol, Vol.247, E21-E28.

Nater, U. M.; Marcaa, R. L.; Florina, L.; Mosesb, A.; Langhansb, W.; Kollerc, M. M. & Ehlert, U. (2006). Stress-induced changes in human salivary alpha-amylase activity – associations with adrenergic activity. Psychoneuroendocrinology, Vol.31, No.1, 49–58.

Nater, U. M.; Rohleder, N.; Schlotz, W.; Ehlert, U. & Kirschbaum, C. (2007). Determinants of the diurnal course of salivary alpha-amylase. Psychoneuroendocrinology, Vol.32, No.4, 392-401.

Winkler, H. & Fischer-Colibrie, R. (1992). The chromogranins A and B: the first 25 years and future perspectives. Neuroscience, Vol.49, No.3 , 497-528.

Saruta, J.; Tsukinoki, K.; Sasaguri, K.; Ishii, H.; Yasuda, M.; Osamura, Y. R.; Watanabe, Y. & Sato, S. (2005). Expression and localization of chromogranin A gene and protein in human submandibular gland. Cells Tissues Organs, Vol.180, No.4, 237-244.

Kanamaru, Y.; Kikukawa, A. & Shimamura, K. (2006). Salivary chromogranin-A as a marker of psychological stress during a cognitive test battery in humans. Stress, Vol.9, No.3, 127-131.

Levine, S. (1993). The psychoendocrinology of stress. Ann N Y Acad Sci, Vol.697, 61-69.

Nozaki, S.; Tanaka, M.; Mizuno, K.; Ataka, S.; Mizuma, H.; Tahara, T.; Sugino, T.; Shirai, T.; Eguchi, A.; Okuyama, K.; Yoshida, K.; Kajimoto, Y.; Kuratsune, H.; Kajimoto, O. & Watanabe, Y. (2009). Mental and physical fatigue-related biochemical alterations. Nutrition, Vol.25, No.1, 51-57.

Akselrod, S.; Gordon, D.; Madwed, J. B.; Snidman, N. C.; Shannon, D. C. & Cohen, R. J. (1985). Hemodynamic regulation: investigation by spectral analysis. Am J Physiol, Vol. 249, H867-875.

Nukui, K.; Matsuoka, Y.; Yamagishi, T.; Sato, K.; Sugino, T. & Kajimoto, O. (2008). Effect of tablet containing Aqua Q10® P40 on physical fatigue in healthy volunteers. Jpn Pharmacol Ther, Vol.36, No.2, 141-152.

10

Quantitative Analysis of Leg Movement and EMG signal in Expert Japanese Traditional Dancer

Woong Choi[1], Tadao Isaka[2], Hiroyuki Sekiguchi[1] and Kozaburo Hachimura[3]
[1]Kinugasa Research Organization, Ritsumeikan University
[2]College of Science and Engineering, Ritsumeikan University
[3]College of Information Science and Engineering, Ritsumeikan University
Japan

1. Introduction

Recently, dance movement has been frequently studied using motion capture, but some movements are unable to be analysed by motion data alone. Systematic research of dance movements using several kinds of data captured by simultaneous measurement of body motion and biophysical information are rarely carried out.

In the research literature there are several studies using the analyses of movement through simultaneous measurement of body motion and biophysical information, for instance, the learning environment for sport-form training (Urawaki, 2005), biomechanical analysis of ballet dancers (Humm et al, 1994), and behaviour capture systems (Kurihara et al, 2002), etc. Although there is one study that extracts a target motion from motion captured dance data (Yoshimura et al, 2001), and another where skillfulness of a dancer is investigated by calculating a typical style of the dancing called *Okuri* (Yoshimura et al, 2004), quantitative analysis on an expert traditional dancer has not been accomplished yet.

We paid attention to leg movements of the lower half of the body. Leg movements of a dancer generate a path of motion, a tempo, and a dance rhythm. In particular, leg movements in Japanese traditional dance allow dancers to express various performances, shift performances, and transfer and retain body weight (Kunieda, 2003).

In the following research, we aim to quantitatively analyse characteristics of leg movement patterns of an expert traditional dancer using simultaneous measurement of body motion and biophysical information (EMG: ElectroMyoGram).

2. Method of experiment

We carried out experiments on the leg movements of expert Japanese traditional dancers with simultaneous measurement of body motion and EMG (Choi, 2007).

2.1 Subject

The subjects who participated in this experiment are two *Hanayagi* style dancers; one has forty years experience (Expert *D*) and the other has twenty years experience (Skilled *S*).

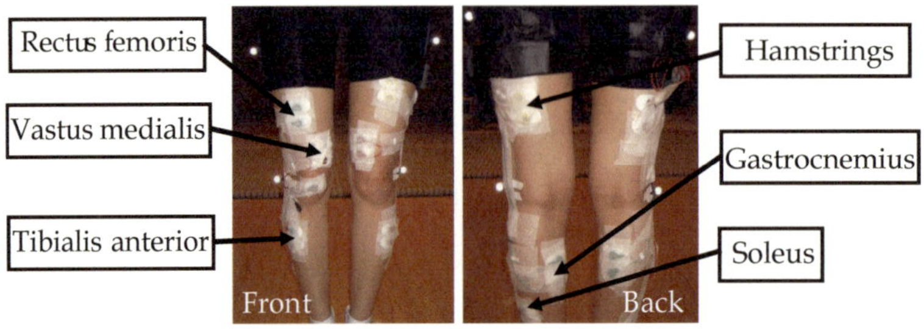

Fig. 1. Attaching place of EMG electrodes.

Performance	Role of subject
Performance 1	Guest
Performance 2	Woman expert entertainer
Performance 3	Man entertainer
Performance 4	Warrior
Performance 5	Coachman
Performance 6	Carpenter
Performance 7	Novice entertainer
Performance 8	Narrator

Table 1. Experiment performances in *Hokushu*.

2.2 Performance

We measured the traditional Japanese dance named *Hokushu* using the constructed system. In *Hokushu*, one dancer plays several roles such as a warrior, a guest, a coachman, a merchant, etc., and acts a total of twenty one performances by oneself. In this research, we measured eight performances from among the twenty-one (see Table 1).

2.3 Simultaneous measurement of body motion and EMG

In this research, 32 markers were attached on the body of a subject in order to capture motion data, and 12 EMG electrodes on the front and back of both legs.

Recording EMG signals needs electrodes, an amplifier and a data recording device. Each EMG signal is obtained by A/D converting data amplified by the amplifier. In this research, we used the SYNA ACT MT11 system (NEC Corp.). The amplitude of an EMG signal is almost proportional to the scale of muscle force. This relationship between EMG signal and muscle force can therefore be used to analyse various human body movements. Because the raw EMG signal obtained by the equipment is corrupted by high frequency noise, we have to employ some noise reduction techniques like low pass filtering. Also, we have to convert the raw signal into a signal that is proportional to the activities of the muscles. Rectification of the signal, or the RMS (Root Mean Square) of the signal is usually used for the analysis.

As per the literature on EMG (Choi, (2007)), the attaching place of EMG electrodes is fixed on the following six muscles (see Fig 1): Rectus Femoris (RF), Vastus medialis (VM), Tibialis Anterior (TA), Hamstrings (HA), Gastrocnemius (GAS) and Soleus (SOL). As shown in Table 2, these muscles have functions associated with leg movement. The SOL, VM, and TA muscles are mono-articular muscles. HA, RF, and GAS muscles are bi-articular muscles.

Muscle	Function
Rectus Femoris (RF)	Extension of knee and flexion of hip
Vastus medialis (VM)	Extension of knee
Tibialis Anterior (TA)	Dorsal flexion of ankle
Hamstrings (HA)	Flexion of knee and extension of hip
Gastrocnemius (GAS)	Plantar flexion of ankle and flexion of knee
Soleus (SOL)	Plantar flexion of ankle

Table 2. Function of muscle (Perotto, (1994)).

To obtain 3D motion data, the Eagle-Hawk system (Motion Analysis Corp.) at Ritsumeikan University was used. This system incorporates 12 infrared cameras detecting small markers attached to a subject who moves in a 4m × 4m area.
We captured data by adjusting the sampling rate of motion capture to 60Hz, and EMG measurement to 1200Hz, and recorded eight performances a total of three times using the simultaneous measurement system.

3. Result and discussion of experiment

In this research, we compared the leg movements of an Expert *D* with that of a Skilled subject *S* by calculating the center of gravity of the subject's body and a co-contraction of the knee and the ankle using a biomechanical method (Winter, 1990).
In the following, we will describe the result of our experiment on a part of Performance 1 of *Hokushu* under the condition of a single support phase.

3.1 Center of gravity

Firstly, we compared the center of gravity of the two subjects under the condition of a single support phase of both legs in Performance 1.

3.1.1 Computation of center of gravity

The center of gravity can be used to indicate transfer and retainment of leg movement. The center of gravity (x_0, y_0, z_0) of Fig. 2 can be calculated by Eq. (1) (Winter, 1990).

$$x_0 = \frac{m_1 x_1 + m_2 x_2 + \cdots + m_n x_n}{M}$$
$$y_0 = \frac{m_1 y_1 + m_2 y_2 + \cdots + m_n y_n}{M} \qquad (1)$$
$$z_0 = \frac{m_1 z_1 + m_2 z_2 + \cdots + m_n z_n}{M}$$

The co-ordinates $(x_1, y_1, z_1) \cdots (x_n, y_n, z_n)$ are the locations of center of gravity in each body segment. These locations in each body segment can be calculated by using anthropometric data (segment weight and segment length) as presented by Matsui (Matsui, (1958)). Fig. 2 (b)

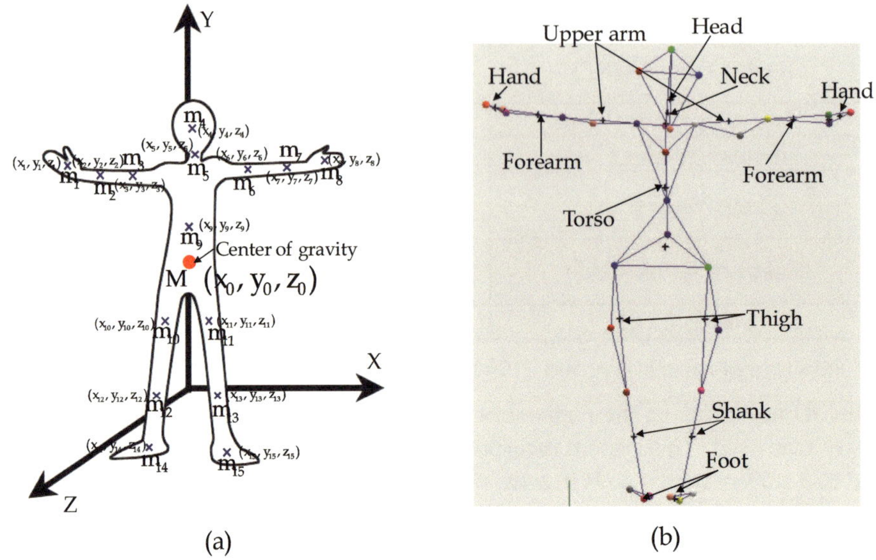

Fig. 2. Center of gravity. (a) Center of gravity in human body. (b) Center of gravity in each segment.

Segment	Segment weight/ Total body weight	Center of gravity/ Segment length
Head	0.037M	0.63
Neck	0.026M	0.50
Torso	0.487M	0.52
Upper arm	0.0255M	0.46
Forearm	0.013M	0.42
Hand	0.006M	0.50
Thigh	0.1115M	0.42
Shank	0.0535M	0.42
Foot	0.015M	0.50

Table 3. Anthropometric data (Matsui, (1958)).

shows the result of our computation for the location of center of gravity in each body segment for subject. The M is a total body weight. M is equal to $m_1 + m_2 + \cdots + m_n$. The values $(m_1, \cdots, m_n)$ are the segment weight in each body segment. In this experiment, we use the anthropometric data of Japanese woman (see Table 3).

3.1.2 Center of gravity on Performance 1

Fig. 3 shows the center of gravity data obtained during Performance 1 of Expert *D* and Skilled *S*.

Fig. 3 (a) and (c) show leg movement under a condition of a single support phase of the right leg during Performance 1. Subjects maintain their body weight with the right leg, while the left leg is swinging. Fig. 3 (b) and (d) show leg movement under a condition of a single support phase of the left leg. Subjects retain their body weight with the left leg, while

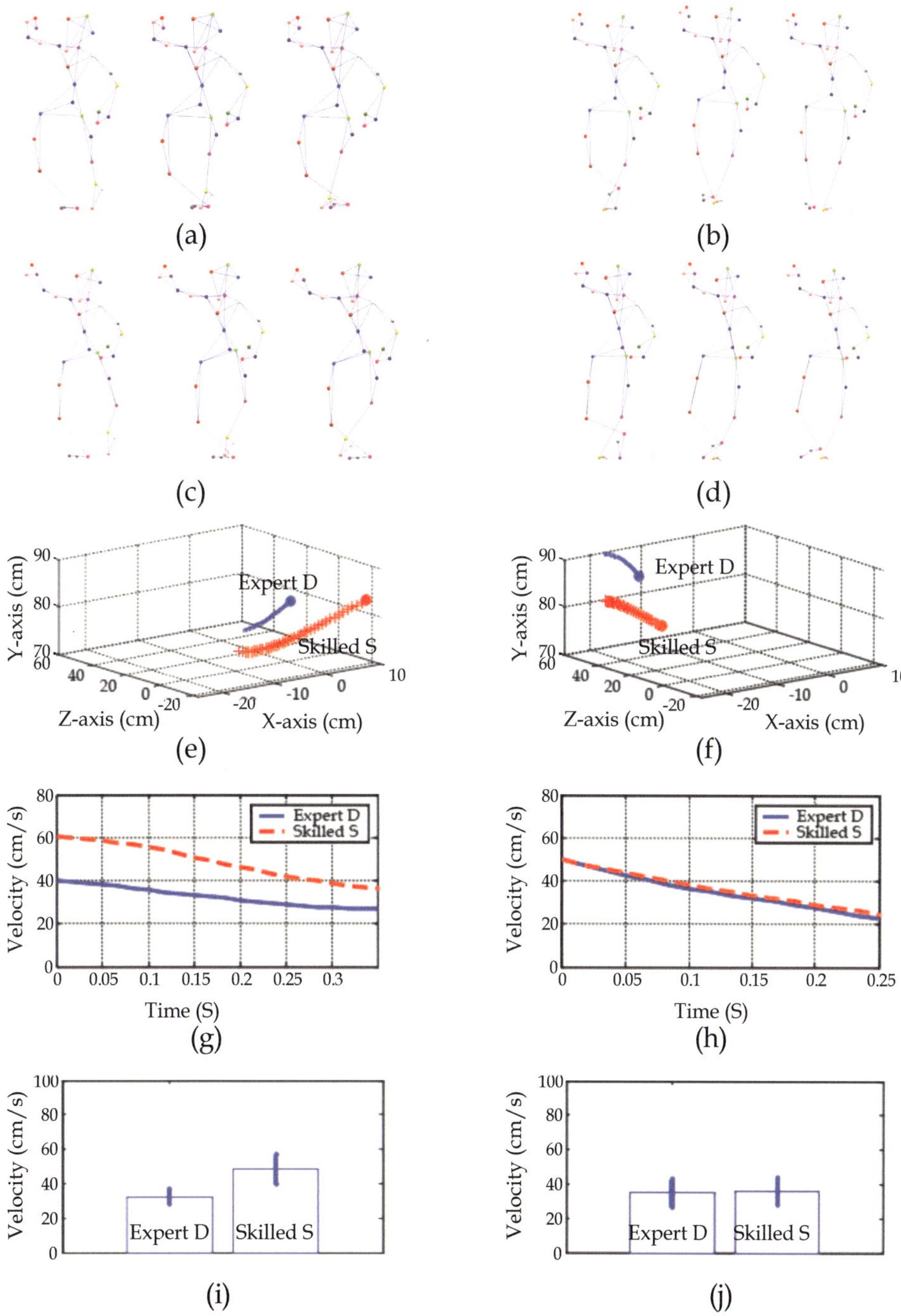

Fig. 3. Center of gravity on Performance 1. (a) Single support phase: *D* (right). (b) Single support phase: *D* (left). (c) Single support phase: *S* (right). (d) Single support phase: *S* (left). (e) Center of gravity in body (right). (f) Center of gravity in body (left). (g) Velocity of CG (right). (h) Velocity of CG (left). (i) Average of velocity of CG (right). (j) Average of velocity of CG (left).

the right leg is swinging. The two subjects have no significant difference in leg movement during the single support phases.

Fig. 3 (e) and (f) show the transfer of the center of gravity of Expert *D* and Skilled *S*. Points indicated by "•" in (e) and (f) show the start point of the single support phase of both legs during Performance 1. The two subjects exhibit leg movement with lower center of gravity under a condition of single support phase of the right leg in (e). Skilled *S* has more transfer of center of gravity than that of Expert *D*. In (f), the two subjects show leg movement which raised the center of gravity. When we consider the fact that the body height of the two subjects are almost the same (about 153cm), we notice that Expert *D* raised her center of gravity approximately 10cm higher than that of Skilled *S*.

Fig. 3 (g) and (h) show the velocity of center of gravity of the two subjects under the single support phase of both legs in Performance 1. In (g), Skilled *S* has a velocity variation of center of gravity of approximately 10-20cm/s greater than that of Expert *D*. In (h), the velocities of center of gravity of both subjects are almost the same.

Fig. 3 (i) and (j) show the average velocity of center of gravity under the single support phase of both legs. In (i), Skilled *S* has an average velocity and a standard deviation larger than those of Expert *D*. In (j), the two subjects have almost the same velocity and standard deviation. Expert *D* dances slowly, about 40cm/s, during the single support phase of Performance 1, but Skilled *S* dances faster at 40-60cm/s velocity.

Based on the above data, we found that Skilled *S* had more center of gravity transfer and velocity variation than Expert *D* during the single support phase of Performance 1.

3.2 Movement of knee and ankle

Secondly, we analysed the characteristics of leg movement of the subjects Expert *D* and Skilled *S* by comparing not only the angles of the knees and ankles but also EMG data of muscles used during their movement in Performance 1.

3.2.1 Knee movement

Fig. 4 shows the angle of the knees and the RMS of the EMG during Performance 1. Fig. 4 (a) and (c) show movements of the right knee of the two subjects under the single support phase of the right leg. Fig.4 (b) and (d) show movements of the left knee during single support phase of the left leg. There is no significant difference in movement of the knees of two subjects during the single support phases.

Fig. 4 (e) and (f) show the angle of the knees of both legs of the two subjects during the single support phase. The angle variation of the knee in (e) indicates that the subjects use knee flexion to lower the leg. The difference of angle variation of the knee between the two subjects was approximately 10-20°. This is not a significant difference. Angle variation of the knees in (f) indicates that the subjects use knee extension to raise the leg.

Fig. 4 (g) and (h) show the RMS values of the RF muscle for Expert *D* and Skilled *S*. During the single support phase of the right leg in (g), the RF muscles of Expert *D* and Skilled *S* discharged approximately 200mV and 400mV, respectively. Compared to Expert *D*, the RF muscle of Skilled *S* discharged approximately twice the EMG level to support the body with lowered center of gravity. During the single support phase of the right leg in (h), the RF muscles of Expert *D* and Skilled *S* discharged approximately 100mV and 200mV, respectively. Once again, the RF muscle of Skilled *S* discharged approximately double the EMG signal than that of Expert *D*.

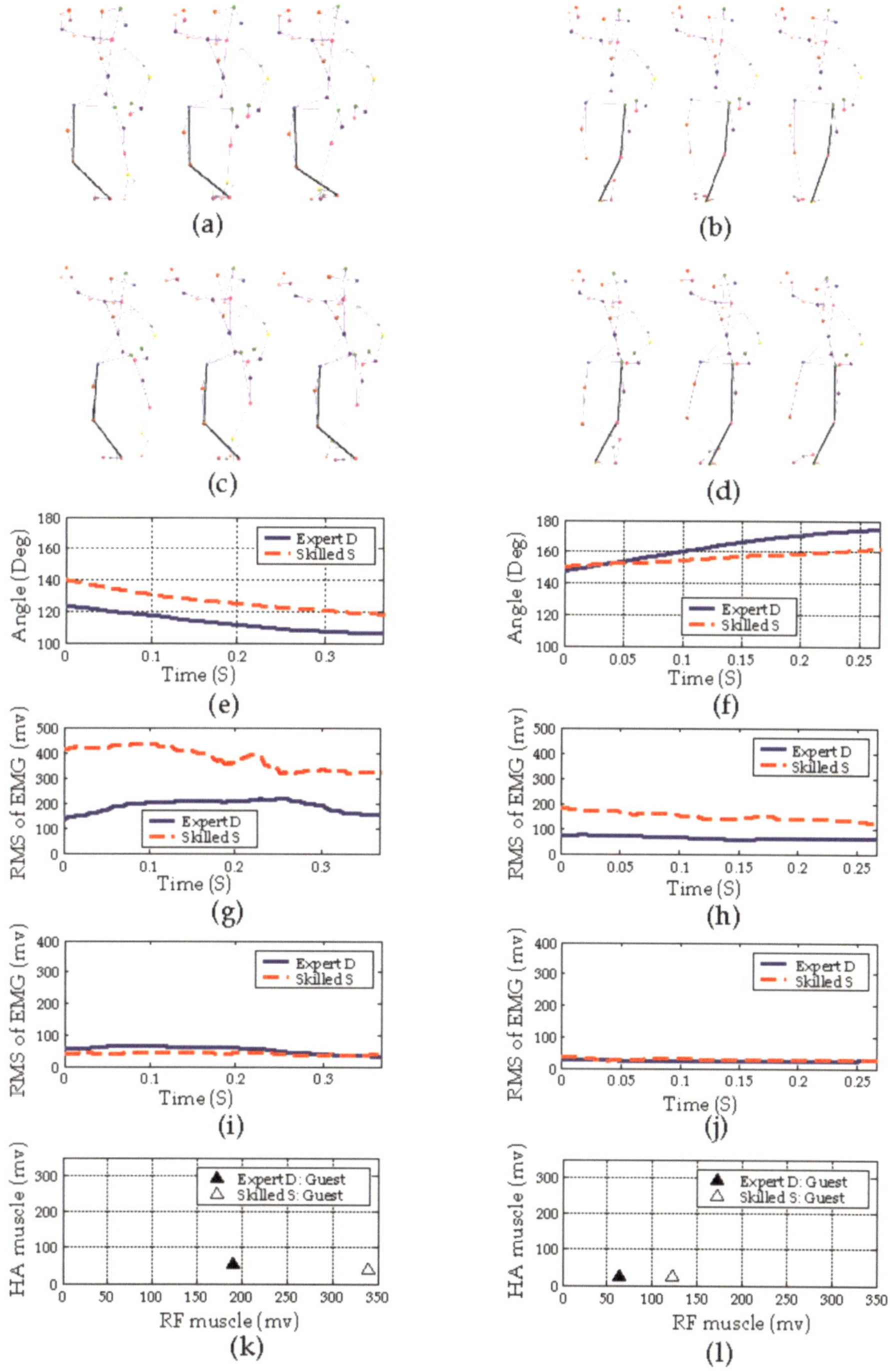

Fig. 4. Angle of knee and RMS of EMG on Performance 1. (a) Knee: *D* (right). (b) Knee: *D* (left). (c) Knee: *S* (right). (d) Knee: *S* (left). (e) Angle of knee (right). (f) Angle of knee (left). (g) RMS of RF(right). (h) RMS of RF (left). (i) RMS of HA (right). (j) RMS of HA (left). (k) Average of RMS (right). (l) Average of RMS (left).

Fig. 4 (i) and (j) show the RMS values of the HA muscles of Expert *D* and Skilled *S*. Under the single support phase of the right leg in (i), the HA muscle produces less EMG than the RF muscle. In order to lower the leg movement, the subjects are able to flex the knee by using a smaller muscle force due to gravity. The RF muscle antagonistic to HA muscle in knee is activated to support the body weight. Also, the HA muscle produces less EMG than the RF muscle during the single support phase of the left leg in (j). The RF muscle is activated to raise the leg with knee extension.

The X and Y axes of Fig. 4 (k) and (l) show the RMS values of EMG signal from the RF and HA muscles. RF and HA muscles are antagonistic muscle pairs of the knee. Expert *D* takes a balance of EMG activity between the two antagonist muscles when compared with Skilled *S* during the single support phase of the right leg in (k). Also, Expert *D* takes balance of EMG activity compared to Skilled *S* during the single support phase of left leg in (l).

Since Skilled *S* has a larger transfer and velocity variation of center of gravity than Expert *D* in (e) of Fig. 3, we noticed that when flexing the knee the RF muscle of Skilled *S* had more EMG activity than that of Expert *D* for supporting the body.

3.2.2 Ankle movement

Next, Fig. 5 shows the angle of the ankle and the RMS of the EMG signal during Performance 1. Fig. 5 (a) and (c) show the movement of the ankle of Expert *D* and Skilled *S* during the single support phase of the right leg. Fig. 5 (b) and (d) show the movement of the ankle during the single support phase of the left leg.

Fig. 5 (e) and (f) show ankle angle of the two subjects during the single support phase of both legs. Ankle angle variation in (e) indicates that the subject used the ankle dorsal to lower the leg. The difference between ankel angle variation between the two subjects was approximately 10°. The angle variation of the knee in (f) indicates that the subjects used ankle plantar flexion to raise the leg.

Fig. 5 (g) and (h) show the EMG RMS value of the TA muscle of Expert *D* and Skilled *S*. The TA muscles of both subjects produced approximately 100mV during the single support phase of the right leg in (g). During the single support phase of the right leg in (h), the TA muscle of Expert *D* and Skilled *S* produced approximately 50mV and 50-200mV, respectively. The TA muscle of Skilled *S* also produced approximately double the EMG signal compared to Expert *D*. After maintaining the EMG discharge of approximately 200mV in the TA muscle during the first 0.1 second, Skilled *S* reduced the discharge of EMG by approximately 50mV during the single support phase of left leg. Expert *D* maintained the EMG discharge of approximately 50mV. Therefore, we conclude that Skilled *S* used more muscle force for acting Performance 1.

Fig. 5(i) and (j) show the RMS value of the SOL muscles of Expert *D* and Skilled *S*. The SOL muscle EMG discharge was maintained at approximately 100mV during the single support phase of the right leg in (i). Also, the EMG discharge of the SOL muscle was maintained at approximately 50mV during the single support phase of the left leg in (j).

The X and Y axies of Fig. 5 (k) and (l) show the EMG RMS values of the TA and SOL muscles. TA and SOL muscles are antagonistic muscles of the ankle. Expert *D* and Skilled *S* took a balance of muscle activity between two antagonistic muscles of ankle during the single support phase of the right leg in (k). However, Expert *D* took a balance of EMG activity of ankle compared to that of Skilled *S* during the single support phase of the left leg in (l). In this result, Expert *D* maintained the EMG activity of the ankle muscle during the single support phase. In particular, Expert *D* takes a balance of EMG activity between two antagonist muscles of the ankle and knee for the single support phase as shown in Figs. 4 and 5.

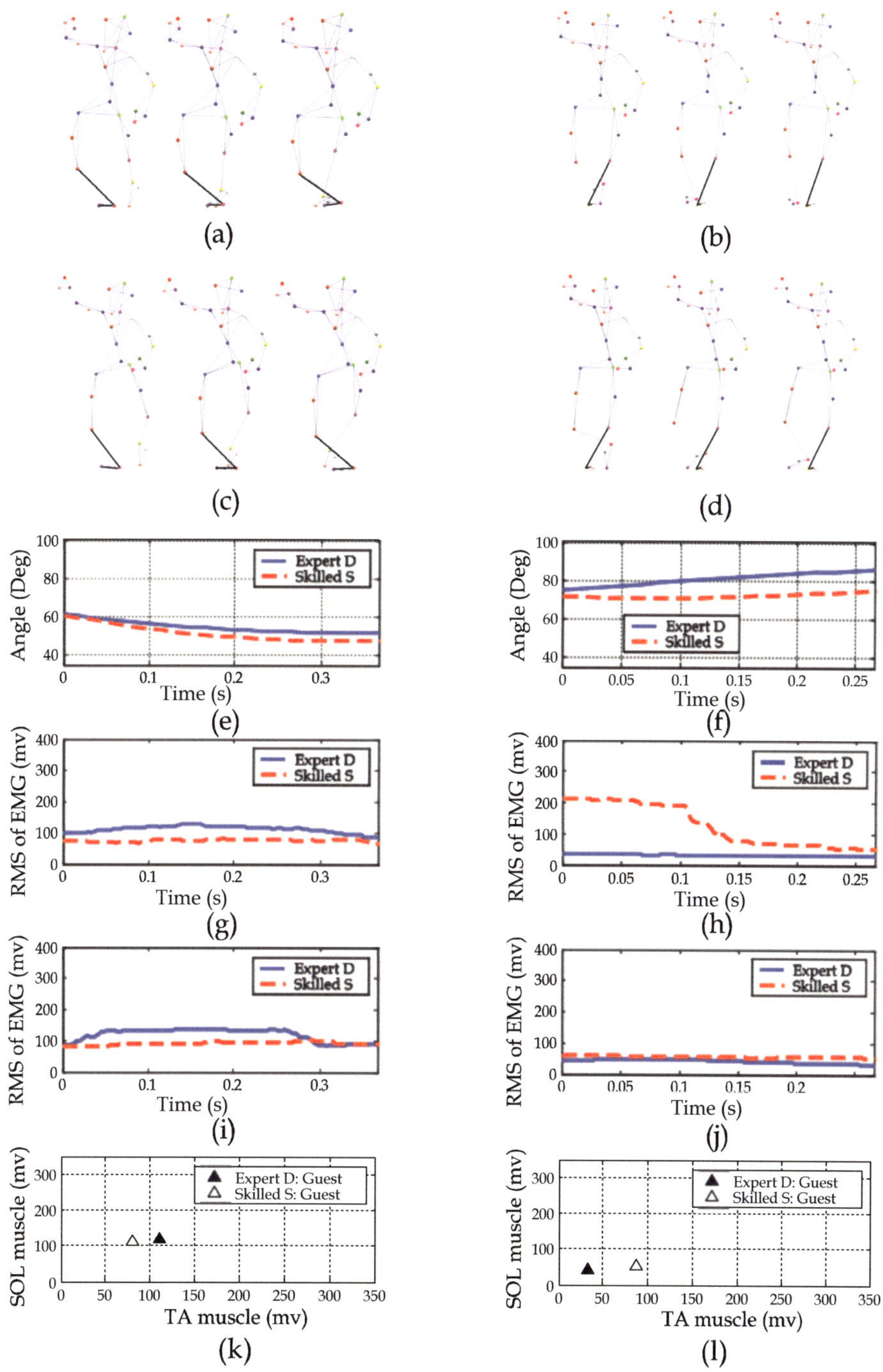

Fig. 5. Angle of ankle and RMS of EMG on Performance 1. (a) Ankle: *D* (right). (b) Ankle: *D* (left). (c) Ankle: *S* (right). (d) Ankle: *S* (left). (e) Angle of ankle (right). (f) Angle of ankle (left). (g) RMS of TA (right). (h) RMS of TA (left). (i) RMS of SOL (right). (j) RMS of SOL (left). (k) Average of RMS (right). (l) Average of RMS (left).

3.3 Efficiency of co-contraction of the knee and ankle

Thirdly, we compared the efficiency of leg movement of the two subjects during the single support phase in Performance 1. The efficiency of leg movement is calculated by observing co-contraction of the two antagonistic muscles of the knee and ankle. The efficiency of co-contraction of antagonistic muscles can be determined by the following equation (Winter, 1990) (see Fig. 6).

$$Co - contraction = 2 \times \frac{A \cap B}{A \cup B} \times 100 \tag{2}$$

We compute the efficiency of leg movement via Eq. (2). Table 4 shows the co-contraction of the knee and ankle of two subjects during Performance 1 of *Hokushu*. Expert *D* had high co-contraction that was approximately 10-20% greater than Skilled *S*. When we take into consideration that the EMG activity of Expert *D* was less than Skilled *S*, we notice that Expert *D* is performing leg movement more efficiently during the single support phase of both legs.

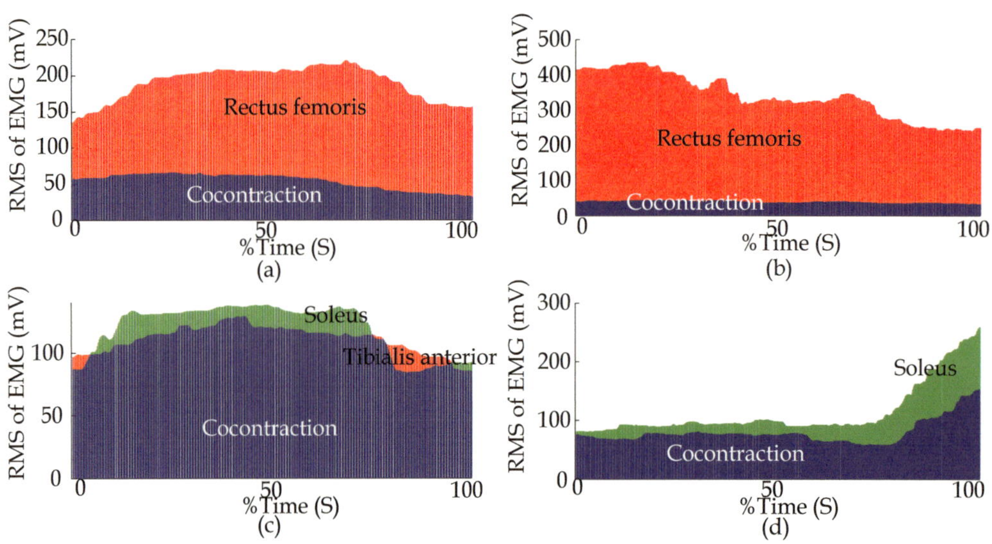

Fig. 6. Co-contraction of antagonistic muscles during single support phase of right leg. (a) Co-contraction of knee (Expert *D*). (b) Co-contraction of knee (Skilled *S*) . (c) Co-contraction of ankle (Expert *D*). (d) Co-contraction of ankle (Skilled *S*).

	Single support phase (right)		Single support phase (left)	
	Knee	Ankle	Knee	Ankle
Expert *D*	41%	77%	53%	86%
Skilled *S*	25%	76%	36%	83%

Table 4. Co-contraction of knee and ankle on Performance 1 of Expert *D* and Skilled *S*.

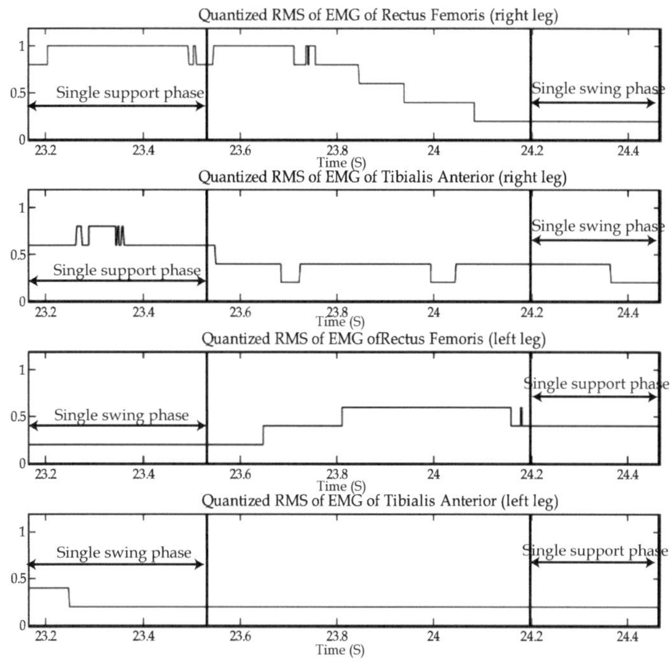

(a)

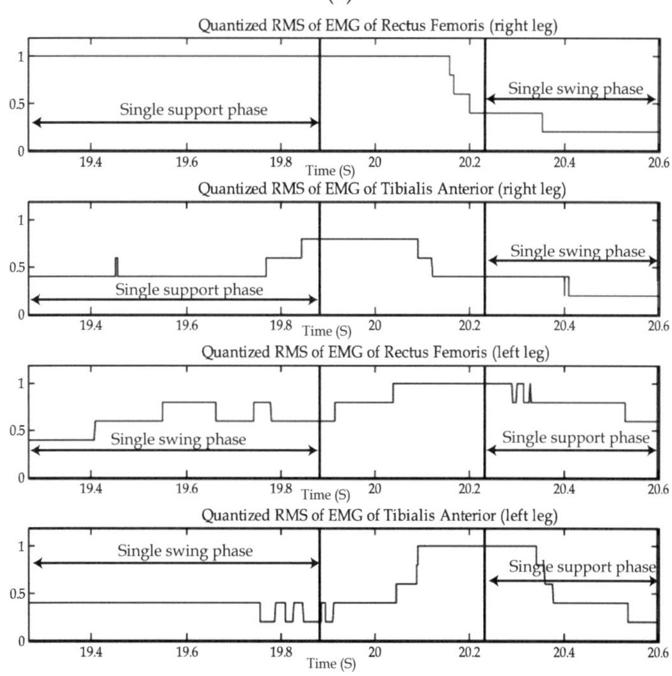

(b)

Fig. 7. Quantized RMS of EMG signal on single support phase during Performance 1. (a) Single support phase of Expert *D*. (b) Single support phase of Skilled *S*.

3.4 Visualization of the single support phase of Performance 1

Finally, we visualize the leg movement of the two subjects during Performance 1 using CG character animation.

Fig. 7 (a) and (b) show the quantized RMS values of the EMG signal for the RF and TA muscles of both legs during single support phase. We used the RMS data of the RF muscle in (g) and (h) of Fig. 4, and the RMS data of the TA muscle in (g) and (h) of Fig. 5. The RMS data is quantized to 5 levels. We then made a CG character animation using an OpenGL program, colouring the character's legs in accordance with the quantized RMS data. At the same time, we show the leg movement of the single swing phase versus the single support phase of both legs in Fig. 7 (a) and (b).

Fig. 8 (a) and (b) show snapshots of the CG character animation with generated colours based on the single support phase of both legs. During high EMG activity, the colour becomes deeper than during low EMG activity, in proportion to the EMG signal level as shown in Fig. 8. We found that the differences in leg movement between the Expert *D* and Skilled *S* were more obvious when displaying EMG information via the CG character.

As shown in Fig. 8 (a) and (b), we notice that the RF and TA muscles of both legs of Skilled *S* on are activated to act Performance 1 compared to Expert *D*. Expert *D* had less EMG activity than Skilled *S* for acting the single swing movement during the single support phase.

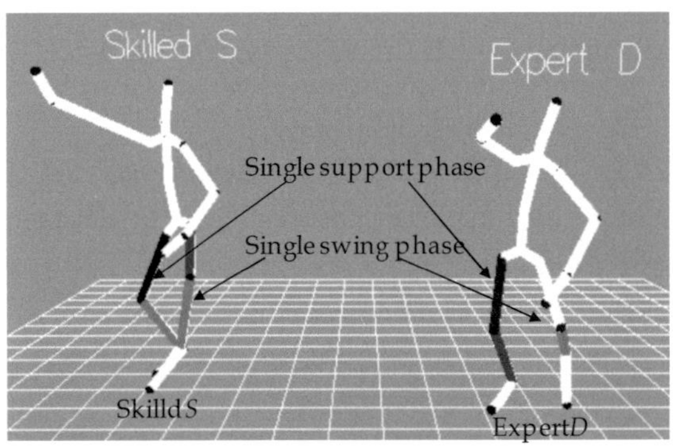

(a)

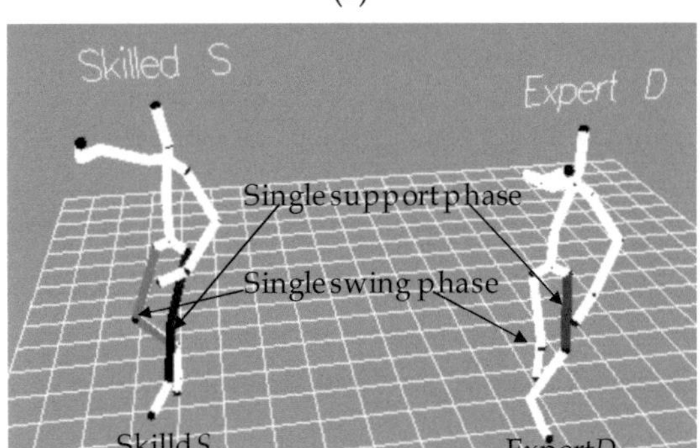

(b)

Fig. 8. CG character animation of body motion and EMG signal on single support phase during Performance 1. (a) Single support phase of right leg. (b) Single support phase of left leg.

4. Conclusion and future work

In this research, we performed quantitative analysis of leg movement patterns of an expert traditional dancer using simultaneous measurement of body motion and leg muscle EMG.
As a result, we verified that Expert *D*, who has a forty-year career as a Japanese traditional dancer, has the effective co-contraction of antagonistic muscles of the knee and ankle and less center of gravity transfer than Skilled *S*, who has only a twenty-year career. Therefore, Expert *D* can efficiently perform dance leg movements with less EMG activity than Skilled *S*. Our research can help dancers and researchers of dance by providing new information on dance movement that cannot be analysed via motion capture alone.
In the future, we will measure the leg movement control of veteran dancers, especially for quantitatively comparing leg movement skills, by recording the leg movements of masters and beginners. Furthermore, we will investigate leg movement skill by simultaneously using EMG equipment and a force plate.

5. Acknowledgment

We would like to thank Ms. Daizo Hanayagi and Ms. Souko Hanayagi for co-operating with us in the motion capturing experiment with EMG measurement. We also thank Prof. Yuka Marumo and Prof. Mamiko Sakata for providing us valuable advice about traditional Japanese dance.
This research has been conducted partly by the support of the Global COE Program, the Open Research Center Program, and the Grant-in-Aid for Scientific Research No. (B)16300035, and No. (C)20500105 all from the Ministry of Education, Science, Sports and Culture.

6. References

Urawaki, K. (2005). A Learing System for Sport Form using Visualization of Biophysical Information, Master's Thesis, *Nara Institute of Science and Technology*, Japan, (in Japanese)

Humm, J.R. ; Harris, G.F. & Raasch, W.G. (1994). A Biomechanical Analysis Of Ballet Dancers On Pointe, *In Proceedings of the 16th Annual International Conference of the IEEE on Engineering in Medicine and Biology Society*, pp. 374-375, 10.1109/IEMBS.1994.411997

Kurihara, K. ; Hoshino, S. ; Yamane, K. & Nakamura, Y. (2002). Optical motion capture system with pan-tilt camera tracking and realtime data processing, *In Proceedings of the IEEE International Conference on Robotics and Automation*, pp. 1241-1248, 10.1109/ROBOT.2002.1014713

Yoshimura, M. ; Mine, N. ; Kai, T. & Yoshimura, I. (2001). Quantification of Characteristic Features of Japanese Dance for Individuality Recognition, *In Proceedings of 10th IEEE on Robot and Human Interactive Communication*, pp. 188-193, 10.1109/ROMAN.2001.981900

Yoshimura, M. ; Kojima, K. ; Hachimura, K. ; Marumo, Y. & Kuromiya, A. (2004). Quantification and recognition of basic motion okuri in Japanese traditional dance, *In Proceedings of 13th IEEE on Robot and Human Interactive Communication*, pp. 205-210, 10.1109/ROMAN.2004.1374757

Kunieda, T. (2003). Body of JIUTA MAI with profound Japanese cul-ture, *In Proceedings of the Inter-Congress of IUAES2002*, pp. 24-31.

Choi, W. ; Isaka, T. ; Sakata, M. ; Tsuruta, S. & Hachimura, K. (2007). Quantification of Dance Movement by Simultaneous Measurement of Body Motion and Biophysical Information, *International Journal of Automation and Computing*, vol. 04, no. 1, pp. 1-7

Perotto, A. O. (1994). *Anatomical Guide for the Electromyographer: The Limbs and Trunk*, Charles C. Thomas Publisher

Wirhed, R. (1984). *Athletic ability and the anatomy of motion*, Wolfe Medical Publications

Winter, David A. (1990). *Biomechanics and Motor Control of Human Movement*, Wiley Interscience

Matsui, H. (1958). *Exercise and center of gravity in human body*, Taiikuno Kagakusha, (in Japanese)

11

A Quantitative Evaluation Method of Handedness Using Haptic Virtual Reality Technology

Tsuneo Yoshikawa, Masanao Koeda and Munetaka Sugihashi
Department of Human and Computer Intelligence,
College of Information Science and Engineering,
Ritsumeikan University
Japan

1. Introduction

Quantitative evaluation of handedness of people will be useful in various situations. For example, handedness is an important factor in designing tools and devices that are to be handled by people using their hands. It will also be useful for knowing the degree of recovery of a person in rehabilitation stage suffering from injury or disease.

A well-known method for evaluating handedness of a person is LQ (laterality quotient)-method (Oldfield, 1971) which is based on the answers to ten questions such as which hand one uses for writing letters. Matsuda et al. (1986) propose to evaluate handedness based on the results of tests of tapping, peg-board, and picking up beans using discriminant function analysis.

There are many researches trying to find functional differences between dominant and non-dominant hands. Fujiwara et al. (2003) use a digital trace method for studying the difference of upper limb coordination between dominant and non-dominant hands. Wu et al. (1996) examine the difference between the behaviors during the operation of touch panel by the dominant and non-dominant hands. Bagesteiro & Sainburg (2002) investigate interlimb differences in coordination through analysis of inverse dynamics and electromyography recorded during the performance of reaching movements. These studies assume that subjects in their experiments can be divided into two groups: right-handed persons and left-handed persons. One possible direction of future research will be to consider the quantitative degree of handedness of each subject.

Haptic virtual reality is a technology which makes it possible for us to see and touch a virtual environment composed by a computer through a haptic display device. Various researches have been done so far in this field (Burdea, 1996). We have proposed a methodology for displaying the dynamics of virtual objects (Yoshikawa et al., 1995). We have also developed a system for observing human skill by using a virtual task space (Yoshikawa & Yoshimoto, 2000).

A method is proposed in this chapter for evaluating quantitatively the handedness and dexterity of a person from his/her performance of some test tasks in the virtual world that are constructed using haptic virtual reality technology. The merits of virtual test tasks over

real tasks are that it is easier to provide a large variety of tasks, to change the values of parameters of these tasks, and to obtain detailed position and force data for evaluation.
We prepare three test tasks: accurate positioning task, accurate force control task, and skillful manipulation task. Performance data for these test tasks taken from a group of subjects are analyzed using the factor analysis. Since the obtained factor scores for the right and left hands of each subject can be regarded as the skillfulness of the right and left hand, it is proposed to define the degree of handedness of the subject based on the difference of these factor scores.

2. Test tasks based on haptic virtual reality

2.1 Outline of handedness evaluation system

An experimental system shown in Fig.1 has been developed for measuring the dexterity of a finger from the viewpoints of position control, force control, and manipulation of objects. The system consists of two force display devices (PHANToM OMNI), a display, and a computer for constructing a virtual task world. The specifications of the computer are shown in Table 1.

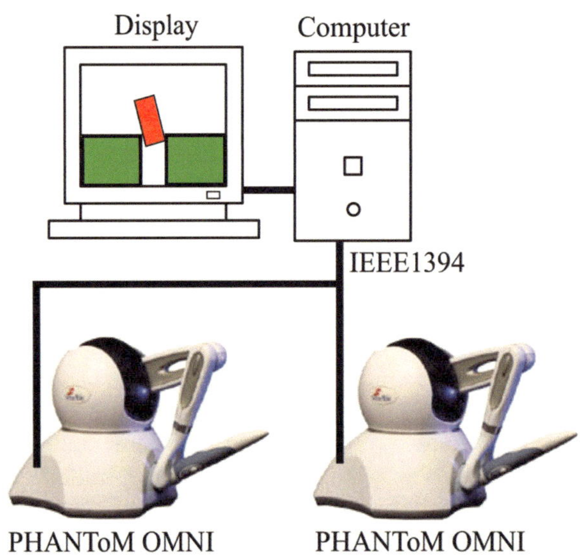

Fig. 1. System configuration

OS	Microsoft Windows XP Professional
CPU	Intel Pentium 4 3.2 [GHz]
Memory	1024 [MB]
Graphic Processor	nVidia GeForce6600
Bus Type	PCI Express × 16

Table 1. Specifications of computer

2.2 Position control test

This test is intended to measure the dexterity in positioning a fingertip accurately. The subject is asked to follow the desired point on the screen which moves along a circle with constant velocity by using his/her index finger. The desired point turns around a circle six times taking 6 seconds for each turn. Fig.2-(a) shows the overview of the task environment and Fig.2- (b) shows the image on the monitor screen. Two tasks are prepared: One is with clockwise rotation and the other is counterclockwise rotation. This is to make the test fair to right-handed and left-handed subjects.

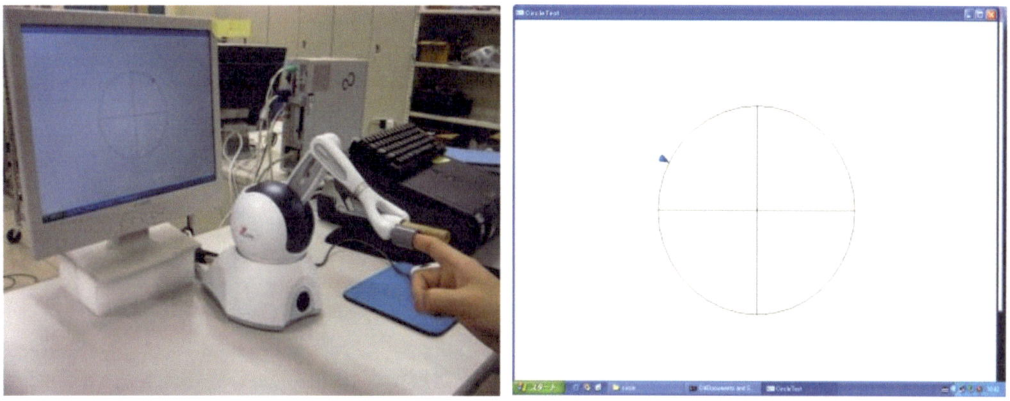

(a) Overview (b) Image on the monitor

Fig. 2. Position control test

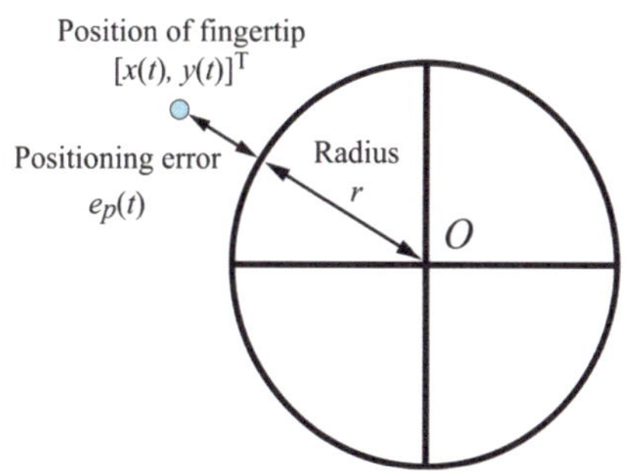

Fig. 3. Positioning error

The average of the tracking error during the five turns from the second to the last turn is taken as the measure of performance of this task. As is shown in Fig.3, the tracking error $e_p(t)$ at time t is given by

$$e_p(t) = |\sqrt{x^2(t) + y^2(t)} - r| \tag{1}$$

where $[x(t),y(t)]^T$ is the position vector of the fingertip on the virtual plane shown by small green circle and r is the radius of the circle. The measure of performance E_p is given by the average magnitude of tracking error, that is,

$$E_p = \frac{\int_0^T e_p(t)dt}{T} \tag{2}$$

where T is the total time (=30 [s]). The smaller the value E_p is, the more dexterous the subject is regarded in position control. A typical trajectory of the tracking error $e_p(t)$ of a subject is shown in Fig.4.

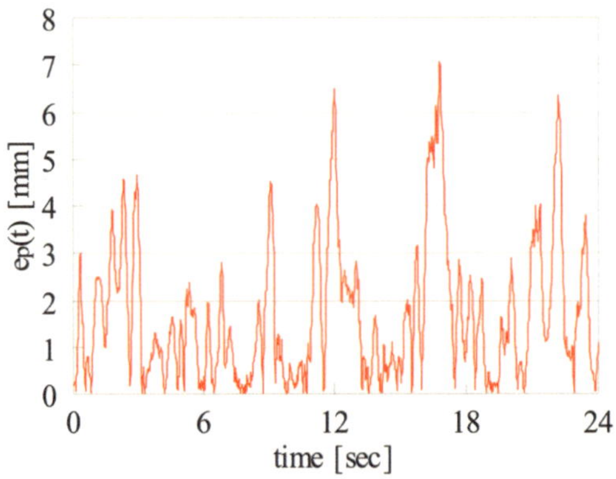

Fig. 4. A trajectory of measured positioning error

2.3 Force control test

This test is intended to measure the dexterity in exerting a certain desired force on an object by a fingertip accurately. The subject is asked to push a square box in the screen with a specified desired force. When the subject pushes the box, he/she can feel the reaction force through the force display device. The reaction force is calculated by using a spring-damper model of the surface of box. The subject can also watch the relative magnitude of the applied force $F(t)$ and the desired force $F_d = 1.0$[N] by the color of the box: The box becomes white when the applied force is close to the desired force ($|F(t) - F_d| \leq 0.1$[N]), it becomes red when the applied force is larger ($F(t) > 1.1$[N]), and green when it is smaller than the desired value ($F(t) < 0.9$[N]). The task continues ten seconds and the data is obtained during 1 through 10 seconds skipping the first 1 second. Fig.5-(a) shows the overview of the task environment and Fig.5-(b) shows the image on the monitor screen.

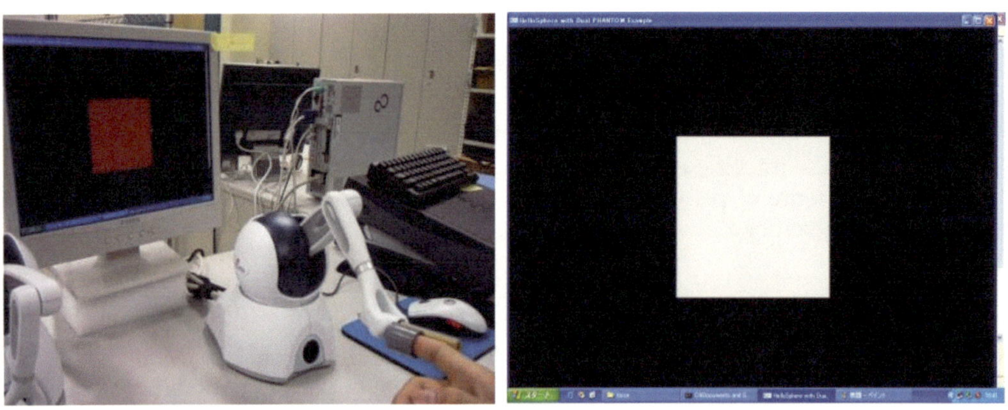

(a) Overview (b) Image on the monitor

Fig. 5. Force control test

The average of the force regulation error during the nine seconds is taken as the measure of performance of this task. The force regulation error at time t is given by

$$e_f(t) = |F(t) - F_d| \tag{3}$$

and the measure of performance E_f is given by

$$E_f = \frac{\int_0^T e_f(t)dt}{T} \tag{4}$$

where T is the total time (=9 [s]). The smaller the value E_f is, the more dexterous the subject is regarded in force control.

2.4 Manipulation test

This test is intended to measure the dexterity of a subject in manipulating objects by his/her hand. The subject is asked to insert a peg into a hole in virtual world, which is constructed by using a dynamics simulator OpenDynamicsEngine. The interaction forces among the fingertips, peg, and hole are calculated based on the intrusion distance among them following the approach described in Yoshikawa & Yoshimoto (2000). The gravitational acceleration is assumed to be 9800[mm/s^2]. The task is specified in the two-dimensional space by constraining the motion of peg in a plane parallel to the monitor screen. The subject is asked to pick up a peg of 50[mm] wide, 100[mm] long, and weighing 100[g], by his/her thumb and index finger and to insert it into a hole of 50[mm] deep and 51[mm] wide, and then to return it to the original position. Fig.6-(a) shows the overview of the task environment and Fig.6-(b) shows the image on the monitor screen. Two tasks are prepared to make a fair evaluation regarding the initial position of the peg: right and left initial positions (see Fig.7). The time E_m[s] needed to perform this insertion task once is taken as the measure of performance.

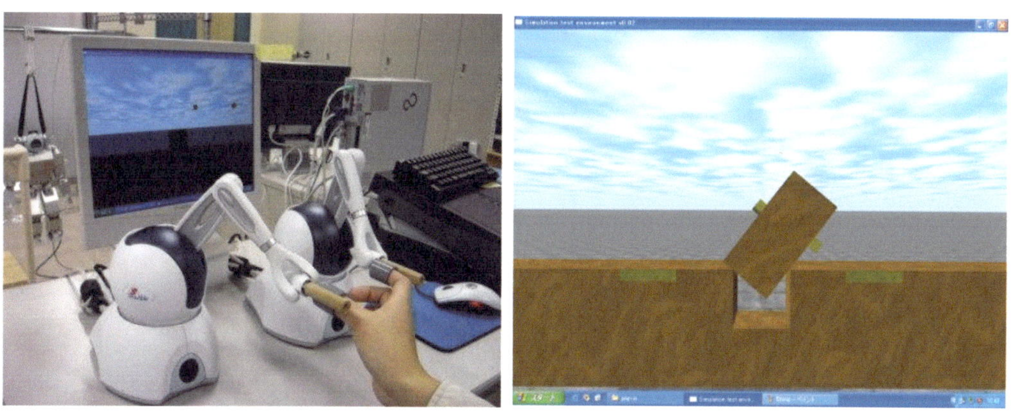

(a) Overview (b) Image on the monitor

Fig. 6. Manipulation test

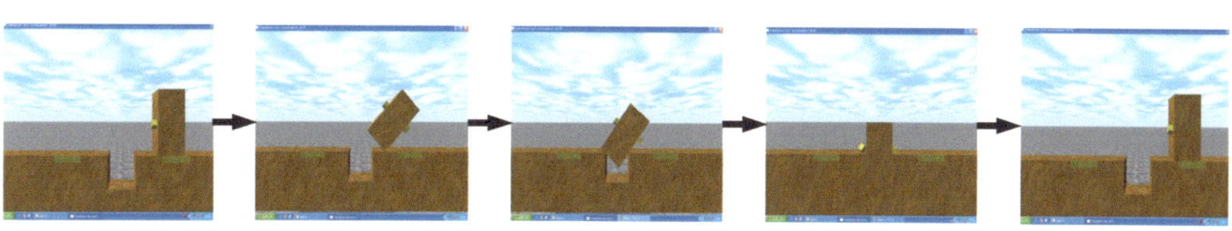

Fig. 7. Peg insertion task from right initial position

3. Experimental results

Ten male subjects of age 22–23 have taken the above described tests. According to the conventional LQ test, nine subjects (Subjects A through I) were right-handed and one subject (Subject J) was left-handed (see Table 2). Tests were repeated three times for the right and left hands of each subject and their averages were regarded as the measured performance data denoted as $\{Z_{ihp}, Z_{ihf}, Z_{ihm}\}$, where subscript i means subject $i = A, B, \dots, J$, subscript h means left hand ($h = l$) or right hand ($h = r$), and subscripts p, f and m mean the position control, force control, and manipulation tests, respectively. Table 3-5 and Fig.8 show the measured data. From the figure it can be seen that, for the nine subjects except subject J, the performance of the right hand was better than the left hand in the position control test and manipulation test. For subject J the left hand was better than the right hand. This is consistent with the result of LQ test.
On the other hand, in the force control test, the left hands of subject J and three others performed better than their right hands.
The correlation matrix R of the performance data in Fig.8 for the three tests is calculated as

$$R = \begin{bmatrix} 1 & 0.189 & 0.657 \\ 0.189 & 1 & 0.279 \\ 0.657 & 0.279 & 1 \end{bmatrix} \tag{5}$$

Subject	LQ value
A	100
B	100
C	100
D	100
E	100
F	100
G	100
H	100
I	90
J	-100

Table 2. Results of LQ value

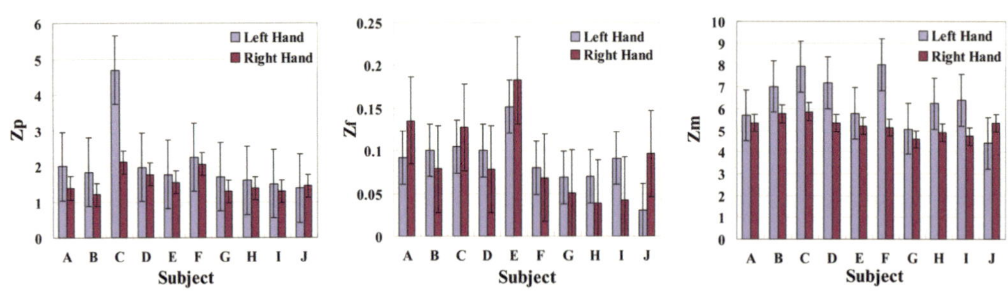

(a) Position control test (b) Force control test (c) Manipulation test

Fig. 8. Results of the three tests

	Left hand (Z_{ilp})		Right hand (Z_{irp})	
	L. T.	R. T.	R. T.	L. T.
A	2.073	1.911	1.480	1.287
B	1.409	2.246	1.153	1.242
C	4.112	5.268	2.263	1.935
D	1.794	2.117	1.767	1.758
E	1.999	1.529	1.432	1.657
F	2.128	2.368	2.051	2.053
G	1.616	1.778	1.258	1.318
H	1.364	1.842	1.448	1.308
I	1.511	1.483	1.243	1.333
J	1.285	1.469	1.364	1.525

Table 3. Results of the position test [mm] (Note: L. T.: left turn, R. T.: right turn. Z_{ilp} and Z_{irp} are given by the means of the values for L. T. and R. T.)

	Left hand (Z_{ilf})	Right hand (Z_{irf})
A	0.0919	0.1355
B	0.1005	0.0787
C	0.1046	0.1276
D	0.0999	0.0785
E	0.1516	0.1828
F	0.0799	0.0681
G	0.0685	0.0501
H	0.0698	0.0385
I	0.0912	0.0422
J	0.0303	0.0965

Table 4. Results of the force test [N]

	Left hand (Z_{ilm})		Right hand (Z_{irm})	
	L. S.	R. S.	R. S.	L. S.
A	6.035	5.344	5.299	5.393
B	6.787	7.254	6.246	5.271
C	7.516	8.341	6.101	5.610
D	8.035	6.319	5.209	5.471
E	5.956	5.594	5.259	5.126
F	7.974	8.057	4.903	5.343
G	4.864	5.266	4.736	4.429
H	5.505	6.954	4.674	5.114
I	5.783	6.998	4.936	4.507
J	4.741	4.067	5.683	5.009

Table 5. Results of manipulation test[s] (Note: L. S.: initial position on left side, R. S.: initial position on right side. Z_{ilm} and Z_{irm} are given by the means of the values for L. S. and R. S.)

From this result, it is seen that the correlation between the position and manipulation tests is large but the correlation between the force test and the other tests is small, implying that the dexterity on force control has a little different tendency from that of position control and manipulation.

4. Definition and evaluation of handedness and dexterity

It is desirable to establish a general quantitative evaluation method of handedness. We propose a quantitative definition of the handedness based on the factor analysis. At the same time, a definition of dexterity for each hand and for each person is also proposed.

To analyze the obtained data by the factor analysis, we first standardize the measured performances for each test as follows. The standardized value z of datum Z is given by

$$z_{iht} = \frac{Z_{iht} - \overline{Z}_t}{v_t}, \quad t = p, f, m \tag{6}$$

where $\overline{Z}_t$ and v_t are, respectively, the average and the standard variation of the data $\{Z_{iht}\}$ for a fixed t.

Let the standardized performance data for hand h of subject i for the position control test be z_{ihp}, that for the force control test be z_{ihf}, and that for the manipulation test be z_{ihm}. Then from the basic formula of the factor analysis we adopt the one-factor model given by

$$z_{ihp} = a_p d_{ih} + e_{ihp} \tag{7}$$

$$z_{ihf} = a_f d_{ih} + e_{ihf} \tag{8}$$

$$z_{ihm} = a_m d_{ih} + e_{ihm} \tag{9}$$

where d_{ih} is the factor score, a_p, a_f, a_m are the factor loading coefficients for the three tests, and e_{ihp}, e_{ihf}, e_{ihm} are the independent errors.

In order to calculate the factor score we first obtain the values of factor loadings. Let the factor loading matrix A be

$$A = [a_p \;\; a_f \;\; a_m]^T \tag{10}$$

then the relation between A and the correlation matrix R is given by

$$R = AA^T + R_e \tag{11}$$

where R_e is the diagonal covariance matrix of the independent errors. Using the Principal Factor Method, factor loading matrix A satisfying (11) is given by

$$A = [-0.668 \quad -0.284 \quad -0.984]^T \tag{12}$$

Now we can obtain the factor score d_{ih} based on the relation

$$d_{ih} = [z_{ihp} \ z_{ihf} \ z_{ihm}] R^{-1} A \qquad (13)$$

Note that, although matrix $-A$ can also be a solution of (11), the above solution with negative components was intentionally chosen. This way, we can obtain the factor score such that the larger the factor score is, the more dexterous the subject is.
The factor scores of the right and left hands of each subject are given in Table 6 and in Fig.9.

Subject	Factor score		Dexterity d_i	Handedness h_i	LQ
	d_{il}	d_{ir}			
A	0.087	0.429	0.258	0.171	R
B	-1.157	0.065	-0.545	0.611	R
C	-2.156	-0.083	-1.120	1.036	R
D	-1.310	0.429	-0.440	0.870	R
E	0.002	0.553	0.278	0.275	R
F	-2.107	0.621	-0.743	1.364	R
G	0.694	1.172	0.933	0.239	R
H	-0.395	0.878	0.241	0.636	R
I	-0.546	1.044	0.249	0.795	R
J	1.340	0.436	0.888	-0.452	L

Table 6. Evaluation results of dexterity and handedness

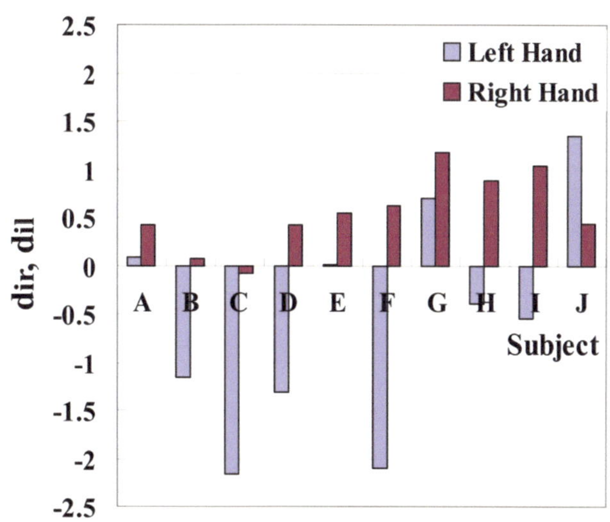

Fig. 9. Factor scores

Based on the above considerations, we define the dexterity d_i and handedness h_i of a subject using the factor score of his/her right hand d_{ir} and left hand d_{il}:

$$d_i = \frac{d_{ir} + d_{il}}{2} \tag{14}$$

$$h_i = \frac{d_{ir} - d_{il}}{2} \tag{15}$$

The dexterity is shown in Fig.10. The handedness and the LQ value of each subject are shown in Fig.11. From the figure we can see that when the value of handedness is positive, the LQ value is also positive, and vice versa, implying that the value of handedness h_i and the conventional LQ value do not contradict to each other. The calculated degrees of handedness, however, differ largely among the right-handed subjects. From this result, it is expected that the proposed method can be used for more detailed quantitative evaluation of handedness.

5. Conclusion

A quantitative evaluation method of dexterity and handedness of a person based on the factor analysis of data from three kinds of performance tests in haptic virtual space has been proposed.

Result of the judgment of handedness from our method for the ten subjects was consistent with that from the conventional LQ method. Hence the proposed approach can be a useful quantitative evaluation method. However, the number of subjects was just ten which is very small. The validity of the method should be examined through tests for a larger group of subjects.

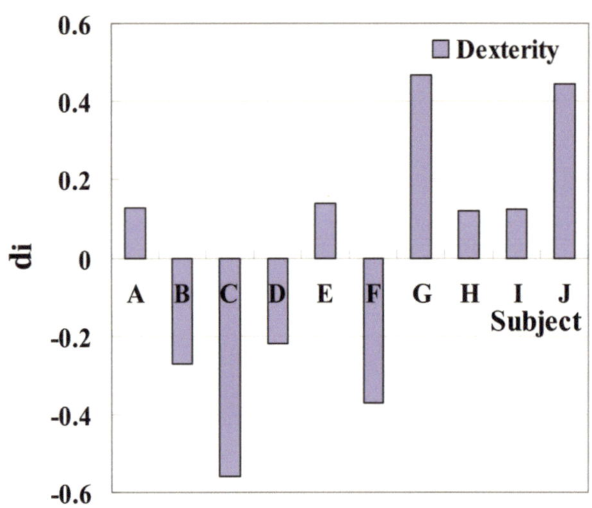

Fig. 10. Dexterity

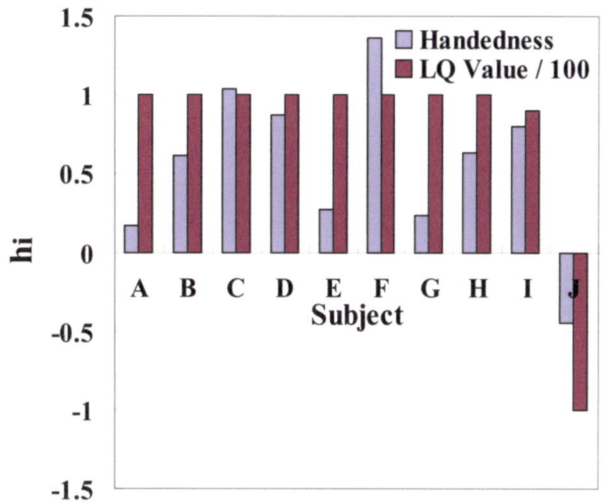

Fig. 11. Handedness

The tendency of force test was a little different from the other two tests. The reason for this difference should be studied in the future.

This chapter has been written based on paper "A Quantitative Evaluation Method of Handedness Using Haptic Virtual Reality Technology" that was presented at the 16th IEEE International Symposium on Robot & Human Interactive Communication, (IEEE RO-MAN 2007, Jeju, Korea, August, 2007).

6. References

Bagesteiro, L.B. & Sainburg, R.L. (2002). Handedness: Dominant Arm Advantages in Control of Limb Dynamics, *Journal of Neurophysiology*, Vol.88, No.5, pp.2408-2421

Burdea, G.C. (1996). *Force and Touch Feedback for Virtual Reality*, A Wiley-Interscience Publication, JohnWiley & Sons, Inc.

Fujiwara, N., Kushida, N., Murakami, T. & Fujimoto, S. (2003). Upper Limb Coordination Differs Among Ages and Between Dominant and Non-dominant Hands Utilizing Digital Trace Test, *Journal of health sciences, Hiroshima University*, Vol.2, No.2, pp.22-28 (in Japanese)

Matsuda, I., Yamaguchi, M. & Yoshida, K. (1986). Quantitative Discrimination of Handedness - Preliminary Study Using Discriminant Analysis Approach -, *Sagyouryouhou (Journal published by Japanese Association of Occupational Therapists)*, Vol.5, pp.40-41 (in Japanese)

Oldfield, R.C. (1971). The Assessment and Analysis of Handedness: The Edinburgh Inventory, *Neuropsychologia*, Vol.9, No.1, pp.97-113

Wu, J., Morimoto, K. & Kurokawa, T. (1996). A Comparison between Effect of Handedness and Non-handedness on Touch Screen Operation, *Transactions of Human Interface Society*, Vol.11, No.4, pp.441-446 (in Japanese)

Yoshikawa, T., Yokokohji, Y., Matsumoto, T. & Zheng, X-Z. (1995). Display of Feel for the Manipulation of Dynamic Virtual Objects, *Journal of Dynamic Systems, Measurement, and Control*, Vol.117, No.4, pp.554-558

Yoshikawa, T. & Yoshimoto, K. (2000). Haptic Simulation of Assembly Operation in Virtual Environment, *Proceedings of the ASME, Dynamic Systems and Control Division–2000*, pp.1191-1198

12

Toward Human Like Walking – Walking Mechanism of 3D Passive Dynamic Motion with Lateral Rolling – Advances in Human-Robot Interaction

Tomoo Takeguchi, Minako Ohashi and Jaeho Kim
Osaka Sangyo University
Japan

1. Introduction

It may not be so science fiction any more that robots and human live in the same space. The robots may need to move like human and to have shape of humanoid in order to share the living space. Some robots may be required to walk along with human for special care. This requires robot to be able to walk like human and to sense how humans walk. Human walks by maximizing walking in between passive walking and active walking in effective manner such as less energy, less time, and so on (Ishiguro & Owaki, 2005). It is important to clarify the mechanisms of passive walking. This study is the first step to decrease the gap between robots and human in motion, advance in human-robot interaction.
Most robots use actuators at each joint, and follow a certain selected trajectory in order to walk as mentioned active walking before. So, considerable power source is necessary to drive and control many actuators in joints.
On the other hand, human swings a leg, leans its body forward, and uses potential energy in order to walk as if human tries to save energy to walk. Walking down the slope is one of the easiest conditions to walk (Osuka, 2002). The application of these human walking to the robots is called passive dynamic walking. A possibility to reproduce passive dynamic walking experimentally is introduced by McGeer (McGeer, 1990). Giving a simply structured walker proper initial conditions, the walker walks down the slope by inertial and gravitational force without any artificial energy externally.
Goswami et al. carry out extensive simulation analysis, and show stability of walking and several other phenomena (Goswami et al., 1998; Goswami et al., 1998). In addition, Osuka et al. reproduce passive dynamic walking and the phenomena experimentally by using Quartet (walker)(Osuka et al., 1999; Osuka et al., 2000).
However, the both studies constrain the yaw and rolling motion in order to simplify the analyses. Also, these analyses are made for legs without knees, so that extra care was necessary to make experimental analyses harder because the swing legs hit the slope at the position that it passes the supporting leg.
In this study, the analyses were made three-dimensional walking with rolling motion. The 3D modeling, and simulation analysis were performed in order to search better walking

condition and structural parameters. Then, the 3D passive dynamic walker was fabricated in order to analyze the passive dynamic walking experimentally.

2. Modelingof 3D passive walker

A compass gait biped model for walking is a model which constrains the motion into a two dimensional plane. The walker for this model has to have four or eight legs to cut off the rolling motion for experimental analyses. In addition, there is foot-scuffing problem at the time when a swing leg is passing the side of support leg.

So, 3D passive walker model is used to solve the problems stated above, and to investigate the stableness of the walker. The modeling and simulation of this study was inspired by Tedrake et al. (Tedrake, 2004; Tedrake et al., 2004).

2.1 3D Model of passive walker

The 3D model of passive walker is shown in Fig. 1. Each parameters used in this model is shown in Table1 and 2.

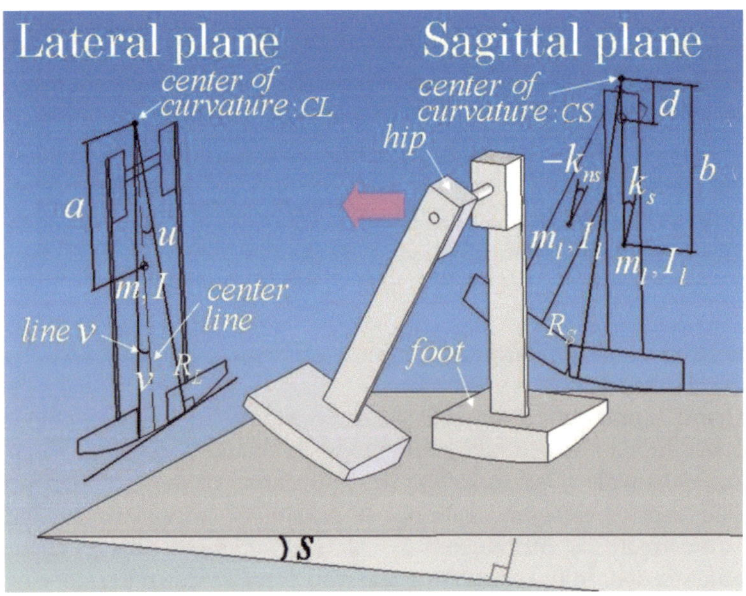

Fig. 1. 3D Model of Passive Walker

Symbol	Lateral Plane	Quantity
M	Mass	2.5 kg
I	Inertia	533 kgcm²
R_L	Radius of foot curve	50 cm
A	Distance between CL and center of gravity	29 cm
U	Angle of rolling	
V	Angle between center line and line v	0.038 rad

Table 1. Parameters for Model in Lateral Plane

Symbol	Sagittal Plane	Quantity
m_l	Mass of a leg	1.25 kg
l_I	Inertia of a leg	47.4 $kgcm^2$
R_s	Radius of foot curve	38 cm
B	Distance CS and center of leg	17 cm
D	Distance between the center of curvature and hip	4.7 cm
k_s	Angle of swing leg	
k_{ns}	Angle of support leg	
S	Angle of slope	0.035 rad

Table 2. Parameters for model in sagittal plane

This model is a 3-D passive walker with two legs connected at hip with simple link structure. Legs do not have knees. Foot with concaved surface allows the rolling motion, so that walking is expanded 3D space. Especially, the rolling motion in lateral plane solves the scuffing problem at the moment when swing leg is passing through supporting leg. In sagittal plane, support leg can be seen as an inverted pendulum, and swing can be seen as simple pendulum for the motion of bipedaling walker.
The assumption that the yaw motion was small enough to ignore was made for simplifying the numerical analysis, and analysis was carried in a way the space is dividing into lateral and sagittal plane.

2.2 Equation of motion for lateral plane

The equation of motion for lateral plane is given. It is assumed that the foot of support leg is on contact and not slipping with surface of slope until becoming swing leg.

$$H(u)\ddot{u} + C(u,\dot{u})\dot{u} + G(u) = 0 \tag{1}$$

$H(u)$ is a matrix for inertial force, $C(u,\dot{u})$ is a matrix for centrifugal force, and $G(u)$ is a vector for gravitational force in (1). For this equation, the component would change according to the angle of rolling, u.
When only supporting leg is on contact on slope ($|u| > v$), the each component is shown in (2).

$$H(u) = I + ma^2 + mR_L^2 - 2mR_L a\cos u$$

$$C(u,\dot{u}) = mR_L a\dot{u}\sin u$$

$$G(u) = mga\sin u \tag{2}$$

When changing the supporting leg ($|u| \le v$), the each component is shown in (3).

$$H(u) = I + ma^2 + mR_L^2 - 2mR_L a\cos(u - w)$$

$$C(u,\dot{u}) = 0$$

$$G(u) = mg(a\sin u - R_L \sin w) \tag{3}$$

Under condition of u>0, w is defined as w=u-v, and under condition of u<0, w is defined as w=u+v in (3).
When the angle of rolling is zero (u=0), the swing leg collides with slope. This collision is assumed to be inelastic collision. The equation of collision can be shown as (4).

$$\dot{u}^{+} = \dot{u}^{-} \cos[2\tan^{-1}\left(\frac{R_L \sin v}{R_L \cos v - a}\right)] \tag{4}$$

Superscripts - and + means before and after collision accordingly in (4).

2.3 Equation of motion for sagittal plane

The equation of motion for sagittal plane is shown as (5).

$$H(q)\ddot{q} + C(q,\dot{q})\dot{q} + G(q) = 0 \tag{5}$$

q is a vector for angle of support and swing leg, H(q) is a 2 by 2 matrix for inertial force, $C(q,\dot{q})$ is a 2 by 2 matrix for centrifugal force in (5). G(q) is a vector for gravitational force in (5). The components of (5) can be expressed in (6).
H(u) is a matrix for inertial force, $C(u,\dot{u})$ is a matrix for centrifugal force, and G(u) is a vector for gravitational force in (1). For this equation, the component would change according to the angle of rolling, u.
When only supporting leg is on contact on slope ($|u|$ >v), the each component is shown in (2).

$$H_{11} = I_1 + m_1 b^2 + m_1 d^2 + m_1 R_s^2 - 2m_1 R_s (b+d)\cos(k_s - s)$$

$$H_{12} = H_{21} = m_1(b-d)\{d\cos(k_s - k_{ns}) - R_s \cos(k_{ns} - s)\}$$

$$H_{22} = I_1 + m_1(b-d)^2$$

$$C_{11} = m_1 R_s (b+d)\sin(k_s - s)\dot{k}_s + \frac{1}{2} m_1 d(b-d)\sin(k_s - k_{ns})\dot{k}_{ns}$$

$$C_{12} = m_1(b-d)\{d\sin(k_s - k_{ns})(\dot{k}_{ns} - \frac{1}{2}\dot{k}_s) + R_s \sin(k_{ns} - s)\dot{k}_{ns}\}$$

$$C_{21} = m_1(b-d)\{d\sin(k_s - k_{ns})(\dot{k}_{ns} - \frac{1}{2}\dot{k}_s) - \frac{1}{2} R_s \sin(k_{ns} - s)\dot{k}_{ns}\}$$

$$C_{12} = \frac{1}{2} m_1(b-d)\{d\sin(k_s - s) + R_s \sin(k_{ns} - s)\}\dot{k}_s$$

$$G_1 = m_1 g\{(b+d)\sin k_s - 2R_s \sin s\}$$

$$G_2 = m_1 g(b-d)\sin k_{ns} \tag{6}$$

The equation for collision can be shown for before and after the collision by the conservation law for angler momentum in (7)

$$Z^{+}(q)\dot{q}^{+} = Z^{-}(q)\dot{q}^{-} \quad (7)$$

Superscripts - and + means before and after collision accordingly in (7). $Z^{+}(q)$ and $Z^{-}(q)$ are matrices for the coefficients of collision. Components in (7) are shown as (8).

$$Z^{-}_{11} = 2bd\cos(k_{ns} - k_s) - (b+d)R_s\cos(k_{ns} - s) - 2bR_s\cos(k_{ns} - s) + 2R_s^2 + b^2 - bd$$

$$Z^{-}_{12} = Z^{-}_{21} = (b-d)\{b - R_s\cos(k_{ns} - s)\}$$

$$Z^{-}_{22} = 0$$

$$Z^{+}_{11} = (b-d)\{d\cos(k_s - k_{ns}) - R_s\cos(k_s - s) + (b-d)\}$$

$$Z^{+}_{12} = -R_s(b-d)\cos(k_s - s) - R_s(b+2d)\cos(k_{ns} - s) + d^2 + 2R_s^2 + bR_s\cos(k_{ns} + s)$$

$$-b^2\cos(2k_{ns}) + d(b-d)\cos(k_s - k_{ns})$$

$$Z^{+}_{21} = (b-d)^2$$

$$Z^{+}_{22} = (b-d)\{d\cos(k_s - k_{ns}) - R_s\cos(k_s - s)\} \quad (8)$$

3. Simulation results

Structural parameters and numerical parameters are searched for stable walking motion. Since there is no effective theory for the stability analysis, the only way is to try the simulations for the conditions those can be realized for the experiments. Some comparisons are made for limit cycles in order to decide the better conditions as shown in Fig. 2 and 8. These results show that limit cycle can be changed drastically in a small difference in two

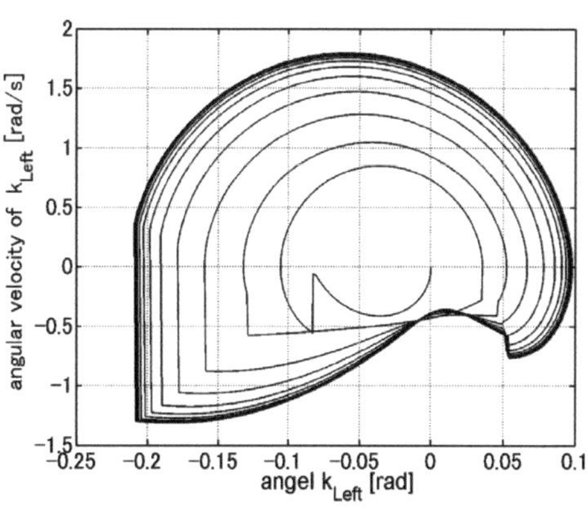

(a) m_l =1.4, I_l =48

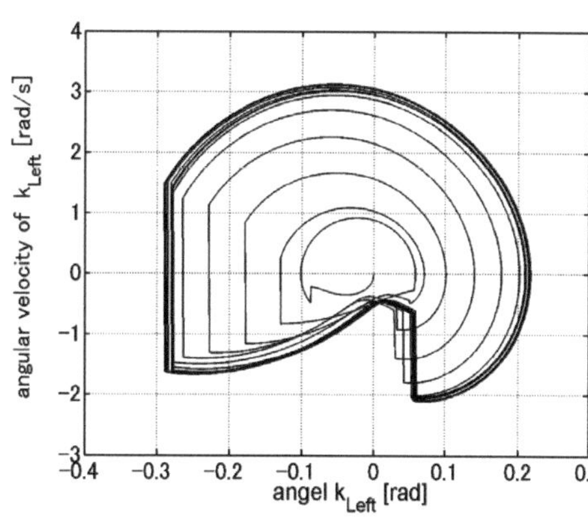

(b) m_l =1.5, I_l =49

(m_l in kg, I_l in kgcm²)

Fig. 2. Limit Cycles around Better Condition

parameters shown. Fig. 2 (a) shows limit cycle. This may be a better condition comparing with Fig. 2 (b) which does not show limit cycle. However, Fig. 2 (a) requires more cycles to converge into the limit cycle comparing with the Fig. 8. The results shown bellow are the ones of better results or better tendency from searching parameters although the method is primitive. Table 1 and 2 show parameters and initial conditions used for better walking results. In order to start walking, initial angle of rolling was applied as 0.18 rad.

3.1 Simulation results for lateral plane

The walking motion in lateral plane is shown schematically in Fig.3. A walking starts from scene 1, and follow the arrows for rolling motion. One cycle of gait is starting from the scene one and just before coming back to scene one again.

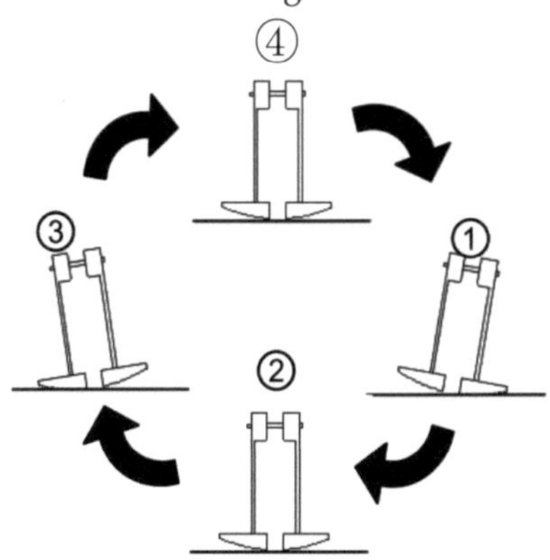

Fig. 3. Motion of Model in Lateral Plane

Fig.4 shows the change in angle of rolling with time. The amplitude of the angle attenuates gradually, and period of walking shortens slowly as time passes.

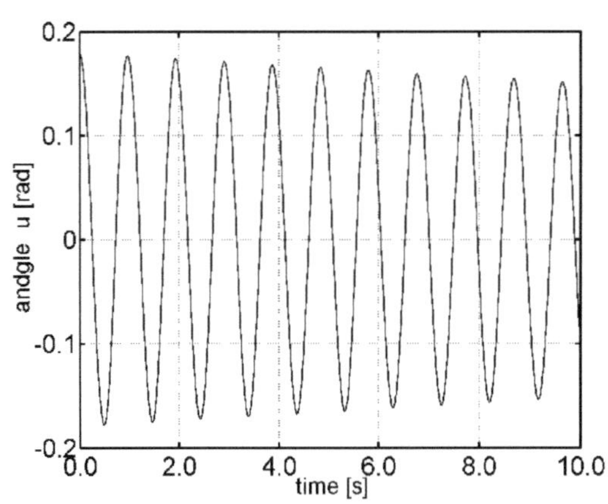

Fig. 4. Angle of Roll in Lateral Plane

Fig. 5 shows the phase plane locus for the angle of rolling for 5 seconds from the beginning of walking. The trajectory starts from the initial condition, $(u, \ddot{u}) = (0.18, 0)$, and converges into the condition, $(u, \ddot{u}) = (0, 0)$. The reason for this phenomenon is the collision at scene 2 and 4 in Fig. 3, and the angular velocity decreases slightly.

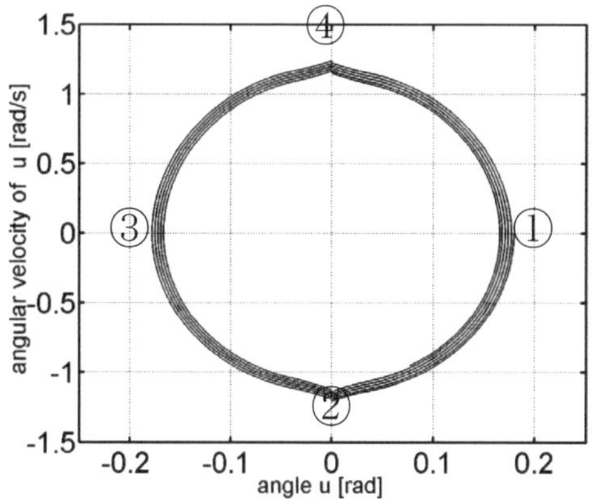

Fig. 5. Phase Plane Locus in Lateral Plane

3.2 Simulation results for sagittal plane

The walking motion in sagittal plane is shown schematically in Fig. 6. A walking starts from scene 1, and follows the arrows as the walker walks down the slope. The motion from scene 1 to just before scene one is defined as one cycle of gait.

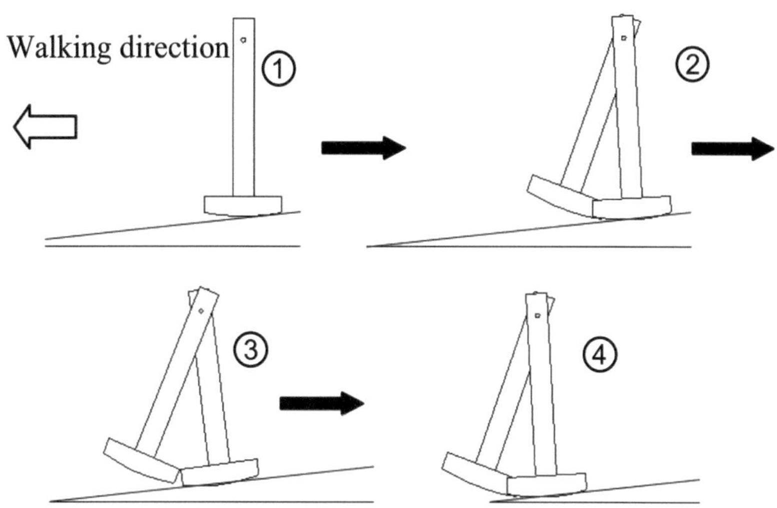

Fig. 6. One cycle of gait for Sagittal Plane Mode

Fig. 7 shows the angle of legs toward waking direction from the beginning of walking for 5 seconds. It seems it will take some time for stable walking. The vertical dotted line in Fig. 7 shows the moment for changing the support leg. The period between changing legs hardly changes even after 30 seconds has passed.

Fig. 8 shows the phase plane locus for angle of legs. The trajectory starts from the initial condition, $(k_{ns}, k_s, \dot{k}_{ns}, \dot{k}_s) = (0,0,0,0)$ shown as scene 1 in Fig. 6, and converges into the same trajectory (the limit cycle) after 7 cycles of gait.

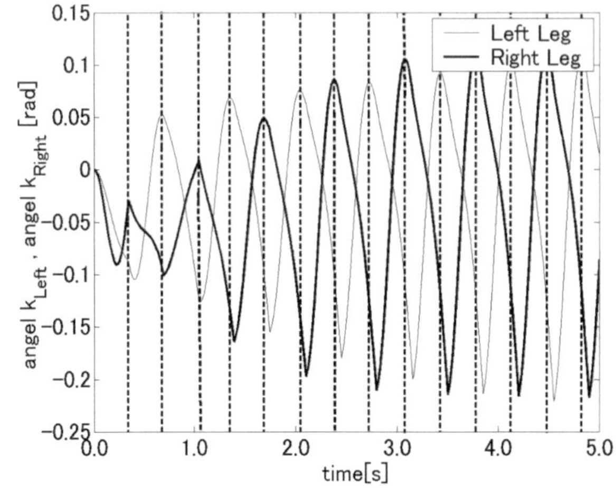

Fig. 7. Leg Angle in Sagittal Plane

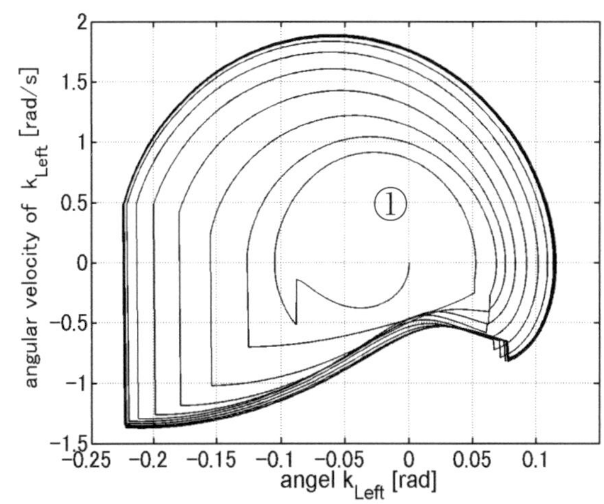

Fig. 8. Phase Plane Locus in Sagittal Plane

3.3 Effects of initial conditions and structural parameters

It is likely that initial conditions and structural parameters are the important factors for stable walking. So, some simulations are performed in this manner.

The limit cycles can be observed under these conditions by changing angle of slope from 0.017 to 0.087 rad shown in Fig. 9. By looking some data from leg angle, the walker is able to walk down the slope. However, some differences are observed in the trajectory of limit cycle as Fig. 9. Places circled are the position where the swing leg is changing to support leg. The length of the vertical line seems to have some effect on the stability of walking. The better condition for stable walking was (c) in Fig. 9. The angle of swing leg to contact the surface of slope seems to be important parameter.

In addition, the effects of structural parameters can be observed in Fig. 10. The ratio of inertia to mass has been changed in order to see phase locus plane. The ratio of stable walking shown above is 38 to 1 in Fig. 10 (a), and all the other conditions are from Table 1 and 2. When ratio decreases to 37 to one, it showed very similar limit cycle. However, the limit cycle starts to change its shape for less stable walking as ratio decreases. When ratio increases, limit cycle is not observed any longer as shown in Fig. 10 (b).

It is also true that the limit cycle is the same as long as the ratio of inertia to mass does not change under same initial conditions. In another word, when the mass and inertia are changed to half without changing the ratio of inertia to mass, the limit cycle is the same as the initial mass and inertia.

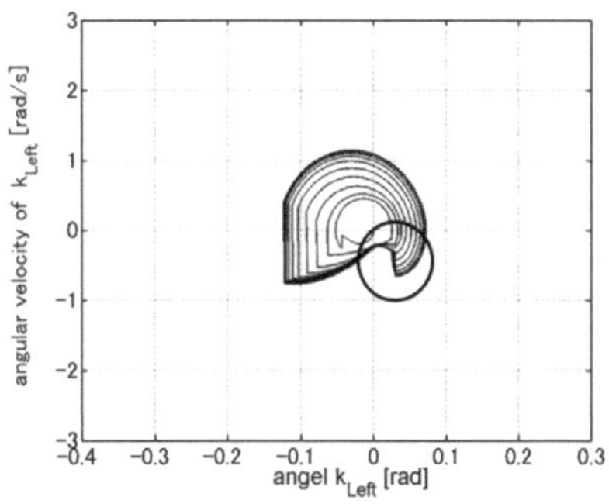

(a) S = 0.017 rad

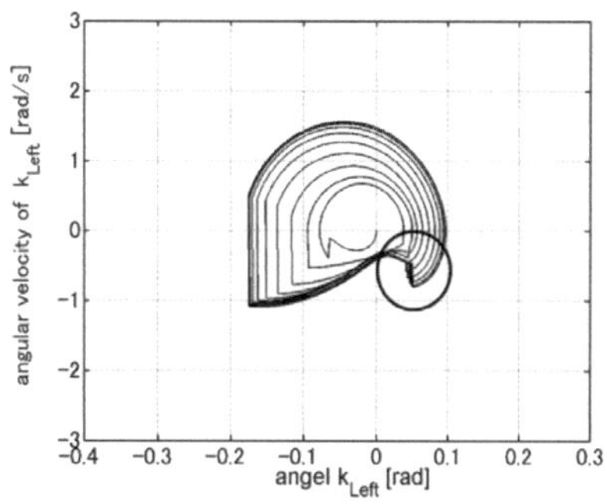

(b) S = 0.026 rad

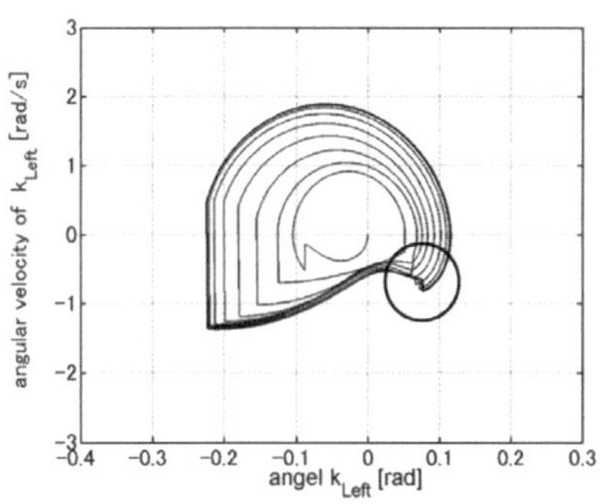

(c) S = 0.035 rad

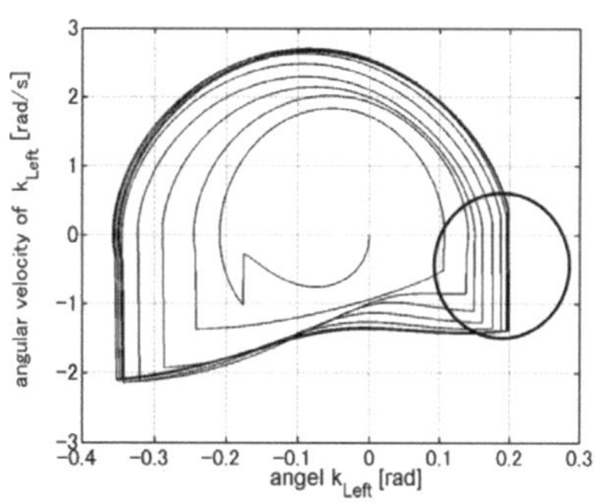

(d) S = 0.070 rad

Fig. 9. Phase Plane Locus by Changing Angle of Slope

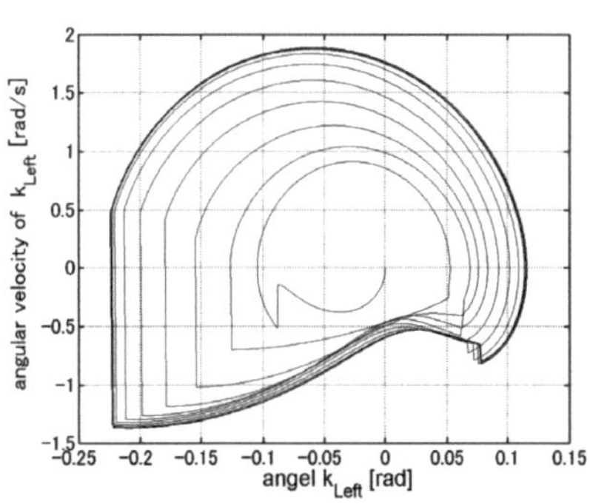

(a) 38:1

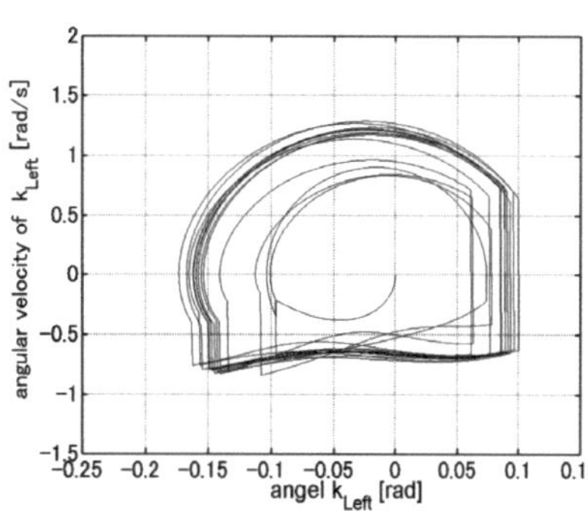

(b) 65:1

Fig. 10. Change in Phase Locus Plane by Changing Ratio of Inertia to Mass (Inertia: Mass)

4. Experimental analyses

For experimental analyses, 3D bipedal passive dynamic walker was build upon the structural parameters from simulation analyses. Experiments were performed around the conditions obtained from the simulation analyses for the walker.

4.1 3D passive walker and experimental method

3D passive walker in this study has two straight legs and two curved foot. The feet have 3D concave up surface with a curvature in each plane, such as 500mm in lateral plane, and 380 mm in Sagittal plane.
A picture of 3D passive walker is shown in Fig. 11. Table 1 and 2 show the other parameters of the walker.
This walker (Fig. 11) has no actuators, and has two legs those are connected together at hip with simple link structure. It is designed after the waking model from Fig. 1. A three dimensional sensor (VC-03, Sensation Inc.) is used. The sensor set on the left hip, as shown in a circle of Fig.11, in order to measure the angle of leg and rolling angle at walk. This sensor can be connected to the computer for real time reading of the angle.
Experiments were performed with 3D passive walker under conditions from the simulation. The initial conditions are used from Table 1 and 2. The angle of slope is set to be 0.035 rad, and $(u, \ddot{u}) = (0.18,0)$ for walking. Some of the initial conditions and structural parameters are varied to see the change in walking. Also, the surface of slope for walking was covered with a rubber sheet for inelastic collision between foot and slope. The rubber sheet may allow the walker decrease yaw motion.

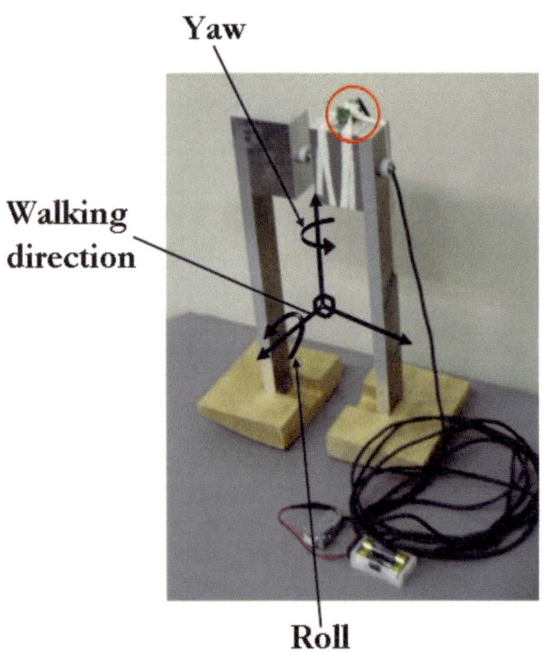

Fig. 11. 3D Passive Walker

4.2 Results

The change in angle of roll is shown in Fig. 12. Although the initial condition is $(u, \ddot{u}) = (0.18, 0)$, the rolling angle shows larger amplitude.

Fig.13 shows the change in angle of left leg with time. Each axis shows time and angle of left leg, horizontal and vertical. This shows the walking motion from the beginning to 6 seconds. However, the yaw motion becomes greater after 6 seconds so that it is hard to measure the angle of left leg correctly.

In addition, the angle of slope is changed from 0.017 to 0.070 rad in order to see effect for walking. The walker is able to walk down the slope for under those angles. However, the gait for waking is different. When the angle is 0.087 rad, the walker can walk down the slop, but falls down from time to time. The better angle for stable walk is around 0.035 rad.

Although the further study is necessary, the changes for other parameters, such as adding weight on foot, cause the change in gait.

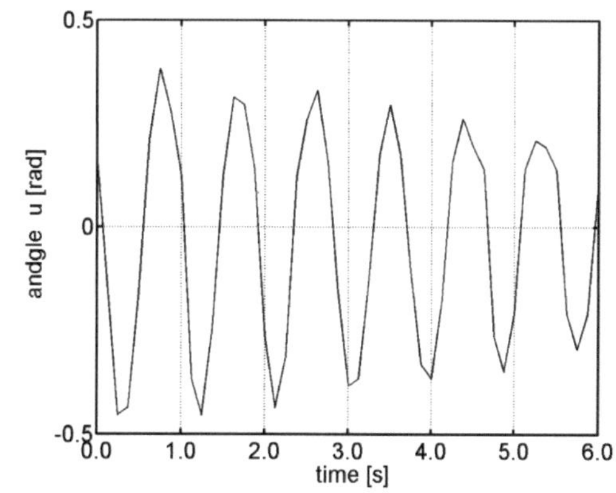

Fig. 12. Change in Angle of Roll

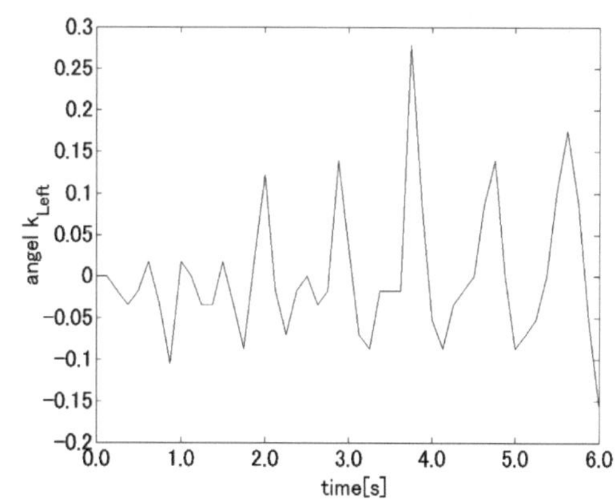

Fig. 13. Change in Angle of Leg

4.3 Discussion

Under one of the best initial conditions (including the structural parameters) for the stable walking, the 3D passive walker showed stable walking. This matching condition is meaningful for further investigation. At the beginning of the walking, the walker shows

very little yaw motion. However, the walker started to show yaw motion greater than expected. The rubber sheet was not enough to compensate the yaw motion.
So, further study is necessary to decrease effects of yaw motion. During human walk, left arm is swung as right leg is stepped forward and right arm is swung as left leg is stepped forward. Arms are attached around hip of 3D passive walker to compensate the yaw motion by swinging arms by imitating human walking.
The other way to decrease yaw motion is also planned as a next study. The leaf spring is made like a body of dinosaur or lizard in order to compensate the yaw motion by spring force and inertia.
Both studies are just started. The further investigations are necessary to be reported.

5. Discussion

Fig.14 shows the comparison of angle of left leg between simulation and experiment according to time in sagittal plane. The vertical axis is for leg angle, and horizontal axis is for time. The solid line is for a result of simulation, and dotted line is for a result of experiment. Both simulation and experiment are continued for 6 seconds.
The initial condition for Fig.14 was derived from the simulation analysis. This condition was one of the best for stable walking. Both results have similar tendency qualitatively. But experimental results seem to have time lag to the simulation result.

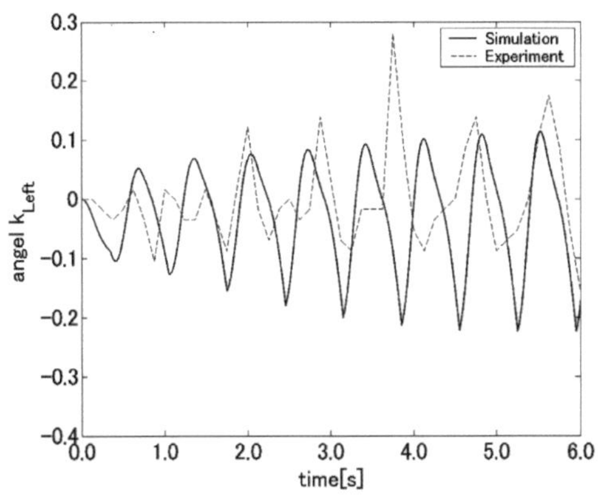

Fig. 14. Angle of Leg by Simulation and Experiment

There are reasons for this time lag to be happened, such as a friction around linkage around hip, friction between foot and surface of floor, and so on. One of the main reasons is from the yaw motion. Because of the yaw motion, the angle of leg cannot be measured correctly for this experiment.
In addition, the change in angle of slope showed similar tendency between simulation and experiment. Especially when the angle of slope is around 0.070 rad, the walker was able to walk down the slope but falls on back very often in experiment. Fig. 9 (d) shows the swing leg becomes to support leg at the point where the swing leg does not become zero angular velocity. This can be read as the reason for the walker fall on back from experiments.
Fig.15 shows change in angle of roll from simulation and experiments. The amplitude is larger for the experiments and the attenuation is much greater in the experiments. The attenuation is probably caused by the rubber sheet, collision to the slope and yaw motion.

The reason for larger amplitude seems to be relating with initial condition for walking experiments.
So, additional analysis was performed in simulation, because the initial condition can be created easily. The initial angular velocity is changed for simulation from 0 to -2.1 rad/s. Fig. 16 shows similar tendency for angle of roll in the beginning. The amplitude of roll becomes similar although attenuation is larger in experiment as before. This gives some attention the initial conditions should be considered carefully especially in experiments.

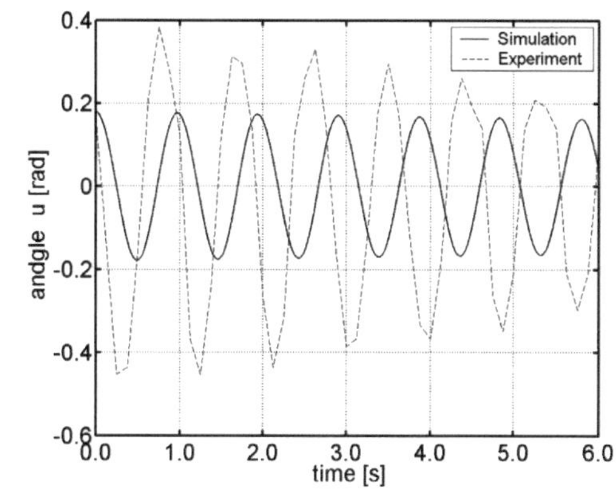

Fig. 15. Angle of Roll by Simulation and Experiment

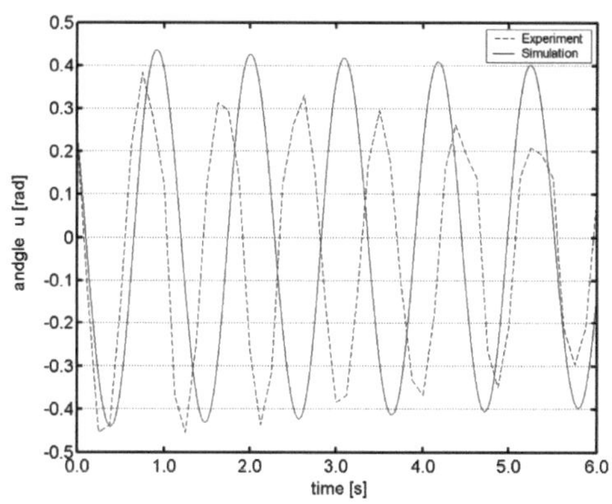

Fig. 16. Angle of Roll by Simulation with Initial Angler Velocity (-2.1rad/sec)

6. Conclusion

As the fist step for the advance in human-robot interaction, it is important to determine the stability of 3D walking model, and to find initial conditions and structural parameters for stable walking as a first step.
The simulation was performed to search of structural parameter for stable walking condition. A 3D walker is build according to the simulation result. Then, the experimental analysis was carried out to search some parameters and compare with simulation result.
Simulation shows some parameters and initial condition would lead stable walking for 3D model in Table 1 and 2. The experimental analysis shows 3D passive walker walks down the

slope under the same condition from simulation result, and angle of legs has similar tendencies as to the simulation results. Although the tendency from the experiments and simulations are similar, the results show some differences such as time lag for leg angle in sagittal plane. One of the main reasons for this seemed to be caused by assumption that the yaw motion is small enough to ignore. So, further trials to decrease or separate the effects from yaw motion would lead better simulation for stable walking and better understanding of passive walking. And more over, the humanoid robot may be able to walk more efficiently. These studies will help interaction between human and robot.

7. References

A. Ishiguro, D. Owaki, "Toward a Well-balanced Control," ISCIE, vol. 49, no. 10, 2005, 417-422. ISSN 0916-1600

K. Osuka, "Legged Robots and Control Scheme based on a Sence of Passive Dynamic Walking," RSJ Journal, vol.20, no.3, 2002, 233-236. ISSN 0289-1824

T. McGeer, "Passive Dynamic Walking," Int. J. of Robotics Research, vol.9, no.2, April, 1990, 62-82. ISSN 0278-3649

A. Goswami, B. Thuilot and B. Espiau, "Compass-Like Biped Robot-Part I: Stability and Bifurcation of Passive Gaits," Technical Report 2996, INRIA, 1998.

A. Goswami, B. Thuilot and B. Espiau, "A Study of the Passive Gait of a Compass-Like Biped Robot: Symmetry and Chaos," The Int. J. of Robotics Research, vol.17, no.12, 1998, 1282-1301. ISSN 0278-3649

K. Osuka, T.Fujitani and T.Ono, "Passive Walking Robot QUARTET," Proc. of the 1999 IEEE Int. conf. on Control Application, 1999, 478-483. ISBN 0-7803-5446-X

K. Osuka and K. Kirihara, "Motion Analysis and Experiment of Passive Walking Robot Quartet II," RSJ Journal, vol.18, no.5, 2000, 737-742. ISSN 0289-1824

R. Tedrake, "Applied Optimal Control for Dynamically Stable Legged Locomotion," PhD thesis, MIT, 2004.

R. Tedrake, T. W. Zhang, M. F. Fong, and H. S. Seung, "Actuating a Simple 3D Passive Dynamic Walking," ICRA, vol.5, April, 2004, 4656-4661. ISBN 0-7803-8232-3

13

Motion Control of Wearable Walking Support System with Accelerometer Based on Human Model

Yasuhisa Hirata, Takuya Iwano, Masaya Tajika and Kazuhiro Kosuge
Department of Bioengineering and Robotics, Tohoku University
Japan

1. Introduction

Many countries of the world including Japan will become a full-fledged aged society. According to report in Japan, the elderly population aged 65 years or over in Japan will number 33 million and will account for more than 25 percent of the population. We have to support the elderly for independence in old age so that a variety of lifestyles is possible. With the development of the robot technologies, robotics researchers have developed various kinds of human assist robot such as walking aid system and manipulation aid system for supporting the elderly.

Especially, the ability to walk is one of the most important and fundamental functions for humans, and enables them to realize high-quality lives. Many researchers focused on a walker-type support system, which works on the basis of the physical interaction between the system with wheels and the user. Walkers are widely used by the handicapped because they are simple and easy to use.

Fujie et al. (1998) developed a power-assisted walker for physical support during walking. Hirata et al. (2003) developed a motion control algorithm for an intelligent walker with an omni-directional mobile base, in which the system is moved based on the user's intentional force/moment. Wandosell et al. (2002) proposed a non-holonomic navigation system for a walking-aid robot named Care-O-bot II. Sabatini et al. (2002) developed a motorized rollator. Yu et al. (2003) proposed the PAMM system to provide mobility assistance and user health status monitoring.

Wasson et al. (2003) and Rentschler et al. (2003) proposed passive intelligent walkers, in which a servo motor is attached to the steering wheel and the steering angle is controlled depending on environmental information. Hirata et al. (2007) developed The RT Walker which has passive dynamics with respect to the force/moment applied. It differs from other passive walkers in that it controls servo brakes appropriately without using any servo motors.

Many researchers have considered improving their functionality by adding wheels with actuators and controlling them based on robot technology (RT), such as motion control technology, sensing technology, vision technology, and computational intelligence. But, the size of the walker-type system is large and the user has to use the both hands for moving it. On the other hand, recently, many robotics researchers focused on wearable walking

support system which could support the motion of the user based on the control of the actuators attached to the body of the human directly.
In U.S., performance augmenting exoskeletons has come from a program sponsored by Defense Advanced Research Projects Agency (DARPA). The goal of the program is to increase the capabilities of ground soldiers beyond that of a human (Garcia et al. (2002)). Kazeroon et al. (2006) developed Berkeley Lower Extremity Exoskeleton (BLEEX). The Sarcos Research Corporation has worked toward a full-body Wearable Energetically Autonomous Robot (WEAR) (Guizzo & Goldstein (2005)). Walsh et al. (2006) also proposed a quasi-passive exoskeleton concept which seeks to exploit the passive dynamics of human walking in order to create lighter exoskeleton devices.
Kiguchi et al. (2003), Naruse et al. (2003), Nakai et al. (2001) and Kawamoto & Sankai (2005) also developed several wearable assist systems for supporting the daily activities of the people such as walking, handling and so on. Some of the conventional wearable human assist systems proposed so far try to identify the motion patterns of the user based on the biological signals such as EMG (electromyogram) signals or hardness of skin surface, and they assist the user based on the identified motions. However, the noises included in these biological signals make it difficult to identify the motions of the user accurately. In addition, since each joint of a human body is actuated with the cooperation of many muscles, the motions of the user could not identify correctly based on the activities of only few muscles observed by EMG signals or hardness of skin surface.
To overcome these problems, our group developed a wearable walking support system which was able to support walking activity without using biological signals (Nakamura et al. (2005)). The system calculates the support moment of the joints of the user by using an approximated human model of four-link open chain mechanism on the sagittal plane and it assists a part of the joint moment by the actuator of the wearable walking support system. In the conventional control algorithm, however, we assumed that the system only supported the stance phase of the gait and we neglected the weight of the support device in the stance phase. We also assumed that the user stood on flat ground and inclination of Foot Link is always parallel to the ground.
When we consider the support of the swing phase of the gait, the conventional control algorithm makes the burden of the user increase, because the user has to lift the support device in the swing phase. Additionally, the inclination of Foot Link always changes widely in the swing phase. In this chapter, we derive the support moment for the knee joint to guarantee the weight of the device. We also propose a method for measuring the inclination of a link of the human model with respect to the vertical direction by using an accelerometer. By using these methods, we derive the support moment of the joint for supporting the user in not only the stance phase but also the swing phase. We applied the proposed methods to the developed wearable walking support system experimentally and the experimental results illustrate the validity of them.

2. Wearable Walking Helper

In this section, we briefly introduce a developed wearable walking support system called Wearable Walking Helper. We developed the smaller and lighter support device for the knee joint than its conventional system proposed by Nakamura et al. (2005). Fig. 1 shows the prototype of the system which consists of knee orthosis, prismatic actuator and sensors. The knee joint of the orthosis has one degree of freedom rotating around the center of the knee joint of the user on sagittal plane. The mechanism of the knee joint is a geared dual hinge joint. The prismatic actuator, which is manually back-drivable, consists of DC motor and ball screw. By translating the thrust force generated by the prismatic actuator to the frames of the knee orthosis, the device can generate support moment around the knee joint of the user.

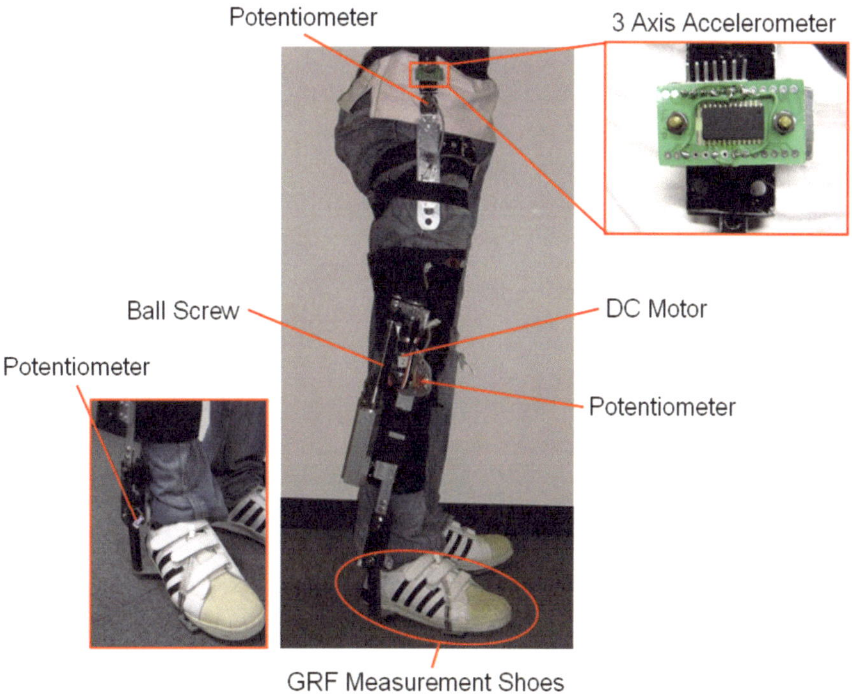

Fig. 1. Wearable Walking Helper with Accelerometer

The system has three potentiometers attached to the ankle, knee and hip joints to measure the rotation angle of each joint. To measure the Ground Reaction Force (GRF), we utilize two force sensors attached to the shoe sole: one is on the toe and the other is on the heel. In addition, a 3-axis accelerometer is attached to near the hip joint to measure inclination of the link. By using measured joint angles, GRFs and the inclination of the link, the control algorithm proposed in this chapter calculates the support moment around the knee joint.

3. Model-based control algorithm

In this section, we describe the control algorithm of the wearable walking support system. Firstly, we derive the knee joint moment based on an approximated human model. Secondly, we also drive the knee joint moment caused by the weight of the device itself. Finally, we determine the support joint moment to be generated by the actuator of the support device.

3.1 Calculation of knee joint moment using human model

To control the Wearable Walking Helper, we use the approximated human model as shown in Fig. 2. Under the assumption that the human gait is approximated by the motion on the sagittal plane, we consider only $Z-X$ plane. The human model consists of four links, that is, Foot Link, Shank Link, Thigh Link and Upper Body Link and these links compose a four-link open chain mechanism.

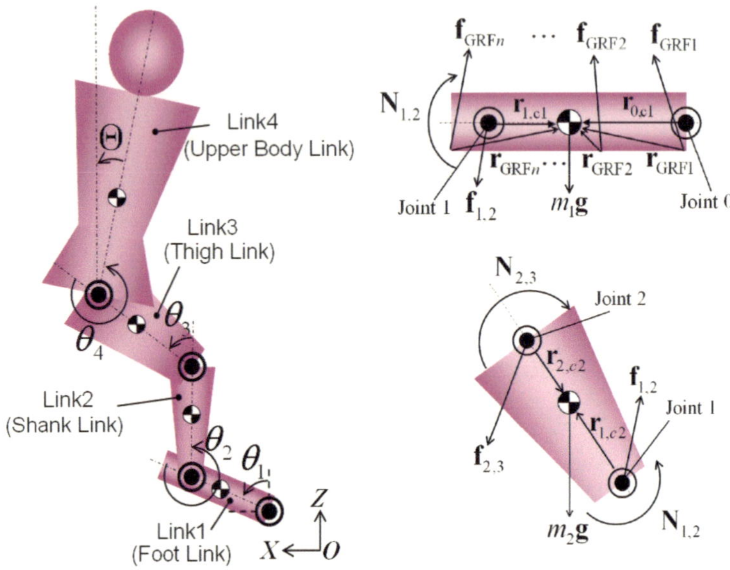

(a) Coordinate Systems b) Foot and Shank Links

Fig. 2. Human Model

To derive joint moments, we first set up Newton-Euler equations of each link. At the link i, Newton-Euler equations are derived as follows:

$$f_{i-1,i} - f_{i,i+1} - m_i g = m_i \dot{v}_{c_i} \tag{1}$$

$$N_{i-1,i} - N_{i,i+1} + r_{i,c_i} \times f_{i,i+1} - r_{i-1,c_i} \times f_{i-1,i} = I_i \frac{d\dot{\theta}_i}{dt} \tag{2}$$

where, $f_{i-1,i}$ and $f_{i,i+1}$ are reaction forces applying to the joint i and $i+1$ respectively. m_i is the mass of the link i, g is the vector of gravity acceleration and $\dot{v}_{c_i}$ is the translational acceleration of the gravity center of the link i. $N_{i-1,i}$ and $N_{i,i+1}$ are the joint moments applying to the joint i and $i+1$ respectively. r_{i,c_i} is the position vector from the joint i to the gravity center of the link i and r_{i-1,c_i} is the position vector from the joint $i-1$ to the gravity center of the link i. I_i is the inertia of the link i and θ_i is the rotation angle of the joint i.

The knee joint moment $N_{2,3}$ can be derived by using the equations of foot link and shank link as follows:

$$\begin{aligned}\tau_k = N_{2,3} = -I_1 \frac{d\dot{\theta}_1}{dt} - I_2 \frac{d\dot{\theta}_2}{dt} - m_1(r_{1,c_1} - r_{1,c_2} + r_{2,c_2}) \times (\dot{v}_{c_1} - g) - m_2 r_{2,c_2} \times (\dot{v}_{c_2} - g) \\ +(r_{1,c_1} - r_{1,c_2} + r_{2,c_2}) \times \sum f_{GRF} - \sum (r_{GRF} \times f_{GRF})\end{aligned} \tag{3}$$

where f_{GRF} is Ground Reaction Force exerted on the foot link.

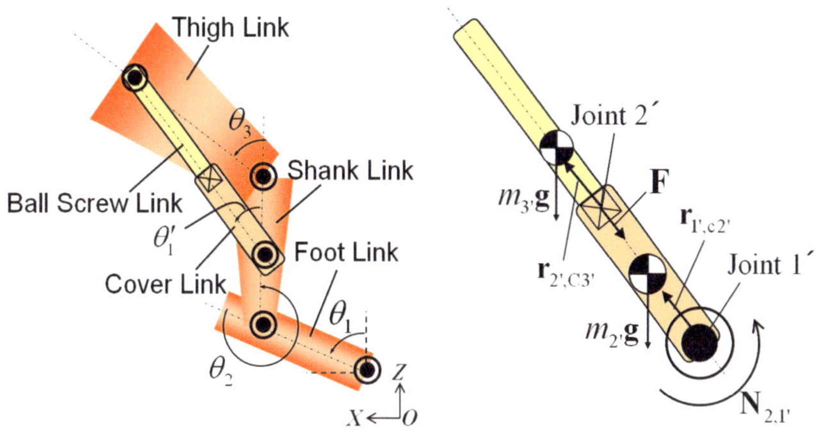

(a) Device Coordinate Systems (b) Ball Screw and Cover Link

Fig. 3. Device Model

3.2 Calculation of knee joint moment considering device model

To derive the knee joint moment affected by the weight of the walking support system, we use the device model as shown in Fig. 3. Since the device model has a closed-loop mechanism, we could not derive the joint moment easily. A variety of schemes for deriving joint torques for robots consisting of closed chain mechanisms have been proposed by Luh & Zheng (1985), Nakamura (1989) and so on. In this research, we apply the method proposed by Luh & Zheng (1985).

First, we define that joint 1′ is the connecting point between the Cover Link and Shank Link, joint 2′ is position of the prismatic joint of the support device as shown in Fig. 3(b) and joint 3′ is the connecting point between the Thigh Link and Ball Screw Link. The closed-chain is virtually cut open at the joint 3′ and we analyze it as virtual open-chain mechanism.

Next, the holonomic constraints are applied to the virtually cut joint. As a result, we can consider the spatial closed-chain linkage as a tree-structured open-chain mechanism with kinematic constraints. Similarly to the method we derived the knee joint moment using human model, the joint moments $N'_{2,3}$ which expresses the joint moment around joint 2 considering the effect of the support device and $N_{2,1'}$ can be derived based on Newton-Euler formulation as follows:

$$\begin{aligned} N'_{2,3} = & -I'_1\frac{d\dot{\theta}_1}{dt} - I'_2\frac{d\dot{\theta}_2}{dt} - I_{2'}\frac{d\dot{\theta}_{2'}}{dt} - m'_1(\mathrm{r}'_{1,c_1} - \mathrm{r}'_{1,c_2} + \mathrm{r}'_{2,c_2}) \times (\dot{\mathrm{v}}'_{c_1} - \mathrm{g}) \\ & - m'_2\mathrm{r}'_{2,c_2} \times (\dot{\mathrm{v}}'_{c_2} - \mathrm{g}) - m_{2'}\mathrm{r}_{2',c_2} \times (\dot{\mathrm{v}}_{c_{2'}} - \mathrm{g}) - m_{3'}\mathrm{r}_{3',c_2} \times (\dot{\mathrm{v}}_{c_{3'}} - \mathrm{g}) \end{aligned} \tag{4}$$

$$N_{2,1'} = I_{2'}\frac{d\dot{\theta}_{2'}}{dt} - m_{2'}\mathrm{r}_{1',c_{2'}} \times (\dot{\mathrm{v}}_{c_{2'}} - \mathrm{g}) - m_{3'}\mathrm{r}_{1',c_{2'}} \times (\dot{\mathrm{v}}_{c_{3'}} - \mathrm{g}) \tag{5}$$

From the Newton equation of Cover Link, the generalized force F shown in Fig. 3(b) can be derived as follows:

$$\mathrm{F} = m_{3'}(\dot{\mathrm{v}}_{c_{3'}} - \mathrm{g}) \tag{6}$$

where $\mathrm{F}=[F_{x2'}F_{z2'}]^T$ is two dimensional vector of generalized force and $F_{x2'}$ is zero since we only consider the gravity direction (z-axis) effected by the weight of the support device.

Now we consider the holonomic constraints for the virtually cut joint. The homogeneous transformation matrix from the joint 1′ to the joint 3′ through the joint 2 is

$$A_{1'}^{2}\ A_{2}^{3'}=\begin{bmatrix}\cos\theta_2 & 0 & \sin\theta_2 & l_3^{'}\sin\theta_2\\ 0 & 1 & 0 & 0\\ -\sin\theta_2 & 0 & \cos\theta_2 & l_2^{'}+l_3^{'}\cos\theta_2\\ 0 & 0 & 0 & 1\end{bmatrix}=\begin{bmatrix}\mathrm{R}_{1'2}^{23'} & \mathrm{P}_{1'2}^{23'}\\ 0 & 1\end{bmatrix} \tag{7}$$

and similarly from the joint 1′ to the joint 3′ through the joint 2′ is

$$A_{1'}^{2'}\ A_{2'}^{3'}=\begin{bmatrix}\cos\theta_1^{'} & 0 & \sin\theta_1^{'} & d\sin\theta_1^{'}+l_b\sin\theta_1^{'}\\ 0 & 1 & 0 & 0\\ -\sin\theta_1^{'} & 0 & \cos\theta_1^{'} & d\cos\theta_1^{'}+l_b\cos\theta_1^{'}\\ 0 & 0 & 0 & 1\end{bmatrix}=\begin{bmatrix}\mathrm{R}_{1'2'}^{2'3'} & \mathrm{P}_{1'2'}^{2'3'}\\ 0 & 1\end{bmatrix} \tag{8}$$

The support device has a closed chain mechanism, and Thigh Link and Ball Screw Link are actually connected at the joint 3′. Therefore, position vectors shown in equations (7) and (8) satisfy the following constraints.

$$\mathrm{c}=\mathrm{P}_{1'2}^{23'}-\mathrm{P}_{1'2'}^{2'3'}=\begin{bmatrix}l_3^{'}\sin\theta_2-(d+l_b)\sin\theta_1\\ l_2^{'}+l_3^{'}\cos\theta_2-(d+l_b)\cos\theta_1^{'}\end{bmatrix}=\begin{bmatrix}0\\0\end{bmatrix} \tag{9}$$

By using the generalized force and moments vector $\o^{o}=[N_{1,2}^{'}\ N_{2,3}^{'}\ F_{z2'}\ N_{2,1'}]^T$ and considering the holonomic constraints, the following equation is satisfied;

$$\mathrm{J(q)\ddot{q}+f(\ddot{q},q)+g(q)}-\o^{o}+\left(\frac{\partial \mathrm{c}}{\partial \mathrm{q}}\right)^T\lambda=0 \tag{10}$$

where

$$\left(\frac{\partial \mathrm{c}}{\partial \mathrm{q}}\right)^T=\begin{bmatrix}0 & 0\\ l_3^{'}\cos\theta_2 & -l_3^{'}\sin\theta_2\\ -\sin\theta_1^{'} & -\cos\theta_1^{'}\\ -(d+l_b)\cos\theta_1^{'} & (d+l_b)\sin\theta_1^{'}\end{bmatrix} \tag{11}$$

Additionally, in the equation (10), the inertia term $\mathrm{J(q)\ddot{q}}$ and the coriolis and centrifugal term $\mathrm{f(\ddot{q},q)}$ can be neglected because we only consider the joint moment occurred by the weight of the support device. Lagrange multiplier vector λ can be derived as follows:

$$\lambda=\left\{\left[\left(\frac{\partial \mathrm{c}}{\partial \mathrm{q}}\right)^T\right]_2\right\}^{-1}\begin{bmatrix}F_{z2'}\\ N_{2,1'}\end{bmatrix}=-\frac{1}{d+l_b}\begin{bmatrix}F_{z2'}(d+l_b)\sin\theta_1^{'}+N_{2,1'}\cos\theta_1^{'}\\ F_{z2'}(d+l_b)\cos\theta_1^{'}+N_{2,1'}\sin\theta_1^{'}\end{bmatrix} \tag{12}$$

where $[(\partial c/\partial q)^T]^2$ is an 2×2 matrix consisting of the last 2 rows of the matrix $(\partial c/\partial q)^T$. With Lagrange multiplier vector λ and generalized moment $\phi^o = [N'_{1,2}\ N'_{2,3}]^T$, the actual joint moment of closed chain mechanism $\phi^c = \begin{bmatrix}\tau_1^c & \tau_2^c\end{bmatrix}^T$ can be derived as follows:

$$\begin{bmatrix}\tau_1^c \\ \tau_2^c\end{bmatrix} = \begin{bmatrix}N'_{1,2} \\ N'_{2,3}\end{bmatrix} - \left[\left(\frac{\partial c}{\partial q}\right)^T\right]^2 \lambda = \begin{bmatrix}N'_{1,2} \\ N'_{2,3}\end{bmatrix} - \begin{bmatrix}0 & 0 \\ l'_3 \cos\theta_2 & -l'_3 \sin\theta_2\end{bmatrix}\lambda \tag{13}$$

where $[(\partial c/\partial q)^T]^2$ is an 2×2 matrix consisting of the first 2 rows of the matrix $(\partial c/\partial q)^T$. Finally, knee joint moment caused by the weight of the device is derived as follows:

$$\tau_g = N'_{2,3} + \frac{l'_3 F_{z2'}(d + l_b)\sin(\theta'_1 - \theta_2) + l'_3 N'_{2,1}\cos(\theta'_1 - \theta_2)}{d + l_b} \tag{14}$$

3.3 Support knee joint moment

To prevent the decrease in the remaining physical ability of the elderly, we calculate the support joint moment τ_{sk} as a part of the derived joint moment τ_k. The joint moment expressed by equation (3) consists of the gravity term τ_{gra} and the GRF term τ_{GRF}. Therfore, we calculate the support joint moment as follows:

$$\tau_{sk} = \alpha_{gra}\tau_{gra} + \alpha_{GRF}\tau_{GRF} + \tau_g \tag{15}$$

where α_{gra} and α_{GRF} are support ratios of the gravity and GRF terms, respectively. By adjusting these ratios in the range of $0 \le \alpha < 1$, support joint moment τ_{sk} can be determined. The gravity term τ_{gra} and the GRF term τ_{GRF} can be expressed as following equations.

$$\tau_{gra} = m_1(r_{1,c_1} - r_{1,c_2} + r_{2,c_2}) \times g + m_2 r_{2,c_2} \times g \tag{16}$$

$$\tau_{GRF} = (r_{1,c_1} - r_{1,c_2} + r_{2,c_2}) \times \sum f_{GRF} - \sum (r_{GRF} \times f_{GRF}) \tag{17}$$

In the conventional control algorithm, we assumed that the term of the weight of the device τ_g could be neglected since we only considered support for the stance phase on flat ground. In this paper, however, we derived the knee joint moment caused by the weight of the device and add the term τ_g to the equation of support joint moment as shown in equation (15). By applying this algorithm to the Wearable Walking Helper, it could support the weight of the device. For determining the appropriate support ratios α_{gra} and α_{GRF}, we have to consider the conditions of the user such as the remaining physical ability and the disabilities. This is our future works in cooperating with medical doctors.

4. Swing phase support using accelerometer

To accomplish the support of swing phase of the gait, the system has to detect the inclination of the link with respect to the vertical direction for calculating the support knee joint moment explained in equation (15). In this section, we first introduce a method to measure the inclination of the link with an accelerometer. Then we verify the effectiveness of the method by preliminary experiments.

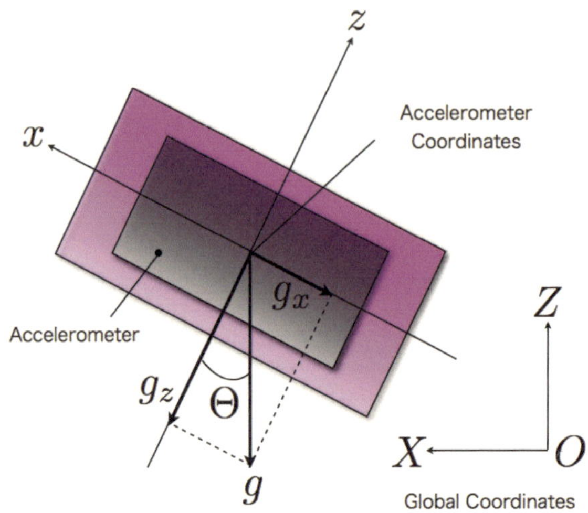

Fig. 4. Measurement of Acceleration of Human Link

4.1 Measuring method of link inclination

As shown in Fig. 4, the gravitational acceleration $g[m/s^2]$ is imposed along the vertical direction. By using the 3-axis accelerometer, the system can measure the gravitational acceleration decomposed in three directions under the condition of no dynamic acceleration. To measure the inclination of the link, we set the $x-z$ plane of the accelerometer coordinate system corresponds to the $X-Z$ plane of the global coordinate system as shown in Fig. 4. Consequently, the system can calculate the inclination of the accelerometer by using the following equation:

$$\Theta = \tan^{-1}\left(\frac{g_x}{g_z}\right) \tag{18}$$

where Θ is inclination of the accelerometer with respect to the vertical direction. g_x and g_z are gravitational accelerations in the direction of x axis and z axis in the accelerometer coordinate system, respectively. By attaching the accelerometer to the support device, the system can measure the inclination of the human links.

4.2 Investigation of influence of dynamic acceleration

With the method for measuring the inclination proposed in the previous section, we can measure the inclination of the link if dynamic acceleration does not arise. Therefore, we should investigate the influence of the acceleration arising from human motions on the accelerometer. In this section, we measure the translational acceleration of each link and investigate which links is better to attach the accelerometer for measuring the inclination of the link with respect to the vertical direction.

In the measurement experiment, we conducted two motions of human: one is standing up and sitting down motions and the other is walking. To calculate translational acceleration of the links, we captured the motion of the subject by using the Motion Capturing System called VICON460. Fig. 5 and Fig. 6 shows the experimental results of two motions.

As shown in Fig. 5, although the translational acceleration of Upper Body Link is largest, it is not so high compared to the gravitational acceleration 9.8 $[m/s^2]$. Similarly, in the case of walking experiment, the translational acceleration of Upper Body Link does not affect the measurement of the accelerometer. In the cases of the other links, the effect of the translational acceleration is too large and it must be difficult to measure the inclination of the like accurately. Especially, dynamic acceleration is highest at Foot Link during the gait, it seems impossible to measure the inclination of Foot Link directly.

Based on these evaluations, we decided to measure the inclination of Upper Body Link instead of Foot Link. Then inclination of Foot Link θ_1 is calculated with the following equation:

$$\theta_1 = \Theta - \theta_2 - \theta_3 - \theta_4 \tag{19}$$

where θ_2, θ_3 and θ_4 are joint angles of ankle, knee and hip joint respectively. Θ is inclination of Upper Body Link measured with the accelerometer.

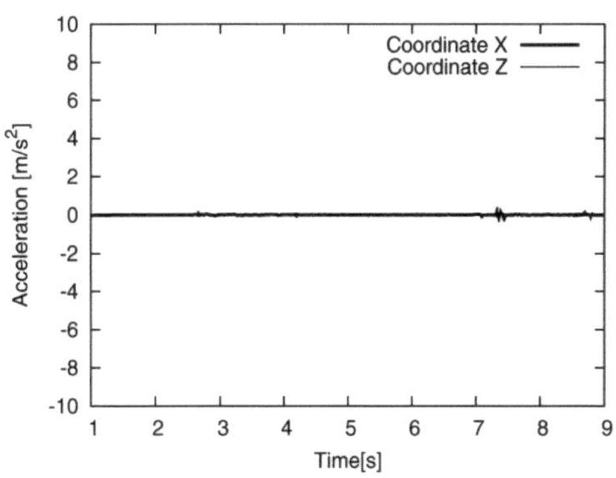

(a) Foot Link

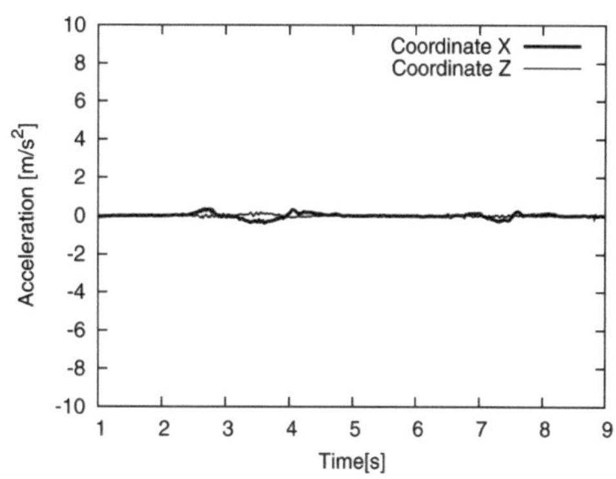

(b) Shank Link

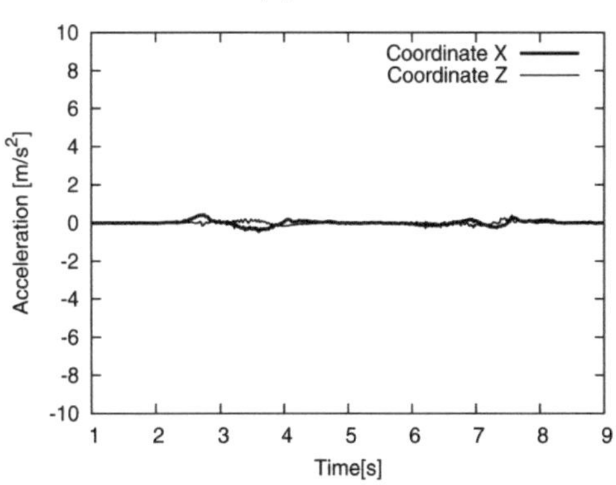

(a) Thigh Link

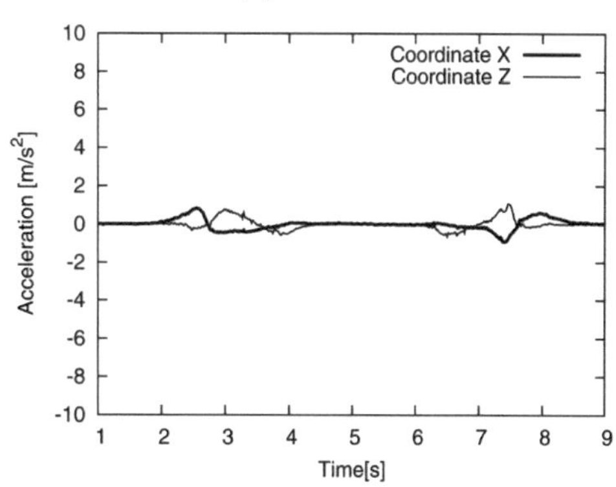

(b) Upper Body Link

Fig. 5. Translational Acceleration During Sit-Stand Motion

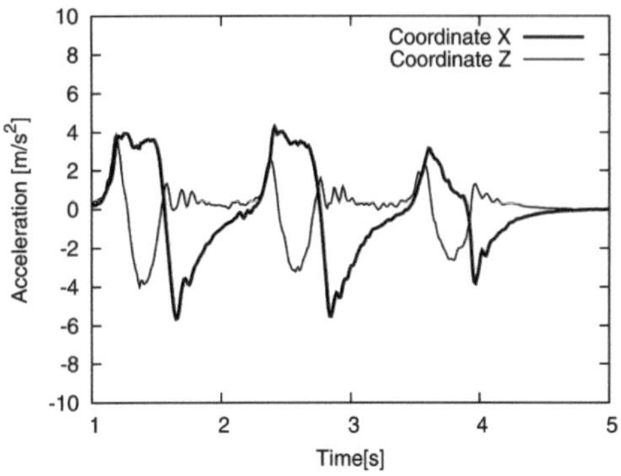

(a) Foot Link

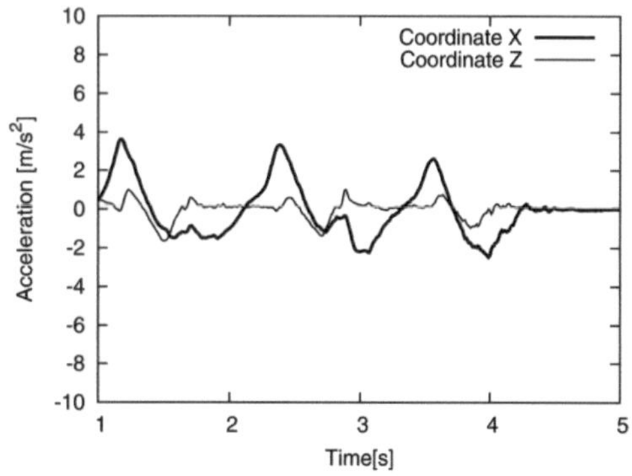

(b) Shank Link

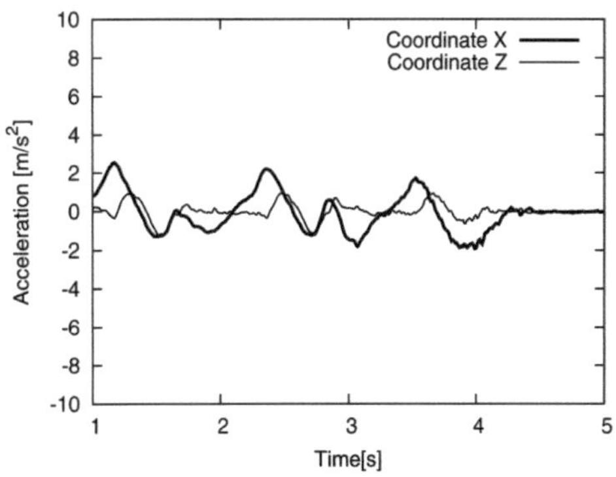

(a) Thigh Link

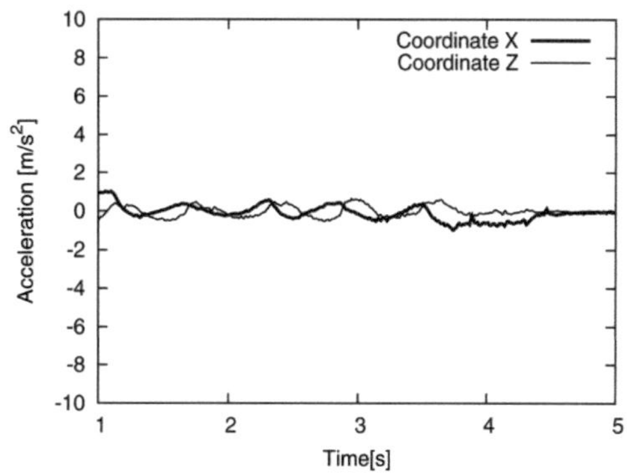

(b) Upper Body Link

Fig. 6. Translational Acceleration During Walking

4.3 Preliminary experiments

To investigate the validity of the proposed method for measuring the inclination of the link, we conducted two preliminary experiments. One is standing up and sitting down motions and the other is walking. During two experiments, we measured the inclination of the Upper Body Link using the accelerometer and joint angles using potentiometers, and then calculated the inclination of Foot Link using measured values. At the same time, we also captured the positions of markers attached to some parts of body of the user by using the Motion Capturing System (VICON460) and calculated the inclination of Upper Body Link for comparing it to the measured inclination using the accelerometer.
Experimental results are shown in Fig. 7 and Fig. 8. As shown in Fig. 7(a), inclinations with the accelerometer and Motion Capturing System are almost the same. Fig. 7(b) shows that inclination of Foot Link is approximately 90 degrees all through the motion. During walking, the inclination of Upper Body Link measured with the accelerometer is close to that of the value with the Motion Capturing System as shown in Fig. 8(a). From Fig. 8(b), the inclination of Foot Link, which was conventionally assumed 90 degrees, can be calculated in real time. From these experimental results, you can see that we measure inclination of Foot Link by using accelerometer and the system could support not only the stance phase but also the swing phase of the gait appropriately.

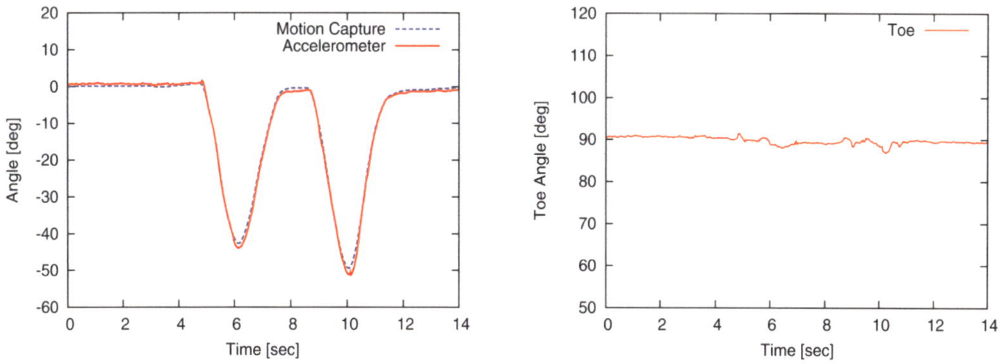

(a) Inclination of Upper Body (b) Inclination of Foot Link

Fig. 7. Experimental Results During Sit-Stand Motion

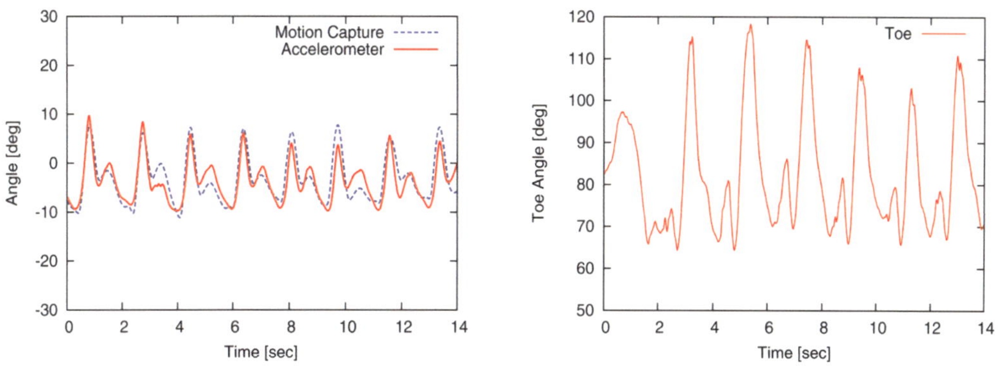

(a) Inclination of Upper Body (b) Inclination of Foot Link

Fig. 8. Experimental Results During Walking

5. Walking experiment

The final goal of this paper is to make it possible to support not only the stance phase but also the swing phase while a user is walking. In this section, by applying the proposed method to Wearable Walking Helper, we conducted experiments to support a user during gait. To show the proposed method is effective for the reduction of burden on the knee joint, we conducted the experiments in three conditions: firstly the subject walked without support control, secondly the subject walked with only stance phase support control, and thirdly the subject walked with both stance and swing phase support control. In addition, during the experiments, we measured EMG signals of muscles conductive to the movement of the knee joint.

In the gait cycle, the Vastus Lateralis Muscle is active in most of the stance phase and the Rectus Femoris Muscle is active in last half of the stance phase and most of the swing phase. Therefore, during the experiments, we measured EMG signals of the Vastus Lateralis Muscle and the Rectus Femoris Muscle. The university student who is 23-years-old man performed the experiments. Support Ratio α_{gra} and α_{GRF} in the equation (15) were set to 0.6, respectively. Note that, for reducing the impact forces applied to the force sensors attached

on the shoes during the gait, we utilized a low pass filter whose parameters were determined experimentally.
Joint angles during the walking experiment with only stance phase support and with both stance and swing phase supports are shown in Fig. 9. Similarly, Fig. 10 shows support moment for the knee joint. From Fig. 9(a), the inclination of Upper Body Link was not measured and the inclination of Foot Link was unknown as the results. On the other hand, with support for both stance and swing phases (Fig. 9(b)), the inclination of Upper Body Link was measured by using accelerometer, and then the system changed the inclination of Foot Link during the gait. From Fig. 10(a), the support moment for the knee was nearly zero in swing phase with conventional method. On the other hand, with the proposed method, support moment for the knee joint was calculated and supported in both stance and swing phases as shown in Fig. 10(b).

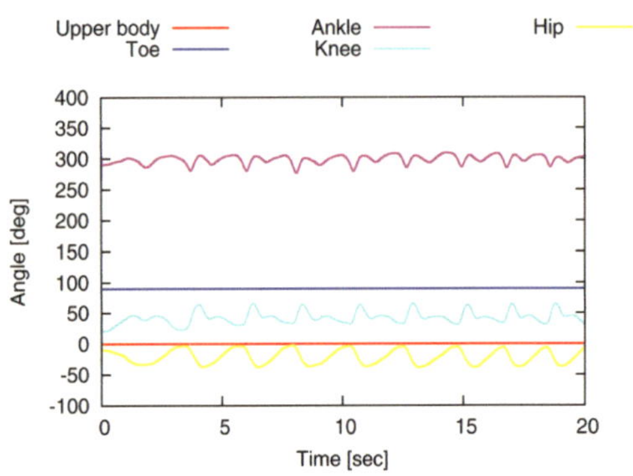

(a) Conventional Method

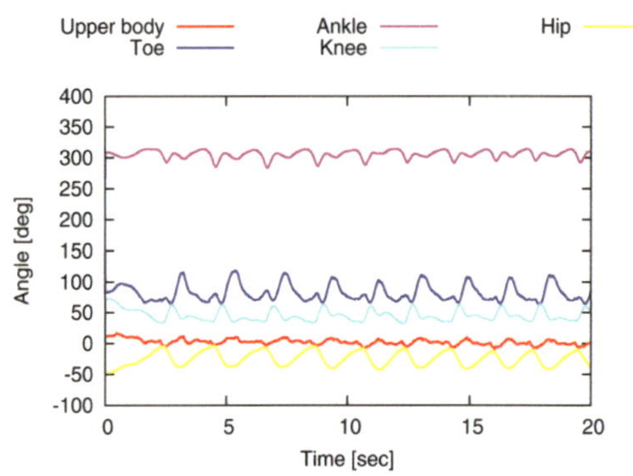

(b) Proposed Method

Fig. 9. Joint Angles During Walking

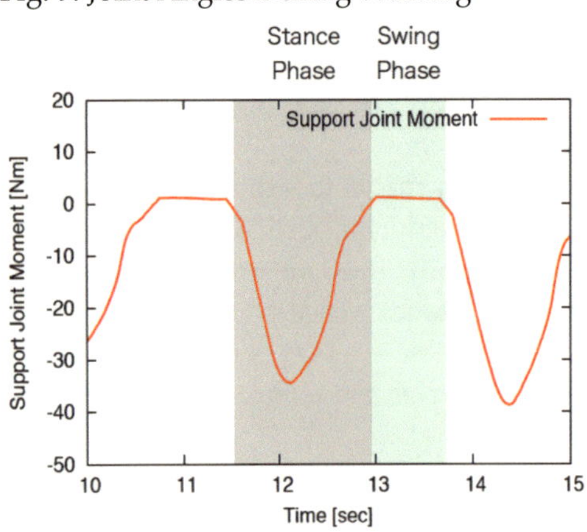

(a) Conventional Method

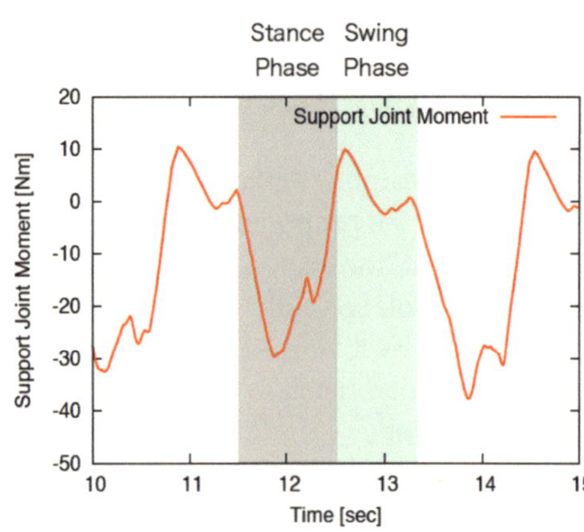

(b) Proposed Method

Fig. 10. Support Knee Joint Moment During Walking

Fig. 11 and Fig. 12 show EMG signals of the Vastus Lateralis Muscle and the Rectus Femoris Muscle during the experiments in three conditions explained above. Fig. 11(d) and Fig. 12(d) shows the integrated values of the EMG signals. From these results, EMG signals of both the Vastus Lateralis Muscle and the Rectus Femoris Muscle have maximum values in the experiment without support and have minimum values in the experiment with both stance and swing phase supports. These experimental results show that the developed system can support both stance and swing phases.

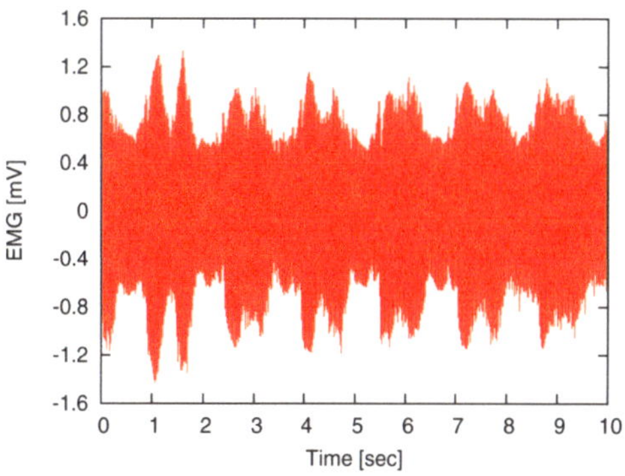

(a) Without Support

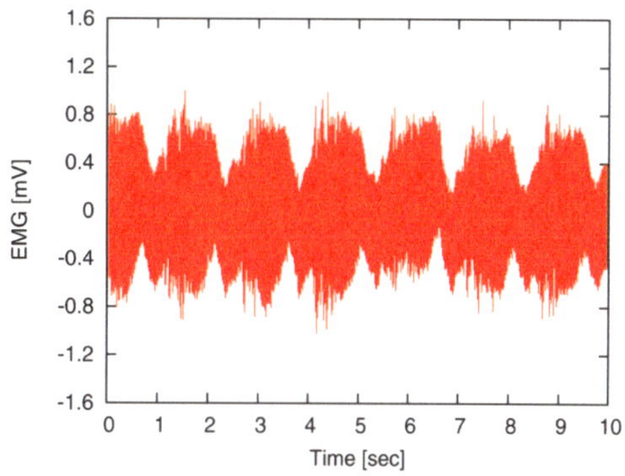

(b) Conventional Method

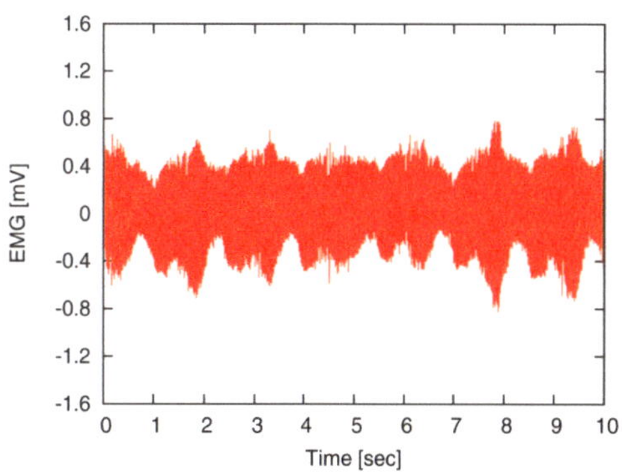

(c) Proposed Method

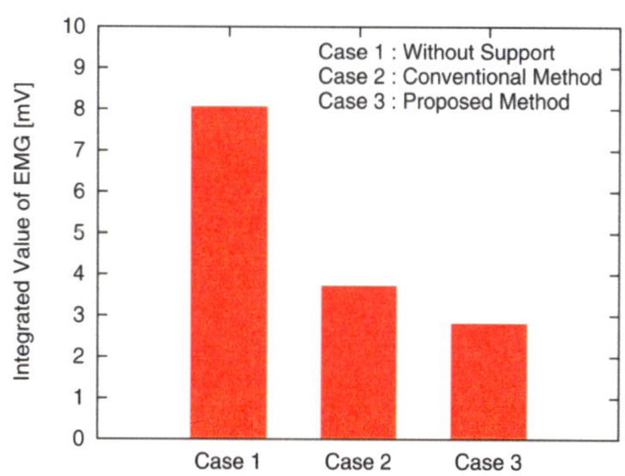

(d) Integrated Values

Fig. 11. EMG Signals of Vastus Lateralis Muscle

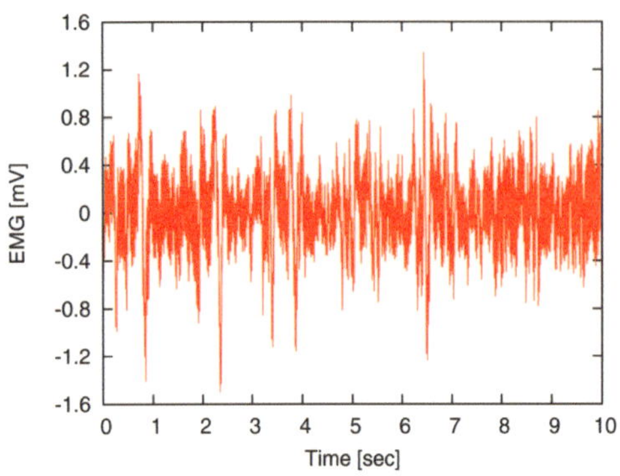

(a) Without Support

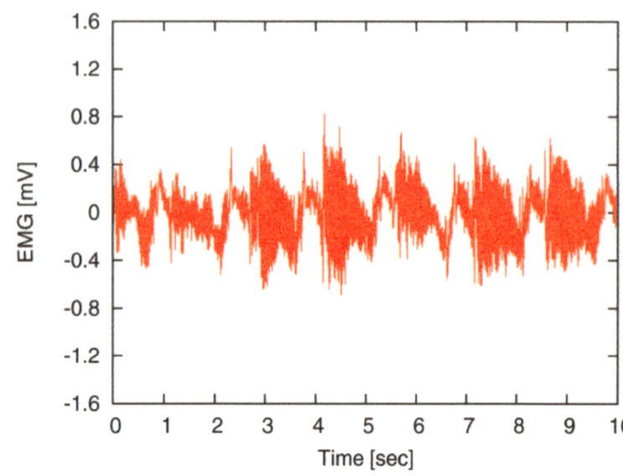

(b) Conventional Method

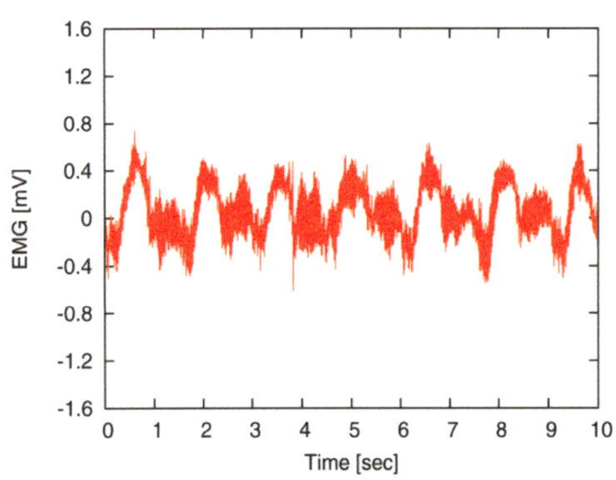

(c) Proposed Method

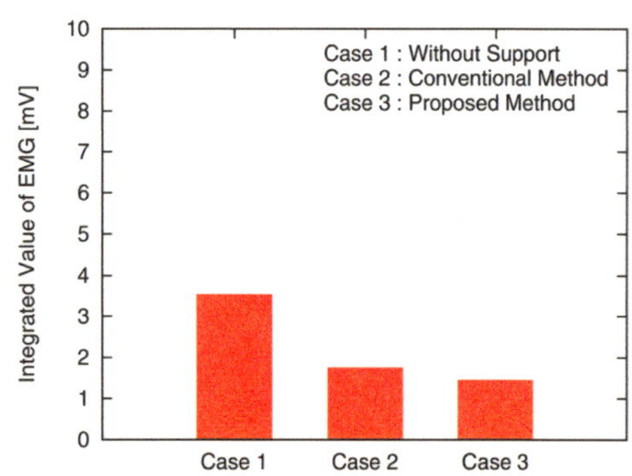

(d) Integrated Values

Fig. 12. EMG Signals of Rectus Femoris Muscle

6. Conclusions

In this paper, we proposed a control method of the wearable walking support system for supporting not only the stance phase but also the swing phase of the gait. In this method, we derived support moment for guaranteeing the weight of the support device and measured an inclination of the upper body of the user with respect to the vertical direction by using the accelerometer. We applied them to the method for calculating the support moment of the knee joint. The validity of the proposed method was illustrated experimentally. Further investigation and experiments based on various motions of subjects including the elderly are important on the next stage of our research. In addition, we will develop a device for supporting the both legs including the knee and hip joints.

7. References

Fujie, M., Nemoto, Y., Egawa, S., Sakai, A., Hattori, S., Koseki, A., Ishii, T. (1998). Power AssistedWalking Support andWalk Rehabilitation, In: *Proc. of 1st InternationalWorkshop on Humanoid and Human Friendly Robotics*

Hirata, Y., Baba, T., Kosuge, K. (2003). Motion Control of Omni-directional typeWalking Support System "Walking Helper", In: *Proc. of IEEE Workshop on Robot and Human Interactive Communication*, 2A5

Wandosell, J.M.H., Graf, B. (2002). Non-Holonomic Navigation System of a Walking-Aid Robot, In: *Proc. of IEEE Workshop on Robot and Human Interactive Communication*, 518-523

Sabatini, A. M., Genovese, V., Pacchierotti, E. (2002). A Mobility Aid for the Support to Walking and Object Transportation of People with Motor Impairments, In: *Proc. of IEEE/RSJ Intl. Conf. on Intelligent Robots and Systems*

Yu, H. Spenko, M., Dubowsky, S. (2003). An Adaptive Shared Control System for an Intelligent Mobility Aid for the Elderly, In: *Auton. Robots*, Vol.15, No.1, 53-66

Wasson, G., Sheth, P., Alwan, M., Granata, K., Ledoux, A., Huang, C. (2003). User Intent in a Shared Control Framework for Pedestrian Mobility Aids, In: *Proc. of the 2003 IEEE/RSJ Intl. Conf. on Intelligent Robots and Systems*

Rentschler, A. J., Cooper, R. A., Blaschm, B., Boninger, M. L. (2003). Intelligent walkers for the elderly : Performance and safety testing of VA-PAMAID robotic walker, In: *Journal of Rehabilitation Research and Development*, Vol. 40, No. 5

Hirata, Y., Hara, A., Kosuge, K. (2007). Motion Control of Passive Intelligent Walker Using Servo Brakes, In: *IEEE Transactions on Robotics*, Vol. 23, No.5, 981-990

Garcia, E., Sater, J. M., Main, J. (2002). Exoskeletons for human performance augmentation (EHPA): A program summary, In: *Journal of Robotics Society of Japan*, Vol. 20, No. 8, 44-48

H. Kazerooni et al. (2006). The Berkeley Lower Extremity Exoskeletons, In: *ASME J. of Dynamics Sys., Measurements and Control*, V128

Guizzo, E., Goldstein, H. (2005). The rise of the body bots, In: *IEEE Spectrum*, Vol. 42, No. 10, 50-56

Walsh, C. J., Pasch, K., Herr, H. (2006). An autonomous underactuated exoskeleton for loadcarrying augmentation, In: *Proc. IEEE/RSJ International Conference on Ingellignet Robots and Systems*, 1410-1415

Kiguchi, K. Tanaka, T., Watanabe, K., Fukuda, T. (2003). Exoskeleton for Human Upper-Limb Motion Support, In: *Proc. of IEEE ICRA*, 2206-2211

Naruse, K. Kawai, S. Yokoi, H. Kakazu, Y. (2003). Development of Wearable Exoskeleton Power Assist System for Lower Back Support, In: *Proc. of IEEE/RSJ IROS*, 3630-3635

Nakai, T. Lee, S, Kawamoto, H., Sankai, Y. (2001). Development of Power Assistive Leg for Walking Aid using EMG and Linux, In: *Proc. of ASIAR*, 295-299

Kawamoto, H., Sankai, Y. (2005). Power Assist Method Based on Phase Sequence and Muscle Force Condition for HAL, In: *Advanced Robotics*, Vol.19, No.7, 717-734

Nakamura, T, Saito, K., Kosuge, K. (2005). Control ofWearableWalking Support System Based on Human-Model and GRF, In: *Proc. of IEEE ICRA*, 4405-4410

Luh, J., Zheng, Y.F. (1985). Computation of Input Generalized Forces for Robots with Closed Kinematic Chain Mechanisms, In: *IEEE J. of Robotics and Automation*, 95-103

Nakamura, Y. Ghodoussi, M.?(1989). Dynamics computation of closed-link robot mechanisms withnonredundant and redundant actuators, In: *IEEE Transactions on Robotics and Automation*, Vol.5, No.3, 294-302

14

Multimodal Command Language to Direct Home-use Robots

Tetsushi Oka
Nihon University
Japan

1. Introduction

In this chapter, I introduce a new concept, "multimodal command language to direct home-use robots," an example language for Japanese speakers, some recent user studies on robots that can be commanded in the language, and possible future directions.
First, I briefly explain why such a language help users of home-use robots and what properties it should have, taking into account both usability and cost of home-use robots. Then, I introduce RUNA (Robot Users' Natural Command Language), a multimodal command language to direct home-use robots carefully designed for nonexpert Japanese speakers, which allows them to speak to robots simultaneously using hand gestures, touching their body parts, or pressing remote control buttons. The language illustrated here comprises grammar rules and words for spoken commands based on the Japanese language and a set of non-verbal events including body touch actions, button press actions, and single-hand and double-hand gestures. In this command language, one can specify action types such as *walk, turn, switchon, push,* and *moveto,* in spoken words and action parameters such as *speed, direction, device,* and *goal* in spoken words or nonverbal messages. For instance, one can direct a humanoid robot to turn left quickly by waving the hand to the left quickly and saying just "Turn" shortly after the hand gesture. Next, I discuss how to evaluate such a multimodal language and robots commanded in the language, and show some results of recent studies to investigate how easy RUNA is for novice users to command robots in and how cost-effective home-use robots that understand the language are. My colleagues and I have developed real and simulated home-use robot platforms in order to conduct user studies, which include a grammar-based speech recogniser, non-verbal event detectors, a multimodal command interpreter and action generation systems for humanoids and mobile robots. Without much training, users of various ages who have no prior knowledge about the language were able to command robots in RUNA, and achieve tasks such as checking a remote room, operating intelligent home appliances, cleaning a region in a room, etc. Although there were some invalid commands and unsuccessful valid commands, most of the users were able to command robots consulting a leaflet without taking too much time. In spite of the fact that the early versions of RUNA need some modifications especially in the nonverbal parts, many of them appeared to prefer multimodal commands to speech only commands. Finally, I give an overview of possible future directions.

2. Multimodal command language

Many scientists predict that home-use robots which serve us at home will be affordable in future. They will have a number of sensors and actuators and a wireless connection with intelligent home electric devices and the internet, and help us in various ways. Their duties will be classified into physical assistance, operation of home electric devices, information service using the network connection, entertainment, healing, teaching, and so on.

How can we communicate with them? A remote controller with many buttons and a graphical user interface with a screen and pointing device are practical choices, but are not suited for home-use robots which are given many kinds of tasks. Those interfaces require experiences and skills in using them, and even experienced users need time to send a single message pressing buttons or selecting nested menu items. Another choice which will come to one's mind is a speech interface. Researchers and componies have already developed many robots which have speech recognition and synthesis capabilities; they recognize spoken words of users and respond to them in spoken messages (Prasad et al., 2004). However, they do not understand every request in a natural language such as English for a number of reasons. Therefore, users of those robots must know what word sequences they understand and what they do not. In general, it is not easy for us to learn a set of a vast number of verbal messages a multi-purpose home-use robots would understand, even if it is a subset of a natural language. Another problem with spoken messages is that utterances in natural human communication are often ambiguous. It is computationally expensive for a computer to understand them (Jurafsky & Martin, 2000) because inferrencess based on different knowledge sources (Bos & Oka, 2007) and observations of the speaker and environment are required to grasp the meaning of natural language utterances. For example, think about a spoken command "Place this book on the table" which requires identification of a book and a table in the real world; there may be several books and two tables around the speaker. If the speaker is pointing one of the books and looking at one of the tables, these nonverbal messages may help a robot understand the command. Moreover, requests such as "Give the book back to me" with no infomation about *the book* are common in natural communications.

Now, think about a *language* for a specific purpose, commanding home-use robots. What properties should such a language have? First, it must be easy to give home-use robots commands without ambiguity in the language. Second, it should be easy for nonexperts to *learn* the language. Third, we should be able to give a single command in a short period of time. Next, the less misinterpretations, false alarms, and human errors the better. From a practical point of view, cost problems cannot be ignored; both computational cost for command understanding and hardware cost push up the prices of home-use robots.

One should not consider only sets of verbal messages but also *multimodal command languages* that combine verbal and nonverbal messages. Here, I define a multimodal command language as a set of verbal and nonverbal messages which convery information about commands. Spoken utterances, typed texts, mouse clicks, button press actions, touches, and gestures can constitute a command generally speaking. Therefore, messages sent using character/graphical user interfaces and speech interfaces can be thought of as elements of multimodal command languages.

Graphical user interfaces are computaionally inexpensive and enable unambiguous commands using menus, sliders, buttons, text fields, etc. However, as I have already pointed out, they are not usable for all kinds of users and they do not allow us to choose among a large number of commands in a short period of time.

Since character user interfaces require key typing skills, spoken language interfaces are preferable for nonexperts although they are more expensive and there are risks of speech recognition errors. As I pointed out, verbal messages in human communication are often ambiguous due to multi-sense or obscure words, misleading word orders, unmentioned information, etc. Ambiguous verbal messages should be avoided because it is computationally expensive to find and choose among many possible interpretations. One may insist that home-use robots can ask clarification questions. However such questions increases time for a single command, and home-use robots which often ask clarification questions are annoying.

Keyword spotting is a well-known and polular method to *guess* the meaning of verbal messages. Semantic analysis based on the method has been employed in many voice activated robotic systems, because it is computationally inexpensive and because it works well for a small set of messages (Prasad et al., 2004). However, since those systems do not distinguish valid and invalid utterances, it is unclear what utterances are acceptable. In other words, those systems are not based on a well-defined command language. For this reason, it is difficult for users to learn to give many kinds of tasks or commands to such robots and for system developers to avoid misinterpretations.

Verbal messages that are not ambiguous tend to contain many words because one needs to put everything in words. Spoken messages including many words are not very natural and more likely to be misrecognised by speech recognisers. Nonverbal modes such as body movement, posture, body touch, button press, and paralanguage, can cover such weaknesses of a verbal command language. Thus, a well-defined multimodal command set combining verbal and nonverbal messages would help users of home-use robots.

Perzanowski et al. developed a multimodal human-robot interface that enables users to give commands combining spoken commands and pointing gestures (Perzanowski et al., 2001). In the system, spoken commands are analysed using a speech-to-text system and a natural language understanding system that parses text strings. The system can disambiguate grammatical spoken commands such as "Go over there" and "Go to the door over there," by detecting a gesture. It can detect invalid text strings and inconsistencies between verbal and nonverbal messages. However, the details of the multimodal language, its grammar and valid gesture set, are not discussed. It is unclear how easy it is to learn to give grammatical spoken commands or valid multimodal commands in the language.

Iba et al. proposed an approach to programming a robot interactively through a multimodal interface (Iba et al., 2004). They built a vaccum-cleaning robot one can interactively control and program using symbolic hand gestures and spoken words. However, their semantic analysis method is similar to keyword spotting, and do not distinguish valid and invalid commands. There are more examples of robots that receives multimodal messages, but no well-defined multimodal languages in which humans can communiate with robots have been proposed or discussed.

Is it possible to design a multimodal language that has the desirable properties? In the next section, I illustrate a well-defined multimodal language I designed taking into account cost, usablity, and learnability.

3. RUNA: a command language for Japanese speakers

3.1 Overview

The multimodal language, RUNA, comprises a set of grammar rules and a lexicon for spoken commands, and a set of nonverbal events detected using visual and tactile sensors on the robot and buttons or keys on a pad at users' hand. Commands in RUNA are given in time series of nonverbal events and utterances of the spoken language. The spoken command language defined by the grammar rule set and lexicon enables users to direct home-use robots with no ambiguity. The lexicon and grammar rules are tailored for Japanese speakers to give home-ues robots directions. Nonverbal events function as altanatives to spoken phrases and create multimodal commands. Thus, the language enables users to direct robots in fewer words using gestures, touching robots, pressing buttons, and so on.

3.2 Commands and actions

In RUNA, one can command a home-use robot to move forward, backward, left and right, turn left and right, look up, down, left and right, move to a goal position, switch on and off a home electric device, change the settings of a device, pick up and place an object, push and pull an object, and so on. In the latest version, there are two types of commands: action commands and repetition commands. An action command consists of an *action type* such as *walk, turn,* and *move,* and *action parameters* such as *speed, direction* and *angle*. Table 1 shows examples of action types and commands represented in character string lists. The 38 action types are categorized into 24 classes based on the way in which action parameters are specified naturally in the Japanese language (Table 2). In other words, actions of different classes are commanded using different modifiers. A repetition command requests the most recently executed action.

Action Type	Action Command	Meaning in English
standup	*standup_s*	Stand up slowly!
moveforward	*moveforward_f_1m* *moveforward_m_long*	Move forward quickly by 1m! Move a lot forward!
walk	*walk_s_3steps* *walk_f_10m*	Take 3 steps slowly! Walk fast to a point 10m ahead!
look	*look_f_l*	Look left quickly!
turn	*turn_m_r_30degrees* *turn_f_l_much*	Turn right by 30 degrees! Turn a lot to the left quickly!
turnto	*turnto_s_back*	Turn back slowly!
sidestep	*sidestep_s_r_2steps*	Take 2 steps to the right!
highfive	*highfive_s_rh*	Give me a highfive with your right hand!
kick	*kick_f_l_rf*	Kick left with your foot!
wavebp	*wavebp_f_hips*	Wave your hips quickly!
settemp	*settemp_aircon_24*	Set the airconditioner at 24 degrees!
lowertemp	*lowertemp_room_2*	Lower the temperature of the room by 2 degrees!
switchon	*switchon_aircon*	Switch on the air conditioner!
query	*query_room*	Give me some information about the room!
pickup	*pickup_30cm_desk*	Pick up something 30cm in width on the desk!
place	*place_floor*	Place it on the floor!
moveto	*moveto_fridge*	Go to the fridge!
clean	*clean_50cm_powerful_2*	Vacuum-clean around you twice powerfully!
shuttle	*shutlle_1m_silent_10*	Shuttle silently 10 times within 1m in length!

Table 1. Action Types and Action Commands

Class	Action Types	Action Parameters
AC1	*standup, hug, crouch, liedown, squat*	*speed*
AC2	*moveforward, movebackward*	*speed, distance*
AC3	*walk*	*speed, distance*
AC4	*look, lookaround, turnto*	*speed, target*
AC5	*turn*	*speed, direction, angle*
AC6	*sidestep*	*speed, direction, distance*
AC7	*move*	*speed, direction, distance*
AC8	*highfive, handshake*	*speed, hand*
AC9	*punch*	*speed, hand, direction*
AC10	*kick*	*speed, foot, direction*
AC11	*turnbp, raisebp, lowerbp, wavebp*	*speed, body part, direction*
AC12	*dropbp*	*body part*
AC13	*raisetemp, lowertemp*	*room, temperature*
AC14	*settemp*	*room, temperature*
AC15	*switchon, switchoff*	*device*
AC16	*query*	*subject*
AC17	*pickup*	*width, height*
AC18	*place*	*height*
AC19	*push, pull*	*object, height, distance*
AC20	*slide*	*object, height, direction,distance*
AC21	*moveto*	*goal*
AC22	*switchcleaner*	*on-off*
AC23	*clean*	*area, repetition, mode*
AC24	*shuttle*	*distance, repetition, mode*

Table 2. Action Classes

3.3 Syntax of spoken commands

There are more than 300 generative rules for spoken commands in the latest version of RUNA (see Table 3 for some of them). These rules allow Japanese speakers to command robots in a natural way by speech alone, even though there are no recursive rules. A spoken action command in the language is an imperative utterance including a word or phrase which determines the action type and other words that contain information about action parameters. There must be a word or phrase for the action type of the spoken command, although one can leave out parameter values. Fig. 1 illustrates a parse tree for a spoken command of the action type *walk* which has *speed* and *distance* as parameters. The fourth rule in Table 3 generates an action command of AC3 in Table 2. The nonterminal symbol P3 correponds to phrases about *speed* and *distance.* There are degrees of freedom in the order of phrases for parameters, and one can use symbolic, deictic, qualitative and quantitative expressions for them (see rules in Table 3).

There are more than 250 words (terminal symbols), each of which has its own pronunciation. They are categorized into about 100 parts of speech, identified by nonterminal symbols (Table 4). One can choose among synonymous words to specify an action type or a parameter value.

No.	Generative Rule	Description
1	S → ACTION	action command
2	S → REPETITION	repetition command
3	ACTION → AC3	class 3 action command
4	AC3 → P3 AT3	parameters and type (class 3)
5	AT3 → AT_WALK	action type *walk*
6	P3 → SPEED	phrase for speed
7	P3 → DIST	phrase for distance
8	P3 → SPEED DIST	speed + distance
9	P3 → DIST SPEED	distance + speed
10	DIST → NUMBER LUNIT PE	number + length unit + *PE*
11	DIST → DISTANCE_AMOUNT PE	short, long
12	P17 → OBJECT17 HEIGHTKARA	parameters for class 17 action
13	HEIGHTKARA → HEIGHTS KARA	height of object to pick up
14	HEIGHTS → PLACE	desk, floor, etc.
15	HEIGHTS → HEIGHT NUMBER LUNIT	height in mm/cm/m
16	HEIGHTS → BODYPARTNO HEIGHT	knee, hips
17	OBJECT17 → OBJWIDTH OBJECT	object for class 17 action
18	OBJWIDTH → WIDTH NUMBER LUNIT NO	width in mm/cm/m
19	OBJWIDTH → OBJSIZE	small, large
20	DIR → DIR_DEICTIC PE	deictic expression for direction
21	REPETITION → REPEAT	repeat last action

Table 3. Example Generative Rules of RUNA

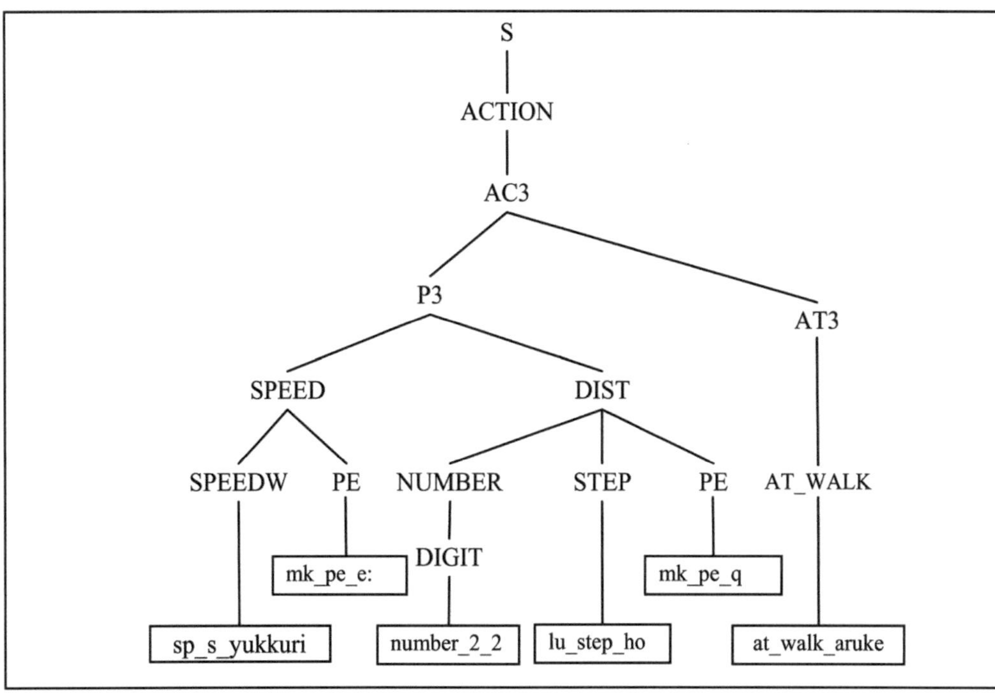

Fig. 1. Parse Tree for a Spoken Command ("Take, uh, two steps ... slowly!")

Part of Speech	Words
AT_WALK	at_walk_aruke, at_walk_hoko, at_walk_hokosihro
GOAL	goal_refrigerator_reizoko, goal_entrance_iriguchi,...
ROOM	home_room_heya
KNEE	bp_knee_hiza
WIDTH	param_width_haba
HEIGHT	param_height_takasa
AROUND	param_around_shui
TIMES	param_times_kai
LUNIT	lu_mm_mm, lu_cm_cm, lu_m_m
TUNIT	tu_degree_do
DIR_LR	dir_r_migi, dir_r_migigawa, dir_r_miginoho, dir_l_hidari, ...
DIR_F	dir_f_mae, dir_f_zenpo
DIR_DEICTIC	dir_deictic_koko, dir_deictic_kocchi, dir_deictic_kochira
DIGIT	number_1_ichi, number_1_iq, number_2_ni, ...
SPEEDW	sp_f_hayaku, sp_f_isoide, sp_s_yukkuri, sp_m_futsuni
DISTANCE_AMOUNT	dst_long_okiku, dst_short_sukoshi, dst_short_chotto, ...
ANGLE_AMOUNT	ang_much_okiku, ang_little_sukoshi, ang_little_chisaku, ...
CLEANER_MODE	mode_powerful_zenryokude, mode_silent_shizukani
NO	joshi_no_no
NI	joshi_ni_ni
WO	joshi_wo_wo
PE (silence or hesitant voice)	mk_pe_q, mk_pe_a:, mk_pe_e:
REPEAT	md_repeat_moikkai, md_repeat_moichido

Table 4. Part of RUNA's Lexicon

3.4 Nonverbal events

In RUNA, a set of *nonverbal events* is defined and used for commanding robots. These events are lists of character strings representing their own type and parameter values. Table 5 shows examples of nonverbal events. These events can be detected using sensors on home-use robots or buttons and sensing devices at users' hand without much hardware and computational cost.

Event Type	Event Parameters	Example
buttonpress	*buttonid , iteration, duration*	*buttonpress_b4_3_124ms*
bodytouch	*position, iteration, duration*	*bodytouch_leftwrist_1_700ms*
singlehandwaving	*direction, iteration, stroke, frequency*	*singlehandwaving_left_3_long_120* *singlehandwaving_up_4_10cm_90*
doublehandgesture	*width, direction, iteration, stroke*	*doublehandgesture_wide_left_3_short*

Table 5. Nonverbal Events

3.5 Semantics

Since the language described above is syntactically unambiguous and simple, it is computationally inexpensive to identify action types and parameters in spoken commands.

As I have already mentioned, each spoken action command in RUNA includes a word specifying an action type, which can be distinguished by its own first string element *at* (Table 4). It can be divided into phrases expressing each parameter value and the action type using words which indicate the end of a parameter phrase, i. e. PE words (Fig. 1, Table 4). Therefore, it is straightforward and computationally inexpensive to identify the action type of a spoken command.

After a spoken command is divided into phrases and its action type is determined, a parameter value can be extracted from each phrase. It is always possible to determine which parameter the phrase is about by finding a keyword of a category such as LUNIT, AUNIT, DIR_LR, WIDTH, HEIGHT, and ANGLE_AMOUNT. If the keyword contains the parameter value, a string for the value of the parameter, *left* or *much*, is constructed. Otherwise, one must find a numerical expression to compose a string such as *1m* amd *2degrees*. Thus, the spoken command in Fig. 1 is converted to a semantic representation *walk_s_2steps*.

Note that in RUNA there are deictic words and some parameter values can be left out in spoken commands. For instance, one may say "Turn slowly" without mentioning the direction or "Look this way" using a deictic expression perhaps with a gesture. In such cases, undecided parameters are resolved by nonverbal events described in the previous subsection. There are rules to map parameter values of nonverbal events (Table 5) to parameter values of action commands (Table 2). Designing these mapping rules is a key to a good multimodal command language that is natural and easy to learn. Table 6 shows examples of event parameters that correspond to action parameters.

If a spoken command has some parameters which cannot be resolved by nonverbal events, those parameter slots are filled with default values. Therefore, a command "Kick" is interpreted as "Kick slowly straight with your right foot" using the default parameter values for the action type *kick*.

Event Type	Event Parameter	Action Type	Action Parameter
button press	*button_id*	*turn / sidestep* *moveforward*	*speed, direction* *speed, distance*
	iteration	*raisetemp* *turn*	*temperature* *angle*
	duration	*turn* *walk*	*angle* *distance*
body touch	*position*	*kick* *raisebp* *turn / sidestep*	*foot* *bodypart* *direction*
single hand waving	*direction*	*turn / sidestep*	*direction*
	stroke	*walk* *turn*	*distance* *angle*
double hand gesture	*width*	*pickup*	*width*
	iteration	*pickup / place*	*height*

Table 6. Mapping between event parameters and action parameters

3.6 Command execution by home-use robots

A complete action command with its type and parameter values is executed by a home-use robot if the action is in the robot's action repertoire. Quantitative parameter values in action commands, e. g. *short*, are converted to quantitative values, e. g. *20cm* when robots execute the commands. The robot starts the action immediately if it has completed the previous command. Otherwise, the robot makes a decision depending on various conditions. It may start the new command immediately after completing the ongoing command, abort it and start the new command, or reject the new command explaining the reason. There is no good theory about the decision making yet, so we describe task specific rules for humanoids, robot cleaners, etc.

4. User studies

4.1 Objectives and methods

In the earlier part of this chapter I pointed out that a multimodal command language to direct home-use robots must have several properties. This opinion arises some fundamental questions:

1. Is the language easy for non-experts to learn and use?
2. How much time does it take to give a command in the language?
3. How expensive are robots that can execute commands in the language without significant delay and frequent misinterpretations?
4. How can the language be improved?

To answer these questions, one must collect data by conducting user studies that record multimodal commands by a wide range of users, speech recognition results, nonverbal events, system interpretations, reactions of home-use robots, user opinions, and so on.

The first question is about learning the command language. One can estimate a user's ability to give multimodal commands in the language (the user's linguistic performance) by giving various tasks. Fluency, human errors, command success rates, and time required for each command, and self-assessments can be indicators of performance. The second question is about the language's efficiency. One must investigate times required for commands by a wide range of users at several stages of learning. The third question can be answered by developing home-use robots and using them in user studies. The last question is related to the other questions and should be answered by finding all sorts of problems including human and system errors. Constructive criticisms by users also play a great role.

My colleagues and I have built a command interpretation system on a personal computer, small real humanoids (Oka et al., 2008), simulated humanoids, and a simulated robot cleaner that can be commanded in different versions of RUNA and conducted some user studies. In these studies, more than a hundred users, mostly young students, commanded one of the robots within 90 minutes. Some of them were asked to give spoken and/or multimodal commands printed in a sheet of paper. Many of them were given one or more goals to be achieved giving spoken or multimodal commands: checking a room, changing the settings of an air conditioner, moving a box, cleaning a dusty area, etc. We video-recorded the users and robots, recorded speech recognition results, nonverbal events, and command interpretations. Each user was asked to fill in a question sheet after commanding the robot.

Before asking each user to command one of the robots, we showed the person a short demonstration movie and handed a leaflet that illustrates how to command each action in diagrams and pictures (Fig. 2).We also prepared some short exercise programs to improve users' success rates and reduce human errors within 20 minutes.

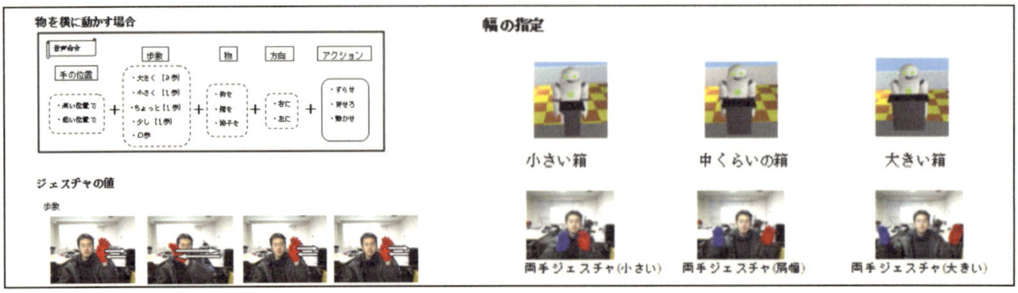

Fig. 2. Parts of one of the leaflets which illustrate RUNA

4.2 Summary of results

In the user studies, the novice users were able to command our robots in RUNA consulting one of the leaflets and complete their tasks. In fact, there were many users who were able to direct the robot without their leaflet later in their tests.

Most of the users spoke clearly and fluently after practice, although there were a small number of hesitations, fluffs, and hashes especially in commands including more spoken phrases. Only several users made word misuses. In the latest studies, 92 - 98 % of spoken messages were correctly recognized with no word misrecognition thanks to the latest version (4.1.1) of an open source grammar based speech recognition engine (Lee et al., 2001).

Most nonverbal messages were given properly after the users learned how to use them. There were few human errors such as pressing a wrong button, touching a wrong part of the robot body, and wrong gestures. However, there are problems in specifying some action parameter values in nonverbal messages. For example, most users made errors in choosing a length value out of five pressing a button, even after some practice to learn durations. There were also failures in specifying action parameters using hand gestures due to errors in our gesture detector using a web camera.

A majority of the users in the latest studies recorded a command success rate higher than 90 %. Most of user commands were completed within 10 seconds and our robots responded to them within a second or so. In fact, there were users who repeatedly gave multimodal commands very quickly without looking at the leaflet. Those users spoke immediately after pressing buttons or moving their hand(s) to the camera. About 77 % of the users who were asked a question about their preference answered that they preferred multimodal commands to speech only commands in RUNA. Those users selected multimodal commands to achieve their tasks more often than the others. In one of the latest studies, all of the 20 users felt that they understood how to direct robots, although some of them did not find it easy.

In the question sheets filled in by the users, there were some important opinions about the language. Some of them pointed out that it was difficult to learn to specify action parameter values in nonverbal messages. There were users who thought speech recognition errors caused problems for them.

4.3 Discussion

Further studies are needed to prove the effectiveness of the language for a wide range of non-experts, but our results imply that the current version of RUNA is fairly easy for Japanese speakers to learn. Although the novice users made some errors, they would not need long time or much effort to fully master the spoken language and the set of nonverbal messages. With more experience, they would be able to give spoken commands specifying three or more action parameters fluently, use default parameter values whenever possible, and choose among nonverbal modes. As even novice users were able to command robots within a short period of time, experienced users would not take unnecessarily long time for a command.

Can users of home-use robots teach themselves the language? A demonstration movie and an introductory leaflet which illustrates examples of multimodal commands would help a novice user to grasp the principles of the language. Although it will take a while to master all types of actions, I suppose that it will be easier and easier to learn a new command.

Multimodal commands in the current version of RUNA can be interpreted using a microphone, a web camera, a controller or a keypad, tactile sensors, and a personal computer. Therefore, home-use robots in future would not need extra hardware for understanding commands in RUNA. Besides, more sophisticated speech recognisers and gesture detectors would reduce misinterpretations of user commands.

One should be able to make the language more natural and easier to learn by both amending the mapping between nonverbal events and action parameters and introducing new types of nonverbal events. In the current version of RUNA, some action parameter values are naturally mapped to event parameter values, and can be specified without acquiring skills. For example, it is easy for anyone to specify a direction by pressing a button, touching the robot, or using a gesture. Likewise, no special skill is necessary to give robots information about body parts, repetition counts, modes, and qualitative values such as *long* and *short*, in nonverbal messages. However, it is difficult for inexperienced users to specify angles, lengths, heights, and temperatures using buttons or gestures. There are three reasons for this. First, users need skills to specify quantities using durations, frequencies, or lengths; how long should I press the button to turn the robot by 30 degrees? Second, users must remember arbitrary mappings; how many times should I wave my hand to get a turn by 180 degrees? Third, our gesture detector cannot measure lengths with precision. This problem can be remedied by making use of a pen tablet, a touch panel, dials, or a screen to display parameter values. Another possible solution is to start an endless action and stop it by pressing a button, touching the robot, raising the right hand, saying "Stop," and so on. One should notice the existing methods are still helpful when users do not need high precision.

Word misuses found in the user studies prove the importance of choice of words for the lexicon of the spoken language. One can prevent word misuses by including as many Japanese words as possible. However, homonyms will increase risks of syntactically or semantically ambiguous utterances and speech recognition errors. Therefore, only frequent word misuses should be removed by adding new words to the lexicon.

5. Future directions

RUNA can be extended by adding grammar rules, spoken words, and types of nonverbal events. Without doubt, multimodal command languages to direct of multipurpose home-use robots in future must have more classes and types of actions. However, its framework based on type and parameter should work well for the purpose of giving home-use robots various kinds of action commands, goals, and missions despite the simplicity and limitations. Certainly, one must avoid syntactically or semantically ambiguous utterances

and select types of nonverbal events suitable for specifying parameter values of actions, goals, and missions taking into account both cost and usability.
Nonverbal messages can help human-robot communications in the same ways that they help human-human communications. They can not only segment and disambiguate verbal messages, but also convey the current status of humans and robots. Eye contacts, hand gestures, postures, body touches, and button press actions can be clues to detect and segment spoken commands, phrases, and words; paralanguage may play important roles in disambiguation; nonverbal messages that inform emotional and physical status may help robots' decision making.
Multimodal languages for responses from home-use robots are also among my interests. Most importantly, robots can send nonverbal messages to convey their status and whether or not they can receive a new command at present. Another interesting future work would be fusing nonverbal and verbal messages. Redundant action parameter values in multiple modes may reduce risks of misinterpretations.

6. Acknowledgment

Development of RUNA was supported by KAKENHI Grant-in-Aid for Scientific Research (19500171). I would like to thank all my colleagues who worked on and discussed the subject with me at Fukuoka Institute of Technology.

7. References

Bos, J. & Oka, T. (2007). Meaningful conversation with mobile robots. *Advanced Robotics,* 21., 1-2, (2007) 209-232, ISSN:0169-1864

Iba, S.; Paredis, C. J. J.; Adams, W. & Khosla, P. K. (2004). Interactive multi-modal robot programming, *Proceedings of the 9th International Symposium on Experimental Robotics (ISER '04)*, pp. 503-512, ISBN:3-54-0288163, Singapore, March 2006, Springer, Berlin

Jurafsky, D. & Martin, H. J. (2000). *Language and speech processing,* ISBN:0-13-122798, 2000, Prentice Hall, Upper Saddle River, New Jersey

Lee, A.; Kawahara, T. & Shikano, K. (2001). Julius --- an open source real-time large vocabulary recognition engine, *Proceedings of the 7th Europian Conference on Speech Communication and Technology,* pp. 1691-1694, Aalborg, September 2001, International Speech Communication Association

Oka, T.; Abe, T.; Shimoji, M.; Nakamura, T.; Sugita, K. & Yokota, M. (2008). Directing humanoids in a multimodal command language, *Proceedings of the 17th IEEE International Symposium on Robot and Human Interactive Communication (RO-MAN '08)*, pp. 580-585, ISBN: 978-1-4244-2213-5, Munich, August 2008, IEEE

Perzanowski, D.; Schultz, A.C.; Adams, W.; Marsh, E. & Bugajska M. (2001). Building a multimodal human-robot interface. *IEEE Intelligent Systems,* 16., 1, (January-February 2001) 16-21, ISSN:1541-1672

Prasad, R.; Saruwatari, H. & Shikano, K. (2004). Robots that can hear, understand and talk. *Advanced Robotics*, 18., 5, (2004) 533-564, ISSN:0169-1864

15

Effectiveness of Concurrent Performance of Military and Robotics Tasks and Effects of Cueing and Individual Differences in a Simulated Reconnaissance Environment

Jessie Y.C. Chen
U.S. Army Research Laboratory - Human Research & Engineering Directorate
United States of America

1. Introduction

1.1 Background

The goal of this research is to examine if and how aided target recognition (AiTR) cueing capabilities facilitates multitasking (including operating a robot) by gunners in a military tank crewstation environment. Specifically, we examine if gunners are able to effectively perform their primary task - maintaining local security - while performing a pair of secondary tasks: (1) managing a robot and (2) communications with fellow crew members. According to Mitchell (2005), who used the Improved Performance Research Integration Tool (IMPRINT) to examine the workload of the crew of a future tank system, the gunner is the most viable option for performing the robotics control tasks compared to the other two positions (i.e. vehicle commander and driver). She found that the gunner had the fewest instances of overload and, therefore, may be able to assume control of the robot. However, she also discovered that there were instances in the model when the gunner dropped his/her primary tasks of detecting and engaging targets to perform robotics tasks, which could be catastrophic for the team and mission during a real operation. If the gunner is the individual who will most likely be assigned the responsibility of robotics control, then it is important to consider what design changes will be necessary to allow successful multitasking without a critical performance decrement in maintaining local security.

Based on Mitchell's modeling work, Chen and Joyner (2009) conducted a simulation experiment and the results showed that, when the robotics operator had to perform robot targeting and local security (i.e. gunner's tasks) at the same time, both workload and performance degraded, compared with a baseline single-task condition. More specifically, as the robotics task became more difficult, the participants' gunnery task performance became worse and their workload assessment also increased. Indeed, past research in dual task performance has shown that operators may encounter difficulties when both tasks involve focal vision. For example, Horrey and Wickens (2004) demonstrated that participants could not effectively detect road hazards while operating in-vehicle-devices. Additionally, Murray (1994) found that as the number of monitored displays increased, the operators' reaction time for their target search tasks also increased linearly. In fact, response times almost doubled when the number of displays increased from 1 to 2 and from 2 to 3 (a slope of 1.94 was obtained). Since both the gunnery and the robotics tasks in Chen and Joyner were heavily visual, we considered tapping into another modality - touch. Our hypothesis was that parsing additional information by using relatively untapped modalities might alleviate the resource demands and could help the operator effectively transition between displays (Wickens, 2002).

1.2 Tactile cueing

In the current study, we examined if and how tactile cueing, which delivered simulated AiTR capabilities (i.e. cues to the direction of a potential target), enhanced gunner's performance in a military multitasking environment. In the first experiment, the simulated AiTR was perfectly reliable; in the second experiment, it was either false-alarm prone (FAP) or miss prone (MP). Sklar and Sarter (1999) found tactile cueing to be particularly useful for target detection and response time with a concurrent visual task, both in conjunction with visual cueing and alone. Terrence et al. (2005) compared spatial auditory and spatial tactile cues and found that participants perceived the tactile cues both faster and more accurately. In another study by Krausman et al. (2005), on the other hand, tactile cueing was not found to be more effective than auditory cueing in terms of response time, although it was more effective than visual cueing. Additionally, participants rated tactile cueing as the most helpful among the three types of alerts.

Spatial attention has been found to have cross-modal links across visual, auditory, and tactile inputs (Spence & Driver 1997). The level of effectiveness of one spatial information display relative to other display modalities may be dependent on the operational context of the experimental procedure (i.e. the demands of the tasks). Ho et al. (2005) found vibrotactile alerts were powerful directors of spatial attention in simulated driving scenarios, with faster responses even when reliability levels made the alerts spatially non-predictive. Clearly, there are potential benefits to offloading information to the relatively underutilized sensory pathways, though the exact nature of the performance gains is in need of further elucidation. With proper implementation, tactile alerts may improve performance when multitasking with man-machine interfaces (Van Erp & Van Veen 2004).

1.3 Imperfect automation and multitasking performance

In the real world, cueing systems are often FAP or MP, based on the threshold settings of the alert. Meyer (2001, 2004) suggests that FAP and MP alerts have distinct effects on operator's usage of the automated systems. Specifically, high FA rates reduce the operator's *compliance* with automation (compliance defined as taking actions based on the alerts). Conversely, high miss rates reduce operator's *reliance* on automation (reliance defined as failure to take precautious actions when there is no alert). Wickens, Dixon, Goh et al. (2005) showed that the operator's automated task performance degraded when the FA rate of the alerts for the automated task was high. On the other hand, when the miss rate was high, the concurrent task performance was affected more than the automated task because the operator had to allocate more visual attention to monitor the automated task. Similarly, Dixon and Wickens (2006) showed that FAs and misses affected compliance and reliance, respectively, and their effects appeared to be relatively independent of each other.

In contrast to Meyer's model and the aforementioned findings, Dixon et al. (2007) showed that FAP automation impaired "performance more on the automated task than did miss-prone automation, (e.g. the "cry wolf" effect) and hurt performance (both speed and accuracy) at least as much as MP automation on the concurrent task (p. 570-571)." FAP automation was found to affect both operator compliance and reliance, while MP automation affected only operator reliance. The authors suggested that the FAP automation had a negative impact on reliance because of the operator's overall reduced trust in the automated system. Similarly, Wickens, Dixon, and Johnson (2005) demonstrated a greater cost associated with FAP automation (than with MP automation), which affected both the automated and concurrent tasks.

Furthermore, Wickens and Dixon (2005) demonstrated that when the reliability level is below approximately 70%, operators often ignore the alerts. In their meta-analytic study, Wickens and Dixon found that "a reliability of 0.70 was the 'crossover point' below which unreliable automation was worse than no automation at all." Although Wickens and his colleagues have done extensive research in this area, their studies were conducted in a different environment (unmanned aerial vehicle control display monitoring), and they did not use tactile cueing. The current study was the first one to examine these issues in the context of combined roles of gunner and robotics operator. Since an AiTR cannot have a perfect reliability rate in foreseeable real world operations, the data from this study should provide useful information to the design community of future military systems, in which AiTR will play an integral role.

1.4 Individual differences in spatial ability and attentional control

In the current study, we also sought to investigate the effects of individual differences in spatial ability (SpA) and perceived attentional control (PAC) on the operators' concurrent performance. SpA has been found to be a significant factor in virtual environment navigation (Stanney & Salvendy, 1995), learning to use a medical teleoperation device (Eyal & Tendick, 2001), target search task (Chen et al., 2008; Chen & Joyner, 2009), and robotics task performance (Cassenti et al., 2009; Lathan & Tracey, 2002; Menchaca-Brandan et al., 2007). For example, Lathan and Tracey (2002) demonstrated that people with higher SpA performed better in a teleoperation task through a maze. They finished their tasks faster and had fewer errors. In a recent study, Cassenti et al. (2009) demonstrated that robotics operators with higher SpA (measured by a mental rotation test) performed robot navigation tasks significantly better than those with lower SpA. Our previous studies (Chen et al., 2008; Chen & Joyner, 2009) also found SpA to be a good predictor of the operator's robotics and gunnery task performance. In the domain of visual spatial displays, Stanney and Salvendy (1995) found that high SpA individuals outperformed those with low SpA on tasks that required visuo-spatial representations to be mentally constructed. While many SpA tests measures focus on visually presented stimuli, the interconnections of sensory modalities at the level of spatial perception may translate into differential effects of multisensory spatial displays across SpA levels (Spence et al., 2004).

In addition to SpA, we also examined the relationship between attentional control and multitasking performance. Several studies show that there are individual differences in multitasking performance, and some people are less prone to performance degradation during multitasking conditions (Rubinstein et al., 2001; Schumacher et al., 2001). There is some evidence that attention-switching flexibility can predict performance of such diverse tasks as flight training and bus driving (Kahneman et al., 1973). There is also evidence that people with better attention control can allocate their attention more flexibly and effectively

(Bleckley et al., 2003; Derryberry & Reed, 2002), and this was partially confirmed by Chen and Joyner (2009). It is likely that operators with different levels of attention switching abilities may react differently to automated systems with FAs and misses. In other words, operators' compliance and reliance behaviors may be altered based on their ability to effectively switch their attention among the systems. For example, the complacency effect may be more severe for poor attentional control individuals compared with those with better attentional control. The current study sought to examine if the compliance vs. reliance effects reported in the literature might be moderated by individual attentional control.

1.5 Current study

In the current study, we simulated a military tank crewstation environment and incorporated AiTR signals (tactile or a combination of tactile and visual) to help participants locate potential threats in the immediate environment while controlling a robot. The primary task of the gunner was to determine which action to take, based on a visual determination of whether a potential threat was hostile or neutral. This task was to be performed while conducting other tasks (including the remote targeting task with the robot and a concurrent communication task). In the first experiment, the simulated AiTR was perfectly reliable; in the second experiment, it was either FAP or MP. For the first experiment, it was hypothesized that tactile signals would improve performance in both the gunnery and the robotics control tasks as they could signal the appropriate times to transition from the robotics control tasks back to the gunner's primary task of maintaining local security around the simulated vehicle. The tactile signals also provide directional information along the azimuth for targets around the vehicle, which may also facilitate performance. Additionally, assisting the gunnery task with the AiTR was expected to enhance the operators' performance of the concurrent tasks, as more mental resources could be directed to these tasks (Young & Stanton, 2007a; Dixons et al., 2004). Past research has shown that automation can help reduce the performance gap between experts and novices (Young & Stanton, 2007a). It is, therefore, reasonable to expect greater performance improvement for the participants with lower SpA when automation is introduced.

For the second experiment, based on the data from Wickens, Dixon, Goh et al. (2005), we expected that the operator's gunnery (automated) task performance would degrade if the FA rate of the AiTR for the gunnery system was high because of reduced compliance with the automation. Conversely, if the cueing was MP, the operator's robotics (concurrent) task performance would be affected more than the gunnery task because of reduced reliance on the automation. More mental and visual resources would be devoted to checking the raw data for the automated task, and therefore, the performance of the concurrent task would be degraded. On the other hand, there was evidence that FAP automation was more detrimental to both the automated and concurrent tasks than MP automation (Dixon et al., 2007). Therefore, it is likely that FAP automation would have a more negative impact on the overall performance than would MP automation. In other words, there have been conflicting results in the literature regarding the independence of the effects of FAP and MP automation on operator compliance and reliance. It is possible that individual differences may be responsible for some of the observed differences in the literature. Therefore, we investigated the effects of individual differences on FAP and MP conditions as a possible explanation for the discrepancies.

2. Experiment 1

2.1 Method

2.1.1 Participants

Twenty college students (4 females and 16 males, mean age = 21.0) participated in this study. Participants were compensated $8 per hour or with class credit for their participation.

2.1.2 Apparatus

2.1.2.1 Simulators.

The experiment was conducted using Tactical Control Unit (TCU) (developed by the U. S. Army Research Laboratory's Robotics Collaborative Technology Alliance) for the robotics control tasks (Figure 1). The TCU is a one-person crew station from which the operator can control several simulated robots, which can either perform their tasks semi-autonomously or be teleoperated. The operator performed the instructed robotics tasks through the use of a 19 in. touch-screen display. A joystick was used to manipulate the direction in which the robotic vehicles moved when in Teleop mode. The robot simulated in our study is the eXperimental unmanned vehicle (XUV) developed by the Army Research Laboratory. The gunnery station was implemented using an additional screen and controls to simulate the out-the-window view and line-of-sight fire capabilities (Figure 1). The interface consisted of a 15 in. flat panel monitor and a joystick. Participants used the joystick to rotate the viewfinder 360 degrees, zoom in and out, and engage targets.

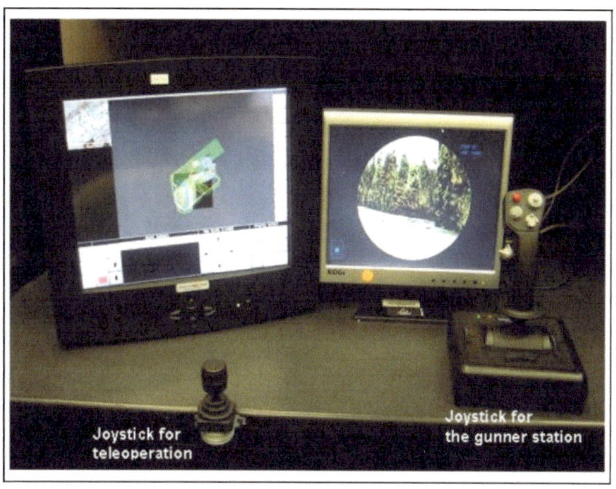

Fig. 1. TCU (left) and Gunnery station (gunner's out-the-window view) (right)

2.1.2.2 AiTR Displays.

To augment target detection in the gunnery component, visual and tactile alerts were used to cue the participant to the direction of a target as determined by the AiTR. The visual alerts were displayed in the lower right area of the screen, with the target icons presented around the overhead-view diagram of the simulated vehicle gunner station. The target icon appeared in one of eight possible locations around the gunner, corresponding to 45° increments along a 360° azimuth. As the gunner rotated the view, the turret portion of the vehicle diagram moved along the eight possible orientations to allow the gunner to place his/her field of view on the cued target.

Tactually, target positions relative to the gunner were presented using eight electromechanical transducers known as 'tactors,' each delivering a 250 Hz sinusoidal, salient (approximately 20 dB above threshold) vibrotactile stimulus harmlessly to the skin. The eight tactors were arranged equidistantly on an elasticized belt worn around the abdomen just above the navel. This configuration was based upon research conducted by Cholewiak et al. (2004) who found that additional tactors within this ring reduced inter-tactor distance and compromised localization performance. The tactile stimulus parameters were programmed onto a battery-powered controller board governing all eight tactors. This board was, in turn, controlled by a computer running the simulation and presenting targets for the visual and tactile conditions. The tactile stimulus had a 300 ms duration, which was determined based upon the simulation's refresh rates for updating AiTR information. To match the visual condition as closely as possible, a target that was directly behind the gunner (6 o'clock position) would cause the tactor on the spine to activate. If the gunner moved the turret to the right, the vibrotactile stimulus would then appear to move along the right side of the body. If the tactor above the navel was active, then this indicated the corresponding hostile target should now be in the gunner's field of view. Participants had an opportunity to familiarize themselves with both types of signals during training.

2.1.2.3 Communication Task Materials.

The communication task was administered concurrently with the experimental scenarios. The questions included simple military-related reasoning tests and simple memory tests. The inclusion of these cognitive tasks was for simulating an environment where the gunner was communicating with fellow crew members in the vehicle. For the reasoning tests, there were questions such as 'if the enemy is to our left, and our UGV is to our right, what direction is the enemy to the UGV?' For the memory tests, the participants were asked to repeat some short statements or keep track of three radio call signs (e.g. "Bravo 83") and they had to report to the experimenter whether the call signs they heard were one of those they were keeping track of. Test questions were pre-recorded by a male speaker and were presented at the rate of one question every 33 seconds via a synthetic speech program, DECTalk®.

2.1.2.4 Questionnaires and Spatial Tests.

A demographics questionnaire was administered at the beginning of the training session. The Cube Comparison (Ekstrom et al., 1976), the Hidden Patterns tests (Ekstrom et al., 1976), and the Spatial Orientation Test (Gugerty & Brooks, 2004) were used to assess participants' SpA. The Cube test requires participants to compare, in 3-minutes, 21 pairs of 6-sided cubes and determine if the rotated cubes are the same or different (only 3 sides of each cube are shown). The Hidden Patterns test measures flexibility of closure and involves identifying specific patterns or shapes embedded within distracting information. The Spatial Orientation test, modeled after the cardinal direction test developed by Gugerty and Brooks (2004), is a computerized test consisting of a brief training segment and 32 test questions. Both accuracy and response time were automatically captured by the program. Participants were designated as high SpA or low SpA based on their composite scores of the three spatial tests (median split).

A questionnaire about attentional control (Derryberry & Reed, 2002) was used to evaluate participants' PAC. The attentional control survey consists of 21 items and measures perceived attention focus and shifting. The scale has been shown to have good internal reliability (α = .88). Derryberry and Reed conducted an experiment to examine the relationship between self-reported (i.e. attentional control survey score) and actual attentional control. They found that participants with a high survey score could better resist interference in a Stroop-like spatial conflict task. In one of our previous studies (Chen and Joyner, 2009), we observed a positive, although somewhat weak, relationship between attentional control survey score and some multitasking performance measures.

Participants' workload was evaluated using the computer-based version of NASA-TLX (Hart & Staveland, 1988). Finally, a usability questionnaire was used to assess participants' reliance on tactile and/or visual cueing for the gunnery task when both types of alerts were available. Participants rated their preference on a 5-point scale (from 1 to 5: entirely visual- predominately visual- both visual & tactile- predominately tactile- entirely tactile).

2.1.3 Experimental design

The overall design of the experiment is a 2 x 2 x 3 mixed design. The between-subject variable is participants' SpA (low vs. high). The within-subject variables are Robotics Task type (Auto vs. Teleop) and AiTR type (Baseline- no alerts vs. Tactile alerts only vs. Tactile + Visual alerts) (see Procedure). There were six within-subject conditions:

- *Auto-BL* (baseline): No alerts + control of a semi-autonomous UGV
- *Teleop-BL*: No alerts + Teleoperating a UGV
- *Auto-Tac*: Tactile alerts + control of a semi-autonomous UGV
- *Teleop-Tac*: Tactile alerts + Teleoperating a UGV
- *Auto-TacVis*: Tactile alerts + Visual alerts + control of a semi-autonomous UGV
- *Teleop-TacVis*: Tactile alerts + Visual alerts + Teleoperating a UGV

The reliability level of the alerts was 100%. However, only hostile targets were cued, not the neutral targets. The participants had to detect the neutral targets on their own. It was decided to not include a visual-cueing condition due to the fact that our simulated environment was heavily visual. Therefore, visual alerts were not expected to be effective if not combined with a non-visual modality.

2.1.4 Procedure

After the informed consent process, participants were administered the surveys and spatial tests. After these tests, participants received training, which was self-paced and was delivered by PowerPoint® slides showing the elements of the TCU, steps for completing various tasks, several mini-exercises for practicing the steps, and 2 exercises for performing the robotics tasks (details presented later). After the tutorial on TCU, participants were trained on the gunnery tasks. The entire training session lasted about 2.5 hrs.

The experimental session took place on a different day but within a week of the training session. Before the experimental session began, participants were given some practice trials and review materials, if necessary, to refresh their memories. After the refresher training, participants completed one combined exercise in which they performed all three tasks (i.e. gunnery, robotics, and communication tasks) at the same time. Participants then changed into one of the laboratory cotton T-shirts in order to standardize how the tactors were applied to the skin. The experimenter then measured the participant around the abdomen just above the navel, adjusted the tactile belt, and arranged the tactors so that they were equidistant for the participant's abdomen. Once fitted with the tactile display, the participant was seated in front of the gunner monitor. A test pattern would confirm that all eight tactors were working properly and that the participant could readily perceive the stimuli. The experimenter then explained the nature of the AiTR system and the corresponding visual or tactile cues that would be provided.

In the experimental trials, participants' tasks were to use their robot to locate targets (i.e. enemy dismounted soldiers) in the remote environment and also find targets in their immediate environment. The tank was simulated as traveling along a designated route, which was approximately 4.3 km and lasted about 15 minutes. There were 10 hostile and 10 neutral targets randomly placed along the route in each gunnery scenario. Hostile targets were enemy soldiers dressed in military uniform and carrying a gun; neutral targets were civilians dressed in typical Middle Eastern attire without any weapons. Participants were instructed to engage the hostile targets and verbally report spotting the neutral targets. Only hostile targets were cued (in the non-baseline conditions), not the neutral targets. The participants had to detect the neutral targets independently. Additionally, the alerts did not occur when neutral targets appeared in the environment. In total, there were six 15-minute scenarios, corresponding to the six experimental conditions, the order of which was counterbalanced according to a Williams Square design.

There were two types of robotics tasks: Auto and Teleop. The Auto control task required the operator to monitor the video feed as the robot traveled autonomously, examine still images generated from the reconnaissance scans, and detect targets. The Teleop task required the operator to manually manipulate and drive the robot (using a joystick) along a predetermined route using the TCU to detect randomly placed targets for each scanning checkpoint. For both the Auto and Teleop tasks, upon detecting a target, participants needed to place the target on the map, label the target, and then send a spot-report.

While the participants were performing their gunnery and robotics tasks, they simultaneously performed the communication task by answering questions delivered to them via DECtalk®. There were two-minute breaks between experimental scenarios. Participants filled out the NASA-TLX after they completed each scenario and the usability survey at the end of the experimental session.

The dependent measures include mission performance (i.e. number of targets detected in the remote environment using the robot and number of targets detected in the immediate environment), communication task performance, and workload assessment.

2.2 Results

2.2.1 Target detection performance

2.2.1.1 Gunnery Task.

Participants were designated as high SpA or low SpA based on their composite SpA test scores (median split). A mixed analysis of variance (ANOVA) was performed to examine the effects of the concurrent robotics tasks on the gunnery task performance (percentage of hostile targets detected), with the Robotics Task condition (Auto vs. Teleop) and the AiTR condition (Baseline vs. Tac vs. TacVis) being the within-subject factors and SpA (High vs. Low) as the between-subject factor. The analysis revealed that AiTR condition significantly affected number of targets detected, $F(2, 36) = 78.6$, $p < .001$. Simple contrasts with the Baseline condition as the reference category showed that target detection in Baseline was significantly lower than in the Tac and TacVis conditions. Participants with higher SpA had significantly higher gunnery task performance than did those with lower SpA, $F(1, 18) = 5.7$, $p < .05$ (Figure 2).

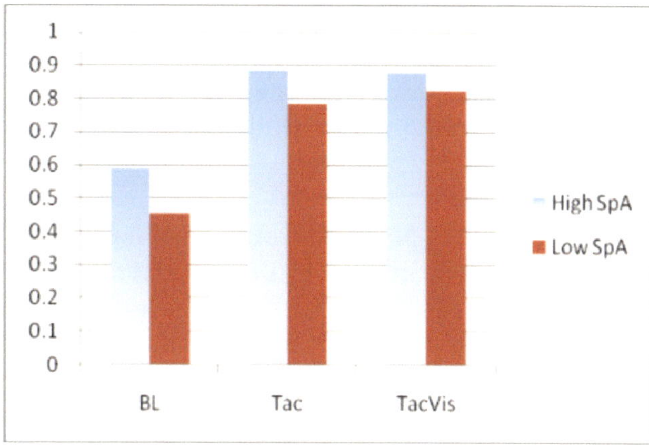

Fig. 2. Gunner's enemy target detection performance and effects of spatial ability (SpA).

Participants' detection of neutral targets was also assessed. Since the AiTR only alerted the participants when hostile targets were present, the neutral target detection could be used to indicate how much visual attention was devoted to the gunnery station. An ANOVA revealed a significant main effect for both Robotics, $F(1, 19) = 13.2$, $p < .005$, and AiTR, $F(2, 38) = 18.1$, $p < .0001$. Post-hoc (LSD) tests showed that Baseline was highest and Tac was lowest, and the differences between each pair were all significant.

2.2.1.2 Robotics Task.

Since participants' task performance in the Auto condition was assisted by the capabilities of the TCU, it was determined that only the performance data from the Teleop condition would be included for the analyses. Performance data from the Tac and TacVis conditions were merged to form the AiTR condition and was compared with the Baseline condition. It was found that the Baseline condition was significantly lower than the AiTR condition, $F(1,18) = 5.3$, $p < .05$. Those with higher SpA outperformed those with lower SpA in the baseline condition, $F(1,18) = 5.9$, $p < .05$, but not in the AiTR conditions (Figure 3).

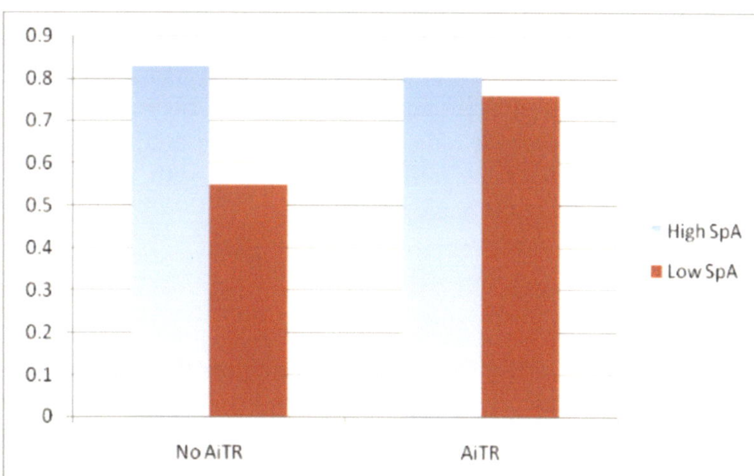

Fig. 3. Robotics (teleoperation) task performance and effects of spatial ability (SpA).

2.2.2 Communication task performance

Performance data from the Tac and TacVis conditions were again merged to form the AiTR condition and was compared with the Baseline condition. The difference between these two conditions was significant, $F(1, 19) = 7.4$, $p < .05$, with the no AiTR condition lower.

2.2.3 Workload assessment

Weighted ratings of the scales of the NASA-TLX were used for this analysis. Participants' perceived workload was significantly affected by the Robotics condition, $F(1, 18) = 5.2$, $p < .05$, as well as the AiTR condition, $F(2, 32) = 4.3$, $p < .05$ (Figure 4). The workload assessment was higher in the Teleop condition ($M = 70.22$) and when the gunnery task was unassisted by the AiTR ($M = 70.5$).

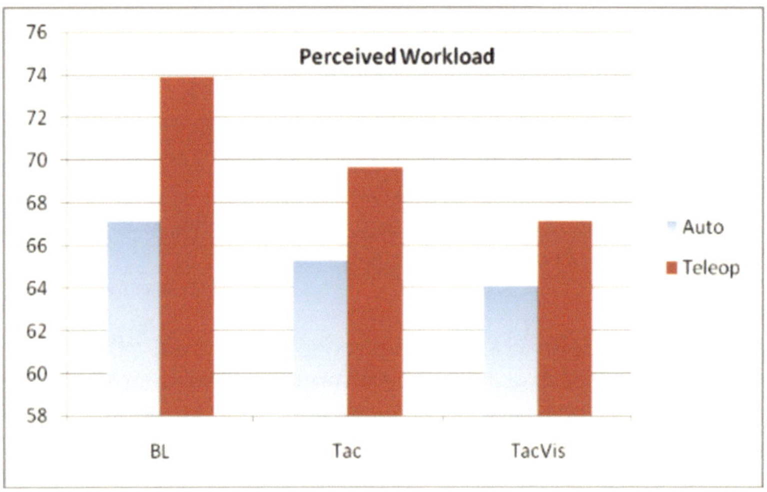

Fig. 4. Workload assessment.

2.2.4 AiTR display usability assessment

A usability questionnaire captured participant preferences for presentation of AiTR information. Following their interaction with the AiTR systems, 65% of participants responded that they either relied predominantly or entirely on the tactile AiTR display. Only 15% responded that they either relied predominantly or entirely on the visual AiTR display. AiTR preference was also significantly correlated with participants' SpA (i.e., composite score of the spatial tests), $r = .53$, $p = .016$.

3. Experiment 2

The goal of this experiment was to examine the effects of unreliable alerts on gunners' concurrent performance of gunnery, robotics, and communication tasks. Both tactile and visual displays were incorporated to provide directional cueing for the gunnery targeting task (based on a simulated AiTR capability). Two types of imperfect AiTR were simulated: false-alarm-prone (FAP) and miss-prone (MP). We were particularly interested in investigating discrepancies in previous research related to compliance and reliance effects as a function of type of AiTR error. Effects of individual differences in SpA and perceived attentional control (PAC) were also evaluated.

3.1 Method

3.1.1 Participants

Twenty-four college students (4 females and 20 males, mean age = 22.3) participated in this study. Participants were compensated $15/hr or with class credit for their participation.

3.1.2 Apparatus

The simulators and cueing displays were identical to those used in Experiment 1. The simulated AiTR was either FAP or MP, with a reliability level at 60%. The low reliability level was deliberately chosen to investigate if the compliance vs. reliance effects as well as the individual differences reported previously in the literature would be amplified in the high workload multitasking environment in the current study. The FAP condition consisted of ten hits (i.e. alerts when there were targets), eight FAs (i.e. alerts when there were no targets), no misses (i.e. no alerts when there were targets), and two correct rejections (CRs) (i.e. no alerts when there were no targets). The MP condition consisted of two hits, no FAs, eight misses, and ten CRs.

The communication task materials, spatial tests, and surveys (i.e., Attentional Control Survey, NASA-TLX, and Usability Survey) were identical to those used in Experiment 1. Participants were also asked to evaluate their trust in the AiTR system using a modified survey by Jian et al. (2000) (items 22-33).

3.1.3 Experimental design

The overall design of the study is a 2 x 3 mixed design. The between-subject variable is AiTR type (FAP vs. MP). The within-subject variable is Robotics Task type (Monitor vs. Auto vs. Teleop) (see Procedure).

3.1.4 Procedure

The preliminary session (i.e., surveys and spatial tests) and the training session were identical to Experiment 1 and lasted about 2.5 hrs. The experimental procedure was also identical to Experiment 1, except that it followed the training session on the same day and the participants were told that the AiTR cueing was unreliable. There were three types of robotics tasks: Monitor, Auto, and Teleop. The Monitor task required the operator to continuously monitor the video feed as the robot traveled autonomously and verbally report detection of targets. There were twenty targets (five hostile and fifteen neutral) along the route. The Auto and Teleop tasks were identical to those in Experiment 1. While the participants were performing their gunnery and robotics control tasks, they simultaneously performed the communication task by answering questions delivered to them via DECtalk®. There were 2-min breaks between experimental scenarios. Participants assessed their workload using the computerized NASA-TLX after each scenario. They also evaluated their perceived utility of and trust in the AiTR at the end of the experiment. The entire experimental session lasted about 1 hr.

The dependent measures include mission performance (i.e. number of targets detected in the remote environment using the robot and number of hostile/neutral targets detected in the immediate environment), communication task performance, and perceived workload.

3.2 Results

3.2.1 Target detection performance

3.2.1.1 Gunnery Task.

A mixed ANOVA was performed to examine the effects of the concurrent robotic control tasks on the gunnery task performance (percentage of hostile targets detected), with the AiTR condition (FAP vs. MP) being the between-subject factor and the Robotics Task condition (Monitor vs. Auto vs. Teleop) as the within-subject factor. The analysis revealed that Robotics condition significantly affected number of targets detected, $F(2, 15) = 4.6$, $p < .05$ (Figure 5). Post hoc (LSD) tests showed that target detection in the Monitor condition was significantly higher than in the Auto and Teleop conditions. Neither AiTR nor the Robotics x AiTR interaction was significant.

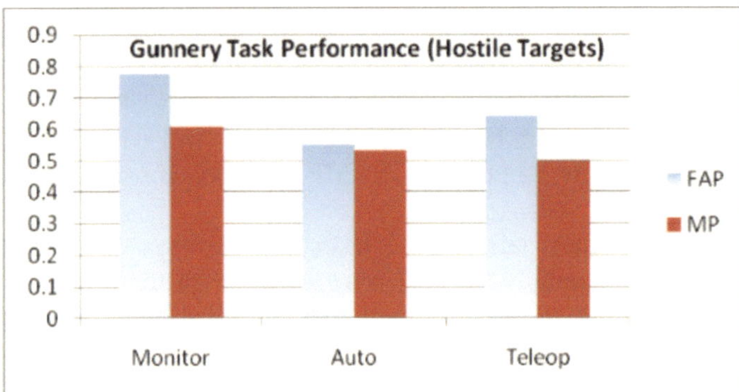

Fig. 5. Gunnery task performance (hostile targets).

Participants with higher SpA had significantly higher gunnery task performance than did those with lower SpA, $F(1, 16) = 6.3$, $p < .05$. When comparable data from both experiments were examined in the same analysis (with only the TacVis condition from Experiment 1 and Robotics and Teleop conditions from Experiment 2), it was found that AiTR reliability contributed significantly to the hostile target detection performance of gunnery task, $F(2,30) = 11.8$, $p = .000$. Post-hoc (LSD) tests show that AiTR with perfect reliability (Experiment 1) was significantly higher than MP, and FAP was also significantly higher than MP, p's < .05.

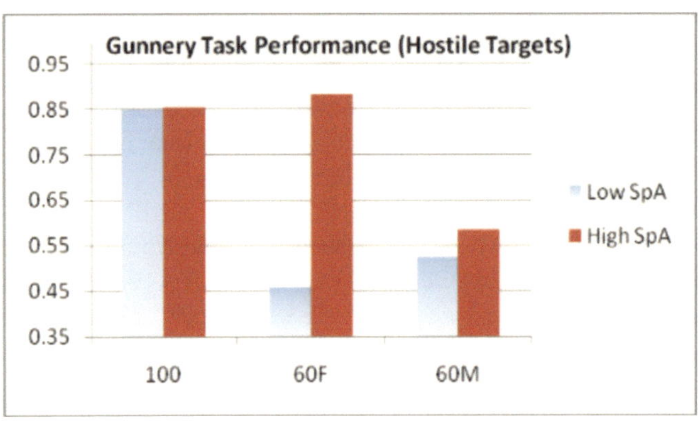

Fig. 6. Gunnery task performance (hostile targets)- effects of AiTR reliability (100 = AiTR with perfect reliability; 60F = FAP; 60M = MP) and SpA.

Participants' SpA was found to affect their gunnery task performance, and there was a significant SpA x AiTR reliability interaction (Figure 6). As Figure 6 shows, there was a large difference between low SpA and high SpA individuals in the FAP condition.

Participants were classified as high or low PAC based on their attentional control survey scores (median split). There was a significant AiTR x PAC interaction, $F(1, 16) = 7.4$, $p < .05$ (Figure 7, upper left). Those with lower PAC performed better with the FAP cueing, whereas those with higher PAC performed at a similar level regardless of the AiTR conditions.

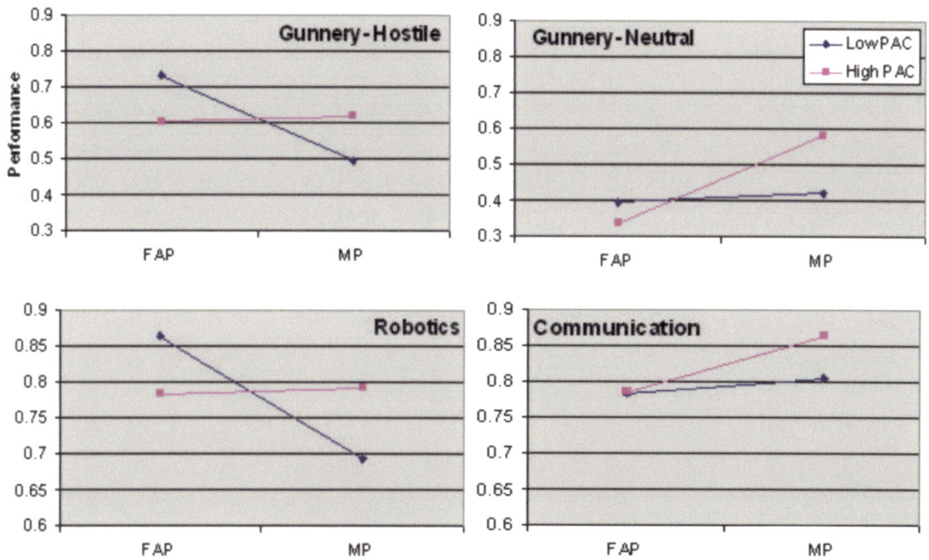

Fig. 7. Interaction between PAC and AiTR unreliability.

In order to further examine the effect of task load on reliance of AiTR, the data of the MP condition were analyzed separately. Due to the small sample size (N = 12), no significant differences were found between those with high vs. low PAC, $F(1, 10) = 1.4$, $p > .05$. However, the trend was evident that, while those with high PAC maintained a fairly stable level of reliance throughout the experimental conditions, those with low PAC became increasingly reliant on the AiTR (and missed more targets), as task load became heavier (i.e. Teleop > Auto > Monitor, based on Chen & Joyner, 2009) (Figure 8). For the low PAC participants, the difference between the Monitor and Teleop conditions was statistically significant, $F(1, 6) = 7.1$, $p < .05$.

Participants' detection of neutral targets was also assessed. Since the AiTR only alerted the participants when hostile targets were present, the neutral target detection could be used to indicate how much visual attention was devoted to the gunnery station. A mixed ANOVA revealed a significant main effect for Robotics, $F(2,15) = 4.4$, $p < .05$. Post hoc tests (LSD) showed that neutral target detection in the Teleop condition was significantly lower than in the Auto condition. The main effect for AiTR failed to reach statistical significance, $F(1, 22) = 3.3$, $p > .05$. There was a significant AiTR x PAC interaction, $F(1, 16) = 3.6$, $p < .05$ (Figure 7, upper right panel). Those with lower PAC performed at about the same level, regardless of the AiTR type, while those with higher PAC had a better performance with the MP cueing

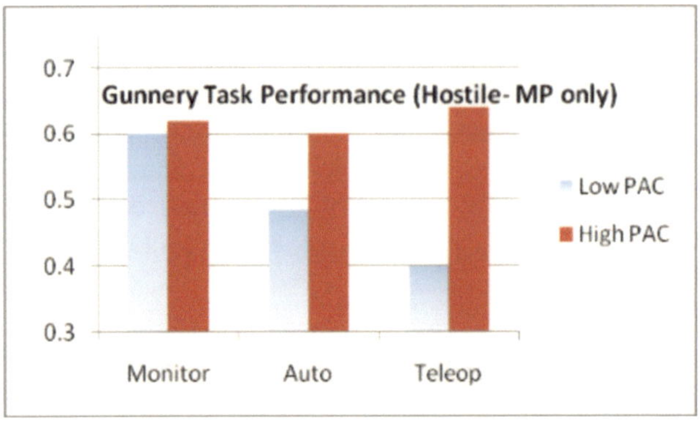

Fig. 8. Effects of PAC on gunnery task performance (hostile targets) in MP conditions.

than with the FAP cueing. When comparable data from both experiments were examined in the same analysis (with only the TacVis condition from Experiment 1 and Robotics and Teleop conditions from Experiment 2), it was found that both the main effect of Robotics and the Robotics x PAC interaction were significant, $F(1,30) = 8.8$, $p = .006$ and $F(1,30) = 4.5$, $p = .04$ respectively (Figure 9). The difference between low PAC and high PAC individuals was larger in the Teleop condition than in the Auto condition.

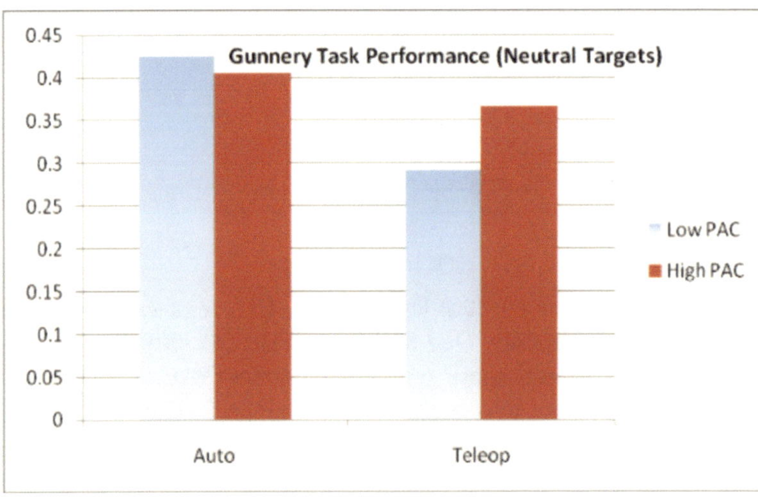

Fig. 9. Gunnery task performance (neutral targets) - effects of Robotics and PAC.

3.2.1.2 Robotics Task.

A mixed ANOVA revealed that there was a significant main effect for Robotics, $F(2,15) = 25.4$, $p < .001$ (Figure 10). The Monitor condition was significantly higher than both the Auto and the Teleop conditions, in terms of percentage of targets detected. The main effect for AiTR was not significant, $p > .05$. There was a significant Robotics x AiTR interaction, $F(2,32) = 4.0$, $p < .05$. The Monitor task performance stayed at the same level regardless of the AiTR types. The Auto task performance was slightly higher with the MP cueing (although the difference failed to reach statistical significance), while the Teleop task performance was significantly higher with the FAP cueing ($p < .05$). There was also a significant AiTR x PAC interaction, $F(1,16) = 4.8$, $p < .05$ (Figure 7, lower left panel). Those with lower PAC had a better performance with the FAP cueing, while those with higher PAC performed better with the MP cueing.

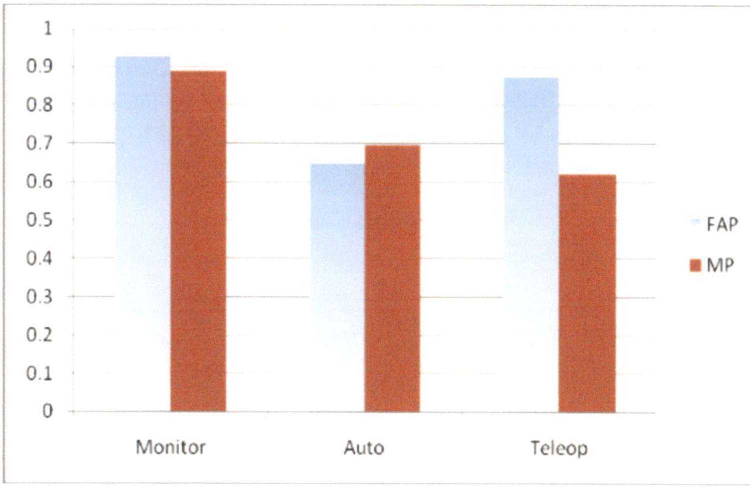

Fig. 10. Robotics task performance.

3.2.2 Communication task performance

A mixed ANOVA revealed that there was a significant main effect for Robotics, $F(2,44) = 3.3$, $p < .05$. The Monitor condition was significantly higher than the Teleop conditions, $F(1,22) = 5.5$, $p < .05$. Neither the main effect for AiTR nor the Robotics x AiTR interaction was significant, p's > .05 (Figure 7, lower right panel). When comparable data from both experiments were examined in the same analysis (with only the TacVis condition from Experiment 1 and Robotics and Teleop conditions from Experiment 2), it was found that the main effect of AiTR reliability was significant, $F(2,29) = 5.3$, $p = .011$ (Figure 11). Post-hoc (LSD) tests showed that communication task performance in Experiment 1 (perfect reliability) was significantly better than either FAP or MP (p's < .05).

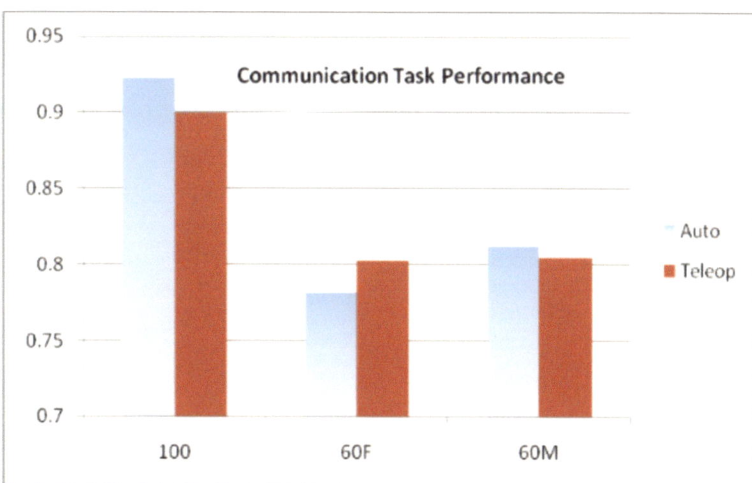

Fig. 11. Communication task performance.

3.2.2 Workload assessment

Participants' self-assessment of workload (weighted ratings of the scales of the NASA-TLX) was significantly affected by Robotic condition, $F(2,15) = 25.1$, $p < .001$ (Figure 12). The perceived workload was significantly higher in the Teleop condition ($M = 77.7$) than in the Auto condition ($M = 69.6$) and the Monitor condition ($M = 61.1$). The difference between Auto and Monitor was also significant. The main effect for AiTR was not significant, $p > .05$. There was a significant Robotics x AiTR interaction, $F(2,15) = 5.5$, $p < .05$.

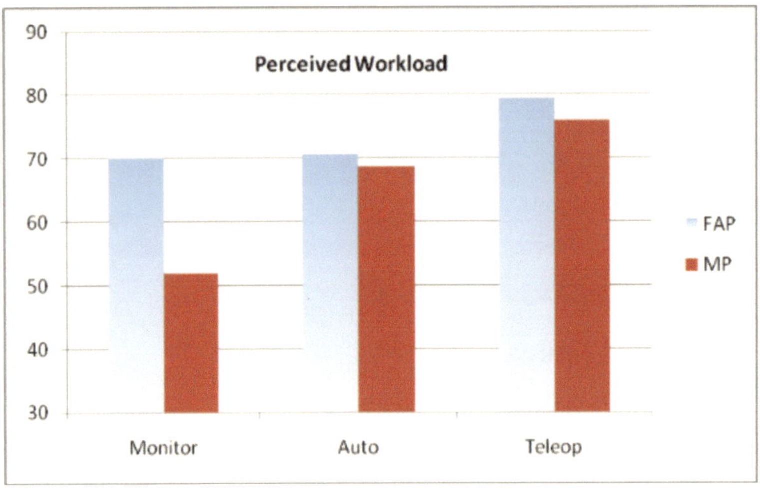

Fig. 12. Perceived workload.

3.2.3 AiTR display usability assessment

Following their interaction with the AiTR systems, 41% of participants responded that they relied predominantly or entirely on the tactile AiTR display, while 36% responded that they relied predominantly or entirely on the visual AiTR display. AiTR preference was also significantly correlated with SpA (composite spatial test scores), $r = .51$, $p < .01$. Those with

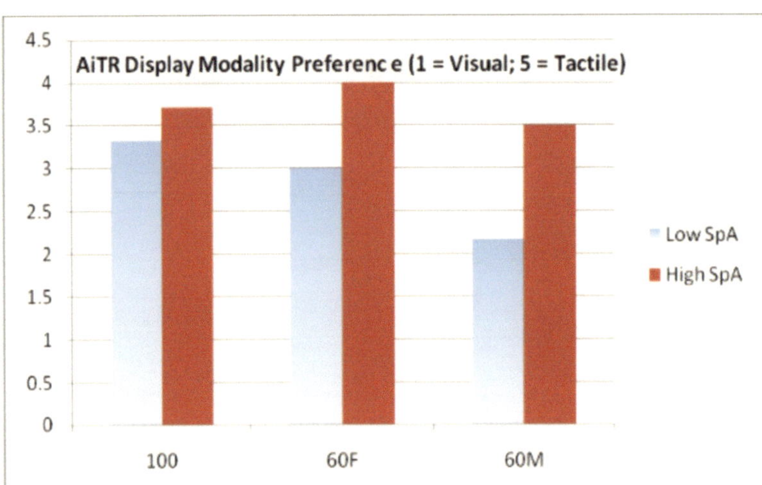

Fig. 13. SpA and AiTR display modality preference.

higher SpA tended to prefer tactile cueing over visual cueing. Conversely, those with lower SpA favored visual cueing over tactile cueing. Figure 13 shows the data from both experiments examined in the same analysis, $F(1,35) = 12.1$, $p = .001$. There was also a significant negative correlation between the participants' ages and their preference of tactile display, $r = -.42$, $p = .003$ (i.e., older participants tended to prefer visual cueing display while younger participants tended to prefer tactile display).

4. General discussion

In this study, we simulated a military tank crewstation environment and examined the performance and workload of the combined position of gunner and robotics operator. More specifically, we investigated the effects of AiTR (with either perfect reliability or imperfect reliability [FAP vs. MP]) on operator's performance of the automated (i.e., gunnery) task as well as the concurrent tasks (i.e., robotics and communication). According to Chen and Joyner (2009), adding a robotics task to the gunner's tasking environment resulted in approximately 30% reduction in target detection for the gunnery task. In Experiment 1, the structural interference for the gunnery task created by concurrent performance of the robotics task was mitigated by augmenting the gunnery task via tactile cueing. Results of Experiment 2 showed that the operator's gunnery task performance in detecting hostile targets was significantly better in the Monitor condition than in the other two robotics task conditions, consistent with the findings of Chen and Joyner (2009). In both Chen and Joyner (2009) and Experiment 2, the workload associated with the Monitor condition was significantly lower than the other robotics conditions. These results suggest that the operator had more visual and mental resources for the gunnery task when the robotics task was simply monitoring the video feed, compared with the other two robotics conditions. Also consistent with past research (Lathan & Tracey, 2002; Vincow, 1998) and Chen and Joyner (2009), participants' SpA was found to be an accurate predictor of their gunnery performance in both Experiments 1 & 2. Thomas and Wickens (2004) showed that there were individual differences in scanning effectiveness and its associated target detection performance. However, Thomas and Wickens did not examine the characteristics of those participants who had more effective scanning strategies. The findings of the current study along with Chen and Joyner indicate that SpA may be an important factor for determining scanning effectiveness. Figure 6 shows that when there was an increased requirement for visual scanning (i.e., FAP), the difference in effectiveness of scanning (i.e., target detection performance) between high SpA and low SpA was especially large. Our findings support the recommendation by Lathan and Tracey that military missions can benefit from selecting personnel with higher SpA to operate robotic devices.

Results of Experiment 2 also showed that there was a significant interaction between types of unreliable AiTR and participants' PAC. For those with high PAC, our data are consistent with the notion that operator reliance on and compliance with automation are independent constructs and are separately affected by system misses and false alarms (Dixon & Wickens, 2006; Meyer, 2001, 2004; Wickens, Dixon, Goh et al., 2005). Based on Figure 7, it is evident that high PAC participants did not comply with alerts in the FAP condition. Since the FAP AiTR had a 0% miss rate, a full compliance should result in a detection rate over 84%, as reported in Experiment 1 (with perfectly reliable AiTR). As predicted, Figure 7 shows that in MP conditions, high PAC participants did not rely on the AiTR and detected more targets than were cued. However, an examination of the data for the low PAC participants revealed a completely opposite trend. Specifically, with the FAP condition, low PAC participants showed a strong compliance with the alerts, which resulted in a good performance in target detection (at a similar level as in Experiment 1). With the MP condition, however, low PAC participants evidently overly relied on the automation and therefore had a very poor performance. Indeed, Figure 8 shows that as task load became heavier, those with low PAC became increasingly reliant on the AiTR (and missed more targets), while those with high PAC maintained a fairly stable level of reliance throughout the experimental conditions. According to Biros et al. (2004), higher task loads tend to induce a higher level of reliance on automated systems. Data of Experiment 2 suggest that this heightened level of reliance is also moderated by PAC. More specifically, only those with low PAC tend to exhibit over-reliance on automation (i.e. complacency) under a heavy task load.

Data of both Experiments 1 and 2 showed that the gunner's detection of neutral targets (which was not aided by AiTR) was significantly worse when s/he had to teleoperate a robot (vs. when the robot was semi-autonomous) or when the gunnery task was aided by AiTR. These findings suggest that participants devoted significantly less visual attention to the gunnery station when their robot required teleoperation or when their gunnery task was assisted by AiTR. On average, in Experiment 1, participants detected 45% of the neutral targets when there was no AiTR; they only detected 28% when there was. These results are consistent with automation research that operators may develop over-reliance on the automatic system and this complacency may negatively affect their task performance (Chen & Joyner, 2009; Dzindole et al., 2001; Parasuraman et al., 1993; Thomas & Wickens, 2004; Young & Stanton, 2007b). It is worth noting that these findings, along with the results of the current study, do not necessarily suggest that manual manipulation of sensor devices be used instead of AiTR devices. However, the issue of over-reliance on these automatic capabilities needs to be taken into account when designing the user interface where these features are present. Data of Experiment 2 also showed that those with lower PAC performed at about the same level, regardless of the AiTR type, while those with higher PAC had a significantly better performance with the MP cueing. This suggests that higher PAC participants devoted more visual attention to the gunnery station (implying a reduced reliance on automation for the gunnery task) when the AiTR was MP than when the AiTR was FAP. Although we did not measure participants' scanning behaviors, the detection rate of neutral targets on the gunnery station provides an estimate of the amount of operator's visual attention on the automated task environment. Again, the data of high PAC participants seem to support the hypothesis that MP automation reduces operator reliance. However, the same phenomenon was not observed for the low PAC participants. Figure 9 shows that, with data from both experiments, the difference in neutral target detection performance between high PAC and low PAC individuals appeared to widen when the robotics task was Teleop, compared with the Auto condition. This finding suggests that high PAC individuals were able to allocate more visual attention to the gunnery tasking environment when the multitasking requirement was more demanding (i.e., Teleop) than did the low PAC individuals.

For the robotics tasks, the results of Experiment 1 showed that participants' teleoperation performance improved significantly when their gunnery task was assisted by AiTR. Therefore, AiTR benefited not only the automated task (i.e., gunnery) but also the concurrent task (i.e., robotics). In the current study, structural interference for the robotics task caused by concurrent performance of the gunnery task was successfully mitigated by providing cues to assist the gunnery task. This finding is consistent with previous research on the effects of automating the primary task on enhancing the concurrent visual tasks (Dixon et al., 2004; Young & Stanton, 2007a). Additionally, it was evident that AiTR was more beneficial for enhancing the concurrent robotics task performance for those with lower SpA than for those with higher SpA. When AiTR was available to assist those operators with low SpA, the performance of their concurrent task was improved to a similar level as those with higher SpA. These results are consistent with other findings showing that vehicle automation helps reduce the performance gap between experts and novices (Young & Stanton, 2007a). These results may have important implications for system design and personnel selection for the future military programs. The data of Experiment 2 showed that participants had the best performance when the task was only monitoring the video feed. Moreover, the Monitor task performance stayed at the same level, regardless of the AiTR types. On the other hand, the Teleop task performance was significantly higher with the FAP cueing. This is consistent with previous studies that MP automation degrades concurrent task performance more than FAP (Dixon & Wickens, 2006; Wickens, Dixon, Goh et al., 2005). However, the same trend was not observed for the other two robotics tasks, which were less challenging than the Teleop task. Therefore, it appears that the adverse effect of MP automation on concurrent tasks is only manifest in more challenging task conditions. The data of Experiment 2 also showed that again, there was a significant interaction between AiTR type and PAC. Consistent with the previous two performance measures (gunnery-hostile and gunnery-neutral), the low PAC participants exhibited a larger performance decrement with the MP conditions. The performance of the high PAC participants, on the other hand, showed a completely opposite trend. These results suggest that the high PAC participants' reduced compliance with the FAP alerts did not help them with their concurrent task, compared with the MP conditions; conversely, their reduced reliance on the MP alerts did not impair their performance. Overall, the low PAC participants showed the most pronounced adverse effect of MP alerts on concurrent performance. In contrast, the FAP alerts not only helped them with their automated task but also their concurrent task.

Taking the three main performance measures together (i.e. Gunnery- Hostile, Gunnery-Neutral, and Robotics), it appears that overall, for high PAC participants, FAP alerts were more detrimental than MP alerts. FAP alerts not only affected their automated task but also the concurrent task. This finding is consistent with the conclusion of Dixon et al. (2007) that FAP degraded overall performance more than MP automation. However, it is worth noting that for low PAC participants, we observed the opposite pattern: MP automation was more harmful than FAP automation. The overall data suggest that low PAC participants had a higher trust in the automation system than did high PAC participants. It is likely that low PAC participants had more difficulty in performing multiple tasks concurrently and had to rely on automation when available. High PAC participants, in contrast, tended to rely on their own multitasking ability to perform the tasks. It is interesting to note that there was no significant difference in the participants' self-assessment of their trust in the AiTR system between high PAC and low PAC groups. This suggests that the participants' self-assessed trust in automation may not truly reflect their actual use (i.e., actual trust) of automation. Our results are consistent with past research (de Vries et al., 2003; Lee & Moray, 1994) that self-confidence is a critical factor in moderating the effect of trust (in automation) on reliance (on the automatic system). Lee and Moray found that when self-confidence exceeded trust, operators tended to use manual control. When trust exceeded self-confidence, automation was used more. Our present data suggest that, this relationship between self-confidence and level of reliance is also moderated by operator's PAC.

Participants' communication task performance improved when their gunnery task was aided by AiTR (Experiment 1) or when their robotics task was Monitor than when it was Teleop (Experiment 2). With data from both experiments examined in the same analysis, it was also found that communication task performance was significantly better when the AiTR was perfectly reliable than when it was either FAP or MP. Again, this result suggests that reliable AiTR not only enhanced the tasks it was designed for, it also benefited concurrent tasks. It also shows that our cognitive communication task was sensitive to the task load manipulations we implemented for the concurrent tasks. Overall, these results are consistent with the conclusion by Young and Stanton (2007a) that a common resource pool feeds separate processing channels. In our case, as the visual channel is assisted, the auditory task is enhanced by the additional resources available in the general pool. This, however, conflicts with the Multiple Resource Theory (Wickens, 2002), which predicts difficulty insensitivity (i.e. changes in the difficulty of one task has little impact on the performance of the concurrent task if different resources are used). According to Naveh-Benjamin et al. (2000), information encoding processes require more attention than retrieval and are more prone to the effects of competing demands of multitasking. It is, therefore, likely that the information-encoding process of the communication task in our study was more disrupted by the concurrent tasks when there was no AiTR or when a more challenging robotics task (i.e., Teleop) was performed.

Participants' workload assessment was found to be affected by the type of concurrent robotics task as well as whether their gunnery task was aided by AiTR. They experienced higher workload when the robot required teleoperation or when their gunnery task was unassisted by AiTR. These results are consistent with Mitchell's (2005) analysis and with the findings of Chen and Joyner (2009) and Schipani (2003), which evaluated robotics operator workload in a field setting. Although many of the ground robots in the Army's future robotics programs will be semi-autonomous, teleoperation will still be an important part of any missions involving robotics (e.g., when robots encounter obstacles or other problems). The higher workload associated with teleoperation needs to be taken into account when designing the user interfaces for the robots (see Chen et al., 2007, for a review of user interface designs for teleoperated robots).

The data of both Experiment 1 and 2 showed significant positive correlations of AiTR preference with SpA, indicating that as AiTR ratings tended toward considerable reliance on the tactile display, there was a concurrent shift with higher SpA. Perhaps those with higher SpA can more easily employ the spatial tactile signals in the dual task setting and therefore have a stronger preference for something that makes the gunner task easier to complete. Individuals with lower SpA, on the other hand, may have not utilized the spatial tactile cues to their full extent and therefore continued to prefer the visual AiTR display. According to Kozhevnikov et al. (2002), visualizers with lower SpA tend to rely on iconic imagery while those with higher SpA tend to prefer using spatial-schematic imagery while solving problems. Therefore, it is likely that in our study, those who preferred visual AiTR displays might be more iconic in their mental representations. However, this preference may have caused degraded target detection performance due to more visual attention being devoted to the visual AiTR display, not to the simulated environment. In contrast, those who were more spatial could take advantage of the directional information of the tactile display to help them with the visually demanding tasks, resulting in a more effective performance. Finally, our data showed that older participants tended to prefer visual cueing display while younger participants tended to prefer tactile display. It is not clear to which extent this shift is related to decline of SpA as people age (Berg et al., 1982).

5. Conclusions

In this study, we conducted two simulation experiments and examined the effectiveness of AiTR capabilities (with either perfect reliability, FAP, or MP) for enhancing the performance of gunners who also had to simultaneously operate a robot and maintain effective communication with fellow crew members. Overall, the findings of these experiments suggest that reliable automation (i.e., AiTR in Experiment 1) for one task benefits not only the automated task but also the concurrent tasks (i.e., robotics and communication in this case). The tactile cues alerted the operator of key moments to transition from the robotics task to the gunnery task, and afforded the operator the ability to timeshare effectively between the two tasks in detecting hostile targets. As searching around the vehicle was normally a task that demanded constant visual resources, the tactile cues alleviated this continuous burden by altering the demand into discrete time increments. Although parsing across available resource types may alleviate some performance decrements, it is still exceedingly difficult to fully insulate the primary task from any impinging secondary task. The automation implemented into the gunnery task via the AiTR must also be closely examined as the nature of the human-system interaction is now markedly different. Operators may develop an over-reliance on the AiTR for their tasks and overlook other developments that are not detected by the system (e.g., the neutral targets in the current study). Additionally, when selecting personnel for simultaneously performing gunnery and robotic tasks, it might be beneficial to take into account their SpA. Chen et al. (2008) and Chen and Joyner (2009) and the current study all demonstrated the superior performance by those with higher SpA. It is especially important if AiTR is not available to assist the operators with their tasks. These data on individual differences can be used in future human performance modeling efforts (e.g., IMPRINT) as input data to modeling tasks and, therefore, enhance future model analyses.

The data of Experiment 2 suggest that there is a strong interaction between the type of AiTR unreliability and participants' PAC for almost all the performance measures. Overall, it appears that for high PAC participants, FAP alerts were more detrimental than MP alerts. FAP alerts affected not only their automated task but also the concurrent task. However, for low PAC participants, MP automation was more harmful than FAP automation. Future research should incorporate performance-based measures of attentional shifting effectiveness (e.g., Synthetic Work Environment) in addition to surveys such as the attentional control survey. In the area of SpA, Experiment 2 replicated the finding of Experiment 1 that the operator's preference of modality of the AiTR display is correlated with his or her SpA. Low SpA individuals prefer visual cueing over tactile cueing, although tactile display would be more effective in highly visual environments (so visual attention can be devoted to the tasks, not to the cues). These findings may have important implications for personnel selection, system designs, and training development. For example, to better enhance the task performance for low SpA individuals, the visual cueing display should be more integrated with the visual scene. Augmented reality (i.e., visual overlays) is a potential technique to embed directional information onto the video (Calhoun & Draper, 2006). Additionally, the capabilities and limits of the automated systems should be conveyed to the operator, when feasible, in order for the operator to develop appropriate trust and reliance (Lee & See, 2004).

6. Acknowledgements

This project was funded by the U.S. Army's Robotics Collaboration ATO. The author thanks Mr. Michael Barnes of ARL - HRED, Dr. Peter Terrence of State Farm Insurance, and MAJ Carla Joyner of U.S. Military Academy for their contributions to this project.

7. References

Berg, C.; Hertzog, C. & Hunt, E. (1982). Age differences in the speed of mental rotation. *Developmental Psychology,* Vol. 18, pp. 95-107.

Biros, D.; Daly, M. & Gunsch, G. (2004). The influence of task load and automation trust on deception detection. *Group Decision and Negotiation,* Vol. 13, pp. 173-189.

Bleckley, M.; Durso, F.; Crutchfield, J.; Engle, R. & Khanna, M. (2003). Individual differences in working memory capacity predict visual attention allocation. *Psychonomic Bulletin & Review,* Vol. 10, pp. 884-889.

Calhoun, G. & Draper, M. (2006). Multi-sensory interfaces for remotely operatedvehicles, In: *Human Factors of Remotely Operated Vehicles,* N. Cooke, H. Pringle, H. Pedersen, & O. Connor, (Eds.), pp. 149-163, Elsevier, Oxford, UK.

Cassenti, D.; Kelley, T.; Swoboda, J. & Patton, D. (2009). The effects of communication style on robot navigation performance, *Proceedings of Human Factors and Ergonomics Society 53rd Annual Meeting,* San Antonio, TX, October 2009, Human Factors & Ergonomics Society, Santa Monica, CA.

Chen, J.Y.C. Durlach, P.; Sloan, J. & Bowens, L. (2008). Human robot interaction in the context of simulated route reconnaissance missions. *Military Psychology,* Vol. 20, No. 3, pp. 135-149.

Chen, J.Y.C.; Haas, E. & Barnes, M. (2007). Human performance issues and user interface design for teleoperated robots. *IEEE Transactions on Systems, Man,and Cybernetics--Part C: Applications and Reviews,* Vol. 37, No. 6, pp. 1231-1245.

Chen, J.Y.C. & Joyner, C.T. (2009). Concurrent performance of gunner's and robotic operator's tasks in a multi-tasking environment. *Military Psychology,* Vol. 21, No. 1, pp. 98 - 113.

Cholewiak, R.; Brill, J. & Schwab, A. (2004). Vibrotactile localization on the abdomen: Effects of place and space. *Perception & Psychophysics,* Vol. 66, pp. 970-987.

Derryberry, D. & Reed, M. (2002). Anxiety-related attentional biases and their regulation by attentional control. *Journal of Abnormal Psychology,* Vol. 111, pp. 225-236.

de Vries, P.; Midden, C. & Bouwhuis, D. (2003). The effects of errors on system trust, self-confidence, and the allocation of control in route planning. *International Journal of Human-Computer Studies,* Vol. 58, pp. 719-735.

Dixon, S. & Wickens, C. (2006). Automation reliability in unmanned aerial vehicle control: A reliance-compliance model of automation dependence in high workload. *Human Factors,* Vol. 48, pp. 474-486.

Dixon, S.; Wickens, C. & Chang, D. (2004).Comparing quantitative model predictions to experimental data in multiple-UAV flight control, *Proceedings of Human Factors & Ergonomics Society 47th Annual Meeting,* pp. 104–108, New Orleans, LA, September, 2004, Human Factors & Ergonomics Society, Santa Monica, CA.

Dixon, S.; Wickens, C. & McCarley, J. (2007). On the independence of compliance and reliance: Are automation false alarms worse than misses? *Human Factors,* Vol. 49, pp. 564-572.

Dzindolet, M.; Pierce, L.; Beck, H.; Dawe, L. & Anderson, B. (2001). Predicting misuse and disuse of combat identification systems. *Military Psychology,* Vol. 13, pp. 147–164.

Ekstrom, R.; French, J. & Harman, H. (1976). *Kit of factor-referenced cognitive tests,* Educational Testing Service, Princeton, NJ.

Eyal, R. & Tendick, F. (2001). Spatial ability and learning the use of an angled laparoscope in a virtual environment, In: *Medicine Meets Virtual Reality 2001,* J. Westwood, H. Hoffman, G. Mogel, D. Stredney & R. Robb, (Eds.), pp. 146-152, IOS Press, Amsterdam.

Gugerty, L. & Brooks, J. (2004). Reference-frame misalignment and cardinal direction judgments: Group differences and strategies. *Journal of Experimental Psychology: Applied,* Vol. 10, pp. 75-88.

Hart, S. & Staveland, L. (1988). Development of NASA TLX (Task Load Index): Results of empirical and theoretical research, In: *Human Mental Workload,* P. Hancock & N. Meshkati, (Eds.), pp. 139-183, Elsevier, Amsterdam.

Ho, C.; Tan, H. & Spence, C. (2005). Using spatial vibrotactile cues to direct visual attention in driving scenes. *Transportation Research Part F: Traffic Psychology and Behaviour,* Vol. 8, pp. 397–412.

Horrey, W. & Wickens, C. (2004). Focal and ambient visual contributions and driver visual scanning in lane keeping and hazard detection, *Proceedings of the Human Factors & Ergonomics 48th Annual Meeting*, pp. 2325-2329, New Orleans, LA, September, 2004, Human Factors & Ergonomics Society, Santa Monica, CA.

Jian, J.; Bisantz, A. & Drury, C. (2000). Foundations for an empirically determined scale of trust in automated systems. *International Journal of Cognitive Ergonomics,* Vol. 4, pp. 53-71.

Kahneman, D.; Ben-Ishai, R. & Lotan, M. (1973). Relation of a test of attention to road accidents. *Journal of Applied Psychology*, Vol. 58, pp. 113-115.

Kozhevnikov, M.; Hegarty, M. & Mayer, R. (2002). Revising the visualizer-verbalizer dimension: Evidence for two types of visualizers. *Cognition & Instruction,* Vol. 20, pp. 47-77.

Krausman, A.; Elliot, L. & Pettitt, R. (2005). *Effects of Visual, Auditory, and Tactile Alerts on Platoon Leader Performance and Decision Making* (Tech Rep. ARL-TR-3633), U.S. Army Research Laboratory, Aberdeen Proving Ground, MD.

Lathan, C. & Tracey, M. (2002). The effects of operator spatial perception and sensory feedback on human-robot teleoperation performance. *Presence,* Vol. 11, pp. 368-377.

Lee, J. & Moray, N. (1994). Trust, self-confidence, and operators' adaptation to automation. *International Journal of Human-Computer Studies,* Vol. 40, pp. 153-184.

Lee, J. & See. K. (2004). Trust in automation: Designing for appropriate reliance. *Human Factors,* Vol. 46, pp. 50-80.

Menchaca-Brandan, M.; Liu, A.; Oman, C. & Natapoff A. (2007). Influence of perspective-taking and mental rotation abilities in space teleoperation, *Proceedings of the ACM/IEEE International Conference on Human-Robot Interaction,* pp. 271-278, Washington, DC, March 2007, ACM Press, New York,

Meyer, J. (2001). Effects of warning validity and proximity on responses to warning. *Human Factors,* Vol. 43, pp. 563-572.

Meyer, J. (2004). Conceptual issues in the study of dynamic hazard warnings. *Human Factors,* Vol. 46, pp. 196-204.

Mitchell, D. (2005). *Soldier Workload Analysis of the Mounted Combat System (MCS) Platoon's Use of Unmanned Assets* (Tech Rep. ARL-TR-3476). U.S. Army Research Laboratory, Aberdeen Proving Ground, MD.

Murray, S. (1994). *Human Performance Studies for Control of Multiple Remote Systems* (Tech Rep. NRaD 1658), SPAWAR, San Diego, CA.

Naveh-Benjamin, M.; Craik, F.; Perretta, J. & Tonev, S. (2000). The effects of divided attention on encoding and retrieval processes: The resiliency of retrieval processes. *Quarterly Journal of Experimental Psychology*, Vol. 53A, pp. 609-625.

Parasuraman, R.; Molloy, R. & Singh, I. (1993). Performance consequences of automation-induced 'complacency'. *International Journal of Aviation Psychology,* Vol. 3, pp. 1-23.

Rubinstein, J.; Meyer, D. & Evans, J. (2001). Executive control of cognitive processes in task switching. *Journal of Experimental Psychology: Human Perception and Performance*, Vol. 27, pp. 763-797.

Schumacher E.; Seymour, T.; Glass, J.; Fencsik, D.; Lauber, E.; Kieras, D. et al. (2001). Virtually perfect time sharing in dual-task performance: Uncorking the central cognitive bottleneck. *Psychological Science*, Vol. 12, pp. 101-108.

Schipani, S. (2003). An evaluation of operator workload during partially-autonomous vehicle operations, *Proceedings of PerMIS 2003*, Gaithersburg, MD, September 2003, NIST, Gaithersburg, MD.

Sklar, A. & Sarter, N. (1999). Good vibrations: Tactile feedback in support of attention allocation and human-automation coordination in event-driven domains. *Human Factors*, Vol. 41, pp. 543-552.

Spence, C. & Driver, J. (1997). Cross-modal links in attention between audition, vision, and touch: Implications for interface design. *International Journal of Cognitive Ergonomics*, Vol. 1, pp. 351–373.

Spence, C.; Pavani, F.; Maravita, A. & Holmes, N. (2004). Multisensory Information visualization; assisting low spatial individuals with information access tasks through the use of visual mediators. *Ergonomics*, Vol. 38, pp. 1184–1198.

Stanney, K. & Salvendy, G. (1995). Information visualization: Assisting low spatial individuals with information access tasks through the use of visual mediators. *Ergonomics*, Vol. 38, No. 6, pp. 1184–1198.

Terrence, P.; Brill, J. & Gilson, R. (2005). Body orientation and the perception of spatial auditory and tactile cues, *Proceedings of the Human Factors & Ergonomics Society 49th Annual Meeting*, pp. 1663-1667, Orlando, FL, September 2005, Human Factors & Ergonomics Society, Santa Monica, CA.

Thomas, L. & Wickens, C. (2004). Eye-tracking and individual differences in off-normal event detection when flying with a synthetic vision system display, *Proceedings of Human Factors & Ergonomics Society 48th Annual Meeting*, pp. 223-227, New Orleans, LA, September 2004, Human Factors & Ergonomics Society, Santa Monica, CA.

Van Erp, J. & Van Veen, H. (2004). Vibrotactile in-vehicle navigation system. *Transportation Research Part F*, Vol. 7, pp. 247-256.

Vincow, M. (1998). *Frame of Reference and Navigation Through Document Visualizations.* Unpublished dissertation, University of Illinois, Urbana-Champaign, IL.

Wickens, C. (2002). Multiple resources and performance prediction. *Theoretical Issues in Ergonomics Science*, Vol. 3, pp. 159-177.

Wickens, C. & Dixon, S. (2005). *Is There a Magic Number 7 (to the Minus 1)? The Benefits of Imperfect Diagnostic Automation: A Synthesis of the Literature* (Tech Rep. AHFD-05-01/MAAD-05-01), University of Illinois, Urbana-Champaign, IL.

Wickens, C.; Dixon, S.; Goh, J. & Hammer, B. (2005). *Pilot Dependence on Imperfect Diagnostic Automation in Simulated UAV Flights: An Attentional Visual Scanning Analysis* (Tech Rep. AHFD-05-02/MAAD-05-02), University of Illinois, Urbana-Champaign, IL.

Wickens, C.; Dixon, S. & Johnson N. (2005). *UAV Automation: Influence of Task Priorities and Automation Imperfection in a Difficult Surveillance Task* (Tech Rep. AHFD-05-20/MAAD-05-6), University of Illinois, Urbana-Champaign, IL.

Young, M. & Stanton, N. (2007a). Back to the future: Brake reaction times for manual and automated vehicles. *Ergonomics*, Vol. 50, pp. 46-58.

Young, M. & Stanton, N. (2007b). What's skill got to do with it? Vehicle automation and driver mental workload. *Ergonomics*, Vol. 50, pp. 1324-1339.

16

Sound Production for the Emotional Expression of Socially Interactive Robots

[1]Eun-Sook Jee, [2]Yong-Jeon Cheong, [3]Chong Hui Kim,
[2]Dong-Soo Kwon, and [4]Hisato Kobayashi
[1]*The Future Robot Research Institute,*
[2]*Human-Robot Interaction Research Center, KAIST,*
[3]*Agency for Defense Development,*
[4]*Graduate School of Art and Technology, Hosei University,*
[1,2,3]*Republic of Korea*
[4]*Japan*

1. Introduction

With the remarkable advancements in the field of robotics, the application of robots is no longer restricted to industrial automation but has been extended to personal home services. Robots are built to interact with humans, since they have not been developed to function as automatic machines, but to coexist as in human society. (Kim et al. 2005) Emotional interaction with humans is an integral function of socially interactive robots like Silbot—an intelligent robot developed in Korea for the purposes of assistance and entertainment geared toward the silver generation. When robots can comprehend human emotion and express their own emotion naturally, an emotional bond between human and robot is established.

Sounds and gestures are the two most basic mediums of emotional communication, and human beings constitute the subject of most studies on emotional communication. Many researches try to investigate the association of human emotion with a voice or facial expression. In recent years, the emotional aspects of music are being studied in both scientific and psychological contexts because of the complexity of emotional experiences in music. (Juslin & Sloboda 2001) In addition, a few researches focus on how to enable a robot to express emotion using speech synthesis, facial expressions, or sound. (Nakanishi & Kitagawa 2006; Jee et al. 2007)

The purpose of this section is to discuss not only the emotional sound design but also the process of emotional sound production aimed to enable robots to express emotion effectively, for facilitating the interaction between humans and robots. To begin with, we use the explicit or implicit link between emotional characteristics and musical parameters to compose six emotional sounds and then analyze them to identify a method to improve a robot's emotional expressiveness.

First, we introduced three emotional sounds—happiness, sadness, and fear—in robots, taking into consideration several musical parameters, namely, mode, tempo, pitch, rhythm, harmony, melody, volume, and timbre. Using the sound samples, we performed an experiment to identify whether the sounds composed convey positive or negative emotions in the robot. Following this, we tested whether three basic emotional sounds coincided with the robot's facial expressions, using the Likert scaling method. This is another approach in the study of emotional expressiveness in robots. The results of experiments using either auditory or visual stimuli will then be compared with the results of experiments using both types of stimuli.

Second, we suggest the idea of incorporating intensity variation in emotional sounds with three different degrees: strong, middle, and weak. For this purpose, we produced additional emotional sounds of joy, shyness, and irritation. We regulate only three musical parameters—tempo, pitch, and volume—because of the technical limitations of the computer system; in other words, robots can control only the tempo, pitch, and volume. Although only three parameters can be regulated and manipulated in our set up, the intensity variation causes more dynamic emotional human-robot interaction.

Finally, we present the idea of synchronization with the emotional sounds of joy, shyness, and irritation. The synchronization of emotional sounds with the behavior of robots, including their movements and gestures, is a key issue in real implementation because it makes a robot's behavior more natural. For the synchronization, we divided the emotional sounds into several segments in accordance with musical structure. Some segments of the emotional sounds are repeatable and robots can control their sound duration for the synchronization.

2. Previous work

Can you ever imagine a movie without sound? Sound is an integral element of human communication and interaction. From the perspective of cognitive science, among human activities related to sound, both language and music share many things in common. For instance, both language and music unfold sound in time. Similar to language, music has a hierarchical structure and it is also believed to have a grammatical structure. (Lerdahl & Jackendoff 1983) What then is the real difference between music and language? Perhaps, the most conspicuous difference is that music has an emotional meaning and induces genuine and deep emotions. (Meyer 1956) There is no language more powerful than the language of music. Music is indeed a language of emotion. (Pratt 1948)

As an emotionally rich medium, music is necessary to express a robot's emotion for human-robot interaction. There exist numerous studies on music and emotion since time immemorial because this topic has always interested people. There are multidisciplinary approaches to understand music and emotion because the emotional experience of music is complex and rich. Several scholars have developed aesthetic and philosophical discussions on music and emotion. (Davies 2001; Kivy 1999; Levinson 1982) Musicologists and music theorists have studied emotional expressiveness not only in western art music but also in pop music. (Cook & Dibben 2001; Meyer 1956) Further, Feld (1982) and Becker (2001) have approached music and emotion through anthropological and ethno-musicological perspectives. DeNora (2001) has applied sociology paradigms to understand the relation between emotion and music. Finally, Bunt & Pavlicevic (2001) have studied music and emotion for therapeutic purposes.

Psychological perspectives on music and emotion can be examined in further detail because emotion is a main concern of psychology. Recently, large-scale investigations on the relation between music and emotion have been performed through psycho-biological or neuropsychological approaches. For instance, using the technique of positron emission tomography (PET), Blood et al. (1999) examined the change in cerebral blood flow during emotional responses to music. They found that music could recruit the neural mechanisms associated with pleasant or unpleasant emotional states. Baumgartner et al. (2006) investigated how music enhances emotions using functional magnetic resonance imaging (fMRI). The brain imaging showed that visual and musical stimuli automatically evoke strong emotional feelings and experiences. Peretz (2006) presented the neural correlates of musical emotion and the existence of specific neural arrangements for certain emotions induced by music. Juslin & Västfall (2008) determined the existence of underlying mechanisms in music that evoke emotions and concluded that these mechanisms are not unique to music. Livingston & Thomson (2009) suggested that music generates emotional experiences by activating the channels related to the audio-visual neuron system.

In addition, some psychologists have studied which musical parameters evoke emotional feelings. For instance, Hevner (1935; 1936; 1937) researched the emotional meanings in music through psychological experiments. She created what she termed the Adjective Circle by categorizing of emotions into eight adjective groups, as shown in Fig. 1.

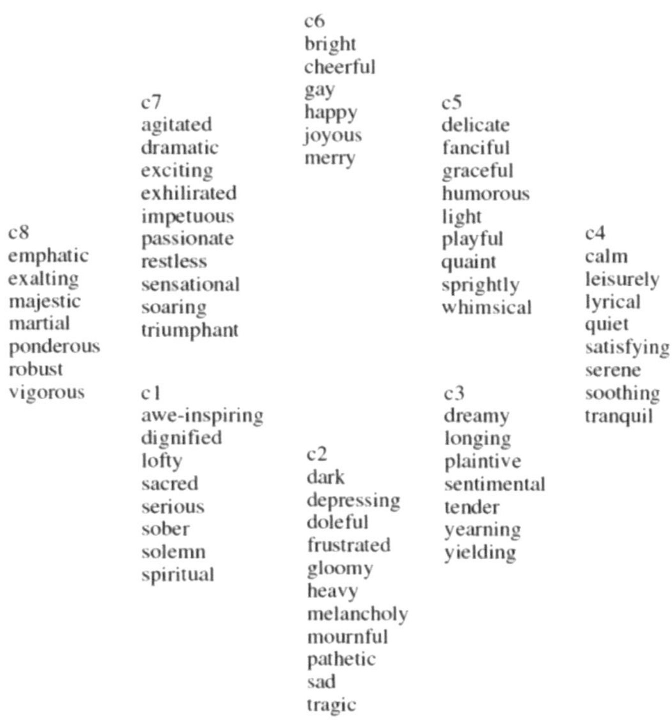

Fig. 1. Hevner's categorization of emotions: the adjective circle

Hevner assumed some associations between musical parameters and emotion. Through experiments, she found that a specific musical parameter was responsible for a particular emotional response. Hevner considered six musical parameters—mode, tempo, pitch, rhythm, harmony, and melody; we have carefully analyzed these during emotional sound production. These parameters and their associations with emotion are briefly summarized as follows.

- Mode is any of the certain fixed arrangements of tones, such as major or minor. Major modes manifest gracefulness (c5) and happiness (c6), while minor modes indicate sadness (c2) and sentimentality (c3).
- Tempo is the speed of music. Fast tempi signify happiness (c6) and excitement (c7), whereas, slow tempi indicate solemnity (c1), sadness (c2), sentimentality (c3), and serenity (c4).
- Pitch is the frequency of sound. Pitches in higher register express serenity (c4) and gracefulness (c5), whereas, pitches in lower register represent sadness (c2) and vigorousness (c8).
- Rhythm is the aspect of music that comprises all the elements that relate to forward movement. A firm rhythm indicates solemnity (c1) and vigorousness (c8). On the contrary, a flowing rhythm expresses sentimentality (c3), gracefulness (c5), and happiness (c6).
- Harmony is the combination of simultaneous musical notes in a chord. A simple harmony represents serenity (c4), gracefulness (c5), and happiness (c6), whereas a complex harmony expresses sadness (c2), excitement (c7), and vigorousness (c8).
- Melody is a succession of single notes that form a tune. Ascending melodies signify solemnity (c1) and serenity (c4), whereas, descending melodies express gracefulness (c5), excitement (c7), and vigorousness (c8).

Hevner's pioneering experimental researches on music and emotion continue to intellectually stimulate researchers today. Interestingly, Juslin (2000) studied the utilization of acoustic cues in the communication of musical emotions between performer and listener and measured the correlation between various emotional expressions and acoustic cues. Gabrielsson & Lindström (2001) presented a historical overview of studies on musical structures and emotion. They suggested more specific musical parameters than Hevner. For example, Gabrielsson & Lindström examined tempo, mode, loudness, pitch, intervals, melody, harmony, tonality, rhythm, timbre, articulation, amplitude envelope, musical form, and the interaction between parameters. They summarized the relation between newly arranged musical parameters and emotion. Juslin & Laukka (2003) modeled the emotional expression of different music performances by means of multiple regression analysis, to clarify the relationship between emotional descriptions and measured parameters such as tempo, sound level, and articulation. Similarly, Schubert (2004) considered different musical parameters of loudness, tempo, melodic contour, texture, and timbre. He investigated the relationship between these parameters and perceived emotion by using continuous response methodology and time-series analysis. In the area of computer entertainment, Berg & Wingstedt (2005) mentioned that the influence of visual aspects on emotional dimensions has been researched more systematically than that of sound. They simulated the relation between musical parameters and expressed emotions by selecting mode, instrumentation, tempo, articulation, volume, and pitch register as musical parameters. Further, through an examination of over 100 empirical studies, Livingstone & Thompson (2006) concluded the corresponding associations between specific emotions and musical parameters. Their results are similar to that of Gabrielsson & Lindström. In addition, Post & Huron (2009) found that the minor mode in Western classical music tends to be slower, based on Hevner's theory and Juslin's cue utilization that the minor mode is associated with sadness (c2) and sentimentality (c3).

As we examined above, the study of emotion and music has a short history. Studies on emotional expression through musical sounds in robotics are even rarer. In the following three sections, we will specify our processes of emotional sound productions in order to enhance a robot's expressiveness through emotional sound coincidence with facial expression, intensity variation of emotional sounds, and sound synchronization with the robot's behavior.

3. Production of basic emotional sounds

In this section, we present the design and production of a robot's emotional sounds. The duration of each emotional sound is two or three seconds. Emotional sounds are produced by MIDI, sound filtering or mixing. The raw audio samples are recorded and filtered through Sound Forge and Cubase software. Some of the filtered audio samples are then mixed with pre-recorded midi sounds by Cubase in order to create emotional sounds in a robot. Fig. 2 shows the process of the emotional sound production.

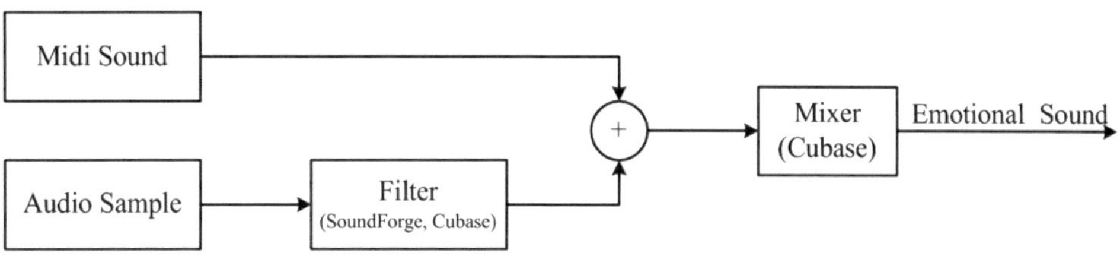

Fig. 2. The design flow of sound production

Basic emotions are defined as a limited number of innate and universal categories or emotions from which all other emotional states can be derived. (Cited in Berg & Wingstedt 2005) Juslin & Sloboda (2001) discussed that basic emotions belong to at least five categories: happiness, sadness, anger, fear, and disgust. We decided to produce two sets of three

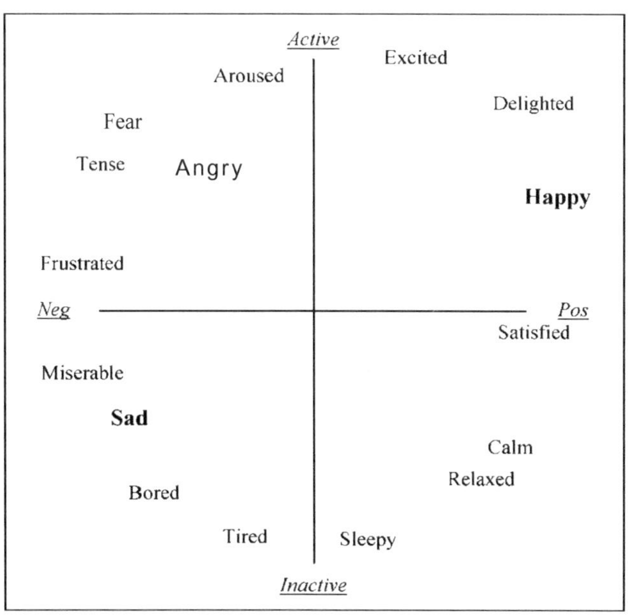

Fig. 3. Two dimensional circumplex model of emotions

emotional sounds: (1) happiness, sadness, and fear and (2) joy, shyness, and irritation. The first set is produced to test the effect of emotional sounds and how these sounds coincide with facial expressions. The second set pertains to the intensity variation of emotional sounds, and the synchronization of the sounds with a robot's behavior. Each emotional sound in both groups is located on three different sections of a two-dimensional circumplex model of emotion, involved in the dimensions of arousal (activity) and valence (positive/negative). (Russell 1980) Figure 4 presents the two-dimensional circumplex model of emotion. With respect to this model, happiness of set 1 and joy of set 2 represent an active and positively valenced emotion, while sadness of set 1 and shyness of set 2 denote an inactive and negatively valenced emotion. Happiness and joy are symmetrically opposite to sadness and shyness. Besides them, we also decided to produce emotional sounds for fear of set 1 and irritation of set 2, which are opposite to happiness and joy on the valence perspective and also opposite to sadness and shyness on the arousal perspective.
On the basis of prior investigations on which musical sound evokes emotion, the following musical parameters will be examined for the three basic emotional sounds of set 1: Hevner's six musical parameters, volume, and timbre. As mentioned above, Hevner considered mode (major or minor), tempo (fast or slow), pitch (high or low), rhythm (firm or flowing), harmony (simple or complex), and melody (ascending or descending). In addition, we examine volume and timbre. As an aside, note that timbre can be defined as an instrumental setting.

3.1 Happiness

The sound of our happiness is in the quasi-major mode. The tempo, at 160 BPM (♩ = 160), is very fast owing to the subdivisions of quarter note (i.e., eight notes, triplets, and sixteenth notes). Most of the notes are in the high pitch range from E4 (ca. 329.6 Hz) to F#6 (ca. 1174.6 Hz). The harmony is simple with major triads, and the rhythm is firm with a vibraphone's quarter notes on beat. Happiness has an ascending melodic contour, and the volume of happiness is 60 dB SPL (10^{-6} watt/m^2). Sounds from the ocarina and vibraphone, produced using a midi keyboard, are used for the timbre of happiness. Fig. 4 shows the score of the sound of happiness.

Fig. 4. Music score for happiness

3.2 Sadness

The sound of sadness is neither in the major nor minor mode. The tempo is 99 BPM (♩ = 99) and very slow because sadness consists of 1 quarter note and 2 dotted half notes. The pitch ranges from G4 (ca. 155.6 Hz) to C7 (ca. 1046.5 Hz). The harmony is complex because of the absence of major or minor triads, and the rhythm is firm with 2 downbeat dotted half notes. The melody of sadness is descending, and the volume of sadness is the same as that of happiness as 60 dB SPL (10^{-6} watt/m^2). The cello and piano are used to determine the timbre. Fig. 5 shows the score of a sadness sound.

Fig. 5. Music score for sadness

3.3 Fear

Similar to sadness, the sound of fear is neither in major nor minor mode because we intend to express the negative valence of sadness and fear by using the same melody line. The tempo is 126 BPM (♩ = 126) but, in reality, it is slower than the tempo of sadness because fear consists of only dotted half notes. Moreover, the duration of the last note is tripled by a tie. The pitch is the lowest among the emotional sounds that we produce. It ranges from G2 (ca. 97.9 Hz) to A3 (ca. 233.1 Hz). The harmony of fear is very simple because only octaves (1:1 ratio) are used. The rhythm is very firm with only downbeat notes, and the melody of fear is descending. The volume of happiness is 70 dB SPL (10^{-5} watt/m^2). In this case, the organ is used to determine the timbre. In the last long note, the vibration that is characteristic of an organ timbre, is fully revealed. Fig. 6 shows the score of the fear sound.

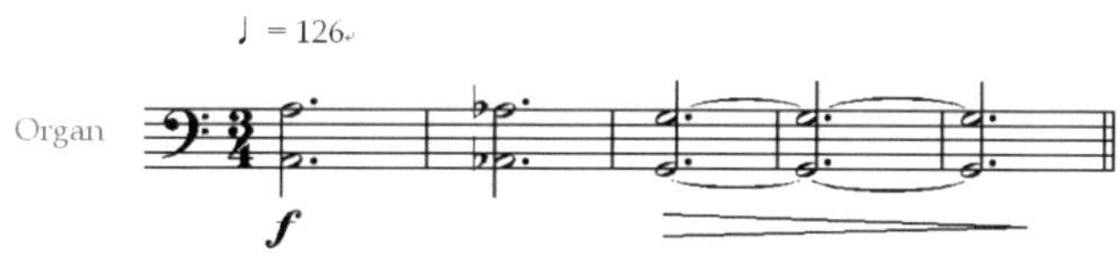

Fig. 6. Music score for fear

3.4 Experiment on basic emotional sounds

We conducted an experiment to test whether emotional sounds evoke or induce happiness, sadness, and fear. We recruited 20 participants, comprising an equal number of men and women. Our participants were asked to rate their emotional states on the Likert five-point scale after listening to randomly presented sounds.

The experiment revealed that 90% made positive responses on our happiness sound; more than half of the participants rated this sound very strongly. On our sadness sound, 65% reported a strong feeling of sadness. Further, 50% of the participants responded positively to the sound of fear, and among them, 15% rated the sound very strongly. Table 1 shows how effectively the sounds express the three basic emotions, from the results of the experiment.

	Happiness	Sadness	Fear
Never			
Weak		2 (10%)	3 (15%)
Moderate	2 (10%)	5 (25%)	7 (35%)
Strong	7 (35%)	13 (65%)	7 (35%)
Very Strong	11 (55%)		3 (15%)
Sum	20 (100%)		

Table 1. Sound validity of the three basic emotions

3.5 Experiment on the coincidence of basic emotional sounds with facial expressions

Nakanishi et al. (2006) proposed a visualization of musical impressions on faces in order to represent emotions. They developed a media-lexicon transformation operator of musical data to extract some impression words from musical elements that determine the form or structure of a song. Lim et al. (2007) suggested the emergent emotion model and described some flexible approaches to determine the generation of emotion and facial mapping. They mapped the three facial features of the mouth, eyes, and eyebrows into the arousal and valence of the two-dimensional circumplex model of emotions.

Even if robots express their emotions through facial expressions, their users or partners could face a problem perceiving the subtle differences in a given emotion. The subtle change of emotion is difficult to perceive through facial expressions, and hence, we selected several representative facial expressions that people can understand easily. Coinciding basic emotional sounds with the facial expression of robots is, hence, an important issue. We performed the experiment to test the whether the basic emotional sounds of happiness, sadness, and fear coincide with the corresponding facial expressions.

We then compared the results of the experiment against either basic emotional sounds or facial expressions with both sounds and facial expression. The experiment on the coincidence of sounds and facial expressions was performed on the same 20 participants. Since the entire robot system is still in its developmental stage, we conducted the experiments using laptops, on which we displayed the facial expressions of happiness, sadness, and fear, following which we played the music composed as part of the preliminary experiment. Figure 8 shows the three facial expressions we employed for the experiment.

Fig. 7. Facial expressions of a preliminary robot

Table 2 shows the results on the coincidence of musical sounds and the facial expressions of happiness, sadness, and fear. The results supported our hypothesis on the coincidence of basic emotional sounds with facial expressions. For instance, a simultaneous simulation of sound and the facial expression of fear show a more positive improvement than that of either sound or facial expression. Therefore, the sounds and facial expressions cooperate complementarily for the conveyance of emotion.

4. Intensity variation of emotional sounds

Human beings are not keenly sensitive to detecting the gradual change in sensory stimuli that evoke emotions. Delivery of delicate changes in emotions through both facial expressions and sounds is difficult. When comparing the conveying of delicate emotional changes, sound is more effective than facial expressions. Cardoso et al. (2001) measured the intensity of emotion through experiments using numerical magnitude estimation (NE) and

	Sound			Facial Expression			Sound with Facial Expression		
	Happiness	Sadness	Fear	Happiness	Sadness	Fear	Happiness	Sadness	Fear
Never						2 (10%)			
Weak		2 (10%)	3 (15%)	1 (5%)	1 (5%)	4 (20%)			
Moderate	2 (10%)	5 (25%)	7 (35%)	7 (35%)	5 (25%)	6 (30%)	4 (20%)	3 (15%)	2 (10%)
Strong	7 (35%)	13 (65%)	7 (35%)	12 (60%)	12 (60%)	8 (40%)	8 (40%)	11 (55%)	10 (50%)
Very Strong	11 (55%)		3 (15%)		2 (10%)		8 (40%)	6 (30%)	8 (40%)
Sum	20 (100%)								

Table 2. Coincidence of emotional sounds and facial expressions

cross-modal matching to line-length responses (LLR) in a more psychophysical approach. We quantized the levels of emotional sounds as strong, middle, and weak, or strong and weak in terms of intensity variation. The intensity variation is regulated on the basis of the result of Kendall's coefficient between NE and LLR. (Cardoso et al. 2001) Through the intensity variation of the emotional sounds, robots can express delicate changes in their emotional state.

We already discussed several different musical parameters for sound production and for displaying a robot's basic emotional state in section 3. Among these, only three musical parameters—tempo, pitch, and volume—are related to intensity variation because of the technical limitations of the robot's computer system. Our approach to the intensity variation of the robot's emotions is introduced with the three sound samples of joy, shyness, and irritation, which are equivalent to happiness, sadness, and fear on the two-dimensional circumplex model of emotion.

First, volume was controlled in the range from 80~85% to 120~130%. When the volume of any sound is changed beyond this range, the unique characteristic of emotional sound is distorted and confused.

Second, in the same way as volume regulation, we controlled the tempo to within the range of 80~85% to 120~130% of middle emotional sounds. When the tempo of the sound changes to slower than 80% of the original sound, the characteristic of the emotional state of the sound disappears. Reversely, when the tempo of the sound accelerates and is faster than 130% of the original sound, the atmosphere of the original sound is modified.

Third, the pitch was also controlled but the change of tempo and volume is more distinct and effective for intensity variation. We only changed the pitch of irritation because the sound of irritation is not based on the major or minor mode. The sound cluster in the irritation sound moves with a slight change in pitch in glissando.

4.1 Joy

Joy shares common musical characteristics with happiness. For the middle joy sound, the mode is the quasi major. The tempo is 116 BPM (♩ = 116) and is quite fast in real life because of the triplets. The pitch ranges from D3 (ca. 146.8 Hz) to C5 (ca. 523.3 Hz). The rhythm is firm with on-beat quarter notes. The harmony is simple owing to major triads, the melody is ascending, and the volume is 60 dB SPL (10^{-6} watt/m^2). The staccato and pizzicato of string instruments determine the timbre of the sound of joy. Figure 8 illustrates wave files depicting strong, middle, and weak levels of joy.

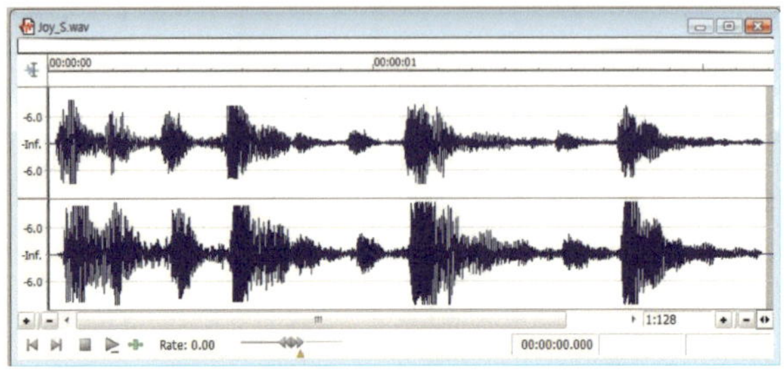

(a) Strong Joy

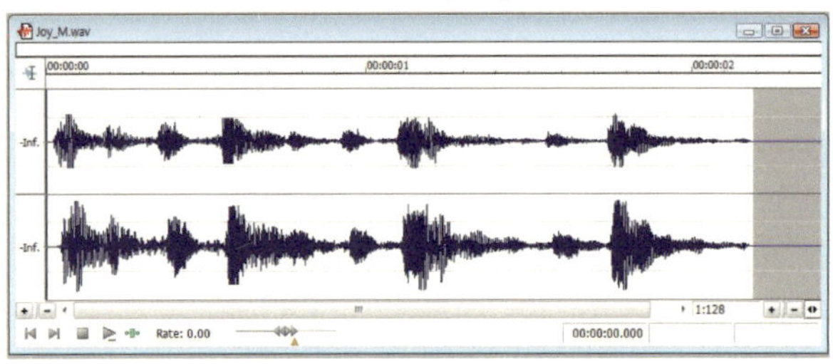

(b) Middle Joy

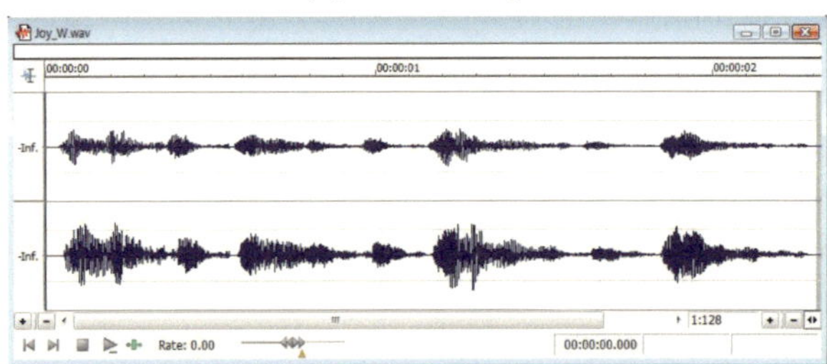

(c) Weak Joy

Fig. 8. Wave file depicting strong, middle, and weak joy sound samples

For the emotion of strong joy, the volume is only increased to 70 dB SPL (10^{-6} watt/m^2). On the other hand, for a weak joy emotion, we decrease the volume down to 50 dB SPL (10^{-7} watt/m^2) and reduce the tempo. Table 3 shows the change in the musical parameters of tempo, pitch, and volume for intensity variation of the sound for joy.

Intensity	STRONG	Middle	Weak
Volume	120% 70 dB SPL	100% 60 dB SPL	80% 50 dB SPL
Tempo	100%	100%	120%
Pitch	146.8~523.3Hz		

Table 3. Intensity variation of joy

4.2 Shyness

Shyness possesses emotional qualities similar to sadness on the two-dimensional circumplex model of emotion. The intensity variation of shyness is performed on two levels: strong and weak. As a standard, a strong shyness sound is composed on the basis of neither a major nor minor mode because a female voice is recorded and filtered in this case. The tempo is 132 BPM (♩ = 132). The pitch ranges from Bb4 (ca. 233.1 Hz) to quasi B5 (ca. 493.9 Hz). The rhythm is firm, the harmony is complex with a sound cluster, and the melody is a descending glissando with an obscure ending pitch point. The volume is 60 dB SPL (10^{-6} watt/m^2) and the metallic timbre is acquired through filtering. Figure 9 shows the wave files of strong shyness and weak shyness.

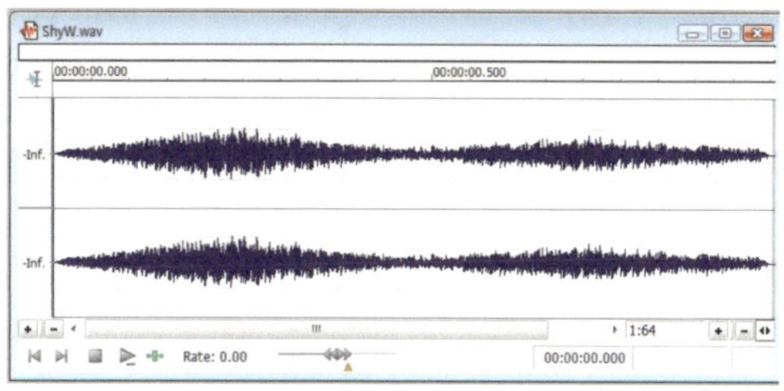

(a) Strong Shyness

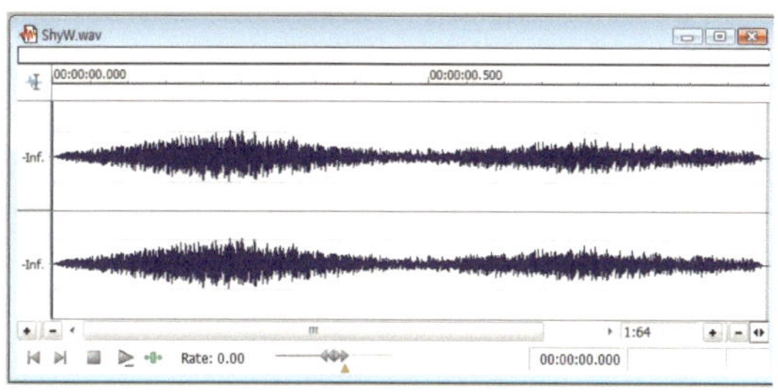

(b) Weak Shyness

Fig. 9. Wave file depicting strong and weak shyness sound samples

For weak shyness, the volume is reduced to 50 dB SPL (10^{-7} watt/m^2), and the tempo is also reduced. Table 4 shows the intensity variation of shyness.

Intensity	STRONG	Weak
Volume	100%	80%
Tempo	100% 60 dB SPL	115% 50 dB SPL
Pitch (Semitone)	233.1~.493.9Hz	

Table 4. Intensity variation of shyness

4.3 Irritation

The emotional qualities of irritation are similar to those of fear. Irritation also only has two kinds of intensity levels. Strong irritation, as a standard sound, is composed on the basis of neither the major nor minor mode because it constitutes a combined audio file and midi featuring a filtered human voice. The tempo is 112 BPM (♩ = 112), and the pitch ranges from C4 (ca. 261.6 Hz) to B5 (ca. 493.9 Hz). The rhythm is firm, and the harmony is complex with a sound cluster. The melody is an ascending glissando, which is the opposite of shyness. It reflects an opposite status on the arousal dimension. The volume is 70 dB SPL (10^{-5} watt/m^2), and the metallic timbre is acquired through filtering, while the chic quality of timbre comes from a midi. Figure 10 shows wave files of strong and weak irritation.

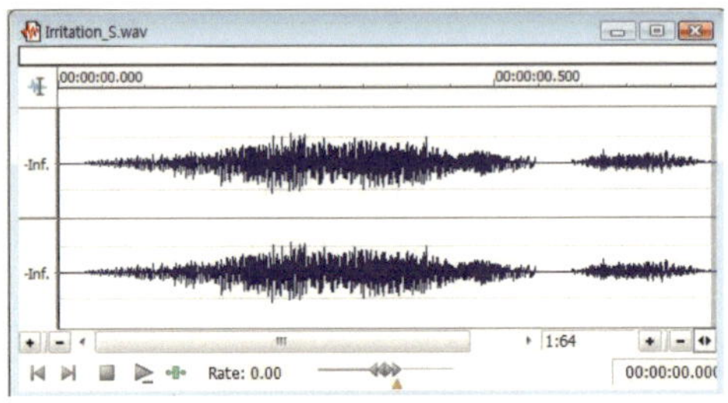

(a) Strong Irritation

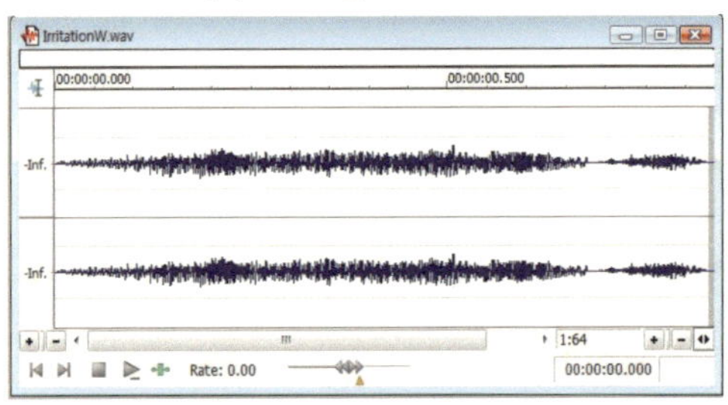

(b) Weak Irritation

Fig. 10. Wave files depicting strong and weak irritation sound samples

For the weak irritation sample, the volume is decreased to 60 dB SPL (10^{-6} watt/m^2) and the tempo is reduced. Table 5 shows how we regulated the intensity variation of irritation.

Intensity	STRONG	Weak
Volume	100% 70 dB SPL	85% 60 dB SPL
Tempo	100%	115%
Pitch	261.6~493.9 Hz	220~415.3 Hz

Table 5. Intensity variation of irritation

5. Musical structure of emotional sounds to be synchronized with a robot's behavior

The synchronization of the duration of sound with a robot's behavior is important to ensure the natural expression of emotion. Friberg (2004) suggested a system that could be used for analyzing the emotional expressions of both music and body motion. The analysis was done in three steps comprising cue analysis, calibration, and fuzzy mapping. The fuzzy mapper translates the cue values into three emotional outputs: happiness, sadness, and anger.

A robot's behavior, which is important in depicting emotion, is essentially continuous. Hence, for emotional communication, the duration of emotional sounds should be synchronized with that of a robot's behavior including motions and gestures. At the beginning of sound production, we assumed that robots could control the duration of their emotional sounds. On the basis of the musical structure of sound, we intentionally composed the sound such that it consists of several segments. For the synchronization, the emotional sounds of joy, shyness, and irritation have musically structural segments, which can be repeated as per a robot's volition. The most important considerations for synchronization are as follows:

1. The melody of emotional sounds should not leap abruptly.
2. The sound density should not be changed excessively.
   - If these two points are not retained, the separation of the segment would be difficult.
3. Each segment of any emotional sound contains a specific musical parameter which is peculiar to the quality of the emotion.
4. Among the segments of any emotional sound, the best segment containing the characteristic quality of the emotion should be repeated.
5. When a robot stretches a sound by repeating one of the segments, both the repetition and the connection points should be connected seamlessly without any clashes or noises.

5.1 Joy

We explain our approach to synchronization by using the three examples of joy, irritation, and shyness, which are presented in section 4. As mentioned above, each emotional sound consists of segments that are in accordance with the musical structure. The duration of the joy sound is about 2.07s, and joy is divided into three segments: A, B, and C. Robots could regulate the duration of joy by calculating the duration of their behavior and repeating any segment to synchronize it. The figure of segment A is characterized by ascending triplets, and its duration is approximately 1.03s. Segment B is denoted by the dotted notes, and the duration of both segments B and C is about 0.52s. Figure 11 shows the musical structure of joy and its duration.

Segment	Duration (s)
A	1.03
B	0.52
C	0.52
Total	2.07

Fig. 11. Musical segments and the duration of joy

5.2 Shyness

The duration of shyness is about 1s. Shyness has two segments, A and B. The figure of segment A is characterized by a descending glissando on the upper layer and a sound cluster on the lower layer. Segment B only has a descending glissando without a sound cluster on the lower layer. The duration of both segments A and B is about 0.52s. Figure 12 shows the musical structure of shyness and its duration.

Segment	Duration (s)
A	0.5
B	0.5
Total	1.0

Fig. 12. Musical segments and the duration of shyness

5.3 Irritation

Irritation has almost the same structure as that of shyness. The duration of irritation is about 1.08s. Irritation has two segments, A and B. The figure of segment A is characterized by an ascending glissando. Segment B has one shouting. The duration of both segments A and B is about 0.54s. Figure 13 shows the musical structure of shyness and its duration.

Segment	Duration (s)
A	0.54
B	0.54
Total	1.08

Fig. 13. Musical segments and the duration of irritation

6. Conclusion

In conclusion, the paper presents three processes of sound production needed to enable emotional expression in robots. First, we consider the relation between three basic emotions of happiness, sadness, and fear, and eight musical parameters of mode, tempo, pitch, rhythm, harmony, melody, volume, and timbre. The survey using the 5-point Likert scale, which was administered to 20 participants, proved the validity of Silbot's emotional sound. In addition, the synchronizing of the robot's basic emotional sounds of happiness, sadness, and fear with facial expressions is tested through the experiment. The results support the hypothesis that the simultaneous presentation of sound samples and facial expressions is more effective than the presentation of either sound or facial expression. Second, we produced emotional sounds for joy, shyness, and irritation in order to determine the intensity variation of the robot's emotional state. Owing to the technical limitations of the computer systems controlling the robot, only three musical parameters of volume, tempo, and pitch are regulated for intensity variation. Third, the synchronization of the durations of sounds depicting joy, shyness, and irritation with the robot's behavior is obtained to ensure a more natural and dynamic emotional interaction between people and robots.

7. References

Baumgartner, T.; Lutz, K.; Schmidt, C. F. & Jäncke, L. (2006). The emotional power of music: How music enhances the feeling of affective pictures, Brain Research, Vol. 1075, pp. 151-164, 0006-8993

Berg, J. & Wingstedt, J. (2005). Relations between selected musical parameters and expressed emotions extending the potential of computer entertainment, In the Proceedings of the 2005 ACM SIGCHI International Conference on Advances in Computer Entertainment Technology, pp. 164-171

Blood, A. J.; Zatorre, R. J.; Bermudez, P. & Evans, A. C. (1999). Emotional responses to pleasant and unpleasant music correlate with activity in paralimbic brain regions, Nature Neuroscience, Vol. 2, No. 4, (April) pp. 382-387, 1097-6256

Cardoso, F. M. S.; Matsushima, E. H.; Kamizaki, R.; Oliveira, A. N. & Da Silva, J. A. (2001). The measurement of emotion intensity: A psychophysical approach, In the Proceedings of the Seventeenth Annual Meeting of the International Society for Psychophysics, pp. 332-337

Feld, S. (1982). Sound and sentiment: Birds, weeping, poetics, and song in Kaluli expression, University of Pennsylvania Press, 0-8122-1299-1, Philadelphia

Hevner, K. (1935). Expression in music: A discussion of experimental studies and theories, Psychological Review, Vol. 42, pp. 186-204, 0033-295X

Hevner, K. (1935). The affective character of the major and minor modes in music, American Journal of Psychology, Vol. 47, No. 4, pp. 103-118, 0002-9556

Hevner, K. (1936). Experimental studies of the elements of expression in music, American Journal of Psychology, Vol. 48, No. 2, pp. 248-268, 0002-9556

Hevner, K. (1937). The affective value of pitch and tempo in music, American Journal of Psychology, Vol. 49, No. 4, pp. 621-630, 0002-9556

Jee, E. S.; Kim, C. H..; Park, S. Y. & Lee, K. W. (2007). Composition of musical sound expressing an emotion of robot based on musical factors, Proceedings of the IEEE International Symposium on Robot and Human Interactive Communication, pp. 637-641, ISBN, Jeju, Aug. 2007, Republic of Korea

Juslin, P. N. (2000). Cue utilization in communication of emotion in music performance: relating performance to perception, Journal of Experimental Psychology, Vol. 16, No. 6, pp. 1797-1813, 0096-1523

Juslin, P. N. & Laukka, P. (2003). Communication of emotions in vocal expression and music performance: Different channels, same code? Psychological Bulletin, Vol. 129, No. 5, pp. 770-814, 0033-2909

Juslin, P. N. & Sloboda, J. A. (Ed.) (2001). Music and emotion, Oxford University Press, 978-0-19-2263189-3, Oxford

Juslin, P. N. & Västfall, D. (2008). Emotional responses to music: The need to consider underlying mechanisms, Behavioral and Brain Sciences, Vol. 31, pp. 556-621, 0140-525X

Kim, H. R.; Lee, K. W. & Kwon, D. S. (2005). Emotional interaction model for a service robot, Proceedings of the IEEE International Workshop on Robots and Human Interactive Communication, pp. 672-678, Nashville, United States of America

Kivy, P. (1999). Feeling the musical emotions, British Journal of Aesthetics, Vol. 39, pp. 1-13, 0007-0904

Lerdahl, F. & Jackendoff, R. (1983). A generative theory of tonal music, MIT Press, 026262107X, Cambridge, Mass.

Levinson, J. (1982). Music and negative emotion, Pacific Philosophical Quarterly, Vol. 63, pp. 327-346, 0279-0750

Livingstone, S. R.; Muhlberger, R.; Brown, A. R. & Loch, A. (2007). Controlling musical emotionality: An affective computational architecture for influencing musical emotions, Digital Creativity, 18, pp. 43-54

Livingstone, S. R. & Thompson, W. F. (2009). The emergence of music from the theory of mind, Musicae Scientiae Special Issue on Music and Evolution in press. 1029-8649

Meyer, L. B. (1956). Emotion and meaning in music. University of Chicago Press, 0-226-52139-7, Chicago

Nakanishi, T. & Kitagawa T. (2006). Visualization of music impression in facial expression to represent emotion, Proceedings of Asia-Pacific Conference on Conceptual Modelling, pp. 55-64

Post, O. & Huron, D. (2009). Western classical music in the minor mode is slower (except in the romantic period), Empirical Musicology Review, Vol. 4, No. 1, pp. 2-10, 1559-5749

Pratt, C. C. (1948). Music as a language of emotion, Bulletin of the American Musicological Society, No. 11/12/13 (September, 1948), pp. 67-68, 1544-4708

Russel, J. A. (1980). A circumplex model of affect, Journal of Personality and Social Psychology, 39, 1161-1178

Schubert, E. (2004). Modeling perceived emotion with continuous musical features, Music Perception, Vol. 21, No. 4, pp. 561-85, 0730-7829

Miranda, E. R. & Drouet, E. (2006). Evolution of musical lexicons by singing robots, Proceedings of TAROS 2006 Conference - Towards Autonomous Robotics Systems, Gilford, United Kingdom

17

Emotoinal System with Consciousness and Behavior using Dopamine

Eiji Hayashi
Kyushu Institute of Technology
Japan

1. Introduction

Recently, the development of robots other than industrial robots, including home robots, personal robots, medical robots, and amusement robots, has been brisk. These robots, however, have required improvements in their intellectual capabilities and manual skills, as well as further increases in user compatibility (Y. Takahashi, M. Asada (2003)). User compatibility in future robots is important for ease of use, non-fatiguing control, robot friendliness (i.e., sympathetic use), and human-like capricious behavior. However, so far the development of the robots has met with problems with regard to their interactions with humans , especially in relation to motion strategies, communication, etc..

The author has developed a superior automatic piano with which a user can reproduce a desired performance as shown in Figure 1 (E.Hayashi, M.Yamane, T.Ishikawa, K.Yamamoto and H.Mori (1993), E.Hayashi, M.Yamane and H.Mori (1994)). The piano's hardware and software has been created, and the piano's action mechanism has been analyzed (E. Hayashi, M. Yamane and H. Mori (2000), Eiji Hayashi. (2006)). The automatic piano employs feedback control to follow up an input waveform for a touch actuator which uses the position sensor of an eddy current to strike a key. This fundamental input waveform is used to accurately and automatically reproduce a key touch based on performance information for a piece of classical music. This automatic piano was exhibited in EXPO 2005 AICHI JAPAN, and a demonstration of its abilities was given.

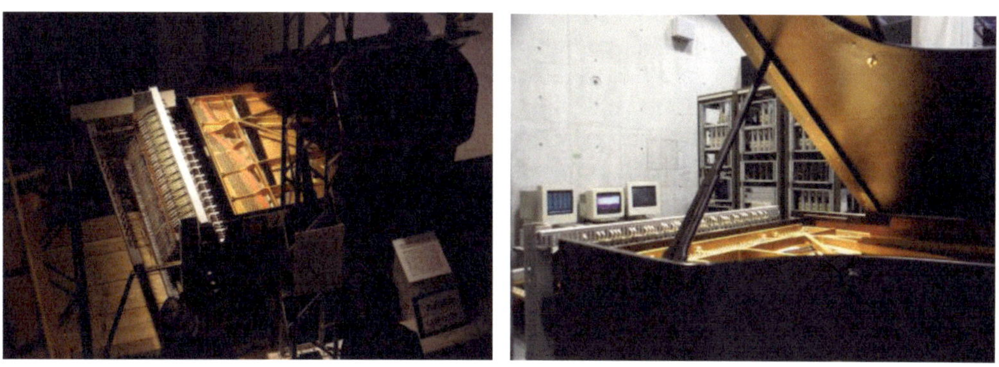

Fig. 1. Automatic Piano : FMT-I

For music to be reproduced by this automatic piano, the user must edit 1000 or more notes in the score of even a short piece of music (K.Asami, E.Hayashi, M.Yamane, H.Mori, and T.Kitamura (Aug. 1998)(Sept. 1998), Y.Hikisaka , E.Hayashi (2007)). However, since the automatic piano can accurately reproduce music, the user can accurately create an emotionally expressive performance according to an idea without action on their part involving fingers, arms, etc. like a pianist.
Although a user can certainly create a desired expression with the automatic piano, the user find or awake variations in the performance when the user listens repeatedly. The user must continue to make changes in their expressive performance. In other words, human seem to like change. These findings suggest that a robot will also need to have slight variation in behavior based to make interactions with them more pleasing.
Macarthy has indicated that a robot will need to consider and introspect in order to operate in the common sense world and to accomplish tasks humans given to it by humans; as such, it will need to have consciousness and introspective knowledges (J. McCarthy (1996)) and some philosohy (J. McCarthy (1995)). In addition, however, he indicates that robots should not be equipped with human-like emotions.
In my laboratory, an animal's adjustment to its environment has been studied in an attempt to emulate its behavior (N. Goto, E. Hayashi (2008), Tadashi Kitamura, Daisuke Nishino (2006)), and attempts have been made to give robots "consciousness" and "emotion" such as that identified in humans and animals to enhance the affinity between humans and robots. These efforts may allow us to meet some of the requirements (E. Hayashi. (2007), E. Hayashi. (2008), S. K. Talwar, S. Xu, E. S. Hawley, S. A. Weiss, K. A. Moxon, and J. K. Chapin (1996), J. Y. Donnart and J. A. Meyyer (1996), R.A. Brooks (1991)) for user compatibility.
Consciousness and behavior are related, and a hierarchical structure model that we call Consciousness-based Architecture (CBA) has been constructed in 5 layers. CBA has been synthesized based on a mechanistic expression model of animal consciousness and behavior advocated by the Vietnamese philosopher Tran Duc Thao (Tran Duc Thao, D.J.Herman, D.V.Morano (1986)). CBA introduces an evaluation function for behavior selection, and controls the robot's behavior. Although the consciousness level is changed in the model, it is difficult for a robot to behave autonomously using only CBA. To achieve such autonomous behavior, it is necessary to continuously produce motion or behavior in the robot, and to autonomously change the consciousness level.
Humans tend to lose interest if a robot continuously gives the same answer or repeats the same motion, but it is not easy for a robot developer to create varied responses and behavioral strategies in a robot. However, if a robot could behave consciously and autonomously, i.e., if a robot had emotional expression, its behaviors appear natural, and the user would not lose interest in it. However, even the human brain does not have a function by which emotions are controlled and managed, nor does a unified system for synthetically administering emotion exist (Joseph LeDoux. (1996)).
In humans and animals, the control or management of emotions depends on the existence of some motivation. The strategy for controlling or managing emotions is carried out as the motivation increases or decreases. Thus, in the present study, a motivation model was been developed to induce conscious, autonomous changes in behavior, and was combined with CBA. CBA was restructured from 5 layers to 4 layers as a retool, and a motivation model was added. Basically, the motivation model is an input to the CBA, and comprises an algorithm with various inputs based on a trace of naturally occurring dopamine in monoamine neurotransmitters (H.Kimura. (2005)).

In this chapter, the expression of emotion by a Conscious Behavior Robot (Conbe-I) that incorporated this motivation model, and the autonomous actions performed to take an object from human's hand were studied. This conscious behavior robot (Conbe-I) which has six degrees of freedom was developed with the aim of providing the robot with the ability to autonomously adjust to a target position. The Conbe-I is a robotic arm with a hand consisting of three fingers in which a small monocular CCD camera is installed. A landmark object is detected in the image acquired by the CCD camera, enabling it to perform holding and carrying tasks. As an autonomy action experiment, CBA including the motivation model was applied to the Conbe-I, and its behavior was then studied.

2. System structure of the Conbe-I

2.1 Hardware

The actuator of the Conbe-I as shown in Figure 2, is basically a robotic arm that was made with Kihara Iron Works. The Conbe-I is 450 mm long and is divided into 2 parts of an arm and a hand. The arm and the hand have 6 degrees and 1 degree of freedom respectively. The Conbe-I thus has a total of 7 degrees of freedom as shown in Figure 3. The hand has 3 fingers, and a CCD camera is fixed on the hand.

Fig. 2. Appearance of Conscious Behavior Robot (Conbe-I)

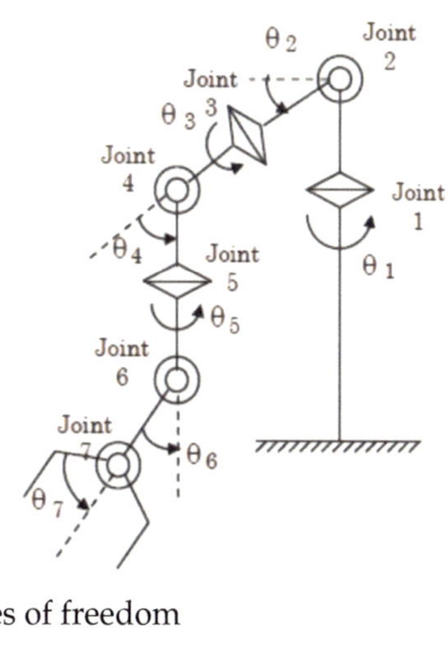

Fig. 3. Arrangement of degrees of freedom

The actuator used a Dynamixel DX-117 manufactured by ROBOTIS CO., LTD for each joint and hand. The DX-117 has a decelerator and an angular sensor, and is able to control position and velocity using a target angle, a torque limit, a speed limit, and so on.

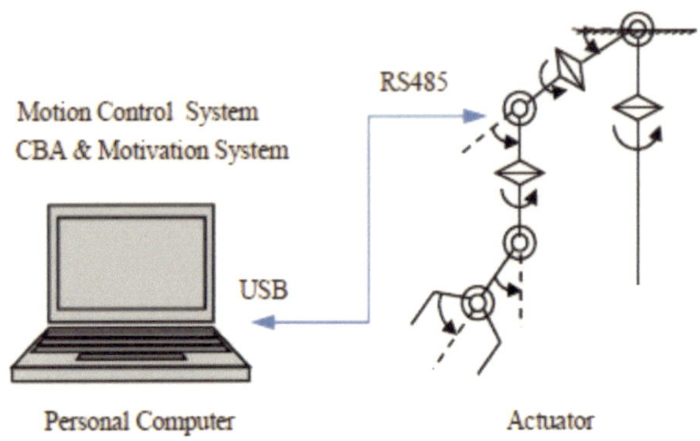

Fig. 4. System of the Conbe-I

The Conbe-I system as shown in Figure 4, consists of a motion control system and CBA with a motivation system in a personal computer, and an actuator. The communication between the personal computer and the actuator uses rs485 for telecommunications. Also, a control driver for a USB in the computer was developed so that the computer could control the actuator while processing the motion control and CBA with the motivation system.

2.2 Motion control system

It is difficult to calculate the angles of all joints from a target position using inverse kinematics since the actuator of the Conbe-I has 6 degrees of freedom of the arm and 1 degree of freedom of the hand. Therefore, the actuator was broken into 4 groups : a shoulder, an elbow, a wrist and a finger, as shown in Figure 5. Each group was then given a role to play in calculating an angle.

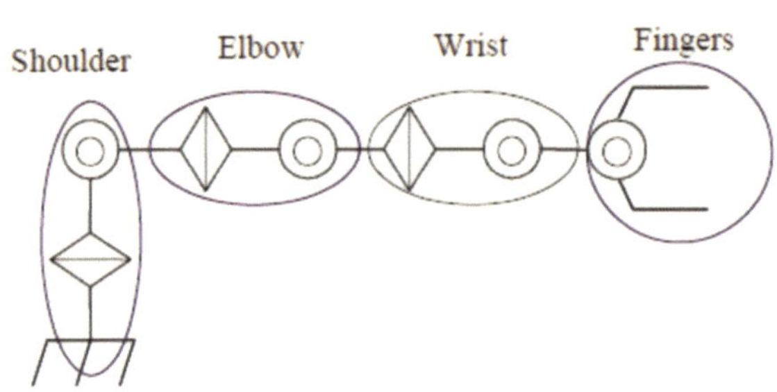

Fig. 5. Actuator divided into 4 groups

Basically, the calculating algorithm is started from θ_6 of the wrist to follow up a target object. But when the calculated angle exceeds the movable range, the angles from the elbow to the shoulder are calculated in turn. Additionally, a total of 81 kinds different patterns are calculated based on the wrist position, and the algorithm is structured so that the posture of the Conbe-I can be chosen such that the distance between the target object and the finger-tip becomes the shortest or the longest in the patterns.

As a result, it is possible to move the Conbe-I immediately toward the target object without inverse kinematics when the Conbe-I finds the target object.

2.3 Consciousness – based architecture

Figure 6 provides a diagram of a hierarchical structure model called CBA (consciousness-based architecture) that hierarchically relates consciousness to behavior. In this model, the consciousness field and the behavior field are built separately.
In a dynamic environment, the model decides on a consciousness level that the Conbe-I must strongly consider, and the Conbe-I selects the behavior corresponding to the consciousness level in the consciousness field and performs a behavior in the behavior modules.
This model is characterized by the consciousness level reaching the highest level. Therefore, the Conbe-I can select advanced behavior when the behavior corresponding to the consciousness level is discouraged by the external environment. Additionally, the mechanism of this model freely selects the most comfortable behavior.

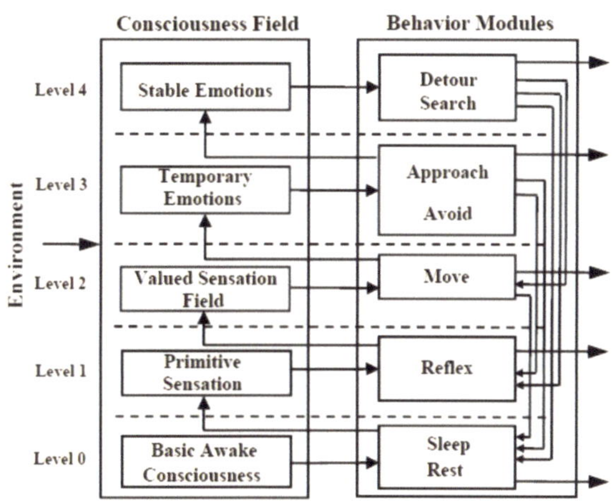

Fig. 6. Model of Consciousness-Based Architecture

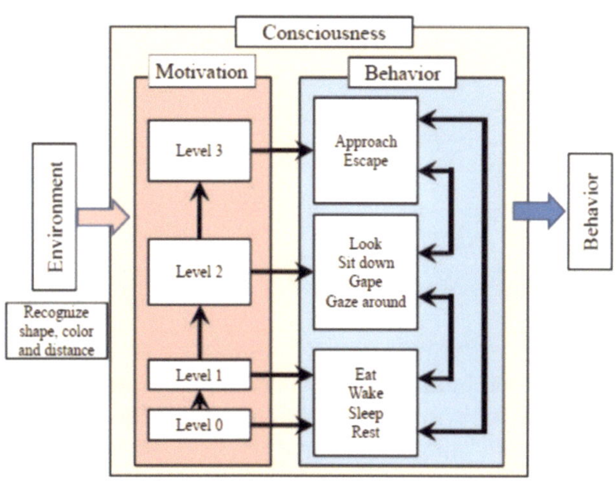

Fig. 7. Autonomous behavior system using 4 layers

Actually, to combine the motivation model with the CBA described in Section 3, the conscious fields and the behavior modules of Figure 6 were restructured from 5 layers to 4 layers with the consciousness up to Level 3. The relation between the consciousness and behavior were given as shown in Figure 7.
We believe that level 4 requires learning, memory and mind based on experiences, but the behavior up to level 3 is instinctive in nature.

3. Motivation model

Even if a robot is pleasing to people when due to its unique movements, people still will lose interest in the behavior, after their initial delight, unless the robot introduces some variations. Although the consciousness and behavior appear not to change significantly when a situation is encountered repeatedly, in actuality they are not the same at all. They continue to change with time, and the consciousness level continues to switch with time.
The CBA is useful for determining the relationship between consciousness and behavior. However, it is not able to continuously change the consciousness and behavior. As a result, the behavior becomes too mechanical.

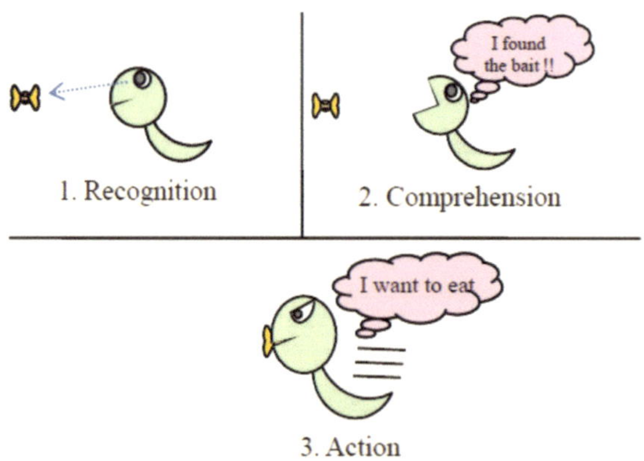

Fig. 8. Motivation in animal taking action

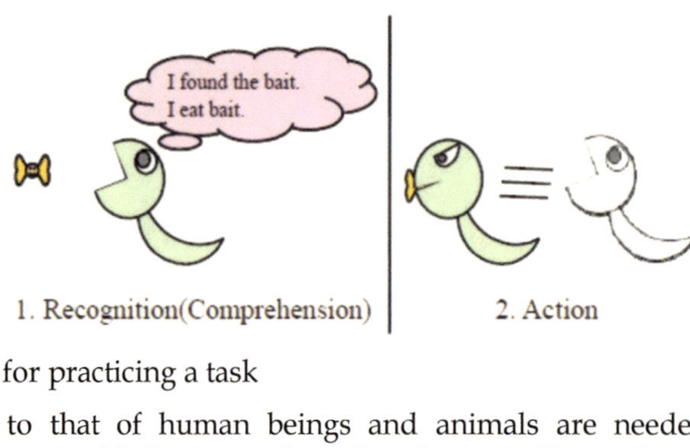

Fig. 9. Simple flow for practicing a task

Behaviors similar to that of human beings and animals are needed to actualize user compatibility. First, animal behavior such as that shown in Figure 8 was considered. When an animal, including a human being, takes some action, it can be represented by a behavior such as "Recognition -> Comprehension -> Action." The behavior will certainly be based on some motivation. Therefore, the emotion-driven behavior of a robot can be directed by a simple flow such as that shown in Figure 9 as the motivation. Thus, we considered this simple flow to be one of the causes of the mechanical action of the robot. The concept of motive was incorporated into the a robot, and a motivation model was constructed to structure an action choice with continuous variation resembling that of human beings and animals.

3.1 Naturally occurring dopamine as an input of motivation

The dopamine in monoamine neurotransmitters was considered in structuring the motivation model. It is thought that dopamine performs functions in the brain, and plays an important roles in behavior, cognition, and motivation. When animals including human beings take various actions, dopamine is secreted in the brain. For that reason, a more natural choice of action would be enabled if the motivation provided by dopamine could be reproduced in a robot.

The motivation model was developed based on an analysis of the effect of a typical-antipsychotic medicine, risperidone, on the release of dopamine in the central nervous system (H.Kimura(2005)). A graph depicting changes in the quantity of dopamine when the author administered a stimulant to a rat showed that dopamine levels in the brain suddenly increased when an accelerator was taken, and then slowly decreased shortly afterwards. Figure 9 shows a trace of the dopamine's variation. The change in the quantity of dopamine depends on the quantity of accelerator.

A waveform of naturally occurring dopamine in Figure 10 was divided into "raise" and "fall" portions. The "rise" and "fall" waveforms are used two types of linear differential equation to show a form in the figure. The "raise" and "fall" parts are adapted "a second-order system" and "a first- order system" respectivelly.

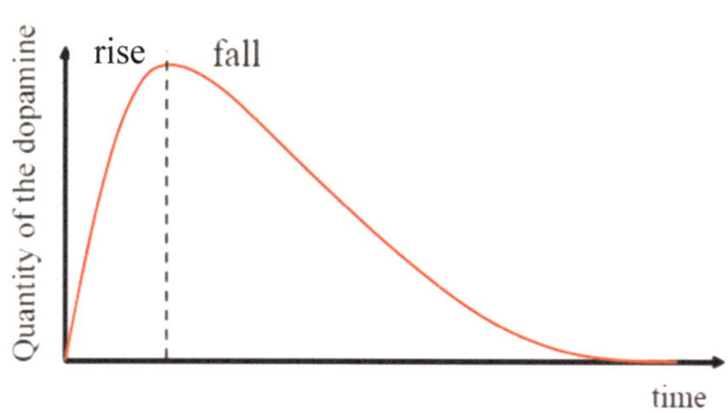

Fug. 10. Trace of naturally occurring dopamine in the case of a rat

When the input $x(t)$ is an accelerator of dopamine and the output $y(t)$ is a naturally occurring dopamine the rise waveform is given by

$$y'' + 2\varsigma\omega_n y' + \omega_n^2 = \omega_n^2 x(t) \tag{1}$$

where ς is the damping factor, and ω_n is the natural frequency.

For the input $x(t)$ and the output $y(t)$, the fall waveform is given by

$$Ty' + y(t) = x(t) \tag{2}$$

where T is the time constant.

The waveform of the naturally occurring dopamine is simulated by calculating the time responses of the respective equations for a step input $x(t)$ as shown in Figure 11.

First, the step response of a second- order system is used for the start of the naturally occurring dopamine. After a peak value is reached, a step response of the first-order system is used. Various traces of the naturally occurring dopamine can be expressed by approporately setting the natural frequency ω_n, damping factor ς, and time constant T of the variable included in the motivation model.

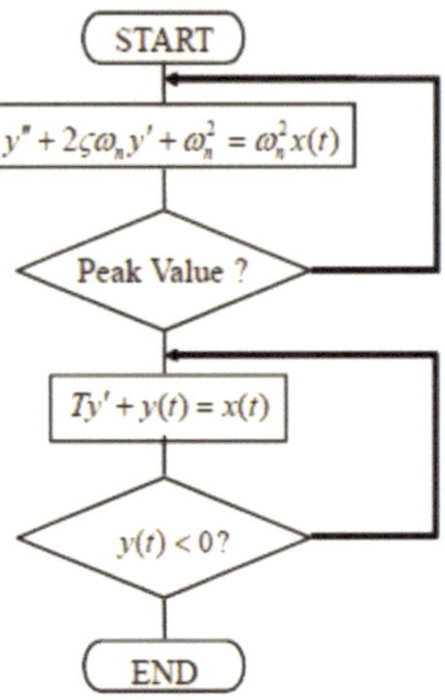

Fig. 11. Calculating the flow of naturally occurring dopamine

Equations (1) and (2) are solved using Runge - Kutta methods to continuously calculate the variation of the input waveform.

3.2 Accelerator of dopamine

To change the consciousness and behavior with time, it is necessary to enable their variation. Also, the quantity of naturally occurring dopamine varies to some extent according to the injecting quantity of an accelerator. Therefore, the injecting quantity of the accelerator was determined by the size of a group of pixels in an image obtained from a ccd camera in the hand of the Conbe-I as shown in Figure 12.

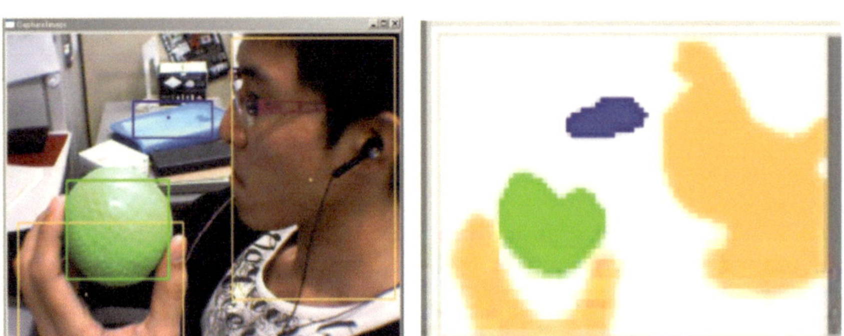

Fig. 12. Process of partitioning

To make multiple segments of grouped pixels, the image obtained from the ccd camera was simplified into four color groups of green, blue, flesh, and others; the green, blue and flesh colors were recognized as objects, and the images could be labeled. To distinguish and recognize objects, the shape, size, and center of the blue and flesh- colored segmentations were calculated as shown in Figure 13. Additionally, from this information and the posture of the robot arm, the Conbe-I could roughly recognize the position and distance of the colored object.

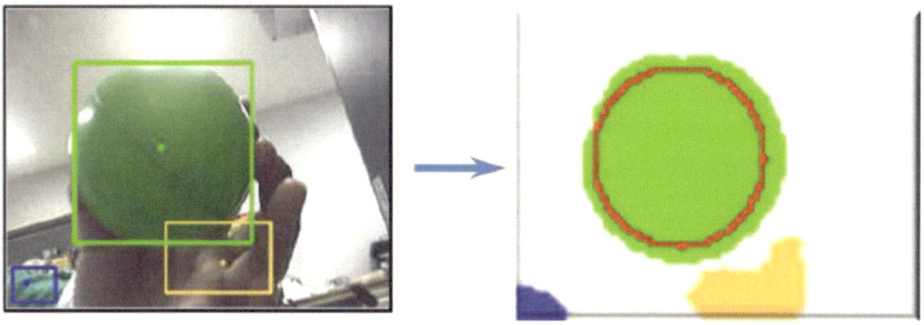

(a) Ball

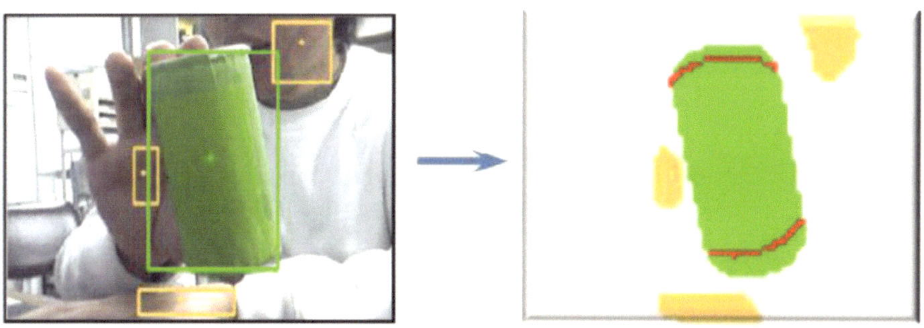

(b) Can

Fig. 13. Distinction and recognition

The objects in Figure 14 were used as means of simulating the naturally occurrence of dopamine in response to the color, shape, and distance of the objects. Hate, pleasure and great pleasure were defined as corresponding to a specific quantity of the naturally occurring dopamine.

(a) Blue: Hate (b) Green: Pleasure (c) Green: Most Pleasure

Fig. 14. Experimental objects representing inclination and disinclination

3.3 Calculating method of naturally occurring dopamine as an input

Each object is located and recognized with time because objects appear and disappear in/from view, at the same time/with a time lag, and also change shape and size, including a distance effect. Hence, each naturally occurring dopamine response (see Eqs. (1) and (2)) is calculated separately, and the quantity of naturally occurring dopamine is determined by the total sum of the positive and negative values as shown in Figure 15. In addition, if a new object is located and recognized, the quantity of naturally occurring dopamine is recalculated according to the variation at that point in time.

The output waveform of a motivation comes to be expressed by an input that is obtained based on the occurrence and the accelerator of dopamine described in the above sections.

The output waveform is estimated using a second- order system of linear differential equations that is similar to the naturally occurring dopamine. The input $y(t)$ is the naturally occurring dopamine, and the output is $Motivation(t)$.

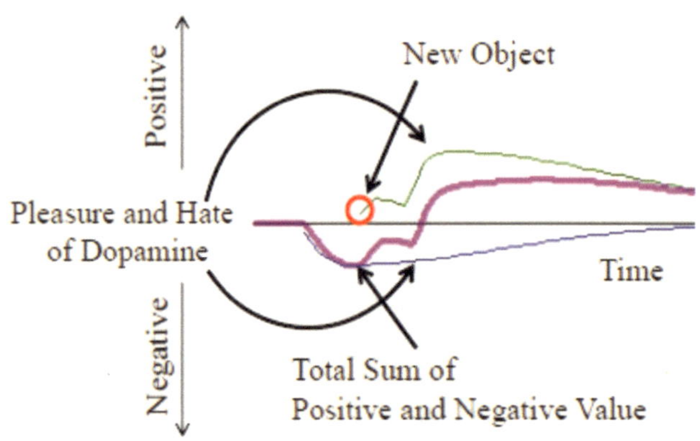

Fig. 15. Waveforms of naturally occurring dopamine

The output waveform of $Motivation(t)$ is given by

$$Motivation''(t) + 2\varsigma\omega_n Motivation'(t) + \omega_n^2 Motivation(t) = \omega_n^2 y(t) \tag{3}$$

where ω_n is the natural frequency, and ς is the damping factor.

Equation (3) is solved using the Runge - Kutta methods to calculate continuously the variation of the input waveform.

The result is shown in Figure 16. Although the motivation waveform has a slight lag relative to the input of the naturally occurring dopamine that is the total sum in this figure, the motivation can be obtained via various variations depending on the variation of the occurring dopamine.

A waveform of the motivation can be determined using such a method, incorporating the natural frequency ω_n, the damping factor ς, and the time constant T. Also, this method can make it is possible for the Conbe-I to behave consciously and autonomously like human beings and animals.

The autonomous behavior system chooses the consciousness level according to the motivation's waveform, and controls the actuators of Conbe-I based on the behavior according to the consciousness level in Figure 17. The boundary between the consciousness levels can be determined freely.

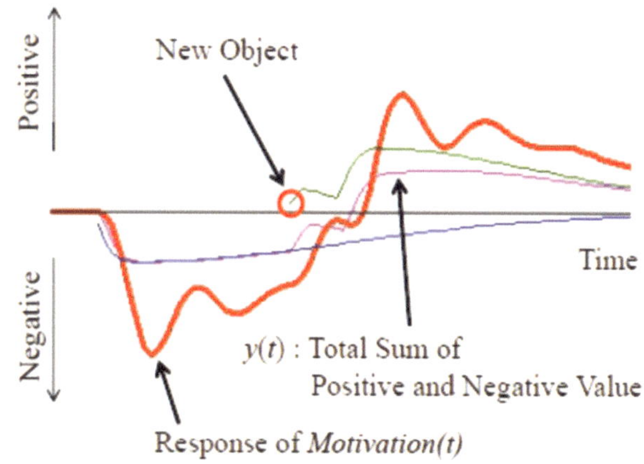

Fig. 16. Waveform of motivation

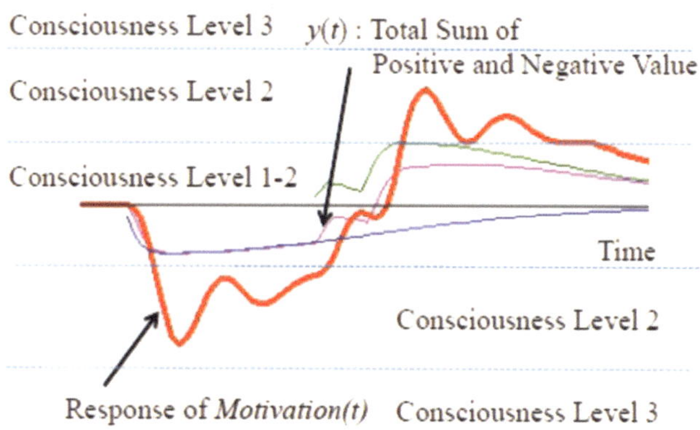

Fig. 17. Relationship between motivation and consciousness

4. Experiment

We confirmed that the Conbe-I could accurately recognize a favorite green ball and a hated blue ball. We observed the action of the Conbe-I until it caught a favored green ball. The transition of the motivation is showed in Figure17. In addition, the actual behavior is shown in Figure 18 (T0-T9), and T0 - T9 in Figure 18 are explained as follows.

The Conbe-I is at rest at T0. Then, when the robot recognizes a green ball, and its motivation increases slightly; the robot begins to run after the ball at T1. The motivation of the robot

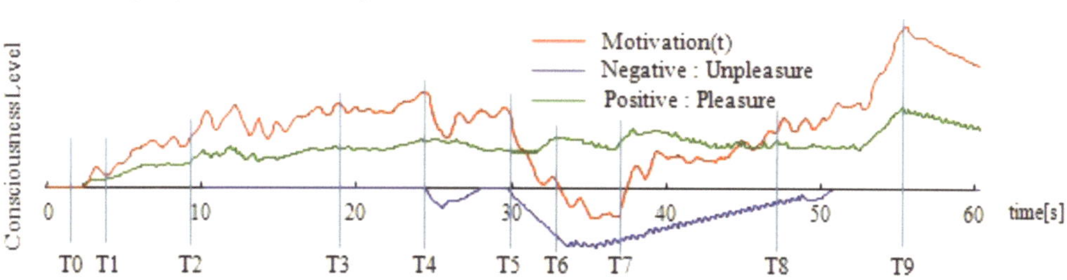

Fig. 17. Transition of the motivation

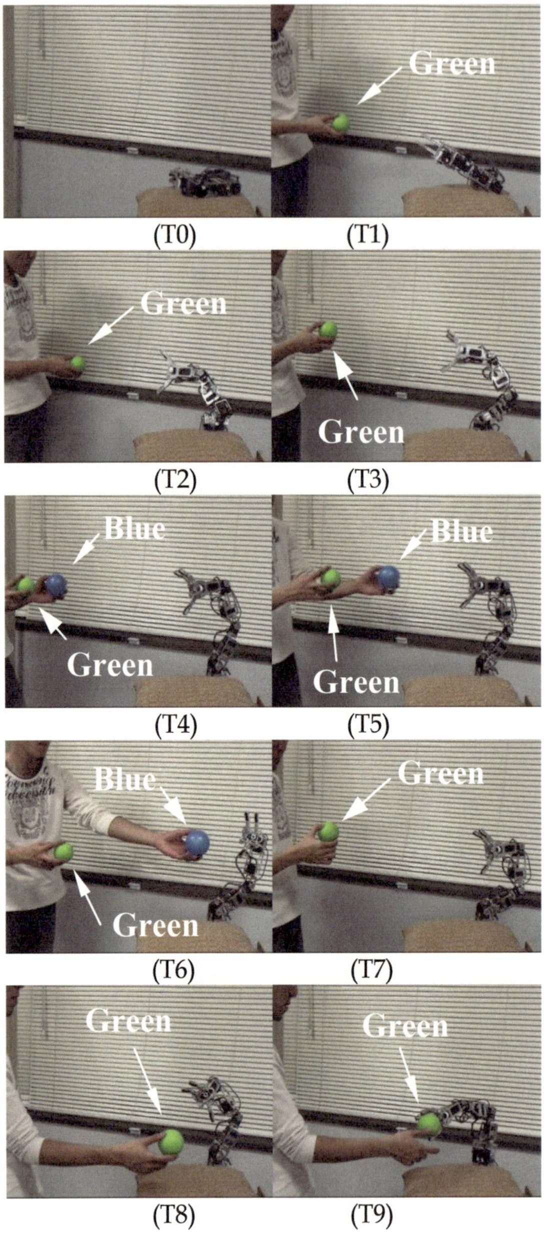

Fig. 18. Behavior of Conbe-I

increases more when the green ball does not move. The robot then recognizes the ball from a higher position at T2. The motivation is sufficiently increased, and the robot begins to approach the green ball at T3. However, when the robot finds a hated blue ball at T4, the motivation of the robot suddenly decreases, and it takes its eyes off of the blue ball. Because the robot has been shown the hated blue ball, the robot exhibits behavior showing that it hates the blue ball at T5 and T6. The robot is no longer beging shown the hated blue ball at T7, and subsequently is only shown the favored green ball. Therefore, its motivation

increases again, and it runs after the green ball at T8. When the motivation increases, it begins to approach the green ball. The robot comes close enough to the green ball to catch it at T9.
This experiment was tried several times. All results for a task in which the Conbe-I took a favored ball were the same. However, the behaviors and motivations up until it took the ball in all the experiments were obviously different.

5. Conclusions

In this chapter, we have described a Conbe-I that was developed to enable autonomous behavior; the Conbe-I was built with an autonomous behavior system combining motivation with consciousness using dopamine. The autonomous behavior system was able to expert effective control of the Conbe-I, and Conbe-I behaved autonomously and freely.
It was difficult to anticipate the movement of the Conbe-I. The robot never repeated the same movement, even when taking a green ball. This was not a mechanically obvious movement. We therefore believe that the Conbe-I displayed choice of action that resembled that of a human being or an animal.
This autonomous behavior system of the Conbe-I does not actually include an emotional component. However, the Conbe-I gives the appearance of a living thing, and the behavior of the Conbe-I seems to show emotion.
In the future a learning system based on experience will be synthesized so that the Conbe-I will be able to control itself by awareness and introspection.

6. Acknowledgement

This research was partially supported by the Ministry of Education, Science, Sports and Culture, Grant-in-Aid for Scientific Research, 2009.

7. References

E.Hayashi, M.Yamane, T.Ishikawa, K.Yamamoto and H.Mori. (1993). Development of a Piano Player, Proceedings of the 1993 International Computer Music Conference, pp.426-427, Sept. 1993, Tokyo, Japan

E.Hayashi, M.Yamane and H.Mori. (1994). Development of Moving Coil Actuator for an Automatic Piano, International Journal of Japan Society for Precision Engineering, Vol.28 No.2, pp.164-169

E.Hayashi, M.Yamane and H.Mori. (2000). Behavior of Piano-Action in a Grand Piano. I: alysis of the Motion of the Hammer Prior to String Contact, Journal of Acoustical Society of America, Vol.105, pp.3534-3544

Eiji Hayashi. (2006). Development of an Automatic Piano that Produce Appropriate -Touch for the Accurate Expression of a Soft Tone-, International Symposium on Advanced Robotics and Machine Intelligence(IROS06), pp.6, Oct. 2006, Beijin Chaina

K.Asami, E.Hayashi, M.Yamane, H.Mori, and T.Kitamura. (1998). Intelligent Edit of Support for an Automatic Piano, Proceedings of the 3rd International Conference on Advanced Mechatronics, pp.342-347, KAIST, Aug. 1998, Taejon,Korea

K.Asami, E.Hayashi, M.Yamane,H.Mori and T.Kitamura. (1998) An Intelligent Supporting System for Editing Music Based on Grouping Analysis in Automatic Piano, IEEE Proceedings of RO-MAN '98, pp.672-677, Sept. 1998, kagawa,Japan

Y.Hikisaka , E.Hayashi. (2007). Interactive musical editing system to support human errors and offer personal preferences for an automatic piano -Method of searching for similar phrases with DP matching and inferring performance expression, Artificial Life and Robotics(AROB 12th '07), pp.4 (CD-ROM), Jan. 2007, Oita Japan.

Y. Takahashi, M. Asada. (2003). Multi-layered learning systems for vision-based behavior acquisition of a real mobile robot, Procceding of SICE Annual Conference, Vol.CD-ROM, pp.2937-2942, Fukui, Japan

J. McCarthy.(1996). Making robots conscious of their mental states," in *Machine Intelligence*, vol. 15, S. Muggleton, Ed. Oxford: Oxford University Press, pp. 3-17,

J. McCarthy. (1995). Proceedings of the Fourteenth International Joint Conference on Artificial Intelligence, IJCAI 95, pp.2041-2044

N. Goto, E. Hayashi. (2008). Design of Robotic Behavior that imitates animal consciousness, Journal of Artificial Life and Robotics Vol.12, Springer, pp97-101

Tadashi Kitamura, Daisuke Nishino. (2006). Training of a Learning Agent for Navigation-Inspired by Brain-Machine Interface, IEEE Transaction on system, man, and cybernetics,Vol.36 No.2, pp.353-365

E. Hayashi. (2008). Navigation system for an autonomous robot using an ocellus camera in indoor environment, Journal of Artificial Life and Robotics Vol.12, Springer, pp346-352

E. Hayashi. (2007). Navigation system with a self-drive control for an Autonomous Robot in Indoor Environment, 16th International Symposium on Robot & Human Interactive Communication (RO-MAN 2007), Aug. 2007, Jedu, Korea.

S. K. Talwar, S. Xu, E. S. Hawley, S. A. Weiss, K. A. Moxon, and J. K. Chapin. (1996). Rat navigation guided by remote control, Nature, Vol.417, pp37-38, 2002

J. Y. Donnart and J. A. Meyyer. (1996) Learning reactive and planning rules in a motivationally autonomous animat, IEEE Trans. System, Man, and Cybernetics, Vol.26 No.3, pp.381-395, 1996.

R.A. Brooks. (1991). Intelligence without representation, Artificial Intelligence, Vol. 47, pp.139-159, 1991.

Tran Duc Thao, D.J.Herman, D.V.Morano.(1986). Phenomenology and Dialectical Materialism Boston Studies in the Philosophy of Science, D Reidel Pub Co, 1986.

Joseph LeDoux. (1996) The Emotional Brain: The Mysterious Underpinnings of Emotional Life, New York, Simon & Schuster, 1996.

H.Kimura. (2005). A trial to anlyze the effect of an atypical antipsychotic medicine, risperidone, on the release of dopamine in the central nervous system, Journal Aichi Medical University Association vol.33 No.1, pp.21-27, 2005.

18

Learning to Understand Expressions of Approval and Disapproval through Game-Based Training Tasks

Anja Austermann and Seiji Yamada
The Graduate University for Advanced Studies (SOKENDAI)
National Institute of Informatics
Japan

1. Introduction

One of the most important factors for infants' learning is positive and negative feedback from their caregiver. In a similar way, learning robots can also use the feedback from their user as a basis for learning and adapting to the user's preferences. A popular example of learning through user feedback is reinforcement learning with a human teacher (Thomaz & Brezeal, 2006), but many applications of learning by positive and negative examples with assistance from a user or behavior adaptation and refinement (Kim & Scassellati, 2007) require an understanding of the user's expression of approval and disapproval. This paper focuses on enabling a robot to learn to understand natural, multimodal approving or disapproving feedback given in response to the robot's moves.

Humans express approval and disapproval toward a robot through different channels, such as words, prosody, gestures, facial expressions and touch. Most work on understanding approval and disapproval has been done with single-modal approaches based on prosodic information from speech signals such as intonation, pitch, tempo, loudness and rhythm (Breazeal, 2002) (Kim & Scassellati, 2007). However, we assume that integrating multiple modalities improves the reliability of the recognition and allows the system to adapt to the individual preferences of the user. We determined the modalities to implement in our system through a user-study. It is described in detail in (Austermann & Yamada, 2008). We found, that speech was by far the most frequently used modality, when giving feedback to an AIBO robot. 78.37% of all feedback was given by speech. It was followed by touch, which was used for 20.92% of the feedbacks. Gesture was applied for giving instructions, but did not play a significant role for giving feedback and was only used in 0.71% of the cases. Therefore, in addition to prosody, we focus on the contents of the speech utterances as well as on interaction through the touch sensors of the robot. We did not integrate the recognition of facial expressions, because we wanted the users to move around freely and interact naturally. A facial expression recognizer would have restricted the users' movements by requiring them to look straight into a camera.

In order to learn to interpret user feedback, our system utilizes a biologically-inspired two-staged learning method which is modeled after basic learning processes in humans and animals. It combines unsupervised training of Hidden Markov Models (HMMs), which models the stimulus encoding occurring in natural learning and clusters similar observed user feedbacks, with an implementation of classical conditioning that associates the trained HMMs with either approval or disapproval. The combination of supervised and unsupervised learning as well as specifically designed training tasks allow our system to learn interaction without requiring any transcriptions of training utterances and without any prior knowledge on the words, language or grammar to be used. As a model of the top-down processes, which occur in human learning, we use the associations learned in the conditioning stage to integrate context information when selecting the best HMM for retraining. This is done by adding a bias on models, that are already associated with approval or disapproval depending on what feedback is expected based on the state of the training task.

Adaptation of a robot to a user is done in a training phase before actually using the robot. The training tasks are designed to allow the robot to anticipate and explore the user's feedback. During the training phase, the robot solves special training tasks in cooperation with the user. The tasks are modeled to resemble simple games. The training phase is inspired by the Wizard-of-Oz principle, aiming at giving the user the feeling that the robot adequately reacts to his or her commands in a stage, where the robot actually does not understand the user. However, the training can be performed without remote controlling the robot because remote controlling would be infeasible for actually training a newly bought service robot. Instead, the tasks are designed to ensure that the robot and the user share the same understanding of whether a move is good or bad. This way, the robot is able to anticipate the user's feedback and instructions and can explore its user's expressions of approval and disapproval by deliberately executing good or bad moves. As a result, natural, situated feedback can be observed and learned.

In the experiment, we use "virtual" tasks. The robot plays on a computer-generated game board which is projected from the back to a white screen. This way, we do not need to rely on the potentially erroneous processing of sensor data for determining the state of the task. Further explanations on the training tasks are given in section 3.

2. Related work

There has been a great deal of work on adapting robots to their users, understanding human expression of affect and emotion (Breazeal, 2002) (Thomaz & Breazeal, 2006) processing natural language (Iwahashi, 2004) (Kayikci et al., 2007) and learning through human feedback in recent years. One example that is particularly related to our work is presented in (Kim & Scassellati, 2007). Kim and Scassellati described an approach to recognize approval and disapproval in a Human-Robot teaching scenario and used it to refine the robot's waving movement by Q-Learning. They employed a single-modal approach to discriminate between approval and disapproval based on prosody.

Learning the connections between words and their meanings through natural interaction with a user has been researched upon in the field of language acquisition

Iwahashi described an approach (Iwahashi, 2004) to the active and unsupervised acquisition of new words for the multimodal interface of a robot. He applied Hidden Markov Models to learn verbal representations of objects and motions, perceived by a stereo camera. The learning component used pre-trained HMMs as a basis for learning and the robot interacted with its user in order to avoid and resolve misunderstandings.

Kayikci et al. (Kayikci et al., 2007) utilized Hidden Markov Models and a neural associative memory for learning to understand short speech commands in a three-staged recognition procedure. First, the system recognized a speech signal as a sequence of diphones or triphones. In the next step, the sequences were translated into words using a neural associative memory. The last step employed a neural associative memory to finally obtain a semantic representation of the utterance.

In the same way as the approaches, outlined above, our learning algorithm attempts at assigning a meaning to an observed auditory or visual pattern using HMMs as a basis. However, our system is not trying to learn the meaning of individual words or symbols, but focuses on learning patterns expressing a feedback as a whole. Moreover, our proposed approach is not limited to a single modality but tries to integrate observations from different modalities.

For learning associations between approval or disapproval and the HMM representations of the observed user behavior, classical conditioning is used in our system. Mathematical theories of classical conditioning were extensively researched upon in the field of cognitive psychology. An overview can be found in (Balkenius & Moren, 1998). The relation of classical conditioning to the phase of learning word meanings in human speech acquisition has been postulated in the book "Verbal Behavior" by B. F. Skinner (Skinner, 1957) and has been adopted and modified by researchers in the field of behavior analysis. An explanation of the processes involved in learning word meanings by conditioning is described by B. Lowenkron in (Lowenkron, 2000).

There have been different approaches to use classical conditioning for teaching a robot, such as in (Balkenius, 1999). However, to our knowledge our proposed approach is the first one to apply classical conditioning to acquire an understanding of speech utterances and integrating multimodal information about user behavior in Human-Robot-Interaction.

3. Training tasks

We propose a training method that allows the robot to explore and provoke approving and disapproving feedback from its user. Our learning algorithm does not depend on the way, training data is recorded. However, we found in an exploratory study (Austermann & Yamada, 2007) that natural feedback, given during actual interaction with a robot in a similar task differs from feedback that a user would record in advance. Therefore, we implemented a training method that uses "virtual" games and allows the robot to explore its user's way of giving feedback and learn actual, situated feedback during realistic interaction.

The robot is supposed to learn to understand the user's feedback in a training phase. This implies that by the time of the training it cannot actually understand its user. However, in order to ensure natural interaction, it needs to give the user the impression that it understands him or her by reacting appropriately. This is done by designing the training task in a way, that the robot can anticipate the user's feedback by knowing which moves are good or bad. If the task ensures, that the user can easily judge whether the robot performed a good or a bad move, the robot can expect approving feedback for good moves and disapproving feedback for bad moves. This way the robot can deal with instruction from the user without actually understanding his or her utterances and can freely explore and provoke its user's approving and disapproving feedback. Our training phase consists of training tasks which were designed based on this principle. The tasks are based on easy

games suitable for young children. In the experiments, the participants were asked to teach the robot, how to correctly play these games using natural feedback.
An issue that we became aware of during preliminary experiments is the very limited ability of the AIBO robot to physically manipulate its environment and to move precisely. The possibility of not detecting errors, such as failing to pick up or move an object, poses a risk for misinterpreting the current status of the task and learning incorrect associations. So we decided to implement the training task in a way that the robot can complete it without having to directly manipulate its environment. We use a "virtual playfield" which is computer-generated and projected from the back to a white screen. The robot shows its moves by motion and sounds. It retrieves information directly from the game server using the AIBO Remote Framework. This way we can ensure that the robot is able to assess its current situation instantly, anticipate the user's next feedback or instruction correctly and associate the observed behavior correctly with approval or disapproval.
The following tasks were selected to be used in our experiments, because they are easy to understand and allow a user to evaluate every move instantly. We selected four different tasks in order to see whether different properties of the task, such as the possibility to provide not only feedback but also instruction, the presence of an opponent or the game-based nature of the tasks influence the user's behavior. We implemented them in a way that they require little time-consuming walking movement from the robot.

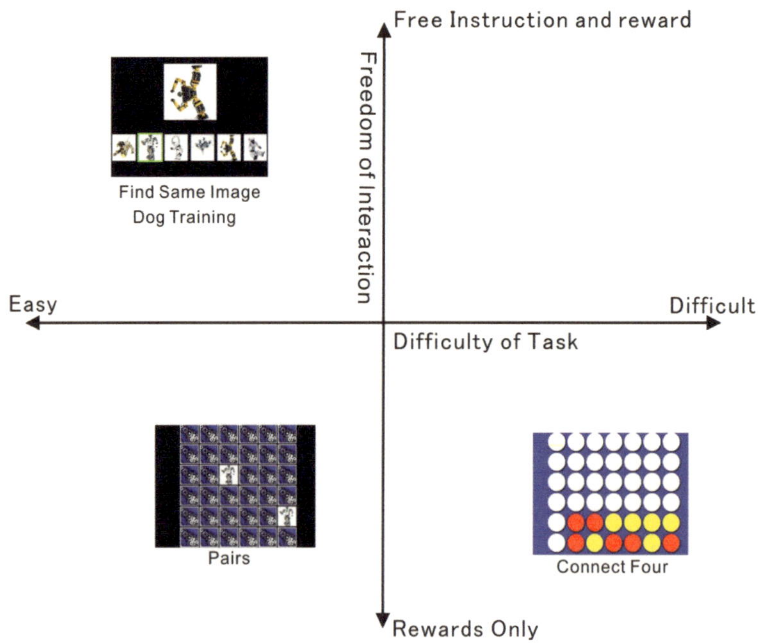

Fig. 1. Properties of the different training tasks

We selected and implemented the different training tasks in a way, that they cover two dimensions which we assume to have an impact on the interaction between the user and the robot.:

- Easy - Difficult: Training tasks can range from ones, that are very easy to understand and evaluate for the user, to tasks where the user has to think carefully to be able evaluate the moves of the robot correctly.

- Constrained - Unconstrained: In the most constrained form of interaction in our training tasks, the user is told to only give positive or negative feedback to the robot but not to give any instructions. In an unconstrained training task, the user is only informed about the goal of the task and asked to give instructions and reward to the robot freely.

The positions of the different tasks in the two dimensions can be seen in Figure 1. There is one task for each of the combinations "easy/constrained", "easy/unconstrained" and "difficult/constrained". The reason, why there is no task for the combination "difficult/unconstrained" is that that in such a situation, the user behavior becomes too hard to predict, so that the robot cannot reliably anticipate positive or negative reward. Screenshots of the playfields can be seen in Figure 2

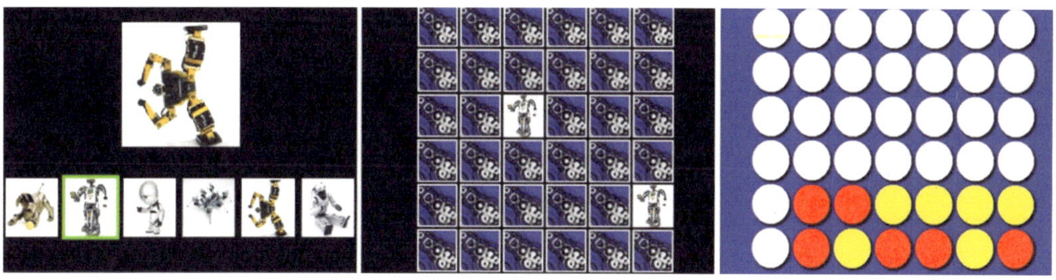

Fig. 2. Game screens of the "Virtual" Training Tasks. (left: Picture Matching, right: Pairs)

3.1.1 Picture matching

On the easy/unconstrained end of the scale, there is the "Find Same Images" task. In this task, the robot has to be taught to choose the image that corresponds to the one, shown in the center of the screen, from a row of six images. While playing, the image that the robot is currently looking or pointing at is marked with a green or red frame to make it easier for the user to understand the robot's viewing or pointing direction. By waving its tail and moving its head the robot indicates that it is waiting for feedback from its user. In this task the user can evaluate the move of the robot very easily by just looking at the sample image and the currently selected image. The participants were asked to provide instruction as well as reward to the robot freely without any constraints to make it learn to perform the task correctly. The system was implemented in a way that the rate of correct choices and the speed of finding the correct image increased over time.

3.1.2 Pairs

As an easy/constrained task, we chose the "Pairs" game. In this task, the robot plays the classic children's game "Pairs": At the beginning of the game, all cards are displayed upside down on the playfield. The robot chooses two cards to turn around by looking and pointing at them. In case, they show the same image, the cards remain open on the playfield. Otherwise, they are turned upside down again. The goal of the game is to find all pairs of cards with same images in as little draws as possible. In this task the user can evaluate easily whether a move of the robot was good or bad by comparing the two selected images.
The participants were asked not to give instruction to the robot, which card to chose but to assist the robot in learning to play the game by giving positive and negative feedback only.

3.1.3 Connect four

As a difficult/constrained task, we selected the "Connect Four" task. In the "Connect Four" game, the robot plays the game "Connect Four" against a computer player. Both players take turns to insert one stone into one of the rows in the playfield, which then drops to the lowest free space in that row. The goal of the game is, to align four stones of one's own color either vertically, horizontally or diagonally.
The participants were asked to not to give instructions to the robot but provide feedback for good and bad draws in order to make the robot learn how to win against the computer player. Judging whether a move is good or bad is considerably more difficult in the "Connect Four" task than in the three other tasks as it requires understanding the strategy of the robot and the computer player.

3.1.4 Dog training

We have implemented the "Dog Training" task as a control task in order to detect possible differences in user behavior between the virtual tasks and "normal" Human-Robot-Interaction. Like the "Find Same Images" task covers the dimensions easy/unconstrained. The user can easily evaluate the robot's behavior and use his/her way of giving instruction and reward freely without restrictions. In the "Dog Training" task, the participants were asked to teach the speech commands "forward", "back", "left", "right", "sit down" and "stand up" to the robot. The "Dog Training" task is the only task that is not game-like and does not use the "virtual playfield". Only in this task the robot was remote-controlled to ensure correct performance.

4. Learning method

We use a biologically inspired approach for learning to classify approval and disapproval using speech, prosody and touch. Our learning method consists of two stages, modeling the stimulus encoding and the association processes, which are assumed to occur in human learning (Burns et al., 2003) (Lowenkron, 2000) (Werker et al., 2005) of associations and word meanings. Details about the biological background of this work are given in section 4.1.
The first learning stage, the feedback recognition learning, is based on Hidden Markov Models. It corresponds to the stimulus encoding phase in human associative learning. Separate sets of HMMs are trained for speech and prosody. The models are trained in an unsupervised way and cluster similar perceptions, e.g. utterances that are likely to contain the same sequence of words or similar prosody. Touch is handled in a different way, because the data returned by the AIBO remote framework does not suffice for HMM based modeling.
The second stage is based on an implementation of classical conditioning. It associates the HMMs which were trained in the first stage with either approval or disapproval, integrating the data from different modalities. As users have different preferences for using speech, prosody and touch when communicating with a robot, the system has to weight the information, coming in through these different channels depending on the user's preferences. Classical conditioning can deal with this problem by emphasizing cues that frequently occur in connection with approving or disapproving feedback for a certain user. It allows the system to weight and combine user inputs in different modalities according to the strength of their association toward approving or disapproving feedback. The data structure, resulting from the learning process, is shown in Figure 3.

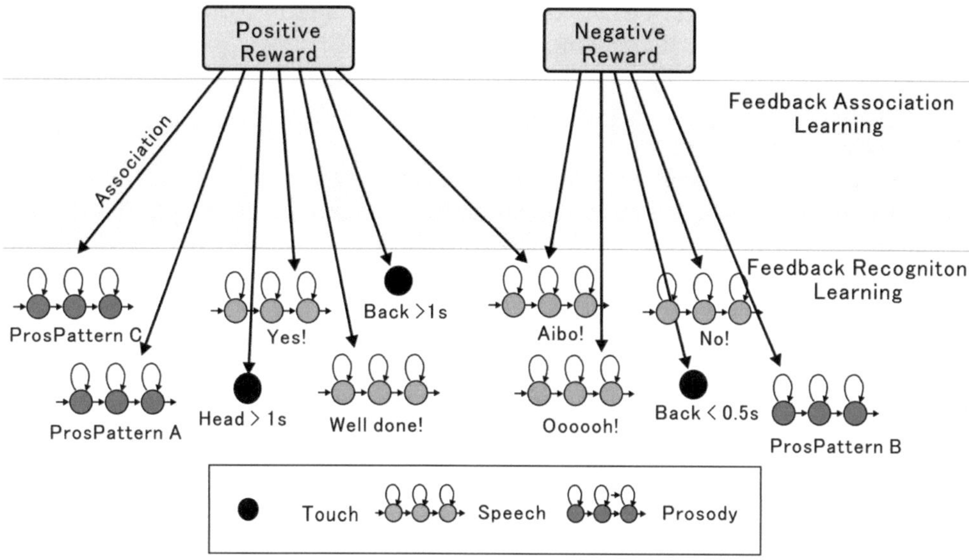

Fig. 3. Data structure, that is learned in the training phase.

4.1 Biological background

Our approach towards understanding feedback from a human is inspired by the biological and psychological processes which are found in human associative learning, speech perception and speech acquisition. However, we do not claim to implement an accurate model of all processes which occur in natural associative learning and understanding of elementary utterances. Instead, we focused on the concepts which appeared most relevant to our research objective of learning to understand human feedback for a robot.

4.1.1 Stimulus encoding for associative learning

Before a human or animal can establish an association between a stimulus and its meaning, the physical stimulus needs to be converted into a representation that the brain can deal with. This process is called *stimulus encoding* (Eysenck & Keane, 2005). Stimulus encoding also enables the brain to abstract from the concrete individual stimuli - which always differ to some extend - to attain a common representation. Evidence of these two stages has been found in experiments on classical conditioning as well as infant word learning (Eysenck & Keane, 2005) (Werker et al., 2005).

For speech, the process of phonological encoding develops and refines in the first months of an infant. Experiments found, that infants' speech acquisition starts from acquiring a proper way of encoding speech-based stimuli (Werker et al., 2005) several months before they are actually able to learn the meaning of words by associative learning.

We adopt this separation between the stimulus encoding and the learning of associations between stimuli and their meanings for our learning algorithm. We combine a stimulus encoding phase based on unsupervised clustering of similar perceptions and an associative learning phase using classical conditioning as a supervised learning method. This allows our system to learn the meaning of feedback from the user during natural interaction because the learning algorithm does not require any explicit information, such as transcriptions of the user's utterances or gestures for stimulus encoding. It only needs the information of whether an utterance means approval or disapproval to associate the HMMs with their correct meanings. This information is given through the training task.

4.1.2 Classical conditioning

The theory of classical conditioning, which was first described by I. Pavlov (Pavlov, 1927) and originates from behavioral research in animals. It models the learning of associations in animals as well as in humans. In classical conditioning, an association between a new, motivationally neutral stimulus, the so-called *conditioned stimulus (CS)*, and a motivationally meaningful stimulus, the so-called *unconditioned stimulus (US)*, is learned (Balkenius & Moren, 1998). In our system, the concepts of approving or disapproving feedback are modeled as *US*. They can, for instance, be interpreted as a positive or negative signal from a reward function used in reinforcement learning. The models of the user's utterances, prosody patterns and touches are *CS* which are associated with approval or disapproval during the feedback association learning phase.

For our task of learning multimodal feedback patterns, the most relevant properties of classical conditioning are blocking, extinction and second-order-conditioning as well as sensory preconditioning:

Blocking

Blocking occurs, when a *CS1* is paired with a *US*, and then conditioning is performed for the *CS1* and a new *CS2* to the same *US* (Balkenius & Moren, 1998). In this case, the existing association between the *CS1* and the *US* blocks the learning of the association between the *CS2* and the *US* as the *CS2* does not provide additional information to predict the occurrence of the *US*. The strength of the blocking is proportional to the strength of the existing association between the *CS1* and the *US*. For the learning of multimodal interaction patterns, blocking is helpful, as it allows the system to emphasize the stimuli that are most relevant. For instance, if a certain user always touches the head of the robot for showing approval, and sometimes provides different speech utterances together with touching the robot, then blocking slows down the learning of the association between approval and these speech utterances if there is already a strong association between touching the head sensor and approval. This way, the more reliable cues are emphasized.

Extinction

Extinction refers to the situation, where a *CS* that has been associated with a *US*, is presented without the *US*. In that case, the association between the *CS* and the *US* is weakened. (Balkenius & Moren, 1998) This capability is necessary to deal with changes in user behavior and with mistakes, made during the training phase, such as a misunderstanding of the situation by the human and a resulting incorrect feedback.

Sensory preconditioning and second-order conditioning

Sensory preconditioning and second-order conditioning describe the learning of an association between a *CS1* and a *CS2*, so that if the *CS1* occurs together with the *US*, the association of the *CS2* towards the *US* is strengthened, too. (Balkenius & Moren, 1998) In sensory preconditioning, the association between *CS1* and *CS2* is established before learning the association towards the *US*, in second-order conditioning, the association between the *US* and *CS1* is learned beforehand, and the association between *CS1* and *CS2* is learned later. Secondary preconditioning and second-order conditioning are important for our learning method, as they enable our system to learn connections between stimuli in different modalities. They also allow the system to continue learning associations between stimuli given through different modalities even when it could not determine whether the robot's move was good or bad, as long as new stimuli, such as new or commands are presented together with stimuli that are already known and associated to a feedback. E.g. a new positive speech feedback is uttered with a typical, known positive/negative prosody pattern.

4.1.3 Top-down and bottom-up-processes in speech understanding

Human perception is not an unidirectional process but involves bottom-up and top-down processes. (Eysenck & Keane, 2005). The *bottom-up processes* are triggered by the physical stimuli, such as audio signals received by the inner ear or light hitting the retina. The *top-down processes*, on the other hand, are based on the context in which a specific stimulus occurs. The context is used to generate expectations about which perceptions are likely to occur. Both, bottom-up and top-down processes, work together in human perception of audio-visual signals to determine the best explanation of the available data.

The interplay of bottom-up processes and top-down processes in speech perception has been investigated in detail by psychologists (Eysenck & Keane, 2005). W. F. Ganong found, that if a person heard an ambiguous phoneme, such as a mixture between "d" and "t", and one of the possible phonemes made a correct word, while the other one didn't, such as "drash"/"trash", the participants were more likely to identify the ambiguous phoneme as the one, that belonged to a correct word. C.M. Connine found that the meaning of the sentence, that an ambiguous phoneme is presented in, has an influence on its identification. These findings suggested that perception is not only driven by the physical stimulus but also depends on expectations generated from the context. Figure 4 shows an overview of bottom-up and top-down processes in human speech perception.

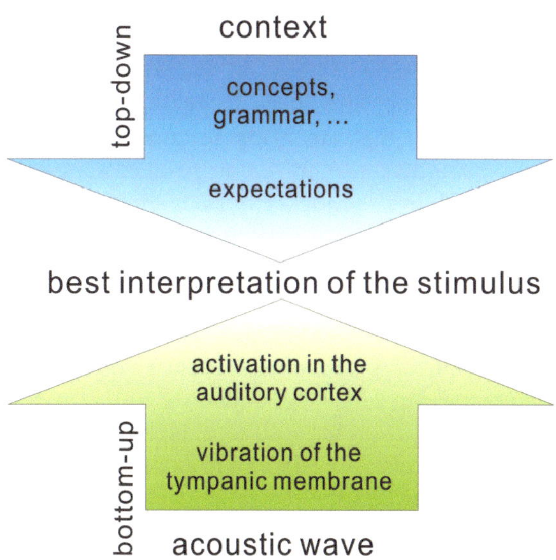

Fig. 4. Bottom-Up and Top-Down Processes in Speech Perception.

In our system, top-down processes are used to improve the selection accuracy when choosing an HMM for retraining. They generate an expectation on which utterances or prosodic patterns are likely to occur, using context information. The context information is calculated from the state of the training task, which suggests whether positive or negative reward is expected, and the learned associations between HMMs and positive or negative feedback. This way HMMs, that have previously been associated with either positive or negative reward, become more likely to be recognized, when another positive or negative reward is expected.

4.2 Feedback recognition learning

The Feedback Recognition learning stage of our learning algorithm clusters and learns the robot's perceptions of the user's feedback. It is based on Hidden Markov Models for speech as well as for prosody and a simple duration-based model for touch.

For each feedback, given by the user, the best matching speech, prosody and touch models are determined according to the methods, described in 4.2.1 to 4.2.3. Then, the most closely matching models are retrained with the data corresponding to the observed feedback. When retraining has finished, the models are passed on to the feedback association learning stage where they are associated with either approval or disapproval based on the situation, that the robot was in, when perceiving the feedback.

In our work, HMMs are employed for the low-level modeling of perceptions. As a standard approach for the classification of time series data, HMMs are widely used in literature. The use of Mel-Frequency-Cepstrum-Coefficients (MFCC) for HMM-based speech recognition is described in (Young et al., 2006). Appropriate feature-sets for emotion and prosody recognition are outlined in (Breazeal, 2002) and (Kim & Scassellati, 2007). We use these tried and tested feature-sets as an input for the HMM-based low-level learning phase.

4.2.1 Speech utterances

To model speech utterances our system trains a user-dependent set of whole-utterance HMMs based on the observed feedback utterances. As a basis for creating utterance models it uses an existing set of monophone HMMs. As the robot learns automatically through interaction, no transcription of the utterances is available. Therefore, an unsupervised clustering of perceived feedbacks that are likely to correspond to the same utterance is necessary. This is done by using two recognizers in parallel. One recognizer tries to model the observed utterance as an arbitrary sequence of phonemes. The other recognizer uses the already trained utterance models to calculate the best-matching known utterance. Every time a feedback from the user is observed, first the system tries to recognize the utterance with both recognizers. Matching is done by HVite, an implementation of the Viterbi Algorithm included in the Hidden Markov Model Toolkit (HTK) (Young et al., 2006). The recognizers return the best-matching phoneme sequence and the best matching utterance out of the utterance models that have been generated up to that point. In addition to that, a confidence level is output by the system for both recognition results.

The confidence levels, which are calculated by HVite as the log likelihood per frame of both results, are compared to determine whether to generate a new model or retrain an existing one. Typically, for an unknown utterance, the phoneme-sequence based recognizer returns a result with a noticeably higher confidence, than the one of the best matching utterance model. For a known utterance, the confidence corresponding to the best-matching utterance

model is either higher or similar to the best-matching phoneme-sequence. Therefore, if the confidence level of the best-fitting phoneme sequence is worse than the confidence level of the best-fitting utterance model or less than 10^{-5} better, then the best-fitting utterance model is retrained with the new utterance.
If the confidence level of the best-matching phoneme sequence is more than 10^{-5} better than the one of the best-fitting whole-utterance model, then a new utterance model is initialized for the utterance. The new model is created by concatenating the HMMs of the recognized most likely phoneme sequence. The new model is retrained with the just observed utterance and added to the HMM-set of the whole-utterance recognizer. So it can be reused when a similar utterance is observed. An overview of the training for speech is shown in Figure 5.

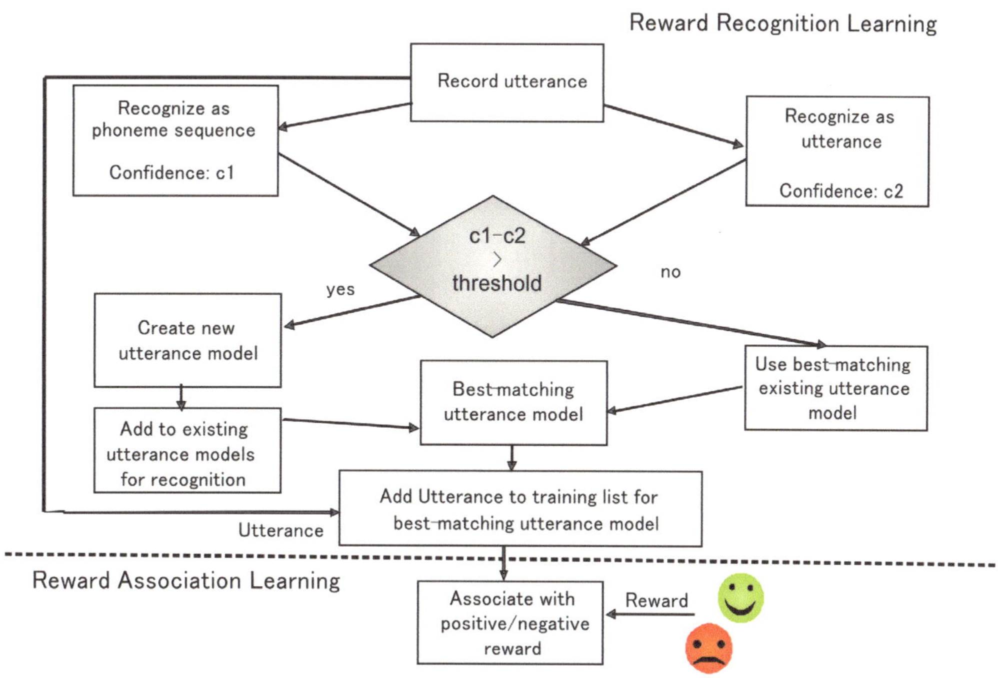

Fig. 5. Algorithm for Recognizing Speech.

The HMM-set for the phoneme-sequence recognizer contains all Japanese monophones and is taken from the Julius Speech Recognition project. We use a simple grammar for the phoneme recognizer that permits an arbitrary sequence of phonemes, not restricted by a language dependent dictionary. A sequence of phonemes may have an optional beginning and ending silence and contain short pauses. The grammar of our utterance model allows exactly one utterance with an optional beginning or ending silence.
During the training phase, utterances from the user are detected by a voice activity detection based on energy and periodicity of the perceived audio signal.

4.2.2 Prosody

We also employ HMMs for recognizing the prosody of speech utterances. The HMMs for interpreting prosody are based on features extracted from the speech signal. First, the signal is divided into frames of 32 ms length with 16 ms overlap. For every frame, the system calculates the pitch, using the YIN Algorithm (Cheveigne & Kawahara, 2002), the overall log energy as well as the frequency spectrum.

Based on this data, a feature vector is calculated consisting of the pitch, the pitch difference to the previous frame, the energy, the energy difference to the previous frame and the energy in frequency bands 1..n. The sequence of feature vectors is written to a file in HTK format to be used for training the HMMs.

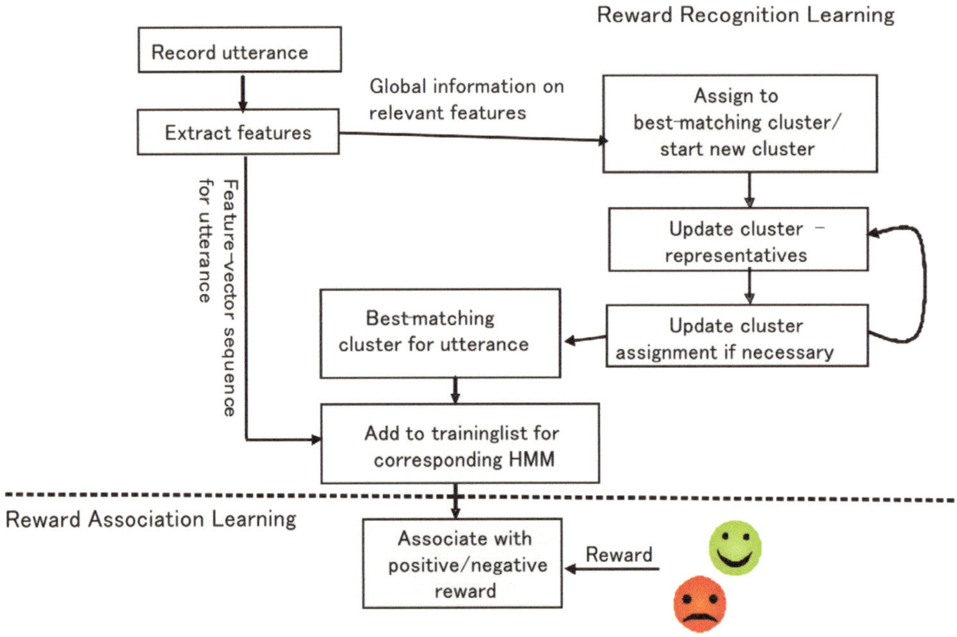

Fig. 6. Algorithm for Learning Prosody.

Additionally, the algorithm calculates some global information based on all frames belonging to one utterance. These are the average, minimum and maximum pitch and energy, the range and standard deviation of pitch and energy as well as the average difference between two adjacent frames of pitch as well as energy. For determining, which HMM is trained with which utterances, the system relies on these global features which have proven to be effective for speech emotion and affect recognition (Breazeal, 2002) (Kim & Scassellati, 2007). A variation of the k-means algorithm which optimizes the number of clusters k between two and ten is used for clustering utterances with similar global features. One HMM is trained for each cluster.

To associate the HMMs with approval or disapproval, every utterance is recognized using the trained HMMs to get the best matching model. This model is then passed to the feedback association learning stage. Figure 6 shows an overview of our prosody recognition.

4.2.3 Touch

We decided not to use HMMs to model touch but a simple duration based model because the output of the touch sensors of the AIBO robot does not suffice for HMM-based modeling. It is binary and does not contain any information on the force applied when touching the sensors. Moreover, the refresh rate when using the AIBO remote framework is quite low.

Therefore, we classified touches of the head sensor and of the back sensor depending on their duration:

- short: less than 0.5 seconds
- medium: between 0.5 seconds and 1 second
- long: one second or longer

Typically, short touches were observed when the user was hitting the robot, while medium and long touches corresponded to caressing or stroking the robot. However, many participants in our user study employed touch only for expressing approval.

4.3 Feedback association learning

In the feedback association learning phase, an association between the HMM or touch pattern model obtained from the feedback recognition learning and either approval or disapproval is created or reinforced. The information of whether the model should be associated with approval or with disapproval is obtained from the current state of the task. If the last move of the robot was a good one, the model, which represents the perceived user feedback, is associated with approval. If the last move was a bad one, it is associated with disapproval.

4.3.1 The Rescorla-Wagner-Model

There are several mathematical theories, trying to model classical conditioning as well as the various effects that can be observed when training real animals using the conditioning principle. The models describe how associations between unconditioned stimuli and conditioned stimuli are learned. In this study, the Rescorla-Wagner model (Rescorla & Wagner, 1972) is used. It was developed in 1972 and most of the more sophisticated newer theories are based on it. In the Rescorla-Wagner model, the change of associative strength of the conditioned stimulus A to the unconditioned stimulus *US(n)* present in trial n, $\Delta V_A(n)$, is calculated as in (1).

$$\Delta V_A(n) = \alpha_A \beta_{US(n)} (\lambda_{US(n)} - V_{all(n)}) \tag{1}$$

α_A and $\beta_{US(n)}$ are the learning rates dependent on the conditioned stimulus A and the unconditioned stimulus US(n) respectively, λUS(n) is the maximum possible associative strength of the currently processed CS to the US(n).

It is a positive value if the CS is present when the US occurs, so that the association between US and CS can be learned. It is zero if the US occurs without the CS. In that case, $\Delta V_A(n)$ becomes negative. Thus, the associative strength between the US and the CS decreases. $V_{all(n)}$ is the combined associative strength of all conditioned stimuli towards the currently processed unconditioned stimulus. The equation is updated on each occurrence of the unconditioned stimulus for all conditioned stimuli that are associated with it.

In this study, the learning rates for conditioned and unconditioned stimuli are fixed values for each modality but can be optimized freely. They determine how quickly the algorithm converges and how quickly the robot adapts to a change in feedback behavior. The maximum associative strength is set to one, in case the corresponding CS is present, when the US occurs, zero otherwise. The combined associative strength of all conditioned stimuli towards the unconditioned stimulus can be calculated easily by summarizing the association values of all the CS towards the US, that have been calculated in the previous runs of the feedback recognition learning.

The major drawback of the Rescorla-Wagner-Model is that it is not able to model the effects of second-order-conditioning and sensory preconditioning directly. We dealt with this issue by running a second pass of the Rescorla-Wagner-algorithm to learn associations between simultaneously occurring CS. In this second pass, the CS1 serves as the US for the conditioning of CS2. In a third pass of the algorithm, we update the relation between the US and all CS2, that have an association to the actually occurred CS1, using a new learning rate $\alpha_{A\ second}$, which is calculated as the product of the original learning rate α_A and the associative strength between the CS1 and the corresponding CS2

4.4 Integration of top-down-processes

Without top-down processes, all HMMs are equally likely to be selected for retraining in the feedback recognition learning phase. The selection of the best-matching model depends only on the perceived signal while the context is not taken into account.

In order to improve the selection of the best-matching speech and prosody models for retraining, we integrated an implementation of top-down processes, which are also present in human audio-visual perception. (Eysenck & Keane, 2005) It uses the associations, learned in the feedback association learning phase to generate expectations about which stimuli, modeled by HMMs, are most likely to occur in a given context.

Knowing through the state of the training task, whether a positive or negative feedback is expected from the user in a given situation, the system uses the learned association matrix to assign a positive or negative bias to each of the existing HMMs. We calculate the bias B_A for an HMM A from the difference of the associative strength V_A of the HMM A towards the expected feedback and the associative strength of it towards the opposite feedback. In case of positive feedback, the factor would be calculated as in (2):

$$B_A = a\, V_{A,positive} - b\, V_{A,\ negative} \tag{2}$$

The constants a and b, which can have values between 0 and 1, determine the impact of the excitatory and inhibitory influences on the calculated bias. A high value a makes the system reuse known HMMs, which are already associated to the present stimulus. A high value b makes the system avoid HMMs, which are already associated to a different stimulus. We found that moderate values for a and high values for b produce best results. In our experiment, we used the values $a=0.2$ and $b=0.8$. The bias B_A is used, if the feedback recognition learning determines that there is more than one HMM that models the stimulus well enough to be a candidate for retraining. In this case, the biases modify the confidence factors returned by the Viterbi algorithm. The biases B_A and the normalized confidence factors C_A are weighted as shown in (3) to select the best HMM for retraining.

$$D_A = c\, B_A - (1\text{-}c)\, C_A, \tag{3}$$

Using this method, HMMs, which are already associated with either positive or negative feedback, become more likely to be selected when a similar feedback is expected. Depending on the constant *c* associations of one HMM with positive and negative reward at the same time, are more or less likely. A value of $c=0.8$ has turned out to increase the quality of the HMM selection, while still allowing HMMs for ambiguous utterances to be associated with both, positive and negative reward.

5. Experimental evaluation

We experimentally evaluated the training method and training tasks as well as the learning algorithm. Ten persons participated in the study. All of them were Japanese graduate students or employees at the National Institute of Informatics in Tokyo. Five of them were females, five males. The age of the participants ranged from 23 to 47. All participants have experience in using computers. Two of them have previous experience in interacting with entertainment robots. Interaction with the robot was done in Japanese. During the experiments, we recorded roughly 5.5 hours of audio and video data.

5.1 Instruction and experimental setting

The participants were instructed to teach the robot in the different training tasks described in section 3. They received explanations of the rules of the game-tasks including whether or not they were expected to give instruction or only feedback. We asked them to use speech, gesture and touch freely in their preferred way and showed them the location of the touch sensors of the AIBO robot, as well as the stereo cameras and the microphone. The experimental setting is shown in Figure 7 and screenshots of the video taken during the experiments is shown in Figure 8.

Fig. 7. Overview of the Experimental Setting.

5.2 Results

We evaluated the performance of the learning algorithm offline with the data recorded within the above described experimental setting. The system was trained and evaluated in a user-dependent way using 10-fold cross evaluation. The average accuracy of our system for classifying between approving and disapproving feedback given by one user based on speech, prosody and touch was 95.97%. The standard deviation between users was 3.30%. As the feedbacks given by the participants showed a slight bias toward approval, the confusion matrix, shown in Table 1 gives a more detailed overview over the performance of our recognizer.

	Positive(actual)	Negative (actual)
Positive (recognized)	52.50%	1.76%
Negative (recognized)	2.27%	43.47%

Table 1. Confusion Matrix

Using speech only we reached a recognition rate of 83.53% with a standard deviation of 8.30%. Using prosody only, the recognition rate was 84.27% with a standard deviation of 8.57%. For touch the recognition rate was 88.17% with a rather high standard deviation of 11.77% as the usage and frequency of touch varied strongly between users. All single-modality recognition rates are considerably lower than the recognition rate for combined feedbacks shown above. This result underlines that combining stimuli given through different modalities is crucial for a reliable recognition.

Without the integration of top-down processes for speech, the recognition rate for speech as a single modality drops to 77.42% with a standard deviation of 13.12%. This degrades the overall recognition rate to 93.95% with a standard deviation of 5.33% if top-down processes are not used.

5.3 Questionnaire based evaluation

In a questionnaire, we asked the participants to evaluate their experience throughout the four different training tasks. The participants could rate their agreement with the statements, shown in table 1, on a scale from 1 to 5, where 1 was the best and 5 the lowest rating.

In the Dog Training task, the robot was remote controlled to react to the user's commands and feedback in a typical Wizard of OZ-Scenario. However, in the Same Image task, the user's instructions and feedback were not actually understood by the robot but anticipated from the state of the training task. This did not have a negative impact on the participants' impression that the robot understood their feedback, learned through it and adapted to their way of teaching, compared to the Wizard of Oz scenario.

The lowest ratings were given for the "Connect Four" task. As the robot's moves could not be evaluated as easily, as in the other tasks, the participants were unsure, which rewards to give and therefore did not experience an effective teaching situation.

5.4 Feedback given by the participants

We analyzed the feedback, given by the participants to find typical similarities and differences in the interaction with AIBO between different users. As for the modalities used for giving reward, we found a strong preference for speech-based reward. Among 2409

	Picture Matching	Pairs	Connect Four	Dog Training
Teaching the robot through the given task was enjoyable	1.81 1.04	1.90 0.83	1.81 0.89	1.63 0.81
The robot understood my feedback	1.27 0.4	1.81 0.74	2.90 0.85	1.81 0.30
The robot learned through my feedback	1.36 0.59	2.81 0.93	3.45 0.95	1.54 0.69
The robot adapted to my way of teaching	1.45 0.66	2.63 1.05	3.45 1.04	1.64 0.58
I was able to teach the robot in a natural way	2.18 0.96	2.09 0.86	2.54 1.12	1.64 0.69
I always knew, which instruction or reward to give to the robot	2.00 0.72	2.09 0.86	2.90 1.02	1.91 0.83

Table 1. (First value: average, second value: standard deviation)

stimuli used for giving reward, 1888 (78.37%) were given by speech, 504 (20.92%) were given by touching the robot and 17 (0.71%) were given by gestures. For the different users, the percentage of speech-based rewards ranged from 52.25% to 97.75%. Gestures were frequently employed by the participants for giving instructions, but we almost did not observe gestures being used for giving positive or negative reward.

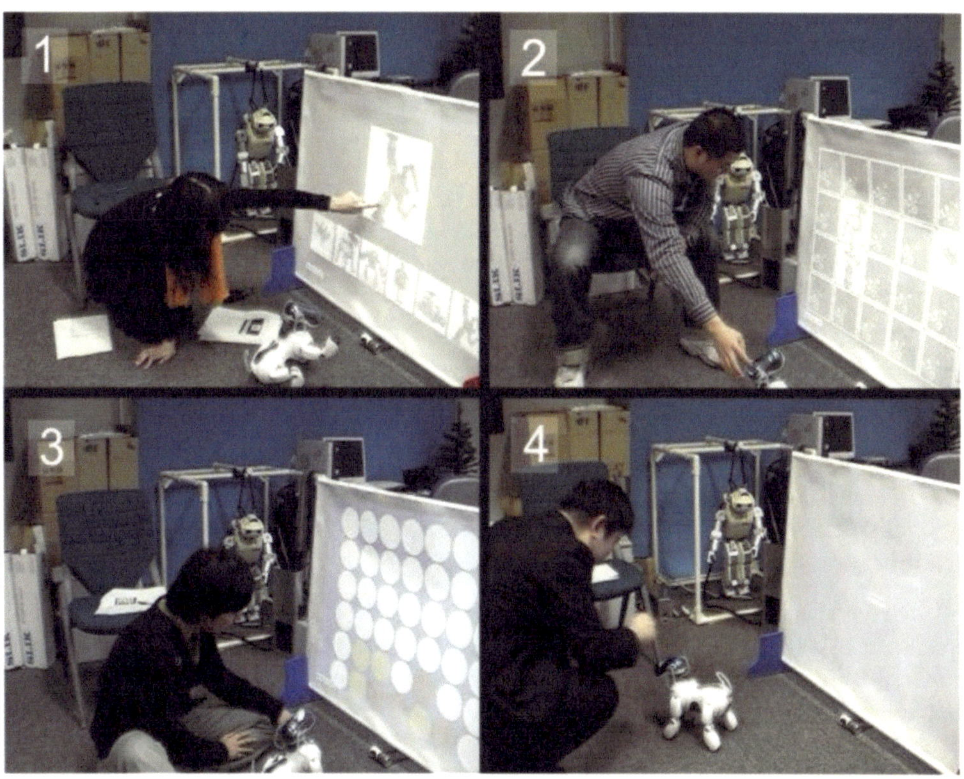

Fig. 8. Experiment scenes: 1: Picture Matching, 2: Pairs, 3: Connect Four, 4: Dog Training

Typically, multiple rewards were given for a single positive or negative behavior of the robot. Counting only the rewards given while n the robot signaled that it was waiting for feedback after an action, 3.43 rewards were given for one action on average, usually including one touch reward and one to four utterances. One utterance was counted as one reward. Repetitions of an utterance were counted as multiple rewards. In case of touch, one or multiple contacts with the robot's touch sensors were counted as one reward, as long as the participant kept his/her hand close to the sensor.
The favorite verbal feedback differed between the users especially in case of positive reward. None of the utterances, used for positive feedback, appeared within the first six most frequently used utterances for all ten participants. On average, each person shared his/her overall most frequently used positive feedback with one other person. In case of negative reward, the feedback, given by the participants was more homogenous. The most frequently used feedback - "wrong" (chigau) - was shared by eight out of ten persons. For the two remaining persons, it was the second and third most frequently used feedback utterance.
As for the variability of the feedback, given to the robot by an individual user: On average, participants used 12.3 different verbal expressions to convey positive feedback and 13.4 different expressions to express negative feedback. However, this number varies strongly between individuals: One person always used the same utterance for giving positive feedback and a second utterance for giving negative feedback while the person with the most variable feedback used 30 different expressions for giving positive and 28 different expressions for giving negative feedback. 55.61% of all verbal feedback was given by the participants using their preferred feedback utterance. 88.73% of a user's verbal feedback was given using one of his/her six most frequently used positive/negative utterances, so understanding a relatively small number of different utterances suffices to cover most of a participant's verbal feedback.
For positive feedback, four out of ten participants had one preferred utterance which did not vary between the four training tasks. In case of negative reward, this was true for five people. For eight out of ten participants in case of positive reward and six participants in case of negative reward, their overall most frequently used feedback utterance was among the top three feedback utterances in each individual task. In the cases, where the preferred feedback was not the same in all tasks, it typically differed for the "Connect Four" task, while in the three other tasks, including the "Dog Training" control task similar feedback was used as described above. As in the "Connect Four" task it was difficult for the users to judge, whether a move was good or bad in order to provide immediate reward, feedback tended to be very sparse and tentative like "not really good" (amari yokunai), "Is this good?" (ii kana?) or "good, isn't it" (ii deshou).

6. Discussion and outlook

In this paper, we described and evaluated a method for learning a user's feedback for human-robot-interaction. The performance based on interpreting speech, prosody and touch feedbacks from a human can be considered sufficiently reliable for being used to teach a robot, for example, by reinforcement learning.
One potential drawback of our approach is that the robot has to complete a training phase with every user who wants to interact with it in order to adapt to the user's way of giving rewards. However, a typical pet robot or entertainment robot only interacts with a very

limited number of persons in a household and usually interacts with the same users frequently and for a long time. Therefore, we assume that user-specific adaptation is desirable even though it needs some initial training effort.

Currently the learning algorithm works offline using the data gathered in the training tasks to generate HMM sets and associations. Main issues that need to be targeted for implementing an online version of the algorithm are the clustering of the training samples for prosody as well as the incremental re-training of the HMMs for speech and prosody.

Our method has only been evaluated for learning feedback, so far. However, it can be used without changes for learning object names as well as simple, non-parameterized commands. However, extensions to the current algorithm are necessary if the robot needs to learn commands with parameters, such as "Can you put {the red ball} {in the box}". While gesture was not necessary for recognizing approval or disapproval, gesture recognition will be helpful to understand commands, so integrating gesture as an additional modality is the current priority of our ongoing research.

One important question that remains open after the study is the similarity of user behavior between virtual tasks and real world tasks. Although we did not observe differences in user feedback between the virtual game tasks and the dog training in our experiment this does not necessarily mean that it is generally possible to train a robot for a real world task using a virtual task. This question will be targeted in a follow-up study.

7. References

A. Austermann, S. Yamada (2008). ""Good Robot, Bad Robot" - Analyzing Users' Feedback in a Human-Robot Teaching Task", *Proceedings of the IEEE International Symposium on Robot and Human Interactive Communication (RO-MAN 08)*,pp. 41-46

C. Balkenius and J. Moren (1998). "Computational models of classical conditioning: a comparative study." *Proceedings of the Fifth International Conference on Simulation of Adaptive Behavior*, pp. 348 - 35

C. Balkenius and J. Moren (1999). "Dynamics of a Classical Conditioning Model", *Autonomous Robots 7*, 41-56

B. Burns, C. Sutton, C. Morrison, P. Cohen (2003), "Information Theory and Representation in Associative Word Learning", *Epigenic Robotics (EpiRob 2003)*

C. Breazeal (2002). "Recognition of Affective Communicative Intent in Robot-Directed Speech" *Autonomous Robots* Volume 12 , Issue 1, 83 - 104

A. de Cheveigne and H. Kawahara (2002): "YIN, a fundamental frequency estimator for speech and music", *The Journal of the Acoustical Society of America*, Vol. 4, pp. 1917 - 1930

M. W. Eysenck, M. T. Keane (2005). "Cognitive Psychology - A Student's Handbook", Psychology Press

N. Iwahashi (2004). "Active and Unsupervised Learning for Spoken Word Acquisition Through a Multimodal Interface", RO-MAN 2004, *13th IEEE international workshop on robot and human interactive communication*, pp. 437 - 442

E. S. Kim, B. Scassellati (2007). "Learning to Refine Behavior Using Prosodic Feedback", *Proceedings of the 6th IEEE International Conference on Development and Learning (ICDL 2007)*, pp. 205-210

Z. K. Kayikci, H. Markert, G. Palm (2007): "Neural Associative Memories and Hidden Markov Models for Speech Recognition", *IJCNN 2007 Conference Proceedings*, pp. 1572 - 1577,

B. Lowenkron (2000). "Word meaning: A verbal behavior account", Presented at the annual convention of the Association for Behavior Analysis, Washington DC, May

I. P. Pavlov (1927). "Conditioned Reflexes: An Investigation of the Physiological Activity of the Cerebral Cortex" (translated by G. V. Anrep), Oxford University Press

R. Rescorla, A. Wagner (1972). "A theory of Pavlovian conditioning: Variations in the effectiveness of reinforcement and nonreinforcement.", *Classical Conditioning II: Current Research and Theory* (Eds Black AH, Prokasy WF) New York: Appleton Century Crofts, pp. 64-99

B. F. Skinner (1957). "Verbal Behavior". Copley Publishing Group, Acton

A. L. Thomaz, and C. Breazeal (2006): "Reinforcement Learning with Human Teachers: Evidence of feedback and guidance with implications for learning performance" *Proceedings of the 21st National Conference on Artificial Intelligence (AAAI 2006)*

J. F. Werker, H. Henny, Yeung (2005). "Infant Speech Perception Bootstraps Word Learning", *Trends in Cognitive Sciences*, Vol. 9, No. 11, pp. 519-527

S. Young et al., (2006) "The HTK Book", HTK Version 3, http://htk.eng.cam.ac.uk/

19

Anticipative Generation and *In-Situ* Adaptation of Maneuvering Affordance in a Naturally Complex Scene

Kohji Kamejima
Osaka Institute of Technology, Japan

1. Introduction

Computational resources combined with advanced mechanical systems rapidly expand the scope of 'informatic vicinity' (Kamejima, 2006) in which machine perception is delegated and networked to support human's situation understanding and decision making. For instance, student knowledge can be expanded by space craft operated interactively from the classroom (Coppin et al., 2000). Final decisions on social safety in large scale natural disasters are determined mainly based upon information gathering and damage evaluation through network systems (Hamada & Fujie, 2001). Recent computer controlled vehicles, in particular, are developing the capability of understanding the situation for supporting human's inherent maneuverability (Özgner & Stiller, 2007).

By expanding the scope of perception to satellite-roadway-vehicle network (Kamejima, 2008), we have an implementation of the informatic vicinity as shown in Fig.1. The latest Earth observation systems can provide a bird's eye view for vehicles to identify themselves as consistent parts of the real world; current vision systems can analyze complex images captured at scene A to control a vehicle mechanism along the roadway specified in one frame of a specific satellite image (Urmson et al., 2009); and by using Global Positioning System (GPS), the vehicle can be localized within a small area in the satellite image in which the roadway pattern at scene A can be matched exactly and extended towards a possible goal, e.g. Scene B, *prior to* physical access (Kamejima, 2007). Therefore, the informatic vicinity can be exploited as a technological basis for the anticipative road following scheme. In addition, through the informatic vicinity, vehicles can mutually provide critical information for analyzing not-yet-accessible scenes, for example, precautionary safety information to human drivers and make effective predictions for machine vision as well.

As a consequence of evolution in the real world filled by uproarious illumination and reflection (Parker, 2003), the range of human's perception is restricted to the physical-geometric perspective from a specific point of view. To facilitate human's inherent perception in complex situations, the view from the vehicle should be located and oriented anticipatively in the informatic vicinity covering all possible transitions from the current scene. Such a cooperative system is expected to act as a substitute for essential parts of humans cognitive ability (Kamejima, 2008). As for playing an essential role in cooperative systems, however, the perceptive delegation is required to maintain on-going conformability

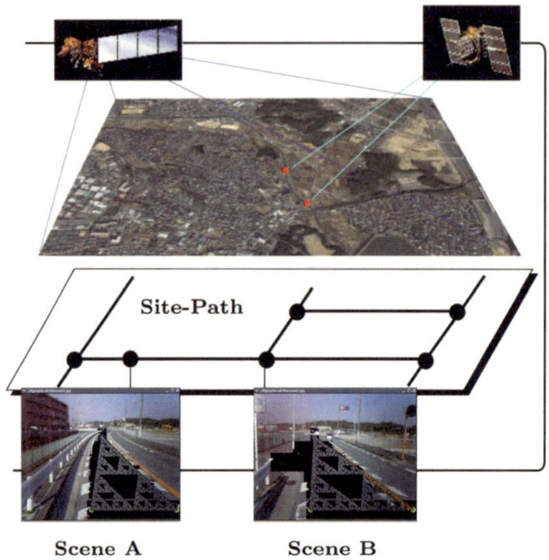

Fig. 1. Anticipative Decision Making in Informatic Vicinity

with human capacity under the schematics of serious contradiction. In other words, subsequent maneuvering processes are anticipatively activated towards scenes beyond the horizon of human's perception.

2. Existence of perceptual invariance

In a naturally complex scene, we are surrounded by optical flux modulating complete information that can afford to induce spontaneous maneuvering processes *preestablishingly*. For anticipative decision making, such *affordance* should be captured and transferred beyond the horizon of perception via a reconfiguration process; the *a priori* orientation of the roadway specified in the bird's eye view should be mapped to the scene image via *a posteriori* adaptation of maneuvering processes. To this end, we introduce a fractal based representation of a roadway pattern in a naturally complex scene.

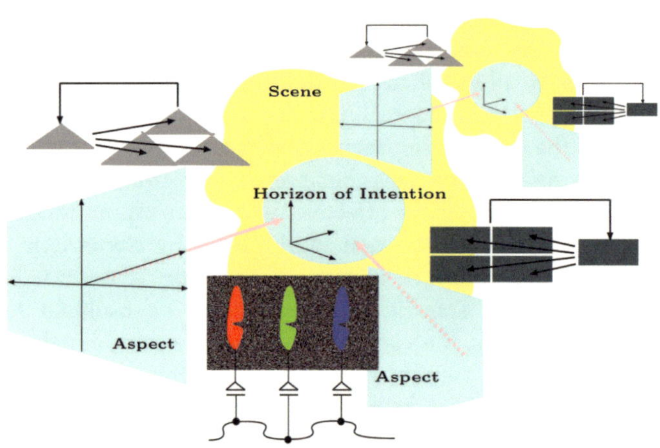

Fig. 2. Multi-Aspect Approach to Complex Scene

Following the collage theorem within the context of multi-fractal modeling (Barnsley, 2006), the expansion of the open space can be associated with the same class of self-similar patterns in multi-viewpoint imagery as illustrated in Fig.2. An approximation of roadway segment can be generated in satellite imagery as a 'carpet' (right aspect); this segment is mapped from the satellite image to associated scene images to yield a skewed 'gasket' (left aspect); through the multi-aspect access to a roadway, the perception process induces anticipative information into a part of the scene called the horizon of intension. This implies that fractal representation of a roadway pattern is transferable through the informatic vicinity as a common basis for mutual mediation of perceptive delegates. In what follows, the fractal coding scheme is introduced on an ineluctable information: noisy pattern covering really existing objects. By combining the randomness, we have robust fractal code for anticipative generation and *in-situ* adaptation of the maneuvering affordance.

3. Randomness-based approach

Suppose that the roadway is segmented in the bird's eye view in terms of a sequence of vectors $\{ \mathfrak{v} \}$ to be 'downloaded' in a scene image. With this anticipative segmentation, we can induce an aspect to be associated with the horizon of intention as shown in Fig.3 where the scope of perception is structured in the scene image in a stochastic sense; the belief on the open space is supported by a probability distribution φ_ρ confined by the estimate of the boundary $(\varphi_\rho^+, \varphi_\rho^-)$; within the horizon of control, the maneuvering process is guided to follow the boundaries under human's spontaneous decision making; and, generated path $\mathfrak{X}_-^+$ is extended towards the scope of perception as a stochastic process susceptive to not-yet-encountered uncertainties. Assume that the image of segment $\mathfrak{v}$ is transferred via inter-viewpoint association and consider anticipative decision making problems in the information structure: how to project $\mathfrak{v}$ in the observed scene; how to evaluate the depth and width of the open space; and, how to adapt the maneuvering process anticipatively to the open space.

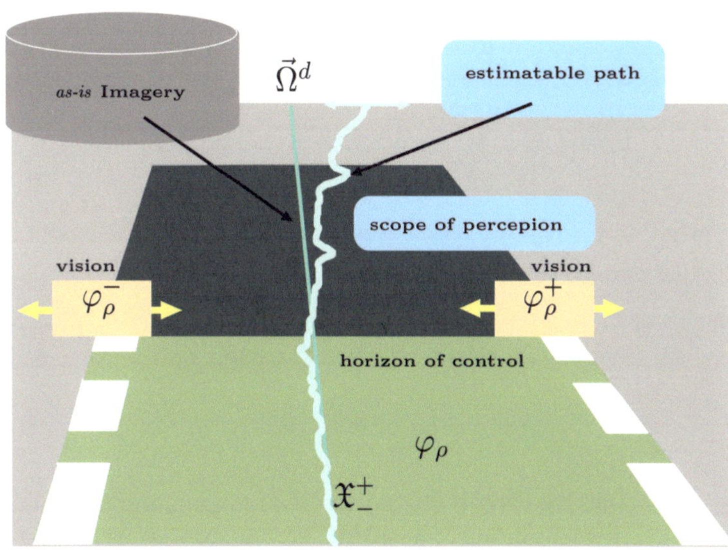

Fig. 3. Information Structure for Anticipative Decision

Let $\vec{\Omega}^d$ be the projection of the vector $\mathfrak{v}$ into the image plane $\Omega = X \times Y$. From the viewpoint of ecological optics, *a priori* basis for spontaneous mobility is provided by random texture mapped onto an image plane Ω. Let $f(\omega)$ be the brightness at the pixel $\omega \in \Omega$ and suppose that views of the objects to be detected are uniquely represented as subsets of Ω and identified within $\mathcal{F}$: the Borel field generated by the subsets of Ω. In the totality of object images, then, we can introduce basic probability space $(\Omega, \mathcal{F}, P)$ where $P(\omega)$ is a uniform probability measure assigned to pixels ω without any *a priori* knowledge. By definition, $P(\omega)$ indexes *a priori* probability for the pixel ω to be a part of an object.

The *a priori* information is transferred to the observation $f(\omega)$ via complex physical, mathematical and cognitive processes. As for the physical complexity, we can utilize various results on geometric-chromatic investigations on optical information transmission. On the other hand, the mathematical complexity for assigning the pixel $\omega \in \Omega$ to a specific part of target object yields combinatorial explosion. However, without serious loss of generality, the combination of the existence theorem (Hutchinson, 1981) with 'collage' theorem (Barnsley et al., 1986) resolves the computational difficulty into the following non-deterministic representation:

$$\Xi = \bigcup_{\mu_i \in \nu} \mu_i(\Xi), \tag{1}$$

where Ξ is a fractal version of the object image; ν denotes a fixed set of contraction mapping of size $||\nu||$:

$$\nu = \{\mu_1, \mu_2, \ldots, \mu_{||\nu||}\}, \qquad \mu_i : \Omega \mapsto \Omega.$$

In this representation, an attractor point $\xi \in \Xi$ can be mapped finally to the entire pattern Ξ through a finite sequence of possible selection $\mu_i \in \nu$. By substituting the iteration of random selection μ_i in a fixed set ν for pattern association (1), we can identify constrained aggregation Ξ with a trajectory of 2D stochastic processes driven by ν. Due to the 'whiteness' in random selection $\mu_i \in \nu$, the expansion of the attractor Ξ of geometric singularity can be visualized as a distribution $\chi_\Xi^{\mathfrak{p}}$ satisfying the following self-similarity

$$\chi_\Xi^{\mathfrak{p}}(\cdot) = \sum_{\mu_i \in \nu} p_{\mu_i} \chi_\Xi^{\mathfrak{p}}[\mu_i^{-1}(\cdot)], \qquad (\cdot) \in \mathcal{F}, \tag{2}$$

with 'coloring probability' $\{p_{\mu_i}\}$ for selecting μ_i in fixed set ν. The existence of the invariant measure implies the possibility for image based association $f \sim \chi_\Xi^{\mathfrak{p}}$.

Being given the invariant measure (2), we can evaluate the probability $\varphi(\omega|\nu)$ for capturing unknown fractal attractor Ξ as the solution to the following equation (Kamejima, 2001):

$$\frac{1}{2}\Delta\varphi(\omega|\nu) + \rho[\chi_\Xi^{\mathfrak{p}} - \varphi(\omega|\nu)] = 0, \tag{3}$$

where $\rho = \log_2 ||\nu||$ denotes the complexity index of the imaging process (1) with (2). By this implicit dependence, the capturing probability $\varphi(\omega|\nu)$ can be generated *prior to* the specification of the mappings $\mu_i \in \nu$.

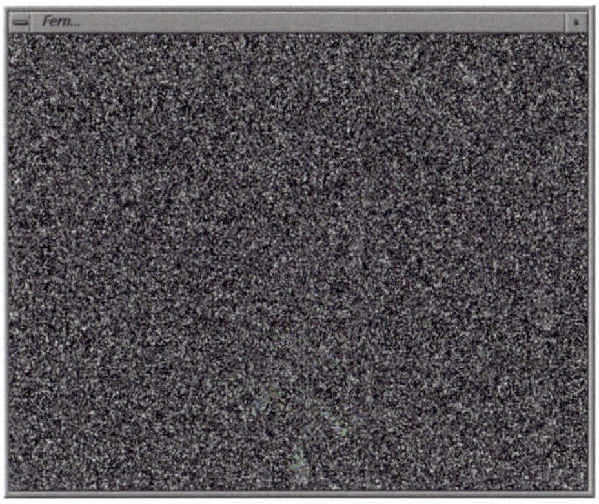

(a) Noisy Observation of $\chi_{\Xi}^{\mathbf{p}}$

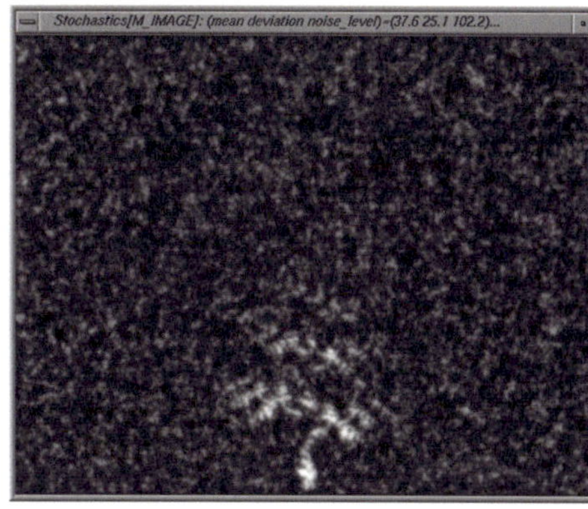

(b) Capturing Probability $\varphi(\omega|\nu)$

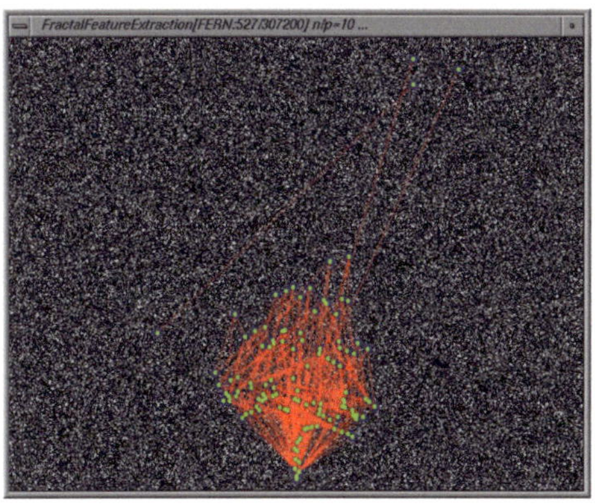

(c) Invariant Feature Θ

(d) Fractal Attractor Regenerated by Θ

Fig. 4. Detection of Fractal Model in Noisy Background

Define the stochastic feature $\tilde{\Theta}$ of fractal attractor Ξ as the totality of local maxima of the capturing probability $\varphi(\omega|\nu)$, i.e.,

$$\tilde{\Theta} = \left\{ \tilde{\theta} \in \Omega \mid \nabla\varphi(\tilde{\theta}|\nu) = 0, \det\left[\nabla\nabla^T\varphi(\tilde{\theta}|\nu)\right] > 0, \Delta\varphi(\tilde{\theta}|\nu) < 0 \right\}. \tag{4}$$

On this discrete set, we can verify the consistency of the mapping set ν through the following computational test:

$$\Theta = \left\{ \theta \in \tilde{\Theta} \mid \exists \mu_i \in \nu : \quad \mu_i^{-1}(\theta) \in \Theta \right\}. \tag{5}$$

By definition, the following random process

$$\xi_{t+1} = \mu_i(\xi_t), \qquad \xi_0 = \theta, \tag{6}$$

expands a point $\theta \in \Theta$ towards the fractal attractor Ξ successively. Therefore, the connectedness of the point set $\tilde{\Theta}$ can be indexed in terms of the distribution of the invariant subset Θ within $\tilde{\Theta}$. This provides a computational basis for the detection and connectedness analysis of the fractal model ν. Figures 4 and 5 demonstrate the detectability of fractal models. In these figures, noisy observations of fractal attractors (a) are identified with the measure $\chi_{\Xi}^{\mathbf{p}}$ to generate the capturing probability $\varphi(\omega|\nu)$ visualized as (b); from the stochastic feature $\tilde{\Theta}$ detected via local analysis of smooth distribution $\varphi(\omega|\nu)$, the invariant feature Θ is extracted as closed links (c); the existence of the invariant feature Θ activates the 2D random process (6) to visualize connected spaces (d). Therefore, we can restore known fractal models corrupted in noisy observation.

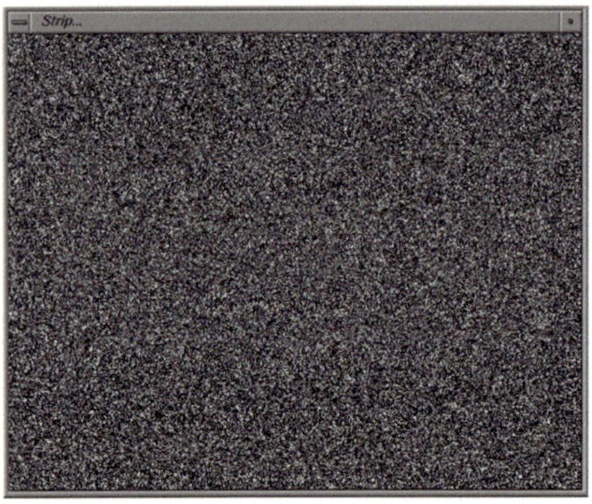

(a) Noisy Observation of $\chi_{\Xi}^{\mathbf{p}}$

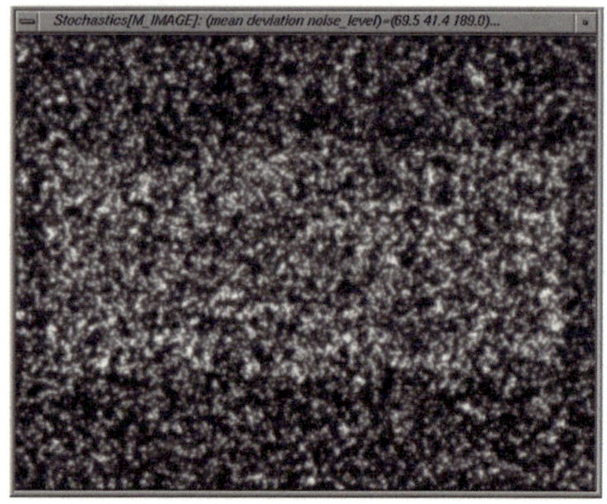

(b) Capturing Probability $\varphi(\omega|\nu)$

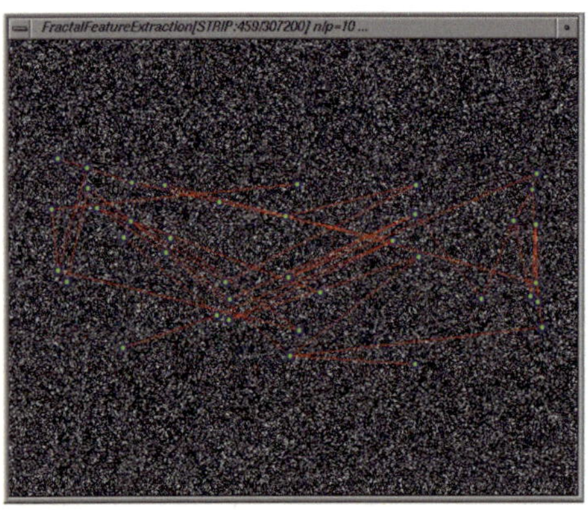

(c) Invariant Feature Θ

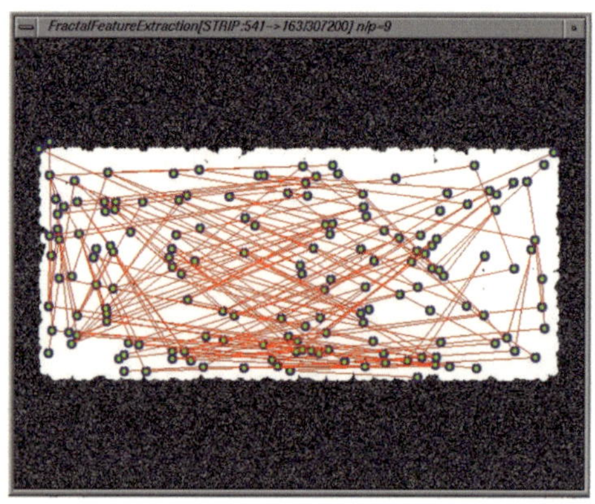

(d) Fractal Attractor Regenerated by Θ

Fig. 5. Detection of a Fractal Model in Noisy Background

Considering the generic rule for associating the not-yet-identified invariant set $\chi_{\Xi}^{\mathbf{p}}$ with observed distribution $f(\omega)$, let a scene indicated in Fig.6 be observed by a viewer with the intentional coordinate system illustrated in Fig.7. By applying a 2D Laplacian filter to the scene, we can extract the noise component which can be utilized as a robust feature of the roadway image. Through the perspective projection, the power spectrum evaluated at the baseline of Δf-image (Fig.8) is expanded in accordance with the line shift towards the vanishing point as shown in Fig.9. Therefore, we can generate a generic representation of an open space in terms of scale information supported by the micro-structure of a roadway area.

Following a multi-scale approach (Jones & Taylor, 1994), the brightness distribution $f(\omega)$ can be decomposed into a function space consisting of class $\mathfrak{F} = \{ f_\sigma, \sigma > 0 \}$ given by

Fig. 6. Shopping Street

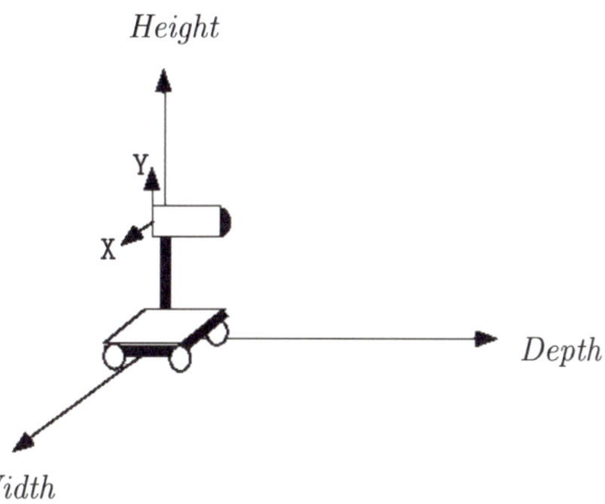

Fig. 7. Intentional Coordinate System

$$f_\sigma(\omega) \sim g_\sigma * \chi_\Xi^{\mathfrak{p}}(\omega) + b(\omega), \tag{7}$$

where g_σ is 2D Gaussian distribution with variance parameter σ; b stands for the aggregation of low frequency components such as $|\Delta b| \ll |\Delta g_\sigma|$. By identifying the measure with an aggregation of 'point images', we can extract component images with specific scales as shown in Fig.10, where a set of Δg_σ-filter with 2D transfer function (see Fig.11) is applied to the point image concentrated at the origin. Noticing the similarity of Δg_σ and g_σ filters near the origin, we have the following local estimates for the scale information $\hat{\sigma}$ at ω (Kamejima, 2005):

$$\hat{\sigma}(\omega) \sim 2\sqrt{|f(\omega)|/|\Delta f(\omega)|}. \tag{8}$$

Let σ_0 be the maximal scale associated with the noise component and define d as the depth parameter indexed along the 'direction of intention' $\vec{\Omega}^d$: the perspective projection of the orientation vector $\mathfrak{v}$ on the scene image. Here we have the following representation of the 'generic' roadway model $\mathfrak{M}(\vec{\Omega}^d, \chi_\Xi^{\mathfrak{p}})$:

$$\bar{\sigma}(d) = \frac{\sigma_0}{d_\infty - d_0}(d_\infty - d), \tag{9a}$$

$$\hat{\chi}_{\Xi}^{\mathfrak{p}} = \frac{1}{\sqrt{2\pi\bar{\sigma}_d^2}} \exp\left[-\frac{|\hat{\sigma}_\omega - \bar{\sigma}_d|^2}{2\bar{\sigma}_d^2}\right]. \tag{9b}$$

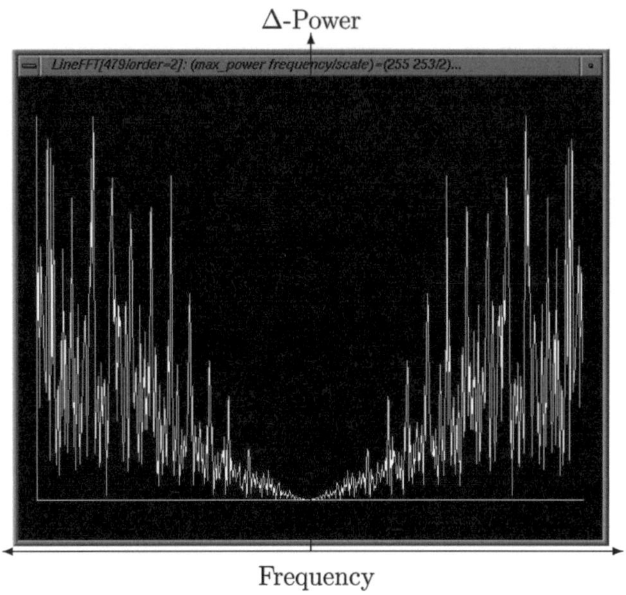

Fig. 8. Power Spectrum of Δf at the Base Line

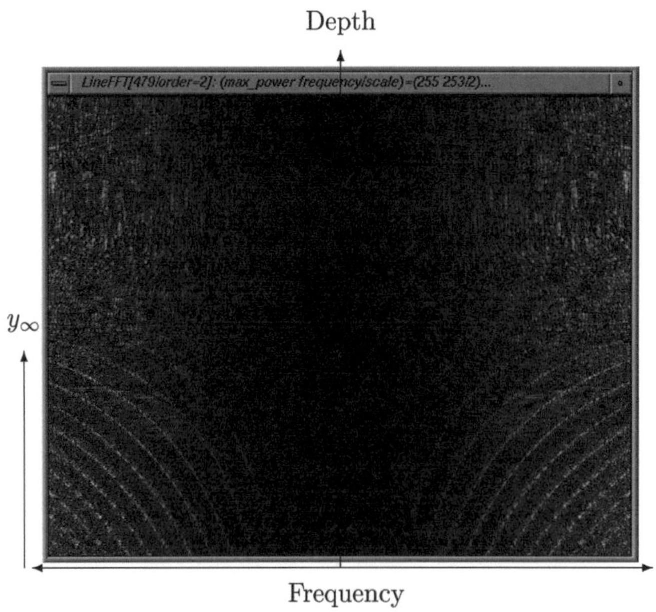

Fig. 9. Directional Fourier Transform of Δf

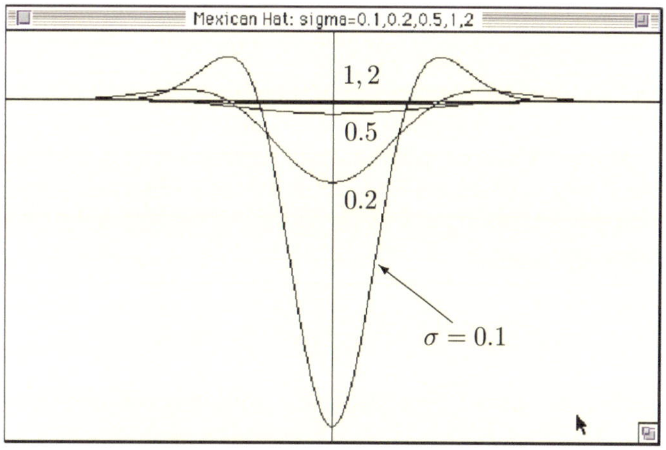

Fig. 10. 2D Δg_σ Filtering of a Point Image

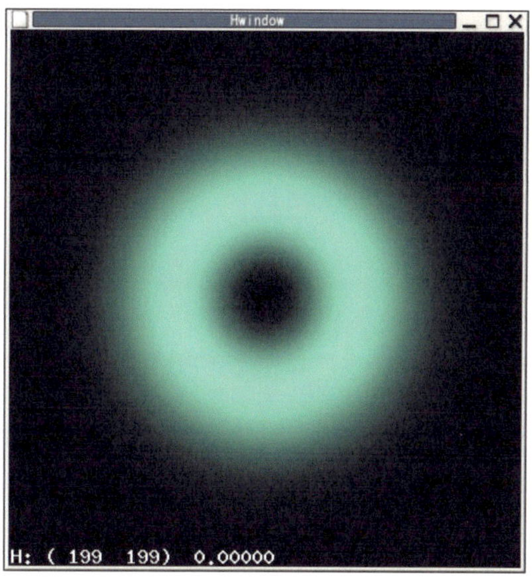

Fig. 11. 2D Power Spectrum of Δg_σ Filter

In (9a), the expansion of the roadway is identified with a pattern $\Xi \in \mathcal{F}$ in which scale information $\hat{\sigma}_\omega$ is regulated by the linear diminishing rule from the bottom of the maneuvering affordance d_0 to the vanishing point d_∞. Hence, we can conclude that the scope of perception is confined in a probabilistic sense (9b) where the estimated distribution $\hat{\chi}^{\mathrm{p}}_{\Xi}$ can be utilized as a 'noisy' observation of the self-similarity (1).

4. Fractal coding of perceptual invariance

Via the self-similarity process (1), an attractor point ξ is allocated to satisfy the following constraint with respect to the not-yet-identified contraction mapping $\mu_i \in \nu$:

$$|\mu_i(\xi) - \omega^f_{\mu_i}| \quad \leq \quad |\xi - \omega^f_{\mu_i}|, \tag{10}$$

where $\omega^f_{\mu_i}$ denotes the fixed point of μ_i. By evaluating the attractive force within the framework of the Hausdorff topology (Kamejima, 1999), we can introduce a simultaneous estimation scheme for model parameters (d_∞, $\vec{\Omega}^d$) with non-unique estimates of fixed points $\Omega^f_{\mu_j}$ associated with not-yet-identified contraction mapping μ_j. To apply the articulation scheme (10) with non-deterministic kinetics, first, a pixel $\omega \in \Omega$ is associated with not-yet-identified attractor Ξ in a stochastic sense. Once we have observed the invariant measure $\hat{\chi}^{\mathfrak{p}}_{\Xi}$, we can evaluate the probability $\varphi(\omega|\nu)$ for capturing unknown fractal attractor Ξ as the solution to the following equation:

$$\frac{1}{2}\Delta\varphi(\omega|\nu) + \rho[\hat{\chi}^{\mathfrak{p}}_{\Xi} - \varphi(\omega|\nu)] \quad = \quad 0. \tag{11}$$

Following this, the image plane is partitioned in accordance with the fractal attractor to be detected. Since various types of attractors are simultaneously observed as object images (Barnsley, 2006) in practical imagery, generated information $\varphi(\omega|\nu)$ is expanded to cover noisy patterns as well. To confine the distribution into a target attractor, let the initial guess for the fixed points $\hat{\Omega}^f = \{\hat{\omega}^f_{\mu_i}\}$ be given as a perspective of the segment $\mathfrak{v}$ and consider the articulation $\Omega \to \{\Lambda_i\}$ as illustrated in Fig. 12:

$$\Lambda_i : \left\{ \omega \in \Omega \mid |\omega - \hat{\omega}^f_{\mu_i}| < |\omega - \hat{\omega}^f_{\mu_j}|, \quad \text{for } \hat{\omega}^f_{\mu_j} \neq \hat{\omega}^f_{\mu_i} \right\},$$

with statistical moments $(\bar{\omega}_i, \Sigma_i)$ conditioned by ν:

$$\int_{\Lambda_i} (\omega - \bar{\omega}_i)\varphi(\omega|\nu)dP(\omega) = 0,$$

$$\Sigma_i \quad = \quad C_i \int_{\Lambda_i} (\omega - \bar{\omega}_i)(\omega - \bar{\omega}_i)^T \varphi(\omega|\nu)dP(\omega),$$

where C_i denotes the normalization constant. In this articulation, the expansion of the domains Λ_i is indexed in terms of the following 'Laplacian-Gaussian basin':

$$\Lambda^{\mathfrak{G}}_i \quad = \quad \left\{ \lambda \in \Lambda_i \mid \left(\frac{1}{2}\lambda^T \Sigma_i^{-1} \lambda - 1 \right) < 0 \right\}. \tag{12}$$

In such a basin $\Lambda^{\mathfrak{G}}_i$, we have the following circumscribing polygon within the context of statistical clustering:

$$\left(\vec{\Omega}^f_{ij}\right)^T R(\pi/2) \left(\partial_\omega - \hat{\omega}^f_{\mu_j}\right) \quad = \quad 0, \tag{13a}$$

$$\left(\vec{\Omega}^\partial_j\right)^T R(\pi/2) \left(\partial_\omega - \bar{\omega}_j\right) \quad = \quad 0, \tag{13b}$$

where ∂_ω is the contact point with $\Lambda^{\mathfrak{G}}_i$; $\vec{\Omega}^f_{ij}$ and $\vec{\Omega}^\partial_j$ are unit vectors associating the fixed point $\hat{\omega}^f_{\mu_j}$ with $\hat{\omega}^f_{\mu_i}$ and $\bar{\omega}_j$, respectively; R denotes the rotation matrix. By adjusting ∂_ω to the boundary of the Laplacian-Gaussian basin (12) along the external normal vector $\vec{\Omega}^\perp_{ij}$, we have the following adaptation scheme of the fixed point estimate:

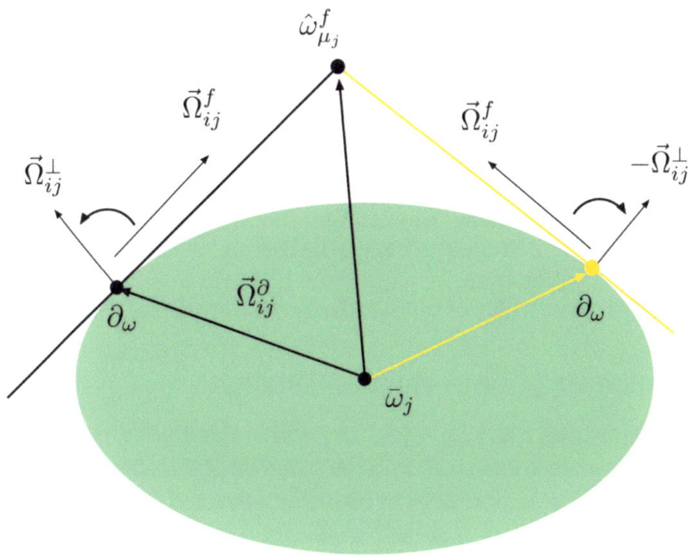

Fig. 12. Laplacian-Gaussian Basin

$$\begin{aligned} d\hat{\omega}^f_{\mu_j} &= -\kappa\phi_j(\hat{\omega}^f_{\mu_j} - \bar{\omega}_j), \\ \phi_j &= \frac{1}{2}(\partial_\omega - \bar{\omega}_j)^T \Sigma_j^{-1}(\partial_\omega - \bar{\omega}_j) - 1. \\ & \partial_\omega - \bar{\omega}_j = -Q_j^{-1} K_{ij} \left(\hat{\omega}^f_{\mu_j} - \bar{\omega}_j\right), \\ & Q_j = \left(\vec{\Omega}^\perp_{ij}\right)^T \Sigma_j \left(\vec{\Omega}^\perp_{ij}\right), \\ & K_{ij} = \Sigma_j \left(\vec{\Omega}^\perp_{ij}\right)\left(\vec{\Omega}^\perp_{ij}\right)^T. \end{aligned} \tag{14}$$

In this scheme, the fixed points $\{\hat{\omega}^f_{\mu_j}\}$ are mutually separated by the expansion of the Laplacian-Gaussian basins (12); on the other hand, the expansion of the fractal attractor to be generated is confined in terms of the contact points $\{\partial_\omega\}$. As a result of this antagonistic dynamics, the update $d\hat{\omega}^f_{\mu_i}$ are coordinated via the integration rule:

$$\sum_j |\phi_j| \quad \rightarrow \quad \min. \tag{15}$$

The statistical clustering is followed by geometric design and computational verification of mapping set $\hat{\nu} = \{\hat{\mu}_i\}$. The self-similarity indicated in Fig.2 combined with the fixed point assignment yields the following description:

$$\hat{\nu} \ni \hat{\mu}_i(\omega): \qquad \mu_i(\omega) = \frac{1}{2}(\omega + \hat{\omega}^f_{\mu_i}), \qquad p_{\mu_i} = \frac{1}{3}. \tag{16}$$

The consistency of fixed point allocation $\hat{\Omega}^f$ should be verified by the self-similarity analysis of the mapping set $\hat{\nu}$ on the fractal attractor to be detected. To this end, we introduce the following computational test on a stochastic representation of the not-yet-identified Ξ (Kamejima, 2001):

Proposition 1 *Let $\hat{\chi}^{\mathfrak{p}}_{\Xi}$ be an invariant measure with respect to the mapping set $\hat{\nu}$. Suppose that $\tilde{\Theta}$ is extracted from the capturing probability $\varphi(\omega|\hat{\nu})$ associated with $\hat{\chi}^{\mathfrak{p}}_{\Xi}$. Then there exists the invariant feature $\Theta \subset \tilde{\Theta}$ satisfying the following constraint*

$$\Theta = \left\{ \theta \in \tilde{\Theta} \mid \exists \hat{\mu}_i \in \hat{\nu} : \hat{\mu}_i^{-1}(\theta) \in \Theta \right\}. \tag{17}$$

The existence of invariant features Θ implies that the range of designed imaging process $\hat{\nu}$ can generate a version of a fractal attractor indicating a connected open space in the roadway area. The combination of equations (9), (11), (12), (14), (17) provides a computational basis for the coding of self-similarity of complex random patterns.

5. *In-situ* adaptation via ground-object separation

By identifying the vanishing point $\omega_\infty = (d_\infty, \vec{\Omega}^d)$ with a fixed point estimate $\hat{\omega}^f_{\mu_j}$ the generic model (9) induces a geometric structure into the scene image as shown in Fig.13. A pixel in a Laplacian-Gaussian basin ω is non-deterministically attracted to one of the fixed points in $\hat{\Omega}^f$ due to the generativity of the self-similarity process. Despite non-deterministic allocation, the structural consistency of the set $\hat{\Omega}^f$ is verified by the existence of the capturing probability $\varphi(\omega|\nu)$ supporting invariant subset Θ. Let $\lceil \xi \rceil$ be the nearest point to the estimate of ω_∞ in the invariant subset Θ. By using the point $\lceil \xi \rceil$, we can specify the horizon of control as well as the depth of the boundary information $(\mathfrak{b}_L, \mathfrak{b}_R)$ to be marked in the scene image. Therefore, the generic model (9) combined with fractal coding yields an estimate of the roadway area *prior to* object identification.
Furthermore, we can design another generic model on the scale space information (8) to detect something perpendicular to the roadway. For this purpose, the mismatch with the generic model (9) is evaluated in terms of the following measure:

$$p(\omega^\uparrow|\omega) = \frac{1}{\sqrt{2\pi\hat{\sigma}^2_\omega}} \exp\left[-\frac{|\hat{\sigma}_{\omega^\uparrow} - \hat{\sigma}_\omega|^2}{2\hat{\sigma}^2_\omega}\right], \tag{18}$$

where ω denotes a pixel selected in the domain confined by the boundary information $(\mathfrak{b}_L, \mathfrak{b}_R)$ and $\lceil \xi \rceil$; $\omega^\uparrow = (\omega_x, \omega_{y+dy})$ is the upward extension of the pixel with the vertical interval dy. This pixel wise evaluation is chained to visualize not-yet-identified objects as follows:

$$\begin{aligned} \chi_{<\omega>} \quad &\sim \quad \prod_{\omega \in <\omega>} p(\omega^\uparrow|\omega) \cdot \varphi(\omega_\downarrow|\nu), \\ <\omega> &= \cdots (\omega_x, \omega_{y+ndy}) \cdots, \end{aligned} \tag{19}$$

where $<\omega>$ denotes the vertical chain of pixels with bottom $\omega_\downarrow$ to be grounded on the maneuvering affordance. The first term of this evaluation indicates the length of the vertical chain; and the second term indexes the probability for the chain to ground somewhere in a plane supporting the roadway area. In equation (19), the probability for the segment $<\omega>$ to be a part of the object is evaluated as the 'breakdown' of the generic model to induce linear scale shift in the scene image.
As shown in equations (9) and (18), roadway area and object images are separated as generic models based on *as-is* information $\hat{\sigma}_\omega$. Noting that the connectedness of the detected roadway area is verified as the existence of a fractal attractor, we can utilize the aggregation

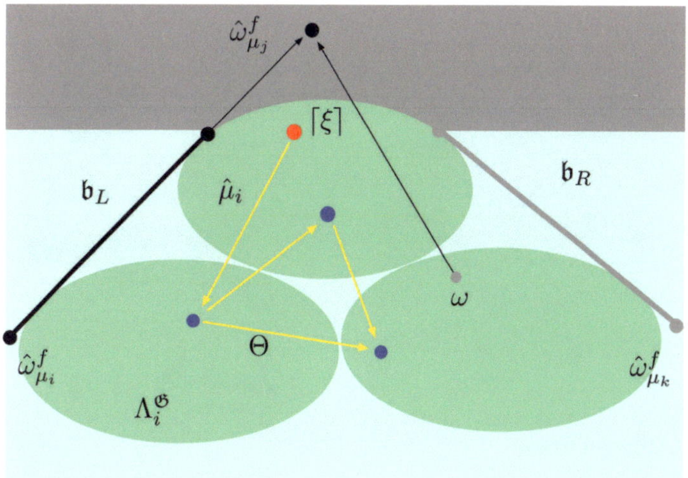

Fig. 13. Fractal Coding of Laplacian-Gaussian Basin

of grounding pixels $\omega_\downarrow$ as an estimate of the boundary of the roadway area confined by a distribution of 'obstacles' to be analyzed in the scene. Hence, we have the following computational scheme for object-ground separation:

- Fractal structure of maneuvering affordance is extracted in terms of 2D allocation of fixed points $\hat{\Omega}^f = \{\hat{\omega}^f_{\mu_i}\}$.
- The imaging mechanism of the randomness distribution $\hat{\chi}^{\mathfrak{p}}_{\Xi}$ is designed in terms of mapping set $\hat{\nu}$ through simultaneous estimation of discrete information $\hat{\Omega}^f$ and induced 2D field $\varphi(\omega|\nu)$.
- The integrity of decentralized estimate $\hat{\Omega}^f$ is visualized as associated attractor Ξ generated by using the imaging process parameter $\hat{\nu}$ on the brightness distribution $f(\omega)$.
- Self-similarity of the imaging process parameter $\hat{\nu}$ based on the estimate $\hat{\Omega}^f$ is verified via computational generation of invariant subset Θ on the local maxima $\tilde{\Theta}$: a pattern sensitive sampling of smooth field $\varphi(\omega|\nu)$.
- As a stochastic basis of the maneuvering affordance, the scale information $\hat{\sigma}_\omega$ provides complementary information; noisy observation of an open space $\hat{\chi}^{\mathfrak{p}}_{\Xi}$ with the distribution of the breakdown $p(\omega\uparrow|\omega)$.
- The boundary of maneuvering affordance can be detected through the aggregation of as the breakdown as 1D imagery $<\omega>$.

The mapping set $\hat{\nu}$ can be designed non-uniquely on the estimate of fixed points $\hat{\Omega}^f$. Such non-unique representation provides computational basis for decentralized perception. The geometry of the maneuvering affordance is transferable via multi-viewpoint imagery and reconfigurable through dynamic interaction with the scene.

The mechanism for the multi-viewpoint integration is illustrated in Fig.14; based on *a priori* information $\mathfrak{v}$ in the bird's eye view, the direction of the roadway $\vec{\Omega}^d$ is transferred to the scene image to specify an initial guess of fixed points $\hat{\Omega}^f$; by articulating the capturing probability $\varphi(\omega|\hat{\nu})$ into the Laplacian-Gaussian basin $\{\Lambda^{\mathfrak{G}}_i\}$, a fractal model is designed in terms of mapping set $\hat{\nu}$; the fractal model is verified via computational detection of invariant feature Θ and adapted to the *as-is* distribution of boundary objects via ground-object separation.

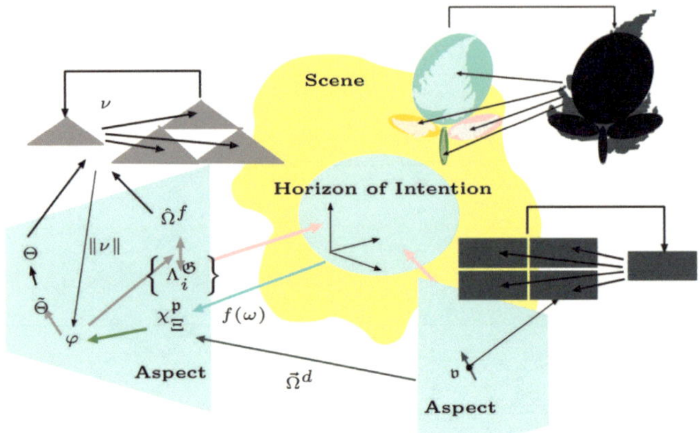

Fig. 14. Adaptive Fractal Code

6. Experiments

Let a fixed point of the Gasket be associated with the vanishing point with a depth parameter d_∞ and suppose that the rest of the fixed points are allocated at both bottoms of the roadway image where maximum scale of random patterns $\hat{\sigma}_{\max}$ maybe detected. By introducing this initial guess, the equations (8) - (17) can be solved via the iteration process:

$$\{\hat{\omega}^f_{\mu_i}\} \to (8) \to (9) \to (11) \to (12) \to (14) \to (17) \to \{\hat{\omega}^f_{\mu_i}\} \cdots \quad (20)$$

Steady state of the iteration process applied on a scene image is indicated in Figs.15 - 18. As an initial guess for starting the iteration (20), the set $\{\hat{\omega}^f_{\mu_i}\}$ is assigned in a scene image displayed in Fig.15; three fixed points are allocated at top-center, left- and right bottom for specifying upper vertex and left-right vertexes of a 'gasket' pattern; as the result of the iteration (20), a mapping set with three fixed points $\{\hat{\omega}^f_{\mu_i}\}$ is designed as a generator of *a priori* gasket model. The *a priori* fractal model based on the fixed point estimates generates the fractal attractor indicated in Fig.16. In this case, the scale of distributed randomness is limited by $\sigma_0 = 2 \cdot \hat{\sigma}_{\min}$. The mapping set $\hat{\nu}$ associated with the gasket model is verified via finite self-similarity analysis as indicated in Fig.17; the consistency of the fractal attractor to be generated is computationally tested via the generation of an invariant subset Θ and indicated as a closed link on a representation of 'most probable' attractor points $\tilde{\Theta}$. By the existence of Θ, the consistency of the measure $\hat{\chi}^{\mathbf{p}}_{\Xi}$ with the randomness distribution is verified as well as the self-similarity of associated attractor Ξ visualized in Fig.18. Thus, the estimate of the vanishing point (d_∞, $\vec{\Omega}^d$) is verified to be consistent with the generic model (9).

In complex scenes where the maneuvering area is clearly indicated as a lane mark as shown in Fig.18, designed mapping set $\hat{\nu}$ specifies the boundary of the fractal model ($\mathfrak{b}_L$, $\mathfrak{b}_R$). Such boundary information is critical in the road following processes. In many practical situations, the boundary is obscured by sign patterns and occluded by obstacles as indicated in Fig.6. In such a scene, we can define the boundary of open space via ground-object separation. To this end, first, the scale shift of distributed randomness was matched with the generic model (9) to design a version of fractal code $\hat{\nu}$. The designed code was verified via a computational consistency test and visualized as shown in Fig.19. By the existence of the

Fig. 15. Roadway Scene to be Analyzed

Fig. 16. Fractal Coding

fractal attractor, the validity of the designed version of fractal code $\hat{\nu}$ was verified as well as the perceptual consistency of the generic model. Hence, we can activate the ground-object separation process; the generic model (9) was applied to entire the scene image; the pixels of inconsistent scale estimate $\hat{\sigma}(\omega)$ were extracted and chained in the scene image as shown in Fig.20. As shown in this figure, resultant chains can separate the image of something perpendicular to the open space supporting the generic rule: the linear scale shift due to perspective projection. Thus, we can define a version of an effective boundary as the vertical chain of the breakdown points with the length over the noise scale: $\| \langle\omega\rangle \| \geq \hat{\sigma}_{\min}$. To confine the fractal model ν within the open space, we re-assign the fixed points $\hat{\Omega}^f = \{\hat{\omega}^f_{\mu_i}\}$ and re-activate the design process. The obtained fractal model was visualized in the scene image as shown in Fig.21. This figure demonstrates that the fractal coding of maneuvering

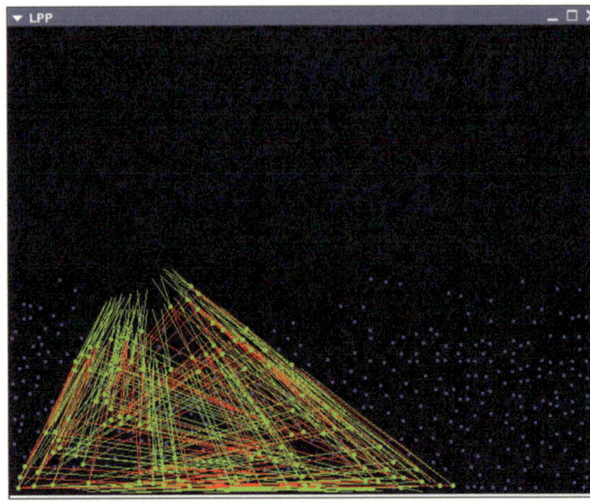

Fig. 17. Computational Verification

Fig. 18. Road Following Process

Fig. 19. Associated Fractal Attractor

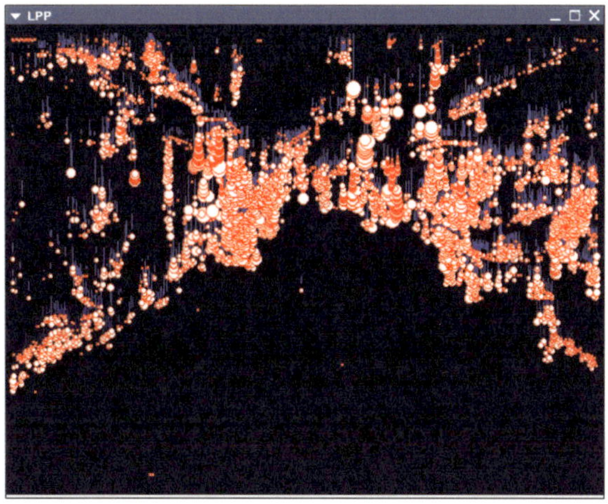

Fig. 20. Object Separation Based on $\hat{\sigma}_\omega$-Model

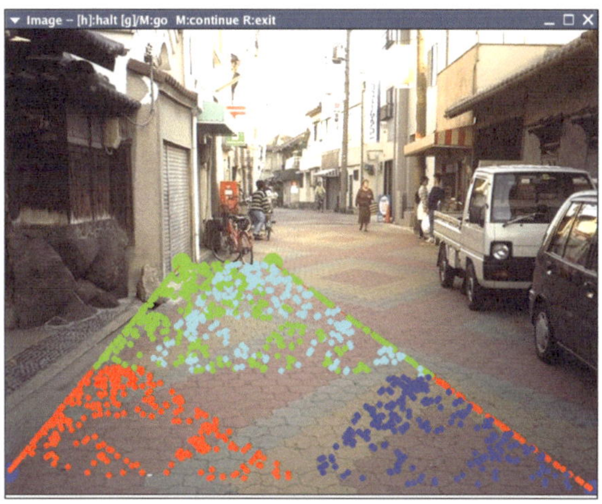

Fig. 21. Fractal Sampling

affordance with breakdown detection yields plausible reference for the visual guidance along a perceptually boundary in a naturally complex scene.
Through these experimental studies, it was demonstrated that the anticipative road following results in the bird's eye view can be applied to an extended class of roadway scenes as an *a priori* model. This implies that the design-and-refine steps of fractal coding can be applied to scenes consisting of objects covered by scale and chromatic randomness. This condition is satisfied in naturally complex scenes consisting of *worn-out* objects on which microscopic damage is expected to be uniformly distributed.

7. Concluding remarks

Fractal representation of the maneuvering affordance has been introduced on the randomness ineluctably distributed in naturally complex scenes. Scale shift of random patterns was extracted from scene image and matched to the *a priori* direction of a roadway. Based on scale space analysis, the probability of capturing not-yet-identified fractal attractors is generated within the roadway pattern to be detected. Such an *in-situ* design process has been demonstrated to yield anticipative models for road following process. The randomness-based approach yields a design framework for machine perception sharing man-readable information, i.e., natural complexity of textures and chromatic distributions. This implies that the fractal roadway model can be used for mental load reduction through human-machine cooperation.

8. References

M. F. Barnsley. *Superfractals*. Cambridge University Press, Cambridge, U.K., 2006.

M. F. Barnsley, V. Ervin, D. Hardin, and J. Lancaster. Solution of an inverse problem for fractals and other sets. *Proceedings of the National Academy of Science, USA*, 83(7):1975–1977, 1986.

P. W. Coppin, R. Pell, M. Wagner, J. R. Hayes, J.-L. Li, L. Hall, K. Fischer, D. Hirschfield, and W. Whittaker. EventScope: Amplifying human knowledge and experience via intelligent robotic systems and information interaction. In *Proceedings of the 9th IEEE International Workshop on Robot and Human Interaction (RoMan2000)*, pages 292–296, Osaka, Japan, 2000. IEEE.

T. Hamada and M. Fujie. Robotics for social safety. *Advanced Robotics*, 15(3):383–387, 2001.

J. E. Hutchinson. Fractals and self similarity. *Indiana University Mathematical Journal*, 30:713–747, 1981.

A. G. Jones and C. J. Taylor. Solving inverse problems in computer vision by scale space reconstruction. In *Proceedings of IAPR Workshop on Machine Vision Applications (MVA'94)*, pages 401-404, Kawasaki, Japan, 1994. IAPR.

K. Kamejima. Generic representation of self-similarity via structure sensitive sampling of noisy imagery. *Electronic Notes in Theoretical Computer Science*, 46: http://www.elsevier.com/wps/find/, 20 pages, 2001.

K. Kamejima. Laplacian-gaussian sub-correlation analysis for scale space imaging. *International Journal of Innovative Computing, Information and Control*, 1(3): 381–399, 2005.

K. Kamejima. Image-based satellite-roadway-vehicle integration for informatic vicinity generation. In *Proceedings of the 15th IEEE International Symposium on Robot and Human Interaction (RoMan2006)*, pages 334–339. IEEE, 2006.

K. Kamejima. Randomness-based scale-chromatic image analysis for interactive mapping on satellite-roadway-vehicle network. *Journal of Systemics, Cybernetics and Informatics*, 5(4):78–86, 2007.

K. Kamejima. Chromatic information adaptation for complexity-based integration of multi-viewpoint imagery - a new approach to cooperative perception in naturally complex scene - *International Journal of Innovative Computing, Information and Control*, 4(1):109–126, 2008.

K. Kamejima. Nondeterministic kinetics associated with self-similarity processes with applications to autonomous fractal pattern clustering. In *Proceedings of 1999 IEEE International Conference on Systems, Man and Cybernetics (SMC'99)*, pages VI:890–895, Tokyo, Japan, 1999. IEEE.

Ü. Özgner and C. Stiller. Systems for safety and autonomous behavior in cars: The DARPA grand challange experience. *Proceedings of the IEEE*, 95(2):397–411, 2007.

A. Parker. *In the Blink of an Eye*. The Free Press, London, U. K., 2003.

C. Urmson, C. Baker, J. Dolan, P. Rybski, B. Salesky, W. Whittaker, D. Ferguson, and M. Darms. Autonomous driving in traffic: Boss and the urban challenge. *AI Magazine*, 30(2):17–28, 2009.

User Intent Communication in Robot-Assisted Shopping for the Blind

Vladimir A. Kulyukin[1] and Chaitanya Gharpure[2]
[1]*Utah State University*
[2]*Google, Inc.*
USA

1. Introduction

The research reported in this chapter describes our work on robot-assisted shopping for the blind. In our previous research, we developed RoboCart, a robotic shopping cart for the visually impaired (Gharpure, 2008; Kulyukin et al., 2008; Kulyukin et al., 2005). RoboCart's operation includes four steps: 1) the blind shopper (henceforth the shopper) selects a product; 2) the robot guides the shopper to the shelf with the product; 3) the shopper finds the product on the shelf, places it in the basket mounted on the robot, and either selects another product or asks the robot to take him to a cash register; 4) the robot guides the shopper to the cash register and then to the exit.

Steps 2, 3, and 4 were addressed in our previous publications (Gharpure & Kulyukin 2008; Kulyukin 2007; Kulyukin & Gharpure 2006). In this paper, we focus on Step 1 that requires the shopper to select a product from the repository of thousands of products, thereby communicating the next target destination to RobotCart. This task becomes time critical in opportunistic grocery shopping when the shopper does not have a prepared list of products. If the shopper is stranded at a location in the supermarket selecting a product, the shopper may feel uncomfortable or may negatively affect the shopper traffic.

The shopper communicates with RoboCart using the Belkin 9-key numeric keypad (See Fig. 1 right). The robot gives two types of messages to the user: synthesized speech or audio icons. Both types are relayed through a bluetooth headphone. A small bump on the keypad's middle key (key 5) allows the blind user to locate it. The other keys are located with respect to the middle key. In principle, it would be possible to mount a full keyboard on the robot. However, we chose the Belkin keypad, because its layout closely resembles the key layout of many cellular phones. Although the accessibility of cell phones for people with visual impairments remains an issue, the situation has been improving as more and more individuals with visual impairments become cell phone users. We hope that in the future visually impaired shoppers will communicate with RobotCart using their cell phones (Nicholson et al., 2009; Nicholson & Kulyukin, 2007).

The remainder of the chapter is organized as follows. In section 2, we discuss related work. In sections 3, we describe our interface design. In section 4, we present our product selection algorithm. In section 5, we describe our experiments with five blind and five sighted, blindfolded participants. In sections 6, we present and discuss the experimental results. In section 7, we present our conclusions.

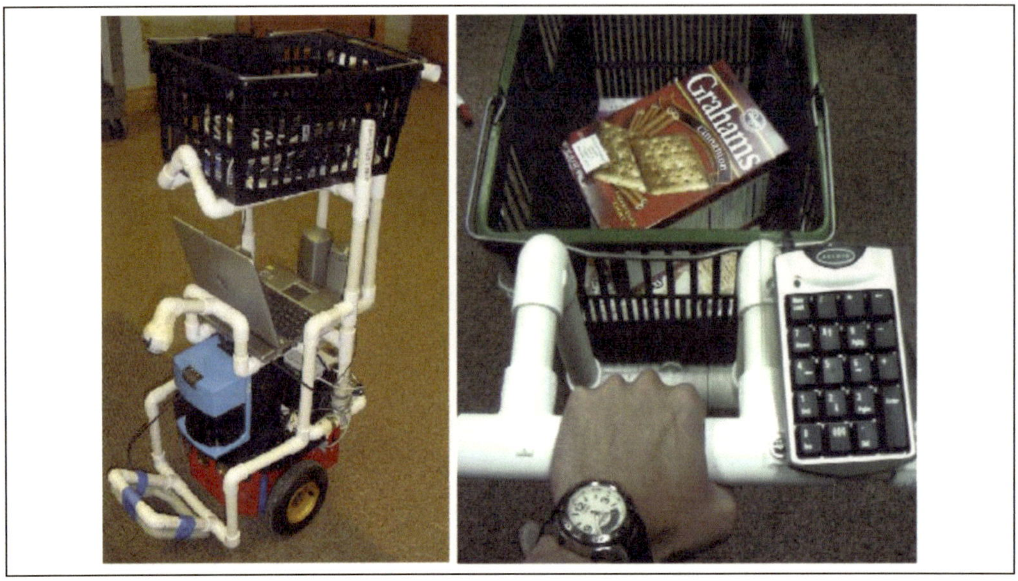

Fig. 1. RoboCart (left); RoboCart's handle with the Belkin 9-key numeric keypad (right).

2. Related work

The literature on communicating user intent to robots considers three main scenarios. Under the first scenario, the user does not communicate with the robot explicitly. The robot attempts to infer or predict user intent from its own observations (Wasson et al., 2003; Demeester et al., 2006). Under the second scenario, the user communicates intent to the robot with body gestures (Morency et al., 2007). The third scenario involves intent communication and prediction through mixed initiative systems (Fagg et al., 2004). Our approach falls under the second scenario to the extent that key presses can be considered as body gestures.

Several auditory interfaces have been proposed and evaluated for navigating menus and object hierarchies (Raman, 1997; Smith et al., 2004; Walker et al., 2006). In (Smith et al., 2004), the participants were required to find six objects from a large object hierarchy. The evaluation was done to check for successful completion of the task, and was not evaluated for time criticality. In (Brewster, 1998), the author investigated the possibility of using nonspeech audio messages, called *earcons*, to navigate a menu hierarchy. In (Walker et al, 2006), the authors proposed a new auditory representation, called *spearcons*. Spearcons are created by speeding up a phrase until it is not recognized as speech. Another approach for browsing object hierarchies used conversational gestures (Raman, 1997), such as *open-object*, *parent*, which are associated with specific navigation actions. In (Gaver, 1989), generic requirements are outlined for auditory interaction objects that support navigation of hierarchies. While these approaches are suitable for navigating menus, they may not be suitable for selecting items in large object hierarchies under time pressure.

In (Divi et al., 2004), the authors presented a spoken user interface in which the task of invoking responses from the system is treated as one of retrieval from the set of all possible responses. The SpokenQuery system (Wolf et al., 2004) was used and found effective for searching spoken queries in large databases. In (Sidner & Forlines, 2004), the authors propose the use of subset languages for interacting with collaborative agents. One advantage of using subset language is that it can easily be characterized in a grammar for a speech recognition system. One disadvantage is that the users are required to learn the subset language that may be quite large if the number of potentially selectable items is in the thousands.

In (Brewster et al., 2003) and (Crispien et al., 1996) the authors present a 3-D auditory interface and head gesture recognition to browse through a menu and select menu items. This approach may be inefficient for navigating large hierarchies because of the excessive number of head gestures that would be required. A similar non-visual interface is also described in (Hiipakka & Lorho, 2003).

Another body of work related to our research is the Web Content Accessibility Guidelines (W3C, 2003) for making websites more accessible. However, since these guidelines are geared toward websites, they are based on several assumptions that we cannot make in our research: 1) browsing a website is not time critical; 2) the user is sitting in the comfort of her home or office; and 3) the user has a regular keyboard at her disposal.

3. Interface design

Extensive research has been done regarding advantages of browsing and searching in finding items in large repositories (Manber et al., 1996; Mackinlay & Zellweger, 1995). It is often more advantageous to combine browsing and searching. However, when the goal is known, query-based searching is found to be more efficient and faster than browsing (Manber et al., 1996; Karlson et al., 2006). Since this case fits our situation, because the user knows the products she wants to purchase, we designed a search-based interface with two modalities: typing and speech. In both modalities, the shopper can optionally switch to browsing when the found list of products is, in the shopper's judgement, short and can be browsed directly. Our interface also supports a pure browsing modality used as the baseline in our experiments. We used the following rules of thumb to iteratively refine our design over a set of user trials with a visually impaired volunteer.

- **Learning:** The amount of learning required to use the interface should be minimal. Ideally, the interface should be based on techniques already familiar to the shopper, e.g. browsing a file system or typing a text message on a mobile phone.
- **Localization:** The shopper must know the state of the current search task. While browsing, the shopper should be able to find out, at any moment, the exact place in the hierarchy. While typing, the shopper should be able to find out, at any moment, what keywords have been previously typed. Similarly, in the speech modality, the shopper should be able to access the previously spoken keywords.
- **Reduced cognitive load:** The cognitive load imposed by the interface should be minimal. For browsing, this can be done by categorizing the products in a logical hierarchy. For typing and speech, continuous feedback should be provided, indicating the effect of every shopper action, e.g. character typed or word spoken.
- **Timestamping:** Every step during the progress of the search task should be timestamped, so that the shopper can go back to any previous state if an error occurs. The shopper should be allowed to delete the typed characters or misrecognized words that returned incorrect results.

3.1 Browsing

The keypad layout for browsing is shown in Fig. 2. The *UP* and *DOWN* keys are used to browse through items in the current level in the hierarchy. The *RIGHT* key goes one level deeper into the hierarchy, and the *LEFT* key - one level up. Visually impaired computer users use the same combination of keys for browsing file systems. Holding *UP* and *DOWN* pressed allows the shopper to jump forward or backward in the list at the current depth in the hierarchy. The length of the jump is proportional to the time for which the key is pressed. A key press also allows the shopper to localize in the hierarchy by informing the shopper the current level and category. The *PAGE-UP* and *PAGE-DOWN* keys allow the shopper to go a fixed number of items up or down at the particular level in the hierarchy. Auditory icons, short and distinct, are provided when the shopper wraps around a list, changes levels, or tries to go out of the bounds of the hierarchy.

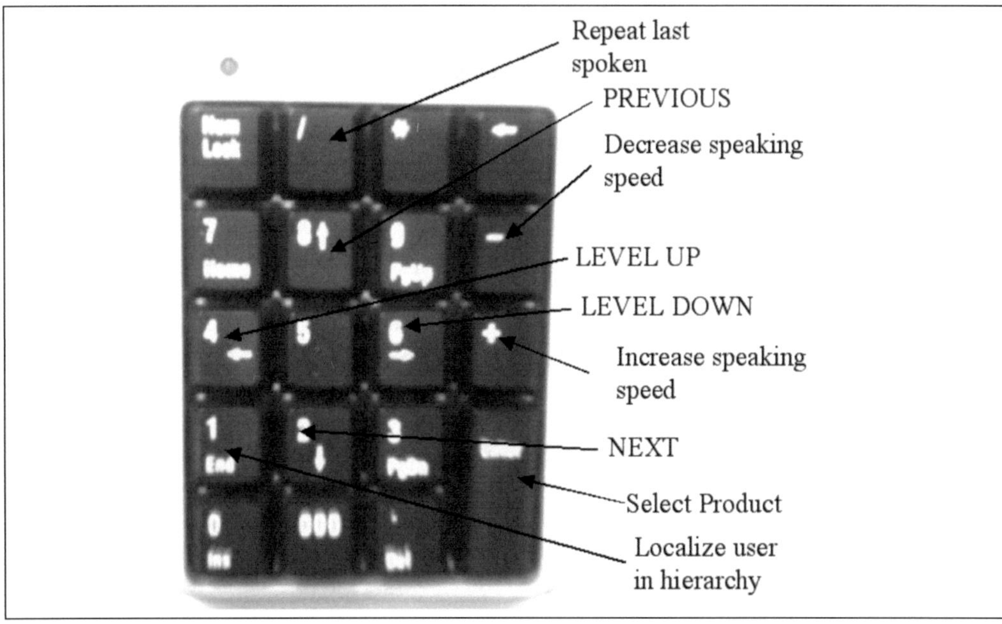

Fig. 2. Keypad layout for the browsing interface.

3.2 Typing

The keypad layout used for the typing interface is shown in Fig. 2. In the typing modality, the shopper is required to type a query string using the 9-key numeric keypad. This query string can be complete or partial. Each numeric key on the keypad is mapped to letters as if it was a phone keypad. Synthesized speech is used to communicate the typed letters to the shopper as the keys are pressed. The *SELECT* key is used to append the current letter to the query string. For example, if the shopper presses key 5 twice followed by the *SELECT* key, the letter *k* will be appended to the query string. At any time the shopper can choose to skip typing the remaining word by pressing the *space* key and continue typing the next word. Every time a new character is appended to the query string, a search is performed and the number of returned results is reported back to the shopper. The partial query string is used to form the prediction tree which provides all possible complete query strings. If the shopper feels that the number of returned results is sufficiently small, she can press *ENTER* and browse through each product using *NEXT* and *PREVIOUS* to look for the desired item.

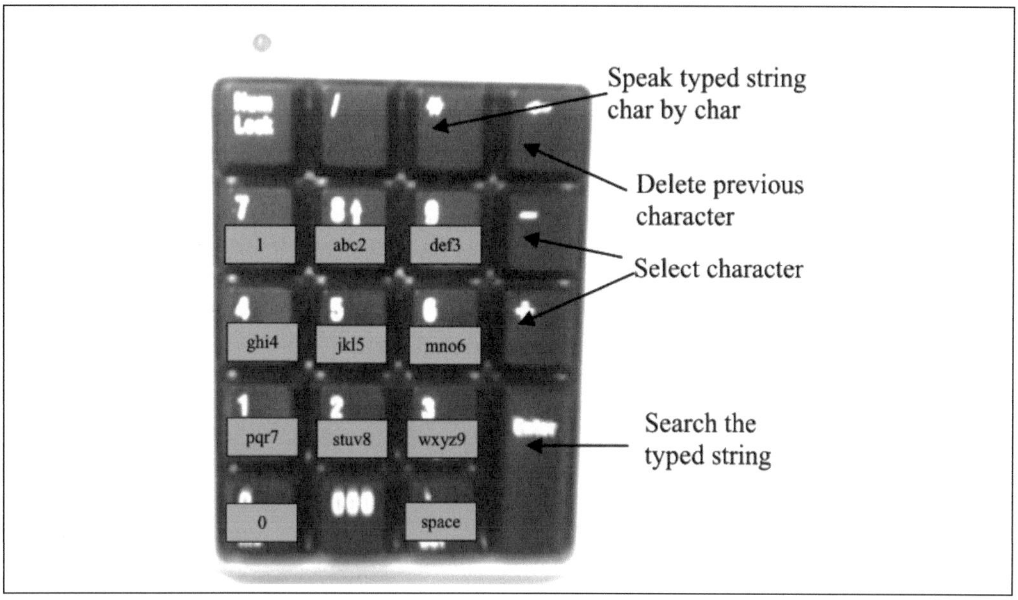

Fig. 2. Keypad layout for the typing interface.

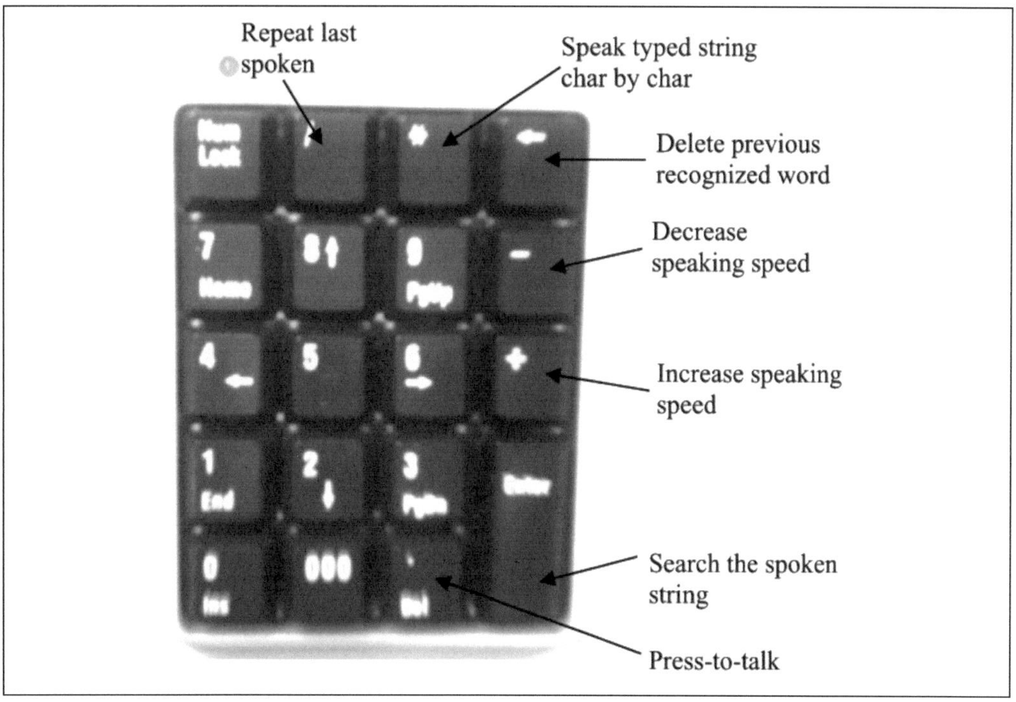

Fig. 3. A partial product hierarchy.

3.2 Speech

Our speech-based modality is a simplified version of the Speech In List Out (SILO) approach proposed in (Divi et al., 2004). The keypad layout for the speech-based modality is shown in

Fig. 3. The query string is formed by the words recognized by a speech recognition engine. The shopper is required to speak the query string into the microphone, one word at a time. A list of results is returned to the shopper, through which the shopper can browse to select the desired item. The grammar for the speech recognition engine consists of simple rules made of one word each, which reduces the number of speech recognition errors. To further reduce the number of false positives in speech recognition due to ambient noise, we provide a press-to-talk key. The shopper is required to press this key just before speaking a word. We use Microsoft's Speech API (SAPI) which provides alternates for the recognized word. The alternates are used to form the prediction tree which, in turn, is used to generate all possible query strings. The prediction tree concept is explained in the next section.

4. Product selection algorithm

Our product selection algorithm is used in the typing and speech modalities. The algorithm can be used on any database of items organized into a logical hierarchy. Each item title in the repository is extended by adding to it the titles of all its ancestors from the hierarchy. For example, in Fig. 4 the item *Kroger Diced Pineapples (0.8lb)* is extended to *Canned Products, Fruits, Pineapple, Kroger Diced Pineapples (0.8lb).*

Each entry in the extended item repository is represented by an N-dimensional vector where N is the total number of unique keywords in the repository. Thus, each vector is an N-bit vector with a bit set if the corresponding keyword exists in the item string. The query vector obtained from the query string is also an N-bit vector. The result of the search is simply all entries i, such that $P_i \,\&\, S = S$, where P_i is the N-bit vector of the i-th product, S is the N-bit query vector, and & is the bit-wise and operation.

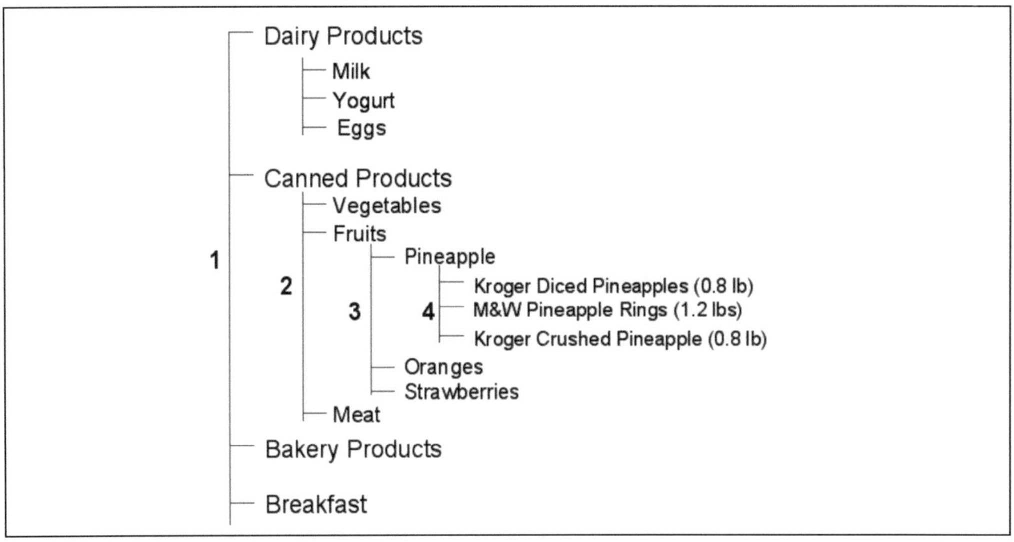

Fig. 4. A partial product hierarchy.

This approach, if left as is, has two problems: 1) the shopper must type complete words, which is tedious using just a numeric keypad or a cell phone; and 2) the search fails if a word is spelled incorrectly. To solve the first problem, we use word prediction where the whole word is predicted by looking at the partial word entered by the shopper. However, instead of having the shopper make a choice from a list of predicted words, or waiting for the user to type the whole word, we search the repository for all predicted options. To solve the second problem, we do not use the spell checker, but instead provide the shopper with continuous audio feedback. Every time the shopper types a character, the number of retrieved results is reported to the shopper. At any point in a word, the user can choose not to type the remaining characters and proceed to the next word.

The predictions of partially typed words form a tree. Figures 5 and 6 show the prediction tree and the resultant query strings when the shopper types "deo so ola." The sharp-cornered rectangles represent the keywords in the repository, also called keyword nodes. The round-cornered rectangles are the partial search words entered by the shopper, also called the partial nodes. Keyword nodes are all possible extensions of their (parent) partial node, as found in the keyword repository.

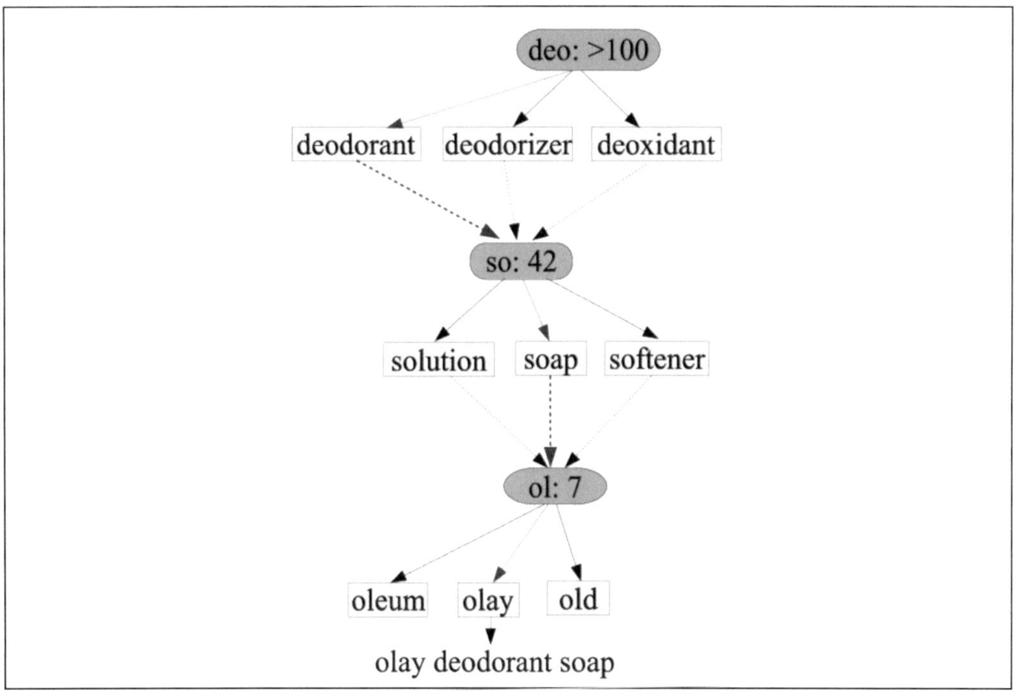

Fig. 5. A sample prediction tree.

Each keyword node is associated with multiple query strings. Every path from the root of the prediction tree to the keyword node forms a query string by combining all keywords along that path. For example, in the prediction tree shown in Fig. 5 there will be three query strings associated with the keyword node solution: deodorant solution, deodorizer solution, and deoxidant solution. The prediction subtree is terminated at the keyword node where the associated query string returns zero results. For example, in Fig. 5, the subtree rooted at solution, along the path deodorant-solution will be terminated since the search string *deodorant solution* returns zero results. Fig. 6 shows the possible query strings for the prediction tree in Fig. 5. The numbers in the parentheses indicate the number of results returned for those search strings. The number after colons in the partial nodes indicates the total results returned by all query strings corresponding to its children (keyword) nodes.

```
Possible search strings
for the Prediction tree
deodorant solution (0)
deodorant soap oleum (0)
deodorant soap olay (2)
deodorant soap old (2)
deodorant softener (0)
deodorizer solution (0)
deodorizer soap oleum (0)
deodorizer soap olay (1)
deodorizer soap old (2)
deodorizer softener (0)
deoxidant solution (0)
deoxidant soap (0)
deoxidant softener (0)
```

Fig. 6. Possible strings for the sample prediction tree.

In addition to implementing the algorithm on a Dell laptop that runs on the robot, we also ported the algorithm to a Nokia E70 cell phone that runs the Symbian 9 mobile operating system. The algorithm was modified when the interface was implemented on the cell phone. The memory and processor speed restrictions on the cell phone made us optimize the algorithm. To reduce space requirements, each word in the product repository was replaced by a number depending upon the frequency of occurrence of that word in the repository. The algorithm for assigning these codes is given in Fig. 7. The procedure SortByFrequency sorts the elements of the set of unique words (W) in the decreasing order of the frequency of occurrence.

```
W = Set of Unique Words
PROD = Set of Products
for each w in W
        FREQ(w) = 0
for each p in PROD
        for each word in W_p
                FREQ(word) = FREQ(word)+1
SortByFrequency(W)
for each word in W
        CODE(word) = INDEX(word)
```

Fig. 7. Frequency-Based Encoding of Words.

The product selection algorithm implemented on the Nokia E70 mobile phone is given in Fig. 8. A set P(w) is a set of indices of products containing word w. Initialized to empty set. PROD is the set of all products. S is the set of keywords in the user query. Q is the set of products containing the word S[i]. 1. R is intersected with Q for each S[i] and eventually the filtered set of products is obtained.

```
W = Set of Unique Words
PROD = Set of Products
for n = 1 to W.length
   P(W[n]) = {}
for i = 1 to PROD.length
   W_p = Set of words in PROD[i]
for j = 1 to W_p.length
   P(W_p[j]) = Union(P(W_p[j]), {i})
R = PROD
S = {keyword1, keyword2, ..., keywordk}
for i = 1 to S.length
   Q = {}
   for j = 1 to W.length
      if W[j] startswith S[i]
            Q = Union(Q, P(W[j])
   R = Intersection(R, Q)
return R
```

Fig. 8. Possible strings for the sample prediction tree.

4.1 Procedure

As mentioned above, we used the product repository of 11,147 products that we obtained from www.householdproducts.nlm.nih.gov. The following procedure was followed for each participant. After arriving at the lab, the participant was first briefly told about the background and purpose of the experiments. Each participant recieved 20 minutes of training to become familiar with the interface and the modalities. As part of the training procedure, the participant was asked to find three products with each modality.

Session 1 started after the training session. Each task was to select a product using a given modality. A set of 10 randomly selected products (set-1) was formed. Each participant was thus required to perform 30 tasks (10 products x 3 interfaces). Because of his schedule, one of the participants was unable to perform the browsing modality tasks due to a scheduling conflict. The product description was broken down into 4 parts: product name, brand, special description (scent/flavor/color), and the text that would appear in the result communicated to the participant with synthetic speech. Table 1 gives an example. In the course of a task, if the participants forgot the product description, they were allowed to revisit it by pressing a key.

PRODUCT NAME	BRAND	DESCRIPTION	RESULT TEXT
Liquid Laundry Detergent	Purex	Mountain Breeze Bleach Alternative	Purex Mountain Breeze with Bleach Alternative Liquid Laundry Detergent

Table 1. A product description.

For Session 2, another 10 products (set-2) were randomly selected. After the initial 30 tasks in Session 1, 20 more tasks were performed by each participant (10 products x 2 interfaces). We skipped the browsing modality in Session 2, because our objective in Session 2 was to check if and how much the participants improved on each of the two modalities, relative to the other. The dependent variables are shown in Table 2. Some variables were recorded by a logging program, others by a researcher conducting the experiment. Since all the tasks were not necessarily of the same complexity, there was no way for us to check the learning effect. All experiments were first conducted with 5 blind participants and then with 5 sighted, blindfolded participants. After both sessions, we conducted a subjective evaluation of the three modalities by administering the NASA Task Load Index (NASA-TLX) to each participant. The NASA-TLX questionnaires were administered to eight participants in the laboratory right after the experiments. Two participants were interviewed on the phone, one day after the laboratory session.

BROWSING	TYPING-BASED	SPEECH-BASED
Time to selection	Typing errors	Recognition errors
Wrong selection	Time to type	Time to speak
Failed search	Time to selection	Time to selection
	Number of returned results	Number of retruned results
	Wrong selections	Wrong selections
	Failed search	Failed search
	Number of chars typed	Number of spoken words

Table 2. Observations for product retrieval interface experiments.

4.2 Data analysis

Repeated measures analysis of variance (ANOVA) models were fitted to the data using the SAS™ statistical system. Model factors were: modality (3 levels: browsing, typing, speech), condition (2 levels: blind, sighted-blindfolded), participant (10 levels: nested within condition, 5 participants per blind/sighted-blindfolded condition), and set (2 levels: set-1 and set-2, each containing 10 products).
The 10 products within each set were replications. Since each participant selected each product in each set, the 10 product responses for each set were repeated measures for this study. Since the browsing modality was missing for all participants for set-2 products, models comparing selection time between sets included only typing and speech modalities. The dependent variable was, in all models, the product selection time, with the exception of analyses using the NASA-TLX workload measure. The overall models and all primary effects were tested using an α-level of 0.05, whenever these effects constituted planned comparisons (see hypotheses). However, in the absence of a significant overall F-test for any given model, post-hoc comparisons among factor levels were conducted using a Bonferroni-adjusted α-level of 0.05/K, where K is the number of post-hoc comparisons within any givenmodel, to reduce the likelihood of false significance.

5. Experiments

Experiments were conducted with 5 blind and 5 sighted, blindfolded participants. The participants' ages ranged from 17 years through 32 years. All participants were males. To avoid the discomfort of wearing a blindfold, for sighted participants the keypad was covered with a box to prevent them from seeing it. The experiment was conducted in a laboratory setting. The primary purpose behind using sighted, blindfolded participants was to test whether they differed significantly from the blind participants, and thus decide whether they can be used in future experiments along with or instead of blind participants. We formulated the following research hypotheses. In the subsequent discussion, H1-0, H2-0, H3-0 and H4-0 denote the corresponding null hypotheses.

Hypothesis 1: (H1) *Sighted, blindfolded participants perform significantly faster than blind participants.*

Hypothesis 2: (H2) *Shopper performance with browsing is significantly slower than with typing.*

Hypothesis 3: (H3) *Shopper performance with browsing is significantly slower than with speech.*

Hypothesis 4: (H4) *Shopper performances with typing and speech are significantly different from each other.}Equations are centred and numbered consecutively, from 1 upwards.*

6. Results

For an overall repeated measures model which included the effects of modality, condition, and participant (nested within condition), and the interaction of modality with each of condition and participant, using only set-1 data, the overall model was highly significant, $F(26,243) = 7.00$, $P < 0.0001$. The main effects observed within this model are shown in Table 3. All the main effects were significant. Interaction of modality x condition, $F(2, 243)=0.05$, $P = 0.9558$ and modality x participant, $F(14, 243)=1.17$, $P = 0.2976$ was observed. Thus, the mean selection time differed significantly among modalities, but the lack of interactions indicated that the modality differences did not vary significantly between blind and sight, blindfolded groups, nor among individual participants. In the ANOVAs, note that the DoF for the error is 243, because one of the participants did not perform the browsing tasks.

SOURCE	MAIN EFFECTS (ANOVA)
Interface	$F(2,243)=42.84$, $P<0.0001$
Condition	$F(1,243)=9.8$, $P=0.002$
Participant	$F(8,243)=9.88$, $P<0.0001$

Table 3. Main effects.

The mean selection time for the group of blind participants was 72.6 secs versus a mean of 58.8 secs for sighted-blindfolded participants, and the difference in these means was significant ($t = 3.13$, $P = 0.0029$). As might be expected, participants differed on mean selection time. However, the majority of the differences among participants arose from blind participant 5, whose mean selection time of 120.9 (s) differed significantly from the mean selection time of all others participants (whose mean times were in the 53-63 secs range) ($P < 0.0001$ for all comparisons between blind participant 5 and all other participants). When blind participant 5 was dropped from the analysis, main effect of both condition and participant (condition) became non-significant ($F(1, 216) = 0.16$, $P = 0.6928$, and $F(6,216) = 0.44$, $P = 0.8545$, respectively). The interactions of modality with condition and participant also remained non-significant. It appears that, on average, when the outlier (participant 5) was removed, blind and sighted-blindfolded participants did not really differ. Thus, there was no sufficient evidence to reject the null hypothesis H1-0.

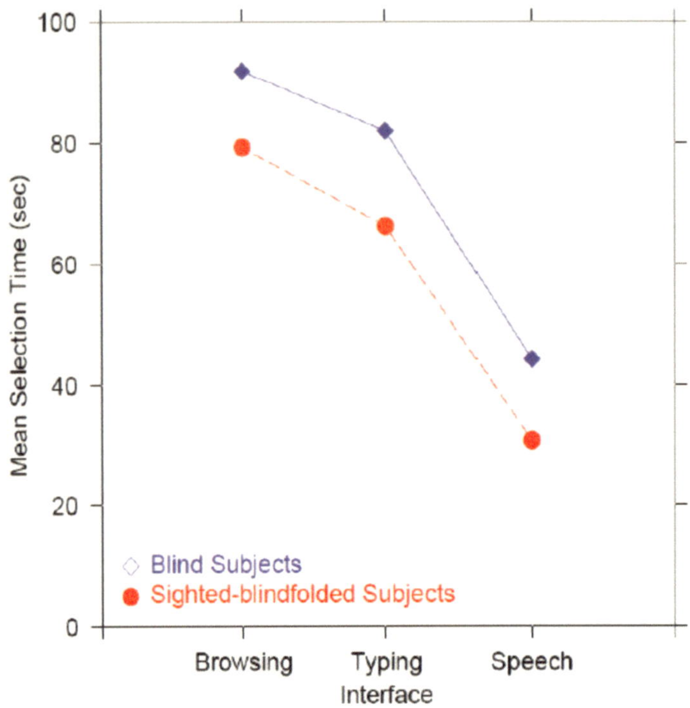

Fig. 9. Mean selection times for blind and blindfolded sighted participants against all interfaces.

A graph of the mean selection times of the blind and the sighted, blindfolded participants for each modality is shown in Fig. 9. The almost parallel lines for the blind and sighted-blindfolded participants suggest that there is no interaction between the modality and the participant type, which is also confirmed by the ANOVA result presented earlier. In other words, the result suggests that the modality which is best for sighted, blindfolded shoppers may also be best for blind shoppers.

The main effect of modality, as shown in Table 3, suggests that, on average (over all participants), two or more modalities differ significantly. Mean selection times for browsing, typing, and speech were: 85.5, 74.1, and 37.5 (seconds), respectively. Post-hoc pairwise t-tests showed that typing was faster than browsing ($t = 2.10$, $P = 0.0364$), although statistical significance is questionable if the Bonferroni-adjusted is used here. We, therefore, were unable to reach a definite conclusion about H2. Both browsing and typing were significantly slower than speech ($t = 8.84$, $P < 0.0001$, and $t = 6.74$, $P < 0.0001$, respectively). This led us to reject the null hypotheses H3-0 and H4-0 in favor of H3 and H4.

Since we were primarily interested in the difference between typing and speech, we decided to compare the modalities on the measures obtained from Session 2. Set-2 was significantly faster than set-1, averaged over the two modalities and all participants ($t = 6.14$, $P < 0.0001$). Since we did not have a metric for the task complexity, we were unable to infer if this result reflected the learning effect of the participants from Session 1 to Session 2. However, a significant interaction of modality x set, $F(1, 382)=13.8$, $P=0.0002$ was observed. The graph of the selection times during Sessions 1 and 2, against the modality type is shown in Fig. 10. It appears from the graph that the improvement with typing was much larger than that with speech. The reduction in selection times from Session 1 to Session 2 varied significantly for typing and speech ($P < 0.0001$). This was probably because the participants were already much faster with speech than typing during Session 1 and had much less room to improve with speech during Session 2.

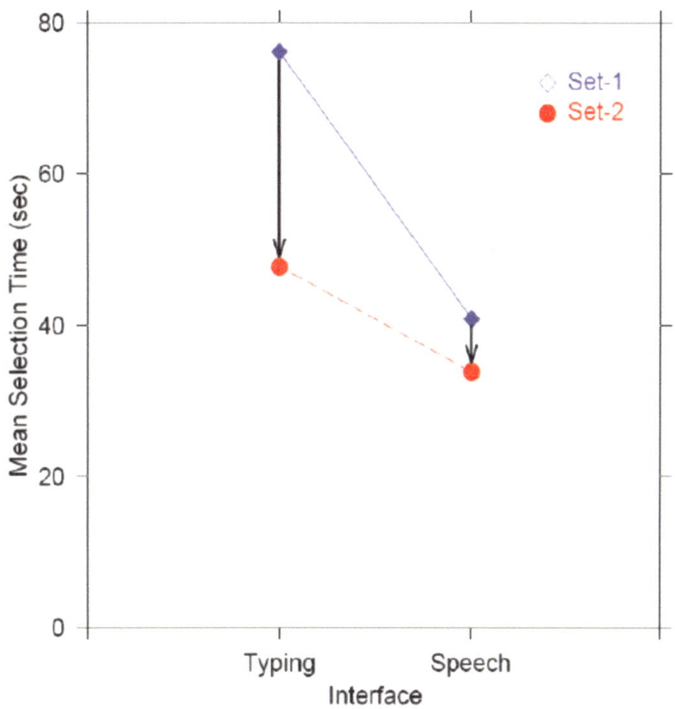

Fig. 10. Change in mean selection times for typing and speech interfaces from Session 1 and Session 2.

A strong Pearson's product moment correlation was found between selection time and query length for both typing and speech, with $r = 0.92$ and $r = 0.82$, respectively. To calculate the PPM correlation, we averaged the selection times over all products having the same query length. This just confirms the obvious that, on average, selection time increases with the number of characters typed or words spoken.

We used a between-subjects design to study the data obtained from the NASA TLX questionaire. The *modality type* was the independent variable and mental *demand*, *frustration*, and *overall workload* were the dependent variables. A one-way ANOVA indicated that there was a significant difference among the three modalities in terms of the mental demand, frustration, and overall workload, ($F(2, 27) = 16.63$, $P < 0.0001$), ($F(2, 27) = 16.63$, $P < 0.0001$), and ($F(2, 27) = 10.07$, $P = 0.0005$) respectively). Post-hoc pair-wise t-tests for the three dependent variables with Bonferoni adjusted α-level of 0.016 are shown in Table 4. The mean values of mental demand, frustration and overall workload for the three modalities are shown in Table 5.

	Browsing x Typing	Browsing x Speech	Typing x Speech
Mental Demand	t=1.075, P=0.2962	* t=3.822, P=0.0012	* t=4.011, P=0.0008
Frustration	* t=6.974, P<0.0001	t=1.348, P=0.1833	* t=4.428, P=0.0004
Overall Workload	*t = 3.369, P=0.0034	* t=4.126, P=0.0006	t=0.9910, P=0.3348

Table 4. Post-hoc t-tests to study workload, mental demand, and frustration imposed by the interfaces (* indicates a significant test).

On the basis of the results reported in the literature we expected browsing to be slower than the other two modalities since the search goal was known. This expectation was confirmed in our experiments. The participants were much slower with typing than speech during Session 1. However, in Session 2, they made a significant improvement with typing.
The improvement was not so significant with speech. We conjecture that, with more trials, typing will improve until it is no longer significantly slower than speech. It is unlikely that this effect will be observed with browsing, because, unlike typing and speech, browsing does not involve any learning. The only part of browsing that may involve learning is the structure of the hierarchy. However, it is unclear how much this knowledge will help the shopper if new tasks are presented to the shopper, i.e., the tasks requiring to use previously unexplored parts of the hierarchy.

	Browsing	Typing	Speech
Mental Demand	45.6	35.9	13.4
Frustration	47.8	1.8	34
Overall Workload	12.88	8.33	7

Table 5. Mean values of mental demand, frustration, and workload.

Unlike browsing, typing and speech involve some learning due to several factors, such as using the multi-tap keypad, speaking clearly into the microphone, and many other search-specific strategies. For example, we observed that while typing and speaking, the participants understood, after a few trials, that using the product's special description for the search narrowed down the results much faster. They also gradually learned they saved time by typing partial keywords, as the trailing characters in a keyword often left the results unchanged.
Though browsing provided features like jumping forward/backward in the current level, localizing, changing speed of text-to-speech synthesis, none of the participants used those features. When the search target is known, pure browsing is cumbersome, because it involves traversing a large hierarchy and guessing the right categories for the target.
The administration of the NASA TLX to the participants revealed that in spite of the significantly slower performance with typing as compared to speech, the workload imposed by the two modalities did not differ significantly. Browsing imposed a significantly higher

workload than either typing or speech. Browsing and typing were significantly more mentally demanding than speech. It was surprising that in spite of the low mental demand, speech caused significantly more frustration than typing. User comments, informally collected after the administration of NASA-TLX, revealed speech recognition errors to be the reason behind the frustration. Though the participants expressed the desire for an hybrid interface, in absence of one, most participants (9 out 10) indicated in their comments that they would prefer just typing.

7. Conclusion

This paper discussed user intent communication in robot-assisted shopping for the blind. Three intent communication modalities (typing, speech, and browsing) are evaluated in a series of experiments with 5 blind and 5 sighted, blindfolded participants on a public online database of 11,147 household products. The mean selection time differed significantly among the three modalities, but the lack of interactions indicated that the modality differences did not vary significantly between blind and sighted, blindfolded groups, nor among individual participants. Though it was seen that speech was the fastest, in real life, the shopper may prefer to use typing as it helps to be more discrete in a public place like a supermarket. A hybrid interface might be desirable. If the exact intention is not known, i.e. when the shopper does not know what she wants to buy, an interface with a strong coupling of browsing and searching is an option. Since it is difficult to evaluate how such a hybrid interface would perform in real life, evaluating the components independently, as was done in this paper, gives us insights into how user intent should be communicated in robot-assisted shopping for the blind.

8. Acknowledgements

This research has been supported, in part, through NSF grant IIS-0346880 award. We would like to thank all participants for volunteering their time for experiments. We are grateful to Dr. Daniel Coster of the USU Department of Mathematics and Statistics for helping us with the statistical analysis of the exeperimental data.

9. References

Gharpure, C. (2008). *Design, Implementation and Evaluation of Interfaces to Haptic and Locomotor Spaces in Robot-Assisted Shopping for the Visually Impaired,* Ph.D. Thesis, Department of Computer Science, Utah State University, Logan, UT, USA.

Kulyukin, V., Gharpure, C., and Coster, D. (2008). Robot-Assisted Shopping for the Visually Impaired: Proof-of-Concept Design and Feasibility Evaluation. *Assistive Technology,* Volume 20.2/Summer 2008, pp. 86-98. RESNA Press.

Kulyukin, V.; Gharpure, C. & Nicholson, J. (2005). Robocart: Toward robot-assisted navigation of grocery stores by the visually impaired, *Proceedings of the IEEE/RSJ International Conference on Intelligent Robots and Systems (IROS),* Edmonton, Canada, July 2005, IEEE.

Nicholson , J. & Kulyukin, V. (2007). Shoptalk: Independent blind shopping = verbal route directions + barcode scans. *Proceedings of the 2007 Rehabilitation Engineering and Assistive Technology Society of North America (RESNA) Conference*, avail. on CDROM, Phoenix, AZ, USA, 2007, RESNA.

Kulyukin, V. and Gharpure, C. (2006). Ergonomics-for-One in a Robotic Shopping Cart for the Blind. *Proceedings of the 2006 ACM Conference on Human-Robot Interaction (HRI 2006)*, pp. 142-149. Salt Lake City, UT, USA, March 2006, ACM.

Kulyukin, V. (2007). Robot-Assisted Shopping for the Blind: Haptic and Locomotor Spaces in Supermarkets (Extended Paper Abstract). *Proceedings of the AAAI Spring Symposium on Multidisciplinary Collaboration for Socially Assistive Robotics Stanford University*, pp. 36-38. Palo Alto, California, March 26-28, 2007, AAAI Press.

Gharpure, C. & Kulyukin, V. (2008). Robot-Assisted Shopping for the Blind: Issues in Spatial Cognition and Product Selection. *International Journal of Service Robotics*, Volume 1, Number 3, July 2008, DOI 10.1007/s11370-008-0020-9, Springer.

Nicholson, J., Kulyukin, V., and Coster, D. (2009). ShopTalk: Independent Blind Shopping Through Verbal Route Directions and Barcode Scans. *The Open Rehabilitation Journal*, ISSN: 1874-9437 Volume 2, 2009, DOI 10.2174/1874943700902010011.

Wasson, G., Sheth, P., Alwan, M., Granata, K., Ledoux A., Ledoux, R., & Huang, C. (2003). User Intent in a Shared Control Framework for Pedestrian Mobility Aids. *Proceedings of the IEEE International Conference on Intelligent Robots and Systems (IROS 2003)*, pp. 2962 - 2967, Las Vegas, NV, USA, October 2003, IEEE.

Demeester, E., Huntemann, A., Vanhooydonck, D., Vanacker, G., Degeest, A., Van Brussel, H., & Nuttin, M. (2006). Bayesian Estimation of Wheelchair Driver Intents: Modeling Intents as Geometric Paths Tracked by the Driver. *Proceedings of the IEEE International Conference on Intelligent Robots and Systems (IROS 2006)*, pp. 5775-5780, Beijing, China, October 2006, IEEE.

Morency, L. P., Sidner, C., Lee, C. & Darrell, T. (2007). Head Gestures for Perceptual Interfaces: The Role of Context in Improving Recognition. Artificial Intelligence, Volume 171, pp. 568-585, Elsevier.

Fagg, A., Rosenstein, M., Platt, R., & Grupen, R. (2004). Extracting user intent in mixed initiative teleoperator control. *Proceedings of the American Institute of Aeronautics and Astronautics Intelligent Systems Technical Conference*, Chicago, IL, USA, September 2004, AIAA.

Raman, T. V. (1997). Auditory User Interfaces, Kluwer Academic Publishers, ISBN: 0-7923-9984-6Boston, USA.

Smith, A., Cook, J., Francioni, J., Hossain, A., Anwar, M., Rahman, M. (2004). Nonvisual tool for navigating hierarchical structures. *Proceedings of the ACM SIGACCESS Accessibility and Computing Conference*, pp. 133-139, Atlanta, GA, USA, October 2004, ACM.

Walker, B., Nance, A. & Lindsay, J. (2006). Spearcons: speech-based earcons improve navigation performance in auditory menus. Proceedings of the 12th International

Conference on Auditory Display (ICAD2006), pp. 63-68, London, UK, 2006, CS Department, Queen Mary, University of London, UK.

Brewseter, S. (1998). Using nonspeech sounds to provide navigation cues, *ACM Transactions on Human-Computer Interaction*, Volume 5, Issue 3, September 1998, pp. 224-259, ISSN: 1073-0516, ACM.

Gaver, W. (1989). The SonicFinder: An interface that uses auditory icons, *Human Computer Interaction*, Volume 4, Number 1, pp. 57-94, July 1989, ACM, ISSN: 0736-6906.

Divi, V., Forlines, C., Gemert, J., Raj, B., Schmidt-Nielsen, B., Wittenburg, K., Woelfel, P., & Zhang, F. (2004). A Speech-In List-Out Approach to Spoken User Interfaces, *Proceedings of Human Language Technologies*, Boston, MA.

Wolf, P., Woelfel, J., Gemert, J., Raj, B., & Wong, D. (2004). *Spokenquery: An alternate approach to choosing items with speech*. Mitsubishi Electric Research Laboratory, TR-TR2004-121., Cambridge, MA, USA, 2004.

Sidner, C. & Forlines, C. (2002). Subset language for conversing with collaborative interface agents. Mitsubishi Electric Research Laboratory, TR-TR2002-36., Cambridge, MA, USA, 2002.

Brewster, S., Lumsden, J., Bell, M., Hall, M., Tasker, S. (2003). Multimodal 'eye-free' interaction techniques for wearable devices, *Proceedings of the SIGCHI conference on Human factors in computing systems*, pp. 473-480, Ft. Lauderdale, Florida, USA, ACM, ISBN: 1-58113-630-7.

K. Crispien, K. Fellbaum, A. Savidis, & C. Stephanidis. (1996). A 3d-auditory environment for hierarchical navigation in non-visual interaction. Proceedings of International Conference on Auditory Displays (ICAD), November 1996, ACM.

Hiipakka, J. & Lorho, G. (2003). A spatial audio user interface for generating music playlists. *Proceedings of the 2003 International Conference on Auditory Display*, Boston, MA, USA, July 2003.

W3C. (2003). Web content accessibility guidelines 1.0. In Web Accessibility Initiative.

Manber, U., B. Gopal, B., & Smith, M. (1996). Combining browsing and searching. *Proceedings of the W3 Distributed Indexing/Searching Workshop*, MIT, Boston, USA.

Mackinlay, J. & Zellweger, P. (1995). Browsing vs search: Can we find a synergy? (panel session). *Proceedings of the International Conference on Computer Human Interaction (SIGCHI)*, Palo Alto, CA, USA.

Karlson, A.; Robertson, G. ; Robbins, D. ; Czerwinski, M. & Smith, G. (2006). Fathumb: A facet-based interface for mobile search. *Proceedings of the International Conference on Computer Human Interaction (CHI)*, Montreal, Quebec, Canada, 2006.

Divi, V.; Forlines, C.; van Gemert, J.V.; Raj, B.; Schmidt-Nielsen, B.; Wittenburg, K.; Woelfel, J.; Wolf, P. & Zhang, F. (2004) A Speech-In List-Out Approach to Spoken User Interfaces, *Proceedings of the Human Language Technology Conference*, May 2004 (HLT 2004), Boston, MA, May 2004, ACM.

Household Product Database. www.householdproducts.nlm.nih.gov, 2004.

Li, B.; Xu, Y. & Choi, J. (1996). Title of conference paper, *Proceedings of xxx xxx*, pp. 14-17, ISBN, conference location, month and year, Publisher, City

Siegwart, R. (2001). Name of paper. *Name of Journal in Italics,* Vol., No., (month and year of the edition) page numbers (first-last), ISSN

Arai, T. & Kragic, D. (1999). Name of paper, In: *Name of Book in Italics,* Name(s) of Editor(s), (Ed.), page numbers (first-last), Publisher, ISBN, Place of publication